THE ARCHEOLOGY OF THE NEW TESTAMENT

THE ARCHEOLOGY OF THE NEW TESTAMENT

The Life of Jesus
and the Beginning of the Early Church

REVISED EDITION

Jack Finegan

PRINCETON UNIVERSITY PRESS
PRINCETON, NEW JERSEY

Library of Congress Cataloging-in-Publication Data
Finegan, Jack, 1908-
The archeology of the New Testament : the life of Jesus and the
beginning of the early church / Jack Finegan.—Rev. ed.
p.   cm.
Includes bibliographical references and indexes.
ISBN 0-691-00220-7 (pbk)
ISBN 0-691-03608-X (cloth)
1. Bible. N.T.—Antiquities. 2. Bible. N.T.—History of
Biblical events. 3. Palestine—Antiquities. I. Title.
BS2375.F5   1992   91-21725
225.9′3—dc20   CIP

PREFACE

THIS BOOK MIGHT properly be dedicated to the remembrance of Melito of Sardis, the first pilgrim to Palestine of whom we are informed. A Christian leader in Asia Minor, in 160 he "went to the East and came to the place (τόπος) where these things were preached and done." Others, unknown to us, may have preceded him in such pilgrimage, certainly many others followed. In 212 Alexander of Cappadocia, earlier a student in the great Christian university in Alexandria, went to Jerusalem "for the purpose of prayer and investigation of the places." The "places" (τόποι), as in the case of Melito, were the sites of sacred history, and the "investigation" was ἱστορία, which means learning by inquiry and is the root of the English word "history." A few years later Origen, who had been a fellow student with Alexander in Alexandria, later head of the Alexandrian school, and after that resident in Palestine, tells how he too "visited the places to learn by inquiry of the footsteps of Jesus and of his disciples." Information he obtained in this way was used by Origen in his scholarly works of exegesis and apology. In this connection he remarks upon occasion that in a given place something "is pointed out" (δείκνυται). Eusebius also uses this word repeatedly in connection with the geographical and historical information which he brings together in his famous Onomasticon, and the use of the identical phrase suggests that in many cases his information comes from far back in the times when the same things were pointed out to many of his predecessors in these investigations.

To these persons, therefore, and to many others also identified in the "Chronological List of Ancient Sources," it was important to learn by investigation, in the very places where events had transpired, as much as possible about the history of Jesus and his early followers, an investigation obviously deemed significant by these persons with respect to the witness that they bore—some to the point of martyrdom—to the facts of the Christian faith. Along with the coming of pilgrims and others of such interest, it is important also to note the continuity of tradition in the early centuries of the church in Palestine, which is indicated by the continuing presence of the Christians of Jewish background described in the section "The Judeo-Christians," the continuous sequence of leaders of the Jerusalem church as outlined in the "List of Bishops of the Jerusalem Church with Explanatory Comments," and the establishment of commemorative observances as noted in the "Outline of Festivals of the Early Church."

In modern times New Testament archeology has also been concerned to conduct investigations in "the place where these things were preached and done." In the Biblical Researches based upon his travels in Palestine in 1838 and 1852, Edward Robinson discussed many New Testament sites as well as Old Testament ones. Likewise the work of the Palestine Exploration Fund and the British School of Archaeology in Jerusalem, of the American School of Oriental Research in Jerusalem, of the Dominican École Biblique et Archéologique Française and of the Studium biblicum Franciscanum, both in Jerusalem, of the Department of Antiquities of Jordan, of the Department of Antiquities and Museums in Israel, of the Department of Archaeology of the Hebrew University, of the Israel Exploration Society, and of other institutions and individuals, has at least in part had to do with sites and objects related to the New Testament and early Palestinian Christianity and to the environment thereof.

In its procedure archeology must be as rigorously scientific as possible. What can be found and dealt with are therefore tangible things, inscriptions, objects, tombs, architectural remains, and the like. These are proper subjects of investigation in their own right. Archeology may be concerned with them simply because they exist, or with respect to their bearing on the history of culture, the history of art, etc. In themselves they are obviously not of the substance of the biblical faith, whether of the Old Testament or of the New Testament. But insofar as the biblical faith both of the Old Testament and of the New Testament has to do with events which happened at particular times and places, the investigation of any and all materials which cast light upon those times and places is of importance and relevance.

The present book has to do, then, with any things which can be found, chiefly in Palestine, which are connected with or cast light upon the life of Jesus and the existence of the early Christian church. The archeological sites and objects are presented in photographs, with some related drawings, maps, and plans, and the ancient sources, such as those mentioned above, are utilized along with the New Testament to help in identifying and interpreting these objects and sites. Since the purpose is the same as that expressed by Origen, namely, "to learn by inquiry of the footsteps of Jesus and of his disciples," the order of presentation is in general the same as that of the records in the New Testament, chiefly in the Gospels, concerning the life of Jesus and of his earliest followers.

Specifically this means that we first investigate sites connected with John the Baptist, then go on to Bethlehem and Nazareth, Samaria and Galilee, Jerash as an example of the Decapolis cities, Caesarea as the Roman capital, Jericho, the Mount of Olives, Jerusalem, and Emmaus. In Jerusalem the climactic sacred site is reached at the Church of the Holy Sepulcher, earlier known as the Anastasis, the Church of the Resurrection. Here the rock of Calvary and the traditional tomb have been so cut away and built upon that it is difficult to see how they may have looked prior to these enterprises, but we try to envision the earlier situation and give a hypothetical reconstruction of the tomb. Then we go on to assemble some additional information on ancient Jewish burial places. This gives perspective with regard to the tomb reconstruction just mentioned, and it also prepares for the last part of our undertaking, namely, to ask if the earliest followers of Jesus have left any tangible signs referring to him. Here we are involved with the history of the cross mark, and the earliest examples of this mark—where the question must at least be raised of possible connection with the Christian faith—are on burial monuments.

Preface to the Revised
Edition
The original edition of this book was published by Princeton University Press in 1969 and the completed manuscript of the present revision was submitted to the publisher in 1990. In the more than twenty years intervening there have been many archeological excavations at relevant sites in historical Palestine and many relevant publications in journals and books. It is the hope in this revision to bring my presentation abreast of the most significant new findings and discussions.

In particular in the present revised volume the new excavations and new discussions of excavated sites which are dealt with include the following among others: At Bethlehem the perimeters of the ancient town and the traditional Field of the Shepherds, the palace-fortress and burial place of Herod the Great at Herodium, and the early synagogue at Herodium. At Nazareth the baptistery under the Church of St. Joseph and the venerated grottoes under the new Church of the Annunciation. In respect of Cana, alternate sites at Khirbet Qana and Kefar Kenna/Karm er-Ras. At Tiberias the Hammath Tiberias synagogue. At Magdala the outlines of the

Roman town and the early Magdala synagogue. At et-Tabgha the status of the plain in the time of Jesus as compared with later time, and new work on the mosaics in the Church of the Multiplication of the Loaves and Fishes. At Capernaum the first century synagogue and the House of Peter. At Kursi the memorial of the Miracle of the Swine. At Caesarea the Promontory Palace and the Mithraeum. At Jerusalem the excavations on the periphery of the Temple Mount, in the Burnt House, and in the Cardo Maximus. At Jerusalem the excavations under the Church of the Holy Sepulcher, among the houses of the wealthy on Mount Zion, and in the Camp of the Essenes on Mount Zion. At Emmaus, alternate sites.

Likewise important subjects are dealt with in the light of recent publications and discussions, including the following among others: New studies of the Dead Sea Scrolls. The place of the Judeo-Christians and the Gentile Christians in remembrance of the life of Jesus and in the history of the Early Church, including the sequence of Jerusalem bishops from the circumcision and bishops from the Gentiles. The festivals of the Early Church in relation to dates in the life of Jesus. Questions of chronology in the life of Herod the Great and the life of Jesus, including both traditional and radical new theories on the dates of the birth, the ministry, and the death of Jesus. Dates derived from the discovery of "micrographics." The walls and areas of ancient Jerusalem. Understanding of the Pool of Bethesda. Location of the Praetorium. Route of Jesus from the Praetorium to Calvary. History of the Rock of Calvary. History of the Tomb of Jesus. History of the Church of the Resurrection (Anastasis). History of the Church of Hagia Sion.

The sites and objects have almost all been seen and studied personally by the author. Many of the photographs he has made himself, others are gathered from the sources to which acknowledgment is made in the notes at the end of the sections. Acknowledgment is also made to Professor Jerry Vardaman formerly of The Southern Baptist Theological Seminary, Louisville, Kentucky and now of The Cobb Institute of Archaeology, Mississippi State University, Mississippi, for a number of photographs and a number of suggestions which have been incorporated into the text and the bibliographies, usually with his name attached. For the cartography of maps and plans Nos. 7, 19, 33, 41, 53, 77, 107, 138, and 143 acknowledgment is made to Evelyn Bingham.

With this book in hand one may go, it is hoped, either in actuality or in imagination and study, "to the East . . . to the place where these things were preached and done."

J.F.

CONTENTS

THE CROSS

CHRONOLOGICAL LIST OF ANCIENT SOURCES

WITH RESPECT to the identification of Gospel sites the following are the most important ancient sources, with approximate dates in parenthesis.

Josephus (90). The Jewish historian was born in 37/38 in Jerusalem, participated in the Jewish War and, after the fall of Jerusalem, settled in Rome. He wrote a long account of *The Jewish War* which probably appeared c. 75, and in the thirteenth year of Domitian (93/94), when he himself was fifty-six years of age, completed his *Jewish Antiquities* (*Ant.* xx 12, 1 §267). His work, *Against Apion*, replied to criticisms on the *Antiquities*, and the *Life* of Josephus responded to another history of the Jewish War by Justus of Tiberias in which Josephus was criticized for his part in the war. In Josephus' *Life* (65 §§359-360), he speaks of Herod Agrippa II as no longer alive, hence must have written this work after the decease of that king. The exact date of Agrippa's death is unknown (see an unpublished paper by Jerry Vardaman). He struck no coins later than 95; no inscription of his (over twenty are known) dates later than 93. He must, however, have lost much, if not all, of his territory before the last year of the emperor Domitian (96), since an inscription from Ahire, under his control formerly, refers to the sixteenth year of Domitian. The date of the death of Josephus himself is also unknown. References are to Josephus' works, ed. H. St. J. Thackeray, Ralph Marcus, Allen Wikgren, and Louis H. Feldman, 9 vols. LCL; for the *War* see also Gaalaya Cornfeld, ed., Josephus, *The Jewish War, Newly Translated with Extensive Commentary and Archaeological Background Illustrations* (Grand Rapids, Mich.: Zondervan, 1982).

THE PROTEVANGELIUM OF JAMES (150). A
legendary account of Mary, daughter of Joachim and Anne, child wife of the widowed Joseph, and mother of Jesus. The oldest manuscript is Papyrus Bodmer v, probably of the third century, ed. M. Testuz, O. Cullmann, HSNTA I, pp. 370-388.

JUSTIN MARTYR (150). Born soon after 100 of a
pagan Greek family at Flavia Neapolis (modern Nablus, cf. No. 62) in Palestine. Justin left Palestine in about 130, became a Christian at Ephesus, founded a school at Rome, and was beheaded under the prefect of Rome, Junius Rusticus, in 165. Eusebius, *Church History* IV,

1ff., mentions eight treatises by Justin. Three are extant in a poor manuscript of 1364, namely, two *Apologies Against the Gentiles*, and a *Dialogue with the Jew Trypho*. The *First Apology* was written c. 150-155; the *Second Apology* was a sort of postscript, and the *Dialogue* was written after the *First Apology*. ANF I.

MELITO OF SARDIS (160). Bishop of Sardis, he
wrote a number of works the titles of which are given by Eusebius (*Ch. Hist.* IV 26). The last which Eusebius mentions, and therefore possibly but not certainly the last which Melito wrote, was an *Apology* addressed to the emperor Marcus Aurelius (161-180). From the quotations given by Eusebius it appears that this was written after the death of the emperor's brother, Lucius Verus, i.e., after the year 169. The work by Melito, which is of particular interest in the present connection, was a treatise in six books named *Extracts*, as both Eusebius (*Ch. Hist.* IV 26, 12 ἐν δὲ ταῖς γραφείσαις αὐτῷ Ἐκλογαῖς) and Jerome (*Lives of Illustrious Men* 24) call it, and addressed to an otherwise unknown Onesimus. It contained a list of the accepted books of the OT canon, and consisted chiefly of quotations from these Scriptures, no doubt quotations believed to have to do with Christ. As he tells of this work Eusebius (*Ch. Hist.* IV 26, 13) quotes from its Preface. In the Preface Melito gives an account of the cause and circumstances of the writing. Onesimus had expressed a wish to have extracts made from the Law and the Prophets concerning the Savior and the Christian faith, and along therewith desired to know accurately the number and order of the ancient books. Melito continues: "Accordingly when I went to the East and came to the place where these things were preached and done (ἀνελθὼν οὖν εἰς τὴν ἀνατολὴν καὶ ἕως τοῦ τόπου γενόμενος ἔνθα ἐκηρύχθη καὶ ἐπράχθη), I learned accurately the books of the Old Testament, and send them to you. . . . From these I have also made the extracts."

Here then was the first pilgrim journey to the East of which we are informed. This bishop in Asia Minor desired to obtain dependable information, particularly concerning the OT canon, in the homeland of the Christian faith. At the same time he desired to see with his own eyes the very place (τόπος) where these things were preached and done, i.e., the actual scene of Gospel history. From this statement we can conclude that the important places in Gospel history were actually being shown to visitors at that time, in the middle of the second century. So the authenticity of the faith was confirmed to Melito and others like him, and they were able to bear witness to it. For the significance of Melito in this respect, see Hans Windisch, "Die ältesten christlichen Palästinapilger," in ZDPV 48 (1925), pp. 145-147.

IRENAEUS (180). Greek writer from Asia Minor, he was bishop of Lyons, and author of *Adversus haereses* ("Against Heresies") and other works (ANF I, pp. 315-578).

ALEXANDER OF CAPPADOCIA (212). Alexander was a friend of Origen and together with him a student under Pantaenus and Clement in Alexandria (Eusebius, *Ch. Hist.* VI 14, 8-9). Later he was bishop in some city in Cappadocia (*Ch. Hist.* VI 11). In the first year of Caracalla (211) Asclepiades was made bishop of Antioch (Eusebius, *Chronicle*, ed. Helm, 2d ed. 1956, p. 213) and Alexander wrote a letter of congratulation (*Ch. Hist.* VI 11) in which he described himself as a prisoner. The next year he went to Jerusalem, where he was made bishop along with the then aged Narcissus (*Chronicle*, p. 213). In Jerusalem he established a library from which Eusebius, a century later, gathered materials (*Ch. Hist.* IV 20). Alexander died a martyr under Decius (250) (Jerome, *Lives of Illustrious Men* 62). When he tells about Alexander's trip to Jerusalem Eusebius (*Ch. Hist.* VI 11, 2) says that he went "for the purpose of prayer and investigation of the places" (εὐχῆς καὶ τῶν τόπων ἱστορίας ἕνεκεν). By the "places" (τόποι) must almost certainly be meant the places that were of special significance in the Christian faith, i.e., the sacred places of Gospel events. Even as the Ethiopian once came to Jerusalem to worship (Ac 8:27), and Paul hastened to be there, if possible, on the day of Pentecost (Ac 20:16), so the bishop desired to pray in Jerusalem and presumably at the sacred places in the city. Furthermore he was concerned with ἱστορία, i.e., investigation in the sense of learning by inquiry, with respect to "the places." Herodotus (II 99) links the same word with seeing and judging when he says that what he writes about Egypt is the outcome "of my own sight and judgment and inquiry" (ὄψις τε ἐμὴ καὶ γνώμη καὶ ἱστορίη). So Alexander desires to conduct "investigation of the places," in order that he may bear witness, as he finally did even unto martyrdom. While neither Melito of Sardis nor Alexander of Cappadocia have left us writings in which are actual descriptions of specific places in the Holy Land, it is evident that both of them undertook to visit the sacred places to confirm the authenticity of the sacred history, and that they might be able to bear witness thereto. Nor were they the only such travelers who had this objective as

early as their times, i.e., in the second and third centuries. What is told by other writers who traveled to the Holy Land later in the third and following centuries was presumably the same sort of information already provided by local traditions in Palestine to Melito and Alexander and their contemporaries. For the significance of Alexander in this respect, see Windisch in ZDPV 48 (1925), pp. 150-151.

ORIGEN (230). Born c. 185, probably at Alexandria, Origen was appointed head of the catechetical school in that city in 202/203. About 212 he traveled to Rome. About 215 he visited Palestine and lectured in Caesarea (Eusebius, *Ch. Hist.* VI 19, 16). In 230 he visited Palestine again and a year later settled permanently in Caesarea where he founded a school. In 218-222 he lectured in Antioch, and in 244 visited Arabia. In the persecution by Decius (250) he was imprisoned and tortured, probably at Caesarea, and died at the age of about seventy, probably in 253/254, at Tyre. During his residence in Palestine, and in connection with his exegetical and text-critical study of the Bible, Origen visited various places of sacred history. This is evident from a statement in his *Commentary on John* (VI 24 GCS Origines IV, p. 149 ANF IX, p. 370) where he gives "Bethabara" as the reading to be preferred in Jn 1:28. Having declared his conviction that we should read not "Bethany" but "Bethabara" in this passage (cf. below No. 9), he adds: "We have visited the places to learn by inquiry of the footsteps of Jesus and of his disciples and of the prophets (γενόμενοι ἐν τοῖς τόποις ἐπὶ ἱστορίαν τῶν ἰχνῶν Ἰησοῦ καὶ τῶν μαθητῶν αὐτοῦ καὶ τῶν προφητῶν)." Here again, as in the case of Melito (above), there is interest in the *topos* or "place" where the things of Christian history were preached and done and, as in the case of Alexander (above), in the *historia* or investigation of these places. In another case Origen appeals to the apologetic significance of an attested site of a Gospel event. Writing *Against Celsus* (I 51 GCS Origenes I, p. 102 ANF IV, p. 418 cf. below No. 25) he says that if anyone wishes to have additional evidence with respect to the birth of Jesus in Bethlehem, let him know that in accordance with the history in the Gospel concerning his birth, the cave in Bethlehem is pointed out where he was born and the manger in the cave where he was wrapped in swaddling clothes (ὅτι ἀκολούθως τῇ ἐν τῷ εὐαγγελίῳ περὶ τῆς γενέσεως αὐτοῦ ἱστορίᾳ δείκνυται τὸ ἐν Βηθλεὲμ σπήλαιον, ἔνθα ἐγεννήθη, καὶ ἡ ἐν τῷ σπηλαίῳ φάτνη, ἔνθα ἐσπαργανώθη). The word δείκνυται, "is pointed out," is very important. It means, almost certainly that in his investigation of the footsteps of Jesus, Origen went himself to Bethlehem and was personally shown, no doubt by the Christians of the place, the evidential cave. To him this was a witness to the truth of the Gospel history. Although Origen is the first Christian to leave explicit eyewitness testimony of this sort to places of the Gospel history, there is little doubt that such places were also "shown" to his predecessors such as Alexander and Melito. After him, Eusebius also uses the same formula, "is pointed out," at a number of points in the *Onomasticon* (see below), namely, with respect to Akeldama (p. 38), Ainon (p. 40), Bethania, Bethabara, Bezatha (p. 58), Jericho (p. 104), Sychar (p. 164), and other places. Since the notations of Eusebius are in much the same style as that of Origen about Bethlehem and employ the characteristic δείκνυται, it is probable that Eusebius derived materials for the *Onomasticon* from these earlier researches of Origen as well as from his own study and knowledge of the country. For Origen's numerous writings see GCS and ANF. For his significance among the early visitors to places of Gospel history, see Windisch in ZDPV 48 (1925), pp. 152-154. As Windisch remarks (ibid., p. 155), the journeys in Palestine of Melito, Alexander, Origen, and other early visitors to places which were shown as places of Gospel history are a testimony to the relatively early date of the traditions attaching to these places. While the genuineness of the sites is not proved by this alone, it is at any rate clear that Melito and the others would not have made their journeys if they had not believed that the places they wished to see were still identifiable and accessible.

EUSEBIUS (325). He was born in Palestine, probably at Caesarea, in 263. At the school which Origen had founded here, the presbyter Pamphilus developed a great library and was the teacher and friend of Eusebius, who called himself Eusebius Pamphili, i.e., the spiritual son of Pamphilus. Eusebius was elected bishop of Caesarea in 313, the same year in which the edict of Constantine brought peace to the church. He was active in the Council of Nicaea (325), took part in the dedication of the Church of the Holy Sepulcher in Jerusalem (335), lectured afterward in the same year in Constantinople (cf. No. 225), and died in 339 or 340. The *Chronicle* of Eusebius was published c. 303 and is extant in late Armenian manuscripts (ed. Karst, GCS), and a Latin version was made by Jerome probably in 381 and is preserved in manuscripts as early as the fifth century (ed. Helm, GCS; cf. Alden A. Mosshammer, *The Chronicle of Eusebius and Greek Chronographic Tradition* [Lewisburg: Bucknell University Press, 1979]). The *Demonstratio Evangelica* was probably written before 311 (ed. Heikel, GCS). The *Church History* may have been composed in a first edition c. 303, but in its completed form it records events down to the victory of Constantine over Licinius (324); thus it may be dated about 325 (ed. Lake and Oulton, LCL; McGiffert, NPNFSS I; cf. Glenn F. Chesnut, *The First Christian Histories: Eusebius, Socrates, Sozomen, Theodoret and Evagrius* [Paris: Beauchesne, 1977]). The *Oration in Praise of Constantine*, whom Eusebius so greatly admired, was pronounced in Constantinople on the thirtieth anniversary (*tricennalia*) of the emperor's reign, July 25, 336 (NPNFSS I, pp. 581-610). The *Life of Constantine* was written after the death of the emperor, May 22, 337, and tells of church buildings that Constantine erected (NPNFSS I, pp. 481-559; LPPTS I-A). The *Onomasticon* (περὶ τῶν τοπικῶν ὀνομάτων τῶν ἐν τῇ θείᾳ γραφῇ) was the fourth part of a work on biblical geography, the writing of which was suggested by Bishop Paulinus of Tyre. Since the latter died in 331, this work was probably composed before that date, say, therefore, about 330, or possibly even earlier, between the *Chronicle* and the *Church History*. The first three parts of the entire work, which are not extant, were an Interpretation of the Ethnological Terms of the Hebrew Scriptures in Greek, a Topography of Ancient Judea, and a Plan of Jerusalem and the Temple. The fourth part, which is extant and is commonly called the *Onomasticon*, is an alphabetical list of place names in the Bible, with notes on the situation and history of these localities. While the work is alphabetically arranged in that it goes through the letters of the alphabet from Alpha to Omega, under each letter it takes up biblical books in order and then in each book takes up place names generally in the order of their occurrence. Under the letter Alpha and in the book of Genesis, for example, we find Ararat (Ἀραράτ) (Gen 8:4), Accad (Ἀχάδ) (Gen 10:10), Ai (Ἀγγαί) (Gen 12:8), and so on, in that order. That the work may rest, at least in part, upon material gathered by Origen, has been pointed out just above. In addition to the Greek text of the *Onomasticon* as written by Eusebius, we also have a Latin translation of the work which was made by Jerome in 390, in which are not a few corrections and additions representing additional information that Jerome is able to supply. Greek and Latin texts, ed. Klostermann, GCS; cf. Peter Thomsen, "Palästina nach dem Onomasticon des Eusebius," in ZDPV 26 (1903), pp. 97-141, 145-168; and *Loca Sancta, Verzeichnis der im 1. bis 6. Jahrhundert n. Chr. erwähnten Ortschaften Palästinas* (Halle a. S.: Rudolf Haupt, 1907); M. Noth, "Die topographischen Angaben in Onomastikon des Eusebius," in ZDPV 66 (1943); T. D. Barnes, "The Composition of Eusebius' Onomasticon," in JTS 26 (1975), pp. 412-415; Robert M. Grant, *Eusebius as Church Historian* (Oxford: Clarendon Press, 1980), pp. 41f. (review by Glenn F. Chesnut in RSR 9 [1983], pp. 118-123); Dennis E. Groh, "The Onomasticon of Eusebius of Caesarea and the Rise of Christian Palestine," in *Studia Patristica* XVIII, Papers of the Ninth International Conference on Patristic Studies, Oxford, 1983, ed. Elizabeth A. Livingstone (Kalamazoo, Mich.: Cistercian Publications, 1985), pp. 23-

31. For Eusebius and Cyril, see P.W.L. Walker, *Holy City, Holy Places* (Oxford: Clarendon Press, 1990).

HELENA (326). This lady was the mother of the emperor Constantine. She began a pilgrimage to the Holy Land in 326 and died not long afterward (c. 327) at the age of eighty. Eusebius tells of her journey in *The Life of Constantine* (III 41-47). Among several of her coins, her portrait and the legend Helena Augusta appear on a coin struck at Ticinum in northern Italy c. 325 (see Barbara Geller Nathanson in BA 49 [1986], p. 30). The example of Helena, and the increased freedom for such travel under the Christian emperors, must have contributed much to the henceforth greatly augmented interest in pilgrimage to Palestine.

THE BORDEAUX PILGRIM (333). This anonymous pilgrim made a journey from Bordeaux to Jerusalem and back by way of Rome to Milan. His is the oldest pilgrim account and is called *Itinerarium a Burdigala Hierusalem usque.* ed. Geyer pp. 1-33; LPPTS I-B; CCSL CLXXV, pp. 1-26; WJP pp. 153-163.

CYRIL OF JERUSALEM (348). Probably born in Jerusalem c. 315, he became bishop of Jerusalem in 347/348 and, in the Easter season of that year, gave a series of twenty-four catechetical lectures in the Church of the Holy Sepulcher, lectures which were afterward published from the shorthand notes of a member of the congregation. NPNFSS VII; LPPTS XI-A.

EPIPHANIUS (367). Born c. 315 in the vicinity of Eleutheropolis near Gaza in Palestine, c. 335 he visited the monks of Egypt, then founded a monastery at Eleutheropolis and headed it for thirty years. In 367 he became bishop of Salamis on the island of Cyprus, but continued in close touch with Palestine personally and through correspondence. He wrote *Ancoratus*, "The Firmly-Anchored Man," in 374; *Panarion*, "Medicine Chest," also cited as *Haereses*, in 374-377; Greek text, ed. K. Holl, GCS 25, 31, 37; vol. 2 and 3, ed. Jürgen Dummer, 1980, 1985; Eng. trans. of Book I (Secs. 1-46) by Frank Williams, NHS 35 (1987); and *De mensuris et ponderibus* ("On Weights and Measures") in 392, a Bible dictionary dealing with canon and versions of the OT, measures and weights in the Bible, and the geography of Palestine, Eng. trans. of the complete Syriac version, ed. James E. Dean, SAOC 11 (1935).

AETHERIA OR EGERIA (381-384). A nun, probably from the north of Spain or the south of France, she was in Jerusalem as a pilgrim from Easter 381 to Easter 384 (Paulus Devos, "La date du voyage d'Égérie," in AB 85 [1967], pp. 165-194). She left a plain record, only a part of which was found in 1884. It also goes under the name of Sylvia and is called *Peregrinatio ad loca sancta,* ed. Geyer pp. 35-101; LPPTS I-C; Hélène Pétré, *Étherie, Journal de voyage* (SC 21) (Paris: Les Éditions du Cerf, 1957); CCSL CLXXV, pp. 37-90; WET (cf. review by A. T. Kraabel in BAR 9.2 [Mar/Apr 1983], pp. 20-23). On her travels she carried with her as a pilgrim guide a Latin translation of the *Onomasticon* of Eusebius, probably the translation by Jerome (J. Ziegler, "Die *peregrinatio Atheriae* und die Hl. Schrift," in *Biblica* 12 [1931], pp. 83f.).

JEROME (385). Born in Dalmatia c. 347, Jerome was educated in Rome and baptized there, and afterwards he lived for a time in Aquileia. In about 373 he went to the East, stayed for two years in Antioch in Syria, then lived among hermits in the Syrian desert of Chalcis to the southwest of Antioch; upon his return to Antioch in 378 or 379 he was ordained by Bishop Paulinus. After study in Constantinople for another two years, he was again in Rome in 382-385, where he was a friend and secretary of Pope Damasus and undertook the revision of the Latin Bible. He also became the center of an ascetical circle in which several ladies of the Roman aristocracy were associated, including the widows Marcella and Paula and the latter's daughter, Eustochium. Soon after the death of Damasus (December 10, 384) Jerome returned to Antioch (August 385), where he was joined by Paula and Eustochium. Together with Bishop Paulinus they traveled in Palestine and Egypt, then in the summer of 386 Jerome settled permanently in Bethlehem, where he lived in a cave at the Church of the Nativity until his death in 420, and Paula and Eustochium chose to live at Bethlehem too. In addition to his translation and revision of the *Onomasticon* of Eusebius, made in 390, as mentioned above, Jerome's own writings were very numerous. CCSL, NPNFSS III, VI.

In his *Letter 46* (NPNFSS VI, p. 65) which he wrote from Bethlehem in 386 in the name of Paula and Eustochium to invite their friend Marcella to visit the Holy Land, Jerome expressed his deep feelings concerning the experiences one would have at the sacred sites. He wrote in part:

Will the time never come when a breathless messenger shall bring the news that our dear Marcella has reached the shores of Palestine, and when every band of monks and every troop of virgins shall unite in a song of welcome? In our excitement we are already hurrying to meet you; without waiting for a vehicle, we hasten off at once on foot. We shall clasp you by the hand, we shall look upon your face; and when, after long waiting, we at last embrace you, we shall find it hard to tear ourselves away. Will the day never come when we shall together enter the Saviour's cave, and together weep in the sepulcher of the Lord with his sister and with his mother? Then shall we touch with our lips the wood of the cross, and rise in prayer and resolve upon the Mount of Olives with the ascending Lord. We shall see Lazarus come forth bound with grave clothes, we shall look upon the waters of Jordan purified for the washing of the Lord. Thence we shall pass to the folds of the shepherds, we shall pray together in the mausoleum of David. We shall see the prophet, Amos, upon his crag blowing his shepherd's horn. We shall hasten, if not to the tents, to the monuments of Abraham, Isaac and Jacob, and of their three illustrious wives. We shall see the fountain in which the eunuch was immersed by Philip. We shall make a pilgrimage to Samaria, and side by side venerate the ashes of John the Baptist, of Elisha, and of Obadiah. We shall enter the very caves where in the time of persecution and famine the companies of the prophets were fed. If only you will come, we shall go to see Nazareth, as its name denotes, the flower of Galilee. Not far off Cana will be visible where the water was turned into wine. We shall make our way to Tabor, and see the tabernacles there which the Saviour shares, not, as Peter once wished, with Moses and Elijah, but with the Father and with the Holy Spirit. Thence we shall come to the Sea of Gennesaret, and when there we shall see the spots where the five thousand were filled with five loaves and the four thousand with seven. The town of Nain will meet our eyes, at the gate of which the widow's son was raised to life. Hermon too will be visible, and the torrent of Endor, at which Sisera was vanquished. Our eyes will look also on Capernaum, the scene of so many of our Lord's signs—yes, and on all Galilee besides. And when accompanied by Christ, we shall have made our way back to our cave through Shiloh and Bethel, and those other places where churches are set up like standards to commemorate the Lord's victories, then we shall sing heartily, we shall weep copiously, we shall pray unceasingly. Wounded with the Saviour's shaft, we shall say one to another: "I have found him whom my soul loveth; I will hold him and will not let him go."

Although Jerome expressed such feelings as these about the visitation of the Holy places, and chose himself to reside at Bethlehem, he also spoke elsewhere about how little the places themselves could mean apart from faith. In his *Letter* 58 (NPNFSS VI, pp. 119-120) written c. 395 to his friend Paulinus of Nola, he declared that access to the courts of heaven was as easy from Britain as from Jerusalem and assured Paulinus that nothing was lacking to his faith although he had not seen Jerusalem, and that he, Jerome, was none the better for living where he did. The Palestinian hermit Hilarion (died 371, Jerome wrote his life in 390, NPNFSS VI, pp. 303-315) provided a good example, Jerome told Paulinus, because although he was a native of and dweller in Palestine he only allowed himself to visit Jerusalem for a single day, "not wishing on the one hand when he was so near to neglect the holy places, nor yet on the other to appear to confine God within local limits." Indeed, said Jerome, "the spots which witnessed the crucifixion and the resurrection profit those only who bear their several crosses, who day by day rise again with Christ, and who thus show themselves worthy of an abode so holy."

PAULA (386). It was after the death of her husband in 380 that this distinguished and wealthy Roman woman became a pupil and companion of Jerome and (as narrated just above) also settled together with her daughter Eustochium at Bethlehem. There she built a convent over which she and Eustochium presided in turn, a monastery of which Jerome was the head, and a hospice for pilgrims, and engaged in many works of charity. She also continued her studies of the Bible with Jerome, having learned Hebrew as well as knowing Greek and Latin. Upon her death in 404 Jerome wrote (*Letter* 108) to Eustochium to console her upon the death of her mother and in the letter described Paula's journey to the East including Egypt and the Holy Land. The tombs of Paula and Eustochium as well as of Jerome are shown adjacent to the cave of the Nativity beneath the Church of the Nativity, and Jerome himself says of Paula that "she was buried beneath the church and close to the cave of the Lord" (108, 33 NPNFSS VI, p. 211). NPNFSS VI, pp. 195-212; LPPTS I-D, E; WJP pp. 47-52.

PAULINUS OF NOLA (403). Born at Bordeaux in 353, Paulinus was a pupil and friend of the Roman rhetorician Ausonius. He adopted the monastic life and lived in Nola in Italy from 394 onward, where he died as bishop in 431. He wrote poems, and letters to Augustine, Sulpicius Severus, and others. MPL 61, CSEL XXIX-XXX.

SOZOMEN (425). Born at Bethelia near Gaza in Palestine, Sozomen became a civil servant at Constantinople. His *Church History* was intended as a continuation of the work of Eusebius and covered the period from 324 to 425. NPNFSS II.

SOCRATES (439). Also a civil servant in Constantinople, in which city he was born c. 380, Socrates wrote a *Church History* in seven books, intended to be a continuation of that of Eusebius, covering the period from the abdication of Diocletian in 305 down to 439. NPNFSS II.

PETER THE IBERIAN (451). The son of a prince in Georgia, he came to Jerusalem in 451 where he was consecrated as a priest. He became bishop of Majuma near Gaza and died there in 485. R. Raabe, *Petrus der Iberer*, 1895 (cited as Raabe, as quoted in Kopp; cf. M.-J. Lagrange in RB 5 [1896], pp. 457-460).

THE JERUSALEM BREVIARY (sixth century). A brief enumeration of the sanctuaries in Jerusalem, probably written in the early sixth century. *Breviarius de Hierosolyma*, ed. Geyer pp. 151-155; LPPTS II-A; CCSL CLXXV, pp. 109-112; WJP pp. 182f.

THEODOSIUS (530). This author is known only from the pilgrim itinerary which he has left, but it is of value for its concise notations on the holy places as they were known in the early sixth century. *Theodosius de situ terrae sanctae*, ed. Geyer pp. 135-150; LPPTS II-B; CCSL CLXXV, pp. 115-125; WJP pp. 62-71.

PROCOPIUS (560). Procopius of Caesarea wrote extensively concerning the reign of the Byzantine emperor Justinian I the Great (527-565) and particularly his widespread and notable building achievements. The treatise on the *Buildings* of Justinian was published in 560 or soon thereafter, trans. H. B. Dewing, LCL; LPPTS II-C.

THE MADABA MOSAIC MAP (560). The ancient Moabite town of Medeba (Num 21:30; Jos 13:9, 16) is today the village of Madaba in Jordan, sixteen miles east and south of where the Jordan flows into the Dead Sea. The place was occupied by Christians from Kerak around 1880, and in 1884 the existence of the mosaic was first reported to the Greek Orthodox Patriarch of Jerusalem, whose librarian visited the site in 1896. The mosaic was the floor of an ancient church, and at the time a new Greek Orthodox church was being built over the old one and the mosaic was already much damaged. The librarian published the first drawings of the map in 1897, and Palmer and Guthe made the first copy in color in 1902. The principal preserved fragment of the map is 10.50 meters long by 5 meters wide. The geographical area represented extends from Aenon (near Scythopolis) in the north to the Canopic branch of the Nile in the south, and from the Mediterranean Sea in the west to Charachmoba (Kerak) on the east. The map is oriented in the literal sense of the word, i.e., the viewer is looking eastward. The inscriptions, which are in Greek, are written so as to be read by one looking in this direction. If a river runs from east to west the letters of its name are written in a vertical line. Buildings normally show the western façade. The intention of the map was obviously to depict the Bible lands and, in its original form, the map must have covered biblical Palestine and parts of adjacent lands connected with the Bible. The principal source was undoubtedly the *Onomasticon* of Eusebius, with which it corresponds in many points. Some other sources must have been used too and one of these may have been an early road map. The center of the map is the city of Jerusalem, shown in a large oval, and most precisely the center is the base of the column shown inside the northern gate of the city, the column no doubt being the point from which road distances from Jerusalem were measured. On the map the sea is deep green, the plains light brown, the mountains dark brown. In the cities, especially in Jerusalem, the normal representation is to use red roofs for churches or monasteries, and yellow or gray roofs for palaces or public buildings. Brown areas appear to be squares. The doors of the principal basilicas are yellow cubes, which may

represent either polished brass or lights shining from inside. The inscriptions are usually in black, but in the mountains where the background is dark they are lettered in white, and in occasional instances an especially important place is indicated in red letters. The neuter article τό is used to signify a sacred place, often one marked by a church. The script of the inscriptions employs an oval alphabet such as is also found, for example, in numerous sixth-century inscriptions in the churches at Gerasa (C. B. Welles in Kraeling, *Gerasa*, p. 367). As may also be seen in some of those inscriptions, omicron and upsilon are often written in a ligature. Some abbreviations and punctuation marks are employed, and consonantal iota is marked with two dots. The date of the map is probably between 560 and 565. Except for the *Tabula Peutingeriana*, a Roman road map of the third century copied in a manuscript of the thirteenth century, the Madaba mosaic map is the only extant ancient cartographical representation of Palestine. P. Palmer and H. Guthe, *Die Mosaikkarte von Madeba*, I, Pls. (Leipzig, 1906); R. T. O'Callaghan, "Madaba (Carte de)," in DB Supplément 5 (1957), cols. 627-704; Michael Avi-Yonah, *The Madaba Mosaic Map with Introduction and Commentary* (Jerusalem: The Israel Exploration Society, 1954); Victor Gold, "The Mosaic Map of Madeba," in BA 21 (1958), pp. 50-71; Herbert Donner and Heinz Cüppers, "Die Restauration und Konservierung der Mosaikkarte von Madeba," in ZDPV 83 (1967), pp. 1-33; and *Die Mosaikkarte von Madaba* I (Abhandlungen des Deutschen Palästinavereins) (Wiesbaden: O. Harrassowitz, 1977); Hans Georg Thümmel, "Zur Deutung der Mosaikkarte von Madeba," in ZDPV 89 (1973), pp. 66-79; Herbert Donner, "Mitteilungen zur Topographie des Ostjordanlandes anhand der Mosaikkarte von Madeba," in ZDPV 98 (1982), pp. 174-191.

THE ANONYMOUS OF PIACENZA (570). The title of this work is *Antonini Placentini Itinerarium*, but it has been shown (Grisar in ZKT 1902, pp. 760-770 and 1903, pp. 776-780) that it describes a pilgrimage not by, but rather under the protection of, Antoninus Martyr, the latter being the patron saint of Placentia, i.e., Piacenza, in Italy, hence the work is now cited as the Anonymous of Piacenza. It describes the sanctuaries, and the legends attaching to them, at the height of the Byzantine period, ed. Geyer pp. 157-218; LPPTS II-D; CCSL CLXXV, pp. 129-174; WJP pp. 78-89.

SOPHRONIUS (634). A native of Damascus, Sophronius became a monk at Jerusalem and also visited Egypt, Rome, and Constantinople. He was made patriarch of Jerusalem in 634. In his time the Persians, i.e., the Neo-Persians or Sasanians, invaded Palestine (614), and he died in the year (638) that Jerusalem was captured by the Muslims under the Caliph 'Umar. Among the many works of Sophronius (MPG 87, 3, cols. 3147-4012) his poems (*Anacreontica*) describe the holy places in Jerusalem and Bethlehem (MPG 87, 3, cols. 3733-3838; LPPTS XI-A, pp. 28-32; WJP pp. 90-92).

THE JERUSALEM CALENDAR (BEFORE 638).
The *Kalendarium Hierosolymitanum*, also known as the Georgian Festival Calendar, is preserved in various manuscripts and lists the stations at which the Georgian Church in Jerusalem celebrated the festivals of the church year prior to the Muslim invasion in 638. H. Goussen, *Über georgische Drucke und Handschriften* in *Liturgie und Kunst*, M.-Gladbach, 1923 (cited as Goussen, as quoted in Kopp).

ARMENIAN DESCRIPTION OF HOLY PLACES (660).
This is a fragmentary Armenian work probably written by an Armenian pilgrim who visited Jerusalem in about A.D. 660, which was not long after the taking of Jerusalem and Palestine by the Muslim Arabs. It is presented as "the faithful account of an eyewitness" and provides a short description of the holy places in Palestine, chiefly in Jerusalem. R. Nisbet Bain, "Armenian Description of the Holy Places in the Seventh Century," in PEFQS 1896, pp. 346-349.

ARCULF (670).
A Frankish bishop and pilgrim, he visited the Near East and stayed nine months in Jerusalem, coming like the Armenian pilgrim just mentioned soon after the rise of Islam. On the return journey Arculf's ship was driven by contrary winds to Britain and he came to Iona. There he related his experiences to Adamnan, Abbot of Iona (679-704), and the latter wrote down the narrative of the journey including ground plans of churches copied from Arculf's wax tablets. The work was in three books, the first concerning Jerusalem, the second about other sites in the Holy Land, and the third about Constantinople. *Adamnai de locis sanctis libri tres*, ed. Geyer pp. 219-297; LPPTS III-A; CCSL CLXXV, pp. 183-234; WJP pp. 93-116.

BEDE (720).
Bede or Baeda, commonly called "the Venerable," lived about 672-735 and spent almost his entire life in the monastery at Wearmouth and Jarrow in Northumbria. About 701 the narrative by Adamnan of the journey of Arculf was presented to the Northumbrian king, Aldfrith the Wise, at York, and became known to Bede. He included some extracts from it in his Ecclesiastical History of the English Nation (731), and founded upon it his own treatise, *De locis sanctis*, which became the standard guidebook to the holy places for the

pilgrims of the Middle Ages. *Baedae liber de locis sanctis*, ed. Geyer pp. 299-324; LPPTS III-A; CCSL CLXXV, pp. 251-280.

WILLIBALD (725).
An English monk, he and two companions arrived in Jerusalem on pilgrimage in 724 and stayed in the Holy Land for two years. Afterward he visited Constantinople and Rome, and eventually became a missionary bishop in Germany. Of several Lives of Willibald, the first was written in about 780 by a nun named Hugeburc. Tobler and Molinier pp. 243-297; WJP pp. 125-135.

EPIPHANIUS, OR EPIPHANIUS MONACHUS HAGIOPOLITA (750-800).
In the title of his "narration" (Διήγησις Ἐπιφανίου Μοναχοῦ τοῦ Ἁγιοπολίτου . . .) he calls himself a monk and a resident of the holy city, i.e., of Jerusalem. His work is an itinerary, written in Greek, and based in part upon an earlier travel account, the latter probably of about the time of Arculf (670). MPG CXX; for other editions and for the date and sources see A. M. Schneider, "Das Itinerarium des Epiphanius Hagiopolita," in ZDPV 63 (1940), pp. 143-154; for critical text and German translation see Herbert Donner, "Die Palästinabeschreibung des Epiphanius Monachus Hagiopolita," in ZDPV 87 (1971), pp. 42-91; for English translation see WJP pp. 117-121.

GEORGIUS (GEORGE) SYNCELLUS (800).
Byzantine chronographer, whose chronicle (*Chronographia*) begins with the creation of the world and extends to the year A.D. 284 (CSHB 30, 31). Syncellus means literally "one who shares a cell" and was the title of several high ecclesiastical officials in the Eastern church; this best-known one is often called by the title alone. After his death (c. 810) his *Chronographia* was continued by his friend Theophanes (CSHB 32, 33).

COMMEMORATORIUM DE CASIS DEI VEL MONASTERIIS (808).
This "commentary" was prepared under Charlemagne and is a catalogue of the most important churches and monasteries of the Holy Land. Tobler and Molinier pp. 301-305; WJP pp. 137-138.

NICEPHORUS (829).
Celebrated Byzantine writer and patriarch of Constantinople (806-815), he was born in Constantinople c. 758 and died in 829. In addition to writings in opposition to the policy of the iconoclasts, his historical works are a short history from 602 (d. of the emperor Maurice) to 769 (*Breviarium Historicum*, MPG 100, cols. 863-994; CSHB 50-C, pp. 3-86), and chronological tables of universal history from the Crea-

tion to the year of his own death (*Chronographia Brevis*, MPG 100, cols. 1002-1056; CSHB 30, pp. 737-788; 31, pp. 549-560).

BERNARD (870). A Frankish monk, he was the last pilgrim from the West to write an account of the holy places before the time of the Crusaders. Tobler and Molinier pp. 309-320; LPPTS III-D; WJP pp. 141-145.

EUTYCHIUS (940). Sa'id ibn al-Bitriq, known as Eutychius or Eutychius of Alexandria, was born in Fustat (Cairo) in 877, became the Greek Orthodox or Melchite patriarch of Alexandria in 935, and died in 940. Around the year 935 he compiled items of history and legend in a world history in Arabic known as the *Annals*, see MPG 111, cols. 907-1156; LPPTS XI-A, pp. 35-70; *Das Annalenwerk des Eutychios von Alexandrien, Ausgewählte Geschichten und Legenden kompiliert von Sa'id ibn Batriq um 935 A.D.*, ed. Michael Breydy, 2 vols. (CSCO 471-472, Scriptores Arabici 44-45) (Louvain: E. Peeters, 1985). Although the attribution is now questioned (Breydy, CSCO 471, p. xi), another work in Arabic has usually been ascribed to Eutychius and is also cited in the present volume under his name, namely, *The Book of the Demonstration* (see Pierre Cachia and W. Montgomery Watt, *Eutychius of Alexandria, The Book of the Demonstration* [*Kitāb al-Burhān*], CSCO 192, 193, 209, 210, Scriptores Arabici 20, 21, 22, 23) (Louvain: Secretariat de Corpus SCO, 1960-1961). In the latter work paragraphs 310ff. describe Christian sanctuaries in Palestine and are probably based upon a much earlier source.

MUQADDASI (985). Shams ad Din Abu Abdallah Muhammad ibn Ahmad, known as al-Muqaddasi, "the Jerusalemite," was an Arabian Muslim traveler and author. Born at Jerusalem in A.H. 336 = A.D. 946, he made his first pilgrimage at the age of twenty in A.H. 356 = A.D. 967 and completed his Description of the Lands of Islam nearly twenty years later in A.H. 375 = A.D. 985. From this work the Description of the Province of Syria, including Palestine, is translated from the Arabic by Guy le Strange in LPPTS III-C.

NASIR-I KHUSRAU (1047). Abu Mu'in Nasir, the son of Khusrau, was born in a village near Balkh in A.H. 395 = A.D. 1003. He was later in government service in that region, but resigned to go on a seven-year pilgrimage (A.D. 1045-1052) to Mecca and Medina. His extended travels included Syria, Palestine, and Egypt, and he was in Jerusalem in the year A.D. 1047. The diary of his travels is called *Safar-nama*, and the long section in it on Syria and Palestine, including Jerusalem, is translated from the Persian by Guy le Strange in LPPTS IV-A.

SAEWULF (1102). Scandinavian pilgrim and later monk in England, his description of Jerusalem and the Holy Land is the first we have to cover the period immediately after the conquest of Jerusalem by the Crusaders on July 15, 1099. LPPTS IV-B.

DANIEL (1106). Daniel was a Russian abbot who made a journey to the Holy Land in 1106/1107. Writing in early Crusader times, his record also reflects traditions preserved by the Greek Orthodox church from before the Crusades. LPPTS IV-C.

PETER THE DEACON (1137). Petrus Diaconus was librarian in Monte Cassino, Italy. In 1137 he compiled a *Book concerning the Holy Places*, utilizing earlier pilgrim writings including the narrative of Aetheria, from which he probably preserves materials otherwise missing. *Petri diaconi liber de locis sanctis*, ed. Geyer pp. 103-121; CCSL CLXXV, pp. 252-280; WET pp. 179-210.

JOHN OF WÜRZBURG (1170). A German priest in the church at Würzburg, he was in the Holy Land between the years 1160 and 1170. His *Descriptio Terrae Sanctae* tells of various sacred sites and especially of the city of Jerusalem. LPPTS V-B.

THEODERICUS (1172). A German priest and pilgrim, and probably the person of the same name who became bishop of Würzburg in 1223. His pilgrimage to the Holy Land (probably in 1172) took place in the time of the Crusaders and before their expulsion from Jerusalem by Saladin in 1187. His work is called *Libellus de Locis Sanctis* ("The Little Book about the Holy Places"). What he saw is clearly described, but what he learned only from hearsay is not so dependable. LPPTS V-D.

WILLIAM OF TYRE (1184). Born in about 1130 in the Crusaders' kingdom of Jerusalem, perhaps in Jerusalem itself, he was chancellor of the Latin kingdom from 1174 and archbishop of Tyre from 1175, both thereafter until his death in 1185. His *History of Deeds Done beyond the Sea* begins at the point of the taking of Jerusalem by the Sasanian Persians in 614 and was completed in 1184 only shortly before the fall of the city to Saladin in 1187. The work is generally regarded as the first comprehensive history of the Crusades. With William's access to the archives of the Church of the Holy Sepulcher, his work is of special value in respect to the history of that church and to the conditions of Christians in Jerusalem. See *A History of Deeds Done beyond the Sea, by William Archbishop of Tyre*, trans. Emily Atwater Babcock and A. C. Krey, 2 vols. (Records of Civilization, Sources and Studies) (New York: Columbia University Press, 1943).

PHOCAS (1185). Joannes Phocas was a Greek monk from Crete who described in some detail his travels from Antioch on the Orontes to Jerusalem and elsewhere in the Holy Land. MPG 133; LPPTS V-C.

ANONYMOUS I (1098), II (1170), III, IV, V, VI, VII (1145), VIII (1185). These are short descriptions of the holy places by unknown authors of the eleventh and twelfth centuries (with more precise dates given when known), i.e., from the time of the Crusades (Jerusalem was taken by the Crusaders in 1099 and by Saladin in 1187). LPPTS VI-A.

ERNOUL (1231). His reports also are from the time of the Crusades, but are preserved only fragmentarily. H. Michelant and G. Raynaud, *Itinéraires à Jérusalem* (Geneva, 1882).

BURCHARD OF MOUNT SION (1283). He was a German Dominican and presumably received his appellation because of extended residence in Jerusalem. His book, entitled "A Description of the Holy Land," is considered the best of its kind from the time of the Crusades. LPPTS XII-A.

BAR HEBRAEUS (1286). He was born at Melitene in Cappadocia (200 miles north of Antioch) in 1226 in a Jewish family that had gone over to Syrian Jacobite (Monophysite) Christianity and was himself known as "Son of the Hebrew." After study in Antioch and Tripoli he served as bishop in several places and in 1264 was made *maphrian* (primate, the rank next to patriarch) of the eastern section of the Syrian church (Chaldea, Mesopotamia, Assyria), with seat at Tagrit (or Karme) on the Upper Tigris. He died in 1286 at Maragha in Azerbaijan (60 miles south of Tabriz) and was buried in a monastery near Mosul, with the inscription, "This is the grave of Mar ('lord,' his title as *maphrian*) Gregory (probably his name adopted when he became bishop), John (his name given at birth)." He wrote both in Arabic and in Syriac. His best-known work in his Syriac *Chronography*, a work in three parts, the first part giving a secular history of the world from Creation to the year of his own death (1286), the second part containing a history of the church from Aaron "the priest" (Ex 31:10) onwards, and the third part recording the history of the Eastern Syrian church from St. Thomas onwards. See *The Chronography of Gregory Abû'l Faraj, The Son of Aaron, The Hebrew Physician Commonly Known as Bar Hebraeus, Being the First Part of His Political History of the World*, trans. Ernest A. Wallis Budge, 2 vols. (London: Oxford University Press, 1932).

QUARESMIUS (1626). Franciscus Quaresmius was born at Lodi in Lombardy in 1583 and died at Milan in 1650. He held high offices in the Franciscan order and in 1616 went to Jerusalem in the position of Guardian. Between 1616 and 1626 he wrote a comprehensive history of the Holy Land and of the custody of the holy places, known as *Elucidatio terrae sanctae*. F. Quaresmius, *Historica, theologica et moralis terrae sanctae elucidatio*, ed. Cypriano da Treviso, 2 vols. (Venice, 1880-1881).

References: William Smith and Henry Wace, *A Dictionary of Christian Biography*, 4 vols. (Boston: Little, Brown and Company, 1877-1887), cited as SWDCB; Johannes Quasten, *Patrology*, 3 vols. (Westminster, Md.: The Newman Press, 1950-1960); Berthold Altaner, *Patrology* (New York: Herder and Herder, 1960); Clemens Kopp, *Die heiligen Stätten der Evangelien* (Regensburg: Friedrich Pustet, 1959) (cited as Kopp 1959), pp. 480-486; Donato Baldi, *Enchiridion Locorum Sanctorum, Documenta S. Evangelii Loca Respicientia* (2d ed., Jerusalem: Franciscan Printing Press, 1954. Reprint, 1982), cited as Baldi.

TABLE OF ARCHEOLOGICAL AND HISTORICAL PERIODS IN PALESTINE

NEOLITHIC PERIOD, BEFORE 4500 B.C.
CHALCOLITHIC PERIOD, 4500-3200 B.C.
EARLY BRONZE AGE, 3200-2100 B.C.
MIDDLE BRONZE AGE, 2100-1500 B.C.
LATE BRONZE AGE, 1500-1200 B.C.
IRON AGE I, 1200-1000 B.C.

IRON AGE II, 1000-586 B.C.

The First Temple period is considered to extend from the tenth to the sixth centuries, more exactly from the fourth year of Solomon (968/967) when he began building the Temple (I K 6:1) to 586 when it was destroyed by the Chaldeans in the nineteenth year of Nebuchadnezzar (II K 25:8).

IRON AGE III, 586-332 B.C. (PERSIAN PERIOD, 539-332)

The Second Temple period began with the completion of the rebuilding of the Temple in the sixth year of Darius (Ezr 6:15) in 515 B.C. and continued through the further reconstruction by Herod the Great down to the final destruction in A.D. 70. Some prefer to call the temple as rebuilt by Herod the Great the Third Temple, but this is not the customary Jewish usage.

HELLENISTIC PERIOD, 332-63 B.C.

Alexander the Great conquered the Middle East, 332
Under the Ptolemies, 323-198
Under the Seleucids, 198-143/142
Independence under the Maccabeans and the Hasmonean Dynasty, 143/142-63 B.C.

ROMAN PERIOD, 63 B.C.-A.D. 324

Pompey captures Jerusalem, 63 B.C.
Roman Emperors

Octavian receives title Augustus on January 16, 27 B.C., d. August 19, A.D. 14
Tiberius made head of state as Tiberius Caesar Augustus on September 17, A.D. 14, d. March 16, A.D. 37

Herodians

Herod the Great is crowned in Rome as king of the Jews, 40 B.C. In 37 B.C. Herod the Great captures Jerusalem, the Romans execute Antigonus, the last of the Hasmoneans, and Herod begins his reign of thirty-seven years from coronation, thirty-four years in fact (Josephus, *War* I 33, 8 §665; *Ant.* XVII 8, 1 §191).

Herod dies between a lunar eclipse (*Ant.* XVII 6, 4 §167, probably the night of March 12/13, 4 B.C.) and the following Passover (*War* II 1, 3 §10; *Ant.* XVII 9, 3 §213, probably April 11, 4 B.C.) and is buried at Herodium (*War* I 33, 9 §673; *Ant.* XVII 8, 3 §199), being succeeded by his sons—Archelaus as ethnarch of Judea (4 B.C.-A.D. 6), Antipas as tetrarch of Galilee and Perea (4 B.C.-A.D. 39), and Philip as tetrarch of Panias and related regions (4 B.C.-A.D. 33/34).

The Herodian period is considered to extend from the time of Herod the Great to the destruction of the Second Temple, therefore from 37 B.C. to A.D. 70.[1]

Jesus Christ, birth in 5, 7, or 12 B.C.[2]

---

1. For the Herodian dates above, see SHJP Vermes/Millar, I, pp. 326-328 n. 165-166, and pp. 336-356. For putting Herod's death as late as 1 B.C., see W. E. Filmer in JTS 17 (1966), pp. 283-298; Ernest L. Martin, *The Birth of Christ Recalculated* (2d ed., Pasadena: Foundation for Biblical Research, 1980); and in CKC pp. 85-92. For putting the death in 3 or 2 B.C., see Ormond Edwards in PEQ 1982, pp. 29-42. For confirmation of 4 B.C. as the correct date, see Timothy D. Barnes in JTS 19 (1968), pp. 204-209; P. M. Bernegger in JTS 34 (1983), pp. 526-531;

Harold W. Hoehner in CKC pp. 101-111; Paul L. Maier in CKC pp. 116-118. Cited as CKC, *Chronos, Kairos, Christos: Nativity and Chronological Studies Presented to Jack Finegan*, ed. Jerry Vardaman and Edwin M. Yamauchi (Winona Lake: Eisenbrauns, 1989), contains discussions of many other dates relating to the life of Jesus.

2. For these and other proposed dates for the birth of Jesus, see the "Outline of Festivals of the Early Church," esp. pp. xlv-xlvi.

The Procurators, A.D. 6-41, 44-66
    Marcus Pontius Pilate, A.D. 26-36 or A.D. 15/16-25/
    26[3]
John the Baptist, A.D. 29 or 15

3. After Archelaus, son of Herod the Great and ethnarch of Judea, was dismissed by Augustus in A.D. 6 for misgovernment, and on down to A.D. 41, and again after the brief rule of Herod Agrippa I, grandson of Herod the Great, in A.D. 41-44, and on down to A.D. 66 (the outbreak of the Jewish war against the Romans), Judea was under the direct rule of Roman governors, known by the titles of *praefectus* (ἔπαρχος) or *procurator* (ἐπίτροπος) (see Josephus, *Ant.* XVIII 2, 2 §§29ff.; XIX 9, 2 §363; XX 1, 1 §§2ff.; *War* II 8, 1 §§117ff.; 11, 6 §§220ff.; cf. below No. 129).

About Pontius Pilate in particular, without specifying the year in which his procuratorship began, Josephus (*Ant.* XVIII 4, 2 §89) relates that his term in Judea was ten years in length and terminated when Tiberius summoned him to Rome to give account about charges against him by the Samaritans, "but before he reached Rome Tiberius had already passed away" (μεταστάς, trans. LCL IX, p. 65). Since Tiberius died on March 16, A.D. 37, and since Pilate's trip to Rome must have occupied several months, we may suppose that Pilate's dismissal was in A.D. 36; with ten years in office, his original appointment would have been in A.D. 26. Furthermore Eusebius (*Ch. Hist.* I 9, 2), although perhaps only by inference since the text of Josephus does not contain the dates, says that the Jewish historian put the appointment of Pilate in the twelfth year of Tiberius (in factual years, Aug/Sept A.D. 25 to Aug/Sept A.D. 26, FHBC p. 265, table 123), and in the *Chronicle* Eusebius lists Pilate as procurator in Tiberius' thirteenth year, equivalent to A.D. 26 (ed. Helm p. 173). The dates usually accepted, therefore, for Pilate's ten-year procuratorship are A.D. 26-36 (E. Mary Smallwood, "The Date of the Dismissal of Pontius Pilate from Judaea," in *JJS* 5 [1954], pp. 12-21; SHJP Vermes/Millar, I, pp. 382-387).

On the other hand Eusebius (*Ch. Hist.* I 9; cf. IX 5, 1) tells of *Acts of Pilate* (circulated in 311 by the emperor Maximinus, regarded by Eusebius as a forgery, HERE IX, p. 748), in which the crucifixion of Jesus was dated in the fourth consulship of Tiberius, which was in the seventh year of his reign, therefore in the spring of the year A.D. 21. In view of this date, together with evidence from the Slavonic version of Josephus' *War*, Robert Eisler (*The Messiah Jesus and John the Baptist* [London: Methuen, 1931], pp. 19, 313) placed the entry of Pilate into office in Judea in late A.D. 18, and Daniel R. Schwartz ("Josephus and Philo on Pontius Pilate," in *The Jerusalem Cathedra* 3 [Jerusalem: Yad Izhak Ben-Zvi Institute; Detroit: Wayne State University Press, 1983], p. 43 n. 22) likewise found reason to support the date of A.D. 18/19 for Pilate's appointment. Now Jerry Vardaman finds "microletters" on ancient coins with various notations significant for chronology (in CKC pp. 66ff., and letters to the present writer in March through May 1990, with permission to cite; for Jewish coins, see A. Reifenberg, *Israel's History in Coins, From the Maccabees to the Roman Conquest* [London: East and West Library, 1953]; Ya'akov Meshorer, *Jewish Coins of the Second Temple Period* [Tel-Aviv: Am Hassefer, 1967]). On a Jewish shekel of "year one" (i.e., the first year of the First Revolt of the Jews against the Romans, A.D. 66) in the British Museum (No. PS139375) Vardaman sees mention of the consul M. Vettius Bolanus, who was only in office September 25 to November 23, A.D. 66 (E. Mary Smallwood, *Documents Illustrating the Principates of Gaius, Claudius and Nero* [Cambridge: Cambridge University Press, 1967], p. 6), which confirms the date of this coin within those two months of the year 66. On the coin Vardaman also finds the information that Pontius Pilate was dismissed from his office as procurator of Judea forty-two years prior to the striking of this coin. This would put Pilate's dismissal late in the year A.D. 25 or possibly early in A.D. 26, and therefore his first year in office was A.D. 15/16. To accord with this date for the dismissal of Pilate the

In the fifteenth year of Tiberius John went into the Jordan region preaching a baptism of repentance (Lk 3:1-3).[4]

statement in Josephus (*Ant.* XVIII 4, 2 §89) usually translated to say that Pilate, dismissed, reached Rome after Tiberius had passed away (μεταστάς), which was on March 16, A.D. 37, may equally well be translated to say that Pilate reached Rome after Tiberius "moved" to Capri, which he did in A.D. 26, for the verb μετατίθημι basically means to transfer to another place, and when Dio Cassius (*Rom. Hist.* 57.12.6) describes Tiberius' move to Capri he uses if not μεταστάς, the closely related form μεταστῆναι (Vardaman letters, April 5 and April 16, 1990, and in CKC p. 79).

Obviously if the procuratorship of Pontius Pilate was in A.D. 15/16-25/26 changes must also be made in hitherto generally accepted dates for other procurators. Pilate's four predecessors and the dates hitherto usually given are (1) Coponius, A.D. 6-9; (2) Marcus Ambibulus, 9-12; (3) Annius Rufus, 12-15; and (4) Valerius Gratus, 15-26 (SHJP Vermes/Millar, I, p. 382 and n. 130, with acknowledgment that the first three cannot be precisely dated). Vardaman (telephone, April 30, 1990) finds on the Jewish shekel of "year one" (A.D. 66) that this year was the fifty-eighth year since the appointment of Annius Rufus, therefore Rufus must have taken office say in midyear A.D. 9, and the successive terms of Coponius and Ambibulus must together have fallen in A.D. 6-9. Josephus (*Ant.* XVIII 2, 2 §32) states that the administration of Annius Rufus was marked by the death of Augustus (August 19, A.D. 14), so Rufus' procuratorship continued into the year 14/15. Between the latter date and the first year of Pilate in A.D. 15 there is only one year for Valerius Gratus, namely 14/15. The statement of Josephus (*Ant.* XVIII 2, 2 §35) that Gratus was in office eleven years was already reduced by Eisler (op. cit., p. 17) to four years on the supposition of an incorrect change of an original Greek character delta (Δ) for the numeral "four" into IA) or "eleven" (iota = 10, alpha = 1), whereas Vardaman supposes that it was an original alpha (= 1) that was misread. (A Greek inscription found at Samaria mentions generals, gives the name Annius Rufus, ΑΝΝΙΟΥΡΟ ΥΦΟΥ, and probably also contained in what is now a gap the name of Valerius Gratus, thus both later procurators evidently served here at an earlier point in their careers, see G. A. Reisner, C. S. Fisher, and D. G. Lyon, *Harvard Excavations at Samaria*, 2 vols. [Cambridge: Cambridge University Press, 1924], I, p. 250, no. 7; II, pl. 59, photo c; and an unpublished paper by Jerry Vardaman and Nikos Kokkinos.) The reconstructed dates of the procurators through Pilate are, therefore, according to the foregoing: (1) Coponius, A.D. 6-9; (2) Marcus Ambibulus, 6-9; (3) Annius Rufus, 9-14; (4) Valerius Gratus, 14/15; and (5) Marcus Pontius Pilate, 15/16-25/26.

4. Since Augustus died on August 15 and Tiberius was named his successor on September 17 in A.D. 14 (see above under Roman Emperors), the fifteenth factual year of Tiberius was Aug/Sept A.D. 28 to Aug/Sept A.D. 29 (FHBC p. 265, table 123); in reckoning by calendar years after accession the fifteenth year would be Jan 1 to Dec 31, A.D. 29 (FHBC p. 268, table 125). Taking Jan 1 to Dec 31, A.D. 29 as the year that would have been meant in usual Roman reckoning, Paul L. Maier (in CKC p. 124, table 1) places the ministry of John as beginning early in that year and extending throughout A.D. 29.

In line, however, with the information noted just above in note 3 that would put the procuratorship of Pontius Pilate in A.D. 15/16-25/26, Jerry Vardaman proposes to emend Lk 3:1 to read in the second year of Tiberius instead of in the fifteenth year (as in all the extant manuscripts). The suggestion is that in the original text the number was "two," which in Greek characters used as numerals would be the character beta, written as B; this was mistakenly copied as EI (epsilon = 5, and iota = 10), and it is interesting to note that in the present

Ministry of Jesus, A.D. 29-33 or 15-21[5]
Herod Agrippa I, A.D. 41-44
Jewish War with Rome (First Revolt), A.D. 66-73
    Destruction of Qumran, 68
    Fall of Jerusalem, 70
    Fall of Masada, 73
    Hadrian, r. 117-138

Orders the rebuilding of Jerusalem as a pagan city, 130
Second Revolt, A.D. 132-135
    Simeon ben Kosiba, called Bar Kokhba, dies at Bethar, 135
    Hadrian proceeds to build Aelia Capitolina, 135[6]

text of Lk 3:1 we have πεντεκαιδεκάτῳ, literally "five and ten," whereas "fifteen" is otherwise more usually written with the reverse order of the words, δεκαπέντε, "ten (and) five" (Ac 27:28). If, then, we read that it was in the second year of Tiberius that John began his work, Tiberius' second factual year began in Aug/Sept A.D. 15 and it could have been in the fall of the year 15 that John received his call and began preaching and baptizing (Vardaman in CKC pp. 59f., 82).

5. After John began his baptismal work in the Jordan region and "all the people were baptized," Jesus also came and was baptized (Lk 3:1) and thereafter began his own public ministry. If John's work began early in A.D. 29 (the fifteenth year of Tiberius) and extended throughout the year (see above note 4), the baptism and start of the public work of Jesus may be put in the fall of the year 29, after many others had been baptized as the text says and also after the summer heat of the Jordan valley (Paul L. Maier in CKC p. 124, table 1). At this time, when he began his ministry, Jesus was about (ὡσεί) thirty years of age (Lk 3:23). If he was born in Nov/Dec 5 B.C. he would have been thirty-two years old in the fall of A.D. 29 and would have reached his thirty-third birthday in Nov/Dec 29, for which "about thirty" is an understandable approximation (Maier in CKC pp. 121f.). If he was born in 7 B.C. (see "Outline of Festivals of the Early Church") and was thus even two years older at this time, the statement of age in Lk 3:23 might still be a reasonable round number. If the beginning of Jesus' ministry was in the fall of A.D. 29, the four ensuing Passovers that are probably indicated in the Fourth Gospel (FHBC p. 284, table 134) would lead to a date for the fourth and final Passover in the spring of A.D. 33, with the crucifixion according to calendrical and astronomical considerations probably on Friday April 3, A.D. 33 (Maier in CKC pp. 120-126; Colin J. Humphreys and W. G. Waddington in CKC pp. 165-181).

If, however, Lk 3:1 is to be emended to read that it was in the second year of Tiberius and thus probably in the fall of A.D. 15 that John the Baptist began to preach and baptize, then the baptism and beginning of the public work of Jesus are probably to be dated after midyear of the same year, A.D. 15, and the first whole year of his ministry would have extended from then until midyear A.D. 16 (Vardaman in CKC pp. 60, 77f.). It is also to be noted, according to Jerry Vardaman (in CKC pp. 56f.), that Josephus refers to Jesus in Ant. XVIII 3, 3 §§63-64 within a context of other historical events that date around A.D. 15-19, while (as noted above in note 3) in microletters on a Jewish shekel of "year one" (A.D. 66) there is information that puts the first year of Pontius Pilate himself as procurator of Judea in A.D. 15/16. Furthermore, in microletters on a coin in the British Museum from Damascus—dated in the year 327 of the Seleucid era (the date was written originally as LZKT, i.e., the sign for "year" followed by zeta = 7, kappa = 20, and tau = 300; and was rewritten as LHKT [eta = 8] or 328), which Seleucid year 327 is the year A.D. 15/16 (FHBC p. 121, table 46), a coin probably struck under Aretas IV (king of Petra and father-in-law of Herod Antipas, Josephus, Ant. XVIII 5, 1 §109; evidently in control of Damascus from this date until Damascus passed from Aretas to Tiberius in A.D. 33/34, cf. II Cor 11:32)—are the words REX JESVS, "King Jesus" (a title not always intended favorably, cf. Mt 27:37 and other passages). Other coins from Damascus, including another with a date of LZKT (= A.D. 15/16), also mention Jesus. From this evidence, therefore, the first year of the "reign" of Jesus, i.e., the first year of his public ministry, is to be placed in A.D. 15/16 (Vardaman in CKC pp. 70-72,

with corrections in letter, March 22, 1990). If Jesus was born in 12 B.C. as Vardaman holds (see "Outline of Festivals of the Early Church," pp. xlv-xlvi), in A.D. 15 Jesus was twenty-seven years of age, and for this "about thirty" (Lk 3:23) is appropriate in the sense of getting relatively close on toward this next round number (CKC p. 57).

In the continuation of the public work of Jesus, Vardaman allows a total length of ministry of six years, with the crucifixion at Passover in A.D. 21 (in CKC p. 78, table 4). Like the Damascus coin with the words "King Jesus," other microletter inscriptions mention Jesus with titles such as "King of the Jews," "Messiah," and the like, and Jesus is also named on Jewish shekels of "year one" (A.D. 66), and even with the title SOTER—ΣΩΤΗΡ ("Savior") in both Latin and Greek spellings (cf. Jn 19:20), but this term is often used in the pagan world as the equivalent of ΒΑΣΙΛΕΥΣ, and on such a nationalistic Jewish coin as this is surely used not as confession but as identification (Vardaman letter, April 16, 1990). Chronologically of the greatest importance along with the information on the "year one" Jewish shekel providing the A.D. 15/16 date of the first year of Pontius Pilate (see above note 3) is the reported discovery of microletters on the rim of the same shekel that read precisely: "Year 6 of the procurator Mar(cus) Pontius Pilate, which is (o και) Year 1 (LA, i.e., the sign for "year" and alpha, the character for the numeral one) of the death (σταυρου, the cross, the crucifixion) of Jesus, the righteous one." On this basis the six years of Pilate and the date of the death of Jesus may be tabulated as follows:

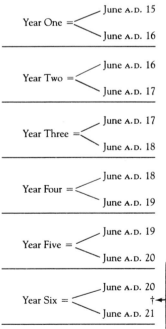

Year One = June A.D. 15 / June A.D. 16
Year Two = June A.D. 16 / June A.D. 17
Year Three = June A.D. 17 / June A.D. 18
Year Four = June A.D. 18 / June A.D. 19
Year Five = June A.D. 19 / June A.D. 20
Year Six = June A.D. 20 / † June A.D. 21 — Jesus dies at Passover in April A.D. 21, while Pontius Pilate is in his sixth year in office [Vardaman letter, April 20, 1990]

Also reported are microletters on a coin struck by Flaccus as governor of Syria in A.D. 26 that indicate this as the sixth year dating from the death of Jesus (Vardaman in CKC p. 60, fig. 1 and letter, March 23, 1990); and microletters on a coin minted by Herod Agrippa I at Cae-

BYZANTINE PERIOD, A.D. 324-638

Constantine the Great

Wins the battle of the Milvian Bridge, 312

Issues Tolerance Edict of Milan with his eastern colleague, Licinius, 313

Reigns as sole ruler of the Roman Empire, 324-337

Takes over Palestine and the East in 324, hence this date as the beginning point of the Byzantine period

Convokes the Council of Nicaea, 325

Founds Constantinople at ancient Byzantium as "New Rome" and capital of the Roman Empire, 330; hence the year 330 is an alternative beginning point of the Byzantine period.

Theodosius I the Great, Roman emperor of the East (r. A.D. 379-395) and of the West (r. 392-395)

He is succeeded by his sons Arcadius in the East and Honorius in the West, marking the permanent division of the empire; hence 379-395 is alternatively taken as beginning point of the Byzantine period.

Theodosius II, Roman emperor of the East (r. A.D. 401-450)

He prefers the study of theology and astronomy to public affairs, which he leaves to his sister Pulcheria and, at times, to his wife, Eudocia.

He decrees that the cross and other Christian symbols may not be used in pavements where they could be walked on, 427.

Issues a codification of Roman law, the Theodosian Code, 428.

Convokes the Council of Ephesus, 431.

Eudocia, empress of the East

Daughter of an Athenian Sophist and originally named Athenais, she was selected by Pulcheria to be the wife of Theodosius II, whom she married (421) after being baptized and taking the name of Eudocia; later she was banished from court, visited Jerusalem in 438, and lived there permanently from 444 until her death in 460, devoting herself to literary and charitable work.

Zeno, Roman emperor of the East (r. A.D. 474-491)

During his reign in the East the Roman Empire in the West came to an end when the Teutonic invaders under Odoacer took Ravenna, the West Roman capital, and deposed Romulus Augustulus as the last Roman emperor of the West, and Zeno reluctantly recognized the rule of Odoacer and granted him the title of patrician.

In Palestine Zeno expelled the Samaritans from Mount Gerizim and built on the mountain the Church of Mary as Theotokos (484).

Justinian I the Great, Byzantine emperor (r. A.D. 527-565)

Based on the Theodosian Code and other sources, he ordered the compilation of the most comprehensive codification of Roman law, the Corpus Juris Civilis.

As described by Procopius (*Buildings*, published c. 560), Justinian built extensively, not only public works but also monasteries, orphanages, hostels, and churches, including Hagia Sophia in Constantinople and the Church of the Nativity in Bethlehem and the Nea Church in Jerusalem.

Heraclius I, Byzantine emperor (r. A.D. 610-641)

In the early years of his reign the Persians (Sasanians) conquered Syria, Palestine, and Egypt; in Palestine, where the Jews had suffered much under Byzantine rule, the invaders were assisted by Jewish soldiers, and many churches were destroyed (A.D. 614).

In campaigns in the years 622-628 Heraclius recovered the lost provinces as well as the "true cross," which the Persians had taken away, but before his reign was over the same areas fell to new conquerors, the Muslim Arabs (629-641).

MUSLIM ARAB PERIOD, A.D. 638-1099

Muhammad, d. 632

Orthodox Caliphs, 632-661

Caliph 'Umar (634-644) receives the surrender of Jerusalem from the Patriarch Sophronius (638) and conquers Caesarea, the capital (640).

Umayyads, 661-750

Muawiyah, the founder, is proclaimed caliph at Jerusalem, but the dynasty is ruled from Damascus.

Caliph Abd al-Malik (r. 685-705) builds the Dome of the Rock at Jerusalem.

Caliph Suleiman (r. 715-717), second son of Abd al-Malik and younger brother of al-Walid (r. 705-715, builder of the Great Mosque at Damascus), establishes a new capital in Palestine at Ramla (probably ancient Arimathea, ten miles northeast of Lod/Lydda) and builds there a palace and a mosque.

Abbasids, 750-1258

They claim descent from al-Abbas, an uncle of Mu-

sarea in A.D. 44 on which are the words JESVS LKΓ MORTV$\frac{S}{M}$, "year twenty-three [kappa = 20, gamma = 3] of Jesus' death," as well as reference to the "reign" (REGNUM) of Jesus as having started in the 327th year (LZKT) of the Seleucid era, i.e., in A.D. 15/16 (Vardaman in CKC pp. 73-76).

6. For Hadrian and Aelia Capitolina, see SHJP Vermes/Millar, I, pp. 541-557; cf. Gedaliah Alon, *The Jews in Their Land in the Talmudic Age* (70-640 C.E.), trans. and ed. Gershon Levi, 2 vols. paged consecutively (Jerusalem: Magnes Press, Hebrew University, 1980-1984), see pp. 442ff. and esp. p. 577 for the date of the end of the Bar Kokhba war against Hadrian, between April and December of 135.

hammad; they rule at Baghdad and generally neglect Palestine.

Fatimids, 909-1171

They claim descent from Fatima, the daughter of Muhammad, and rule from Egypt.

Caliph al-Hakim (r. 996-1021) destroys churches and synagogues in Palestine and elsewhere (1009).

CRUSADER PERIOD, A.D. 1099-1291

Crusaders take Jerusalem, July 15, 1099

Crusaders defeated by Saladin in battle at the Horns of Hattin, 1187

MAMLUK PERIOD, A.D. 1250-1517

Originally slaves (as the name means), chiefly Turks and Circassians, brought to Egypt under the Fatimids, they were converted to Islam and ruled as sultans (literally "with authority") from capitals at Cairo and Damascus, waging bitter war with the last of the Crusaders.

Fall of Acre (Acco, Accho) and departure from Palestine of the last of the Crusaders, 1291

The Franciscan Order is charged with the Custody of the Holy Land (*Custodia Sanctae Terrae*), c. 1342.

OTTOMAN PERIOD, A.D. 1517-1918

Descendants of Uthman or Osman, leader of a Turkish tribe and sultan of Turkey c. 1300, the Muslim Ottomans capture Constantinople in 1453 and become the heirs of the Byzantine Empire.

Suleiman I the Magnificent (r. 1520-1566), in c. 1540 builds the walls that still surround the Old City of Jerusalem.

BRITISH PERIOD, A.D. 1918-1948
STATE OF ISRAEL, A.D. 1948-PRESENT

Note: Dates in the earlier periods in the foregoing table are approximate, cf. BAR 15.6 (Nov/Dec 1989), pp. 70f.

TABLE OF MONTHS IN THE ROMAN, EGYPTIAN, MACEDONIAN, AND HEBREW CALENDARS

ROMAN (JULIAN)

		Number of Days
1.	Januarius	31
2.	Februarius	28
3.	Martius	31
4.	Aprilis	30
5.	Maius	31
6.	Junius	30
7.	Julius	31
8.	Augustus	31
9.	Septembris	30
10.	Octobris	31
11.	Novembris	30
12.	Decembris	31
		365

Kalends, first day of month

Ides, fifteenth day in March, May, July, and October, thirteenth day in other months

Nones, ninth day before Ides, therefore seventh day in March, May, July, and October, fifth day in other months

Source: FHBC pp. 75f., table 31

EGYPTIAN (JULIAN REFORM)

		First Day of the Month in a Common Year
1.	Thoth	Aug 29
2.	Phaophi	Sept 28
3.	Hathyr	Oct 28
4.	Choiak	Nov 27
5.	Tybi	Dec 27
6.	Mecheir	Jan 26
7.	Phamenoth	Feb 25
8.	Pharmuthi	Mar 27
9.	Pachon	Apr 26
10.	Pauni	May 26
11.	Epeiph	June 25
12.	Mesore	July 25

five or six epagomenal days

Source: FHBC p. 29, table 8

MACEDONIAN (EQUATED WITH ROMAN)

		First Day of the Month
1.	Peritios	Feb 1
2.	Dystros	Mar 1
3.	Xanthikos	Apr 1
4.	Artemisios	May 1
5.	Daisios	June 1
6.	Panemos	July 1
7.	Loos	Aug 1
8.	Gorpiaios	Sept 1
9.	Hyperberetaios	Oct 1
10.	Dios	Nov 1
11.	Apellaios	Dec 1
12.	Audynaios	Jan 1

Source: FHBC p. 69, table 25

MACEDONIAN (EQUATED WITH HEBREW)

1.	Peritios	Shebat (Jan/Feb)
2.	Dystros	Adar (Feb/Mar)
3.	Xanthikos	Nisan (Mar/Apr) (Josephus, *Ant.* I 3, 3 §81; III 10, 5 §248)
4.	Artemisios	Iyyar (Apr/May)
5.	Daisios	Sivan (May/June)
6.	Panemos	Tammuz (June/July)
7.	Loos	Ab (July/Aug)
8.	Gorpiaios	Elul (Aug/Sept)
9.	Hyperberetaios	Tishri (Sept/Oct)
10.	Dios	Marheshvan or Heshvan (Oct/Nov) (*Ant.* I 3, 3 §80)
11.	Apellaios	Kislev (Nov/Dec) (*Ant.* XI 5, 4 §148; XII 5, 4 §248; 7, 6 §319)
12.	Audynaios	Tebeth (Dec/Jan)

HEBREW (BABYLONIAN)

11.	Shebat	(Jan/Feb)
12.	Adar	(Feb/Mar)
1.	Nisan	(Mar/Apr) 14, Slaying of Passover Lamb, Ex 12:6 14-21, Feast of Unleavened Bread, Ex 12:18
2.	Iyyar	(Apr/May)
3.	Sivan	(May/June) Fiftieth Day, Lv 23:16
4.	Tammuz	(June/July)
5.	Ab	(July/Aug)
6.	Elul	(Aug/Sept)
7.	Tishri	(Sept/Oct) 10, Day of Atonement, Lv 16:29 15-21, Feast of Tabernacles, Lv 23:34
8.	Marheshvan or Heshvan	(Oct/Nov)
9.	Kislev	(Nov/Dec)
10.	Tebeth	(Dec/Jan)

Source: FHBC p. 30, table 9

NOTE ON MEASURES OF LENGTH AND STATEMENTS OF DIRECTION

IN THE ANCIENT sources such as have been listed above there are various references to distances and directions. The most important measures of length are: אמה.

HEBREW

CUBIT, THE ENGLISH word is derived from Greek κύβιτον and Latin *cubitum* which mean "elbow," hence is a measure approximately equal to the distance from the elbow to the finger tips. The usual Hebrew word is אמה which means "forearm" and "cubit," and this is usually rendered in the LXX by the Greek word πῆχυς which has the same two meanings. Dt 3:11 mentions the "cubit of a man" which RSV renders as the "common cubit." As the etymology of "cubit" suggests, the length of this ordinary cubit was presumably the average length of the forearm, say about 17.5 inches or in round numbers 18 inches, i.e., one and one-half English feet. Ezk 40:5 refers to a cubit which was a cubit and a handbreadth in length. RSV calls this a "long cubit." If the additional handbreadth be taken as nearly three inches additional this would make a long cubit of about 20.4 inches. The Siloam Tunnel (No. 176) is 1,749 feet long by Vincent's measurement, and the Hebrew inscription found in it says that it was 1,200 cubits in length. This gives a cubit 17.49 inches in length. Other evidence makes it probable that this same value of very close to seventeen and one-half inches is that of Josephus and of *Middoth* as they give measurements of the Jerusalem temple. R. B. Y. Scott in BA 22 (1959), pp. 22ff.; O. R. Sellers in IDB IV, pp. 837f.; R. Pearce S. Hubbard in PEQ 1966, p. 131.

GREEK

FOOT, πούς, ATTIC 295.7 MILLIMETERS, Olympic 320.5 mm., as compared with English 304.8 mm., say approximately one English foot.

Stadion or Stade, στάδιον, 600 feet, no matter what the length of the foot, Attic stadion 607 English feet, Olympic stadion (as measured from the race course at Olympia) 630.8 English feet, say approximately 600 English feet.

ROMAN

FOOT, PES, 296 MILLIMETERS, say approximately one English foot.

Pace or Step (probably actually a double pace), *passus*, five *pedes*, say approximately five English feet.

Stadium, *stadium*, 125 *passus*, 625 *pedes*, say approximately 600 English feet.

Mile, *mille passus*, a thousand paces, indicated by a *miliarium* or milestone, also called a *lapis* or (mile) stone (in Greek *mille* is used as a loan word in the form μίλιον, and a milestone is called a σημεῖον, literally a mark or sign), 5,000 Roman feet, eight *stadia*, approximately 4,854 English feet, two Roman miles = approximately 1.8 English miles, five Roman miles = approximately 4.5 English miles.

League, *leuca*, sometimes defined as 1,500 Roman paces or 1.5 Roman miles, is also otherwise reckoned, depending upon the source, from about 2.5 to 4.5 Roman miles.

ENGLISH AND METRIC EQUIVALENTS

12 inches = 1 foot
5,280 feet = 1 mile
1 millimeter = 0.039 inches
1 centimeter = 0.39 inches
1 meter = 39.37 inches
1 kilometer = 0.62 miles

EXAMPLES OF THE USE of some of the foregoing measures: Josephus says that the façade of the Temple edifice was of equal height and breadth, each dimension being a hundred cubits (ἀνὰ πήχεις ἑκατόν), i.e., about 150 feet (*War* v 5, 4 §207); Origen states that Bethany was fifteen stadia from Jerusalem (ἀπέχει τῶν Ἱεροσολύμων σταδίους δέκα πέντε), i.e., about 1.7 miles from the city (*Commentary on John* vi 24 GCS Origenes iv p. 149); Eusebius and Jerome locate Bethany at the second mile from Aelia (ἐν δευτέρῳ Αἰλίας σημείῳ; *in secundo ab Aelia miliario*), i.e., about 1.8 miles from Jerusalem (*Onomasticon*, pp. 58-59), and place Bethennim (the Ain of Jos 15:32) two miles from a certain terebinth tree (ἀπὸ β′ σημείων τῆς τερεβίνθου; *in secundo lapide a terebintho*) (*Onomasticon*, pp. 24-25); and the Bordeaux Pilgrim states that the spring of the prophet Elisha is 1,500 paces from the city of Jericho (*a ciuitate passos mille quingentos*), i.e., slightly less than a mile and one-half (Geyer p. 24; CCSL CLXXV, p. 18; WET p. 160).

As for directions it is often customary, as in the *Onomasticon*, to distinguish only the four cardinal directions, and "to the east" (πρὸς ἀνατολάς or πρὸς ἡλίου ἀνατολάς; *ad orientalem plagam*), for example, can mean east or anywhere in the eastern quarter such as northeast (*Onomasticon*, p. 20 line 16, p. 64 line 25).

With the above tabulation of measures readily available references are often allowed to stand in our text to cubits, stadia, etc., without giving conversion into English units. Also it is the case that some archeological reports use centimeters and meters while others employ inches, feet, and yards, and it has been deemed simpler and more accurate to reproduce the reported figures in whatever system is employed rather than to convert all into a single system, and again it is assumed that this will cause no difficulty.

LIST OF BISHOPS OF THE JERUSALEM CHURCH WITH EXPLANATORY COMMENTS

BISHOPS OF THE CIRCUMCISION

"THE FIRST BISHOPS that presided there [i.e., at Jerusalem] are said to have been Jews, and their names are preserved by the inhabitants of the country" (Eusebius, *Dem. Evang.* III 5, 103 GCS Eusebius VI p. 131). "The chronology of the bishops of Jerusalem I have nowhere found preserved in writing. . . . But I have learned this much from writings [presumably records preserved by the Jerusalem church], that until the siege of the Jews, which took place under Hadrian [in the Bar Kokhba revolt, 132-135], there were fifteen bishops in succession there, all of whom are said to have been of Hebrew descent" (Eusebius, *Ch. Hist.* IV 5; *Chron.* ed. Helm pp. 175-199; cf. Epiphanius, *Pan. haer.* 66, 20 GCS Holl/Dummer III, pp. 44f.; Syncellus, CSHB 30, pp. 620-661, 764f.; Nicephorus, *Chronographia Brevis*, MPG 100, cols. 1035-1040, also cols. 1039-1056 for the bishops of Rome, Constantinople, Alexandria, and Antioch).

With such information as is available about only a few of them, the list of the fifteen follows:[1]

1. James the Just, the brother of the Lord (Eusebius, *Ch. Hist.* II 1, 2-4). When Peter "departed and went to another place" after imprisonment by Herod Agrippa I (A.D. 44), he left a parting word for "James and . . . the brethren" (Ac 12:17) and thus apparently recognized James as the head of the Jerusalem church. Likewise when Paul came back at the end of his third missionary journey (A.D. 54 or 55) with the contribution collected among the Gentiles for the "poor" at Jerusalem, he and his party presented themselves to James and the elders,

and it was they—presumably with James as the head and the spokesman—who said to Paul, "You see, brother, how many thousands there are among the Jews of those who have believed; they are all zealous for the law" (Ac 21:20). Eventually, when the procurator Festus was dead and his successor Albinus was still en route (Josephus, *Ant.* xx 9, 1 §200), the high priest Ananus took this as a favorable opportunity to kill James, whose death is therefore dated in the year 61 (Eusebius, *Chron.* ed. Helm pp. 182f.).

2. Simeon, the son of the Lord's uncle Clopas and thus a cousin of the Lord (*Ch. Hist.* III 32, 6; IV 22, 4; *Chron.* ed. Helm p. 194). The choice of Simeon as the second bishop was "after James the Just had suffered martyrdom" (*Ch. Hist.* IV 22, 4), thus presumably in the year 61 (*Chron.* ed. Helm p. 183). Another statement places the event "after the martyrdom of James and the conquest of Jerusalem which immediately followed" (*Ch. Hist.* III 11), but the conquest of Jerusalem (in 70) did not follow the death of James (in 61) "immediately," so this statement is presumably incorrect not only in its apparent compression of the sequence of events, but also in its implication of such a long gap in the leadership of the Jerusalem church. Assuming the earlier date for the accession of Simeon, it must have been he who, in the time of the Jewish war against the Romans (66-73), led the people of the church to dwell in Pella, a city in Jordan and thus outside of Judea (*Ch. Hist.* III 5, 3) and then, after the war, led the return to Jerusalem, to which

---

1. Archbishop Dowling, "The Episcopal Succession in Jerusalem from c. A.D. 30, a Notitia of Fifteen Early (Hebrew) Bishops of Jerusalem, Twenty-six (Gentile) Bishops of Jerusalem, Ninety-four (Orthodox) Patriarchs of Jerusalem," in PEFQS 1913, pp. 164-177, 1914, pp. 33-40. For other dates and differences in names in lists of the Je-

rusalem bishops, see Adolf Harnack, *Geschichte der altchristlichen Literatur bis Eusebius*, II, *Die Chronologie*, 1, *Die Chronologie der Literatur bis Irenäeus nebst einleitenden Untersuchungen* (2d ed., Leipzig: J. C. Hinrichs, 1958), pp. 218-230.

Epiphanius (*On Weights and Measures* 14-15 [54d-55a] ed. Dean pp. 30f.) refers when he speaks of "such as had come back from the city of Pella to Jerusalem and were living there and teaching," the language suggesting that while some returned to Jerusalem others remained in Pella.

3. Justus
4. Zacchaeus
5. Tobias
6. Benjamin
7. John
8. Matthias
9. Philip
10. Seneca[2]
11. Justus
12. Levi
13. Ephres[3]
14. Joseph
15. Judas

BISHOPS OF THE GENTILES

WHEN THE BAR KOKHBA revolt was finally suppressed in A.D. 135 in the eighteenth year of Hadrian, the emperor proceeded with his plan to rebuild Jerusalem as a Roman city and colony under the name of Colonia Aelia (Hadrian's family name) Capitolina (referring to the Capitoline Jupiter, the chief Roman god), a municipal area in which no Jew would be permitted. As Eusebius relates (*Ch. Hist.* IV 6, 3), "the whole nation (τό πᾶν ἔθνος) [of the Jews] was prohibited from this time on by a decree, and by the commands of Hadrian, from ever going up to the country about Jerusalem. For the emperor gave orders that they should not even see from a distance the land of their fathers. Such is the account of Ariston of Pella." This Ariston of Pella is known as the author of a lost *Dialogue of Jason* (a Jewish Christian) *and Papiscus* (an Alexandrian Jew) *concerning Christ*, Ariston himself probably being a Judeo-Christian of around A.D. 140, and it may well have been from this *Dialogue* that Euse-

bius derived the information about Hadrian's action of exclusion of the Jews from Aelia Capitolina.[4]

From this and other ancient references to Hadrian's action it is supposed that the emperor's orders took the form of a resolution adopted at his recommendation by the Roman Senate (*senatus consultum*), a resolution which decreed that it was forbidden henceforth for all circumcised persons to enter and to stay within the territory of Aelia Capitolina, and that any person contravening this prohibition should be put to death. That the prohibition was enforced by the death penalty is confirmed by Justin (*Apology* I 47; cf. *Dialogue with Trypho* 16 and 92), who remarks that "death is decreed against a Jew apprehended entering it [Jerusalem]." The interdict applied not just to the city proper but to the entire municipal territory of Aelia Capitolina, which included the mountains immediately surrounding the city, known as Oreine ("the hill country," Lk 1:65), and extended northward to Gophna and southward to Herodium and Bethlehem. The inclusion of Bethlehem in the forbidden area is confirmed in his time (A.D. c. 200) by Tertullian (*An Answer to the Jews* 13, ANF III, p. 169), when he writes that "none of the race of Israel has remained in Bethlehem; and (so it has been) ever since the interdict was issued forbidding any one of the Jews to linger in the confines of the very district."[5]

Whether the exclusion edict of Hadrian applied equally to the Judeo-Christians as well as to the Jews of the Jewish religion is not entirely clear. As to the attitude of Hadrian to the Christians in general, Eusebius (*Ch. Hist.* IV 3 and 9; *Chron.* ed. Helm p. 199) tells us that when Hadrian was in Athens in the year 125, both Quadratus "a disciple of the apostles," and Aristides "an Athenian philosopher," presented "apologies" (i.e., defenses) for Christianity to the emperor, and there is a brief quotation from Quadratus in Eusebius. A full Syriac version of the Apology of Aristides was found in the Monastery of St. Catherine at Mount Sinai, in which Aristides contrasts the Christians favorably in regard to their knowledge of the truth in comparison with the "barbarians," the Greeks, and the Jews (ANF IX, pp. 259-279). Eusebius (*Ch. Hist.* IV 9) quotes a letter of Hadrian to Minucius Fundanus, proconsul of Asia, in which he wishes the Christians to be protected by law from tumul-

---

2. Seneca is a Latin name, but it was common for Jews to bear a Latin or Greek name as well as a Hebrew name, and even to use one of the former instead of the latter.

3. For Ephres, Syncellus (CSHB 30, pp. 661, 765) gives Ephraim, which is the Hebrew form of this name.

4. Rendel Harris, "Hadrian's Decree of Expulsion of the Jews from Jerusalem," in HTR 19 (1928), pp. 199-206. For Ariston, see Harnack, *Geschichte der altchristlichen Literatur bis Eusebius*, II, 1 (2d ed., 1958), pp. 268f.

5. Michael Avi-Yonah, a work published in Hebrew in 1946, Ger. ed., *Geschichte der Juden in Zeitalter des Talmud in den Tagen von Rom*

und Byzanz (Studia Judaica, Forschungen zur Wissenschaft des Judentums, II) (Berlin: Walter de Gruyter, 1962); Eng. eds., *The Jews of Palestine: A Political History from the Bar Kokhba War to the Arab Conquest* (New York: Schocken Books, 1976); and *The Jews under Roman and Byzantine Rule: A Political History of Palestine from the Bar Kokhba War to the Arab Conquest* (New York: Schocken Books, 1984), pp. 50f.; Peter Schäfer, *Geschichte der Juden in der Antike: Die Juden Palästinas von Alexander dem Grossen bis zur arabischen Eroberung* (Stuttgart: Katholisches Bibelwerk; Neukirchen-Vluyn: Neukirchener Verlag, 1983), p. 174.

tuous and illegal proceedings against them. It is also the case that the Christians did not join in the Bar Kokhba war against Hadrian, and Eusebius (*Chron.* ed. Helm p. 201) records that Bar Kokhba killed them in all kinds of persecutions because they were not willing to help him against the Romans, while Justin (*Apol.* I 31 ANF I, p. 173) says: "In the Jewish war which lately raged, Bar Kokhba . . . gave orders that Christians alone should be led to cruel punishments, unless they would deny Jesus Christ and utter blasphemy." It is possible, therefore, that a distinction was made between the Judeo-Christians, as belonging to the category of Christians, and the Jews of the Jewish religion, and the former were allowed to return quickly to Jerusalem.[6]

On the other hand, the edict of Hadrian was directed against all circumcised persons and the whole nation of the Jews, which terms would seem plainly to include all Jews whether converted to Christianity or not; therefore it must be judged more probable that Judeo-Christians as well as Jews of the Jewish religion were excluded by Hadrian's ban from his new city.[7] Gentiles had no doubt been increasing in numbers in Jerusalem after the First Revolt of the Jews against Rome as well as now after the Second Revolt, and thus the Christian church in Jerusalem became a church from the Gentiles and, from Hadrian on, its leaders were a line of Gentile bishops.

Officially, at least, the interdiction of Jewish presence in Jerusalem inaugurated by Hadrian continued in effect for some two hundred years. Antoninus Pius (138-161), Hadrian's immediate successor, lifted an even earlier ban by Hadrian on the practice of circumcision to the extent that this rite was again made permissible for sons born to Jewish parents (but was not permissible for other nationalities, i.e., it was not permitted to make proselytes), but

the exclusion of all Jews from Aelia Capitolina was continued.[8]

Nevertheless, it may be supposed that as time went on the ban instituted by Hadrian and probably continued by Antoninus Pius and his successors was not always enforced with a full degree of strictness. As seen in the several following examples, it appears from Talmudic sources that some Jews managed to visit Jerusalem possibly already in the second century and certainly in the third. According to a story with obviously legendary features, Rabbi Jose ben Halafta (in the fourth generation of the Tannaim, c. 140-c. 165, JE VII, pp. 241f.; XII, p. 49) related: "I was once traveling on the road, and I entered into one of the ruins of Jerusalem in order to pray," and he went on to declare that he heard a divine voice, cooing like a dove, which said, "Woe to the children, on account of whose sins I destroyed My house and burnt My temple and exiled them among the nations of the world," whereupon the prophet Elijah appeared to him and told him that this voice exclaimed thus three times every day (*Berakoth* 3a, SBT I, pp. 6f.). References to "the holy community in Jerusalem," which was studying questions of the Law during the patriarchate of the patriarch Judah I (c. 135-c. 220, JE VII, p. 333), suggest that a group of rabbis was actually resident there in that time. Another story concerns a donkey driver named Simeon bar Kantra (in the time of the fifth generation of the Tannaim, in the first half of the third century), who asked the rabbis if, during his business travels, he would have to rend his garments every time he passed Jerusalem, a ritual required of those who looked upon the desolation of the Temple. Similarly Rabbi Johanan (a scholar of the second generation of the Amoraim, in the second half of the third century) contrasted the earthly

---

6. Bellarmino Bagatti, *The Church from the Circumcision: History and Archaeology of the Judaeo-Christians* (PSBFSS 2) (Jerusalem: Franciscan Printing Press, 1971), p. 10; and *The Church from the Gentiles in Palestine: History and Archaeology* (PSBFSS 4) (Jerusalem: Franciscan Printing Press, 1971), p. 11.

7. Teddy Kollek and Moshe Pearlman, *Jerusalem, A History of Forty Centuries* (Rev. ed., New York: Random House, 1972. Reprint, 1974), p. 140; E. Mary Smallwood, *The Jews under Roman Rule: From Pompey to Diocletian* (Studies in Judaism in Late Antiquity, ed. Jacob Neusner, vol. 20) (Leiden: E. J. Brill, 1976), p. 460; Avi-Yonah, *The Jews under Roman and Byzantine Rule*, pp. 50f.

8. Amnon Linder, *The Jews in Roman Imperial Legislation* (Detroit: Wayne State University Press; Jerusalem: Israel Academy of Sciences and Humanities, 1987), pp. 99-102; SHJP Vermes/Millar, pp. 539, 555; Smallwood, *The Jews under Roman Rule*, p. 478. In the early Aramaic work *Megillat Taanit* (scroll of fasting), which gives a list of thirty-six days on which there were happy events in the history of the Jews during the Second Temple period, on the anniversaries of which fasting was therefore forbidden, an item in the month of Adar reads: "On the 28th day thereof (Adar) the good news reached the Jews that they were not to be restrained from the study of the Law. It is not permitted to mourn thereon." In much later Hebrew scholia appended to the work, this

day is explained as marking the abrogation of Hadrian's harsh decree. Heinrich Graetz (*History of the Jews* [Philadelphia: Jewish Publication Society of America, 1941], II, pp. 432f.) accepts the scholiast's explanation and dates the event celebrated in *Megillat Taanit* in A.D. 139/140, but notes that Antoninus Pius did not repeal the law forbidding the Jews to enter Jerusalem. Frédéric Manns ("L'histoire du Judéo-Christianisme," in *Studia Oecumenica Hierosolymitana* I, Papers, read at the 1979 Tantur Conference on Christianity in the Holy Land, ed. D.-M. A. Jaeger, p. 142) also cites *Megillat Taanit* and thinks that the action of Antoninus Pius allowed both Jews and Judeo-Christians to return to Jerusalem at once. All the other items in the list in *Megillat Taanit*, however, pertain to events prior to the destruction of the Second Temple (A.D. 70), and it may therefore be judged more probable that the item for the twenty-eighth day of Adar also refers to some earlier event prior to A.D. 70. If this is so, the scholiast's explanation must be incorrect and there can be no connection with Hadrian and Antoninus Pius (Solomon Zeitlin, *Megillat Taanit as a Source for Jewish Chronology and History in the Hellenistic and Roman Periods* [Philadelphia, 1922], pp. 79f.; Hans Lichtenstein, "Die Fastenrolle, Eine Untersuchung zur jüdisch-hellenistischen Geschichte," in HUCA VIII-IX [1931-1932], p. 279).

Jerusalem with the heavenly city by saying, "(To) Jerusalem of the present world, anyone who wishes goes up, but to that of the world to come only those invited will go" (*Baba Bathra* 75b, SBT XXI, p. 302).[9]

In the fourth century under Constantine the old edict of Hadrian was still, as far as we know, in effect, even if often evaded in practice, but the emperor made two changes.[10] For one thing, it was now apparently only the city of Jerusalem itself and not its whole territory in which Jewish presence was prohibited; thus during the earlier years of his life at Bethlehem (A.D. 386 and following) Jerome had a Jew named Bar Aninas as a teacher, the latter for fear of other Jews coming to Jerome by night, like "a second edition of Nicodemus" (Jn 3:2; Jerome, *Letter* 84 NPNFSS VI, p. 176). For another and important matter, it was now under Constantine that the Jews were permitted to go to Jerusalem once a year, on the anniversary of the destruction of the city (reckoned by the rabbis as having been on the ninth day of the month of Ab in both 586 B.C. and A.D. 70), for the purpose of lamentation at the site of the Temple.

This annual event of lamentation is described by both the Bordeaux Pilgrim (333) and Jerome. The Bordeaux Pilgrim mentions two statues in the Temple area (understood by the pilgrim to be statues of Hadrian) and says (Geyer p. 33; LPPTS I-B, p. 22; CCSL CLXXV, p. 16; WET p. 157): "and not far from the statues there is a perforated stone (*lapis pertusus*, probably the sacred rock under the present Dome of the Rock, in which various holes are still to be seen, No. 180) to which the Jews come every year and anoint it, bewail themselves with groans, rend their garments, and so depart." Jerome speaks of the ban of the Jews from entering Jerusalem as continuing "up to the present day . . . except for lamentation" (*usque ad praesentem diem . . . excepto planctu*, the last word meaning in particular a beating of the breast, arms, and face in mourning), and goes on to portray a sad spectacle that to him exhibits divine punishment: "On the (anniversary of the) day on which Jerusalem was captured and destroyed by the Romans, you can see a mournful people come together, decrepit women and old men marked by rags and years, showing in their bodies and in their clothes the wrath of the Lord" (*Commentary on Zephaniah* i 15-16; SHJP Vermes/Millar i, p. 557; Peters, *Jerusalem*, pp. 144f.).

Only in the fifth century, through the intervention of the empress Eudocia (wife of Theodosius II, living in Je-

rusalem 444-460), was the 200-year-old ban finally canceled and Jews again allowed to settle in the city.[11]

Returning now to the time when Hadrian first instituted his ban on the presence of all those of the race of the Jews (probably including Christians of Jewish descent) in his newly founded Aelia Capitolina, Eusebius (*Ch. Hist.* IV 6, 4) goes on with his account: "And thus when the city had been emptied of the Jewish nation and had suffered the total destruction of its ancient inhabitants, it was colonized by a different race. . . . And as the church there was now composed of Gentiles, the first one to assume the government of it after the bishops of the circumcision was Marcus." Beginning with this Marcus, Eusebius later (*Ch. Hist.* v 12; *Chron.* ed. Helm pp. 201-209; cf. Epiphanius, *Pan. haer.* 66, 20 GCS Holl/Dummer III, pp. 46f.; Syncellus, CSHB 30, pp. 661-670, 765f.) gives a list of fifteen bishops of the Gentiles, as follows (here numbered in sequence from the fifteen bishops of the circumcision):

16. Marcus
17. Cassianus
18. Publius
19. Maximus
20. Julian
21. Gaius
22. Symmachus
23. another Gaius
24. another Julian
25. Capito
26. another Maximus
27. Antoninus
28. Valens
29. Dolichianus
30. Narcissus. In A.D. 212 Bishop Alexander of Cappadocia (see above under "Chronological List of Ancient Sources") came to Jerusalem and became bishop along with Narcissus. Alexander is quoted by Eusebius (*Ch. Hist.* VI, 11, 4) as saying that Narcissus was then 116 years of age.

Beyond this point the episcopal names continue to be noted in Eusebius down to Macarius (314-333), the thirty-ninth in the succession from James, during whose rule Helena visited the Holy Land (d. c. 327) and with whom Constantine corresponded (for *Ch. Hist.* references, NPNFSS I, p. 402; *Chron.* ed. Helm p. 230). Of later bishops of Jerusalem the second successor of Macarius was Cyril I, who is especially known for his *Catechet-*

9. Avi-Yonah, *The Jews under Roman and Byzantine Rule*, pp. 80f.; and *Geschichte der Juden*, p. 81 n. 146 for Talmudic references; Smallwood, *The Jews under Roman Rule*, p. 500 (both Avi-Yonah and Smallwood cite S. Safrai in *Scripta Hierosolymitana* 23 [1972], pp. 62-78); FDI p. 54.

10. Avi-Yonah, *The Jews under Roman and Byzantine Rule*, p. 164.

11. Kollek and Pearlman, *Jerusalem, A History of Forty Centuries*, p. 140. For edicts of Theodosius II in the years 420 and 423 ruling in the name of public law that Jewish synagogues and private houses should not be burned or wrongfully damaged, although new synagogues should not be built, see Linder, *The Jews in Roman Imperial Legislation*, pp. 283-295.

ical Lectures delivered in 348 (NPNFSS VII, pp. 1-183). In turn, Cyril's third successor and thus the forty-fourth in succession from James was Juvenal (422-458), and it was in his time that the empress Eudocia lived in Jerusalem (444-460). At the Council of Chalcedon (451) Juvenal obtained for the church of Jerusalem the dignity of a patriarchate, with jurisdiction over the three provinces of Palestine, and Juvenal became the first patriarch of Jerusalem, the title thereafter borne by the head of the Jerusalem church (NSH VI, pp. 287f.).

THE JUDEO-CHRISTIANS

THE MODERN TERM *Judeo-Christians* is used for the early Christians who were of Jewish descent, in contrast with those of Gentile descent, and thus it is necessary to distinguish in Palestine "the church from the circumcision" and "the church from the Gentiles."[1] Like the many thousands (RSV) or more probably many tens of thousands (πόσαι μυριάδες, literally "myriads," a very large number, not exactly defined, cf. the identical words in Josephus, *Ant.* VII 13, 1 §318, trans. "many tens of thousands," LCL V, p. 531) described to Paul at Jerusalem (Ac 21:20), the Judeo-Christians "believed" and at the same time were "zealous for the law." The belief was plainly belief in Jesus as Messiah (Christ), and the zeal for the law meant observance of the precepts of the Torah concerning such matters as circumcision, dietary requirements, and special days.

In the Greek-speaking Gentile church belief in Jesus as Christ (Χριστός) led to the name Christian (Χριστιανός), attested first at Antioch (Ac 11:26) and found in Ac 26:28 in the words of King Agrippa to Paul and in 1 Pet 4:16. The Judeo-Christians, however, were called by other names, of which the most widely used were Nazarenes and Ebionites. Jesus is the Nazoraean or Nazarene (Ναζωραῖος, Ναζαρηνός) as a resident of Nazareth (Ναζαρέτ) and as the fulfillment of prophecy (Mt 2:23, perhaps alluding to the "shoot [נצר] from the stump of Jesse," Isa 11:1, cf. Erich Klostermann in HZNT 4, p. 19); and in Ac 24:5 Paul is himself accounted a leader of the sect (αἵρεσις) of the Nazarenes (Ναζωραῖοι). In Rom 15:26 and Gal 2:10 the people of the Jerusalem church are the "poor" (πτωχοί) as well as the "saints" (ἅγιοι),

and the former name reflects the very frequent Old Testament mention of the humble "poor" (אביונים) as the recipients of favor and help from God (Ps 86:1; Isa 25:4, cf. Hans Lietzmann in HZNT 8, p. 123); hence from the Hebrew the name Ebionites, and the designation of the Judeo-Christians by this name.

Both names, Nazarenes and Ebionites, are used by later writers of the Gentile church (see below) for the Judeo-Christians, and for them these writers also often use the term *sect* (αἵρεσις) in the later disapproving sense of "heresy." In Talmudic sources the term מין (*min*, plural *minim*) also describes persons who are sectarians or heretics in the sense that they are within the Jewish community but are false to it, and in most of its occurrences it probably refers to the Judeo-Christians ("Minim" literally means "Kinds," that is of a different "Kind" from Jews [Vardaman]). In their observance of the precepts of the Torah the Judeo-Christians were certainly still living within the acceptable framework of Jewish life, and even their belief that Jesus was the Messiah was not necessarily ground for ostracism, even as in his time Rabbi Akiba seems to have been free to believe that Bar Kokhba was the Messiah, and early relations between Jews and Jewish Christians were not necessarily unfriendly. An example is in a conversation that took place in Sepphoris probably in the early second century between Rabbi Eliezer and a Judeo-Christian, Jacob of Kefar Sekaniah, in which the rabbi listened with pleasure to the interpretation of a verse in the Torah (Dt 23:18), which Jacob said he had received from Jesus (*Abodah Zarah* 16b-17a SBT XXV, p. 85; *Midrash Rabbah*,

1. Bellarmino Bagatti, *The Church from the Circumcision: History and Archaeology of the Judaeo-Christians* (PSBFSS 2) (Jerusalem: Franciscan Printing Press, 1971); and *The Church from the Gentiles in Palestine: History and Archaeology* (PSBFSS 4) (Jerusalem: Franciscan Printing Press, 1971). For the Judeo-Christians, see also: E. Testa, *Il simbolismo dei Giudeo-Cristiani* (PSBF 14) (Jerusalem: Franciscan Printing Press, 1962) (for criticism of this work, see Erich Dinkler in JAC 5 [1962], pp. 108f.); Jean Daniélou, *Primitive Christian Symbols* (Baltimore: Helicon Press, 1964); and *The Theology of Jewish Christianity* (Philadelphia: Westminster Press, 1977); Albert Storme, "L'église de la circoncision," in AJBA 1 (1968), pp. 29-40; Ignazio Mancini, *Archaeological Discoveries relative to the Judaeo-Christians* (PSBFCM 10) (Jerusalem: Franciscan Printing Press, 1970); Bruce J. Malina, "Jewish Christianity: A Select Bibliography," in AJBA 2.2 (1973), pp. 60-65; Frédéric Manns, *Essais sur le Judéo-Christianisme* (PSBFA 12) (Jerusalem: Franciscan Printing Press, 1977); and *Bibliographie du judéo-christianisme* (PSBFA 13) (Jeru-

salem: Franciscan Printing Press, 1979); and "L'histoire du judéo-christianisme," in *Studia Oecumenica Hierosolymitana* I, Papers read at the 1979 Tantur Conference on Christianity in the Holy Land, ed. D.-M. A. Jaeger (Tantur, Jerusalem: Ecumenical Institute for Theological Research, 1981), pp. 1131-145; James F. Strange, "Diversity in Early Palestinian Christianity, Some Archaeological Evidences," in ATR 65 (1983), pp. 14-24; Stephen Goranson in BA 51 (1988), pp. 70f.; Eric M. Meyers, "Early Judaism and Christianity in the Light of Archaeology," in BA 51 (1988), pp. 69-79; Eric M. Meyers and L. Michael White, "Jews and Christians in a Roman World," in *Archaeology* 42 (Mar/Apr 1989), pp. 28f.; Ray A. Pritz, *Nazarene Jewish Christianity, From the End of the New Testament Period Until Its Disappearance in the Fourth Century* (Studia Post-Biblica 37) (Jerusalem: The Magnes Press, The Hebrew University; Leiden: E. J. Brill, 1988); Solomon Landers, *The Church That Disappeared*, f. BR 7, 4 (Aug. 1991), p. 2, not available at present writing.

Ecclesiastes, I 8 SMR VIII, p. 27; cf. below, No. 87). When, however, along with Gentile Christians, Judeo-Christians ascribed to Jesus a position that seemed to infringe on the divine unity there was controversy, and sometime after A.D. 80 under Rabbi Gamaliel a prayer against them as *minim* was inserted in the collection known as the Eighteen Benedictions (*Shemenoh 'Esreh*, JE XI, p. 281).[2]

In the preceding section on the bishops of the Jerusalem church we have seen that when Hadrian rebuilt Jerusalem as Aelia Capitolina (A.D. 135) he prohibited the whole nation of the Jews from coming there, a ruling which probably excluded the Judeo-Christians as well, so that from then onward the Jerusalem church "was composed of Gentiles" and its heads were Gentiles (Eusebius, *Ch. Hist.* IV 6, 4). Nevertheless in Palestine as a whole the Judeo-Christians certainly continued to exist, and there are many examples that reflect their continuing presence and significance.

A question on which there was much discussion was whether Easter should be celebrated on the fourteenth day of Nisan (the date of the Jewish Passover, Ex 12:6, which could fall on any day of the week) or only on the Lord's day (Sunday). The former view was undoubtedly held especially by the Judeo-Christians and the latter by the Gentile Christians, and Epiphanius (*Pan. haer.* 70.9.9 P821 GCS Epiphanius III, p. 242) says that controversy over this subject arose "after the time of the bishops of the circumcision." In A.D. 196 the matter was under discussion at a council in Palestine over which Theophilus bishop of Caesarea and Narcissus bishop of Jerusalem (see "List of Bishops of the Jerusalem Church") presided (*Ch. Hist.* V 23, 2; *Chron.* ed. Helm p. 211),[3] and with the dominance of the Gentile bishops the decision was for the Sunday usage, as it was also finally affirmed by the Council of Nicaea (325), which addressed a letter to "the brethren" about its decisions and reported: "We have also gratifying intelligence to communicate to you relative to unity of judgment on the subject of the most holy feast of Easter: for this point also has been happily settled through your prayers; so that all the brethren in the East who have heretofore kept this festival when the Jews did, will henceforth conform to the Romans and to us, and to all who from the earliest

time have observed our period of celebrating Easter" (Sozomen, *Ch. Hist.* I 9 NPNFSS II, p. 13).[4]

Other examples indicative of continuing Judeo-Christian presence and significance in Palestine include the following: For his study of the Old Testament (the results embodied in his *Hexapla* and biblical commentaries) Origen (living at Caesarea c. 230) learned the Hebrew language (Eusebius, *Ch. Hist.* VII 16, 1), probably from Judeo-Christians, and discussed scriptural passages with persons of that background. On Isaiah 6:3 Origen writes (*On Principles* I 3, 4 ANF IV, p. 253): "My Hebrew master used to say that those two seraphim in Isaiah which are described as . . . calling to one another, and saying, 'Holy, holy, holy, is the Lord God of hosts,' were to be understood of the only-begotten Son of God and of the Holy Spirit," an exegesis certainly not Jewish but Jewish-Christian. About the meaning of the Hebrew letter taw Origen (*Selecta in Ezechielem* 9 MPG XIII cols. 800-801) asked three Jews, among whom was "one of those who believe in Christ," and this one provided the obviously Judeo-Christian explanation that the taw symbolizes the Cross (cf. p. 786). Jerome recalls his earlier time in the desert when he betook himself "to a brother who was a believer from among the Hebrews" (*fratri, qui ex Hebraeis crediderat*) in order to learn the Hebrew language (*Letter* 125, 12 MPL XXII col. 1079), and again he speaks of another, who is apparently also a believer, as simply a Hebrew (*Hebraeus*) (*Commentary on Habakkuk* II 3 MPL 25 col. 1311). At Jerusalem, according to Eusebius (*Ch. Hist.* VI 19), "the chair (θρόνος) of James," believed to be the episcopal seat of the first bishop of Jerusalem, was preserved until Eusebius' own time, another indication of the continuity of Christian tradition in the city in spite of the transition from Judeo-Christian to Gentile leadership in the church. Archeological remains attributable to the Judeo-Christians are discussed below (e.g., the synagogue-church at Nazareth [No. 46] and the house-church at Capernaum [No. 99]).

Literary descriptions of Judeo-Christian practices and beliefs are found chiefly in writers of the larger church and are often directed against them or some of them.[5]

In his *Dialogue with Trypho* (46-48 ANF I, pp. 217-219) Justin Martyr is asked by the Jew whether someone who believes that Jesus is the Christ but at the same time

---

2. R. Travers Herford, "The Problem of the 'Minim' Further Considered," in *Jewish Studies in Memory of George A. Kohut*, ed. Salo W. Baron and Alexander Marx (New York: Alexander Kohut Memorial Foundation, 1935).

3. The *Libellus Synodicus* (also called the *Synodicon*, it contains brief notices of 158 councils of the first nine centuries) makes the Caesarea council into two synods, one at Jerusalem under Narcissus and one at Caesarea under Theophilus (Karl Joseph von Hefele, *A History of Councils of the Church from the Original Documents*, 5 vols. [Edinburgh: T. and T. Clark, 1876-1896], I [2d ed., 1883], p. 80).

4. The approved time was that which had been established at Al-

exandria, namely the first Sunday after the first full moon following the vernal equinox (March 21). See Louis Duchesne, *Early History of the Christian Church* (4th ed., New York: Longmans, Green, 1922), II, p. 111.

5. A. F. J. Klijn and G. J. Reinink, *Patristic Evidence for Jewish-Christian Sects* (SNT 36) (Leiden: E. J. Brill, 1973); Igino Grego, *La reazione ai Giudeo-Cristiani nel IV secolo negli scritti patristici e nei canoni conciliari* (Quaderni de "La Terra Santa") (Jerusalem: Franciscan Printing Press, 1973). For extant written works that reflect or are the direct product of Jewish Christian thought, see Daniélou, *The Theology of Jewish Christianity*, pp. 11-54.

wishes to observe the Mosaic ordinances (which amounts to a concise definition of a Judeo-Christian) will be saved, and Justin replies that in his opinion such a person will be saved, provided he does not try to impose the same ordinances on Gentiles. "I hold," says Justin, "that we ought to join ourselves to such, and associate with them in all things as kinsmen and brethren." Of course, if one such falls back and denies that Jesus is the Christ, he will not, in Justin's opinion, be saved. When Trypho raises a further question, however, in connection with Justin's belief "that this Christ existed as God before the ages, then that he submitted to be born and become man," Justin makes it plain that he does not agree with those who do not hold this belief but hold instead that Jesus was a man who only became Christ when he was chosen and anointed. There were thus evidently two kinds of Judeo-Christians, distinguishable in terms of Christological belief, and Justin cannot agree with those who do not hold the doctrine that he considers orthodox.

In his work *Against Heresies* (I 26, 2 ANF I, p. 352; Klijn and Reinink pp. 104-105) Irenaeus (180), bishop of Lyons, describes Judeo-Christians whom he must have known elsewhere than in Palestine[6] under the name of Ebionites. With obvious disapproval Irenaeus says that the Ebionites use only the Gospel according to Matthew and have nothing to do with the apostle Paul; they practice circumcision and observe the customs enjoined by the Law; they are so Jewish in their manner of life that they even adore Jerusalem as if it were the house of God (probably meaning that like the Jews they even face in that direction in prayer [cf. Epiphanius, *Pan. haer.* I 19, 3, 5; Williams NHS 35, p. 46]).[7]

Like Justin Martyr, Origen (230) also recognizes two kinds of Judeo-Christians. In his work *Against Celsus* (V 61 ANF IV, p. 570; Klijn and Reinink pp. 134-135) Origen speaks of some who accept Jesus but regulate their lives like the multitude of Jews in accordance with the Jewish law and says: "And these are the twofold sect of the Ebionites, who either acknowledge with us that Jesus was born of a virgin, or deny this, and maintain that he was begotten like other human beings." Here Origen evidently uses the name Ebionites as inclusive of both of these two kinds of Jewish Christians.

Eusebius (325) also uses the name Ebionites as inclusive of two kinds of Judeo-Christians, but his description of the two kinds does not distinguish them very clearly (*Ch. Hist.* III 27; Klijn and Reinink pp. 140-141). Speaking of them all, he says that they were called Ebionites "because they held poor and mean opinions concerning Christ," which opinions consisted in considering Jesus a plain and ordinary man who achieved righteousness only because of his superior character and had been born naturally from Mary and her husband. Some of the same name, however, did not deny that Jesus was born of a virgin and of the Holy Spirit, but nevertheless they did not acknowledge his preexistence. They rejected the epistles of Paul and used the Gospel according to the Hebrews. "Wherefore . . . they received the name of Ebionites, which signified the poverty of their understanding. For this is the name by which a poor man is called among the Hebrews." Elsewhere, in his *Commentary on Psalms* (MPG 23, cols. 1008-1009) Eusebius quotes Psalm 84:4 (LXX 83:5)—"Blessed are those who dwell in thy house"—and then goes on to speak against those who are obviously Judeo-Christians: "He did not say: blessed are the circumcised nor those who observe the Sabbath, nor those who keep the Mosaic sacrifices and the other commandments of the corporal law; also not those who are descended from Abraham, neither the Israelite nor the Jewish people, but simply all those who dwell in the house of the Lord."

Cyril of Jerusalem (348) is evidently making a distinction from Judeo-Christian usage when he emphasizes the importance of correct terminology for the church that he himself represents. He says (*Catechetical Lecture* XVIII 26 MPG 33, col. 1048; NPNFSS VII, p. 140): "When you are a sojourner in any city, do not ask simply where the Lord's house (κυριακός) is, for the other sects of the impious also give this name to their own caves (σπήλαια), nor ask merely where the church (ἐή κλησία) is, but where is the catholic church (ἡκαθολικὴ ἐκκλησία)." From this we also learn that the Judeo-Christian place of worship was often a cave or an edifice focused upon a cave, and when we remember that the *Protevangelium of James* (19.2 James p. 46; HSNT I, p. 384) says that at the time of the birth of Jesus in the cave at Bethlehem the cave was overshadowed by a bright cloud, it is not surprising to find that such a sacred grotto is called a "most luminous cave" (*spelunca lucidissima*, e.g., at Nazareth, No. 53), i.e., a grotto illuminated by the divine presence. So in turn Gentile churches might also rise later over these same "mystic caves" (μυστικὰ ἄντρα), as Eusebius calls them (*Life of Constantine* III 43), referring to the grotto at Bethlehem and also the grotto on the Mount of Olives.[8]

Of these church writers Epiphanius (367) is the first to give the name of the Nazoraeans (Nazarenes), and in his *Panarion* (I 29, 1, 1-9, 5; Williams NHS 35, pp. 112-119; Klijn and Reinink pp. 168-169) he speaks at length of and against them. They did not name themselves after Christ or with Jesus' own name, but "Nazoraeans" (Ναζ-

---

6. Klijn and Reinink, op. cit., p. 69.

7. John Wilkinson, "Orientation, Jewish and Christian," in PEQ 1984, p. 17.

8. E. Testa, "Le 'Grotte dei Misteri' Giudeo-Cristiane," in LA 14 (1964), pp. 65-144; Bagatti, *Church from Circumcision*, pp. 133-136.

ωραῖοι, i.e., Nazarenes). At that time, Epiphanius goes on to say, all Christians were called Nazarenes (cf. Ac 24:5). For a short while they were also called "Jessaeans," either from Jesse the father of David or from the name of Jesus (although he had previously said that they did not name themselves with Jesus' own name). They use both the Old Testament and the New Testament. They acknowledge the resurrection, the divine creation of all things, and that God is one and that his son is Jesus Christ. They are different from both Jews and Christians, from Jews because they have faith in Christ, and from Christians because they are still bound by the Law in observance of circumcision, the Sabbath, and the rest. In spite of this adherence to the Law, they are hated by the Jews themselves because they preach that Jesus is the Christ, and the Jews utter imprecations against them three times a day. The Nazarenes have the Gospel according to Matthew in its entirety in Hebrew. They live in Beroea near Coelesyria (east of Antioch), at Cochaba in Bashanitis (north of Pella and east of Mount Hermon), and near Pella in the Decapolis, where they settled after they left Jerusalem in the Jewish war against the Romans.[9]

Epiphanius also tells us that the Nazoraeans (Nazarenes) wished to be called only by this name and not by the name Christian: "For this group did not name themselves after Christ or with Jesus' own name, but 'Nazoraeans' " (*Pan. haer.* XXIX 1, 2 GCS I, p. 321; Williams NHS 35, p. 112). Likewise, Epiphanius says, the Ebionites did not wish to call their places of worship "churches" but "synagogues" (cf. Jas 2:2): "Ebionites . . . call their church (ἐκκλησία) a synagogue (συναγωγή), not a church" (*Pan. haer.* XXX 18, 2 GCS I, p. 357; Williams NHS 35, pp. 133f.).

Not to be confused with the Nazoraeans/Nazarenes is another group that Epiphanius names and describes separately (*Pan. haer.* I 18, 1, 1-3, 5; 29, 6, 1; Williams NHS 35, pp. 42-44, 116), namely, the Nasaraeans (Ναασαραῖοι), a pre-Christian Jewish sect. Although they were originally from Gileaditis, Bashanitis, and Jordan—regions much like those attributed to the Judeo-Christians—they are certainly not in any sense Christians, for Epiphanius says flatly that "the Nasaraean sect was before Christ, and did not know Christ." They are Jews who practice Judaism "in all respects." They acknowl-

edge the Jewish patriarchs and fathers and Moses, and they observe circumcision, the Sabbath, and the Jewish feasts. On the other hand they do not accept the Pentateuch, nor will they offer sacrifice or eat meat. The later Mandaeans, it may be added, used the similar name, Nasoraeans, but are hardly the same people, for the Mandaeans opposed Judaism and did not practice it "in all respects," and were distinguished by baptismal practices of which Epiphanius says nothing in connection with the Nasaraeans (FMM pp. 259ff.).

As for the Ebionites ('Εβιωναῖοι), whose name was first mentioned by Irenaeus, Epiphanius writes a long chapter against them (I 30, 1, 1-34, 9; Williams NHS 35, pp. 119-151; Klijn and Reinink pp. 174-192). They are said to have gotten their start after the fall of Jerusalem, when the believers had settled in Pella, and their territory is much the same as that of the Nazarenes (Cochaba, Bashanitis, etc.) A certain Ebion is presented as their founder, and he is said to have "emerged" from the Nazoraeans; although the personal name may be only an imaginary construction from the name of the group (see above, p. xxxix), the statement may preserve a recollection of the "emergence" of the Ebionites from the early Jerusalem community that withdrew to Pella. Although this Ebion was, Epiphanius says, of the Nazoraeans' school, he preached and taught differently. The Nazoraeans called Jesus Christ the son of God; Ebion declared that he was begotten of the seed of a man, Joseph, and Christ only entered into him in the form of a dove. The Nazoraeans had the Gospel of Matthew in its entirety in Hebrew; the Ebionites have the same gospel but in corrupt and mutilated form.

Turning to Jerome, in 375 he began a period of life in the wilderness of Chalcis, and here he was only about fifteen miles southwest of Beroea, which Epiphanius named as one of the centers of the Nazoraeans (Nazarenes). So Jerome must have had good opportunity to obtain information about the Nazarenes, and the "brother who was a believer from among the Hebrews," from whom Jerome learned Hebrew (as mentioned above), may well have been one of them. The Gospel of Matthew, which Epiphanius says the Nazarenes had in its entirety in Hebrew, is mentioned by Jerome as preserved in the library at Caesarea, and he also says that it was in use by the Nazarenes in Beroea in Syria, from

9. According to a proposed but not universally accepted interpretation of the find, there is illustration of the continuing existence of a Judeo-Christian community at Pella in the discovery there of a sarcophagus, concerning which various lines of evidence suggest that it dates around A.D. 60 to 150—the time in which otherwise Judeo-Christianity was most prominent—and was the burial place at that time of a Jewish-Christian leader in Pella. See Robert Houston Smith, "A Sarcophagus from Pella: New Light on Earliest Christianity," in *Archaeology* 26.4 (Oct 1973), pp. 250-256. For the excavations at Pella

see Robert Houston Smith, "Pella of the Decapolis," in *Archaeology* 34.5 (Sept/Oct 1981), pp. 46-53; A. W. McNicoll et al., "Preliminary Report on the University of Sydney's Seventh Season of Excavation at Pella (Ṭabaqat Faḥl) in 1985," in ADAJ 30 (1986), pp. 155-198, with bibliography on p. 197; Robert Houston Smith and Leslie Preston Day, *Pella of the Decapolis, 2, Final Report on The College of Wooster Excavations in Area IX, The Civic Complex, 1979-1985* (The College of Wooster, 1989).

whom he received the opportunity to copy the book, and this is evidently the same as the Gospel according to the Hebrews, which Jerome says he translated into Greek and Latin and which he cites many times in his own various writings (*Lives of Illustrious Men* 2, 3 NPNFSS III, p. 362; Klijn and Reinink pp. 208-211). Where Jerome describes the Nazarenes he says that they accept Christ in such manner that they do not cease to keep the old Law (*Commentary on Isaiah* 8.11; Klijn and Reinink p. 221), and he writes about them as follows (*Letter to Augustine* [A.D. 404] 112.13 NPNF I, p. 338; Klijn and Reinink pp. 200-201):

> What shall I say of the Ebionites, who make pretensions to the name of Christians? In our own day there exists a sect among the Jews throughout all the synagogues of the East, which is called the sect of the Minaeans, and is even now cursed by the Pharisees. The adherents of this sect are commonly known as Nazarenes. They believe in Christ the Son of God, born of the Virgin Mary; and they say that he who suffered under Pontius Pilate and rose again, is the same as the one in whom we believe. But while they desire to be both Jews and Christians, they are neither the one nor the other.

In addition to his disparaging mention of the Ebionites at the beginning of the passage just quoted, Jerome also elsewhere speaks of Ebionites as another kind of Jew and the heirs of Jewish error, being persons who called themselves "poor ones" because of the lowness of their understanding (*Commentary on Daniel*, prologue; *Commentary on Isaiah* 66.20; Klijn and Reinink pp. 218-219, 226-227).

Although the preceding patristic references are not devoid of confusion between the Nazarenes and the Ebionites, we may conclude that there were indeed two kinds of Judeo-Christians (Justin Martyr, Origen, Eusebius): the Nazarenes, whose name originally applied to all the Christians of Jewish background and practice (Ac 24:5; Epiphanius), and the Ebionites who "emerged" from the Nazarenes (Epiphanius). Both were alike in their continuation in the Jewish way of life, but later the Nazarenes were viewed as substantially orthodox in their belief in Christ as the Son of God (Epiphanius, Jerome),[10] whereas the Ebionites were of "poor" understanding because they considered Jesus an ordinary man, both naturally, and only made Christ through attainment in character and by the descent of the dove (Eusebius, Epiphanius). Both Nazarenes and Ebionites were describable, however, as neither Jews nor Christians (Jerome), so all were eventually condemned by the Jews (Eighteen Benedictions) and opposed by the Gentile Christians, and thus they gradually dwindled in numbers and finally disappeared. Jerome is witness to the fact that both Nazarenes and Ebionites were still known in his time, i.e., toward the very end of the fourth century. When Augustine wrote his *Reply to Faustus the Manichaean* (XIX 17 NPNF IV, p. 246; Klijn and Reinink pp. 236-237) in about 400, he said of the Nazarenes that they were in existence until that time, or at least until recently, but always in the same small number. When Theodoret, bishop of Cyrus east of Antioch—in the midst of former Ebionite territory—wrote his *History of Heresies* (II 11 MPG 83, col. 397; Klijn and Reinink pp. 350-351) in about 453 he named the Ebionites among the sects of which not even a small remnant remained.

But in the Church of Santa Sabina in Rome (erected by the priest Peter under the pontificate of Celestine I [422-432] as is evident from the dedicatory *titulus* inscription in mosaic still in place over the door of the entrance wall) there is in mosaic on either side of the inscription the figure of a woman, each robed in purple and holding an open book in her hand, the one at the left labeled Ecclesia ex Circumcisione, and the one at the right labeled Ecclesia ex Gentibus.[11] Thus viewers may be reminded that if a feminine personification of the church is appropriate then two women must be shown and not just one, and of the two the first in sequence of time is not the one who represents the Gentile church but the one who represents the Judeo-Christian church.

10. Pritz, *Nazarene Jewish Christianity*, p. 82.
11. Walter Fraser Oakeshott, *The Mosaics of Rome, from the Third to the Fourteenth Centuries* (Greenwich, Conn.: New York Graphic Society, 1967), pp. 89f.

OUTLINE OF FESTIVALS OF THE EARLY CHURCH

EVEN AS JESUS at the age of twelve went with Joseph and Mary to Jerusalem for the feast of the Passover (Lk 2:41-51) and also in the course of his own ministry went there at an unnamed feast (Jn 5:1), at the feast of Tabernacles (Jn 7:2, 10), and at the feast of Passover (Jn 2:13; Mt 26:2ff., etc., Jn 12:1ff.), so also afterward some of his followers are spoken of as going to the temple at the hour of prayer (Ac 3:1), and no doubt the Judeo-Christians in general continued many of the Jewish fasts and feasts. Such events of the Jewish calendar were no doubt especially in mind when Paul protested the observance by the Galatians of "days, and months, and seasons, and years" (Gal 4:10), and along this line there was evidently such an abandonment of the older observances that the Jewish speaker in Justin's *Dialogue with Trypho* (10 ANF I, p. 199) could object about the Christians: "You observe no festivals or sabbaths."

The need for common devotional festivals continued, however, and in fact the Jewish festal observances of the Sabbath (Ex 20:8), the Passover (Ex 12:1ff.), and the Weeks (the fiftieth day, Lv 23:15-16; Dt 16:9-10) provided precedents for corresponding weekly and annual dates in the Christian calendar, new connotations of course being attached to the related Christian observances.

The weekly Christian observance was now on "the first day of the week" (Ac 20:7) as "the Lord's day" (Rev 1:10), in remembrance of the resurrection on the first day of the week (Mt 28:1, etc.; *Apostolic Constitutions* [latter half of the fourth century], VIII 33 ANF VII, p. 495: "the Sabbath is on account of the creation, and the Lord's day [on account] of the resurrection). That this was also "the day of the Sun" (Justin Martyr [c. 150], *Apol.* I 67 ANF I, p. 186) or "the venerable day of the Sun" (Constantine's edict in 321 making the day a public holiday, NSH XI, p. 147) was not inappropriate inasmuch as Christ is himself "the Sun of righteousness" (Mal 4:2, cf. Hippolytus [170-236], *Treatise on Christ and Antichrist* 61 ANF V, p. 217; Cyprian [200-258], *Treatise* IV 35 ANF V, p. 457).

Likewise the Passover was now for Christians "the Passover of the Lord" (τὸ κυρίου πάσχα, *Epistle to Diog-netus* XII 9 ANF I, p. 30) and became the later Christian Easter, the festival commemorating the resurrection of Jesus Christ, with the Christians of Jewish descent holding to observance at the Passover date (the fourteenth of Nisan), regardless of the day of the week, the Christians of Gentile descent putting the observance always on the first day of the week, the Lord's day, Sunday (see above on the Judeo-Christians, p. xl).

Both before and after Passover/Easter there were related Christian observances. During the prior period "in which the bridegroom was taken away" (Mt 9:15, etc.), i.e., in the time when Jesus was moving toward death, there was fasting (Tertullian, *On Fasting* 2 ANF IV, p. 103). Then came the paschal supper, in which the injunction "Do this for a remembrance of me" (Lk 22:19) was observed. Afterward the events of the death and the resurrection were remembered too, and "thenceforward," the *Apostolic Constitutions* (V 19 ANF VII, p. 447) instruct, "leave off your fasting, and rejoice, and keep a festival, because Jesus Christ, the pledge of our resurrection, is risen from the dead." Tertullian also, writing *On Baptism* (19 ANF III, p. 678), pictures the Passover as a more than usually solemn day for baptism, "when, withal, the Lord's passion, in which we are baptized, was completed," but says also, "After that, Pentecost is a most joyous space for conferring baptisms; wherein the resurrection of the Lord was repeatedly proved [by the frequent appearances of the risen Christ] among the disciples."

According to Ac 1:3, however, the appearances of the risen Christ continued for forty days until his ascension (Ac 1:9) rather than the full fifty days to the day of Pentecost, and therefore there also came to be an observance of an Ascension day on the fortieth day. The *Apostolic Constitutions* (V 19 ANF VII, pp. 447f.) instruct: "From the first Lord's day, count forty days, from the Lord's day till the fifth day of the week, and celebrate the feast of the ascension of the Lord." As for the day of Pentecost itself, it was now in the Christian church the memorial of the descent of the Holy Spirit upon the apostles at Jerusalem (Ac 2:1ff.).

In contrast with the foregoing, the Christian festivals

of Epiphany and Christmas were not connected with feasts of Israel (cf. Chrysostom, *Discourses against Judaizing Christians* [in Antioch, A.D. 386/387], IV 3, 9 FCNT 68, p. 80: "Did the Jews . . . ever share with us the day of the Epiphanies?") and did have some associations with pagan observances. In contrast with the primary Christian feasts of Easter in celebration of the resurrection, and of the Lord's day as the weekly return of the resurrection day, there was evidently at first, at least in some quarters, no concern for an annual remembrance of the day of Jesus' birth, and in other quarters there were given varying dates for the year and for the day of the event. Origen (c. 230), although he almost certainly visited the Bethlehem cave of the Nativity in person, seems to have thought that a birthday observance was a pagan ritual, and he claimed that only such persons as Pharaoh and Herod had their birthdays celebrated (Benoit, *Christmas*, p. 12).

Origen's predecessor, Clement of Alexandria, however, writing his *Stromata* in about A.D. 194, cites a number of different year and day dates that were current and himself gives an exact date for the year and the day: "Our Lord was born in the twenty-eighth year . . . in the reign of Augustus. . . . From the birth of Christ . . . to the death of Commodus are, in all, a hundred and ninety-four years, one month, thirteen days" (*Stromata* I 21, 145 ANF II, p. 333). The reign of Augustus in Egypt, to which Clement would naturally refer, began in August in the year 30 B.C., so the indicated year is 3/2 B.C. (FHBC p. 219, table 98). The murder of the emperor Commodus took place on December 31, A.D. 192, so the precisely indicated date is November 18, 3 B.C.

As for the year date of the year 3/2 B.C., this date is also given by other writers of the early church (FHBC p. 229, table 107), but it was very possibly arrived at by counting back (Paul L. Maier in CKC p. 147) on the basis of Lk 3:1, 23 exactly thirty years from the fifteenth year of Tiberius (A.D. 28/29 in the factual years of the emperor's reign, FHBC p. 265, table 123). Lk 3:23, however, only says that Jesus was "about" thirty years of age at the time, which allows some leeway, and the 3/2 B.C. date can hardly be correct, for the birth of Jesus must have been before the death of Herod the Great, and the death of Herod was almost certainly in the spring of 4 B.C. (see "Table of Archeological and Historical Periods in Palestine"), and various factors involved can suggest a date for the birth perhaps late in the year 5 B.C. (Maier in CKC p. 124, table 1). The Star of Bethlehem (Mt 2:1-12) is also involved in the reckoning of the birth date, however, and the best astronomical explanation of the star is probably that which sees it as the conjunction of Jupiter and Saturn in 7 B.C., when their stationary points were over Palestine and on November 12 would have appeared as if over Bethlehem to the Magi riding from Je-

rusalem, astronomical phenomena which Babylonian planetary theories and cuneiform texts show were calculated many decades in advance by Babylonian astronomers (Konradin Ferrari-D'Occhieppo in CKC pp. 41-53). As to the date of the birth in relation to the planetary date of 7 B.C., Justin Martyr (*Dialogue with Trypho* 88) says that the Magi came "as soon as the child was born"; but the *Protevangelium of James* (in Papyrus Bodmer V, Ferrari-D'Occhieppo, op. cit., pp. 52f.) represents the child as old enough when the Magi came that they saw him "standing by his mother Mary's side"; while both Origen (*Commentary on Matthew*, frag. 23, ed. Erich Klostermann III, GCS 41, p. 25) and Eusebius (*Questiones ad Stephanum*, XVI, 2 MPG 22, col. 934) state that Jesus was two years old when the wise men came; and Epiphanius (*Pan. haer.* 51, 22, 13 Holl/Dummer II, p. 287) says that the star appeared in its evening rising (ἐν τῇ ἀνατολῇ, literally "in the rising," the same phrase as in Mt 2:2) in the hour when Jesus was born and two years before the wise men arrived in Jerusalem and Bethlehem.

Two other reckonings point to the year 12 B.C. for the birth of Jesus, but arrive at their conclusions by mutually irreconcilable paths. In CKC pp. 133-163 Nikos Kokkinos notes from the Gospels and Josephus (*Ant.* XVIII 5, 1-3 §§109-124) that Herod Antipas put away his wife the daughter of Aretas and married Herodias, which was criticized by John the Baptist leading to John's death, and which led Aretas to make war on Herod Antipas and led the Roman emperor Tiberius to send Vitellius against Aretas, an expedition which was terminated by the death of Tiberius in A.D. 37. Therefore the war of Aretas with Herod Antipas was in 36, and the death of John the Baptist, while Herodias was living with Herod, was in 35. Since the death of John preceded the death of Jesus, the crucifixion of Jesus was in A.D. 36 (the last possible year within the procuratorship of Pilate, A.D. 26-36). Taken literally, Jn 2:20-21 makes Jesus forty years of age at his first Passover in Jerusalem (in A.D. 34), therefore his birth was in 12 B.C. (with Halley's Comet as the Star of Bethlehem, CKC pp. 158-162).

In CKC pp. 56-64 Jerry Vardaman cites the Aemilius Secundus inscription (FLAP p. 260), references in Dio Cassius (*Rom. Hist.* 54.28.4; 35.1ff.), and other evidence, for a first Roman census by Quirinius as governor of Syria (Lk 2:2) in 12/11 B.C. (with a second census in A.D. 6/7, Josephus, *Ant.* XVIII 1, 1 §1, Ac 5:37), and this together with the data about Tiberius, Herod the Great, John the Baptist, and the ministry of Jesus (see "Table of Archeological and Historical Periods in Palestine") points to the birth of Jesus in 12 B.C. (with Halley's Comet as the Bethlehem Star, CKC p. 66). Vardaman and Kokkinos thus agree on the date of Jesus' birth in 12 B.C. and the identification of the Star of Bethlehem (and also on the existence of microletters, CKC p. 66), but

Kokkinos' chronology is otherwise largely different from that of Vardaman (e.g., the date of Herod Antipas' marriage to Herodias: Kokkinos, A.D. 34, CKC p. 146; Vardaman, A.D. 17/18, CKC p. 71). Thus Kokkinos and Vardaman agree that 12 B.C. is the birth year of Jesus, but differ widely on dates relating to Jesus' ministry and death, as well as the time of Paul's conversion (Kokkinos, A.D. 36; Vardaman, A.D. 25).

As for the day date of November 18, the day of the death of Commodus on the last day of the year in A.D. 192 was only about two years before Clement was writing and must have been very well known, and the date of Jesus' birth—which Clement reckons from that point—is the earliest and most exactly stated day date for the birth given by an early church writer (Meier in CKC p. 129), and it also looks in general to the midwinter season of the year as do the other most important dates still to be considered below.

In the same passage (*Stromata* I 21, 145 ANF II, p. 333) Clement goes on to other dates, and writes:

> And there are those who have determined not only the year of our Lord's birth (γένεσις), but also the day; and they say it took place in the twenty-eighth year of Augustus, and in the twenty-fifth day of Pachon. And the followers of Basilides hold the day of his baptism as a festival, spending the night before in readings. And they say that it was the fifteenth year of Tiberius Caesar [Lk 3:1], the fifteenth day of the month Tybi; and some that it was the eleventh of the same month. And treating of his passion, with very great accuracy, some say that it took place in the sixteenth year of Tiberius, on the twenty-fifth of Phamenoth; and others the twenty-fifth of Pharmuthi and others say that on the nineteenth of Pharmuthi the Savior suffered. Further, others say that he was born on the twenty-fourth or twenty-fifth of Pharmuthi.

In consideration of these data we will note first the statement that the followers of Basilides (a Christian Gnostic teacher in Alexandria [Eusebius, *Ch. Hist.* IV 7, 3] c. 117-138) celebrate the festival of Jesus' baptism on the fifteenth or eleventh of Tybi. In the standard Egyptian calendar (Julian reform), the month of Tybi began on December 27 and the eleventh day, counted inclusively, was January 6, while Tybi 15 was the same date in an earlier form of the calendar (Konradin Ferrari-D'Occhieppo in CKC pp. 51f.).

In his *Panarion* Epiphanius (367) repeatedly gives this very same date of January 6 as the date of the birth of Jesus, which he speaks of under the term Epiphany/Epiphanies (ἐπιφάνεια, ἡ or τά, *Pan. haer.* 51, 18, 1 Holl/Dummer II, p. 270) and the like-meaning Theophany or Theophanies (θεοφάνεια, ἡ or τά, *Pan. haer.* 51, 29, 4 Holl/Dummer II, p. 284). In *Pan. haer.* 51, 22, 3-4 (Holl/Dummer II, p. 284) he cites the forty-second

year of Augustus (with the reign reckoned as beginning after the assassination of Julius Caesar on March 15, 44 B.C., this is 3/2 B.C., the same as the twenty-eighth year of Augustus' Egyptian rule given by Clement of Alexandria) and also specifies the consular date *Augusto XIII et Silvano* which is 2 B.C. (FHBC p. 100, table 39; p. 175, table 81; p. 96, table 38), and then writes: "Christ was born on the eighth day before the Ides of January, thirteen days after the winter solstice and the beginning of the increase of the light and the day." Counted inclusively, eight days before the Ides (the thirteenth) of January is January 6. The same date is thirteen days after December 25, which was thus at that time accepted as the date of the winter solstice.

In *Pan. haer.* 51, 24, 1 (Holl/Dummer II, pp. 292f.) Epiphanius gives the same date of the eighth day before the Ides of January, explains that the exact time, according to Roman reckoning, was between the evening of January 5 and the morning of January 6, and adds the equivalent dates in no less than eight other calendars including the Egyptian Tybi 11.

In yet another passage (*Pan. haer.* 51, 22, 9-11 Holl/Dummer II, pp. 285-287) Epiphanius tells us that this same exact time of the night of January 5 and the morning of January 6 was also when a ceremony was held in the temple of Kore in Alexandria, in which the participants stayed awake all night, making music to the idol with songs and flutes, then in the early morning descended by torchlight to a subterranean shrine and brought forth a wooden image marked with the sign of a cross and a star of gold; this they carried in procession, and they explained that the date thus observed was when Kore, the virgin, gave birth to the deity Aion. This makes it not unlikely that the identical date of January 6, reported by Clement for the festival of the baptism of Jesus among the Basilidian Gnostics, was fixed upon by way of syncretism and/or rivalry with this pagan festival reported by Epiphanius (Kirsopp Lake in HERE V, p. 332). For Epiphanius, however, the January 6 date is first of all that of the Epiphany/Theophany in the birth of Jesus.

Among the other dates cited by Clement of Alexandria (in the same passage, above) we may note that there were those who put the birth of Jesus on the twenty-fifth day of Pachon in the twenty-eighth year of Augustus (3/2 B.C.). In the standard Egyptian calendar (Julian reform) the month of Pachon began on April 26 and the twenty-fifth day, counted inclusively, was May 20. It may be noted that there is still a trace of this date in the Coptic calendar in Egypt, which celebrates the entry of the child Jesus with his parents into Egypt on the same date (Kirsopp Lake in HERE III, p. 605; cf. Otto F. A. Meinardus, *The Holy Family in Egypt* [The American

University in Cairo Press, 1986], pp. 6, 43, for the Coptic Feast of the Coming of our Lord into Egypt on the twenty-fourth/twenty-fifth of Bashons, now June 1/2).

Almost this same date is found in what Epiphanius tells about the Alogi (Ἄλογοι), a group in Asia Minor around A.D. 180 who opposed the Montanists and the Johannine doctrine of the Logos to which the Montanists adhered. According to Epiphanius (*Pan. haer.* 51, 29, 1-5 Holl/Dummer II, p. 300) the Alogi put the birth of Jesus in the fortieth year of Augustus (5/4 or 4 B.C., FHBC p. 175, table 81; p. 219, table 97), or contradictorily under the consuls S. Camerinus and B. Pompeianus and, assuming that the latter name means Poppaeus Sabinus, these were the consuls of A.D. 9 (*Camerino et Sabino*, FHBC p. 96, table 38). At any rate, as for the day, it was the twelfth day before the Kalends or first day of July or of June; counting inclusively, the two dates are June 20 and May 21. The latter date is close to the May 20 date given by Clement of Alexandria in the preceding paragraph, but here Epiphanius says that this was given as the day of the conception (σύλληψις) as announced by Gabriel to Mary (Lk 1:26ff.) rather than the day of the birth of Jesus, and perhaps in Clement's statement too γένεσις (cf. γεννάω, to beget) means conception rather than birth. From this point Epiphanius reckons with the birth in Mary's seventh month (the same period given by the Egyptians for the birth of Osiris) and comes to the Egyptian date Tybi 11, equivalent to the eighth day before the Ides or thirteenth day of January, which, counted inclusively, is January 6 (cf. Kirsopp Lake in HERE III, p. 605).

That both birth and baptism continued to be remembered in Egypt on January 6 we learn when the monk John Cassian makes two visits there between 380 and 400 and writes of "Epiphany . . . which the priests of that province regard as the time, both of our Lord's baptism and also of his birth in the flesh, and so celebrate the commemoration of either mystery not separately as in the Western provinces but on the single festival of this day" (NPNFSS XI, p. 401; cf. E. O. James in EB 1966, p. 704).

The rationale for the commemoration of both events in the single festival of this day lay in the thought that the baptism itself marked a spiritual birth. This was expressed in two Latin homilies ascribed variously to Ambrose of Milan (fourth century) or Maximus of Turin (fifth century), in which January 6 is declared to be the birthday of the Lord Jesus "whether he was born of the Virgin on that day or was born again in baptism." It is his "nativity both of flesh and of spirit." As thirty years before he "was given forth through the Virgin," so on the same day he was "regenerated" and "sanctified" "through the mystery" (NSH III, p. 47). Later the visit of the Magi

(Mt 2:1ff.), which was a manifestation to the wider world, and the miracle at Cana in which he also "manifested his glory" (Jn 2:1ff.) were also associated with the same date of January 6.

In the Jerusalem church the Epiphany celebration of the physical and spiritual birthdays of Christ together continued until in the sixth century when the Egyptian monk, Cosmas Indicopleustes, writing between c. 535 and c. 547, says: "The Christians of Jerusalem, as if on the authority of the blessed Luke, who says that Christ was baptized 'when he began to be about thirty years of age' (Lk 3:21-23 KJV), celebrate his nativity on Epiphany. . . . for on the day of his nativity fell also his baptism" (J. W. McCrindle, *The Christian Topography of Cosmas, An Egyptian Monk* [London: Hakluyt Society, 1897], p. 143; Cosmas Indicopleustès, *Topographia Chrétienne*, ed. Wanda Wolaska-Conus [sc 141, 59, 197], 3 vols. [Paris: Les Éditions du Cerf, 1968, 1970, 1973], II, pp. 23f.). Finally, however, it was only the Armenian Orthodox church that maintained the Epiphany coincidence of nativity and baptism, and only in that church is the birth of Christ still celebrated on January 6 and not on December 25 (Oscar Cullmann, *Der Ursprung des Weihnachtsfestes* [2d ed., Stuttgart: Zwingli Verlag, 1960], p. 33).

As in Alexandria and the East, so also in Rome and the West there were varying calculations of the date of Jesus, and of these the first of which we know were those of Hippolytus (c. 165-c. 235) (Roger T. Beckwith in SL 13 [1979], p. 11). In his *Chronicle* the tables are carried to the thirteenth year of Severus Alexander (234/235), which is counted as year 5738 from Adam, and the birth of Christ is assigned to the year 5502, which must have been equivalent to 3/2 B.C. (*Hippolytus Werke*, GCS IV, 2d ed., Rudolf Helm, 1955, pp. 193-196). In a revision known under the name of Hippolytus of Thebes (ed. Jo. Albertus Fabricius, 1716, p. 46) the figures are adjusted to come to year 5500 from Adam (3/2 B.C.), the same as in the *Chronographies* of the contemporary Julius Africanus (FHBC pp. 146ff., tables 59A, 59B). An anonymous Latin tractate, *De Pascha Computus*, written in North Africa in 243 and found among the works of Cyprian, has been shown to be based very closely on a lost work of Hippolytus (Kirsopp Lake in HERE III, p. 606). Here the writer also begins with Creation. He notes that creation began with the separation on Sunday, the first day, of light from darkness (Gen 1:3), and since the two were apparently an equal pair this must have been when day and night were equal. In the Roman calendar the spring equinox, when day and night are equal, was on March 25; therefore March 25 was the first day of creation. The sun was created on Wednesday, the fourth day (Gen 1:16), which was March 28, and it follows that

Christ, who is to Christians "the sun of righteousness" (Mal 4:2), was born on Wednesday March 28 (Cullmann, *Der Ursprung des Weihnachtsfestes*, pp. 10f.).

In his own *Commentary on Daniel*, probably composed in 202, of which only a fragment survives, Hippolytus says, with a gap in the extant text (ANF v, p. 179; Hermann Usener, *Das Weihnachtsfest* [Bonn: H. Bouvier, 1969], pp. 369-375), that the first appearance of our Lord in the flesh took place in Bethlehem "on the fourth day before the . . . of April, on the eighth day before the Kalends of January on a fourth day (of the week, i.e., Wednesday)" (πρὸ τεσσάρων ἀπριλίων ἐγένετο πρὸ ὀκτὼ καλανδῶν Ἰανουαρίων ἡμέρᾳ τετράδι). Likewise in the cycle of Easter dates inscribed on the sides of the marble statue chair of Hippolytus (discovered in 1551 at the burial place of Hippolytus on the Via Tiburtina, now in the Lateran Museum) one item contains the abbreviated words π(ρὸ) ὅ νω(νῶν) ἀπρει(λίων), "the fourth day before the Nones of April," against which is the notation γένεσις Χ(ριστο)ῦ, "birth of Christ." Therefore the text in Hippolytus' *Commentary on Daniel* may be completed as reading "on the fourth day before the Nones of April," and since the Nones are the fifth day of the month the date, counted inclusively, is the second day of April. The words that follow this date, "on the eighth day before the Kalends of January," i.e., on the twenty-fifth day of December, are obviously in contradiction to the first date and must be an interpolation to insert here the date later accepted in Rome but certainly therefore not yet current in the time of Hippolytus. At the same point in the *Commentary on Daniel* Hippolytus goes on to say that this date of the birth of Christ was in the forty-second year of Augustus and in year 5500 reckoned from Adam, which should mean 3/2 B.C. (FHBC p. 218, table 97, and pp. 143f.). But Hippolytus also goes on to say that Jesus suffered in his thirty-third year of life on the eighth day before the Kalends of April (i.e., on March 25), in the eighteenth year of Tiberius (i.e., in A.D. 31/32, FHBC p. 265, table 123), when Gaius (Caligula) was consul for the fourth time together with Gaius Cestius Saturninus. This consular date indicates the year A.D. 41 (FHBC p. 96, table 35), and if Jesus was then thirty-three years of age Hippolytus is saying that he was born in A.D. 8, which is not in agreement with the references to the forty-second year of Augustus and the eighteenth year of Tiberius.

The date of the birth of Jesus on the eighth day before the Kalends or first day of January, i.e., December 25, which was obviously an interpolation in the text of Hippolytus' *Commentary on Daniel* and was apparently unknown to Hippolytus, appears as the officially accepted date in the Roman city calendar (an almanac for the use of Christians) edited by Furius Dionysius Filocalus (later

the calligrapher of Pope Damasus, 366-384) in the year 354, but based at this point on a list probably compiled in the year 336. The entry reads: *VIII Kal. Ian. natus Christus in Betleem Iudeae*, "December 25, Christ was born in Bethlehem of Judea" (KLT 2, p. 4; FHBC pp. 95, 255f.).

Here the date for the birth of Christ is the same as the date of the winter solstice, "after which is the beginning of the increase of the light and the day," accepted at that time as on December 25 (see the quotation above from Epiphanius, *Pan. haer.* 51, 22, 4). The worship of the sun was then widespread in the Roman Empire (FMM pp. 209-212) and this date was naturally of great importance. Already in A.D. 274 the emperor Aurelian declared the "unconquered sun" the official deity (*deus sol invictus*) of the Roman Empire and set the birthday celebration of the sun (*natalis solis invicti*) on December 25 (EB 1966, v, p. 704). Note also that Mithras too was called *sol invictus* (David Ulansey, *The Origin of the Mithraic Mysteries* [New York and Oxford: Oxford University Press, 1989], pp. 107, 110f.), and that Manichaean prayers were uttered facing the sun (EB 1966, XIV, p. 784; cf. FMM pp. 209-212, 305).

The even earlier occupation of Christian thought with the solar year (noted above) suggests that the December 25 date for the birth of Jesus could have been arrived at independently (Kirsopp Lake in HERE III, p. 608), but like the January 6 date in Egypt, the exact coincidence in date with the Roman festival of the sun must have allowed for syncretism and/or rivalry and was certainly used by way of both comparison and contrast (Cullmann, *Der Ursprung des Weihnachtsfestes*, pp. 29f.). Augustine (354-430), for example, in a sermon in which he cites Eph 4:26, "let not the sun go down upon your wrath" (KJV), says: "Let then your wrath at length pass away also, now that we are celebrating the days of the great Sun, of that Sun of which Scripture says, 'Unto you shall the Sun of righteousness arise with healing in his wings' [Mal 4:2 KJV]. . . . That Sun riseth upon the righteous only; but this sun which we see, God 'maketh' daily 'to rise upon the good and evil' [Mt 5:45]. The righteous attain to the seeing of that Sun; and that Sun dwelleth now in our hearts by faith" (*Sermon* VIII 7 NPNF VI, p. 286). Again in an anti-Manichaean writing (A.D. 397), Augustine speaks of "the difficulty of curing the eye of the inner man that he may gaze upon his Sun,—not that sun which you worship, and which shines with the brilliance of a heavenly body in the eyes of carnal men and of beasts,—but that of which it is written through the prophet, 'The Sun of righteousness has arisen upon me' " (*Against the Epistle of Manichaeus called Fundamental* 2 NPNF IV, pp. 129f.).

Ultimately the full equation with the solar year was

completed by the belief that the crucifixion as well as the conception took place on March 25, and the birth on December 25. Thus Augustine, writing *On the Trinity* (A.D. 400-428), says: "For he is believed to have been conceived on the twenty-fifth of March, upon which day he also suffered. . . . But he was born, according to tradition, upon December the twenty-fifth" (IV 5 NPNF III, p. 740).

In the West, therefore, there were the two festivals of Christmas celebrating the birthday of Christ on December 25 and of Epiphany on January 6 commemorating other events in which Christ was "manifested," most notably his baptism, and the two were observed separately, as the words of John Cassian (A.D. c. 400), quoted above, show. From the West the December 25 date spread gradually into the East and was accepted there in many quarters but not in all for the birthday observance. This will appear in the following references.

In the year 376 Gregory of Nyssa (in Cappadocia) gave a sermon "On the Baptism of Christ" for the Day of Lights (baptism was often called Illumination and observed with lighted torches and candles), in which he said that the Nativity had been celebrated shortly before ("Christ . . . was born as it were a few days ago," NPNFSS V, p. 518 and p. xiii for the date), thus Christmas (December 25) was recently past and he was speaking at Epiphany (January 6).

In the year 380 in Constantinople, Gregory of Nazianzus delivered an oration (no. 38) "On the Theophany, or Birthday of Christ," and although he uses a word (θεοφάνεια) that is virtually synonymous with "epiphany," it is plain that he is speaking just of the birthday celebration (on December 25) for he says that they will shortly be thinking of the baptism ("A little later on you will see Jesus submitting to be purified in the River Jordan," sec. 16, NPNFSS VII, p. 350), and indeed the latter is the subject of his immediately following orations (no. 39) "On the Holy Lights" and (no. 40) "On Holy Baptism," in which he refers back to the preceding festival ("At his birth we duly kept festival," no. 39, sec. 14, NPNFSS VII, p. 357), thus is speaking now at Epiphany, January 6, A.D. 381.

Of the greatest influence for the acceptance in the East of December 25 rather than January 6 for the birthday festival of Christ were no doubt the sermons of the famous John Chrysostom (c. 347-407) delivered in Antioch in the Christmas season in the year 386 (Usener, *Das Weihnachtsfest*, pp. 221-234; Hans Lietzmann, "Über das Datum der Weihnachtspredigt des Johannes Chrysostomos," ibid., pp. 379-384). In his *Homily on Philogonius*, delivered on December 20 on the memorial day of this former bishop of Antioch, Chrysostom tells his hearers that the festival will soon take place which is

the holiest of the entire church year because it celebrates the birth of Christ, without which he would not have been baptized (Epiphany), nor crucified and risen (Easter), nor would he have sent the Spirit (Pentecost).

In his actual Christmas-day sermon on December 25 (*in diem natalem Domini nostri Jesu Christi*) Chrysostom declares that it would be wonderful if the sun could come down from heaven and send forth its light on earth, and it is more wonderful that in the incarnation "the sun of righteousness" (Mal 4:2) does in fact send forth its light from human flesh. As to the date of the festival on December 25, Chrysostom says that this date was known earlier in the West but has been known among them in Antioch for less than ten years (p. 355 MPG 49, col. 351). Since the date was so newly known to his hearers it was important to show that it was the correct date, and Chrysostom offers three proofs: (1) Remembering what Gamaliel said (in Ac 5:38-39) about the failure or success of the apostolic cause, one can say that the new date would not have spread and been accepted so rapidly if it were not true; (2) The date is confirmed by the census (Lk 2:1-7), of which there is public record in Rome (to which record Justin, *Apology* I 34 ANF I, p. 174, and Tertullian, *Against Marcion* IV 7 ANF III, p. 352, also refer).

(3) Exegesis of scripture confirms the date (pp. 358-362 MPG 49, cols. 351-358). In Lk 1:5ff. the announcement to Zechariah, a priest of the division of Abijah, that his wife Elizabeth would bear a son to be named John came when it was Zechariah's lot to enter the Temple and burn incense. Chrysostom evidently assumes (incorrectly as far as we know) that Zechariah was high priest, and the occasion was the Day of Atonement (the one day of the year when the high priest entered the Holy of Holies, on the tenth day of the seventh month, Lev 16:29, i.e., Tishri 10), followed shortly by the Feast of Tabernacles (on the fifteenth day of the seventh month, and continuing for seven days, Lev 23:34, i.e., Tishri 15-21). This feast, says Chrysostom, the Jews celebrate toward the end of the month Gorpiaios. In A.D. 386 there was a new moon on September 10. Since the month Tishri falls normally in September/October this new moon presumably marked Tishri 1. Tishri 10, the Day of Atonement, was therefore September 20 in that year, and Tishri 15-21, the Feast of Tabernacles, was September 25-October 1. In the calendar of Macedonian origin used in Syria in this time the month of Gorpiaios began on September 1 (FHBC p. 69, table 25 and pp. 257f.), and the Feast of Tabernacles was therefore celebrated toward the end of Gorpiaios exactly as Chrysostom says, and the first day of the Feast of Tabernacles was September 25. This was when the announcement came to Zechariah. After that, Elizabeth was in her sixth month when Mary came to her (Lk 1:36ff.), and Chry-

sostom carefully names and counts six intervening months (Hyperbereteaios, Dios, Apellaios, Audynaios, Peritios, and Dystros), bringing us to March 25. From this point Mary's nine intervening months extend from Xanthikos (April) to Apellaios (December), and so we come to December 25.

Although some of Chrysostom's assumptions were no doubt incorrect, some modern studies have followed somewhat similar lines by trying to establish when Zechariah's priestly division was on duty, and counting from there. In the organization of the priesthood there were twenty-four divisions or courses (KJV), of which the first was that of Jehoiarib and the eighth was that of Abijah, to which Zechariah belonged (Lev 24:7-18). Each course served one week at a time beginning on the sabbath (II Ch 23:8; Josephus, *Ant.* VII 14, 7 §365) and if the sequence were followed through twice it would make forty-eight weeks, but it is not known how the remaining weeks of a fifty-two week year were covered (M. Avi-Yonah in *The Teacher's Yoke, Studies in Memory of Henry Trantham*, ed. Jerry Vardaman [Waco, Tex.: Baylor University Press, 1964], p. 54). Some think that the courses followed each other in unbroken succession without regard to the beginning and ending of years, others that the sequence began afresh at the first month Nisan or the seventh month Tishri (Roger T. Beckwith, "St. Luke, The Date of Christmas and the Priestly Courses at Qumran," in RQ 9 [1977], pp. 79f.).

In the Talmud (*Ta'anith* 29a SBT 9, p. 154) it is stated that the First Temple was destroyed on the ninth day of Ab (July/August) and the course of Jehoiarib was on duty at the time, and it was the same with the Second Temple (destroyed in A.D. 70). Counting backward from this point one study finds that in the year (A.U.C. 748 = 6 B.C.) before the birth of Jesus the course of Abijah would have been on duty the week of October 2-9. From this point, fifteen months (six for Elizabeth and nine for Mary) would come toward the end of December (and quite reasonably to December 25) in the following year (5 B.C.) (Alfred Edersheim, *The Life and Times of Jesus the Messiah*, 2 vols. [Grand Rapids, Mich.: Eerdmans, 1945], I, pp. 135, 187 and n. 3; II, p. 705), and this reckoning is not far from that by Chrysostom.

Noting that the first day of the seventh month (the months always being numbered from Nisan) or Tishri 1 was the New Year's Day of the Israelite year beginning in the fall, was the first day of the month in which the First Temple was dedicated (I K 8:2; II Ch 5:3), and was the day when the priests commenced their duties at the rebuilt altar after the exile (Ezr 3:1-6), another study holds that the sequence of the courses always began afresh on the sabbath on or next before Tishri 1, so as to be on duty on Tishri 1 itself, and finds that the course of Abijah would have been on duty each year in the month

Heshvan (October/November) and again in the month Iyyar (April/May), and the fifteen months thereafter would come to the month Shebat (January/February) or to the month Ab (July/August), and the former of these termini is not far from the traditional dates (January 6 and December 25) for the Nativity (Beckwith in RQ 9 [1977], pp. 90f.).

Uncertainty of course remains in all such calculations, especially in view of the observational basis of the Jewish calendar and of the Babylonian calendar on which it was based and of the necessity in these calendars for intercalation to keep lunar months in line with the solar year (Ben Zion Wacholder, *Essays on Jewish Chronology and Chronography* [New York: Ktav, 1976], p. 62 and table 1 on p. 64; Roger T. Beckwith in CKC pp. 185-205; for reconstructed Babylonian tables in which some dates "may be wrong by one day," see Richard A. Parker and Waldo H. Dubberstein, *Babylonian Chronology 626 B.C.-A.D. 75* [Providence, R.I.: Brown University Press, 1956], p. 25) and approximation is safer than exact dates in some conclusions, nevertheless there are several pointers in the foregoing toward the midwinter for the season of the birth of Jesus, and it may be thought not impossible that there was authentic tradition to that effect at least, while in respect to the later ministry of Jesus as well as to his birth astronomical and calendrical data may allow greater exactitude.

Along with the Christmas date of December 25, Epiphany continued to be celebrated in Antioch and elsewhere in the East, and in a sermon on January 6, 386 (*de baptismo Christi et de Epiphania*, pp. 358-363 MPG 49 cols. 351-358) Chrysostom discusses the baptism of Christ, in which he was made "manifest" to all; thus Epiphany is the proper name of this festival, he says, and should not be applied to Christmas as some still did (cf. EB 1966, V, p. 705).

Likewise the *Apostolic Constitutions*, which also reflect conditions at Antioch in the latter part of the fourth century, call for observance of both the festival of the birth, "because on it the unexpected favor was granted . . . that Jesus Christ . . . should be born of the Virgin Mary, for the salvation of the world," and "the festival of Epiphany, because on it a manifestation took place of the divinity of Christ, for the Father bore testimony to him at the baptism, and the Paraclete, in the form of a dove, pointed out to the bystanders him to whom testimony was borne" (ANF VII, p. 495).

In her time in the Holy Land (381-384) the pilgrim Aetheria participated in various services held at sacred sites at special times of remembrance, and she provides a firsthand description of events. Information is also available from the Old Armenian Lectionary, which is of special value as a supplement where portions of Aetheria's record are missing. This Armenian list of readings for the divine services is preserved in three versions, namely, the Armenian Codex Jerusalem 121 of the Convent of Saint James in Jerusalem, the Paris manuscript of the Bibliothèque Nationale in Paris, and the Erevan manuscript 985 in the Matenadaran in Erevan, which appear to reflect conditions in Jerusalem in the early fifth century and to derive from a Greek original. According to Armenian tradition the original lectionary was prepared by James the first bishop of Jerusalem and was completed by Cyril his successor in the fourth century (Athanase Renoux, *Le Codex Arménien Jérusalem 121*, in PO 35, 1, 1969; 36, 2, 1971; WET pp. 253ff.).

As seen in Aetheria and the Armenian Lectionary, and as far as the life of Jesus is concerned, the church year in Jerusalem begins with Epiphany (January 6) (cf. below, No. 25), while December 25 is the date of an observance on Mount Sion in memory of James (James the Just, the first bishop) and of David (the king, cf. Ac 2:29), although in some other towns they keep the birth of Christ on the same day, i.e., on December 25 (Renoux, *Le Codex Arménien Jérusalem 121*, pp. 73-78, 367 no. LXXI; WET p. 275).

After Epiphany there are some five further major observances:

(1) The Fortieth Day after Epiphany (February 14) commemorates the presentation of Jesus in the Temple (cf. Lv 12:2, 4 for the period of time from the birth) and was observed with the highest honor (Geyer p. 77; LPPTS I-C, pp. 52-53; CCSL CLXXV pp. 72-73; WET p. 128).

(2) Quadragesima or Lent is a period of fasting and especially of instruction preparatory to baptism, extending for a considerable time before Easter. Although the original name means "The Forty Days" or "The Fortieth" (*quadragesima*, the name of the Sunday at the beginning of the period), there was much variation in the length of the period as observed in different times and places (cf.

Irenaeus, quoted by Eusebius, *Ch. Hist.* v 12-13). In the fifth century Socrates (*Ch. Hist.* v 22) remarks on the surprising variety in the number of days and reports that in Rome the fasting was for three successive weeks before Easter, except on Saturdays and Sundays; while Sozomen (*Ch. Hist.* VII 19) says that the period consisted of six weeks in Palestine, although seven at Constantinople. In her time in Palestine (381-384), however, Aetheria records as follows (Geyer p. 78; LPPTS I-C, pp. 52-53; CCSL CLXXV pp. 72-73; WET p. 128):

> Then comes the Easter season, celebrated in this manner. Now with us we observe forty days before Easter (*quadragesimae ante pascha*), but here they keep eight weeks (*octo septimanae*). It makes eight weeks because they do not fast on the Lord's Day or on the Sabbath with the exception of one Sabbath day, which is the vigil of Easter, on which it is necessary to fast. So subtracting from these eight weeks, eight Lord's Days and seven Sabbaths—for they must fast on one Sabbath, as I said above—there remain forty-one fast days, which are here called Feasts (ἑορταί, a plural word with a singular meaning as the name for the quadragesimal fast).

(3) Easter is the supreme festival of the resurrection, and the entire week beginning with the previous Sunday, which is the Day of Palms, is "The Great Week" (Geyer p. 82; LPPTS I-C, pp. 57-58; CCSL CLXXV p. 76; WET p. 132).

(4) The Fortieth Day after Easter commemorates the Ascension (Ac 1:3; for Aetheria see below, No. 25; for the Old Armenian Lectionary see WET p. 273, no. 57 and cf. pp. 49-53, 77-78).

(5) The Fiftieth Day or Pentecost (πεντηκοστή) commemorates the descent of the Spirit (Ac 2:1; Geyer p. 93; LPPTS I-C, p. 69; CCSL CLXXV p. 84; WET p. 141; cf. below, No. 204).

LIST OF
ABBREVIATIONS

AAA *Acta apostolorum apocrypha*, ed. C. Tischendorf (1851). Vol. 1, ed. R. A. Lipsius (1891); vols. 2, 1 and 2, ed. M. Bonnet (1898 and 1903). 3 vols., reprint (1959).

AASOR *Annual of the American Schools of Oriental Research.*

AB *The Anchor Bible.*

ABEL, *GÉOGRAPHIE* F.-M. Abel, *Géographie de la Palestine.* Vol. I, 1933; Vol. II, 1938 (Paris: J. Gabalda et Cie).

ADAJ *Annual of the Department of Antiquities of Jordan.*

AJA *American Journal of Archaeology.*

AJBA *The Australian Journal of Biblical Archaeology.*

AJPA *Archaeology of Jerusalem*, First Temple, Second Temple and Byzantine Periods, Major Archaeological Remains Visible Today (with numbers), published as part of The Wide Screen Project, Historical Geography of the Bible Lands, by *Pictorial Archive* (P.O. Box 19823, Jerusalem, distributed by Zondervan Publishing House).

ANB *Analecta Bollandia.*

ANEP James B. Pritchard, *The Ancient Near East in Pictures Relating to the Old Testament* (Princeton: Princeton University Press, 1954).

ANET James B. Pritchard, ed., *Ancient Near Eastern Texts Relating to the Old Testament*, 2d ed. (Princeton: Princeton University Press, 1955); *Supplementary Texts and Pictures Relating to the Old Testament* (Princeton: Princeton University Press, 1969).

ANF Alexander Roberts and James Donaldson, eds., rev. by A. Cleveland Coxe, *The Ante-Nicene Fathers, Translations of the Writings of the Fathers down to A.D. 325*, 10 vols. (1885-1887).

ARAB Daniel D. Luckenbill, *Ancient Records of Assyria and Babylonia*, 2 vols. (Chicago: University of Chicago Press, 1926-1927).

ASR *Anatolian Studies presented to Sir William Mitchell Ramsay*, edited by W. H. Buckler and W. M. Calder (Manchester: University Press, 1923).

ASSEMANI Joseph Assemani, *Ephraem Syri Opera omnia quae exstant Graece, Syriace, Latine*, 6 vols. (Rome: Typographia Pontificia Vaticana, 1732-1746).

ASV *American Standard Version.*

ATR *Anglican Theological Review.*

AVIGAD, *DISCOVERING JERUSALEM* Nahman Avigad, *Discovering Jerusalem* (Nashville and New York: Thomas Nelson, 1983).

AVI-YONAH, *ABBREVIATIONS* Michael Avi-Yonah, *Abbreviations in Greek Inscriptions (The Near East, 200 B.C.-A.D. 1100)*. QDAP 9 (1940) Supplement.

AVI-YONAH, *GAZETTEER* Michael Avi-Yonah, *Gazetteer of Roman Palestine.* Qedem 5 (Jerusalem, 1976).

AVI-YONAH, *HOLY LAND* Michael Avi-Yonah, *The Holy Land from the Persian to the Arab Conquests (536 B.C. to A.D. 640), A Historical Geography* (Grand Rapids: Baker Book House, 1966).

AVI-YONAH, *MADABA MOSAIC* Michael Avi-Yonah, *The Madaba Mosaic Map, with Introduction and Commentary* (Jerusalem: The Israel Exploration Society, 1954); with this cf. the same author's *Map of Roman Palestine*, 2d ed. (London: Oxford University Press, 1940).

BA *Biblical Archaeologist.*

BABCOCK AND KREY Emily Atwater Babcock and A. C. Krey, *A History of Deeds Done Beyond the Sea, by William, Archbishop of Tyre*, 2 vols. (New York: Columbia University Press, 1943).

BAC *Bullettino di archeologia cristiana.*

BADÈ, *TOMBS* William F. Badè, *Some Tombs of Tell en-Nasbeh discovered in 1929* (Berkeley: Palestine Institute Publication no. 2, 1931).

BAGATTI AND MILIK Bellarmino Bagatti and J. T. Milik, *Gli scavi del "Dominus flevit"* (*Monte Oliveto-Geruselemme*). Part I, *La necropoli dei periodo romano.* PSBF 13 (Jerusalem: Franciscan Printing Press, 1958).

BAGATTI, *ANTICHI VILLAGI* Bellarmino Bagatti, *Antichi Villagi Cristiani di Galilea.* PSBFCMI 13 (Jerusalem: Franciscan Printing Press, 1971).

BAGATTI, *CHURCH FROM CIRCUMCISION* Bellarmino Bagatti, *The Church from the Circumcision, History and Archaeology of the Judaeo-Christians.* PSBFSS 2 (Jerusalem: Franciscan Printing Press, 1971).

BAGATTI, *CHURCH FROM GENTILES* Bellarmino Bagatti, *The Church from the Gentiles in Palestine.* PSBFSS 4 (Jerusalem: Franciscan Printing Press, 1971).

BAGATTI, *EXCAVATIONS NAZARETH* Bellarmino Bagatti, *Excavations in Nazareth.* Vol. 1, *From the Beginning till the XII Century.* PSBF 17 (Jerusalem: Franciscan Printing Press, 1969).

BAGATTI, *TOMB OF VIRGIN MARY* Bellarmino Bagatti, M. Piccirillo, and A. Prodomo, *New Discoveries at the Tomb of Virgin Mary in Gethsemane.* PSBFCM 17 (Jerusalem: Franciscan Printing Press, 1975).

BAHAT, *PLANS* Dan Bahat, *Jerusalem, Selected Plans of Historical Sites and Monumental Buildings* (Jerusalem: Ariel Publishing House, 1980).

BAIAS *Bulletin of the Anglo-Israel Archaeological Society* (London).

BALDI Donato Baldi, *Enchiridion Locorum Sanctorum, Documenta S. Evangelii Loca Respicientia*, 2d ed. (Jerusalem: Franciscan Printing Press, 1954. Reprint, 1982).

BAR *Biblical Archaeology Review.*

BARROIS A.-G. Barrois, *Manuel d'archéologie biblique* (Paris: A. et J. Picard et Cie. Vol. I, 1939; Vol. II, 1953).

BASOR *Bulletin of the American Schools of Oriental Research.*

BCH *Bulletin de correspondance hellénique.*

BEN-DOV, *SHADOW OF TEMPLE* Meir Ben-Dov, *In the Shadow of the Temple, The Discovery of Ancient Jerusalem* (New York: Harper and Row, 1985).

BENOIT, *CHRISTMAS* Pierre Benoit, ed., *Christmas, A Pictorial Pilgrimage* (Nashville: Abingdon Press, 1969).

BENOIT, *JESUS AND GOSPEL* Pierre Benoit, *Jesus and the Gospel.* Vol. I (New York: Seabury Press, 1973).

BI *Biblical Illustrator* (Nashville, Tenn.).

BIBLICA *Biblica* (Pontifical Biblical Institute, Rome).

BJRL *Bulletin of the John Rylands Library.*

BR *Bible Review.*

BREYDY Michael Breydy, *Das Annalenwerk des Eutychios von Alexandrien, Ausgewählte Geschichten und Legenden kompiliert von Sa'id ibn Baṭrīq um 935 A.D.* CSCO 471-472, Scriptores Arabici 44-45 (Louvain: E. Peeters, 1985). Vol. 1, Arabic text; Vol. 2, German translation. All references are to the translation.

BRIAND Gaultier Briand, *Nazareth Judéo-Chrétienne.* Cahiers de "La Terre Sainte" (Jerusalem: Franciscan Printing Press, n.d.).

BYZANTION *Byzantion, Revue Internationale des Études Byzantines.*

CAGNAT René Cagnat, *Cours d'épigraphie latine*, 4th ed. (Paris: Fontemoing, 1914).

CAP R. H. Charles, ed., *The Apocrypha and Pseudepigrapha of the Old Testament in English with Introductions and Critical and Explanatory Notes to the Several Books*, 2 vols. (Oxford: Clarendon Press, 1913).

CASEY *The Excerpta ex Theodoto of Clement of Alexandria edited with Translation, Introduction, and Notes,* by Robert P. Casey. Studies and Documents, I (London: Christophers, 1934).

CCSL *Corpus Christianorum Series Latina.*

CEMA K. A. C. Creswell, *Early Muslim Architecture* (Oxford: Clarendon Press, Vol. I, 1932; Vol. II, 1940).

CH. HIST. *Church History.*

CIG *Corpus inscriptionum graecarum* (Berlin: G. Reimer, 1828-1897).

CIL *Corpus inscriptionum latinarum* (Berlin: G. Reimer, 1893-1943).

CKC *Chronos, Kairos, Christos: Nativity and Chronological Studies Presented to Jack Finegan,* ed. Jerry Vardaman and Edwin M. Yamauchi (Winona Lake: Eisenbrauns, 1989).

CLERMONT-GANNEAU Charles Clermont-Ganneau, *Archaeological Researches in Palestine during the Years 1873-1874* (London: Palestine Exploration Fund, Vol. I, 1899; Vol. II, 1896).

CNI *Christian News from Israel.*

CORNFELD Gaalyah Cornfeld, *Archaeology of the Bible: Book by Book* (London: Adam and Charles Black, 1977, © 1976).

CORBO, *SANTO SEPOLCRO* Virgilio C. Corbo, *Il Santo Sepolcro di Gerusalemme,* 3 vols. PSBFCM 29. (Jerusalem: Franciscan Printing Press, 1981).

COÜASNON Charles Coüasnon, *The Church of the Holy Sepulchre in Jerusalem.* The Schweich Lectures of the British Academy, 1972 (London: Oxford University Press, 1974).

CRAI *Comptes rendus des séances de l'Académie des Inscriptions et Belles-Lettres.*

CRAMER Maria Cramer, *Das altägyptische Lebenszeichen im christlichen (koptischen) Ägypten, Eine kultur- und religionsgeschichtliche Studie auf archäologischer Grundlage,* 3d ed. (Wiesbaden: Otto Harrassowitz, 1955).

CROWFOOT, *EARLY CHURCHES* J. W. Crowfoot, *Early Churches in Palestine.* The Schweich Lectures of the British Academy, 1937 (London: The British Academy, 1941).

CSCO *Corpus Scriptorum Christianorum Orientalium.*

CSEL *Corpus scriptorum ecclesiasticorum latinorum.*

CSHB *Corpus Scriptorum Historiae Byzantinae.*

DACL *Dictionnaire d'archéologie chrétienne et de liturgie* (1924ff.).

DALMAN, *JERUSALEM* Gustaf Dalman, *Jerusalem und sein Gelände* (Gütersloh: C. Bertelsmann, 1930).

DALMAN, *SACRED SITES* Gustaf Dalman, *Sacred Sites and Ways, Studies in the Topography of the Gospels.* trans. Paul P. Levertoff (New York: Macmillan, 1935).

DB *Dictionnaire de la Bible.*

DEAN *Epiphanius' Treatise on Weights and Measures, The Syriac Version,* ed. by James E. Dean. SAOC 11 (Chicago: University of Chicago Press, 1935).

DE ROSSI G. B. de Rossi, *La Roma sotterranea cristiana* (1864-1877).

DIEHL E. Diehl, ed., *Inscriptiones latinae christianae veteres,* 3 vols. (Berlin: Weidmann, 1961).

DJD *Discoveries in the Judaean Desert.*

DM *The Mishnah translated from the Hebrew with Introduction and Brief Explanatory Notes,* by Herbert Danby (London: Humphrey Milford, Oxford University Press, 1933; rev. ed. 1964).

DÖLGER Dölger, ΙΧΘΥC (Münster in Westf.: Aschendorf. Vol. I, Das Fisch-Symbol in frühchristlicher Zeit, 2d ed. 1928; Vol. IV, Die Fisch-Denkmäler in der frühchristlichen Plastik, Malerei und Kleinkunst, Tafeln, 1927).

EAEHL *Encyclopedia of Archaeological Excavations in the Holy Land,* ed. Michael Avi-Yonah and Ephraim Stern, 4 vols. (Jerusalem: Israel Exploration Society and Massada Press, 1975-1978).

EB *Encyclopaedia Britannica.*

EBIB *Encyclopaedia Biblica*, ed. T. K. Cheyne and J. Sutherland Black, 4 vols. (New York: Macmillan, 1899-1903).

EI *The Encyclopaedia of Islam*, new edition (Leiden: E. J. Brill; London: Luzac, 1960ff.).

EUSEBIUS, *ONOMASTICON* ed. Erich Klostermann, GCS Eusebius 3:1.

EXPLOR *Explor, A Journal of Theology* (Evanston: Garrett-Evangelical Theological Seminary).

FAWR Jack Finegan, *The Archeology of World Religions: The Background of Primitivism, Zoroastrianism, Hinduism, Jainism, Buddhism, Confucianism, Taoism, Shinto, Islam, and Sikhism* (Princeton: Princeton University Press, 1952; paperback edition in three volumes, 1965).

FCNT *The Fathers of the Church, A New Translation* (Washington, D.C.: The Catholic University of America Press, 1947f.).

FDI Jack Finegan, *Discovering Israel: An Archeological Guide to the Holy Land* (Grand Rapids, Mich.: Eerdmans, 1981).

FHBC Jack Finegan, *Handbook of Biblical Chronology, Principles of Time Reckoning in the Ancient World and Problems of Chronology in the Bible* (Princeton: Princeton University Press, 1964).

FHRJ Jack Finegan, *Hidden Records of the Life of Jesus* (Philadelphia: United Church Press, 1969).

FLAP Jack Finegan, *Light from the Ancient Past; The Archeological Background of Judaism and Christianity*, 2d. ed. (Princeton: Princeton University Press, 1959).

FMM Jack Finegan, *Myth and Mystery, An Introduction to the Pagan Religions of the Biblical World* (Grand Rapids, Mich.: Baker Book House, 1989).

FREY Jean-Baptiste Frey, *Corpus Inscriptionum Iudaicarum, Recueil des inscriptions juives qui vont du IIIe siècle avant Jésus-Christ au VIIe siècle de notre ère* (Città del Vaticano: Pontificio Istituto di Archeologia Cristiana. Vol. I, Europe, 1936; Vol. II, Asie-Afrique, 1952).

GALLING, "NEKROPOLE" K. Galling, "Die Nekropole von Jerusalem," in PJ 32 (1936), pp. 73-101.

GALLING, *REALLEXIKON* Kurt Galling, *Biblisches Reallexikon* (Handbuch zum Alten Testament, ed. Otto Eissfeldt, 1) (Tübingen: J. C. B. Mohr [Paul Siebeck], 1937).

GBT Lazarus Goldschmidt, *Der babylonische Talmud*, 9 vols. (Leipzig: Otto Harrassowitz, 1899-1935).

GCS *Die griechischen christlichen Schriftsteller der ersten drei Jahrhunderte, herausgegeben von der Kirchenväter-Commission der königl. preussischen Akademie der Wissenschaften.*

GEFFCKEN Joh. Geffcken, ed., *Die Oracula Sibyllina* (Leipzig: J. C. Hinrichs, 1902).

GEYER P. Geyer, *Itinera Hierosolymitana saeculi IIII-VIII.* CSEL 39 (Vindobonae: F. Tempsky; Lipsiae: G. Freytag, 1898).

GOODENOUGH Erwin R. Goodenough, *Jewish Symbols in the Greco-Roman Period* (New York: Pantheon Books, Inc., Bollingen Series XXXVII, 1953ff.).

GOUSSEN H. G. Goussen, *Über georgische Drucke und Handschriften; the Festordnung und die Heiligenkalendar des altchristlichen Jerusalems betreffend* (photographic reproduction from *Liturgie und Kunst*, 1923) (München-Gladbach; B. Kühlen, 1923).

HARRIS AND MINGANA Rendel Harris and Alphonse Mingana, *The Odes and Psalms of Solomon* (Manchester: University Press, Vol. I, 1916; Vol. II, 1920).

HERE James Hastings, ed., *Encyclopaedia of Religion and Ethics*, 12 vols. (1910-22).

HOLLIS AND BROWNRIGG Christopher Hollis and Ronald Brownrigg, *Holy Places, Jewish, Christian, and Muslim Monuments in the Holy Land* (New York: Frederick A. Praeger, 1969).

HSNTA Edgar Hennecke, *New Testament Apocrypha*, ed. Wilhelm Schneemelcher, trans. R. McL. Wilson, Vol. I, *Gospels and Related Writings*, 1963; Vol. II, *Writings Relating to the Apostles; Apocalypses and Related Subjects*, 1965. (Philadelphia: The Westminster Press).

HTR *Harvard Theological Review.*

HUCA *Hebrew Union College Annual.*

HZNT *Handbuch zum Neuen Testament,* ed. Hans Lietzmann.

IB *The Interpreter's Bible,* 12 vols. (New York and Nashville: Abingdon Press, 1951-1957).

IDB *The Interpreter's Dictionary of the Bible,* 4 vols. (New York and Nashville: Abingdon Press, 1962).

IDB-S *The Interpreter's Dictionary of the Bible. Supplementary Volume* (Nashville: Abingdon Press, 1976).

IEJ *Israel Exploration Journal.*

JAC *Jahrbuch für Antike und Christentum.*

JANT Montague Rhodes James, *The Apocryphal New Testament* (Oxford: Clarendon Press, 1924).

JAOS *Journal of the American Oriental Society.*

JBL *Journal of Biblical Literature.*

JE *The Jewish Encyclopedia,* ed. Isidore Singer, 12 vols. (New York and London: Funk & Wagnalls Company, 1901-1905).

JEA *The Journal of Egyptian Archaeology.*

JERUSALEM REVEALED *Jerusalem Revealed,* ed. Y. Yadin (Jerusalem: Israel Exploration Society, 1975).

JJS *Journal of Jewish Studies.*

JPOS *Journal of the Palestine Oriental Society.*

JQR *Jewish Quarterly Review.*

JRS *Journal of Roman Studies.*

JSS *Journal of Semitic Studies.*

JTC *Journal for Theology and the Church.*

JTS *Journal of Theological Studies.*

KENYON, JERUSALEM Kathleen M. Kenyon, *Jerusalem, Excavating 3000 Years of History* (London: Thames and Hudson, 1967).

KJV *King James Version.*

KLIJN A. F. J. Klijn, *The Acts of Thomas.* Supplements to Novum Testamentum, V (Leiden: E. J. Brill, 1962).

KLIJN AND REININK A. F. J. Klijn and G. J. Reinink, *Patristic Evidence for Jewish-Christian Sects.* SNT 36 (Leiden: E. J. Brill, 1973).

KLT *Kleine Texte für theologische und philologische Vorlesungen und Übungen,* ed. Hans Lietzmann.

KOPP Clemens Kopp, *Die heiligen Stätten der Evangelien* (Regensburg: Friedrich Pustet, 1959). The condensed English edition is: *The Holy Places of the Gospels* (New York: Herder and Herder, 1963).

KRAELING, BIBLE ATLAS Emil G. Kraeling, *Rand McNally Bible Atlas* (Chicago: Rand McNally and Company, 1956).

KRAELING, GERASA *Gerasa, City of the Decapolis,* ed. Carl H. Kraeling (New Haven: American Schools of Oriental Research, 1938).

KROLL Gerhard Kroll, *Auf den Spuren Jesu,* 10th ed. (Stuttgart: Verlag Katholisches Bibelwerk, 1988).

LA *Liber Annus* (Jerusalem: Studium Biblicum Franciscanum).

LAGRANGE M.-J. Lagrange, *L'Évangile de Jésus-Christ,* new ed. Études bibliques (Paris: J. Gabalda et Cie., 1954).

LCL *The Loeb Classical Library.*

LEFEBVRE Gustave Lefebvre, *Recueil des inscriptions grecques-chrétiennes d'Egypte* (Cairo: Imprimerie de l'Institut Français d'Archéologie Orientale, 1907).

LEVANT *Levant, Journal of the British School of Archaeology in Jerusalem.*

LPPTS *The Library of the Palestine Pilgrims' Text Society,* 13 vols. (London, 1890–97). For contents and manner of citation, see Aziz S. Atiya, *The Crusade, Historiography and Bibliography* (Bloomington: Indiana University Press, 1962).

LXX The Septuagint. Henry Barclay Swete, ed., *The Old Testament in Greek according to the Septuagint.* I, 4th ed. (1909); II, 3d ed. (1907); III, 3d ed. (1905).

Alfred Rahlfs, ed., *Septuaginta, id est Vetus Testamentum Graece iuxta LXX interpretes.* 2 vols. (1935). *Septuaginta, Vetus Testamentum Graecum auctoritate Societatis Litterarum Gottingensis editum* (1931ff.).

MACKOWSKI Richard M. Mackowski, *Jerusalem City of Jesus: An Exploration of the Traditions, Writings, and Remains of the Holy City from the Time of Christ.* Photography by Garo Nalbandian (Grand Rapids: Eerdmans, 1980).

MEISTERMANN Barnabas Meistermann, *Guide to the Holy Land* (London: Burns Oates and Washburne, 1923).

MEYERS AND STRANGE Eric M. Meyers and James F. Strange, *Archaeology, The Rabbis and Early Christianity* (Nashville: Abingdon, 1981).

MPG Jacques Paul Migne, *Patrologiae cursus completus. Series graeca.*

MPL Jacques Paul Migne, *Patrologiae cursus completus. Series latina.*

MÜLLER-BEES *Die Inschriften der jüdischen Katakombe am Monteverde zu Rom entdeckt und erklärt von D. Dr. Nikolaus Müller, nach des Verfassers Tode vervollständigt und herausgegeben von Dr. Nikos A. Bees.* Schriften herausgegeben von der Gesellschaft zur Förderung der Wissenschaft des Judentums (Leipzig: Otto Harrassowitz, 1919). Cf. Harry J. Leon in AJA 31 (1927), pp. 392-394.

MURPHY-O'CONNOR Jerome Murphy-O'Connor, *The Holy Land: An Archaeological Guide from the Earliest Times to 1700,* 2d ed. (Oxford: Oxford University Press, 1986).

NAEHL Avraham Negev, *Archaeological Encyclopedia of the Holy Land* (New York: G. P. Putnam's Sons, 1972).

NAZARETH TODAY *Nazareth Today: Souvenir of the New Basilica of the Annunciation Recently Opened for Worship* (Jerusalem: Franciscan Printing Press, n.d.).

NBAC *Nuovo bulletino di archeologia cristiana.*

NG *National Geographic.*

NHS *Nag Hammadi Studies.*

NÖTSCHER Friedrich Nötscher, *Biblische Altertumskunde* (Die Heilige Schrift des Alten Testaments) (Bonn: Peter Hanstein, 1940).

NPNF Philip Schaff, ed., *A Select Library of the Nicene and Post-Nicene Fathers,* First Series. 14 vols. (1886-1889).

NPNFSS Philip Schaff and Henry Wace, eds., *A Select Library of Nicene and Post-Nicene Fathers of the Christian Church,* second series. 14 vols. (1890-1900).

NSH *The New Schaff-Herzog Encyclopedia of Religious Knowledge,* 12 vols. (New York and London: Funk and Wagnalls, 1908-1912).

NT *New Testament.*

NTAM *New Testament Archaeology Monographs,* ed. Jerry Vardaman (Louisville, Ky.: Southern Baptist Theological Seminary).

NTS *New Testament Studies.*

O'CALLAGHAN R. T. O'Callaghan, "Madaba (Carte de)," in DB Supplément 5 (1957), cols. 627-704.

OESTERLEY W. O. E. Oesterley, *II Esdras (The Ezra Apocalypse)* (London: Methuen and Co. Ltd., 1933).

OIP *Oriental Institute Publications,* University of Chicago.

OP *The Oxyrhynchus Papyri,* ed. Bernard P. Grenfell and Arthur S. Hunt, *et al.* (London: Egypt Exploration Fund, 1898ff).

OT *Old Testament.*

OVADIAH, CORPUS Asher Ovadiah, *Corpus of the Byzantine Churches in the Holy Land.* Theophaneia 22 (Bonn: Peter Hanstein, 1970).

OVADIAH, CORPUS SUPPLEMENTUM Asher Ovadiah and Carla Gomez de Silva, "Supplementum to the Corpus of the Byzantine Churches in the Holy Land," in *Levant* 13 (1981), pp. 200-261.

PACK Roger A. Pack, ed., Artemidorus, *Onirocriticon* (Leipzig: B. G. Teubner, 1963).

PARROT, GOLGOTHA André Parrot, *Golgotha and the Church of the Holy Sepulchre.* Studies in Biblical

Archaeology no. 6 (New York: Philosophical Library, 1957).

PEARLMAN AND YANNAI Moshe Pearlman and Yaacov Yannai, *Historical Sites in the Holy Land* (2d ed., Tel Aviv-Jerusalem: Massadah-P.E.C. Press Ltd., 1965; rev. ed., Valley Forge: Judson Press, 1985).

PEFQS *Palestine Exploration Fund Quarterly*, embodying the *Quarterly Statement of the Palestine Exploration Fund.*

PEQ *Palestine Exploration Quarterly.*

PETERS, *JERUSALEM* F. E. Peters, *Jerusalem: The Holy City in the Eyes of Chroniclers, Visitors, Pilgrims, and Prophets, from the Days of Abraham to the Beginnings of Modern Times* (Princeton: Princeton University Press, 1985).

PJ *Palästinajahrbuch des Deutschen evangelischen Instituts für Altertumswissenschaft des Heiligen Landes zu Jerusalem.*

PO *Patrologia Orientalis.*

PREISIGKE, *Namenbuch* Friedrich Preisigke, *Namenbuch, enthaltend alle griechischen, lateinischen, ägyptischen, hebräischen, arabischen und sonstigen semitischen und nichtsemitischen Menschennamen, soweit sie in griechischen Urkunden (Papyri, Ostraka, Inschriften, Mumienschildren usw.) Ägyptens sich vorfinden* (Heidelberg, 1922).

PSBF *Publications of the Studium Biblicum Franciscanum* (Jerusalem).

PSBFA *Publications of the Studium Biblicum Franciscanum, Analecta.*

PSBFCM *Publications of the Studium Biblicum Franciscanum, Collectio Maior.*

PSBFCMI *Publications of the Studium Biblicum Franciscanum, Collectio Minore.*

PSBFSS *Publications of the Studium Biblicum Franciscanum, Smaller Series.*

PWRE Pauly-Wissowa, *Real-Encyclopädie der classischen Altertumswissenschaft.*

QADMONIOT *Qadmoniot, Quarterly for the Antiquities of Eretz-Israel and Biblical Lands* (Jerusalem: Israel Exploration Society) (in Hebrew).

QDAP *Quarterly of the Department of Antiquities in Palestine.*

QEDEM *Qedem, Monographs of the Institute of Archaeology, The Hebrew University of Jerusalem.*

RABIN Chaim Rabin, *The Zadokite Documents*, 2d ed. (Oxford: Clarendon Press, 1958).

RAC *Rivista di Archeologia Cristiana.*

RAMSAY, *PHRYGIA* W. M. Ramsay, *The Cities and Bishoprics of Phrygia* (Oxford: Clarendon Press, Vol. I, 1895; Vol. I, Part II [cited as II], 1897).

RAO C. Clermont-Ganneau, *Recueil d'archéologie orientale* (Paris: Ernest Leroux, 1888-1924).

RB *Revue Biblique.*

RECENT ARCHAEOLOGY *Recent Archaeology in the Land of Israel*, ed. Hershel Shanks and Benjamin Mazar (Washington, D.C.: Biblical Archaeology Society; Jerusalem: Israel Exploration Society, 1984).

REJ *Revue des Études Juives.*

RFAC *Reallexikon für Antike und Christentum*, ed. Theodor Klauser (Stuttgart: Hiersemann Verlag, 1950ff).

RIVB *Rivista Biblica.*

ROBINSON, *BIBLICAL RESEARCHES* Edward Robinson, *Biblical Researches in Palestine, Mount Sinai and Arabia Petraea*, 3 vols. (Boston: Crocker and Brewster, 1841); Vol. 4, *Later Biblical Researches in Palestine and in the Adjacent Regions* (Boston: Crocker and Brewster, 1857).

RQ *Revue de Qumran.*

RSR *Religious Studies Review.*

RSV *Revised Standard Version.*

SALLER, *SECOND CATALOGUE* Sylvester J. Saller, *Second Revised Catalogue of the Ancient Synagogues of the Holy Land.* PSBFCMI 6 (Jerusalem: Franciscan Printing Press, 1972).

SAOC *Studies in Ancient Oriental Civilization.*

SBT I. Epstein, ed., *The Babylonian Talmud* (London: The Soncino Press, 1935ff.).

SC *Sources Chrétiennes.*

SCHWARTZ Eduard Schwartz, *Eusebius Werke, Die Kirchengeschichte*, 3 vols. GCS IX 1-3 (Leipzig: J. C. Hinrichs, 1903-1909).

SHANKS, *JUDAISM IN STONE* Hershel Shanks, *Judaism in Stone, The Archaeology of Ancient Synagogues* (New York: Harper and Row; Washington, D.C.: Biblical Archaeology Society, 1979).

SHJP Emil Schurer, *A History of the Jewish People in the Time of Jesus Christ*, 5 vols. (New York: Charles Scribner's Sons, 1896). Revisions of the German edition 1901-1909, and photographic reprint by George Olms Verlagsbuchhandlung (Hildesheim, 1964). New revised version, ed. Geza Vermes, Fergus Millar, Matthew Black, and Martin Goodman, *The History of the Jewish People in the Age of Jesus Christ (175 B.C.-A.D. 135)*, 3 vols. in 4 (Edinburgh: T. and T. Clark, 1973-87), cited as SHJP Vermes/Millar.

SIMONS, *JERUSALEM* J. Simons, *Jerusalem in the Old Testament: Researches and Theories* (Leiden: E. J. Brill, 1952).

SJLA *Studies in Judaism in Late Antiquity*, ed. Jacob Neusner.

SL *Studia Liturgica: An International Ecumenical Quarterly for Liturgical Research and Renewal.*

SNT *Supplements to Novum Testamentum.*

SMITH, *GEOGRAPHY* George Adam Smith, *The Historical Geography of the Holy Land* (London: Hodder and Stoughton, 25th ed., 1931. Reprint in Fontana Library, London: Collins, 1966).

SMITH, *JERUSALEM* George Adam Smith, Jerusalem, *The Topography, Economics and History from the Earliest Times to A.D. 70*, 2 vols. (New York: A. C. Armstrong and Son, 1908).

SMR H. Freedman and Maurice Simon, eds. *Midrash Rabbah* (London: Soncino Press, 1939ff).

STIASSNY M. J. Stiassny, with photographs by David Harris, *Nazareth* (Vienna: St. Gabriel-Verlag, 1967).

STUDIA HIEROSOLYMITANA *Studia Hierosolymitana in onore di P. Bellarmino Bagatti, I, Studi archeologici.* PSBFM 22 (Jerusalem: Franciscan Printing Press, 1976).

STYGER Paul Styger, *Die römischen Katakomben* (Berlin: Verlag für Kunstwissenschaft, 1933).

SWDCB William Smith and Henry Wace, *A Dictionary of Christian Biography*, 4 vols. (Boston: Little, Brown and Company, 1877-1887).

SYNAGOGUE IN LATE ANTIQUITY *The Synagogue in Late Antiquity*, ed. Lee I. Levine (Philadelphia: American Schools of Oriental Research, 1987).

SYNAGOGUES REVEALED *Ancient Synagogues Revealed*, ed. Lee I. Levine (Jerusalem: Israel Exploration Society; Detroit: Wayne State University, 1982).

TELL EN-NASBEH *Tell en-Nasbeh Excavated under the Direction of the Late William Frederic Badè*, by Chester C. McCown *et al.*, 2 vols. (Berkeley and New Haven: The Palestine Institute of Pacific School of Religion and The American Schools of Oriental Research, 1947).

TESTA Emmanuele Testa, *Il simbolismo dei giudeo-cristiani.* PSBF 14 (Jerusalem: Franciscan Printing Press, 1962).

TESTA, *NAZARET GIUDEO-CRISTIANA* Emmanuele Testa, *Nazaret Giudeo-Cristiana: Riti, Iscrizioni, Simboli.* PSBFCMI 8 (Jerusalem: Franciscan Printing Press, 1969).

THEOPHANEIA *Theophaneia, Beiträge zur Religions- und Kirchengeschichte des Altertums.*

TOBLER AND MOLINIER Titus Tobler and Augustus Molinier, *Itinera Hierosolymitana et descriptiones terrae sanctae*, 2 vols. (Geneva: J.-C. Fick, 1879 (all of the references here are to vol. I).

VC *Vigiliae christianae.*

VINCENT, *JÉRUSALEM* L.-Hugues Vincent and M.-A. Steve, *Jérusalem de l'Ancien Testament, re-*

cherches d'archéologie et d'histoire (Paris: Librairie Lecoffre, J. Gabalda et Cie, Éditeurs, 3 parts, 1954-1956).

VINCENT, *JÉRUSALEM NOUVELLE* *Jérusalem recherches de topographie, d'archéologie et d'histoire.* Vol. ii, *Jérusalem nouvelle* by Hugues Vincent and F.-M. Abel, 4 fascicules and volume of plates (Paris: Librarie Lecoffre, J. Gabalda, Éditeur, 1914-1926).

VOGEL, *BIBLIOGRAPHY* *Bibliography of Holy Land Sites compiled in Honor of Dr. Nelson Glueck* by Eleanor K. Vogel, Part i, and Part ii by Eleanor K. Vogel and Brooks Holtzclaw, Offprints from HUCA Vols. XLII (1971) and LII (1981) (New York: Hebrew Union College—Jewish Institute of Religion; Part i, 2d printing, 1974; part ii, 1981).

VT *Vetus Testamentum.*

WATZINGER Carl Watzinger, *Denkmäler Palästinas, Eine Einführung in die Archäologie des Heiligen Landes.* Vol. i, *Von den Anfängen bis zum Ende der israelitischen Königszeit,* 1933. Vol. ii, *Von der Herrschaft der Assyrer bis zur arabischen Eroberung,* 1935 (Leipzig: J. C. Hinrichs).

WET John Wilkinson, *Egeria's Travels Newly Translated with Supporting Documents and Notes* (London: S.P.C.K., 1971).

WJJK John Wilkinson, *Jerusalem as Jesus Knew It: Archaeology as Evidence* (London: Thames and Hudson, 1978).

WJP John Wilkinson, *Jerusalem Pilgrims before the Crusades* (Warminster: Aris and Phillips, 1977).

WILPERT, "LA CROCE" G. Wilpert, "La croce sui monumenti delle catacombe," in NBAC 8 (1902), pp. 5-14.

YADIN, *MASADA* Yigael Yadin, *Masada, Herod's Fortress and the Zealots' Last Stand* (London: Weidenfeld and Nicolson, 1966).

YCS *Yale Classical Studies.*

YJS *Yale Judaica Series.*

ZÄS *Zeitschrift für ägyptische Sprache und Alterthumskunde.*

ZAW *Zeitschrift für die alttestamentliche Wissenschaft.*

ZDPV *Zeitschrift des Deutschen Palästina-Vereins.*

ZHT *Zeitschrift für die historische Theologie.*

ZKT *Zeitschrift für katholische Theologie.*

ZNW *Zeitschrift für die neutestamentliche Wissenschaft.*

ZTK *Zeitschrift für Theologie und Kirche.*

Selected bibliographies in the present book may be supplemented by Vogel, *Bibliography.* For maps and plans, see *Holy Land,* Supplement to NG 176.6 (Dec 1989), p. 713A; *Archaeology of Jerusalem* published by Pictorial Archive, Jerusalem (cited as AJPA, above); Bahat, *Plans.*

THE ARCHEOLOGY
OF THE
NEW TESTAMENT

THE LIFE OF JOHN THE BAPTIST

1. A View of Ain Karim and the Church of St. John the Baptist

THE FORERUNNER OF JESUS was known as John the Baptist and was the son of a priest Zechariah and his wife Elizabeth. When Mary visited the home of Zechariah and Elizabeth she went "into the hill country, to a city of Judah" (Lk 1:39); and when John was born and named the events were the subject of conversation "through all the hill country of Judea" (Lk 1:65). The word here rendered "hill country" is ὀρεινή. In the *Natural History* (v 15), which was completed in A.D. 77, Pliny uses the same word in Latin as the name of the district in which, he says, Jerusalem was formerly (*Orinen, in qua fuere Hierosolyma*). Certainly the name was appropriate to the mountainous region in which Jerusalem was located.

Therefore the home of Zechariah and Elizabeth, which was the birthplace of John, was somewhere in the hilly area around Jerusalem. About A.D. 150 *The Protevangelium of James* (22:3; JANT p. 48; HSNTA I, p. 387) represents Elizabeth as fleeing to save John when Herod slaughtered the children, and as going up into the hill country where a mountain was rent asunder and received her. Legendary as this is, the reference is at any rate also to the hill country. Theodosius (530) (Geyer p. 140; LPPTS II-B, p. 10; CCSL CLXXV, p. 117; WJP p. 65) states that it was a distance of five miles from Jerusalem to the place where Elizabeth, the mother of John the Baptist, lived. This agrees with the distance (7.50 kilometers) from Jerusalem westward to the village of Ain Karim ("Spring of the Vineyard"). This village is mentioned by name in the Jerusalem Calendar (before 638) when it

1. A View of Ain Karim and the Church of St. John the Baptist

3

gives this as the place of a festival, celebrated on the twenty-eight of August, in memory of Elizabeth: "In the village of Enquarim, in the church of the just Elizabet, her memory" (Goussen p. 31/Kopp 1959 p. 133). In the *Book of the Demonstration* (312), ascribed to Eutychius of Alexandria (940), it is said: "The church of Bayt Zakariya in the district of Aelia bears witness to the visit of Mary to her kinswoman Elizabeth" (CSCO 193, p. 135). When Jerusalem was rebuilt by Hadrian (135) it was called Aelia Capitolina, so the church just referred to "in the district of Aelia" was in the vicinity of Jerusalem and probably at Ain Karim. Whether the church of Elizabeth mentioned in the Jerusalem Calendar and the church of Zechariah spoken of by Eutychius were two different churches or were one and the same is not fully clear, but the latter will appear more probable in the light of what follows from Daniel. Daniel (1106) describes two separate churches that were evidently at Ain Karim. Proceeding from the monastery of the Holy Cross west of Jerusalem it was, he says (LPPTS IV-C, pp. 51ff.), four versts (the Russian verst equals 3,500 feet or about two-thirds of an English mile) to the house of Zacharias, the house where the holy Virgin came to greet Elizabeth. "A church now occupies this place," he writes; "on entering it there is, to the left, beneath the low altar, a small cavern, in which John the Forerunner was born." Half a verst from there, Daniel continues, is the mountain that gave asylum to Elizabeth and her son when the soldiers of Herod were pursuing them, and this place is also marked with a small church. The church described by Daniel at the site of the house of Zacharias is presumably the same as the church of Zakariya mentioned by Eutychius; it may well be also the same as the church of Elizabeth listed in the Jerusalem Calendar since it marks the place, according to Daniel, where Mary visited Elizabeth. The second church, where the rock received Elizabeth and John, was obviously related to the narrative in *The Protevangelium of James* rather than to the account in the canonical Gospels.

The spring that provides water for the village of Ain Karim must have encouraged settlement in this region from an early time, and pottery from the Middle Bronze Age has been found at or near Ain Karim (G. Ernest Wright in BASOR 71 [Oct. 1938], pp. 28f.). The town may be the same as the Karem (Καρέμ) listed in Jos 15:59 LXX among the cities of the tribe of Judah.

The photograph shows the village as it lies in the hill country, with the Church of St. John the Baptist near the center of the picture. The church has been in the hands of the Franciscans since 1674. In 1941-1942 they conducted excavations in the area immediately west of the church and the adjoining monastery. In the area were uncovered several rock-cut chambers and graves as well as wine presses with mosaic floors and small chapels with mosaic pavements. The southern rock-cut chamber contained pottery of a type which has been found elsewhere around Jerusalem in association with coins of the Herodian dynasty and belongs therefore to the period from about the first century B.C. up to A.D. 70. This chamber must have existed, then, in about the first century B.C., and it is evidence for a community here at the very time of Zechariah, Elizabeth, and John. The other finds show a continuity of the community not only during Roman but also Byzantine and early Arab times. As for St. John's church itself, the present structure may be mainly from the eleventh century (Abel, *Géographie* II, pp. 295f.) but lower portions of the walls probably still remain from the Byzantine period (fourth-seventh centuries). At the front end of the left aisle is a grotto which must correspond with the small cavern mentioned by Daniel.

Sylvester J. Saller, *Discoveries at St. John's, 'Ein Karim, 1941-1942.* PSBF 3 (Jerusalem: Franciscan Press, 1946); Donato Baldi and Bellarmino Bagatti, *Saint Jean-Baptiste dans les souvenirs de sa Patrie.* PSBFCMI 27 (Jerusalem: Franciscan Printing Press, 1980). Photograph: courtesy École Biblique et Archéologique Française.

2. The Church of the Visitation at Ain Karim

THE OTHER ANCIENT church at Ain Karim is known as the Sanctuary of the Visitation. It is located across the village to the southwest from St. John's. In the vicinity are two rock-cut chambers with ledges around the walls, tombs therefore of a type known in Palestine from the end of the Late Bronze Age and in use even in the Roman period (see No. 253). In 1938 the Franciscans conducted excavations in the ancient ruins at the Visitation Church. The early sanctuary was built against a rocky declivity, and both Byzantine and medieval walls were found. In the crypt a recess contains an oval gray rock, 91 by 104 by 70 centimeters in size, with a natural depression in the center. It is venerated as the *pietra del nascondimento*, the "stone in which John was concealed," in obvious dependence on *The Protevangelium of James* (cf. above No. 1).

QDAP 8 (1939), pp. 170-172; Bellarmino Bagatti, *Il santuario della Visitazione ad 'Ain Karim (Montana Judaeae), esplorazione archeologica e ripristino.* PSBF 5 (Jerusalem: Franciscan Press, 1948). Photograph: courtesy École Biblique et Archéologique Française.

3. Marble Statue of Aphrodite from Ain Karim

IN THE EXCAVATIONS at Ain Karim this marble statue of Aphrodite or Venus was found in two broken pieces. As joined together again the total height of the figure is 72 centimeters. The statue appears to be a copy

2. The Church of the Visitation at Ain Karim

of a work of Praxiteles (340 B.C.) and, with its strong and vigorous lines, is thought to belong to the first century of the Christian era. According to Herodotus (I 105) the goddess Aphrodite was worshiped in a temple in Ascalon as early as in the time of Psammetichus (Psamtik I, 663-610 B.C.) of Egypt. According to Jerome (*Letter 58 to Paulinus*, 3) there was from the time of Hadrian to the reign of Constantine—a period of about 180 years—on the rock at Jerusalem, where the cross had stood, a marble statue of Venus that was an object of worship. This was done away with when the Church of the Holy Sepulcher was built and dedicated in 335 (Eusebius, *Life of Constantine* III 26). The statue here shown, made of marble as was the one Jerome describes at Calvary, presumably stood at Ain Karim during the Roman period too, and was also overthrown in the Byzantine period, perhaps somewhat later than the one in Jerusalem.

While the evidence noted thus far seems to point to Ain Karim, there were other traditions. Among the Christian sanctuaries of the Arab period (seventh-tenth centuries) there were two churches of St. John the Baptist of Jerusalem, one on the summit of the Mount of the Olives, the other at the foot of the Mount. Concerning the latter a Slavonic text (*Archives de l'Orient Latin*, II, p. 392; J. T. Milik in RB 67 [1960], p. 562 cf. p. 357) earlier than Daniel (1106) says that the place at the foot of the Mount was that of the house of Zechariah where John was born and from which Elizabeth went into the mountains with her child.

Saller, *Discoveries at St. John's, 'Ein Karim,* pp. 108-115, 190 n. 1, pl. 30, 1 a-c. Photograph: courtesy Palestine Archaeological Museum.

3. Marble Statue of Aphrodite from Ain Karim

4. A View of the Wilderness of Judea

ALTHOUGH JOHN was born in a city in the "hill country" of Judah (No. 1), it is stated of him in Lk 1:80 that he was in the wilderness or, literally, in the deserts (ἐν ταῖς ἐρήμοις) till the day of his manifestation to Israel, i.e., until the day of his public appearance. Like the Hebrew מדבר, which it generally translates in the LXX, the Greek ἔρημος is the desolate, empty, lonely land. It may be stony or sandy, or it may be a grassland. It may be the haunt of nomads. But it is not cultivated, and it is not permanently settled.

Since the birthplace of John was in the land of Judea, the wilderness in which he spent his youth was presumably the wilderness of Judea. The latter is definable from biblical references. Num 21:20 states that Mount Pisgah looks down upon Jeshimon. The latter name means desolated or deserted and probably describes the barren terraces of marl on either side of the Jordan above the Dead Sea and the steep hills behind Jericho and on the west side of the Dead Sea. Jos 15:61-62 lists six "cities" which were in the wilderness of Judah. Among them are the following, whose probable locations are in the area just described and whose names are obviously characteristic for desert sites: Beth-arabah, "House of the Arabah (i.e., the 'arid region' containing the Jordan and Dead Sea and extending to the Gulf of Aqabah)," probably to be identified with Ain Gharba, southeast of Jericho; 'Ir-hammelah, "City of Salt," probably the later Qumran; and En-gedi, "Spring of the Kid," still today a hot spring called Ain Jidi on the west shore of the Dead Sea twenty miles south of Qumran. In all, the area of this wilderness (see map, No. 7) is some thirty-five miles from north to south and fifteen miles from east to west.

This view in the wilderness of Judea is taken from the road between Jerusalem and Jericho. In the distance an ancient trail runs across the hills.

Smith, *Geography*, pp. 312-316. Photograph: JF.

5. Khirbet Qumran and the Dead Sea Scrolls

BECAUSE ZECHARIAH and Elizabeth were already of advanced age at the birth of John, it may be supposed that the child was left without father and mother at a relatively early time. How this child could live "in the wilderness" (Lk 1:80) is difficult to understand, unless there were those there who received him and helped him. In fact there was a community of men living in the Judean wilderness at Qumran, of whom it was said that, although they did not marry, they adopted children and raised them in their own teachings, and it is at least possible that John was taken in here as a child. The possibility encounters problems, of course, since an antipathy is known to have existed between the people of Qumran and the regular temple priests (Vardaman), and Zechariah, John the Baptist's father, was of the priestly family of Abijah (Lk 1:5), one of the regular line of priestly courses or families.

As for Qumran, this is the name of a *wadi* or watercourse that cuts down through the limestone cliffs and through a marl terrace on the northwestern shore of the Dead Sea. On the marl terrace beside Wadi Qumran is the site of Khirbet Qumran (*khirbet* means a ruined place). In 1873-1874 a large ancient cemetery was noted here by Charles Clermont-Ganneau; beginning in 1947 ancient manuscripts and fragments of manuscripts were found in caves in the marl terrace and in the cliffs above by Bedouins and by archeologists, and beginning in 1951 Khirbet Qumran was excavated by archeologists.

Of the architectural remains excavated at Khirbet Qumran the earliest is a rectangular building and a long wall, which are attributed on the basis of the associated pottery to the eighth-seventh centuries B.C. (in Iron Age II) and are thought to represent an Israelite fort of that time. At this point Khirbet Qumran may very probably be identified with the 'Irhammelah or the City of Salt of Jos 15:62.

According to the numerous coins found in Khirbet Qumran, the main buildings may have been constructed under John Hyrcanus (135-104 B.C.) and were certainly occupied under Alexander Janneus (103-76 B.C.). In the reign of Herod the Great the place was probably abandoned for a time, for only few of the coins of this king were found. Such abandonment may well have been due to the great earthquake that Josephus says struck Judea in the seventh year of Herod, 31 B.C. (*Ant.* xv 5, 2 §122; *War* I 19, 3 §370). There is probable evidence of this earthquake in discernible damage in the great tower at Khirbet Qumran and in a large diagonal crack running down through the steps into a large pool. Moreover, in E. Netzer's excavations of the Maccabean period buildings and palaces at Jericho, eight miles north of Qumran, widespread evidence came to light of extensive earthquake damage which brought their occupation to an end at this same time, 31 B.C. (Vardaman).

The coins suggest that Qumran was reoccupied under Herod's son Archelaus (4 B.C.-A.D. 6), during which time some repairs and minor modifications were probably made. Occupation continued from then on until the time of the Jewish war against the Romans. Josephus states that in the spring of A.D. 68 Vespasian set out with his army from Caesarea to finish the conquest of Palestine and on the second day of the month Daisios reached and took Jericho, most of whose inhabitants had already fled to the hill country (*War* IV 8, 1-2 §§443-452). Since Khirbet Qumran is not far from Jericho, it is most prob-

4. A View of the Wilderness of Judea

5. Khirbet Qumran and the Dead Sea Scrolls

able that the Qumran community was also destroyed at this time, i.e., in June A.D. 68. Evidence of the Roman conquest and destruction was found in Khirbet Qumran in Roman arrowheads of iron and a layer of burnt ash in the ruins. For a few years afterward some Roman soldiers may have been quartered at Qumran, and some coins of the Second Revolt of the Jews against Rome suggest that Jewish forces were there at that time. After that Qumran was no longer occupied.

The buildings excavated at Khirbet Qumran suggest that this was an important center of a community but not the place of residence of most of the members of the community, who lived perhaps in more temporary dwellings and also in adjacent caves. The main building was a large rectangular room about 100 by 120 feet in size, fortified with a massive two-story tower at the northwest corner. In the southwest corner were a court and several large rooms. A low bench around the four sides of one room suggests that this was a place of assembly. Fragments from an upper story in this area fitted together to make a plastered table and bench, which together with two Roman period inkwells, one of copper and one of terra cotta, appear to be from a scriptorium, in all probability the very place where many of the scrolls were copied. In an extension of the main building to the south a room twenty-two feet long may have provided a common dining room, for in an adjacent smaller room were found more than one thousand bowls stacked against the wall.

Water was brought down by a stone aqueduct from natural reservoirs at the base of the cliffs above Khirbet Qumran and collected in cisterns and basins, perhaps as many as forty in all. In many cases a flight of steps leads down into the basin, often with low partitions to form several parallel descents. While the steps could make it easier to draw water at different levels, in at least some cases the basin may have been intended for bathing and perhaps for bathing as a ritual act.

As for the cemetery adjacent to the east, it contains about 1,100 tombs. As the excavated examples show, the usual type consisted of a vertical shaft with a place for the body in a recess, closed by stones or mud bricks, under the eastern wall. Burials were very simple, with almost no pottery or jewelry. Potsherds in the earth fill agree in type and date with the pottery found in the nearby building ruins.

The ancient manuscripts and manuscript fragments found in the caves in the Qumran area—commonly known as the Dead Sea Scrolls—are presumably of the same date as the community settlement, and such a date is confirmed by pottery in the caves in which the manuscripts were found and by carbon-14 dating of the linen scroll wrappers at a median date of A.D. 33 ± 200 years (DJD I, pp. 18-38). In the citation of these texts an internationally accepted system of abbreviations is employed. First, the material on which the writing is found is indicated, no sign meaning leather, "p" standing for papyrus, "cu" for copper, and "o" for ostracon. Second, the place of discovery is shown, 1Q, for example, meaning Cave 1 at Qumran. Third, the contents of the document are shown. Biblical and apocryphal books are designated with customary abbreviations. Commentaries are indicated with the letter "p" standing for *pesher* or commentary. New works are marked with a letter corresponding to the first letter of their Hebrew title as known or as supposed. Thus the work commonly called the Manual of Discipline is designated 1QS, the "S" standing for the

word סרק (*serek*) meaning the "Order" or "Rule" of the community; and The War of the Sons of Light with the Sons of Darkness is 1QM from מלחמה (*milhamah*) meaning "War." Among the scrolls almost all the books of the Old Testament are represented as well as some commentaries, apocryphal books, and the like. Notable are an almost complete copy of Isaiah (1QIsᵃ) and a Commentary on Habakkuk (1QpHab). There are also new compositions including the just-mentioned Manual of Discipline and War book. Similar in language and ideas to the Manual of Discipline is the so-called Zadokite Document, which was found in Cairo in 1896, of which a fragment was found in Cave 6 at Qumran (6QD).

As to the people for whom Qumram was a community center and from whom the scrolls come, it is the prevailing opinion that they were more or less closely related to the Essenes of whom we learn from Josephus, Philo, and Pliny. Josephus (*Ant.* XVIII 1, 5 §§18-22; *War* II 8, 2 §§119-161) says that the Essenes live simply and have their property in common. They disdain marriage but adopt children to raise in accordance with their own principles; one order, however, allows marriage. They settle in various towns. They clothe themselves in white. They pray before sunrise, labor in the morning and in the afternoon, bathe in cold water, and eat their meals in common. They take an extraordinary interest in the writings of the ancients. One desiring to join the order is proved for a year, then allowed to share in the waters of purification, but tested yet two years more before being admitted to take the common food.

Philo (*Every Good Man is Free* 75-91, LCL IX [1941], pp. 53-63) describes the Essenes in much the same way as Josephus does; he says that they are characterized by frugality, simple living, contentment, humility, love of men, and the spirit of fellowship, and he adds that they are indeed "athletes of virtue." Pliny (*Natural History* V, xv) calls the Essenes a "solitary tribe" located on the west side of the Dead Sea and says that they are remarkable for having no women, no money, and only palm trees for company.

The correspondence of these descriptions with what is found at Khirbet Qumran in terms of location and arrangements for ablutions, communal eating, and scribal activity goes far to support the identification of the people of Qumran with the Essenes. Likewise the large number of biblical and other ancient texts preserved in the Dead Sea Scrolls agrees with the extraordinary interest the Essenes were said to have in the writings of the ancients. In particular, too, the community life described in the Manual of Discipline (1QS) exhibits characteristic features like those attributed to the Essenes. Thus the manual speaks about living in "the order of the community (יחד, *yahad*)" (I 1), into which the members shall bring all their property (I 12). No one may be admitted who prefers to walk in his own stubbornness of heart, nor can he be sanctified by any washing (III 4-6), but those who turn from wickedness and are cleansed form together a holy congregation (עדה, 'edah) (v 20). In other information about the Qumran community in the manual we learn that in public gathering the "session of the many (רבים , rabbim)" is presided over by a supervisor (מבקר , mebaqqer) or overseer (פקיד , paqid) (VI 8, 12, 14), and in the Zadokite Document we likewise hear of the mebaqqer and of the "assembly" (קהל , qahal). All of this organizational terminology is also of interest in connection with the organization of the early Christian church. The emphasis upon community (yaḥad) makes one think of the "fellowship" (κοινωνία) of the Jerusalem church (Ac 2:42), and at both Qumran and Jerusalem there was actual community of property. The word "congregation" ('edah) is that usually translated συναγωγή, "synagogue," in the Septuagint (Ex 12:3, etc.), and this word is used for the Christian assembly in Jas 2:2. The "many" (rabbim) of the Qumran community are designated by a word (rab) to which in the Septuagint the term πλῆθος, "multitude," often corresponds (Gen 16:10, etc.), and the latter word is used for the Christian group in Ac 6:2, 5; 15:12, 30. The two titles of supervisor (mebaqqer) or overseer (paqid) seem to have about the same meaning and the latter, paqid, is translated in the Septuagint by ἐπίσκοπος (Jg 9:28; Neh 11:9, 14, 22), while in the New Testament the same word appears in the Revised Standard Version as "guardian" (Ac 20:28; I P 2:25) and "bishop" (Phil 1:1; I Tim 3:2; Tit 1:7). As for the word "assembly" (qahal) used in the Zadokite Document, it is usually translated by ἐκκλησία in the Septuagint (Dt 31:30, etc.), and this is the word for "church" in the New Testament.

Charles Clermont-Ganneau, *Archaeological Researches in Palestine during the Years 1873-1874*, 2 vols. (London: Committee of the Palestine Exploration Fund, 1896-1899), II (1896), pp. 14-16; Millar Burrows, *The Dead Sea Scrolls of St. Mark's Monastery* (New Haven: American Schools of Oriental Research, 1950); William H. Brownlee, *The Dead Sea Manual of Discipline*. BASOR Supplementary Studies 10-12 (1951); E. L. Sukenik, *The Dead Sea Scrolls of the Hebrew University* (Jerusalem: Magnes Press, 1955); Theodor H. Gaster, *The Dead Sea Scriptures in English Translation* (Garden City, N.Y.: Doubleday, 1956); John C. Trever, *Scrolls from Qumrân Cave I* (Jerusalem: Albright Institute of Archaeological Research and the Shrine of the Book, 1972); R. De Vaux, *Archaeology and the Dead Sea Scrolls* (London: Published for the British Academy by Oxford University Press, 1973); Géza Vermès, *The Dead Sea Scrolls in English*, 3d ed. (London and New York: Penguin, 1987); Joseph Fitzmyer, *The Dead Sea Scrolls: Major Publications and Tools for Study* (Missoula, Mont.: Scholars Press, 1977, new edition to come); *Discoveries in the Judean Desert* (abbreviated DJD); *Revue de Qumran* (abbreviated RQ). For the City of Salt, see M. Noth, "Der alttestamentliche Name der Siedlung auf chirbet ḳumrân," in ZDPV 71 (1955), pp. 111-123. On delay and progress in publication of the Dead Sea Scrolls see BAR 16, 4 (July/Aug 1990), pp. 44-49. One as yet unpublished text was found in six copies in Cave 4 and from the phrase *miqsat ma'aseh ha-Torah*, meaning "some of the legal rulings of [i.e., pertaining to] the Torah," is identified as 4QMMT. It is in the form of a letter that was either written or purported to have been written to the priestly establishment at Jerusalem about some twenty religious laws (*halakhah*, pl. *halakhot*), on which Qumran differed from Jerusalem, this being at least in part the reason for the separation from Jerusalem of the Qumran group. It is expected that when 4QMMT is published and studied further it will cast new light on the origin of the Qumran community and, some think, will require reconsideration of the theory of Essene origin of the sect as presently generally accepted. See Stephen Goranson, "Pharisees, Sadducees, Essenes, and 4QMMT," in BA 53 (1990), p. 70f.; Lawrence H. Schiffman, "The New Halakhic Letter (4QMMT) and the Origins of the Dead Sea Sect," in BA 53 (1990), pp. 64-73; and "The Significance of the Scrolls," in BR 6, 5 (Oct 1990), pp. 18-27; Hershel Shanks, "The Difference between Scholarly Mistakes and Scholarly Concealment, The Case of MMT," in BAR 16, 5 (Sept/Oct 1990), pp. 64f. Against Schiffman and in favor of the Essene hypothesis, see James C. Vanderkam, "The People of the Dead Sea Scrolls, Essenes or Sadduces?" in BR 7, 2 (Apr 1991), pp. 42-46. For the Essenic character of the Qumran community and the probability that John the Baptist was at Qumran in his early life, see William H. Brownlee in *Interpretation* 9 (1955), p. 73; Otto Betz, "Was John the Baptist an Essene?" in BR 6, 6 (Dec 1990), pp. 18-25. Photograph: JF.

6. Column VIII of the Manual of Discipline

IN THEIR CENTER above the Dead Sea the Qumran community was located on the edge of the wilderness of Judea, the limestone hills of which fall off precipitously to the marl terrace on which their buildings were constructed (No. 5). In Israelite experience and thought the wilderness was of great importance. It was a place of political refuge and a base for revolutionary action. When Saul pursued David, David took refuge in the wilderness of En-gedi (I Sam 24:1). When Antiochus Epiphanes persecuted the Jews, "Many who were seeking righteousness and justice went down to the wilderness to dwell there, they, their sons, their wives, and their cattle, because evils pressed heavily upon them" (I Macc 2:29), and there in the wilderness, when they were hunted out by the enemy and refused to defend themselves on the sabbath, they died. Judas Maccabeus kept himself and his companions alive in the wilderness (II Macc 5:27). An Egyptian led four thousand *sicarii* into the wilderness (Ac 21:38).

The wilderness was also unforgettably associated with the thought of the exodus. The first exodus, from Egypt, was across the wilderness of Sinai. The second exodus, from Babylon, was across the wilderness between Babylonia and Palestine and, in connection with it, Isaiah (40:3) heard a voice crying: "In the wilderness prepare the way of the Lord,/make straight in the desert a highway for our God."

This passage in Isaiah was of decisive importance in the thought of the Qumran community. In Column VIII of the Manual of Discipline (1QS), shown in the present photograph (No. 6), in the middle of the column the text states that, according to these rules, the men of the community will separate themselves from the midst of perverse men to go to the wilderness to prepare the way, i.e., to do what the Scripture instructs when it says, "In the wilderness prepare the way of. . . ./make straight in the desert a highway for our God." This is an exact quotation of Is 40:3 except that, as may be seen in line 14 of Column VIII, four dots stand in the place of the four letter name of the Lord (YHWH), which was too holy to write or pronounce. Then it is further explained that this reference really means to study the Law which God commanded through Moses, so as to do, as occasion arises, according to all that was revealed in it and according to what the prophets also revealed through God's Holy Spirit. It was, therefore, with deliberate intent that the Qumran community established itself in the wilderness, there to study and do the Law, and thus to prepare the way of the Lord. The purpose was, as it were, to make a third exodus and a third conquest of the promised land, a conquest which would be both "concurrent with, and instrumental in, the ushering in of the Kingdom of God" (Williams). Significantly enough, the same crucial pas-

sage in Isaiah is cited in all four Gospels (Mt 3:3; Mk 1:3, Lk 3:4; Jn 1:23) to describe the work of John the Baptist as he made his public appearance, and according to Jn 1:23, he himself cited the passage with respect to his own work. The relationship of John in his public work with Qumran was, therefore, not only one of geographical nearness but also of similarity of thought form. Yet the work to which John addressed himself was not that deemed most important at Qumran, namely, the study of the Law, but rather something that was distinctively different, namely, the preaching of a baptism of repentance.

Millar Burrows, *The Dead Sea Scrolls of St. Mark's Monastery*, Vol. II, Fascicle 2, *Plates and Transcription of the Manual of Discipline* (New Haven: The American Schools of Oriental Research, 1951); William H. Brownlee, *The Dead Sea Manual of Discipline, Translation and Notes.* BASOR Supplementary Studies Nos. 10-12, pp. 32-33; Theodor H. Gaster, *The Dead Sea Scriptures in English Translation* (Garden City, N.Y.: Doubleday, 1956), p. 56; George H. Williams, *Wilderness and Paradise in Christian Thought* (New York: Harper & Brothers, 1962), p. 19. Photograph: Burrows, *op. cit.*, pl. VIII, courtesy American Schools of Oriental Research.

7. Map of the Lower Jordan Valley

WHEN JOHN THE BAPTIST came on the scene of his public work he was found in "the region about the Jordan" (Lk 3:3) and was baptizing people in the Jordan (Mt. 3:6, Mk 1:5). The sketch map shows sites on the Lower Jordan and in the adjacent valley as far westward as Jericho.

Map: JF, cf. Kopp 1959, p. 141.

8. The Jordan River near the Monastery of St. John

WHEN JOHN CHOSE to baptize in the Jordan River it was presumably first of all because this stream provided adequate water for the ceremony of immersion ($\beta\alpha\pi\tau\iota\zeta\omega$ Mt 3:6, etc., in LXX for טבל IV K 5:14, "to dip"). It is also true that a connection was recognized between John and Elijah (Mk 1:2 cites Mal 4:5; see also Mt 11:14; 17:12; Mk 9:13), and John clothed himself in the same garb as Elijah (Mt 3:4; Mk 1:6; cf. II K 1:8). At the close of his life (II K 2) Elijah was at Jericho and Gilgal and then went across the Jordan; therefore it could be that John's choice of a Jordan locale in which to work was related to his enactment of the role of Elijah. Since all the people, as it seemed, of Jerusalem and Judea went out to John (Mt 3:5; Mk 1:5), it is probable that his place of preaching and baptizing was at a point on the river to which a main road or roads came down. As may be seen on the preceding Map of the Lower Jordan Valley (No.

6. Column VIII of the Manual of Discipline

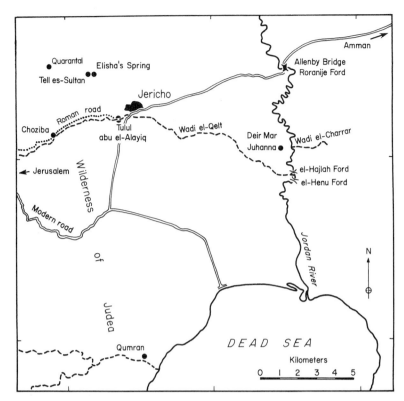

7. Map of the Lower Jordan Valley

8. The Jordan River near the Monastery of St. John

7), the main road east from Jericho to Amman crosses the river today by a bridge at what used to be the Roranije ford. This point is five miles on the road from Jericho and about nine miles on the river upstream from where the Jordan enters the Dead Sea. Below the Roranije ford there were three other ancient crossings. The next was about four and one-half miles downstream where the Deir Mar Juhanna or Monastery of St. John stands on a low hill seven hundred yards west of the river and, on the other side, the Wadi el-Charrar comes in from the east. The photograph shows the river in this area. Another mile below was the el-Hajlah ford, near where the Wadi el-Qelt comes in from the west. Half again as far southward was the el-Henu crossing. The circumstances of John's work noted above make it probable that his activity was somewhere in this general area.

Photograph: JF.

9. Baptism in the Jordan River near the Monastery of St. John

IN JN 1:28 (cf. Jn 10:40) there is reference to a specific point for John's work when it is stated that he was baptizing "in Bethany beyond the Jordan." In the NT the well-known Bethany is the village on the slope of the Mount of Olives near Jerusalem, and this Bethany beyond the Jordan is not mentioned except in the Fourth Gospel. While in Jn 1:28 the best and earliest manuscripts read Bethany (βηθανία), there is also a variant reading of Bethabara (βηθαβαρά). The latter reading is now preserved only in some relatively late manuscripts (Π = 041 ninth century, Ψ = 044 eighth-ninth centuries, Sinaitic and Curetonian Syriac, etc.), but Origen was acquainted with it and was convinced that it was correct. Bethany, he explains in his *Commentary on John* (VI 24 GCS Origenes IV, p. 149; ANF IX, p. 370), was the town of Lazarus, Martha, and Mary, only fifteen stadia (less than two miles) from Jerusalem, but the river Jordan is about 180 stadia (over twenty miles) distant and there is no place named Bethany in its neighborhood. "They say," however, Origen declares, "that Bethabara is pointed out on the banks of the Jordan, and that John is said to have baptized there." His further contribution to the subject is the suggestion that in etymology Bethany means "House of obedience," and Bethabara "House of preparation," the latter obviously being the more appropriate to the work of the one who prepared the way before the face of the Christ. Eusebius also, in the *Onomasticon* (p. 58), lists Bethany as the village of Lazarus at the Mount of Olives and gives Bethabara (βηθααβαρά) as the place where John baptized and where even until now, as he says, many of the brethren aspire to receive the washing. Yet one other textual variant appears in Jn 1:28 in the hand of the second correc-

9. Baptism in the Jordan River near the Monastery of St. John

tor of Codex Sinaiticus and the margin of the Harklean Syriac, namely, Betharaba, (βηθαραβά). This can be explained as a simple error for Bethabara or as an equation of the place with the Betharabah listed in Jos 15:6, which was probably located southeast of Jericho (cf. above No. 4).

In the itinerary of the Bordeaux Pilgrim (333), after a description of the Dead Sea, it is said (Geyer p. 24; LPPTS I-B, p. 26; CCSL CLXXV, p. 19; WET p. 161): "From there to the Jordan, where the Lord was baptized by John, is five miles. Here there is a place by the river, a little hill on the far bank, where Elijah was caught up into heaven." The distance of five Roman miles, or about four and one-half English miles, upstream from the Dead Sea would have brought the pilgrim to about the point of the Monastery of St. John. The little hill on the east side would be the Jebel Mar Elyas or Mount of St. Elijah, which is less than a mile and one-half up the Wadi el-Charrar. Jewish tradition must have pointed to this as the place where Elijah was taken up. According to II K 2:4, 6, 8-11, the place of that event was indeed east of the Jordan across from Jericho. By the hill are abundant springs and the waters here might well have been used for baptizing when the Jordan was in flood.

Theodosius (530) (Geyer pp. 145-146; LPPTS II-B, pp. 14-15; CCSL CLXXV, pp. 121-122; WJP p. 69); also says that it was five (Roman) miles from the Dead Sea to the place where the Lord was baptized and declares that the place was marked by a marble column with an iron cross. He also says that there was a Church of St. John the Baptist here, but does not make it plain whether the church was on the west bank or the east. It could have been where the Monastery of St. John is now. As to the place where the Lord was baptized, however, he says explicitly that it was on the east side (trans Iordanem) and he mentions there a little mountain where Elijah was taken up, obviously identical with the hill mentioned by the Bordeaux Pilgrim.

The Anonymous of Piacenza (570) mentions (Geyer p. 165; LPPTS II-D, pp. 8-9; CCSL CLXXV, p. 134) the same hill and the spring, two Roman miles (slightly less than one and one-half English miles) from the Jordan, where John used to baptize. The valley itself is where Elijah was found when the raven brought him bread and meat. Wadi el-Charrar was, accordingly, identified with "the brook Cherith that is east of the Jordan" (I K 17:5), and with this identification, it appears more clearly than ever that John chose to do his work in surroundings associated with Elijah. The place where Jesus himself was baptized (Geyer pp. 166-168; LPPTS II-D, pp. 10-12; CCSL CLXXV, pp. 135-136; WJP p. 82), however, was at the Jordan. At the place a wooden cross stood in the water and above the Jordan, not far from the river, was the Monastery of St. John. At Epiphany, says the Anonymous, many peo-

ple come here to the river to be baptized. The photograph pictures the preparation for the conduct of baptism by the Greek Orthodox Church at this traditional place on the Jordan River near the Monastery of St. John.

Photograph: JF.

10. The Region of Jericho on the Madaba Mosaic Map

THE AREA WHICH has just been under discussion is depicted in detail on the Madaba Mosaic map. We will now show this area in photographs of three slightly overlapping sections (Nos. 10-12). The first photograph reproduces the area around Jericho. Extending up a little above the middle of the picture are the dark mountains of the wilderness of Judea. Beyond is the lighter plain of the Jordan and in the extreme upper right-hand corner the curve of the shore of the Dead Sea. On the edge of the plain and near the mountains are, from left to right: Archelais (Αρχελαις) (Josephus, Ant. XVII 13, 1 §340; XVIII 2, 2 §31); the place of Saint Elisha (Τὸ τοῦ ἁγίου Ελισαιου), undoubtedly the spring cleansed by Elisha (II K 2:19-22) and visited by the Bordeaux Pilgrim (Geyer p. 24; LPPTS I-B, p. 25; CCSL CLXXV, p. 18; WET pp. 160f.) at 1,500 paces from Jericho, shown here with a sanctuary from under the southern tower of which a stream flows toward the city; and Jericho (·Ι· εριχω). Farther out in the plain are Galgala, the place which is also called the Twelve Stones (Γαλγαλα τὸ καὶ Δωδεκαλιθον), marking the site of Jos 4:20, located by Eusebius (Onomasticon pp. 64-67) two miles from Jericho in an eastward direction (πρὸς ἡλίου ἀνατολάς Jos 4:19 LXX) and shown here with a wall in which are embedded twelve white stones; and the Threshing Floor of Atad which is now Bethagla ("Αλων 'Ατὰθ ἡ νῦν βηθαγλά), the site of Gen 50:10-11, located by Eusebius (Onomasticon p. 8) three miles from Jericho and two miles from the Jordan, i.e., on the west side as shown here. The fact that the passage in Genesis puts the place "beyond the Jordan" can be explained by supposing that the statement is phrased from the point of view of Joseph's party as they came up from Egypt. On the other hand, the site may have been originally in Jordan and transferred to the west side for the convenience of visiting pilgrims. It is not, however, mentioned in any of the ancient pilgrim itineraries. From Archelais to Bethagla many palm trees are shown and they are particularly numerous around Jericho. Both Josephus (Ant. XVIII 2, 2 §31) and Pliny (Nat. Hist. XIII 9, 44) mention the date palms at Archelais, and Josephus (Ant. XVII 13, 1 §340) tells of a whole plain planted with palm trees at Jericho.

Photograph: courtesy Victor R. Gold.

10. The Region of Jericho on the Madaba Mosaic Map. North is at *left* on Madaba mosaic.

11. The Lower Jordan River on the Madaba Mosaic Map. North is at *left* on Madaba mosaic.

11. The Lower Jordan River on the Madaba Mosaic Map

THIS PHOTOGRAPH OVERLAPS the east edge of the preceding section and repeats in whole or in part the legends for Galgala and Bethagla (see No. 10). Looking beyond these legends, we see the Jordan River flowing down through the plain and into the Dead Sea. In the river are several fish and the one farthest downstream is turning back, evidently in distaste, from the salt water of the Dead Sea, in which are no living creatures. Upstream there is a contruction that reaches across the river, with a boat beneath it. This is perhaps a ferry guided by a rope across the river. On the west bank at this point is a tower built upon an arch and approached by a ladder. Eusebius (*Onomasticon* p. 154) mentions a certain Magdalsenna (Μαγδαλσεννά), which marked the border of Judea and was eight miles north of Jericho; since Magdal can be Hebrew "tower" (מגדל) and the location is approximately correct, this tower may mark that site. On either side of the river crossing is a large desert shrub, perhaps a thorn bush, and these mark the plains of Jericho on this side of the river and the plains of Moab in Jordan. In Jordan a lion, the representation of which is badly damaged, is chasing a gazelle. Also partly damaged are two unidentified villages with many date palms.

Coming to the banks of the river and the names associated with the work of John the Baptist, we have on the west side the name Bethabara and, under it, a legend in red letters (partly obscured by the leg of the photographer's tripod) identifying the place of St. John (and) of the baptism (Βεθαβαρὰ τὸ τοῦ ἁγίου Ἰωάννου τοῦ βαπτίσματος), and a church building. In Jn 1:28 Bethany (or Bethabara) is located beyond the Jordan, and both the Bordeaux Pilgrim and Theodosius (cf. above No. 9) mention the place of the baptism of Jesus in some connection with the hill from which Elijah was caught up, which was on the east side of the river. If John was working thus on the east side of the river and if Jesus was baptized in the river itself (Mk 1:9), the actual place would presumably have been near the east bank. The transfer of Bethabara and of the traditional place of the baptism to the west bank, as shown here in the Madaba Mosaic, would make the spot more convenient for pilgrims to visit, and this may account for the change.

On the map we see on the east side of the river at about the place where we would have expected to find Bethabara and the hill of Elijah, a site with an inscription reading "Aenon, there now Sapsaphas" (Αἰνὼν ἔνθα νῦν ὁ Σαπσαφάς). Since the map shows the Aenon identified as near Salim (Jn 3:23) farther up the river (cf. No. 12) this is not that Aenon, at least in the opinion of the mapmaker, although his use of the name here may mean

that one tradition did localize the other Aenon at this place. Since the name Aenon is doubtless derived from the Hebrew word for "springs" (עינים), it could refer here to the springs by the hill from which Elijah was supposed to have been taken up, springs which could have been used for baptism by John as well as the Jordan itself, and which are probably to be identified with the spring where John was said to baptize, two miles from the Jordan, as mentioned by the Anonymous of Piacenza (Geyer p. 199: LPPTS II-D, p. 9; CCSL CLXXV, p. 134; WJP p. 81 and cf. above No. 9). Sapsaphas may mean "willow" (Avi-Yonah in IDB I, p. 52). A Sapsas is mentioned by John Moschus (MPG 87, col. 2851), who also says that the patriarch Elias of Jerusalem (494-518) built a church and monastery there. No buildings are shown at this site on the Madaba Map, but there is an object on the right side which may be a tree, and a representation on the left side which could stand for a cave. Around 840 Epiphanius Monachus (MPG 120, col. 272; WJP p. 120) mentions a cave of the forerunner about a mile beyond the Jordan (πέραν τοῦ Ἰορδάνου ὡς ἀπὸ μιλίου ἑνός ἐστι τὸ σπήλαιον τοῦ προδρόμου), which may be what is meant here.

F.-M. Abel in RB 41 (1932), pp. 248-252 and pl. v facing p. 240; Sylvester J. Saller and Bellarmino Bagatti, *The Town of Nebo (Khirbet el-Mekhayyat), with a Brief Survey of Other Ancient Christian Monuments in Transjordan.* PSBF 7 (Jerusalem: Franciscan Press, 1949), p. 226 no. 59 and pl. 54 no. 1; Wolfgang Wiefel "Bethabara jenseits des Jordan (Joh. 1, 28)," in ZDPV 83 (1967), pp. 72-81. Photograph: courtesy Victor R. Gold.

12. Upper Portion of the Jordan River on the Madaba Mosaic Map

THIS IS THE UPPERMOST part of the river preserved in the fragmentary mosaic map at Madaba. As also in the lower course of the river (see No. 11), there is a boat in the stream and a construction across the river, probably a ferry. Below this, a tributary river, evidently the Jabbok (Wadi Zerqa), comes in from the far side and creates a disturbance in the Jordan. On the west bank at this point is a village labeled Κορεους, Coreus. This is doubtless the Coreae (Κορέαι) that Josephus (*War* I 6, 5 §134; IV 8, 1 §449; *Ant.* XIV 3, 4 §49; 5, 2 §83) mentions as below Scythopolis and on the border of Judea, a point through which Pompey marched in 63 B.C. and Vespasian in A.D. 68. It is identified with Tell el-Mazar at the lower end of Wadi Far 'ah (BASOR 62 [Apr. 1936], p. 14). Upstream on the west side opposite the ferry is a place labeled Αἰνὼν ἡ ἐγγὺς τοῦ Σαλήμ, clearly intended to be the Aenon near Salim Αἰνὼν ἐγγὺς τοῦ Σαλίμ of Jn 3:23. The location is in agreement with Eusebius (*Onomasticon* p. 40) who places the Aenon in Jn 3:23 at eight miles

12. Upper Portion of the Jordan River on the Madaba Mosaic Map. North is at *left* on Madaba mosaic.

south of Scythopolis, and also with a description given by Aetheria (Geyer pp. 56-58; LPPTS I-C, pp. 30-32; CCSL CLXXV, pp. 54-56; WET pp. 108-111). The latter came down into the Jordan valley to a village called Sedima, which, she was given to understand, had been the Salem of King Melchizedek. Two hundred paces from there she was shown a garden called the Garden of St. John. Here was a spring that flowed into a pool and in this, she says, it appeared that John had baptized. On the Madaba Map the pool may be represented by the row of bluish-greenish cubes above the name Aenon. In the area indicated, some twelve kilometers south of Tell el-Husn (ancient Beth-shean and Scythopolis), there is in fact a region of abundant springs (Ain ed-Deir and others) (RB 22 [1913], pp. 222-223). The marches of Pompey and Vespasian down the Jordan valley and through this region, referred to above, show that this was on a main route of travel. If John the Baptist worked here as well as at the lower fords of the Jordan (cf. above No. 8), he was in both cases in regions where large numbers of people would have passed.

Photograph: courtesy Victor R. Gold.

13. Baptismal Pool and Apse in the Byzantine Church in the Desert of St. John near Hebron

WHILE THE AREA dealt with in the preceding sections (Nos. 4-12) appears best to correspond with the indications in the Gospels as to where the work of John the Baptist was centered, there are also other but later traditions. In the pilgrim record known as Anonymous II (1170), there is mention of returning from Hebron toward Jerusalem and of passing the Church of St. John the Baptist, where he preached baptism and repentance and where there was an unfailing spring of water in the midst of the desert (LPPTS VI-A, p. 11). The combination of church and desert and spring in the vicinity of Hebron corresponds with a valley five miles west of that city, in which are a spring still called Ain el-Ma'mudiyyeh, "spring of baptism," and the ruins of a small Byzantine church. The church was probably built in the time of Justinian (527-565). As shown in the photograph, there is in the apse a circular baptistery over four feet deep, with four marble steps leading down into it. A conduit opens in the wall at one side, which conducts water to the baptistery from the spring. Another location for the "desert of John," for which the attestation is even later, is about a mile and one-half west of Ain Karim at Ain el-Khabis, the "Spring of the Hermit." It is mentioned first by Ulrich Brunner, who made a trip from Würzburg to Jerusalem in 1470 (ZDPV 29 [1906], p. 43). At the place there are now a church and monastery built by the Franciscans.

"Le désert de Saint Jean près d'Hébron," in RB 53 (1946), I, "La tradition," by Clemens Kopp, pp. 547-558; II, "Les monuments," by A.-M. Steve, pp. 559-575; "Die Jerusalemfahrt des Kanonikus

13. Baptismal Pool and Apse in the Byzantine Church in the Desert of St. John near Hebron

Ulrich Brunner vom Haugstift in Würzburg (1470)," ed. Reinhold Röhricht, in ZDPV 29 (1906), pp. 1-50. Photograph: RB 53 (1946), pl. IX, courtesy École Biblique et Archéologique Française.

14. Machaerus

THE DEATH OF John the Baptist is related in Mt 14:3-12 and Mk 6:17-29. The king who ordered John beheaded was Herod Antipas, tetrarch of Galilee and Perea from 4 B.C. to A.D. 39. At his birthday banquet, it is stated in Mk 6:21, there were present "the leading men of Galilee." This could suggest that the banquet was held in the city of Tiberias, which Herod Antipas built as his capital on the Sea of Galilee (Josephus, *Ant.* XVIII 2, 3 §36). Josephus (*Ant.* XVIII 5, 2 §119), however, states

that John was brought in chains to Machaerus and there put to death. The site of Machaerus, shown in this photograph, is some fifteen miles southeast of the mouth of the Jordan, in the wild and desolate hills that overlook the Dead Sea from the east. The fortress on this site was built originally by the Hasmonean king Alexander Jannaeus (104-78 B.C.) in about the year 90 (*War* VII 6, 2 §171), destroyed by Pompey's general Gabinius in 57 B.C. (*War* I 8, 5 §167), then rebuilt very splendidly by Herod the Great. Upon the death of the latter it passed into the hands of Herod Antipas, and his relations with Nabatea doubtless made the place, strategically located in the direction of Nabatea, of special importance to him. After the death of Herod Antipas (A.D. 39) his tetrarchy was given to Herod Agrippa I, who then ruled over Machaerus. After Agrippa's death (A.D. 44); however, the Romans occupied the country, and only in A.D.

14. Machaerus

68 early in the First Revolt were the Jews of the village of Machaerus able to dispossess the Roman garrison and occupy the fortress (*War* II 18, 6 §§485-486). Finally, after the destruction of Jerusalem (A.D. 70), Lucilius Bassus, the new Roman commander and governor of Judea, having first easily defeated the Jewish garrison at Herodium (A.D. 71), besieged, took, and destroyed Machaerus (A.D. 72).

It is at this point that Josephus (*War* VII 6, 1ff. §§164ff.) gives a full description of Machaerus. The site had great natural strength, being a rocky eminence entrenched on all sides within deep ravines. The valley on the west extends sixty stadia to Lake Asphaltitis, as Josephus calls the Dead Sea; the valley on the east falls away to a depth of a hundred cubits (150 feet). Particularly because of its proximity to Arabia, Herod the Great regarded the place as deserving the strongest fortification. He enclosed an extensive area with ramparts and towers and founded a city; on top of the mountain, sur-

rounding the crest, he built a wall with corner towers each sixty cubits (90 feet) high, and in the center of this enclosure he built a magnificent palace. At convenient spots numerous cisterns were provided to collect rain water.

In Arabic the ruins of the Machaerus fortress are called Qalat el-Mishnaqa and the village on the plateau to the east of the mountain is Meqawer. The site was visited in 1807 by the German explorer Ulrich Seetzen, and the name of the village reminded him of the name of Machaerus in Greek (Μαχαιροῦς). The archeological excavation of Machaerus was begun in 1968 by Jerry Vardaman, then of the Southern Baptist Theological Seminary, Louisville, Kentucky, and later director of the Cobb Institute of Archaeology, Mississippi State University; in 1973 the German scholar August Strobel identified and studied the wall of circumvallation by which the Romans encircled the defenders within the fortress; and in 1978-1981 excavations were carried out

18

by Virgilio Corbo, together with Stanislao Loffreda and Michele Piccirillo, all of the Franciscan Biblical Institute, Jerusalem.

On the summit of the hill, 1,100 meters above the level of the Dead Sea, the area of the fortress is about 100 meters long and 60 meters wide and is surrounded by a polygonal wall, strengthened by three large rectangular towers. The towers and at least part of the wall were built by the Hasmoneans, but many of the structures were reused in the Herodian period. Within the fortified area are the ruins of the Herodian palace, including rooms, a large courtyard, and an elaborate bath, with fragments of floor mosaic still remaining. Farther down the eastern slope of the hill are other walls and towers, perhaps representing the "lower town," of which Josephus also speaks (*War* VII 6, 4 §191). Traceable also, coming from the east, is the aqueduct that brought water to the cisterns of the fortress. Pottery found in the area extends from Late Hellenistic to Roman and confirms the two main periods of occupation, namely, Hasmonean (90-57 B.C.) and Herodian (30 B.C.-A.D. 72), with a brief reoccupation soon after A.D. 72 and then nothing further—so complete and systematic was the destruction visited upon the site by the Romans.

G. A. Smith in PEFQS 1905, pp. 229ff.; DB Supplément, "Machéronte," V, 613-618; SHJP Vermes/Millar, I, pp. 345-348; Jerry Vardaman, "Machaerus: Project for Excavation," and "Preliminary Report on Results of the 1968 Excavations at Machaerus," in the Archives of the Department of Antiquities of Jordan; August Strobel, "Observations about the Roman Installations at Mukawer," in ADAJ 19 (1974), pp. 101-127; and "Das römische Belagerungswerk um Machärus, Topographische Untersuchungen," in ZDPV 90, 2 (1974), pp. 128-184; M. Piccirillo, "First Excavation Campaign at Qal'at el-Mishnaqa-Meqawer," in ADAJ 23 (1979), pp. 177-183; S. Loffreda in RB 86 (1979), pp. 122-125; and "Preliminary Report on the Second Season of Excavations at Qal'at el-Mishnaqa Machaerus," in ADAJ 25 (1981), pp. 85-94; Virgilio Corbo, "La Fortezza di Macheronte," in LA 28 (1978), pp. 217-231; and "Macheronte la Reggia-Fortezza Erodiane," in LA 29 (1979), pp. 315-326; and "La Fortezza di Macheronte (Al Mishnaqa)," in LA 30 (1980), pp. 365-376; S. Loffreda, "Alcuni vasi ben datati della Fortezza di Macheronte," in LA 30 (1980), pp. 403-414; M. Piccirillo, "Le monete délla Fortezza di Macheronte," in LA 30 (1980), pp. 403-414. See esp. the plans in ADAJ 23 (1979), p. 181 fig. 1; and in LA 30 (1980), p. 71. Photograph: courtesy Jerry Vardaman.

15. The Church of John the Baptist at Samaria-Sebaste

WHILE THE DEATH of John the Baptist probably took place at the remote and gloomy fortress of Machaerus (No. 14), it is stated in Mt 14:12 and Mk 6:29 that his disciples came and took his body and buried it. Therefore, his grave was evidently in some place other than at Machaerus and might well have been at some place out-

side of the jurisdiction of Herod Antipas. The fame of John the Baptist (cf. Ac 19:3, etc.) was such that he was remembered at many places. Possession of his head was claimed by several cities, including Damascus and Constantinople; and in Aleppo, Baalbek, Beirut, Byblos, Gaza, Homs, and Tripoli the principal mosque or church is connected either with John or with his father, Zechariah. The oldest available tradition, however, points to Samaria-Sebaste as the place of his tomb. Rufinus of Aquileia (d. 410) (*Ch. Hist.* II 28; MPL XXI, col. 536) and Theodoret of Cyrus (d. c. 466) (*Ch. Hist.* III 3; NPNFSS III, p. 96) relate that under Julian the Apostate (361-363) pagan rioters despoiled the tomb of John the Baptist at Sebaste, which makes it likely that it had already been a holy place for a long time. It is true that Eusebius does not mention the tomb of John the Baptist when he lists Samaria (Σομερών) in the *Onomasticon* (p. 154), but he is only discussing the place in connection with Jos 12:20 and 1 K 16:24. Jerome, however, adds at this point in the *Onomasticon* that Samaria was where the remains of St. John the Baptist were buried. Likewise in his *Letter 108, 13 to Eustochium* (NPNFSS VI, p. 201) Jerome tells how Paula saw at Samaria-Sebaste the last resting places of the prophets Elisha and Obadiah and John the Baptist (cf. *Letter 46, 13 Paula and Eustochium to Marcella*, NPNFSS VI, p. 65) and also encountered many demonized persons who had evidently been brought to the holy tombs in the hope of healing (cf. II K 13:21). Recalling the probable connections that appear at the beginning of his work between John the Baptist and Elijah (cf. above No. 8), it may be judged not purely accidental if the disciples of John chose to inter him not beside Elijah, which would of course have been impossible according to II K 2:11, but in the place where rested the man who had inherited the spirit and mantle of Elijah, namely, Elisha. If the Obadiah in question here is the Obadiah of 1 K 18:3-16 who assisted the prophets in the days of Elijah, then he who fearlessly challenged Herod and Herodias, and was slain by them, was given a resting place related to the remembrance of the courageous opponents of Ahab and Jezebel. In Samaria-Sebaste today the grave of John the Baptist, together with those of Elisha and Obadiah, is supposed to be just outside the Roman city wall at the east end of the village. A church was built over the grave at this place, probably in the fourth century, of which some stones may remain. The Crusaders found the earlier church in ruins and built a new cathedral in the second half of the twelfth century, and of this an arch and other portions are extant. Later a mosque was built here too. In the photograph the minaret of the mosque rises prominently above the walls that now surround the entire site. As for the tomb itself, it is described as of an ordinary Roman type of the third or second century if not earlier, i.e., it can be as early as the

15. The Church of John the Baptist at Samaria-Sebaste

first century, which would be necessary if its traditional identification with the last resting place of John the Baptist is to be accepted.

R. W. Hamilton, *Guide to Samaria-Sebaste* (Amman: Hashemite Kingdom of Jordan Department of Antiquities, 1953), pp. 34-40; André Parrot, *Samaria.* Studies in Biblical Archaeology 7 (1958), pp. 122-126; Joachim Jeremias in ZNW 52 (1961), pp. 96-98. Photograph: The Matson Photo Service, Alhambra, Calif.

16. The Church of the Finding of the Head of John the Baptist at Samaria-Sebaste

ON THE ACROPOLIS at Samaria-Sebaste Herod the Great built a large temple in honor of the emperor Augustus. Running past the acropolis on the south was a broad columned street that was probably built at the end of the second century when Septimius Severus made Sebaste a Roman colony. Between the acropolis and the columned street is the small ruined church shown in this photograph. These ruins were found, almost by chance, by the Joint Expedition of Harvard University, the Palestine Exploration Fund, the Hebrew University, and the British School of Archaeology in Jerusalem in their excavations of Samaria in 1931. The oldest building here

may be of the sixth century. It was a small basilica, with nave and two aisles, projecting apse, and mosaic floor, of which some portions remain. This church was destroyed, but was replaced in the eleventh century by a church with a round dome carried on four granite columns; in the photograph three of the columns may be seen still standing, one fallen. This church was rebuilt once again, probably in the second half of the twelfth century at about the same time that the Latin cathedral was being built at the east end of the city (No. 15). The ruins correspond with a description by Phocas who visited Sebaste in 1185 (LPPTS V-C, p. 16). He mentions first a church that is evidently the cathedral at the east end of the city, and then writes: "In the midst of the upper part of the city stands a hill, upon which in ancient times stood Herod's palace, where the feast took place, and where that wicked damsel danced and received the sacred head of the Baptist as the reward of her dancing. At the present day, however, the place has become a Greek monastery. The church of this monastery is domed. On the left side of the altar is a little chapel in the middle of which is a marble circle lying over a very deep excavation wherein was made the discovery of the sacred head of the Forerunner, revered by angels, which had been buried in that place by Herodias."

16. The Church of the Finding of the Head of John the Baptist at Samaria-Sebaste

Theodosius (530) says that Sebaste was the place where John the Baptist was beheaded (Geyer p. 137; LPPTS IIB, p. 7; CCSL CLXXV, p. 115; WJP p. 63), and the probability is that the ruins of the temple of Augustus on the acropolis had by then been taken for the remains of the palace of Herod Antipas where the famous events connected with the death of John had taken place. It was then natural to suppose that the head of John had been buried nearby by Herodias, and this legend led to the building of the church which, as we have seen, goes back to the sixth century and was so unmistakably described in the light of these assumed connections by Phocas in the twelfth century. In his day Burchard (1283) also saw two churches in honor of John the Baptist at Sebaste, one the cathedral on the side of the mountain, the other a building on the brow of the hill where the king's palace (as he also calls the ruins of Herod's temple to Augustus) once stood. At the second church the Greek monks showed him where John was imprisoned and beheaded, but Burchard rightly points out that this is not correct because better authorities, including Josephus, agree that John was beheaded at Machaerus beyond Jordan, and because Herod as tetrarch of Galilee and Perea had no authority in Samaria, which was in the jurisdiction of Pilate even as were Jerusalem and Judea (LPPTS XII-A, pp. 50-51).

J. W. Crowfoot, *Churches at Bosra and Samaria-Sebaste* (London: British School of Archaeology in Jerusalem, Supplementary Paper 4, 1937), pp. 24-39 and pl. 13(a); Ovadiah, *Corpus*, pp. 157-159, nos. 158-159. Photograph: courtesy Department of Antiquities, Amman, Jordan.

THE LIFE OF JESUS

BETHLEHEM

17. The Terraced Slopes of Bethlehem

MT 2:1 AND LK 2:4-7 STATE that Jesus was born in Bethlehem. The town of Bethlehem is on a ridge about 2,500 feet high some six miles south and slightly west of Jerusalem (cf. Eusebius, *Onomasticon* p. 42). The pho-tograph looks toward the southeastern end of the ridge, on the northern slope of which is the Church of the Nativity. The rocky hill, originally isolated from the village but now incorporated in it, contains caves and looks down on the fields steeply below to the east. In the four-teenth century B.C. Abdi-Heba, governor of Jerusalem,

17. The Terraced Slopes of Bethlehem

speaks of "the 'Apiru people" who are taking many places and mentions "a town of the land of Jerusalem, Bit-Lahmi by name" (ANET p. 489 and n. 21). This is an almost certain reference to Bethlehem, the latter part of the name perhaps being that of a Canaanite deity. In Hebrew, however, the name (בית לחם, spelled Βη-θλέεμ) means "House of Bread," and Jerome (*Letter*, 108 NPNFSS VI, p. 199) reports that upon her visit to Bethlehem Paula saw with the eyes of faith the slaughtered innocents, the raging Herod, and Joseph and Mary fleeing to Egypt, and with a mixture of tears and joy cried: "Hail Bethlehem, house of bread, wherein was born that Bread that came down from heaven" (Jn 6:51).

In OT history Bethlehem was the home of David (Ru 4:11; I Sam 16) and therefore the city of David (I Sam 20:6; Lk 2:4), but the famous king chose to make his capital at Jerusalem, and Bethlehem remained a "village" (κώμη) as it is called in Jn 7:42. The prophet Micah, however, thought of Bethlehem as of great potential importance when he wrote of it as the home of the future messianic ruler (Mic 5:2), and this prophecy was quoted by Mt (2:5-6) in his narrative of the birth of Jesus. In his narrative Luke (2:7) states that the mother Mary laid the child in a manger because there was no place for them in the inn.

Photograph: JF.

18. Bethlehem from the South

THIS PHOTOGRAPH OF Bethlehem looks back at the town from the south. It also shows the olive groves of the countryside, and the rock walls that fence the fields.

Photograph: The Matson Photo Service, Alhambra, Calif.

19. Plan of the Fortress-Palace at Herodium near Bethlehem

IN THE PHOTOGRAPH of the terraced slopes of Bethlehem (No. 17) there is seen rising as a truncated cone against the horizon at the left the artificially heightened hill, 5 kilometers southeast of Bethlehem and 12 kilometers south of Jerusalem, which was the Herodium, the fortress-palace and finally the burial place of Herod the Great, the king at whose grim threat Joseph and Mary fled with Jesus from Bethlehem (Mt 2:13ff.).

In all, on the borders of his kingdom for external defense and at strategic points within for internal control, Herod the Great had no less than eleven fortresses (the Antonia in Jerusalem is dealt with separately below, No. 215). Of the eleven, Herodium near Bethlehem and a second Herodium in Jordan were Herod's own constructions, whereas most of the others were built originally by

18. Bethlehem from the South

the Maccabean and Hasmonean leaders and rebuilt by Herod. The eleven were: (1) Alexandrium (Khirbet Sarbata), in the Jordan valley fifteen miles southeast of Shechem; (2) Cypros (Tell el-Akabe), above the Wadi el-Qelt west of Jericho; (3) Hyrcania (Khirbet Mird), in the wilderness southwest of Qumran; (4) Zif (Khirbet Ziph) and (5) Carmel (Khirbet Kermal), both in the wilderness above En-Gedi; (6) Adora (Dura) and (7) Oresa (Khirbet Istabul or Khirbet Harrissah), both south of Hebron; (8) the second Herodium, at el-Hubbeisa in Jordan; (9) Herodium, near Bethlehem; (10) Machaerus, on the east side of the Dead Sea; and (11) Masada, on the west shore of the Dead Sea. Of these the last three named—Herodium (near Bethlehem), Machaerus, and Masada—were palaces as well as fortresses, and also continued to figure prominently in events after Herod the Great (Machaerus has already been described above, No. 14).

Concerning the Herodium here near Bethlehem, Josephus (*War* I 21, 10 §§419-21; cf. *Ant.* xv 9, 4 §§323-325) says that it was on an artificial rounded hill and was elaborately decorated by Herod:

The crest he crowned with a ring of round towers; the enclosure was filled with gorgeous palaces, the magnificent appearance of which is not confined to the interior of the apartments, but outer walls, battlements, and roofs, all had wealth lavished upon them in profusion. He had, at immense expense, an abundant supply of water brought into it from a distance, and provided an easy ascent by two hundred steps of the purest white marble; the mound, though entirely artificial, being of a considerable height. Around the base he erected other palaces for the accommodation of his furniture and his friends. Thus, in the amplitude of its resources this stronghold resembled a town, in its restricted area a simple palace.

As we learn further from Josephus, the site was where in 40 B.C. Herod, fleeing with his family to Masada from Antigonus the last Hasmonean king of the Jews and going on to Rome to receive the kingship for himself, fought an important battle with the Hasmoneans and their Parthian supporters, and it was to commemorate his victory on that occasion that he founded this Herodium at this spot (*War* I 14, 8 §265). From other references in Josephus Herodium was probably built between 22 and 15 B.C., the latter the year in which Marcus

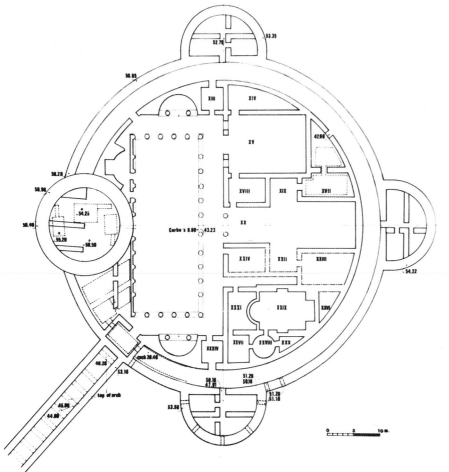

19. Plan of the Fortress-Palace
at Herodium near Bethlehem

Agrippa visited Judea and Herod showed him Herodium and other of his constructions (*Ant.* xv 2, 1 §§12-13).

Herod died at Jericho (probably in the spring of 4 B.C., see the Table of Archeological and Historical Periods in Palestine), and the body was taken to Herodium for burial. The initial march was for eight stades (roughly one mile) out of Jericho, with troops and servants forming a solemn and splendid cortege (*Ant.* xvii 8, 3 §§196-199; *War* i 33, 9 §§670–673; cf. Douglas Johnson in CKC pp. 98f.); the total distance was about 200 stades (150 stades from Jericho to Jerusalem, *War* iv 8, 3 §474, and 60 stades from Jerusalem to Herodium, *War* i 21, 10 §419).

In Arabic the name of the hill in question is Jebel Fureidis, a name that has been understood as a diminutive of a word signifying Paradise, but which may actually preserve the name Herodis, as Herodium was called in the time of Bar Kokhba. The site was first identified as that of Herodium by Edward Robinson, who visited Jebel Fureidis on May 8, 1838, and said that there was "scarcely a doubt" that this was the fortress and city described by Josephus.

Excavations on the summit of the mound were conducted by Virgilio Carbo of the Studium Biblicum Franciscanum in Jerusalem in 1962-1967, with subsequent works of preservation by G. Foerster for the Israel Department of Antiquities and the National Parks Authority in 1969. Further excavations in the subterranean cisterns and tunnels and in the complex of buildings at the foot of the hill to the north were conducted by Ehud Netzer on behalf of the Hebrew University and the Israel Exploration Society in 1972 and following.

Edward Robinson, *Biblical Researches in Palestine, Mount Sinai and Arabia Petraea, A Journal of Travels in the Year 1838*, II, pp. 169-174; E. Jerry Vardaman, "The History of Herodium," in E. Jerry Vardaman and James L. Garrett, Jr., eds., *The Teacher's Yoke: Studies in Memory of Henry Trantham* (Waco, Tex.: Baylor University Press, 1964), pp. 58-81; Virgilio Corbo, "L'Herodion di Gebel Fureidis," in LA 13 (1962-1963), pp. 219-277; 17 (1967), pp. 65-121; G. Foerster, "Herodium," in IEJ 19 (1969), pp. 123f.; A Segal, "Herodium," in IEJ 23 (1973), pp. 27-29; E. J. Vardaman, "Herodium: A Brief Assessment of Recent Suggestions," in IEJ 25 (1975), pp. 45f.; "Symposium: Herod's Building Projects," in *The Jerusalem Cathedra*, ed. Lee I. Levine (Jerusalem: Yad Izhak Ben-Zvi Institute; Wayne State University Press, 1981), pp. 48-80; Ehud Netzer, *Greater Herodium*, in *Qedem* 13 (1981); and "Searching for Herod's Tomb," in BAR 9, 3 (May/June 1983), pp. 30-51; *Herodium, An Archaeological Guide* (Jerusalem: Cana, 1987); and "Jewish Rebels Dig Strategic Tunnel System," in BAR 15, 4 (July/Aug 1988), pp. 18-33. Plan: Ehud Netzer, *Greater Herodium*, in *Qedem* 13 (1981), p. 80 ill. 107, courtesy The Institute of Archaeology, Hebrew University of Jerusalem.

20. Looking Down into the Excavated Fortress-Palace at Herodium

AS REVEALED in the excavations, Herod's fortress-palace on the summit of Jebel Fureidis was a circular structure with two concentric rings of walls, 3.5 meters apart and an outer diameter of 63 meters. At the cardinal points of the compass were four towers. The tower set into the walls on the east side (shown in this photograph) is completely round, with an external diameter of 18 meters; the towers on the west, north, and south are semicircular and project outward from the outer wall. Under the walls and towers is a system of vaults that extended the area of the upper hill. An earth and stone fill against the walls and towers left only their tops showing above, and thus the whole appeared as a great tumulus, the mausoleum of Herod the Great (but his actual burial place has not yet been found).

The circular area inside the walls, comprising the palace proper and its grounds, was laid out in two main sections. The eastern half was laid out as a garden surrounded by a colonnade (at the foot of the round tower in this photograph). Opening onto the garden are a vaulted entrance passage and gate chamber, presumably once reached from the base of the hill by the 200 marble steps mentioned by Josephus (see above, No. 19). The western half contains a large dining hall (*triclinium*) and an elaborate bathhouse, with dressing room (*apodyterium*), warm room (*tepidarium*), hot room (*caldarium*), and cold room (*frigidarium*), the floors paved with white and black mosaics and the walls decorated with frescoes in various colors. Above, there was probably at least one more story to provide living quarters.

At the foot of the hill to the north was a whole complex of structures. A very large palace or audience hall was 130 meters in length and 54 meters in width, with a ground area of about 7,000 square meters (more than twice as large as the palace area on the summit of the hill above, which was about 3,000 square meters in area), and there were other buildings as well as a Roman bath. Overlooked by the large palace was a "course," first thought to have been a hippodrome but too narrow for that purpose, although perhaps an athletic course, a promenade, or a funeral course for Herod's own funeral. Likewise uncertain as to original usage was a "monumental building" at the end of the course. Yet below was a huge rectangular pool complex. Water was brought to the pool by an aqueduct from the vicinity of Urtas (or Artas), a village in Wadi Urtas, less than two miles southwest of Bethlehem, but for the upper palace the water still had to be carried up to cisterns in the mount above.

In all, then, Greater Herodium, as the fortress-palace above and the whole complex below may be called, ex-

20. Looking Down into the Excavated Fortress-Palace at Herodium

21. The Synagogue at Herodium

IN THE FIRST REVOLT of the Jews against Rome all three fortress-palaces—Herodium, Machaerus, and Masada—were occupied by the revolutionaries (*War* iv 9, 9 §555) and of these, after the fall of Jerusalem (A.D. 70), Herodium was the first to be taken (A.D. 71) by the Romans under Lucilius Bassus (*War* vii 6, 1 §163). During the Second Revolt (132-135) Herodium also served as a stronghold of the forces of Bar Kokhba. This is shown by a fragmentary Hebrew text found along with other documents of the Revolt in the caves of Wadi Murabbaʻat (a defile which begins in the vicinity of Herodium and runs down to the Dead Sea, some 12 miles below Qumran), this text beginning, "On the twentieth of (the month of) Shebat, Year Two of the Liberation of Israel by Simeon ben Kosiba [whom Rabbi Akiba named Bar Kokhba, Son of a Star, Num 24:17], President of Israel. In the camp which is at Herodium. . . ."

In the opinion of the excavator (Corbo in LA 17 [1967], pp. 101-103), it was during the First Revolt that the Jewish occupants of Herodium converted the *triclinium* (dining hall) into a synagogue, the ruins of which are shown in the present photograph, looking southwest. Using some architectural elements from elsewhere in the Heodium, this was a rectangular building (10.5 by 15 meters) with an entrance on the east, stone columns dividing the hall, and at least in a second phase of construction, stone benches along the walls. In general the synagogue is much like the synagogue at Masada (No. 23), where the excavator (Yadin, *Masada*, pp. 181-189) finds reason to believe that this was a synagogue already under Herod the Great and was then reconstructed by the revolutionaries during the First Revolt. The same earlier origin may therefore also be possible for the synagogue at Herodium (Saller, *Second Catalogue*, pp. 40f., no. 43). The entrance from the east to these early synagogues at Herodium and also at Masada accords with a rabbinic text (*T. Megillah* iii 22, Levine, *Synagogues Revealed*, p. 29) which states: "One should only place the entrance to synagogues in the east, for we find that in the Temple the entrance faced the east." That the two synagogues were planned with an orientation like that of the Temple agrees with the other evidence that they were built while the Second Temple was still standing. Adjacent to the eastern wall of the Herodium synagogue there was a Jewish ritual bath (*mikvah*). The Jewish revolutionaries also occupied the bathhouse of Herod, and later, in the Byzantine period and down into the seventh century, monks established a monastery there and erected a chapel in a room south of the bathhouse.

tended over an area of approximately 45 acres, and the construction involved earth and building works on a grand scale. Thus Herod memorialized a crucial battle in his own career, provided himself with a retreat center separate from Jerusalem yet not far away, and planned an imposing monument for his own burial place.

From this high mountaintop at Herodium Herod was able to look down upon Bethlehem, and it need hardly be surprising if a man who put to death his best-loved wife, Mariamne, his sons Alexander, Aristobulus, and Antipater, and other persons, and who especially toward the end of his life "became quite savage and treated everyone with uncontrolled anger and harshness" (*Ant.* xvii 6, 1 §148), should have been led by the report to him of the birth of a king of the Jews in Bethlehem to order the wholesale slaughter of the small children of the Bethlehem region (Mt 2:16).

> Near Urtas (Artas) are the "Pools of Solomon," fed by several springs in the vicinity and by conduits from springs in Wadi Arrub and Wadi Biar (5 miles farther south), and it was water from these sources that was carried not only to Herodium by Herod's aqueduct but also to Jerusalem by the "Low Level Aqueduct," which may well have been constructed by Herod too, and by the "High Level Aqueduct," which may have been even older. The statements by Josephus (*Ant.* xviii 3,2 §60; *War* ii 9, 4 §175) that Pilate constructed an aqueduct to bring water to Jerusalem from a distance of 200 stades (about 23 miles) or 400 stades should probably be understood to refer to restoration of Herod's aqueduct rather than to initial construction. For the water systems leading to Herodium and to Jerusalem, see C. Schick, "Die Wasserversorgung der Stadt Jerusalem," in ZDPV 1 (1878), pp. 132-176, especially pp. 167f. for the aqueduct to Herodium; George Adam Smith, *Jerusalem, The Topography, Economics and History from the Earliest Times to A.D. 70*, 2 vols. (New York: A. C. Armstrong, 1908), i pp. 124-131. For maps, see ZDPV 19 (1896), at end; *Qadmoniot* 5, 3-4 (1972), facing p. 124. Photograph: JF.

G. Foerster, "The Synagogues at Masada and Herodium," in *Synagogues Revealed*, pp. 24-29; Levine, in *Synagogue in Late Antiq*

21. The Synagogue at Herodium

uity, pp. 10-12. For the text from Wadi Murabba'at, see Yigael Yadin, *Bar-Kokhba, The Rediscovery of the Legendary Hero of the Second Jewish Revolt against Rome* (New York: Random House, 1971), p. 182. Photograph: from *Qadmoniot* I, 4 (1968), p. 133, courtesy Israel Exploration Society, Jerusalem.

22. Masada from the Western Wilderness

LIKE MACHAERUS (No. 14) and Herodium (Nos. 19-21), Masada was also the site of a fortress-palace of Herod the Great. The great rock, which rises precipitously 1,300 feet above the western shore of the Dead Sea, and the happenings which took place here are described at some length by Josephus (*War* VII 8, 1-9, 2 §§252-406):

> A rock of no slight circumference and lofty from end to end is abruptly terminated on every side by deep ravines, the precipices rising sheer from an invisible base and being inaccessible to the foot of any living creature, save in two places where the rock permits of no easy ascent. Of these tracks one leads from Lake Asphaltitis [the Dead Sea] toward the sun-rising [i.e., on the east], the other, by which the approach is easier, from the west. The former they call the snake, seeing a resemblance to that reptile in its narrowness and continual windings. . . . After following this perilous track for thirty stadia, one reaches the summit, which, instead of tapering to a sharp peak, expands into a plain (§§280-284).

The first to build a fortress at Masada was the high priest Jonathan, the brother of Judas Maccabeus and his successor as the leader of the Jews (161-143 B.C.). Even-

tually Herod the Great obtained the place and when he went to Rome to receive the kingship left his family here for safety. Then when he came to rule in fact he proceeded with great building works (§285). He enclosed the entire summit with a wall of stone, on which stood thirty-seven towers. Good soil on the summit was reserved for cultivation. Large tanks were cut in the rock as reservoirs for water. Beneath the ramparts on the crest and inclining toward the north he built a magnificent palace (§§286-291). After the death of Herod the Great (4 B.C.) the fortress-palace was held by his son and successor in the rule of Judea, Archelaus (4 B.C.-A.D. 6), then by the Romans from A.D. 6 to 66, except for the years 41-44 when Herod Agrippa I was king.

Finally the Sicarii (named from the *sicae* or short daggers they carried) under Eleazar the son of Jairus (a descendant of Judas the Galilean or Gaulanite, founder of the "fourth philosophy" of the Jews, usually identified with Zealots, Ac 5:37 [A.D. 6/7]; *Ant.* XVIII 1, 1 §4; 1, 6 §23; *War* II 8, 1 §116; 17, 2 §408; VII 8, 1 §252-253, 268; SHJP Vermes/Millar, I, p. 382) took Masada at the outset of the First Revolt (A.D. 66), and it was they who, in the end, besieged by the Romans under Flavius Silva (successor of Lucilius Bassus as governor of Judea), took their own lives rather than fall into the hands of their enemies (*War* VII 8, 2ff. §§275ff.). The tragedy and the taking of Masada by the Romans ensued on the fifteenth day of the month Xanthikos (March/April) in a year probably to be identified as A.D. 74 (*War* VII 9, 1 § 401; inscriptions show that Silva cannot have come to Judea as governor before A.D. 73, therefore the fall of Masada must have been in the spring of A.D. 74 at the earliest,

SHJP Vermes/Millar, I, pp. 512, 515, citing W. Eck, *Senatoren von Vespasien bis Hadrian* [1970], pp. 93-111).

The site of Masada, called es-Sebbe by the Arabs, was tentatively identified by Edward Robinson and his companion E. Smith in 1838 (Robinson, *Biblical Researches*, III, pp. 240-242) and was studied with particular reference to the Roman camps and siege wall by the German scholars Adolf Schulten and Adolf Lammerer in 1932 (ZDPV 56 [1933], pp. 1-179). After preliminary Israeli surveys in 1953 and 1955-1956, full-scale excavations were conducted in 1963-1965 by Yigael Yadin, with volunteer workers from many countries.

Three main periods are represented in the finds: the period of Herod the Great (37-4 B.C.), the period of the First Revolt (A.D. 66-74), and the Byzantine period (fifth and sixth centuries). Most of the actual structures belong to the first of these periods. A casemate wall (a double wall with chambers between the walls) extends for 1,500 yards around the entire summit and has thirty towers and four gates. Herod's palace, which Josephus described as "inclining towards the north," was built on three descending terraces at the narrowest north end of the mountain, and portions of mosaic floors, painted walls, and columns with Corinthian capitals are still in place. On the summit are capacious storerooms, a luxurious bathhouse, a large western palace, with a swimming pool nearby, and also some smaller palaces. Water was brought from dams in wadis to the west by conduits that led to reservoirs hewn in the side of the rock, then was carried by hand to cisterns on the summit.

In the period of the First Revolt Masada was occupied by the Sicarii, as Josephus states. From arrows and other weapons, coins, and other finds, it appears that the revolutionists used the northern palace as their military headquarters and the western palace as an administrative center, while families lived in the smaller palaces and rooms in the casemate wall and the towers. Among the coins are many shekels with dates from all the years of the revolt from year one to year five, the last year when shekels were struck, the year (A.D. 70) of the destruction of Jerusalem (Yadin, *Masada*, pp. 108, 168). There are also fragments of manuscripts, including biblical books (Gen, Lv, Pss) and books of the apocrypha and pseudepigrapha (Ben Sira, Jubilees), as well as a text identical with a text discovered in Cave 4 at Qumran, which can suggest that after the destruction of Qumran (A.D. 68) some of the Essenes joined the revolutionists at Masada (Yadin, *Masada*, pp. 173f.). Some seven hundred ostraca are written in Hebrew and Aramaic, and some have single names on them, including the name of Ben Yair, probably the Eleazar ben Yair (son of Jairus) named by Josephus as commander of the Sicarii at Masada (Yadin, *Masada*, p. 201). Roman coins and several Latin papyri confirm the fact that Silva left a Roman garrison at Masada for some time (*War* VII 10, 1 §407).

In the fifth and sixth centuries Christian monks lived on Masada. They built a small church, which had a long hall with an apse in the eastern wall and a floor of colored mosaics (Ovadiah, *Corpus*, pp. 137-138, no. 139).

In the present photograph the terraces on which Herod the Great built his northern palace are at the left. At the right is the rock ridge, which Josephus calls Λευκή (*War* VII 8, 5 §305), "White (Cliff)," above which the Romans built a yet higher embankment and raised a stone platform and iron-enclosed tower to support the great battering ram with which they finally breached the wall on the summit of Masada. In the background distance are the Dead Sea and the Mountains of Moab.

22. Masada from the Western Wilderness

Adolf Schulten, "Masada, die Burg des Herodes und die römischen Lager," in ZDPV 56 (1933), pp. 1-179; R. W. Funk in IDB III, pp. 293f. Yigael Yadin, *Masada, Herod's Fortress and the Zealots' Last Stand* (London: Weidenfeld and Nicolson, 1966); and in IDB-S pp. 577-580; Shaye J. D. Cohen, "Masada: Literary Tradition, Archaeological Remains, and the Credibility of Josephus," in *Essays in Honour of Yigael Yadin*, ed. Geza Vermes and Jacob Neusner, in JJS 33 (1982), republished for the Oxford Centre for Postgraduate Studies (Totowa, N.J.: Allanheld, Osman, 1983), pp. 385-405; *The Masada Reports* (Israel Exploration Society, Hebrew University of Jerusalem, 1989ff.). Photograph: JF.

23. The Synagogue at Masada

ON THE SUMMIT of Masada, built against the northwestern wall and facing toward Jerusalem, is a rectangular structure (12 by 15 meters), with an opening on the east, with pillars, and with benches along the inner walls. Excavation indicated two stages of construction, with the benches added in the second phase. Found in two pits under the floor of the building were fragmentary portions of parchment scrolls of the biblical books of Deuteronomy and Ezekiel. The conclusion is that at least in its second phase, i.e., in the time of the Sica ii/Zealots, who were strong adherents of the Law, this was a synagogue, and the place under the floor where the scrolls were found was a sort of *genizah* (depository for Hebrew books that were out of use), in which perhaps the manuscripts were hidden when Masada was about to fall. But already in its first phase as well as later the structure was oriented toward Jerusalem, and this fact together with the strong conservative tradition of keeping a house of worship on the site of its predecessor make it not unlikely that this was a synagogue already in the time

of Herod the Great. Thus it is well possible that this and the similar structure already described at Herodium (No. 21) are two of the oldest synagogues in the Holy Land. As at Herodium so also here at Masada there is a ritual bath (*mikvah*) not far from the synagogue.

Y. Yadin, "The Synagogue at Masada," in *Synagogues Revealed*, pp. 19-23; and *Masada*, pp. 181-189; Levine, in *Synagogues Revealed*, pp. 24-26; Saller, *Second Catalogue*, pp. 62-64. Photograph: JF.

24. Plan of Bethlehem

AFTER THE FOREGOING brief survey of several of the fortress-palaces of Herod the Great, one of which—the Herodium—looms over Bethlehem, we return now to Bethlehem itself.

In exploration in 1969 for the Israel Archaeological Survey, S. Gutman and A. Berman found pottery of the Iron Age in the area marked on the plan by shaded diagonal lines, to the east and south of the Church of the Nativity (marked in solid black), suggesting that this area was that of the *tell* of ancient Bethlehem. Roman and Byzantine objects were found chiefly in the built-up region to the southwest of the church, while the present town extends on to the northwest (note that the direction north is to the right side of the plan).

Immediately north of the Church of the Nativity is the Franciscan Monastery with the Church of Saint Catherine (built in 1881), and when a site north of the monastery was being prepared is 1962 for the erection of a new school by the Custody of the Holy Land, two tombs were found, one of which contained objects of

23. The Synagogue at Masada

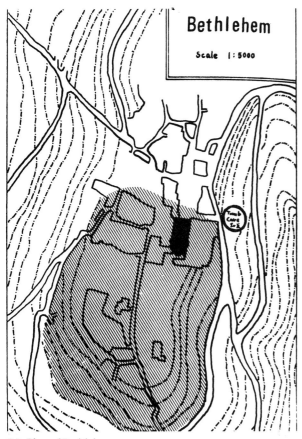

24. Plan of Bethlehem

Iron Age II, while the other was of Byzantine date and was associated with walls, mosaics, and a Greek inscription, evidently the remains of a Byzantine chapel.

The Church of the Nativity is located, therefore, at the western summit of the Iron Age *tell* of Bethlehem, with the slopes of the hill descending to the north and the south, and if the town of the Roman period (i.e., of the time of the birth of Jesus) was similarly situated, the traditional site of the birth of Jesus marked by the church was indeed at the village of that time.

S. Gutman and A. Berman, "Communication," in RB 77 (1970), pp. 583-585; Sylvester Saller, "Iron Age Remains from the Site of a New School at Bethlehem," in LA 18 (1968), pp. 153-180; and "The Byzantine Chapel Found at Bethlehem in 1962," in LA 22 (1972), pp. 153-168. Plan: from RB 77 (1970), p. 584, courtesy *Revue Biblique*, Jerusalem.

25. Plan of the Church of the Nativity at Bethlehem

LATER TRADITION STATES that the place of the birth of Jesus in Bethlehem was a cave. In such traditions there was a recognizable tendency to localize events in caves; on the other hand, caves have actually provided habitation and shelter for persons and beasts in Palestine from ancient times until now. Justin Martyr, born soon after 100 in Neapolis and writing his *Dialogue with the Jew Trypho* shortly after the middle of the century, says: "But when the Child was born in Bethlehem, since Joseph could not find lodging in the village, he took up his quarters in a certain cave near the village; and while they were there Mary brought forth the Christ and placed him in a manger, and here the Magi who came from Arabia found him" (*Dialogue* 78). Like wise *The Protevangelium of James* (second century) refers to the cave which Joseph found, which was the place of the birth, and says that at the time there was "a bright cloud overshadowing the cave" (18.1; 19.2 James p. 46; HSNTA I, pp. 383f.).

Origen, who was in Palestine frequently from 215 onward and wrote *Against Celsus* about 248, reports what is evidently the same tradition as that given by Justin and *The Protevangelium of James* and speaks as if he himself were one of those to whom the cave had been shown: "In accordance with the narrative in the Gospel regarding his birth, there is pointed out at Bethlehem the cave where he was born, and the manger in the cave where he was wrapped in swaddling clothes. And this sight is greatly talked of in surrounding places, even among the enemies of the faith, it being said that in this cave was born that Jesus who is worshiped and reverenced by the Christians" (*Against Celsus* I 51).

It was undoubtedly the cave to which the foregoing references point, over which the original Church of the Nativity was built. In his work on *The Life of Constantine* (III 25-43, 51-53) Eusebius tells us that the emperor caused four churches to be built in Palestine at sacred sites connected with Christ. Three sites were obvious choices, namely, the places of birth at Bethlehem, of crucifixion and resurrection at Jerusalem (Nos. 225ff.), and of ascension on the Mount of Olives (Nos. 154-155), while the fourth was at Mamre where "the self-same Savior who erewhile had appeared on earth had in ages long since past afforded a manifestation of his divine presence to holy men of Palestine near the oak of Mamre" (cf. Gen 18:1). The church at Calvary and the Holy Sepulcher is credited to Constantine alone (although Socrates, *Ch. Hist.* I 17, gives a share of the credit to Helena), while the churches at Bethlehem and on the Mount of Olives are attributed to Constantine's mother Helena, who made a visit to the Holy Land and the eastern provinces only shortly before her death (c. 327) at the age of eighty (*Life of Constantine* III 46). The suggestion for the church at Mamre was made by another member of the imperial family, Constantine's mother-in-law Eutropia, the mother of his empress Fausta (for Eutropia, see Louis Duchesne, *Early History of the Christian Church*, 4th ed. [New York: Longmans, Green, 1922-25], II, pp. 65f.; for the church at Mamre, see Ovadiah, *Corpus*, pp. 131-132, no. 135). For guidance in identification of the traditional sites and in carrying out of the work on the churches at Jerusalem and Bethlehem, there was no doubt help for Helena and Constantine from Marcarius bishop of Jerusalem (314-333), for we know that he was present at the Council of Nicaea (325) and that afterward Constantine wrote a long letter to him about the building of the Church of the Holy Sepulcher (No. 225).

Eusebius, writing the account of the Bethlehem church, says (*Life of Constantine* III 43) that it was dedicated by Helena "at the grotto which had been the scene of the Savior's birth," and that both Helena and Constantine beautified the sacred cave with rich gifts. Only a few years later the Bordeaux Pilgrim (333) says of Bethlehem: "There a basilica has been built by order of Constantine" (Geyer p. 25; LPPTS I-B, p. 27; CCSL CLXXV, p. 20; WET p. 162). This sounds as if the church were already finished at that time, although in fact the final dedication did not take place until May 31, A.D. 339 (J. T. Milik in RB 67 [1960], p. 572), which was after the death (in 337) of Constantine himself.

The Bethlehem cave and the basilica erected over it naturally became the focus of special attention at the time of special remembrance of the birth of Jesus. As to the date, Jerome, who came from Rome and lived (385-420) in a cave under the Bethlehem church (No. 32) supported the Roman date of December 25 (Benoit, *Christmas*, p. 13), but for the Jerusalem church the proper date of the observance was Epiphany, January 6 (see Outline of Festivals of the Early Church), and in the year 383 the pilgrim Aetheria was at Bethlehem on that date for the Epiphany celebration. In her record there is a considerable gap at this point, but from what remains and from the Old Armenian Lectionary we can follow the events (Geyer pp. 75-77; LPPTS I-C, pp. 50f.; CCSL CLXXV, pp. 71f.; WET p. 128; Renoux, *Le Codex Arménien Jérusalem 121* [PO 36, 2], pp. 211-225, nos. I-IX). The observances began on the afternoon of January 5 with a gathering involving readings and prayers at the traditional place near Bethlehem where the shepherds received the angelic announcement (Nos. 38f.) and then continued in the Cave of the Nativity, concluding with the celebration of the Eucharist at midnight. Then the bishop and the Jerusalem monks returned to Jerusalem, arriving just before dawn (at which point Aetheria's narrative resumes), but the Bethlehem celebrants continued their hymns until day and thereafter maintained the observance for eight days continuously.

Aetheria also describes another observance at Bethlehem, which took place on the fortieth day after Easter (Geyer p. 93; LPPTS I-C, p. 69; CCSL CLXXV p. 84; WET p. 41; Renoux, *Le Codex Arménien Jérusalem 121* [PO 36, 2], pp. 337-339): "The fortieth day after Easter (*pascha*) is the fifth day of the week (Thursday). On the fourth day

of the week (Wednesday) all go to Bethlehem to celebrate vigils. For vigils are held in the church in Bethlehem, in which church is the cave where the Lord was born. On the next day, which is the fifth day of the week, the fortieth day after Easter, Mass is celebrated in due order, with the presbyters and the bishop preaching on subjects appropriate to the day and place (*apte diei et loco*), and finally they all return to Jerusalem in the evening."

We know (Apostolic Constitutions V 19 ANF 7, pp. 447f.; Renoux, *Le Codex Arménien Jérusalem 121* [PO 36, 2], pp. 337-339, no. LVII) that there was a festival of Ascension Day on the fortieth day after Easter, and it is possible that the place where Jesus was born was also thought of as a fitting place in which to celebrate the Ascension, so that this was the nature of the observance that Aetheria describes (J. G. Davies, "The Peregrinatio Egeriae and the Ascension," in VC 8 [1954], pp. 93-100). Aetheria, however, says that the sermons on this

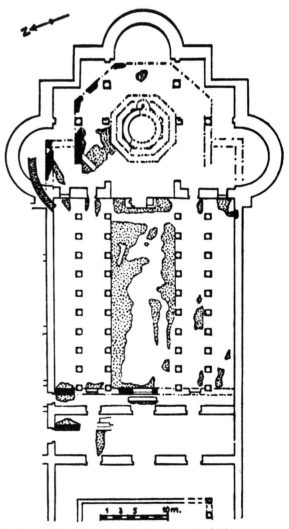

25. Plan of the Church of the Nativity at Bethlehem

occasion were appropriate "to the day and place," and the most appropriate place to celebrate the Ascension was surely on the Mount of Olives and not here at Bethlehem. Therefore it is possible that it was a different event at Bethlehem that was commemorated in the observance of which Aetheria speaks. In fact we learn from the Old Armenian Lectionary (according to Paris manuscript 44) that there was a commemoration of the Children Killed by King Herod at Bethlehem on May 18, and it is well possible that in the year (383) when Aetheria was at Bethlehem for the celebration this date coincided with the fortieth day after Easter (Renoux, *Le Codes Arménien Jérusalem 121*, p. 335, no. LV; Paulus Devos, "Égérie à Bethléem, Le 40ᵉ jour après Pâques à Jérusalem en 383," in AB 86 [1968], pp. 87-108).

Turning now to the Bethlehem church itself, the presently existing structure is substantially the church as rebuilt by the emperor Justinian in the sixth century, but under it are almost certainly the remains of the Constantinian basilica of the fourth century. The archeological history of the church was investigated by William Harvey for the Department of Antiquities of Palestine in 1932 and 1934, and by Bellarmino Bagatti for the Franciscan Custody of the Holy Land in 1949-1950.

According to these studies and especially according to the revisions by Bagatti of earlier conclusions, the Constantinian church was approached through a forecourt or atrium, doubtless open to the sky and surrounded by a colonnade, which was in the area of the present courtyard in front of the present church (No. 36). Between the atrium and the basilica proper was a narthex, marked by two parallel walls and with a portion of white mosaic floor still remaining. Within the basilica proper the main longitudinal area was divided by rows of columns into a central nave and two aisles on either side, and the floor was covered with mosaics. Further, according to Bagatti, there was a polygonal apse at the east end and a raised octagonal platform, which supported the altar; the altar was directly over the cave below, and there was an entry at one side to descend to the venerated grotto.

In the plan, which is drawn according to the excavations of 1932-1934 and 1949-1950, the remains of Constantinian walls are in black, and the supplied parts of the same area are in short lines and dots, while dotted areas are mosaics. Plain white lines outline the Justinian church of the sixth century.

H. Vincent and F.-M. Abel, *Bethléem Le sanctuaire de la Nativité* (Paris: J. Gabalda, 1914); R. W. Hamilton, "Excavations in the Atrium of the Church of the Nativity, Bethlehem," in QDAP 3 (1934), pp. 1-8; William Harvey, *Structural Survey of the Church of the Nativity, Bethlehem* (London: Oxford University Press, 1935); E. T. Richmond, "Basilica of the Nativity, Discovery of the Remains of an Earlier Church," in QDAP 5 (1936), pp. 75-81; "The Church of the Nativity, The Plan of the Constantinian Church," in QDAP 6 (1938), pp. 63-66; J. W. Crowfoot, *Early Churches* (1941) pp. 22-30 and fig. 2 on p. 18; Bellarmino Bagatti, *Gli antichi edifici sacri de Betlemme in seguito agli scavi e restauri praticati dalla Custodia di Terra Santa* (1948-1951) PSBF 9 (Jerusalem: Franciscan Printing Press, 1952); and Bagatti, *Church from Gentiles*, pp. 175-184; Gregory T. Armstrong, "Imperial Church Building in the Holy Land in the Fourth Century," in BA 30 (1967), pp. 90-102; Edward J. Yarnold, "Who Planned the Churches at the Christian Holy Places in the Holy Land?" in *Studia Patristica* XVIII, I, Historica-Theologica-Gnostica-Biblica, Papers of the Ninth International Conference on Patristic Studies, Oxford, 1983, ed. Elizabeth A. Livingstone (Kalamazoo, Mich.: Cistercian Publications), pp. 105-109; Pierre Benoit, *Christmas, A Pictorial Pilgrimage* (Nashville: Abingdon Press, 1969), pp. 20f.; Ovadiah, *Corpus*, pp. 33-37; and *Corpus Supplementum*, p. 128. Plan: Bagatti, *Church from Gentiles*, p. 176, fig. 48, courtesy Studium Biblicum Franciscanum, Jerusalem.

26. Interior of the Church of the Nativity at Bethlehem

IN THE EXAMINATION of the Church of the Nativity at Bethlehem, portions of floor mosaic were found in the nave and aisles at a level about 75 centimeters below the present floor, and other portions were in the apse and also in the narthex (No. 25). Although attributed by some (Crowfoot) to the fifth century, they may probably be accepted from their position as belonging to the Constantinian basilica (Bagatti). This photograph shows the interior of the church at the time when the floor of the nave was broken through to expose the mosaics. Afterward, wooden trap doors were put in place through which, when opened, portions of the mosaics can be seen.

L.-H. Vincent in RB 45 (1936), pp. 544-574; Crowfoot, *Early Churches*, pp. 26, 120; Bagatti, *Church from Gentiles*, p. 177, fig. 49, and p. 183. Photograph: The Matson Photo Service, Alhambra, Calif.

27. Floor Mosaic in the Nave of the Church at Bethlehem

THE PATTERN of the floor mosaics in the nave of the church consists of geometrical designs. The entire mosaic may be thought of as having been, in a way, like a great carpet covering the floor of the basilica.

Photograph: The Matson Photo Service, Alhambra, Calif.

28. Detail of Mosaic in the Church at Bethlehem

THE CONSIDERABLE COMPLEXITY of the geometrical designs may be seen in this more detailed photograph of another portion of the nave mosaics.

Photograph: The Matson Photo Service, Alhambra, Calif.

26. Interior of the Church of the Nativity at Bethlehem

27. Floor Mosaic in the Nave of the Church at Bethlehem

28. Detail of Mosaic in the Church at Bethlehem

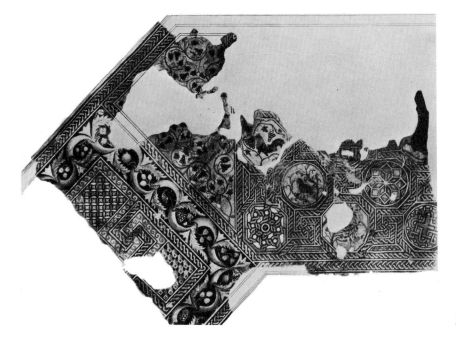

29. Floor Mosaic in the Octagon

29. Floor Mosaic in the Octagon

AT THE EAST END of the nave in the Constantinian basilica, steps led up to the octagonal platform, around which was an octagonal band of mosaic pavement. A portion of the mosaic that survives is shown in the photograph: an acanthus border, geometrical patterns, various flowers and fruits, a bird in one medallion and a cock in another.

Bagatti, *Gli antichi edifici sacri de Betlemme*, p. 2; Crowfoot, *Early Churches*, pp. 23-24, 120f. Photograph: Crowfoot, *Early Churches*, p. XI.

30. Floor Mosaic with the Word IXΘYC

ON EITHER SIDE of the octagonal band of mosaic pavement in the apse was a small panel of mosaic, and at the left side is the mosaic panel shown in this photograph (for the location see Bagatti, *Church from Gentiles*, p. 179, fig. 51). In addition to geometrical designs, the Greek word IXΘYC is inscribed in the center of the panel. In Greek the word means "fish," a term of multiple possible Christian allusions, and the individual characters make a famous early Christian acrostic, taken as the initials of the words Jesus Christ, God's Son, Savior (FLAP p. 535 and fig. 193; cf. below, No. 99). In A.D. 427 the emperor Theodosius II forbade the use of the cross and other Christian symbols in pavements where they would be walked on (M. Avi-Yonah in QDAP 3 [1933], p. 63 n. 17), but at this earlier time the placement of the sacred word in the mosaic pavement was ev-

idently unobjectionable, and at all events the spot was where no one would ordinarily have walked. To the right of this mosaic, however, remnants of stairs have been discovered, and these were evidently the old entry to the venerated grotto below.

Bagatti, *Church from Gentiles*, p. 182. Photograph: from Harvey, *Structural Survey of the Church of the Nativity* (Bethlehem, 1935), fig. 97.

30. Floor Mosaic with the Word IXΘYC

31. Column and Capital in the Church of the Nativity

THIS PHOTOGRAPH SHOWS the upper part and capital of one of over fifty columns that still stand in the Church of the Nativity, most of them in the two double rows that mark the central nave and the four side aisles. The columns are of red limestone, probably quarried near Bethlehem. The capitals are of the Corinthian order, with acanthus leaves and curved scrolls at the top. As with respect to the mosaics (No. 26), there is difference of opinion about the date of the columns. Some (e.g., Harvey and Crawfoot) believe they were first cut in the sixth century for Justinian's church, but more probably (Kroll p. 42, col. 3) columns, bases, and Corinthian capitals all come from the Constantinian basilica and were raised when Justinian raised the floor of the church, for they stand on blocks of stone that rest in turn upon low longitudinal walls or stylobates, place having been made for the latter by cutting through the mosaics. In addition ten new columns and four corner columns were made in the same style to fit the enlarged size of the hall.

The paintings that are now seen on the columns were done by the Crusaders and show the figures of various saints with names written in Greek and Latin, as well as a Madonna and Child. Remains of mosaic decoration on the walls of the church also date from the Crusader period. From what is still to be seen and from detailed description by Quaresmius (1628) we know that the ancestors of Jesus were depicted according to Mt 1:1-16 on the south wall and according to Lk 3:23-38 on the north wall, while other registers contained the decisions of important church councils: on the west wall were prophets holding texts believed to refer to Christ; and in the transept were scenes from the life of Jesus (Kroll p. 47, cols. 2-3).

E. T. Richmond in QDAP 6 (1938), p. 68; Crowfoot, *Early Churches*, p. 25 and n. 2, pp. 151-153; R. W. Hamilton in QDAP 13 (1948), p. 113 and n. 1; Bagatti, *Gli antichi edifici sacri di Betlemme*, pp. 48, 51-52, 79-106. Photograph: courtesy École Biblique et Archéologique Francaise.

32. Statue of Jerome near the Church of the Nativity

IN 385 JEROME MOVED to Bethlehem and lived there in a cave adjacent to the grotto of the Church of the Nativity until his death in 420. in his *Letter 58 to Paulinus* (NPNFSS VI, p. 120), written in 395, he refers to the fact that in Jerusalem from the time of Hadrian to that of Constantine the spot which had witnessed the resurrection was occupied by a figure of Jupiter and the rock where the cross had stood bore a marble statue of Venus. Thus, he explains, the original persecutors "supposed

31. Column and Capital in the Church of the Nativity

that by polluting our holy places they would deprive us of our faith in the passion and in the resurrection." In a similar way he reports concerning Bethlehem: "Even my own Bethlehem, as it now is, that most venerable spot in the whole world of which the psalmist sings: 'the truth hath sprung out of the earth' (Ps 85:11), was overshadowed by a grove of Tammuz, that is of Adonis; and in the very cave where the infant Christ had uttered his earliest cry lamentation was made for the paramour of Venus."

Tammuz was the Babylonian god who died and rose annually in the death and rebirth of vegetation. He was equated with Adonis who, in Greek mythology, was the lover of Aphrodite, i.e., Venus. The liturgical wailings of his worshipers are referred to in Ezk 8:14. This god was worshiped, according to Jerome's statement, in the grotto where Christ was born and in the grove of trees above it. The parallelism with pagan defilement of the places of the crucifixion and resurrection in Jerusalem shows that this spot in Bethlehem, to which Christian tradition had already attached special meaning, was also a deliberate choice. That this understanding of the meaning of Jerome is correct is confirmed by the probably independent and even more explicit statement of Paulinus of Nola (*Epistle* 31, 3 CSEL XXIX-XXX, p. 270): "For the emperor Hadrian, in the belief that he could destroy the Christian faith by the dishonoring of a place, dedicated a statue of Jupiter on the place of the passion, and Bethlehem was profaned by a grove of Adonis." From both Jerome and Paulinus, then, we have evidence that the identification of the Bethlehem cave as the place of the birth of Jesus was already older than the time of Hadrian, i.e., it must go back into the first century and therefore to Judeo-Christian tradition.

No doubt the erection of the church involved the elimination of the grove of Tammuz installed by Hadrian, and there may be a reference to this when Cyril of Jerusalem (348) says of Bethlehem that "a few years ago the place was woody" (NPNFSS VII, p. 77). On the other hand this statement is made in connection with citation of Ps 132:6 (cf. KJV), "Lo, we heard of it in Ephratah [ancient name of Bethlehem, cf. Below No. 34], we found it in the plains of the wood," and the reference by Cyril could just be to longer-standing woods at Bethlehem.

Adjacent to the grotto of the nativity and extending under the Franciscan Church of St. Catherine, which is beside the Church of the Nativity on the north, are several other subterranean chambers. The place where Jerome lived and worked, his tomb which the Anonymous of Piacenza (Geyer p. 178; LPPTS II-D, p. 23; CCSL CLXXV p. 143; WJP p. 85) says Jerome carved out of the rock at the mouth of the cave where the Lord was born, and also the tombs of his friends Paula (d. 404, cf. Jerome, *Letter*

108, 34), Eustochium (d. 419), and Eusebius of Cremona (d. c. 423) are believed to be located in these chambers. Above ground in a cloister of the Church of St. Catherine the statue of Jerome shown in this photograph stands on a granite column.

Bagatti, *Gli antichi edifici sacri di Betlemme*, pp. 50, 195. For a critical view of the Jerome/Paulinus references, see Peter Welten, "Bethlehem und die Klage um Adonis," in ZDPV 99 (1983), pp. 189-203. Photograph: JF.

32. Statue of Jerome near the Church of the Nativity

33. Plan of the Church of Justinian at Bethlehem

AFTER THE COUNCIL of Chalcedon (451) the Christian church was divided between the Orthodox (who accepted the Chalcedonian belief that Christ had two separate natures, human and divine) and the Monophysites (who believed in "one nature" that was both human and divine), and the emperor Justinian (527-565) undertook to repress all "heretics," a term he redefined to include

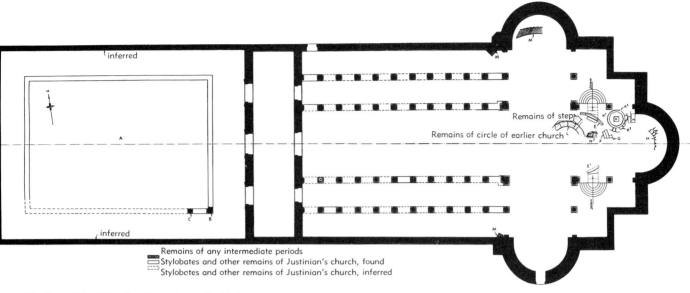

inferred

inferred

Remains of step
Remains of circle of earlier church

Remains of any intermediate periods
Stylobates and other remains of Justinian's church, found
Stylobates and other remains of Justinian's church, inferred

33. Plan of the Church of Justinian at Bethlehem

not only Christians who disagreed with the established church (therefore the Monophysites in particular) but also all who were not Orthodox, which included the Jews and Samaritans. Accordingly, he reaffirmed old laws and issued new regulations that imposed severe restrictions upon Jews and Samaritans, and this led to uprisings of the Samaritans against the Byzantines, which took place in 529, 556, and 578 (the last under Justinian's successor, Justin 565-578), in the last two of which the Jews also joined with the Samaritans.

In the Samaritan revolt many Christian churches were destroyed and burned, and damage was probably done to the Bethlehem church at this time, for a layer of charred material has been found over a part of the mosaic floor in the nave. Afterward Justinian was instrumental in building or rebuilding many churches in the Holy Land (as well as at Constantinople and elsewhere), and this he did at Bethlehem. In his *Book of the Demonstration* (313, trans. Watt, I, p. 135) Eutychius (940) speaks of the church at Bethlehem as bearing witness to the birth of Christ from Mary the Virgin in a cave in that place, and in his *Annales* (MPG 111, cols. 1070f., 159f.; Breydy 2, p. 88) he speaks of the Samaritan revolt and then tells of what Justinian did: "The emperor Justinian ordered his envoy to pull down the church of Bethlehem, which was a small one, and to build it again of such splendor, size, and beauty that none even in the Holy City should surpass it." In the end, however, Eutychius relates, the emperor was displeased with what his representative did and had him beheaded. The new building must have been completed at least by 532, for Cyril of Scythopolis records that John Hesychastes prayed in the narthex of the church that year (A. M. Schneider in RFAC II, col. 226).

The examination of the Church of the Nativity by Harvey in 1934 (cf. above, No. 25) showed that the present church is in plan that of Justinian. In comparison with the earlier Constantinian church, that of Justinian likewise included atrium and narthex, but the main hall was longer, now a rectangle instead of a square (33 meters long instead of 26.5 meters previously), and the nave was widened (10.26 meters) and the side aisles narrowed in proportion. Further, the east end of the church was now enlarged with a large eastern apse and a north-south transept with an apse on either end. Access to the sacred grotto below was now by stairs leading down from the north and south, and the great bronze doors through which one still passes are from the rebuilding by Justinian.

E. T. Richmond, "The Church of the Nativity, The Alterations carried out by Justinian," in QDAP 6 (1938), pp. 67-72; EAEHL 1, pp. 204f. Plan: QDAP 6 (1938), fig. 2 following p. 72, courtesy Palestine Archaeological Museum.

34. Bethlehem on the Madaba Mosaic Map

BETHLEHEM APPEARS on the Madaba Mosaic Map south of Jerusalem (see No. 229). The name is in red letters as used for important places: Βηθλεεμ, Bethlehem. The red-roofed building beneath the name is evidently the Church of the Nativity. Since the church must have been rebuilt by Justinian by 532 (No. 33) and since the Madaba Map dates about 560, it is presumably the church of Justinian that is represented. Correspondence of detail with the plan of Justinian's church (No. 33) is not altogether easy to see, but it may be taken that the attempt is made to show a basilica with three apses.

34. Bethlehem on the Madaba Mosaic Map

Bagatti, *Gli antichi edifici sacri di Betlemme*, pp. 2, 4. Photograph: courtesy Victor R. Gold.

35. The Tomb of Rachel near Bethlehem

BELOW THE BETHLEHEM church on the Madaba Mosaic Map (No. 34) are the legends: Ἐφραθᾶ, Ephrathah; and Ῥαμά. φωνὴ ἐν Ῥαμὰ ἠκούσθη, Ramah. A voice was heard in Ramah. This is a quotation of Jer 31: 15, in connection with which the following explanation is necessary.

Gen 35:19 and 48:7 state that the burial place of Rachel was "on the way to Ephrath (that is, Bethlehem)." The wording suggests that Ephrath or Ephrathah was an older village that was absorbed into Bethlehem and in Mic 5:2 the two names are put together, Bethlehem Ephrathah. I Sam 10:2, however, places the tomb of Rachel in the territory of Benjamin, and the site of er-Ram five miles north of Jerusalem probably corresponds with a Ramah at this place. Indeed the Madaba Map shows another Ῥαμά, Ramah, north and slightly east of Jerusalem (this may be seen on Nos. 10 and 62). It was presumably to the northern Ramah that Nebuzaradan in 588 B.C. took Jeremiah and the captives of Jerusalem and Judah who were being exiled to Babylon (Jer 40:1). Rachel was the mother of Joseph and Benjamin, and Joseph's son Ephraim became synonymous with northern Israel (Jer 31:9). So Jeremiah (31:15) hears a voice in Ramah and it is Rachel weeping for her children, perhaps with reference to the earlier deportation (722 B.C.) of the northern Israelites by the Assyrians (II K 18:11) as well as to the present carrying into exile by the Babylonians. Between the two locations, Matthew is evidently thinking of Ramah and Rachel's tomb as near Bethle-

hem, and as he quotes Jer 31:15 he is hearing the ancient lementation of Rachel echoing in that of the mothers of Bethlehem at the slaughter of the innocents by Herod the Great (Mt 2:18).

As seen in the present photograph the traditional tomb of Rachel, corresponding with the location "on the way to Ephrath" (that is, Bethlehem), is on the old road leading into Bethlehem from Jerusalem. The Pilgrim of Bordeaux (333) (Geyer p. 25; LPPTS I-B, pp. 26-27; CCSL CLXXV, pp. 19-20; WET p. 162) describes the location exactly: "Four miles from Jerusalem on the right is the tomb (*monumentum*) in which Rachel, Jacob's wife, was laid. Two miles further on, on the left, is Bethlehem." The same site is mentioned by Jerome as he tells of the visit of Paula to the Holy Land and says at this point that "she proceeded to Bethlehem stopping only on the right side of the road to visit Rachel's tomb" (*Letter* 108, written in A.D. 404, NPNFSS VI, p. 199). In his time Arculf (670) (Geyer pp. 258f.; LPPTS III-A, p. 31; CCSL CLXXV, pp. 208-209; WJP p. 105) saw the tomb as shaped like a pyramid. Over the years the building has been modified, and as the tomb now exists it represents renovation by the Jewish philanthropist Moses Montefiore, who obtained the keys to the grave for the Jews in 1841 (Meistermann pp. 300f.).

Today the tomb of Rachel is the object of veneration by Jews, Christians, and also Muslims, for Rachel is honored in their history too. She is not mentioned by name in the Quran, but there may be indirect reference to her in Sura IV 27 (22) and XII 77 (Maulana Muhammad Ali, *The Holy Qur'ān* [Lahore, 1973], p. 476 n. 1247). In later tradition it is related that Joseph (Yūsuf), sold by his brothers, comes by the tomb of Rachel (Rāḥīl), throws himself from his camel upon her grave, and cries: "O mother, look on thy child, I have been deprived of my coat, thrown into a pit, stoned and sold as a slave."

35. The Tomb of Rachel near Bethlehem

Then he hears a voice: "Trust in God" (EI III, pp. 1103f.; also the Shorter Encyclopaedia of Islam [1953], p. 467).

Photograph: JF.

36. View of the Church of the Nativity

WRITING ONE of his *Anacreontics* in 603/604, Sophronius (LPPTS XI-A, p. 29) describes the church of Justinian with its three splendid apses (ἐκπρεποῦς τρικόγχον [κόγχος = anything like a mussel-shell]) and its

paneled ceiling which shone as if with the light of heavenly bodies (καλάθωσιν ἀστροφεγγῆ). When the Sasanian Persians under Chosroes II (590-628) invaded Palestine in 614, they destroyed the sanctuaries in Jerusalem and came on to Bethlehem. Although Justin Martyr (*Dialogue* 78, see No. 25 above) says that the Magi "came from Arabia," Clement of Alexandria (*Stromata* I 15, 71 ANF II, p. 316) attests the belief that the Magi were Persians. At the Bethlehem church the visit of the Magi of the Christ child (Mt 2:1) appears to have been depicted, probably in a mosaic, with the Magi in Persian costume. A Greek communication of the Synod of Jerusalem in

36. View of the Church of the Nativity

836 states that when the Persians arrived at Bethlehem they were amazed to see the figures of the Magi, observers of the stars and their own compatriots, and therefore they spared the church. When the Caliph 'Umar took Jerusalem in 638 he also came to Bethlehem and prayed in the south apse where he could face toward Mecca. Eutychius (*Annales*, MPG 111, col. 1100; LPPTS XI-A, p. 67; Breydy, CSCO 472, p. 120) tells of this and in the same connection mentions the mosaic work in the church. By agreement with Sophronius, then the patriarch of Jerusalem, the Muslims were allowed to continue to pray where 'Umar had prayed, and it was probably because of this Muslim usage that the Bethlehem church was spared the general demolition of churches in the Holy Land ordered by the Fatimid Caliph al-Hakim in 1009.

The Crusaders arrived in 1099 and Tancred raised his flag over the basilica; Baldwin was crowned king of the Latin Kingdom there on Christmas Day, 1100. On the north side of the church the Crusaders built a cloister and monastery, which were given to the Canons of St. Augustine, and both the church and monastery were protected with a high wall and towers, making it a veritable fortress. Later the Franciscans received the basilica, established themselves in the deserted Augustinian monastery, and built the Church of St. Catherine, which they still own. After repeated transfers of possession between the Latins and the Greeks, the latter held the basilica permanently and also built a monastery on the southeast side, while the Armenians established a monastery to the southwest. In the photograph, showing the church as it appears today, the rectangular paved square in front of the basilica occupies in part the area of the former atrium. The medieval facade of the church is directly ahead, a modern graveyard and the Franciscan convent are at the left, and the Armenian convent at the right.

Bagatti, *Gli antichi edifici sacri di Betlemme*, pp. 12-13. Photograph: The Matson Photo Service, Alhambra, Calif.

37. The Entrance to the Church of the Nativity

OF THE THREE doors that gave access to the narthex, only the central one remains in use and, as seen in this photograph, it has long since been for the most part walled up in order to keep out animals and give protection in wartime. The rectangular doorway is the modern entrance. The arch is from the medieval period. The beam which runs straight across much higher up is the cornice and corbel of the great door of the once magnificent church of Justinian. The courses of stonework above are also medieval.

Bellarmino Bagatti, *L'archeologia cristiana in Palestina*. Civiltà orientali (Florence: G. C. Sansoni, 1962), p. 88 no. 6. Photograph: courtesy École Biblique et Archéologique Française.

38. Floor Mosaic in the Sacred Cave at the Field of the Shepherds near Bethlehem

AFTER THE CAVE of the Nativity, Christian tradition was most interested at Bethlehem in the place of the angelic announcement of the birth of the Savior to "shepherds out in the field, keeping watch over their flock by night" (Lk 2:8-20). Although in respect of Bethlehem the record of Aetheria (381-384) is incomplete, a letter in praise of the pilgrim's life by the seventh-century monk Valerius makes it certain that Bethlehem was among the places she visited (WET p. 174), and also the relevant statement in the *Book concerning the Holy Places* by Peter the Deacon (1137) is probably based upon Aetheria, as Peter writes that in the vicinity of Bethlehem "there is the church called At the Shepherds (*Ad Pastores*), where there is now a large garden which is carefully enclosed by a wall all around, and also there is a most luminous (*lucidissimus*) cave with an altar in the place where an angel appeared to the shepherds (*pastoribus*) as they kept watch and announced to them the birth of Christ" (Geyer pp. 109f.; WET pp. 185f.). Likewise as he writes (in the year 386) in the name of Paula and Eustochium to invite Marcella to visit the Holy Land, Jerome holds out the prospect that, among many other sacred places, they shall visit "the folds of the shepherds" (*Letter* 46 NPNFSS VI, p. 65); and when he writes (404) to console Eustochium upon the recent death of Paula, her mother, he recalls how, upon her initial visit (385/386) to the cave of the Nativity in Bethlehem, "Paula went a short distance down the hill to the tower of Edar, that is 'of the flock,' near which Jacob fed his flocks, and where the shepherds keeping watch by night were privileged to hear the words: 'Glory to God in the highest and on earth peace, goodwill toward men' " (*Letter* 108 NPNFSS VI, p. 200). Hebrew Migdal Eder (or Edar) means "tower of the flock" (as the same words are translated in Mic 4:8), and in Gen 35:21 Jacob is said to have journeyed on from Rachel's tomb "and pitched his tent beyond the tower of Eder" (the location presumably having been in the vicinity of Bethlehem); hence at the point of Jerome's reference it was evidently supposed that the place where Jacob pastured his flocks was the same as that where the later shepherds heard the angel's message.

In the course of time it was yet further believed that the New Testament shepherds, by then thought to have been three in number, were buried at the same place, and Arculf (670) went to visit the site. Adamnan records:

37. The Entrance to the Church of the Nativity

Arculf gave us a short account of the tombs of those shepherds, around whom, on the night of the Lord's birth, the heavenly brightness shone. "I visited," he said, "the three tombs of those three shepherds who are buried in a church near the Tower of Gader, which is about a thousand paces [about a mile] to the east of Bethlehem. When the Lord was born, the brightness of the angelic light surrounded them at that place that is near the Tower of the Flock, where the church has been built, containing the sepulchers of those shepherds" (Geyer p. 258; LPPTS III-A, pp. 30f.; CCSL CLXXV, p. 208; WJP p. 105).

The traditional Field of the Shepherds to which the foregoing references point, about a mile east of Bethlehem, is near the Arabic village of Beit Sahur. As elsewhere, a cave provided a specific focus of the tradition. The site is under the jurisdiction of the Greek Orthodox Patriarchate of Jerusalem, and archeological excavation was conducted in 1972 and thereafter by Vassilios Tzaferis. Five phases in the history of the site have been identified: (1) the Sacred Natural Cave (second half of the fourth century A.D.); (2) the Cave Church (fifth century); (3) the Roof chapel (fifth century); (4) the Basilica (sixth century); (5) the Monastery Church (seventh century). Portions, at least, of floor mosaics remain from the first four phases and, together with three Greek inscriptions, provide clues to the dating.

38. Floor Mosaic in the Sacred Cave at the Field of the Shepherds near Bethlehem

41

The Sacred Cave was most probably a natural rock cave, and it was evidently considered and used as a sacred place, for which reason the rock floor was leveled and a mosaic pavement laid down upon it. In this mosaic the main motif (found twice and shown in one example in the present photograph) is that of an eight-pointed star made of two interlaced squares, enclosed within a circle, with the circle enclosed within a square. Between the two star design are scattered small equilateral crosses (one seen in the lower left-hand corner in this photograph). While both the eight-pointed star and the equilateral cross are found in various contexts in the early centuries, their occurrence in this particular place is most probably to be taken as symbolic rather than just decorative, i.e., the star alludes to the star of Bethlehem (Mt. 2:2) and the cross is also of Christian significance. In terms of archeological and literary evidence, the mosaic is assigned to a date in the second half of the fourth century, and this appearance of the crosses in a floor mosaic is congruent with a date before the decree of Theodosius II in A.D. 427 forbidding the placement of the cross in pavements (cf. No. 30). Stylistically the mosaic is considered transitional between Roman and Byzantine styles, which also fits such a date. Given the date thus indicated in the second half of the fourth century, this is one of the earliest Christian mosaics discovered in the Holy Land.

Photograph: LA 25 (1975), pl. 1, 2 (cf. *Archaeology* 30 [1977], p. 89), courtesy Studium Biblicum Franciscanum, Jerusalem.

39. Floor Mosaic in the Roof Chapel at the Field of the Shepherds near Bethlehem

IN THE SECOND phase (fifth century) at the Field of the Shepherds an actual small church was built within the sacred cave. This cave church is a rectangular building, 11 by 15 meters, consisting of a main hall with a narrow narthex in the west and a semicircular apse within the hall in the east, and there are two adjacent rooms on the north. The walls are of well-cut stone and the hall was roofed with large limestone blocks. Except for the upper part, which projected above the surface of the earth, the entire complex was underground. The hall was paved with mosaics of black and red terrace, laid out about 0.3 meters above the mosaic pavement of the cave itself, but of these mosaics only small fragments remain. As a whole the underground church was so well preserved that it was used as a parish church for the Greek Orthodox community of Beit Sahur until 1955, when a new church was built in the village and the archeological exploration of the older site became possible.

On the top of the roof of the cave church was found the mosaic pavement shown in the present photograph, and this apparently belonged to a small chapel of some sort built here in a third phase of construction (also attributed to the fifth century). The mosaic is in a semielliptical shape. The border is decorated in black and red; in the upper scene vines (cf. Jn 15:1) issue from an amphora (cf. M. Avi-Yonah in ZDPV 3 [1933], p. 62), on

39. Floor Mosaic in the Roof Chapel at the Field of the Shepherds near Bethlehem

either side of which are also branches with flowers, while above a round medallion contains red flowers with red and blue leaves. Below were two inscriptions in Greek, the one on the right badly damaged, the one on the left reading

Μνήσθητι Κ(ύρι)Λ ε τοῦ δοῦλου σοῦ
Δααζάρου καὶ πάσης τῆς
καρποφορίας αὐτοῦ † Ἀμήν

Remember, O Lord, your servant
Laazarus and all his
contributions. † Amen.

The spelling of Laazarus with two alphas suggests the Hebrew pronunciation of the name; the "contributions" are presumably the generous offerings of this Christian to the church at the Shepherds' Field; a cross separates the dedicatory sentence from the concluding Amen. As a Byzantine mosaic of the fifth century, this is one of only a few known Christian mosaics dating to this period.

The fourth phase is perhaps datable in the first half of the sixth century and in the reign of Justinian (527-565), when most of the churches were built in the Holy Land and when large numbers of pilgrims were coming. The entire area surrounding the cave church, some 60 by 40 meters, was now enclosed by a wall of heavy limestone blocks. Whatever chapel was on the roof of the cave church was removed, leaving only the mosaic pavement just described, and a whole new basilica was constructed. The new basilica measured 30 by 15 meters, with atrium, narthex, nave, two aisles, and apse, as well as colorful mosaic floor, but the architectural elements including marble columns and Corinthian capitals were largely scattered or reused and of the mosaics only small fragments remain. There are signs of burning, and the destruction was probably by the Persians in A.D. 614.

In the fifth phase, probably not long later in the seventh century, yet another church was built on the same site which for the most part followed the plan of the preceding basilica, the chief difference being that instead of the marble columns that had previously supported the roof, massive stone pillars were now built. Around the church were also various living quarters and other installations. It is probable that after the Arab conquest (A.D. 640) few pilgrims came, and this was a monastery and its monastery church, as it continued until final destruction and abandonment in the tenth century.

Vassilios Tzaferis, "The Archaeological Excavation at Shepherds' Field," in LA 25 (1975), pp. 5-52; and "Byzantine Mosaics in Israel," in *Archaeology* 30 (1977), pp. 87-90. Photograph: LA 25 (1975), pl. 2, 1 (cf. *Archaeology* 30 [1977], p. 88), courtesy Studium Biblicum Franciscanum, Jerusalem.

NAZARETH

40. Nazareth

THE TOWN OF NAZARETH, a portion of which is shown in this photograph down a cactus-lined path, is in the hills of Galilee at an elevation of 1,150 feet. From the heights there is a view south across the Plain of Esdraelon, west to Mount Carmel, east to Mount Tabor, and north to Mound Hermon. In the OT Jos 19:10-15 gives a list of the towns of the tribe of Zebulun and (v.13) names Japhia, which may be the Japha that is on a yet higher hill one and one-half miles southwest of Nazareth, but does not mention Nazareth. Josephus, who was responsible for military operations in this area in the Jewish War, settled at Japha (*Life* 52 §270) and fortified the place (*War* II 20, 6 §573), and also used Sepphoris, three miles north of Nazareth, as headquarters (*Life* 12 §63, etc.). In his writings he gives the names of forty-five towns in Galilee, but does not say anything about Nazareth. The Talmud also, although it refers to sixty-three Galilean towns, does not mention Nazareth. In spite of this silence of the OT, Josephus, and the Talmud, excavations shortly to be mentioned (No. 43) show that it was certainly a settled place at an early date, and Nazareth is also named in an inscription of the end of the third century or beginning of the fourth century found at Caesarea (No. 44), as well as by both Julius Africanus (170-240) cited by Eusebius and in the *Onomasticon* of Eusebius (No. 45). Lack of earlier mention, therefore, does not suggest doubt that there was a city called Nazareth in Jesus' time (Cheyne in EB III, cols. 3358-3362), but only attests the relative insignificance of the city, which may also be reflected in the disparaging comment quoted in Jn 1:46. According to Lk 2:51 Jesus must have grown up in Nazareth; according to Mk 1:9 at his baptism he came from Nazareth. He was therefore "the one from Nazareth" (ὁ ἀπὸ Ναζαρέθ) (Mt 21:11; Jn 1:45; Ac 10:38), "the Nazarene" (ὁ Ναζαρηνός) (Mk 1:24, etc.), or "the Nazoraean" (ὁ Ναζωραῖος) (Mt 2:23, etc). Both of the last terms probably derived linguistically from Nazareth and mean "inhabitant of Nazareth."

In the light of recent archeological evidence (see No. 43 below) that Nazareth was an old established site long before the Early Roman period and during it, Vardaman remarks that there is little reason to question the Gospel record that Jesus grew up there. For representative older skepticism on this matter, he cites, besides Cheyne above, Champlin Burrage, *Nazareth and the Beginnings of Christianity* (Oxford: University Press, 1914), pp. 6f., 26, 27, 29, etc.; Arthur Drews, *The Christ Myth*, (Chicago: Open Court Publishing Co., 1911, rev. 3d ed., pp. 59-60; J. Z. Lauterbach, "Jesus in the Talmud," *Rabbinic Essays by Jacob Z. Lauterbach* (Cincinnati: Hebrew Union College Press, 1951), p. 483;

40. Nazareth

and A. Powell Davies, *The Meaning of the Dead Sea Scrolls*, Signet Key Books (New York: New American Library, 1956), pp. 117ff. For the linguistic question see W. F. Albright, "The Names 'Nazareth' and 'Nazoraean,'" in JBL 65 (1946), pp. 397-401; Albrecht Alt, *Where Jesus Worked* (London: Epworth Press, 1961), pp. 12-17; Willibald Bösen, *Galiläa als Lebensraum und Werkungsfeld Jesu, Eine zeitgeschichtliche und theologische Untersuchung* (Freiburg, Basel, Wien: Herder, 1985), pp. 97-145. Photograph: JF.

41. Plan of Nazareth

THIS SKETCH PLAN of Nazareth shows the chief places that are mentioned in the following discussion.

Plan: JF, cf. B. Bagatti, "Ritrovamenti nella Nazaret evangelica," in LA 5 (1954-1955), p. 7 fig. 1; and in DB Supplément VI, cols. 319-320 fig. 599.

42. The Fountain of Mary at Nazareth

AT NAZARETH the main supply of water even into the twentieth century and presumably from the earliest times was from the spring known as the Spring or Fountain of Mary (Ain Maryam). This spring rises in the hill above the Greek Orthodox Church of Mary's Fountain, also know as the Church of St. Gabriel (No. 55), and from there it was long since conducted into the grounds of the

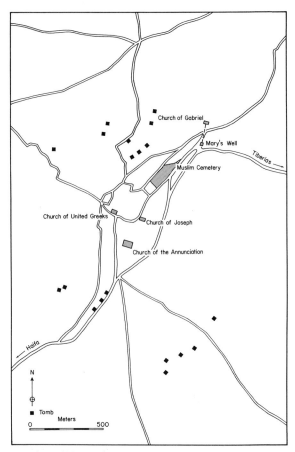

41. Plan of Nazareth

church and then piped on down the hill to the southeast, nearly 500 feet from the source, to an outlet built in 1862 beside the road leading from Nazareth to Tiberias and now rebuilt in new form. The photograph shows the outlet enclosure in the days when the women of Nazareth still came to it, with their water vessels on their heads.

Asad Mansur, " 'The Virgin's Fountain,' Nazareth," in PEFQS 1913, pp. 149-153; Clemens Kopp in JPOS 19 (1939-1940), pp. 253-258; Bagatti, *Antichi Villagi*, p. 25 fig. 8 for a sketch of the water conduits leading from the spring. Photograph: The Matson Photo Service, Alhambra, Calif.

43. An Ancient Grotto Habitation Adjacent to the Church of the Annunciation

THE OLDEST KNOWN human life in the region of Nazareth is attested by the skull found in 1934 by R. Neuville in a cave about one and one-half miles southeast of the city, a skull which may be older than that of Neandertal man. In Nazareth itself a complex of burial caves was found in the upper city in 1963, in which there was pottery of the first part of the Middle Bronze Age (RB 70 [1963], p. 563; 72 [1965], p. 547).

42. The Fountain of Mary at Nazareth

43. An Ancient Grotto Habitation Adjacent to the Church of the Annunciation

Down in the area of the Latin Church of the Annunciation there was certainly an ancient village of long continuance. Archeological investigation in and around this church was conducted by Benedict Vlaminck in 1892, by Prosper Viaud in 1889 and 1907-1909 and by Bellarimo Bagatti in 1955 and thereafter when the previously standing eighteenth-century (1730) church was demolished to make way for the new and larger Basilica of the Annunciation (No. 49). The area under and around the church, as well as at the Church of St. Joseph not far away, was plainly that of an agricultural village. There were numerous grottoes, silos for grain, cisterns for water and oil; presses for raisins and olives, and millstones. While the silos are of a type found at Tell Abu Matar as

early as the Chacolithic Age (IEJ 5 [1955], p. 23) the earliest pottery found in them here at Nazareth is of Iron II (900-600 B.C.). Vardaman calls attention to the characteristic large jar with a small "funnel" beside the mouth; this appendage, though designed like a funnel, is simply attached to the shoulder, and does not actually pierce the wall of the jar (for an illustration of this jar, see Bagatti in DB Supplément VI, col. 323, Fig. 601). Other pottery of the site comprises a little of the Hellenistic period, more of the Roman, and most of all of the Byzantine period. Of the numerous grottoes at least several had served for domestic use and had even been modified architecturally for this purpose. One of these, where walls were built against a grotto to make a habitation,

45

had already been found by Viaud under the convent adjoining the Church of the Annunciation and is shown in the photograph. Twenty-three tombs have also been found, most of them at a distance of something like 250 to 750 yards from Church of the Annunciation to the north, the west, and the south. Since these must have been outside of the village proper, their placement gives some idea of the limits of the settlement. Eighteen of the tombs are of the kokim type, which was known in Palestine from about 200 B.C. (cf. No. 255), and became virtually the standard type of Jewish tomb. Two of the tombs, one (PEFQS 1923, p. 90) only 60 yards and the other (QDAP 1 [1932], pp. 53-55) 450 yards southwest of the Church of the Annunciation, still contained objects such as pottery lamps and vases and glass vessels, and these date probably from the first to the third or fourth centuries of the Christian era. Four of the tombs were sealed with rolling stones, a type of closure typical of the late Jewish period up to A.D. 70 (Nos. 274, 281). From the tombs, therefore, it can be concluded that Nazareth was a strongly Jewish settlement in the Roman period (cf. also No. 45).

R. Köppel, "Das Alter der neuentdeckten Schädel von Nazareth," in *Biblica* 16 (1935), pp. 58-73; Clemens Kopp in JPOS 18 (1938), pp. 191-207; Lagrange, pp. 14-15; *Nazareth Today*, trans. Gerard Bushell (Jerusalem: Franciscan Printing Press, n.d.); B. Bagatti in DB Supplément VI, cols. 318-329; and in EAEHL III, pp. 911-922; and Bagatti, *Excavations Nazareth*. For a photograph of the Jewish grave with a rolling stone at the Convent of the Sisters of Nazareth, see Stiassny, p. 70. Photograph: courtesy École Biblique et Archéologique Française.

44. Inscription from Caesarea Mentioning Nazareth

THE FINDINGS in excavations already referred to (No. 43) provide positive evidence of the existence of a town at Nazareth in the time of Jesus. Fragments of an inscription found at Caesarea in 1962, in the excavations of the Hebrew University assisted by the Southern Baptist Theological Seminary, now provide the first known occurrence of the name Nazareth in an inscription and the earliest occurrence of the name in Hebrew. Two fragments were found at this time and a third, found some years previously, was recognized as evidently belonging with them. The first fragment, with which we are here specially concerned, shown in the photograph, is of dark gray marble, 153 by 124 mm. in size, and inscribed in square Hebrew characters with portions of four lines remaining. From the three fragments together and by comparison with materials in Talmudic and liturgical sources, it has been possible to show that the complete inscription was a list of the twenty-four priestly courses (cf. 1 Ch 24:7-19; Neh 12:1-21), giving the name of each course (or family) in its proper order and the name of the town or village in Galilee where it was settled. This

44. Inscription from Caesarea Mentioning Nazareth

transfer of the courses of priests to residences in Galilee must have taken place after the destruction of the Temple of Jerusalem in A.D. 70 and the subsequent expulsion of the Jews from the territory of Aelia Capitolina by Hadrian (cf. No. 184). The inscription fragments were found in the northern part of Caesarea where the Jewish synagogue was located, and the whole stone tablet was probably once fixed on the synagogue wall. In the ruins of the Caesarea synagogue a hoard of 3,700 bronze coins was found which was apparently hidden in 355/356, and it is believed that the synagogue was built at the end of the third or beginning of the fourth century (cf. No. 132). The inscription is judged to be of about the same date. In the fragment shown in the photograph the name Nazareth (נצרת) is to be seen in line 2; also in line 4, assuming only that the initial Mem is missing, we have the name Migdal (מ]גדל), probably referring to Migdal Nunaiya or Magdala (No. 73).

M. Avi-Yonah, "A List of Priestly Courses from Caesarea," in IEJ 12 (1962), pp. 137-139; *Archaeology and Caesarea* (Louisville: The Southern Baptist Theological Seminary, 1963), p. 7; E. Jerry Vardaman, "Introduction to the Caesarea Inscription of the Twenty-four Priestly Courses," pp. 42-45, and M. Avi-Yonah, "The Caesarea Inscription of the Twenty-four Priestly Courses," pp. 46-57, in *The Teacher's Yoke: Studies in Memory of Henry Trantham*, ed. by E. Jerry Vardaman and James L. Garrett, Jr. (Waco, Tex: Baylor University Press, 1964). Photograph: courtesy The Southern Baptist Theological Seminary.

45. Plan of the Church of the Annunciation at Nazareth

WITH RESPECT to the possible remembrance of any particular location in Nazareth associated with the life of Jesus, it is important to recall that, according to positive evidence, members of the family of Jesus were still living in Palestine, some of them perhaps in Nazareth, until the end of the first century and the beginning of the second, and further descendants were probably there much longer than that. The Jewish Christian writer Hegesip-

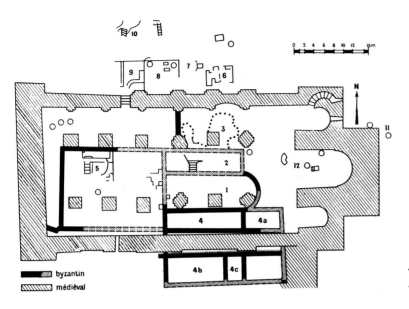

byzantin
médiéval

45. Plan of the Church of the
Annunciation at Nazareth

pus (c. 180), quoted by Eusebius (*Ch. Hist.* III, 11 and 32), says that Symeon (who succeeded James, the brother of the Lord, as head of the church in Jerusalem, and was himself a cousin of Jesus, being son of Clopas who was brother of Joseph) lived to the age of 120 and suffered martyrdom under Trajan (in the latter's tenth year of reign, i.e., 107, according to the *Chronicle* of Eusebius [ed. Helm p. 194]); and (*Ch. Hist.* III, 20) that two grandsons of Jude, the brother of Jesus, were brought before Domitian (in his fifteenth year of reign, i.e., 96, according to Eusebius, *Ch. Hist.* III, 18) because of suspicion attaching to them as descendants of David, but were freed and lived on till the time of Trajan (98-117). In their examination before the emperor these two men admitted that they were indeed of the house of David, but declared possession between them of only a piece of land thirty-nine quarter-acres (πλέθρων λθ') in extent and worth 9,000 denarii, which they worked to pay their taxes and support themselves, and they confirmed their statement by showing their toil-calloused hands, so in the end the imperial suspicions were entirely allayed. They were, therefore, farmers, and since they were undoubtedly brought from Palestine to Rome for the examination, they may very well have been living at Nazareth, in an area the agricultural nature of which was abundantly demonstrated by the archeological finds cited above (No 43). Upon release the two men also became leaders of the churches, both because they were witnesses (μάρτυρας) and because they were relatives of the Lord. With such members of the family, and undoubtedly others after them, living on in Palestine and very probably in Nazareth itself, it is possible to believe that remembrance of at least some particular sites in the home town of Jesus would long be preserved.

Like the Jewish-type tombs (No. 43), the Caesarea inscription reporting the settlement of priests in Nazareth (No. 44) also suggests the strongly Jewish character of the town. Along the same line Julius Africanus (c. 200), cited by Eusebius (*Ch. Hist.* I 7, 14), speaks of Nazareth and Cochaba as Jewish villages. Epiphanius (*Pan. haer.* I 29, 7, 7; 30, 2, 8-9 GCS I, pp. 330, 335; Williams, NHS 35, pp. 118, 121) mentions a place called Cochaba in Jordan (cf. M. Avi-Yonah, *The Holy Land from the Persian to the Arab Conquests* (Grand Rapids: Baker, 1966), p. 168 and map p. 169), but this Cochaba which is associated with Nazareth may be identified with modern Kaukab, north of Nazareth, in the Battof Valley (S. Liebermann and M. Avi-Yonah in QDAP 5 [1936], p. 171). Cochaba also seems to be referred to in a newly discovered geographical source from Cave 5 among the Dead Sea Scrolls (see DJD III, no. 9, p. 179, and other references there, cited by Vardaman). Along with speaking of Nazareth and Cochaba as Jewish villages, Africanus in the same passage also tells of the δεσπόσυνοι, or relatives of the Lord, who come from both towns and keep the records of their descent with great care. Also a martyr named Conon, who died in Pamphylia under Decius (249-251), declared at his trial: "I belong to the city of Nazareth in Galilee, and am a relative of Christ whom I serve, as my forefathers have done" (Kopp 1959, p. 90; SWDCB I, p. 621).

Later, Constantine authorized Joseph of Tiberias, a Jewish priest who had become a Christian and had the dignity of a count (SWDCB III, p. 460), to build churches in Galilee. In about 359 Epiphanius met this man, then seventy years of age, in Scythopolis and quotes (*Pan. haer.* I 30, 11, 9f. GCS I, p. 347; Williams, NHS 35, p. 128) Joseph as saying that no one had ever been able to build churches in the towns of Galilee (presumably he means before he himself did so), because no Greek or

Samaritan or Christian was among them (ἔνθα τις οὐδέ-ποτε ἴσχυσεν οἰκοδομῆσαι ἐκκλησίας, διὰ τὸ μήτε Ἕλληνα, μήτε Σαμαρείτην, μήτε Χριστιανὸν μέσον αὐτῶν εἶναι). This matter of having no Gentiles among them was especially true, Joseph added, in Tiberias and Diocaesarea, which is also called Sepphoris, and in Nazareth and Capernaum. Absent in Nazareth, therefore, according to Joseph, were Gentile Christians and any Gentile church (ekklesia), but we remember (from the introductory section on the Judeo-Christians) that the Judeo-Christians (Ebionites and Nazarenes) did not wish to be called "Christians" and wished to call their places of worship a "synagogue" and not a "church"; therefore what Joseph says does not exclude the presence in Nazareth of believers from among the Jews (see the evidence just above of Jesus' family members continuing to live at Nazareth), nor the existence of a synagogue-church (see below the evidence of such).

As for the work of Joseph himself, Epiphanius reports that in Tiberias, where a pagan temple had been left unfinished since the time of Hadrian, Joseph rebuilt it into a church, and he also built churches in Sepphoris "and in other towns." The "other towns" could have included Nazareth, but of the four towns earlier named (Tiberias, Sepphoris, Nazareth, Capernaum) only the first two are specifically named here, so whether Joseph built also at Nazareth and/or at Capernaum remains uncertain but is by no means impossible. Allowing for the fact that Joseph was seventy years old when Epiphanius met him in the year 359, Joseph's active church building work may be provisionally dated around A.D. 330.

It is some time before a church is actually mentioned at Nazareth. In the *Onomasticon* (ed. Klostermann, GCS Eusebius III 1, pp. 138-141) Eusebius locates Nazareth in Galilee fifteen miles east of Legio (which was near Megiddo) and near Mount Tabor (from which it is in fact only five miles to the west), and Jerome adds in his version that it was a *viculus* or mere village, but neither writer mentions a church in the place, a fact explainable as set forth just above. The extant portions of the Madaba Mosaic Map also do not extend far enough to show Nazareth, so what may have appeared in that source can no longer be ascertained. In 570, however, the Anonymous of Piacenza reports coming from Diocaesarea (Sepphoris) to Nazareth, speaks of the fertility of the region, refers to the beauty of the Hebrew women of the city, who say that St. Mary was a relative of theirs, and records: "The house of St. Mary is a basilica" (Geyer p. 161; LPPTS II-D, p. 5; CCSL CLXXV, p. 131; WJP pp. 79f.).

In the already mentioned (No. 43) archeological work of Benedict Vlaminck and of Prosper Viaud in the last years of the nineteenth century and the first years of the twentieth century at the then still-standing eighteenth-century Church of the Annunciation, the walls of a pre-ceding Crusader church were uncovered and some of its capitals found, while under it the remains of a Byzantine church were also discovered, as well as various mosaics and graffiti. Then when the small eighteenth-century church was demolished in 1955 in preparation for the erection of the new Basilica of the Annunciation, mosaic pavements were lifted to allow full examination, and Bellarmino Bagatti (1955-1968) carried excavation down to the rock level below (Bagatti, *Excavations Nazareth*, pp. 114-173; and Bagatti, *Church from Circumcision*, pp. 122-128; *Nazareth Today*, pp. 11-13).

Looking now at the plan (No. 45), the larger outline is that of the Crusader church. This edifice was 75 meters long and 30 meters wide, and was oriented directly to the east. Two rows of columns marked out the nave and two side aisles, and the hall terminated in three apses at the eastern end. As for the Crusader capitals that Viaud found, they had never been installed, but were elaborately carved with figures of Christ and the Apostles and are now in the Monastery Museum (Stiassny, pictures on pp. 114-117). Enclosed within the precincts of the Crusader church, underneath the north side aisle, was a rock cavern with two grottoes, one larger and one smaller (no. 3 in the plan), the veneration of which the erection of the church above was evidently intended to continue.

As to the building of the church by the Crusaders, when they arrived at the end of the eleventh century the preceding church was in ruins. The historian William of Tyre (1095-1184, Babcock and Krey, I, p. 399) tells us that under Godfrey of Bouillon, Prince Tancred was given the charge of Galilee (1099) and made his capital at Tiberias, in which territory he devoted much attention to establishing richly adorned churches, namely, at Nazareth, Tiberias, and on Mount Tabor. The date of the Crusader church at Nazareth is therefore in the very early twelfth century. Soon after, the Russian abbot Daniel (1106) visited Nazareth and wrote (LPPTS IV-C, pp. 69f.):

A large and lofty church rises in the midst of the town. It has three altars [i.e., in the three apses]. Upon entering it there is to the left side [i.e., at the north side aisle], before a little altar, a small but deep cavern with two small doors, one east and the other west, through which the grotto is reached; entering by the western door one has on the right hand a cell [i.e., the larger grotto, no. 3 in the plan], with a narrow entrance, in which the holy Virgin lived. . . . On entering the same cavern by the western door, one has on the left hand the sepulcher of St. Joseph, spouse of Mary [i.e., the smaller grotto, see below No. 48 for this misidentification]. . . . In the same cavern, near the west door, is the place where the holy Virgin Mary sat spinning purple, that is a scarlet thread, when the archangel Gabriel, sent by God, presented himself before her (cf. below No. 55).

In view of this traditional identification of the larger grotto as marking the residence of Mary and the place of the Annunciation, note some of the other items marked in the plan. Immediately to the north but outside the wall of the Crusader church, a large artificial cavern (no. 6 in the plan) was an ancient wine press (Bagatti in DB Supplément VI, col. 325). Like many other such presses found in Palestine (Saller, *Discoveries at St. John's, 'Ein Karim* [PSBF 3], pp. 96-100), this is probably from the Roman period and is one of the remains of ancient agricultural Nazareth (cf. No. 43). Other remains nearby include an oven (no. 8 in the plan) and grain silos (no. 10) (see Bagatti in DB Supplément VI, col. 326 and fig. 604). Such were some of the surroundings where tradition remembered the home of Mary.

In the same plan, the smaller rectangular structure, of which the actually preserved walls are shown in black, was the church of the Byzantine period, which was the predecessor of the Crusader church. Like its successor, the Byzantine church had nave and two side aisles and was oriented directly to the east, but had only a single apse at the eastern end, while at the western end there was a large atrium. The atrium was nearly 21 meters long and 16 meters wide; the central nave (no. 1 in the plan) was about 19 meters long and 8 meters wide; and the two side aisles (nos. 2 and 4) were about 3 meters wide. At the east end of the south side aisle there was a sacristy (no. 4a), and outside the church on the south side there was a small monastery (nos. 4b and 4c). This church also was laid out in relation to the two venerated grottoes, one larger and one smaller (no. 3 in the plan), but being a smaller structure than the Crusader church that encompassed the grottoes, the caves remained outside and below the north aisle. In what follows (No. 48) is will be seen that this church was probably built about A.D. 427 and perhaps thanks to a certain deacon Conon of Jerusalem. Although damaged and repaired several times, it remained in use from the fifth century to the twelfth century, when it was finally replaced by the Crusader structure (*Nazareth Today*, p. 14). This, therefore, must have been the church to which the Anonymous of Piacenza (570) referred in the above-quoted statement, "The house of St. Mary is a basilica."

Prosper Viaud, *Nazareth et ses deux églises de l'Annunciation et de Saint-Joseph* (Paris: Alphonse Picard, 1910); Kopp in JPOS (1938), pp. 210-216; 19 (1939-1940), pp. 82-116; Kopp 1959, pp. 92-106; B. Bagatti, "Ritrovementi nella Nazaret evangelica," in LA 5 (1954-1955), pp. 5-44; and in DB Supplément VI, cols. 329-332; and *Excavations Nazareth*, pp. 9-26, 114-173; and *Church from Circumcision*, pp. 122-128; and "Il nuovo santuraio di Nazaret e l'archeologia," in *Antichi Villaggi*, pp. 20-22; Gaultier Briand, *Nazareth Judéo-Chrétienne* (Jerusalem: Franciscan Printing Press, n.d.); *Nazareth Today*, trans. Gerard Bushell (Jerusalem: Franciscan Printing Press, n.d.); Stiassny, pp. 80-82; Testa, *Nazaret Giudeo-Cristiana*; Benoit, *Christmas*, pp. 16f.; Ovadiah, *Corpus*, pp. 144f.; Ernest Saunders, "Christian Synagogues and Jewish Christianity in Galilee," in *Explor* 3 (1977), pp. 70-78, esp. pp. 74f.; James F. Strange, "Diversity in Early Palestinian Christianity, Some Archaeological Evidences," in ATR 65 (1983), pp. 14-24. Plan: Bagatti in DB Supplément VI, cols. 321-322, fig. 600, courtesy Terra Santa.

46. Plan of the Area of the Venerated Grottoes under the Church of the Annunciation

THE PRESENT PLAN (turned for convenience 90° from plan No. 45) represents the subterranean area of the two venerated grottoes, the larger outlined in the upper left-hand corner, and the smaller marked F. Aligned with the grottoes is the wall marked G. This was the south wall of an edifice underlying the Byzantine church above, and the stones of this wall were reused in the double row of stones that made the stylobate (a low wall supporting a row of columns) between the nave and the south aisle of the Byzantine church (Bagatti, *Excavations Nazareth*, p. 83 fig. 42), a plain proof of the priority of the building below, which was destroyed to make way for the Byzantine church. In addition to the wall (G), many other architectural elements of the same pre-Byzantine structure were found, including columns, column bases, plain capitals, cornices, jambs of doors and windows, and other dressed stones. Stylistically these elements are similar to what has been found in stratigraphically excavated Jewish synagogues in Galilee and the Golan Heights, which are dated to about the middle of the third century A.D., so this edifice must have been erected at about that time and in synagogal form (Bagatti, *Church from Circumcision*, p. 125; Strange in ATR 65 [1983], p. 17, with references to Meyers).

The architectural fragments just mentioned were covered with Byzantine plaster, on which many graffiti were written in charcoal or cut in with a sharp instrument. Included are many signs of the cross and other signs and short inscriptions understandable as of Judeo-Christian import. On the plaster remaining on one column, along with many crosses a partially preserved inscription incised in large letters contains the words, "under the holy place of M . . . I wrote . . ." (ΥΠΟ ΑΓΙΩ ΤΟΠΟ Μ . . . ΕΓΡΑΨΑ . . .). Here, asking for remembrance in this holy place, some pilgrim probably wrote the pilgrim's own name and/or the name(s) of some dear one(s), as the Anonymous of Piacenza did at Cana, where that pilgrim said, "I, unworthy though I am, wrote the names of my parents" (Geyer p. 161; LPPTS II-D, p. 4; CCSL CLXXV, p. 130; WJP p. 79; cf. No. 57). As for "the holy place of M . . .," where only the initial letter "M" of the personal name survives, it is at least possible and even probable that that name was Mary. At any rate that name is very plainly found in the inscription on the base

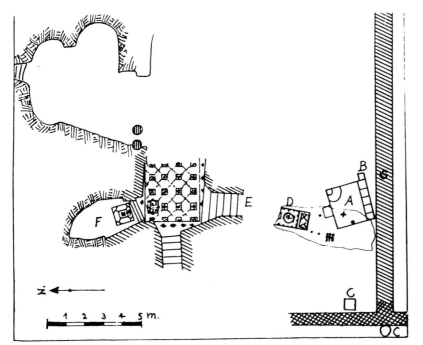

46. Plan of the Area of the Venerated Grottoes under the Church of the Annunciation

of another column: "XE//MAPIA." The abbreviation in the first line is often used for χριστέ as an address to "Christ" (Mt 26:68), but in the present context the excavator very convincingly thinks it stands for χαῖρε, "hail," and is intended to repeat the angelic salutation to Mary in Lk 1:28 (Bagatti, *Excavations Nazareth*, pp. 156-158; and *Church from Circumcision*, pp. 62f., 125f.; Briand pp. 22f.).

Together the architectural elements and the graffiti just described allow the conclusion that we see here the remains of a pre-Byzantine synagogue-church dating in the third-fourth century (Strange in ATR 65 [1983], p. 17) and continuing in use until replaced by the Byzantine church in the early fifth century.

Located as it was in closes proximity to the venerated grottoes, there is little doubt that it was the larger of these which was especially associated with Mary, the mother of Jesus. This grotto (no. 3 in plan No. 45, and in the upper left-hand corner in the present plan) is about 16 by 19 feet in size. Although no ornamentation survives from the time of the synagogue-church which was focused upon the cave, there is a rock-hewn apse in the east wall of the grotto, and this can be taken as indication of a liturgical connection.

The grotto need not itself have been a habitation, but like many other grottoes nearby, it might have been connected as an underground storeroom or other facility with a dwelling that has long since disappeared (Benoit, *Christmas*, p. 17). In view of the attested presence of members of the family of Jesus down at least into the middle of the third century (such as the martyr Conon, see No. 45), remembrance of a specific place is surely not

impossible. The excavator himself (Bagatti, *Excavations Nazareth*, p. 173) finds no difficulty in thinking that persons who belonged to Nazareth and were relatives of Christ had continued to live on their own property, had been at the head of the Judeo-Christian church in Nazareth, and had erected the religious edifice just described.

See review of Bagatti, *Excavations Nazareth*, by Renate Rosenthal in IEJ 21 (1971), p. 181 for the opinion that "much room is left for discussion and varying interpretations." But for recognition of the Jewish-Christian synagogue-church at Nazareth and the "Hail Mary" inscription as evidence of Jewish-Christian veneration of Mary already in the very first centuries, see Cornfeld, pp. 308f. Plan: Briand, *Nazareth, Judéo-Chrétienne*, p. 38, courtesy Studium Biblicum Franciscanum, Jerusalem.

47. The Mosaic of the Crown in the Church of the Annunciation

WHEN THE REMAINS of the Byzantine church were discovered (No. 46), surviving portions of mosaic pavement were found in its adjacent monastery (nos. 4b and 4c in plan No. 45), in the church's south side aisle and sacristy (nos. 4 and 4a), and in the area shown in plan No. 46 (Bagatti, *Excavations Nazareth*, p. 94 fig. 49).

The mosaic marked as D in plan No. 46 and shown in the present photograph is known as the Mosaic of the Crown. It was discovered originally by Viaud and was in the middle of the nave of the Byzantine church but on a slightly lower level than the rest of the floor (Bagatti, *Excavations Nazareth*, p. 95 fig. 50), and it faced northwards rather than in the east-west direction of the nave

47. The Mosaic of the Crown in the Church of the Annunciation

and aisles of the church. The entire section, with part of the top damaged and missing, is about 5.3 meters long and 2 meters wide. Against a white background, a crown is formed of red and black tesserae in three concentric circles, and terminates in two ribbons. Set within the crown is an equal-armed cross, with the letter rho worked into it to make much the equivalent of a tao-rho or cross-monogram (cf. below p. 354). In making a fill under the mosaic, old materials were sealed in, and in this case the date of the mosaic appears to be in the fourth century, so that it is prior to the building of the Byzantine church, and this agrees with its difference in level and difference in orientation (Strange in ATR 65 [1983], p. 15). As being earlier than the Byzantine church and of fourth-century date, the Mosaic of the Crown represents a late phase in the history of the synagogue-church and agrees with dating the Judeo-Christian edifice in the third-fourth centuries all together (Bagatti, *Excavations Nazareth*, pp. 97-100, no. 1; Strange in ATR 65 [1983], pp. 15-17; see Cornfeld p. 309 for this as the cosmic cross on a mosaic symbolizing the celestial abode).

Photograph: Prosper Viaud, *Nazareth et ses deux églises de l'Annonciation et de Saint-Joseph* (Paris: Alphonse Picard, 1910), p. 89 fig. 44.

48. Mosaic and Inscription of Conon in the Church of the Annunciation

DIRECTLY AHEAD FROM the Mosaic of the Crown (No. 47) six rock-cut steps (E in plan No. 46) lead down to the lower level in front of the two venerated grottoes, about four feet below the level of the nave of the church above. In front of the entrance to the smaller grotto there is a large mosaic pavement (outlined in plan No. 46), which was found originally by Vlaminck, was still preserved to the extent of about 9 meters square, and perhaps originally extended a like distance eastward in front of the larger grotto. The mosaic field is divided into squares and lozenges; in four out of fifteen squares are equal-armed crosses; other crosses are around the borders. In the northwest corner of the field at the entrance to the grotto a large square encloses the following inscription (M. Avi-Yonah in QDAP 3 [1934], pp. 36f., no. 271, 2; Bagatti, *Excavations Nazareth*, pp. 100-102, no. 2):

ΠΡΚΩΝΩ
ΝΟCΔΙΑΚ
ΙΕΡΟCΟΛ
ΥΜΩΝ

The initial abbreviation ΠΡ can stand for παρά, with the genetive meaning "from," or perhaps here for προσφορά, "gift" or "offering"; ΔΙΑΚ is plainly to be completed as the word for "deacon" (διάκονος) in the genitive; thus the text is to be filled out and translated: προσφορὰ Κώνωνος διακόνου Ἱεροσολύμων, "Gift of Conon, Deacon of Jerusalem."

Just inside the entrance of the smaller grotto there is also a small section of mosaic that has likenesses to the Mosaic of Conon, but also is like the Mosaic of the Crown (No. 47) in that it too exhibits a cross-monogram but in somewhat different form (Bagatti, *Excavations Nazareth*, pp. 102f., no. 3).

Since all three mosaics just described have the cross in different forms, it must be supposed that they are prior to the edict of Theodosius II in A.D. 427 (cf. No. 30), which forbade the use of the cross and other Christian symbols in pavements to be walked on. If the Mosaic of the Crown is fourth century in date it was certainly prior to the edict. The Conon inscription, however, may be much closer to the time when the emperor's edict became known in Nazareth, because based on the lettering the inscription is usually placed toward the middle of the fifth century (Kroll p. 88, col. 1). In contrast, however, with these mosaics, in the mosaics of the monastery on the south side of the Byzantine church there are circles that look as if they might have been intended to include crosses but in fact are left empty. Inasmuch as the tesserae of the mosaics in other parts of the church and the

48. Mosaic and Inscription of Conon in the Church of the Annunciation

tesserae in the convent are the same, the excavator surmises that the imperial edict of A.D. 427 became known here while the artists were still working, thus the presumed date of the Byzantine church is in the first half of the fifth century, spanning the time both before and after A.D. 427 (Bagatti, *Excavations Nazareth*, p. 94, fig. 49, Room "i"; p. 105, no. 9; p. 106, fig. 61; p. 108; and *Church from Circumcision*, pp. 124f.; Kroll p. 85, col. 1 no. 2). Since the Conon inscription probably dates to about the same time, this allows the further supposition that it was the Jerusalem deacon himself who provided for the building of the Byzantine church (Stiassny p. 83; *Nazareth Today*, p. 14).

From the mosaic of Conon we go on into the smaller grotto (F). As seen in the quotation from the abbot Daniel (1106, see above No. 45), some visitors thought this was the burial place of Joseph, the spouse of Mary; others have surmised it to be the grave of Joseph of Tiberias, who did much for the churches of Galilee (No. 45, cf. Kopp 1963, pp. 64f.), but archaeological investigation tells a different story. The grotto is a cavern about 15 feet long and half as wide, and its walls were plastered up to six times, one coat over the other, in ancient time. In the third coat of plaster from the beginning there was a coin of the young Constantine, hence the first and second plaster coats must have been earlier than the fourth century. On the earliest plaster there is a painting with an inscription in red, and the shapes of the letters are held to indicate a third-century date (Bagatti, *Church from Circumcision*, p. 127; Strange in ATR 65 [1983], pp.

15f.). We see here the remnant of a crown and a series of flowering branches, while among the branches the painted inscription seems to have been made by the same hand as the painter of the accompanying scene. The inscription has been translated as follows (Bagatti, *Excavations Nazareth*, pp. 196-199; Testa, *Nazaret Giudeo-Cristiana*, pp. 64-70; Briand pp. 20-31):

The memorial
I made for the light

	ω
A	ω

Lord Christ, save your servant Valeria. Here we praised the death of [name missing]. And give to suffering the palm which (it is customary to give) to one who died for Christ. Amen.

It is evidently a pilgrim named Valeria who has come to this place, where a martyr was honored, and has made a "memorial . . . for the light," that is, has decorated the grotto with the painting in honor of the martyr. In the painting, therefore, the crown is the crown of life that is given to the one who is "faithful unto death" (Rev 2:10), and the flowering branches represent the garden of paradise in which the victor will find reward. The grotto is, therefore, at this time a martyrium. That the martyr here honored was Conon, who was from Nazareth and of the family of Jesus and died in Asia Minor in about A.D. 250 (No. 45), is probable, especially inasmuch as the Jerusalem deacon Conon, whose mosaic and inscription are in front of the grotto, was a namesake and possibly even a descendant of this famous hero of the faith.

When the mosaic with the cross-monogram in the middle of the nave of the Byzantine church (D in plan No. 46) was lifted, there was discovered, underneath, the basin marked A in the same plan (Bagatti, *Excavations Nazareth*, pp. 115-130, figs. 70-72; Strange in ATR 65 [1983], p. 16). This is a rock-cut cubical tank about two meters in length, breadth, and depth, with seven steps (B) descending westward into it on the south side. Five steps were cut in the rock; two, above ground, were constructed of stones and mortar. Thus at some time care was evidently taken to reach the number seven. A quarter-round sump is in the northeast corner of the basin floor, and not far away are two cisterns (C in the plan).

In respect to the date of the basin, it is to be noted that it is immediately beside the wall (G) that was the south wall of the synagogue-church of the third century (No. 46) and was reused in the south stylobate of the Byzantine church of the fifth century. The basin, however, is not in alignment with that wall but is turned 11°-12° northward, therefore goes back to an earlier date. As to its origin, the basin has been variously thought to have been at first a wine press (Kroll p. 90, col. 2) or a Jewish ritual bath (*mikvah*) (Strange in ATR 65 [1983], pp. 15f.). As it was found, however, the walls of the basin were plastered and marked with signs cut in the plaster while it was still fresh, therefore probably by the original workmen who installed the plaster. The signs are understood as of Judeo-Christian character—a small plant, a cross with three points, small boats, a network with 400 meshes. The careful provision of exactly seven steps for descent and ascent at the basin can also accord with Judeo-Christian thought about the descent and ascent of the Redeemer and the redeemed (cf. Irenaeus, "that the Word should descend to the creature, and that, on the other hand, the creature should contain the Word, and ascend to him, passing beyond the angels, and be made after the image and likeness of God" [*Adv. haer.* v 36 ANF I, p. 567]; for the seven heavens, see *Testament of Levi* 3 CAP II, pp. 305f.; and cf. the cosmic ladder, based on Gen 28:12 [Bagatti, *Church from Circumcision*, pp. 209f., 279ff.]). Therefore this may be seen as the baptistery of the Judeo-Christian community of Nazareth and the baptistery of their synagogue-church of the third-fourth century (Bagatti, *Church from Circumcision*, p. 126; Kroll p. 90, no. 3).

In addition the small grotto (F in plan No. 46), which became the martyrium of Conon, is near the basin and the cisterns, and at an early time it may well also have been used in relation to baptism, so that the cisterns provided water, the grotto was for preliminary rites, and the basin for the water ceremony itself. A very similar baptismal basin is also found under the Church of St. Joseph, where likewise a cistern and a grotto are adjacent (No. 54). In fact the Judeo-Christians are believed to have held that there are no less than three baptisms—namely, a baptism of fire, a baptism of water, and a baptism of Spirit (Testa, *Nazaret Giudeo-Cristiana*, pp. 22-53). In addition to references to water and the Spirit in the Gospels (Mt 3:16, etc.) there is reference to fire in Justin, *Dialogue with Trypho* 88: "When Jesus had gone to the river of Jordan . . . and when he had stepped into the water, a fire was kindled in the Jordan"; as well as reference to light in the Gospel of the Ebionites, which records about the baptism, "And immediately a great light shone round about the place" (HSNTA I, p. 157; Epiphanius, *Pan. haer.* I 30, 13, 6; Williams, NHS 35, p. 130); and Cyril of Jerusalem urges in his *Catechetical Lecture* II 15 (NPNFSS VII, p. 12): "Turn and bewail thyself, shut thy door, and pray to be forgiven, pray that he may remove from you the burning flames." For the three baptisms of fire, water, and Spirit, action in more than one place may well have been involved.

Photograph: Bagatti, *Excavations Nazareth*, p. 98, fig. 52, courtesy Studium Biblicum Franciscanum, Jerusalem.

49. The New Latin Basilica of the Annunciation at Nazareth

IN SEQUENTIAL SUMMARY of the complex history hypothetically reconstructed in the foregoing sections, in the first-third centuries the family of Jesus lived on in Nazareth (No. 45). Under their leadership in the second-third centuries they built a place of worship of synagogal type adjacent to the grotto that remained to mark the place of Mary's home (Nos. 46-47), and at the same time an older rock-cut water basin with adjacent cisterns was made into their baptistery (No. 48). In the third century a nearby smaller grotto became a shrine in memory of the martyr Conon (d. c. 250), who was from Nazareth and of the family of Jesus. In the fourth century floor mosaics with cross-monograms pointed out this martyrium. In the first half of the fifth century a Byzantine church took the place of the earlier synagogue-church, and the Jerusalem deacon Conon, whose name is in the mosaic in front of the smaller grotto, may have been the donor of the building (No. 48).

The Byzantine church probably continued in use down into the seventh century, but was probably damaged in the Sasanian Persian invasion (614) and again under the Fatimid Caliph al-Hakim (1009), so that this structure was in ruins when the Crusaders arrived at the end of the eleventh century, and it was the Crusaders who built the great twelfth-century basilica that has already been described (No. 45).

53

49. The New Latin Basilica of the Annunciation at Nazareth

In the following centuries many more disastrous events transpired, including destruction of buildings and massacre of Christians in Nazareth in 1263 by Sultan Baibars, and the Crusader church was in ruins when the Franciscan Custody of the Holy Land finally obtained possession of the site in 1620. This was in the period of Turkish rule (1517 and following), and it was not until 1730 that permission was obtained by the Franciscans resident in Nazareth to build a new church, the fourth in the continuing series.

For the work of building this church only six months were allowed—the length of time for the Muslims to go on their pilgrimage to Mecca and back—and the resultant structure was of modest size, and only in 1877 was somewhat enlarged (*Nazareth Today*, p. 17). In contrast with the Byzantine and Crusader buildings the Franciscan church was oriented not from west to east but from south to north and lay across the older buildings and over the venerated grottoes. It formed a rectangle 22 meters long and 17 meters wide, and was divided by two rows of large pillars into nave and two side aisles. At the north end of the central nave steps led down to the Grotto of the Annunciation, while two other flights of steps on the right and the left led up to the high altar, which was directly above the most sacred grotto (Kroll p. 85, no. 4).

It was this Franciscan church that was demolished in 1955 to make way for the fifth church, which is the new Basilica of the Annunciation, and at the same time to allow the archeological investigations described above. A preliminary plan for the new church was by Antonio Barluzzi, who otherwise built many of the finest modern churches in the Holy Land; the finally approved plan was by Giovanni Muzio; construction began in 1960, and its dedication was in 1969 (*Nazareth Today*, pp. 17-19). In the present view of a portion of Nazareth the new basilica appears in the center. It is the largest Christian church edifice in the Middle East.

Stiassny, passim. Photograph: Courtesy Government Press Office, State of Israel.

50. Looking Toward the Grotto of the Annunciation in the Basilica of the Annunciation

THE GROTTO of the Annunciation and the Chapel of the Angel in front of it are in the place of honor in the center of the lower level of the Basilica of the Annunciation, with an eight-sided light-opening (*oculus*) allowing illumination from the upper church above. In the picture the arch is the rock in which the grotto was ex-

50. Looking Toward the Grotto of the Annunciation in the Basilica of the Annunciation

51. Our Lady of the Flowers, from Japan, in the Basilica of the Annunciation

cavated; masonry is from the Byzantine church, and the granite columns flanked the grotto in the Franciscan work of 1730.

For the appearance of the grotto during excavations in 1966, see Bagatti, *Excavations Nazareth*, p. 179, fig. 140. Photograph: JF.

51. Our Lady of the Flowers, from Japan, in the Basilica of the Annunciation

THE NEW BASILICA of the Annunciation stands in a large elevated square of 800 square meters, which protects remains of the dwellings of ancient Nazareth that have been excavated in the ground below. The basilica itself is a double church, the upper to provide the place of contemporary worship, the lower church for private devotion and to display the archeological remains of the preceding structures. The outer walls follow the lines of

52. The Church of St. Joseph in Nazareth

the walls and foundations of the Crusader basilica except on the west side where the new wall is set back about five meters to allow for a plaza in front of the main entrance. The lofty cupola of the church rises to a height of 55 meters and from within appears like an inverted lily of Nazareth, the town which was "the flower of Galilee" (Jerome, *Letter* 46). The star-shaped opening in the roof of the lower church, which admits light to the most sacred spot in front of the Grotto of the Annunciation, is situated exactly under the dome of the upper church. Decoration throughout is in bronze, stained glass, and mosaic, and the inner walls of the nave are lined with large paintings of the Mother and Child, contributed from countries around the world, each in the style of the country, such as for example, Our Lady of the Flowers by Luke Hasegawa and Yoshi Yamauchi from Japan.

Hollis and Brownrigg pp. 103ff., with plan on p. 106; *Nazareth Today*, pp. 19ff. Photograph: JF.

52. The Church of St. Joseph in Nazareth

THE CHURCH of St. Joseph is located 100 meters to the north of the Church of the Annunciation, with the Franciscan convent (erected in 1930) between the two churches. As we have seen, this whole area was the central part of the ancient agricultural village of Nazareth, and ancient grottoes, cisterns, a wine press (Bagatti in DB Supplément VI, cols. 325-326, figs. 602 B, and 603), and the like are found under and around the Church of St. Joseph, as at the Church of the Annunciation (No. 45).

Photograph: The Matson Photo Service, Alhambra, Calif.

53. Plan of the Church of St. Joseph

AT THE SITE just described (No. 52), the Franciscans began to acquire property in 1754 and built a small chapel which, destroyed by earthquake in 1837, was rebuilt in the following year (Meistermann p. 492). In 1889 and following and again in 1908 and following, Prosper Viaud conducted excavations and uncovered the walls, still standing in some places to a height of two meters, of a Crusader church of the twelfth century. Upon these foundations the new Church of St. Joseph was built and completed in 1914.

As shown in the plan, drawn originally by Viaud (*Nazareth et ses deux églises*, p. 134, fig. 64), the Crusader church was 29 meters long and 16 meters wide. Orientation was to the east, the entrance was in the middle of the western façade (as in the restored Crusader Church of St. Anne in Jerusalem), and the edifice terminated in three apses at the eastern end.

Underneath the ruins of the Crusader church were also found a fragment of Byzantine mosaic pavement made of white cubes, a water basin with steps down into it like the one at the Church of the Annunciation, and

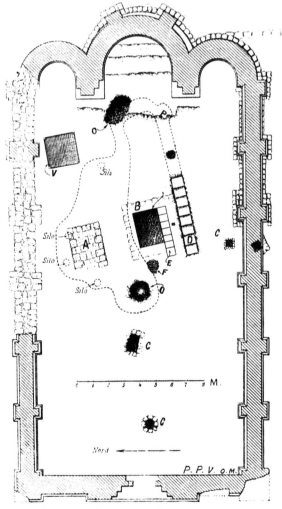

53. Plan of the Church of St. Joseph

subterranean grottoes that had been use also in archeologically earlier periods. Thus the Crusaders had evidently rebuilt an earlier existing church of the Byzantine period (RB 2 [1893], p. 241).

Here the underlying rock of the hill slopes from west to east, and to some extent the Byzantine church floor followed that slope, for the fragment of Byzantine mosaic found in abut the middle of the church (F in the plan) is 1.6 meters below the level of the threshold, and on at the east end the hill drops off by as much as five meters even more steeply (Viaud, *Nazareth et ses deux églises*, p. 135, fig. 65). The other early installations shown on the plan are: A, the base of a pillar; B, a basin, with E, seven steps leading down into it; C, three cisterns situated to the west and south of the basin; D, stairs leading down to P, a rock-cut passage that curves in a semicircle to make an entrance to a large rock-grotto; O, openings that allow light to enter the grotto, once mouths of silos, with several other silos also marked on the plan; V, a rectangular depression. It is notable that the several main items just enumerated are turned by about 25° to the northeast in comparison with the east-west long axis of the Crusader church, and together with the fragment of Byzantine mosaic this confirms the conclusion that an earlier, differently oriented edifice underlay the Crusader church. This earlier orientation was evidently in relation to the main grotto, which is outlined in the plan, and was a room over 2 meters high, 9-10 meters long, and 4-5 meters wide.

In 1970 Bellarmino Bagatti excavated along the north wall of the Crusader church and in some of the grottoes under the wall. When the medieval church was excavated in 1892 much debris was piled here, and in the piles of debris Bagatti found in inverse order (as thrown out in the excavations) pottery fragments from the Iron Age to the Roman, Byzantine, and Crusader periods; and in the grottoes likewise he found Roman as well as Crusader pottery, thus the site was certainly inhabited in the first century B.C. and the first century A.D. as well as earlier and later.

As to the identification and significance of the successive churches on this site, Arculf (670, quoted by Adamnan, 679-704) (Geyer p. 274; LPPTS III-A, pp. 83-84; CCSL CLXXV, p. 219; WJP p. 109) says that Nazareth has two large churches (*ecclesiae*). One of these is "where the house was in which the archangel Gabriel came to the blessed Mary, and spoke to her there, finding her alone," and this presumably refers to the Church of the Annunciation (No. 45). The other church to which Arculf refers he describes as follows:

One [church] in the middle of the city (*in medio ciuitatis*)
is founded on two vaults, where once there was the house in
which our Lord and Savior was brought up (*nutritus*, literally

nourished). This church . . . is raised on two mounds, with
arches interposed, having down below among these mounds
a very clear fountain (*fons*), from which all the population
draw their water in vessels by means of pulleys.

The description of this church as being where the
house was in which Jesus was brought up (*nutritus*, nourished) in infancy, corresponds with the mention of "Nazareth, where he had been brought up" in Lk 4:16, which
reads in Latin, *Nazareth, ubi erat nutritus*, and leads to
the name, the Church of the Nutrition. The statement
that this church was in the middle of the city agrees with
the location of the Church of St. Joseph, which like the
nearby Church of the Annunciation was indeed in the
central part of ancient Nazareth (No. 43). That the
church was also "founded on two vaults" and "raised on
two mounds, with arches interposed" can also agree with
the situation of the Church of St. Joseph, for the great
difference in the level of the underlying rock between
the west and the east could well have required the provision of arches to sustain the mosaic pavement of the
Byzantine church at its eastern end (Bagatti in RB 78
[1971], p. 587; and in LA 21 [1971], p. 32).

There is a problem, however, in the statement of Arculf that in the church in question there was a very clear
fountain from which all the population drew water in
vessels by means of pulleys. Although the word *fons* can
mean not only fountain or spring but also well-source or
even cistern, the "very clear" fountain that was adequate
for the entire population would appear to be the Fountain of Mary (No. 42) at the Church of St. Gabriel (No.
55), which as far as known has always been the main
spring of Nazareth. On the other hand, as far as known,
that location was not in the center of ancient Nazareth,
as was the location of the Church of St. Joseph together
with the Church of the Annunciation, and thus there is
a dilemma (Stiassny p. 96; Kroll p. 439 n. 118).

Another passage that comes into consideration is
found in Peter the Deacon (1137):

> The cave in which she lived (*spelunca . . . in qua habitauit*,
> presumably meaning Mary the mother of Jesus, although
> Kopp 1963, p. 79, reads "he" and refers this to Jesus) is large
> and most luminous (*lucidissima*), where an altar has been
> placed, and there inside the cave itself is the place (*locus*)
> from which she drew water. Inside the city, where the syna-
> gogue was where the Lord read the book of Isaiah (Lk 4:17),
> there is now a church. But the spring (*fons*) from which Mary
> used to take water is outside the village (Geyer p. 112; WET
> p. 193).

Since Peter drew some of his materials from Aetheria
(381-384), the first sentence and one-half of this passage
is sometimes supposed to derive from Aetheria, while the
remainder is from some other source. The idea of the
"most luminous cave," however, would seem more likely

to have come from the realm of Judeo-Christian thought
than to have been used by Aetheria, and if this is true
the author of this language remains unknown (Bagatti,
Excavations Nazareth, p. 23). Taking the passage as a
whole, it appears to speak of two places where Mary obtained water, one in the cave where she lived and the
other a spring outside the village (presumably the Fountain of Mary at the Church of St. Gabriel), and it can be
suggested that Peter the Deacon confused the two (WET
p. 193 n. 3, 4). On the other hand, if there were indeed
a place from which Mary drew water in the cave where
she lived (at the Church of the Annunciation or the
Church of St. Joseph), it might have been Arculf (or
Adamnan, his copyist) who confused such a "family
well" at the Church of St. Joseph with the "public fountain" at the location of the Church of St. Gabriel (cf.
Briand p. 54; Bagatti, *Excavations Nazareth*, p. 24). In
this case the most important item in Arculf's description
of the church in which Jesus was brought up would remain the statement that it was in the middle of the city,
pointing to identification of the present Church of St.
Joseph as representing the Church of the Nutrition.

Quaremius, writing in 1616-1626, is plainly referring
to the place of the present Church of St. Joseph and of
the Crusader church that stood there in his time, when
he says (Baldi p. 38, no. 6; Kopp 1963, p. 82): "If you
proceed as much as a stone's throw northwards (*quantum
jactus est lapidis ad aquilonem*) from the Church of the
Annunciation, you will come upon a place (*locus*) which
from antiquity to the present day has been called 'the
house and workshop of Joseph (*domus et officina Joseph*).'" That Joseph was a carpenter (τέκτων) is indicated in Mt 13:55, and in Mk 6:3 Jesus himself is also
called a carpenter. The *Childhood Gospel of Thomas* (11,
JANT p. 63; HSNTA I, p. 396) says that Joseph was a carpenter and describes him as making ploughs and yokes
and a bed; and Justin (*Dialogue with Trypho* 88 ANF I, p.
244) likewise speaks of Jesus, considered to be the son of
Joseph the carpenter, as working as a carpenter and making ploughs and yokes. That the place where Joseph
lived with Mary as his wife and where Jesus was brought
up after the return from Egypt (Mt 2:19-23) was Joseph's
house, where was also his workshop, is surely possible,
and thus Arculf's Church of the Nutrition and Quaresmius' Church of the House and Workshop of Joseph can
be successive designations of the successive (Byzantine
and Crusader) churches in the location of the present
Church of St. Joseph. The evidence of even earlier veneration of the site in connection with the baptistery under the church (No. 54) suggests Judeo-Christian tradition and the possibility of authentic remembrance.

Prosper Viaud, *Nazareth et ses deux églises de l'annonciation et de
Saint-Joseph* (Paris: Alphonse Picard, 1910); Kopp in JPOS 19
(1939-1940), pp. 277-285; and Kopp 1963, pp. 82-86; Briand pp.

50-62; Stiassny pp. 93, 96; Bagatti, *Excavations Nazareth*, pp. 221-227 for grottoes, etc., under the Church of St. Joseph; and in RB 78 (1971), p. 587; and "Scavo presso la Chiese di S. Giuseppe a Nazaret (Agosto 1970), " in LA 21 (1971), pp. 5-32; Ovadiah, *Corpus Supplementum*, p. 248, no. 61. Plan: from Bagatti in LA 21 (1971), p. 7, fig. 2, courtesy Studium Biblicum Franciscanum, Jerusalem.

54. Baptistery under the Church of St. Joseph

THE BASIN MARKED as B in plan No. 53 was cut in the rock and partly built in masonry. It is virtually identical with the basin already described at the Church of the Annunciation (No. 48) in size (about 2 meters in length, breadth, and depth) and in the arrangement of seven steps (E in plan No. 53) to lead down into it. Here, as found by the excavators (Bagatti, *Church from Circumcision*, pp. 243-245), there were traces of mosaic on the steps, on the floor of the basin were six rectangles of mosaic, and on the north side there is a circular sump and an irregular black basalt stone is set into the floor. In the wall alongside the steps there is a small water channel also decorated with mosaic, but without any outlet. Like the basically similar baptistery at the Church of the Annunciation, this was probably also a baptistery of the Judeo-Christians and probably of the same early date, say second-third century.

The architectural features just enumerated are understandable as symbolic reflections of Judeo-Christian ideas (Briand pp. 39-50). As explained in connection with the baptistery at the Church of the Annunciation, the stair-way of seven steps, descended on the way to baptism and ascended afterward, recalls the mystery of the descent of the Word through the seven heavens and past their angels, and the subsequent ascent of the redeemed. The black stone here set in the floor recalls the Rock that was Christ, which Paul mentions in connection with the mention of baptism (I Cor 10:1-4), and together with the six rectangles of mosaic are reminiscent of the description in the *Shepherd of Hermas* of the tower that was built on the water (*Vis.* III 2.4) and raised on a great rock (*Sim.* IX 4.2), with many other stones built into it (*Vis.* III 2.5), until the tower became one solid stone with the rock (*Sim.* IX 13.5). The building was done by six young men (*Vis.* III 2.5), and a glorious and great man was in their midst (*Sim.* IX 12.7), who was himself the Lord of the tower (*Sim.* IX 7.1). The tower is the Church (*Sim.* IX 13.1), the six men are glorious angels and the glorious man is the Son of God (*Sim.* IX 12.8), while otherwise stated the rock is itself the Son of God (*Sim.* IX 12.1). The reason the tower, which is not yet completed (*Sim.* IX 5.1), is built on the water is "because your life was saved and shall be saved through water [i.e., baptism]" (*Vis.* III 4,5). So also the channel without outlet must be symbolic and suggests the Jordan as the place of baptism and of crossing to the Promised Land. As at the Church of the Annunciation so also here the baptistery is adjacent to cisterns and grottoes and all may have been of baptismal use—the cistern for baptismal water, the grotto for preliminary rites, and the basin as the baptistery proper.

54. Baptistery under the Church of St. Joseph

According to Eric M. Meyers and James F. Strange (*Archaeology, The Rabbis and Early Christianity* [Nashville: Abingdon, 1981], pp. 107, 137), it is possible to think that the basin at the Church of the Annunciation "may be one of the earliest pieces of Jewish-Christian architecture," but such a conclusion about this basin and the other at the Church of St. Joseph "remains speculative." For criticism of supposed insistence on "producing archaeological data that will confirm presupposed traditions," see Graydon F. Snyder, *Ante Pacem, Archaeological Evidence of Church Life Before Constantine* (Mercer University Press, 1985), p. 6. For appreciation of "highly scientific . . . Italian methodology," as shown by Bagatti's study of the traditional sites of the House of Mary and the House of Joseph at Nazareth, see E. Stockton in AJBA 1, 2 (1968-1971), p. 87. Photograph: JF.

55. The Church of St. Gabriel at Nazareth

AS NOTED ABOVE (NO. 42), the spring that was, as far as we know, from the earliest times the main source of water at Nazareth is just above the present Greek Orthodox Church of St. Gabriel and is piped into the crypt of the church. It has also been noted (No. 53) that when Arculf (670) describes "a very clear fountain" from which the population of Nazareth draw their water, it sounds like this spring and can point to the Church of St. Gabriel as standing for Arculf's Church of the Nutrition, although Arculf's other statement that the place is "in the middle of the city" sounds more like the location of the Church of St. Joseph, which also therefore has claim to represent both the Church of the Nutrition and the Church of the House and Workshop of Joseph.

Another association of the Church of St. Gabriel has basis in the apocryphal *Protevangelium of James* (c. second century), in which there is mention of a spring in connection with the angel Gabriel and the Annunciation to Mary (Lk 1:26ff.). According to this account (JANT pp. 41-43; HSNTA I, pp. 378-380) Joachim and Anna, the parents of Mary, gave Mary into the keeping of priests in the Temple at the age of three, where she remained until she was twelve years old. Then the priests gave her into the care of Joseph, who took her into his house while he went away to build his buildings. In time the priests undertook to make a veil for the Temple, and the lot fell to Mary to weave the purple and scarlet for this purpose.

> . . . and she took them and went into her house. At that time Zacharias became dumb, and Samuel took his place until the time when Zacharias was able to speak (again) (Lk 1:20, 64). But Mary took the scarlet and began to spin it.
>
> And she took the pitcher and went forth to fill it with water, and lo, a voice saying: "Hail, thou that art highly favored among women" (Lk 1:28). And she looked about her on the right hand and on the left, to see whence this voice came. And trembling she went to her house and set down the pitcher, and took the purple and sat down on her seat

> and drew out (the thread). And behold, an angel of the Lord stood before her saying: "Fear not, Mary, for you have found grace before the Lord of all things and shall conceive of his Word" (Lk 1:30-31).
>
> . . . And she made the purple and the scarlet and brought them to the priest. And the priest blessed her and said: "Mary, the Lord God has magnified your name, and you shall be blessed among all generations of the earth."

According to this passage, the angel spoke to Mary twice and in two separate places, the first time when she had gone forth to fill her pitcher with water, presumably at a fresh-water spring, and the second time when she was back in her house again. The spring was presumably the main spring at Nazareth, near the present Church of St. Gabriel, and her house from which she went forth and to which she came back could have been in the same vicinity, but equally well could have been down in what we know to have been the central part of ancient Nazareth, i.e., at the Latin Church of the Annunciation or the Church of St. Joseph.

When the Russian abbot Daniel (1106) came, he visited two churches at Nazareth and understood them respectively in exactly the terms of the narrative in *The Protevangelium of James*. The two churches are plainly the predecessors of the present Church of the Annunciation and the Church of St. Gabriel (LPPTS IV-C, pp. 69-

55. The Church of St. Gabriel at Nazareth

71). One is "a large and lofty church . . . in the midst of the town." A cave under the church is where Mary sat spinning purple when the archangel Gabriel came and spoke to her, and thus the church is dedicated to the Annunciation; it was formerly destroyed but the Franks have restored it, and a Latin bishop lives there (cf. No. 49).

Then Daniel left the town and went for the distance of a good bow-shot toward the summer sunrising (i.e., to the northeast), where he found a very deep well with very cold water, to which one descends by several steps.

> This well is covered by a round church dedicated to the archangel Gabriel. . . . It is near this well that the holy Virgin received the first announcement from the archangel. She had come to draw water, and had filled her pitcher, when the voice of the invisible angel was heard, saying, "I salute you, O full of grace, the Lord is with you" (Lk 1:28). Mary looked all round, and seeing no one, but having heard only the voice, took up her pitcher again and returned astonished, saying to herself, "What does this voice mean that I have heard without having seen anyone?" (cf. Lk 1:29). On returning to her house at Nazareth she sat down at the spot previously mentioned, and began to spin purple; it is then that the archangel Gabriel appeared to her, standing on the place mentioned above, and announced to her the birth of Christ (Lk 1:30).

With this understanding of the unfolding of the Annunciation in two phases, first at the well (at the present Church of St. Gabriel) and then at Mary's home (at the present Church of the Annunciation), the Church of St. Gabriel can also be called the Church of the First Annunciation.

Photograph: JF.

56. The Outlet from the Spring in the Crypt of the Church of St. Gabriel

IN HIS TIME the Scandinavian pilgrim Saewulf (1102) found the city of Nazareth destroyed by the Saracens, but of the famous spring he wrote: "the fountain near the city bubbles out most clearly, still surrounded as it used to be with marble columns and slabs. From this fountain it was that the Child Jesus, together with other boys, oftentimes drew water for the use of his Mother" (LPPTS IV-B, p. 25). At the place of the spring the first church was built by the Greeks (Meistermann p. 496) and is first mentioned by the Greek monk Phocas (1185). As in *The Protevangelium of James* and in the account by Daniel (No. 55), Gabriel came to Mary first at the fountain and then again back at the house, which is here identified as the house of Joseph, therefore was at the place of the Church of St. Joseph rather than the Church of the An-

nunciation. Phocas writes in part as follows (MPG 133, col. 936; LPPTS V-C, pp. 12f.):

> At the entering in the first gate of this large village [Nazareth] you will find a church of the Archangel Gabriel; and there is to be seen a little grotto on the left side of the altar in this church, in which a fountain (πηγή) wells up, pouring forth a transparent stream, wherein the immaculate Mother of God (Θεοτόκος), when she was given by the priests to the just Joseph, and was kept in his house, used to come daily and drew water; but in the sixth month (Lk 1:26) of the Forerunner (Πρόδρομος), when she was about to draw water as usual, she received the first greeting (ἀσπασμός) from Gabriel, and, being disturbed in mind, went back trembling to the house of Joseph, where she heard the angel say, "Hail, O favored one" (Χαῖρε, κεχαρι τωμένη), and answered, "Behold the handmaid of the Lord. . . ." After this, the house of Joseph was altered into a beautiful church.

As for the present Church of St. Gabriel near the spring, it was begun in 1767. The axis of the church runs from east to west, while six steps lead down from the nave into the vaulted north transept of the older church, the roof of which is level with the ground. It is in this crypt that the spring water empties.

Since the earlier years of Jesus' life were spent in Nazareth (Lk 2:39f., 51), the Nazareth synagogue was no doubt the place where he received religious instruction, as it was later the place where he himself taught (Mt 13:54, etc.). As to secular training, the *Childhood Gospel of Thomas* tells that Joseph took Jesus to a teacher who practiced the alphabet with him for a long time (JANT p. 53; HSNTA I, p. 397), but rabbinic sources show that at

56. The Outlet from the Spring in the Crypt of the Church of St. Gabriel

least later a synagogue was a place where, perhaps in adjacent space, children received elementary instruction (I. Sonne in IDB IV, p. 491), so the synagogue at Nazareth could have been the place for Jesus' early studies of that sort too.

In the war with the Romans in the year 67 Japha, only a mile and a half southwest of Nazareth, was the scene of fierce fighting and its inhabitants were massacred by the Romans (Josephus, War III 7, 31 §§289-306), and its synagogue was destroyed (RB 30 [1921], pp. 434-438), and Nazareth was undoubtedly wiped out as well (Kopp 1963, p. 53) and its synagogue destroyed too. Like the Japha and other Galilean synagogues (No. 89), the Nazareth synagogue must have been built again at a later time. The Anonymous of Piacenza (570), who found the house of Mary in Nazareth made into a basilica (No. 45), also tells us that in the synagogue was the bench on which Jesus sat with the other children, and also the book in which he wrote his ABCs (Geyer p. 161; LPPTS II-D, p. 5; CCSL CLXXV, pp. 130-131; WP p. 79). In his time Peter the Deacon (1137) (quoted above, No. 53) speaks of the synagogue as the place where Jesus read from the book of Isaiah and records that the synagogue had been made into a church, and Burchard of Mount Sion (1283) says the same thing (LPPTS XII-A, p. 42).

As to the site of the synagogue, Quaresmius (1626) (II 632 Kopp 1959, p. 119) says: "If you go from the Church of St. Joseph farther northward you will come to a church which is dedicated to the Forty Martyrs, and farther beyond that to a spring and a church." Then, concerning the Church of the Forty Martyrs, he raises the question whether it was the place of the synagogue that the Lord formerly visited. In the Muslim cemetery in Nazareth, which is on the way north to Mary's Fountain, there is a small shrine still called the Place of the Forty (maqam el-arba'in), which may preserve remembrance of the church to which Quaresmius refers. And four gray granite columns, found here but now moved to another place in the city, may be remains of a Byzantine church on the site, since they are like others in the Church of the Annunciation. This site may have the best claim to be that of the synagogue and is pointed to as such by the Orthodox Greeks. In modern times the Church of the United Greeks, which is nearer to the Church of the Annunciation, is accepted by some (Dalman) as marking the place of the synagogue. This church, in use since 1741, incorporates a room with a barrel-vaulted roof, which is probably the structure mentioned by Surius (1644, Kopp 1959, p. 120) as being a portion of the synagogue and used in his time as a stall for camels. As a site for the synagogue, however, the place has no earlier attestation.

For the Church of St. Gabriel: Kopp in JPOS 19 (1939-40), pp. 258-277; and Kopp 1963, pp. 75-82; Bagatti, "La Chiesa della Prima Annunziazione a Nazaret," in Antichi Villaggi, pp. 23-29. For the synagogue, the Place of Forty, and the Church of the United Greeks: Dalman, Sacred Sites, p. 68; Kopp in JPOS 20 (1946), pp. 29-42; Kopp 1959, pp. 116-122; Kopp 1963, p. 55; Bagatti in LA 14 (1963-64), p. 53; and Bagatti, Excavations Nazareth, pp. 233f. See also Donato Baldi, "Nazaret ed i suoi santuari," in LA 5 (1954-55), pp. 213-260. Photograph: JF.

57. On the Road from Nazareth Looking Toward the Traditional Village of Cana in Galilee

IN THE GOSPEL records Jesus was born at Bethlehem (Nos. 17ff.), brought up at Nazareth (Nos. 40ff.), and baptized by John in the Jordan River (Nos. 8ff.). Afterward he performed his first and second signs at Cana in Galilee, then worked repeatedly in Judea (Jn 2:13, etc.; cf. Mt 23:37; Lk 13:34)(Nos. 143ff.) and intensively in Galilee (Nos. 69ff.).

The first sign at Cana was the miracle of the wine at the marriage feast (Jn 2:1-11); the second was the healing from this distance of the son of the official who came from Capernaum to ask for help (Jn 4:46-54; cf. Mt 8:5-13; Lk 7:1-10). The disciple Nathanael was also from Cana in Galilee (Jn 21:2).

The indication in the narrative of the second sign at Cana that one would "come down" from Cana to Capernaum (Jn 4:47) places the Cana in question somewhere in the hill country above the Sea of Galilee; otherwise there are no further geographical details in the Gospel to show the location. The identification of this Cana as "in Galilee" (Jn 2:1, 11; 4:46), however, clearly distinguishes it from "Kana, as far as Sidon the Great" (Jos 19:28), which was on the northern border of the territory of the tribe of Asher and is represented by the modern Qana, six miles southeast of Tyre. Nevertheless in the Onomasticon (ed. Klostermann, GCS p. 116) Eusebius cites "Cana (Κανά), as far as the great Sidon, of the lot of Asher," as the place of the miracle of the wine and of the home of Nathanael, which identification by Eusebius has to be incorrect.

In the search for the Cana of the Gospel two sites come into consideration. Both have present-day names reminiscent of Cana, both are in the hill country above the Sea of Galilee as required by the consideration just noted, and the two are in fact only six miles apart. Khirbet Qana is an unoccupied place of ruins on a hill overlooking a fine plain known as Sahel el-Buttauf, identifiable with the ancient Plain of Asochis (for the Plain of Asochis, see Josephus, Life 42 §§207; LCL Josephus I, p. 79 n. a, and map of Galilee facing p. 412; Meistermann pp. 519f.); the location is six miles north of the important city of Sepphoris (Saffuriya) and nine miles north of

57. On the Road from Nazareth Looking Toward the Traditional Village of Cana in Galilee

Nazareth. Survey in 1982 of the ruins on the summit of the hill traced streets, plazas, foundations of houses, and many cisterns; habitation was especially considerable in the Roman period (Kroll p. 180, col. 3). This must be the Cana that Josephus mentions when, at the outbreak of the Jewish war against the Romans (A.D. 66), he marched in one night with 200 men from Cana to Tiberias (*Life* 16-17 §§86-90). Only a mile to the northwest of Cana was Jotapata, which was the last place of refuge of the Galileans in the same war (*War* III 7, 3 §§141ff.).

The second site under consideration is Kefar Kenna, which is a still inhabited village (*kefar* means village), as shown in the present photograph, located less than four miles northeast of Nazareth on the road to Tiberias.

In his Latin translation of the *Onomasticon* (GCS p. 117) Jerome allows the reference to the Cana of Jos 19:28 to stand, but inserts an explanation of why that Cana is called "great," in which he reveals his knowledge of a "smaller" Cana—"because there is another smaller one, and to distinguish them this one is called the greater"—and it is probably this lesser village that he himself thinks of as that of the Fourth Gospel (Kopp 1963, p. 149). At any rate, when Jerome invites Marcella to visit the Holy Land (A.D. 386) and describes the places they will visit, he says: "We shall go to see Nazareth, as its name denotes, the flower of Galilee. Not at all far off we will see Cana (*haud procul cernetur Cana*),

where the water was turned into wine" (*Letter* 46, 13 CSEL LIV, p. 344; NPNFSS VI, p. 65). Likewise when he describes the visits by Paula (d. 404) to sacred sites, he writes: "She passed quickly through Nazareth where the Lord grew up, through Cana and Capernaum" (*Letter* 108, 13 NPNFSS VI, p. 202). Between Khirbet Qana and Kefar Kenna, the latter would seem to accord better with what Jerome says, for it was probably always a small village and it was the nearer of the two sites to Nazareth. Especially if Jerome's Latin is translated as "Not far off [from a standpoint in Nazareth] Cana will be visible" (NPNFSS VI, p. 65), Kefar Kenna would seem to be indicated.

The first to speak of a shrine at Cana is the Anonymous of Piacenza (570). This pilgrim traveled from Ptolemais (Acre) on the coast to Diocaesarea (Sepphoris), and then: "Three miles (*milia tria*) farther we reached Cana, where the Lord was present at the wedding, and we actually reclined on the couch [*accubitum*, a couch on which guests reclined at a meal], where I (unworthy though I am) wrote the names of my parents. Of the water pots two are still there, and I filled one of them with wine and lifted it up when full onto my shoulder and carried it to the altar; and we washed in the spring for a blessing. Then we reached the city of Nazareth" (Geyer p. 161; LPPTS II-D, p. 4; CCSL CLXXV, p. 130; WJP p. 79). Kefar Kenna is two and one-half miles east of Sepphoris, which is approximately the three Roman miles stated by the Anonymous of Piacenza as the distance from Sepphoris to Cana, so Kefar Kenna is almost certainly the place that is here in mind. Also Kefar Kenna has a good spring, which Khirbet Qana does not (Kopp 1963, p. 150).

The mention of the altar by the Anonymous of Piacenza attests to the existence at that time of a church commemorative of the miracle of the wine at Kefar Kenna, and it is most probably the same church in the same town that Willibald (725) and his companions saw when they came from Nazareth to the village that they understood to be Cana (Latin *Chanam*). They were in Nazareth, and then "they came to the village of Cana, where the Lord turned water into wine. There is a large church (*ecclesia magna*) there, and in the church on the altar there is one of the six water-pots which the Lord commanded to be filled with water, and it was turned into wine; and from it they drank wine [*de illo communicaverunt vino*, probably meaning that Willibald and his companions received communion]" (Tobler and Molinier p. 260; WJP p. 128). As the account continues, they stayed in Cana one day, then went on and came to Mount Tabor, and such an itinerary of Nazareth—Cana—Tabor fits well with Kefar Kenna as Cana.

Epiphanius the Monk (750-800) appears to stand in the same series of pilgrims of these times who visited Kefar Kenna as the Cana of the wine miracle, for at this point he followed the same itinerary as Willibald, but in reverse, going in one day's journey from Tabor to Cana. Epiphanius the Monk also adds mention of a monastery at Cana: "It is a journey of one day from Tabor to the great city of Cana of Galilee, in which the marriage took place at which Christ made the water wine. A monastery (μοναστήριον is there in which the miracle took place" (ZDPV 87 [1971], p. 80; WJP p. 121). No doubt the monastery and the church comprised one architectural unit, so there is no essential difference in reference to the one or the other.

In the *Commemoratorium de casis Dei* (808) the catalogue of churches and monasteries regularly includes the number of ecclesiastics at the various places, so although in this case the surviving text breaks off without this item, the statement, "In Cana of Galilee, where the Lord (made) wine of water" (Tobler and Molinier p. 303; WJP p. 138), there was no doubt given such a number, and therefore it may be concluded that a church and monastery still existed at that time at Cana, and that on the basis of the earlier testimonies this was at Kefar Kenna.

In 1654 Jean Doubdan visited Kefar Kenna and found that the ancient church was still preserved almost intact, but was in use as a mosque. In his work *Le voyage de la Terre Sainte* Doubdan describes the church at Cana as follows:

It is a very ancient building made throughout of cut stones, and consists of two large main buildings, of which the one on the right is the church, which is a vaulted structure about forty paces long and twenty paces wide, supported in the middle by a row of columns, and (with) some windows that admit the light. It is quite deserted but nevertheless still quite entire, and serves as a mosque for the people of the country, and underneath it is a chapel which is said to be on the same place where our Savior performed this miracle. The other part is a large dwelling-house which used to be the residence of the ecclesiastics, where at present dwell *santons* [religious persons of the Muslim faith], and between these two buildings is a very spacious court, on the door and entrance of which is a large stone which serves as a lintel, on which are cut in relief three pots or pitchers with some ancient writing half effaced, which sets forth that it is the very place where the great miracle was wrought (Baldi p. 212, No. 263; Meistermann p. 520; Bagatti in LA 15 [1964-1965], pp. 270f.).

How long it was before this description was written that the church at Kefar Kenna had been taken over for a mosque Doubdan does not say, but it could have been long before, and this could have led to avoidance of Kefar Kenna by Christian pilgrims. At any rate by the Crusader period the alternate site of Khirbet Qana was being visited. Saewulf (1102), the first to prepare a pilgrim record after the Crusader conquest of Jerusalem (1099), is the first to point to Khirbet Qana for Cana in Galilee, as he apparently does in view of the distance and the hill location, which he cites in this passage: "From Nazareth, Chana of Galilee—where our Lord changed water into wine at the marriage—is distant about six miles (*sex miliariis*) to the north, situated on a hill. There is nothing there except the monastery, which is called *Architriclinii* (House of the Ruler of the Feast)" (Baldi p. 208, no. 247; LPPTS IV-B, p. 26; Bagatti in LA 15 [1964-1965], p. 252).

Likewise Burchard of Mount Sion (1283) writes about Cana of Galilee: "The place is shown at this day where the six water-pots stood, and the dining-room wherein the tables were. . . . To the north Cana of Galilee has a tall round mountain, on whose slope it stands. At its foot, on the south side, it has a very fair plain, which Josephus calls Carmelion; it reaches as far as Sepphoris, and is extremely fertile and pleasant. . . . Two leagues to the south of Cana of Galilee is Sepphoris" (Baldi pp. 209f., no. 255; LPPTS XII-A, pp. 38f., 41). Here too Cana is plainly identified with Khirbet Qana by the distance north of Sepphoris and the hill location (as in Saewulf) overlooking a fine plain.

In his *Elucidatio terrae sanctae*, however, Quaresmius (1626) discusses the respective claims for the two Canas. The one, Khirbet Qana, he describes as about six Roman miles from Sepphoris and ten from Nazareth, with no church; the other, Kefar Kenna, he describes as four miles from Nazareth, with a church and even with a spring from which, it was said, the water was drawn which was turned into wine (Baldi pp. 211f., no. 262). In conclusion he found Kefar Kenna the true site, and in 1641 the Franciscans purchased a house next to the mosque, then in 1879 acquired the mosque structure itself and built a small church, which was enlarged in following years and stands now, together with its monastery, in the center of the village. In 1556, while the mosque was still in use as described by Doubdan (1654), a Greek Orthodox church was built somewhat farther away, was rebuilt in 1886, and stands now near the highway on the edge of the village. It too was intended to do honor to the miracle at Cana.

In the years after 1879 when the small Franciscan church was being enlarged, and Father Egidius Geissler was the priest in charge, some excavations were made, and two feet under the level of the new building some remains of an older edifice were found. Most importantly, a portion of mosaic pavement was discovered in 1901 in the region near the altar, and it contains an Aramaic inscription that is translated: "Honored be the memory of Yoseh, son (Aramaic *bar*) of Tanhum, son of Butah, and his sons, who made this *tabula* (טבלה): may it be a blessing for them. Amen" (Clermont-Ganneau in PEFQ 1901, pp. 251, 374-389; 1902, pp. 132-134; QDAP 2 [1933], pp. 178f., no. 167; Saller, *Second Catalogue*, pp. 51f., no. 59). The word that is similar to the Latin *tabula* probably means "section of the floor" (Levine in *Synagogues Revealed*, p. 80) and thus refers to the mosaic itself and may be translated here as "mosaic." The nature of the inscription is that of a blessing upon a donor or donors, such as is found in many synagogue inscriptions, e.g., the phrase "may he be blessed" in the synagogue at Hammath Tiberias (Dothan, *Hammath Tiberias*, p. 54; cf. No. 72), and we may conclude that the mosaic belonged to a synagogue that was an earlier structure upon the site. Paleographically the inscription is assigned to the third or fourth century A.D.

At Sepphoris (Saffuriya) Prosper Viaud excavated in the ruins of the unfinished Crusader church of St. Anna in 1908 and found remnants of a mosaic floor that contained a Hebrew inscription that is almost identical with the inscription of Kefar Kenna in that it also honors a son of Tanhum, and, as far as preserved, uses the same language: "Honored be the memory of Rabbi Yudan, son (Hebrew *ben*) of Tanhum, son of . . ." (QDAP 3 [1933], pp. 39f., nos. 295, 296; Dalman, *Sacred Sites*, p. 76; Saller, *Second Catalogue*, pp. 75f., no. 111). Paleographically, also, this inscription is very similar to the inscription at Kefar Kenna and is likewise attributed to the third-fourth centuries. Inasmuch as Sepphoris is specifically named by Epiphanius (*Pan. haer.* GCS I, p. 347; NHS 35, p. 128; cf. above no. 45) as among the places where the Judeo-Christian Count Joseph of Tiberias built churches, it may be reasonably surmised that it was Jo-

seph who here at Sepphoris around A.D. 330 built a church over the ruins of the synagogue, and that he did the same at Kefar Kenna, only three Roman miles distant to the east (Meistermann p. 522).

In 1955-1956, 1965, and 1969 archeological excavations were conducted by Bellarmino Bagatti and Stanislao Loffreda at Kefar Kenna and also at nearby Karm er-Ras, the two probably anciently forming one village. Ceramics indicate habitation in the Roman and Byzantine periods and coins date from Herod the Great (37-4 B.C.) to Constantine (A.D. 326). The third-fourth century synagogue inscription at the Franciscan church in Kefar Kenna has already been discussed. At Karm er-Ras architectural elements were found that may have belonged to a second synagogue (Saller, *Second Catalogue*, p. 52). The existence of two synagogal edifices can suggest that there were two communities here, one of Jews with its synagogue, and one of Judeo-Christians with its synagogue-church, as in other villages of Galilee; thus here too Judeo-Christian traditions may have been preserved from early times (Bagatti in LA 15 [1964-1965], pp. 290, 292; Cornfeld p. 309).

Bellarmino Bagatti, "Le antichita' di Kh. Qana e di Kefr Kenna in Galilee," in LA 15 (1964-65), pp. 251-292; Bagatti, *Antichi Villaggi* pp. 42-48; Bagatti, *Church from Circumcision* p. 132; Stanislao Loffreda, "Scavi a Kafr Kanna," in LA 19 (1969), pp. 328-348. Photograph: JF.

SAMARIA

58. The Landscape of Samaria

BETWEEN GALILEE and Judea on the west side of the Jordan lay the territory of Samaria. Because of the hostility between Jews and Samaritans reflected in Jn 4:9, it is probable that Jews ordinarily went around Samaria rather than through it on journeys between Judea and Galilee. On the occasion recorded in Jn 4:3-43, however, Jesus went from Judea to Galilee through Samaria. The territory is named for its city, on a prominent hill forty miles north of Jerusalem and capital of Israel for a time in the OT period (1 K 15:24); in the NT period it was rebuilt and renamed Sebaste by Herod the Great (Josephus, *War* I 21, 2 §§403). The territory itself varied in its boundaries at different times, but comprised mainly the hill country of the central highlands. The photograph shows the landscape of Samaria from the road north from Jerusalem.

André Parrot, *Samaria the Capital of the Kingdom of Israel*. Studies in Biblical Archaeology 7 (London: SCM Press, Ltd., 1958). Photograph JF.

58. The Landscape of Samaria

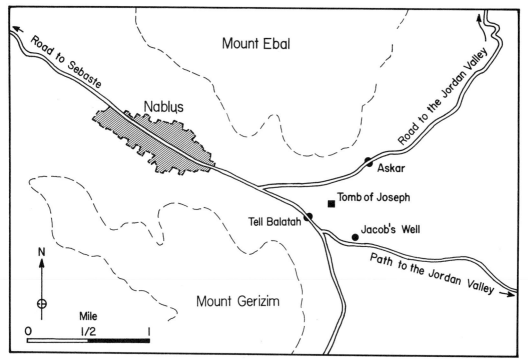

59. Map Showing Jacob's Well and Environs

59. Map Showing Jacob's Well and Environs

THIRTY-FIVE MILES NORTH of Jerusalem the road from Jerusalem to Samaria/Sebaste is joined by another road that comes up from the Jordan valley past Corea and through Wadi Far'ah (Josephus, *War* IV 8, 1 §§449; BA-SOR 62 [1936], p. 14), and the two proceed as one through the pass between Mounts Gerizim and Ebal and on another five miles to Samaria/Sebaste. Immediately prior to his journey from Judea to Galilee through Samaria (Jn 4:3-4) Jesus had been engaged in baptizing (Jn 4:1) and had had certain relationships with John the

Baptist (Jn 3:25f.), therefore it is probable that he came up at this time from the Jordan valley. The road just mentioned, or a path which took some shortcuts but followed a more or less parallel route, would have been the probable way. The sketch map shows where these routes converge in the vicinity of Jacob's well and proceed through the pass between Mounts Gerizim and Ebal.

Map: JF, cf. Kopp 1959, p. 199.

60. Mount Gerizim

JESUS (Jn 4:5-6) CAME to a city of Samaria called Sychar (Συχάρ, spelled Σιχάρ in a few manuscripts and Sichar in the vulgate) or Shechem (in the Sinaitic and Curetonian Syriac manuscripts the name would correspond to Greek Συχέμ, i.e., שכם in Hebrew), which was near the field that Jacob gave to his son Joseph. Jacob's well (πηγή, literally "spring") was there and, as Jesus conversed beside it with a woman of Samaria, the latter referred to an adjacent mountain of which she said, "Our fathers worshiped on this mountain" (Jn 4:5-7, 20). The mountain on which the Samaritans had long worshiped and on which, indeed, their descendants worship until today, Mount Gerizim (גרצים , LXX Γαριζίν, Dt 11:29, etc), known in Arabic as Jebel et-Tor. It rises 2,890 feet above sea level and 700 feet above the narrow valley between it and Mount Ebal, the latter reaching 3,085 feet above sea level. At the time of the schism between the Samaritans and the Jews, Sanballat built on Mount Garizein (Γαριζείν or Γαριζίν) a temple like the one in Jerusalem, an event which Josephus (Ant. XI 8, 2 and 4 §§310, 324) puts at the time of Alexander the Great. It has hitherto been supposed that Josephus is in error in

this dating, for the well-known Sanballat who is mentioned in the OT was a contemporary of Nehemiah (Neh. 4:1, etc.), and is also named in a letter dated in the seventeenth year of King Darius II, 408 B.C. (ANET p. 492); thus he lived something like a century earlier than Alexander. With the discovery of the Samaria Papyri in Wadi Daliyeh (Frank M. Cross, Jr., in BA XXVI [4 Dec. 1963], pp. 110-121), however, it has become known that at least three different governors of Samaria bore the name of Sanballat, and Josephus may be quite correct as to the date of the Sanballat who built the Mount Gerizim temple (ibid., p. 121 n. 27). Josephus (Ant. XIII 9, 1 §§255f.; cf. War I 2, 6 §63) also records that this temple was destroyed by John Hyrcanus (135-104 B.C.) at the same time that he destroyed Shechem. From recent excavations it appears that this destruction of Shechem took place in 108/107 B.C. (G. Ernest Wright, Shechem. 1964, pp. 183-184).

After A.D. 135 Hadrian built a temple of Jupiter on Mount Gerizim, which appears on Roman coins from the Neapolis mint beginning in the reign of Antoninus Pius (138-161) and continuing for nearly a century (BASOR 180 [Dec. 1965], p. 40). The coins show a colonnaded street at the foot of the mountain and a long stairway that leads up to the temple on the summit. It is evidently this stairway to which the Bordeaux Pilgrim (333) refers when he notes concerning Mount Gerizim (mons Agazaren) (Geyer p. 20; LPPTS I-B, p. 18; CCSL CLXXV, p. 13; WET p. 154): "Here the Samaritans say that Abraham offered sacrifice, and one reaches the summit of the mountain by steps, three hundred in number." The reference shows that the Samaritans identified Mount Gerizim with Mount Moriah (Gen 22:2), whereas for the Jews (Josephus, Ant. VII 13, 4 §333) the place of Abraham's sacrifice was the threshing floor of Araunah, where

60. Mount Gerizim

David built an altar (II S 24:18) (also cf. below No. 230). It would also seem from the language about the steps that the Samaritans were still using some part of the mountaintop for worship at that time. In 484, however, the Samaritans fell upon the Christians in their church in Neapolis while they were celebrating Pentecost and wounded their bishop, Terebinthius (for the name cf. the terebinth in Gen 35:4); in response the emperor Zeno (474-491) drove the Samaritans from the mountain and built on it an octagonal church dedicated to Mary as the Mother of God (Θεοτόκος), a church for which Justinian (527-565) contributed fortifications (Procopius, *Buildings* V 7, 7).

The ruins of the Theotokos church and its fortifications are on the higher southern peak of Mount Gerizim, were excavated by A. M. Schneider in 1928, and reported on by him in 1951 (*Beiträge zur biblischen Landes- und Altertumskunde hervorgegangen aus der* ZDPV 68 [1951], pp. 211-234). The ruins of the Hadrian temple are on a *tell* on the northern spur of the mountain known as Tell er-Ras. The temple was excavated by the Drew-McCormick expedition in 1966 (NTS 13 [1967], pp. 401-402), and the great stairway was traced down the mountain from the temple to the eastern edge of Neapolis in the valley below. Also under the temple were found the walls of another and different type of building, with which were associated fragments of Hellenistic pottery. This could have been the Samaritan temple of about the fourth century B.C. If this is correct then Hadrian chose, here as well as at Bethlehem (No. 32) and Jerusalem (Nos. 183, 225), to erect one of his temples on a site already held sacred. As for the Samaritans of the present day, they continue to offer their annual Passover sacrifice just to the west of the higher southern peak, where they also make their encampment (No. 61) during the seven days of the feast (RB 31 [1922], p. 435). This view is from the present village of 'Askar, probably ancient Sychar, on the slope of Mount Ebal, and shows Mount Gerizim and the Samaritan shrine on the summit.

J. Creten, "La pâque des Samaritains," in RB 31 (1922), pp. 434-442; Moses Gaster, *The Samaritans, Their History, Doctrines and Literature*. The Schweich Lectures, 1923 (London: Oxford University Press, 1925); Joachim Jeremias, *Die Passahfeier der Samaritaner*. ZAW Beiheft 59 (Giessen: Alfred Töpelmann, 1932); P. Antoine, "Garizim (Le Mont)," in DB Supplément III cols. 535-561; A. M. Schneider, "Römische und Byzantinische Bauten auf dem Garizim," in *Beiträge zur biblischen Landes- und Altertumskunde hervorgegangen aus der* ZDPV 68 (1951), pp. 211-234; Harold H. Rowley, *Sanballat and the Samaritan Temple*, reprinted from BJRL 38 (1955), pp. 166-198; Robert J. Bull in BASOR 180 (Dec. 1965), pp. 37-41; Howard C. Kee, "Tell-er-Ras and the Samaritan Temple," in NTS 13 (1967), pp. 401-402; Robert J. Bull, "A Preliminary Excavation of an Hadrianic Temple at Tell er-Ras on Mount Gerizim," in AJA 71 (1967), pp. 387-393; "The Excavation of Tel er-Ras on Mt. Gerizim," in BA 31 (1968), pp. 58-72; in RB 75 (1968), pp. 238-243; and in PEQ 1970, p. 110 and pl. XVIB for

drawing of coin showing temple, stairway, and colonnaded street; Ovadiah, *Corpus*, pp. 140-142, no. 143; Alan David Crown, "The Biblical Samaritans in the Present Day," in BAIAS 7 (1987-1988), pp. 40-49. Photograph: The Matson Photo Service, Alhambra, Calif.

61. Encampment of the Samaritans on Mount Gerizim

THE PHOTOGRAPH SHOWS an encampment of the Samaritans on Mount Gerizim in the area adjacent to the enclosure in which they conduct their Passover sacrifice, as mentioned in No. 60.

Photograph: The Matson Photo Service, Alhambra, Calif.

61. Encampment of the Samaritans on Mount Gerizim

62. The Region of Jacob's Well on the Madaba Mosaic Map

THE CITY of Samaria to which Jesus came in Jn 4:5 was near the field that Jacob gave to Joseph, and Jacob's well was there. When Jacob returned from paddan-aram he came to the city of Shechem (שכם), camped before the city, and purchased for money the piece of land on which he had pitched his tent (Gen 33:18-19). About to die in Egypt, Jacob told Joseph that he had given him Shechem, which he took with sword and bow (Gen 48:22), which sounds as if, at some point, an actual conquest had been involved. The passage just cited contains the word שכם, which may be taken as the name of the city (e.g., *An American Translation*: "I hereby give you Shechem"), or may be translated as a word meaning "shoulder" or "slope" (RVS: "I have given to you . . . one mountain slope"). This suggests that the city derived its name from its location on the slope of a mountain. According to Jg 9:7 this mountain would be Mount Gerizim. Ultimately the mummy of Joseph (Gen 50:26) was buried at Shechem in the portion of ground that his father had purchased (Jos 24:32). After playing an important part in many phases of OT history, Shechem was destroyed by John Hyrcanus in 108/107 B.C. at the same time that he destroyed the Samaritan temple on Mount Gerizim (Josephus, *Ant.* XIII 9, 1 §255; *War* I 2, 6 §63; cf. above No. 60). The new city that arose in this area was Flavia Neapolis. Pliny (*Nat. Hist.* V 14, 69) mentions Neapolis and says it was formerly called Mamortha; Josephus (*War* IV 8, 1 §449) mentions it and gives the native name as Mabartha. Like the name Shechem which refers to the "shoulder" of Mount Gerizim, this old name probably comes from *maʿabarta* (מעברתא), meaning "pass" or "passage," and refers to the pass between Mounts Gerizim and Ebal. Justin Martyr, who was born here, says that his father and grandfather were natives of Flavia Neapolis in Syria Palestina (or Palestinian Syria) (ἀπὸ Φλαυίας Νέας πόλεως τῆς Συρίας Παλαιστίνης) (*Apology* I 1; cf. Eusebius, *Ch. Hist.* IV 12, 1), and this makes it probable that the city was founded by Vespasian (69-79), the founder of the Flavian dynasty. Coins put the epoch of the era of the city in A. D. 72/73 (SHJP Vermes/Millar, I, p. 520). Neapolis is the modern Nablus, lying in the narrow valley between Gerizim and Ebal. Since Josephus (*Ant.* IV, 8 44 §305) says that Shechem (he spells the name Σίκιμον or Σίκιμα) is "between two mountains, the Garizaean on the right and that called 'Counsel' (the Hebrew Ebal [עיבל], Dt 11:29, etc., LXX Γαιβάλ, is here Hellenized as βουλή) on the left," it might be thought that Shechem had occupied the same site as Flavia Neapolis and present-day Nablus, directly between the two mountains. Jerome (*Letter* 108, 13 NPNFSS VI, p. 201) also says that Shechem "is now called Neapolis." In the *Onomasticon* (pp. 158-159, 164-165), however, Eusebius says that Shechem (Συχέμ), where the bones of Joseph were buried, was near Neapolis (πλησίον Νέας πόλεως) rather than at it, and here Jerome repeats rather than changes the information (*iuxta Neapolim*). In the section of the Madaba Mosaic Map shown in the photograph, in the rather obscured area in the upper lefthand portion, but also visible on No. 10, Neapolis (Νεάπολις) appears plainly labeled

62. The Region of Jacob's Well on the Madaba Mosaic Map

and represented as a large city. From the eastern gate at the top, a colonnaded street runs westward. In the southern part of the city is a basilica, facing eastward, with red roof. Presumably this is the episcopal basilica attacked by the Samaritans in 484 (cf. No. 60), and the site is occupied today by the Main Mosque in Nablus. At the intersection of the east-west street with a north-south street is a dome on columns; this is where the en-Nasr Mosque is now. At the south end of the north-south street are semicircular steps, probably representing a nympheum at the Ain Qaryun spring where a Roman structure has been found. South of Neapolis is Tur Garizin (Τουρ Γαριζιν) and, across the valley to the east (with only the bottom of the legend visible at the extreme upper edge of this photograph), Tur Gobel (Τουρ Γωβηλ). These are Mounts Gerizim and Ebal with the names given in the Aramaic form, using Aramaic טור, tur, for "mountain" instead of Hebrew הר, har.

The section of the Madaba Mosaic Map shown in the present photograph overlaps with the bottom part of the section shown in No. 10, and in the latter place the names of both mountains can be read plainly, Τουρ Γαριζιν and Τουρ Γωβηλ. In the section in No. 10, however, we also see that the map made place for a second and evidently alternate tradition about the location of the two mountains. There, on the edge of the mountain range west of Archelais and the place (i.e., the spring) of Saint Elisha, and not far northwest of Jericho, are smaller labels for the two mountains, using the form of their names as found in the Septuagint, Γεβαλ and Γαριζειν.

In the *Onomasticon* (pp. 64-65) Eusebius and Jerome also record the two traditions according to which the two mountains were either adjacent to Jericho (*iuxta Iericho*) or, as the Samaritans say, adjacent to Neapolis (*iuxta Neapolim*). Eusebius, followed by Jerome, thinks the Samaritan tradition unlikely because the two mountains at Neapolis are so far apart that the blessings and curses of Dt 11:29 could not have been heard back and forth. Actually, of course, the Samaritan tradition was correct and is verified by Josephus, who mentions Sichem and Argarizin (Σίκιμα καὶ Ἀργαριζίν) together (*War* I 6 §63), and is recognized by the Bordeaux Pilgrim who, as we have seen (No. 60) cites what the Samaritans say about *mons Agazaren*, and also locates *Sechim* at the foot of the mountain (Geyer p. 20: LPPTS I-B, p. 18; CCSL CLXXV, p. 13; WET p. 154). The rise of the Jericho tradition, on the other hand, was no doubt made possible by ambiguity in the language of Dt 11:30 and an exegesis thereof inspired by Jewish hostility to the Samaritans.

Between Tur Gobel and Tur Garizin on the map (No. 59) is Shechem. The label reads: Συχὲμ ἡ κ(αὶ) Σίκιμα κ(αὶ) Σαλήμ, Sichem which is also Sikima and Salem.

The words are almost identical with the listing of Shechem in the *Onomasticon* (p. 150), where Eusebius writes: "Shechem which is also Sikima or also Salem (Συχὲμ ἡ καὶ Σίκιμα ἡ καὶ Σαλήμ). A city of Jacob now deserted (ἔρημος). The place is shown in the environs (ἐν προαστείοις—the space in front of a town) of Neapolis; there also the tomb of Joseph is shown."

As for the identification or association of the name Salem with Shechem, this is doubtless a reflection of the same tradition attested by Epiphanius when he writes, "But others say that the Salem of Melchizedek was opposite Shechem in Samaria, whose grounds are seen (lying) waste" (*On Weights and Measures* 74 [75a] ed. Dean p. 75; cf. *Pan. hear.* 55, 2 GCS II, Holl/Dummer p. 326); and it agrees with the existence of ruins and a village east of Shechem to which the same Salim still attaches. As for Shechem itself, the site has been identified with almost complete certainty with Tell Balatah, beside the village of Balatah, and excavated by G. Ernest Wright beginning in 1956. The site is on the edge of the plain one and one-half miles southeast of Nablus, corresponding with the placement by Eusebius "in front of" Neapolis and with the location on the Madaba Map, and at the foot of Mount Gerizim, corresponding with the statement of the Pilgrim from Bordeaux and again with the location on the Madaba Map.

Just north of Shechem on the Madaba Mosaic is a building and the legend Τὸ τοῦ Ἰωσήφ, literally "The of Joseph." What is meant is quite certainly "The (monument, i.e., tomb) of Joseph." This is mentioned by Eusebius (as quoted above), and also by the Bordeaux Pilgrim, who writes (Geyer p. 20; LPPTS I-B, p. 18; CCSL CLXXV, pp. 13-14; WET pp. 154f.): "At the foot of the mountain is the place which is named Sechim. Here is a tomb (*monumentum*) where Joseph is laid in the estate (*villa*) which Jacob his father gave him." Today the Tomb of Joseph is shown as a stone-built grave inside a domed Muslim building (*Maqam en-Nebi Yusuf*) on the northeastern outskirts of the village of Balatah.

East of the Tomb of Joseph on the Madaba Map is a village adjacent to Tur Gobel, and under it a partially effaced legend which is probably to be restored to read: [Συ]χαρ ἡ νῖν [Σ]υχωρα, Sychar which is now Sychora. This is no doubt the En Soker or "spring of Sychar" mentioned in the Mishna (*Menahoth* 10, 2 DM p. 505) and represented by the present-day village of 'Askar which, with its spring, is on the slope of Mount Ebal a mile east of Nablus. South of Shechem, with its legend to the southeast, very plainly visible in the photograph, is a red-roofed church labeled: Ὅπου ἡ πηγὴ τοῦ Ἰακώβ, Here (is) the Well of Jacob. This corresponds with the deep well that is still today on the southeastern outskirts of the village of Balatah.

It has been noted above (No. 60) that in the Sinaitic and Curetonian Syriac manuscripts the city of Samaria in Jn 4:5 was Shechem. The excavation of Tell Balatah confirms that the city on the tell came to an end about the end of the second century B.C., in agreement with the literary evidence that Shechem was destroyed by John Hyrcanus in 108/107 B.C. (cf. above Nos. 60, 62). The excavators believe, however, that a village probably continued to exist where the village of Balatah is now (G. Ernest Wright, *Shechem, The Biography of a Biblical City* [New York and Toronto: McGraw-Hill, 1964], p. 244 n.6). This would allow the supposition that the city from which the woman of Samaria came out to draw water (Jn 4:7) and to which she went back (Jn 4:28) was none other than Shechem itself, in the form of a village which continued after the destruction of the city on the ancient tell. The distances involved would be very reasonable, for it is only some three hundred yards from the Tomb of Joseph on the northeastern edge of Balatah to the Well of Jacob on the southeastern edge. The name Sychar in Jn 4:5, in this case, would be a textual corruption of Sychem or Shechem which found its way into many of the manuscripts normally regarded as most dependable.

If, however, Sychar is the correct reading of Jn 4:5 then it must be supposed that the woman of Samaria came from the city now represented by the village of 'Askar. In this case the distance is one kilometer south from 'Askar to Jacob's Well. In spite of the greater distance, ancient writers as well as the major manuscripts tend to point to Sychar rather than to Shechem as the city connected with the event at the well. Eusebius (*Onomasticon* p. 164) gives this entry for Sychar: "Sychar (Συχάρ). In front of Neapolis near the field which Jacob gave to Joseph his son. In which Christ, according to John, conversed with the Samaritan woman at the well. And it is shown until now."

Likewise the Bordeaux Pilgrim, having spoken of Sichem and the tomb in which Joseph was laid, writes (Geyer p. 20; LPPTS I-B, pp. 18-19; CCSL CLXXV, p. 14; WET p. 155): "A thousand paces from there is the place which is named Sechar, from which the Samaritan woman came down (*descendit*) to the place where Jacob dug the well in order to draw water from it, and our Lord Jesus Christ talked with her; where there are plane trees which Jacob planted, and a bath (*balneus*, probably a baptistery, since the same word [*balneum*] is used a little later for the baptistery behind the Church of the Holy Sepulcher in Jerusalem [Geyer p. 23; LPPTS I-B, p. 24; CCSL CLXXV, p. 171; WET p. 158]) which is filled from this well."

To complete consideration of the presently relevant portions of this part of the Madaba Mosaic Map it will suffice to notice the text written in red in the area otherwise blank on the west side of Tur Garizin. The text is:

·Ἰωσὴφ εὐλόγησέν σε
ὁ Θεὸς εὐλογίαν γῆς
ἐχούσης πάντα καὶ
πάλιν ἀπ' εὐλογίας Κ(υρίο)υ
ἡ γῆ αὐτοῦ

Joseph "God blessed thee
with the blessing of the earth
possessing all things" and
again "Of the blessing of the Lord
is his land"

The two LXX quotations, separated by "and again," are from the blessings of Joseph by Jacob in Gen 49: 25 and by Moses in Dt 33:13. The word "Lord" is abbreviated.

F.-M. Abel, "Naplouse, Essai de topographie," in RB 32 (1923), pp. 120-132; Albrecht Alt, "Salem," in PJ 25 (1929), pp. 52-54; Abel, *Géographie* I, pp. 360f., "Garizim et Ébal." Photograph: courtesy Victor R. Gold.

63. Jacob's Well

THIS PHOTOGRAPH SHOWS the mouth of Jacob's well and the manner of lowering a water vessel into its depths.

Photograph: The Matson Photo Service, Alhambra, Calif.

64. Tell Balatah

THIS VIEW is from Mount Ebal and looks down upon Tell Balatah, site of the ancient city of Shechem, in the middle foreground. The modern village and refugee camp are just beyond. To the right can be seen the lower slope of Mount Gerizim.

For the excavation of Tell Balatah, see G. Ernest Wright, *Shechem, The Biography of a Biblical City* (New York and Toronto: McGraw-Hill, 1964). Photograph: Jerry Vardaman.

65. Sychar

THIS IS A VIEW of the village of 'Askar, probably ancient Sychar, on the lower slope of Mount Ebal.

Photograph: Jerry Vardaman.

63. Jacob's Well

64. Tell Balatah

65. Sychar

66. Plan of the Church over Jacob's Well according to Arculf

AS EXPLAINED ABOVE (NO. 62), the reference by the Pilgrim from Bordeaux (333) to a bath (*balneus*) that was filled with water from the Well of Jacob suggests that there was then already a baptistery at Jacob's Well. If the baptistery was associated with a church, this church would have been of Constantinian date. The Bordeaux Pilgrim does not mention a church, however, and neither does Eusebius when he tells about the well in the *Onomasticon* (p. 164). But in his description of the pilgrimage of Paula (386) Jerome (*Letter* 108, NPNFSS VI, p. 201) says that "she entered the church built upon the side of Mount Gerizim around Jacob's Well"; and in his translation of the *Onomasticon* (p. 165) he adds at the point of the mention of the well the words, "where now a church has been built." At least by around 380, therefore, there was a church at the well.

The account of the pilgrimage of Arculf (670), written by Adamnan, contains this passage (Geyer p. 270; LPPTS III-A, pp. 41-42; CCSL CLXXV, p. 216; WJP p. 108) concerning the site: "Arculf . . . passed through the district of Samaria, and came to the city of that province which is called in Hebrew Sichem, but in Greek and Latin custom is named Sicima; it is also often called Sichar, however improperly. Near that city a church (*ecclesiam*) built beyond the wall, which is four-armed, stretching towards the four cardinal points, like a cross, a plan of which is drawn below. In the middle of it is the Fountain of Jacob (*fons Iacob*)."

Arculf also drank water from the well and obtained a figure as to its depth. Using the Greek unit orgyia (ὄργυια), which was the length of the outstretched arms. or some six feet, he reported that the well had a depth of twice twenty orgyiae. The plan of the church that accompanied the description by Arculf is reproduced from Codex Parisinus (Latin 13048), a ninth-century manuscript of *De Locis sanctis* preserved in the Bibliothèque Nationale, Paris. Since Arculf came to Palestine after the Persian invasion (614) and the Muslim conquest (638) it is possible that by then the upper church had been destroyed and what he saw and drew was only a cruciform crypt immediately over the well. His language, however, appears intended to say that the church itself was in existence and in this form at that time.

Photograph: Arculfus De Locis Sanctus, Codex Parisinus Lat. 13048, courtesy Bibliothèque Nationale. Paris.

67. Plan of the Crusader Church over Jacob's Well

BEFORE THE CRUSADERS came the church of Jacob's Well was probably in ruins; at any rate, they built a new church there. The Crusader church is attested as in existence around 1150 and was dedicated to the Savior of the world, in evident allusion to Jn 4:42. In this connection Vardaman suggests that it is of interest that a hoard of 35 Ptolemaic silver tetradrachmas was found in the 1960 excavations of Shechem. Many of these coins mention Ptolemy II as "Savior" (ΣΩΤΗΡΟΣ), which was used as a title for the emperor Augustus at a

66. Plan of the Church over Jacob's Well according to Arculf

later period, of course (see Sellers, "The Coins of Shechem," in BA 25 [1962], pp. 90f.). The Crusader church at Jacob's Well was also ruined. In 1882 the *Memoirs of The Survey of Western Palestine* (II, pp. 172-178) describe only a broken vault and a massive stone of local white limestone with a round hole directly over the well, the stone deeply grooved from the ropes with which water pots were drawn up. Concerning the well the *Memoirs* (pp. 174, 176) state:

> The site is acknowledged by Jews, Moslems, and Christians. The existence of a well sunk to a great depth in a place where water-springs on the surface are abundant is sufficiently remarkable to give this well a peculiar history. It is remarkably characteristic of the prudence and forethought of the great Patriarch, who, having purchased a parcel of ground at the entrance of the vale [of Shechem], secured on his own property, by dint of great toil, a perennial supply of water at a time when the adjacent water-springs were in the hands of

unfriendly, if not actually hostile, neighbors. . . . The well was undoubtedly sunk to a great depth for the purpose of securing, even in exceptionally dry seasons, a supply of water, which at great depths would always be filtering through the sides of the well and would collect at the bottom.

In 1885 the Greek Orthodox church purchased the property of Jacob's Well and, in due time, began certain excavations. The ruins uncovered appear to have been entirely from the Crusader period. They were sufficient to allow the drawing of a partially hypothetical plan of the Crusader church as shown in the illustration. The church had a nave and two side aisles, was oriented to the east, and had three apses. From the nave two staircases ran down at the right and the left to the crypt at the well, the church being positioned so that the well was under the central apse.

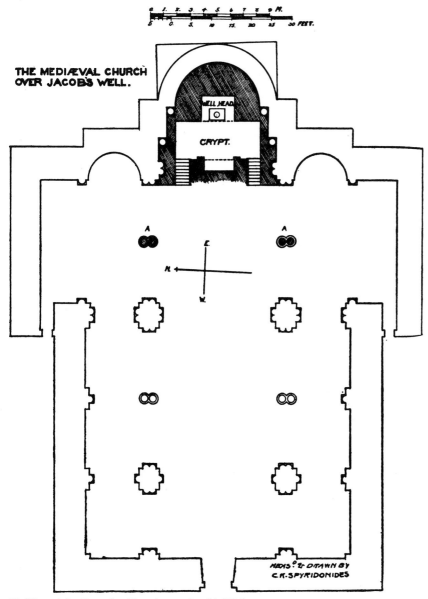

67. Plan of the Crusader Church over Jacob's Well

RB 2 (1892), pp. 242-244; 4 (1895, pp. 619-622 (Paul-M. Séjourné); PEFQS 1881, pp. 212-214 (Charles W. Barclay); 1893. pp. 255-256 (G. Robinson Lees); 1894, pp. 108-112 (F. J. Bliss); 1895, p. 89; 1900, pp. 61-63 (Conrad Schick); 1908, pp. 248-253 (C. K. Spyridonidis); 42 (1933), pp 384-402 (F.-M. Abel, "Le puits de Jacob et l'eglise Saint-Sauveur"); Ovadiah, *Corpus Supplementum*, pp. 244-246, no. 59. Plan: C. K. Spyridonidis, "The Church over Jacob's Well," in PEFQS 1908, plan on p. 252, courtesy Palestine Exploration Fund.

68. The Unfinished Greek Orthodox Basilica over Jacob's Well

IN 1903 THE GREEK ORTHODOX CHURCH began to build a new basilica over Jacob's Well and in 1959-1960 the structure stood at the point shown in this photograph. The two small temporary shacks at the head of the nave give access to the two staircases that lead down to the crypt and the wellhead.

Photograph: JF.

68. The Unfinished Greek Orthodox Basilica over Jacob's Well

GALILEE

69. The Southern End of the Sea of Galilee

THE HEBREW NAME for Galilee, גליל, transliterated in Greek as Γαλιλαία, means "circle," hence signifies "region" or "district." Lying in the northern part of Palestine, Galilee was more exposed to foreign influences than the rest of the land and had a pagan as well as a Jewish population. Is 9:1 (Heb. 8:23) identifies the area as that of the tribes of Zebulun and Naphtali and calls it "Galilee of the nations," equally well translatable as "the district of the nations." Mt 4:14-16 cites the passage in Isaiah in connection with the residence of Jesus at "Capernaum by the sea" and includes Is 9:2 (Heb. 9:1) as relevant to the effect of the work of Jesus: "the people who sat in darkness have seen a great light, and for those who sat in the region and shadow of death light has dawned." Josephus (*War* III 3, 1-2 §§35-43) delimits the area of Galilee as enveloped by Phoenicia and Syria on the west and north, and bounded by Samaria and the territory of Scythopolis on the south and the territory of Hippos, Gadara, and Gaulanitis on the east. He writes, perhaps not without exaggeration: "the land is everywhere so rich in soil and pasturage and produces such variety of trees, that even the most indolent are tempted by these facilities to devote themselves to agriculture. In fact, every inch of the soil has been cultivated by the inhabitants; there is not a parcel of waste land. The towns, too, are thickly distributed, and even the villages, thanks to the fertility of the soil, are all so densely populated that the smallest of them contains above fifteen thousand inhabitants."

The large lake, which is an outstanding feature of Galilee, is called the Sea of Chinnereth or Chinneroth in the OT (Num 34:11; Jos 12:3; 13:27), Gennesar in 1 Macc 11:67 and Josephus, and the Lake of Gennesaret (Lk 5:1), the Sea of Tiberias (Jn 6:1; 21:1), and the Sea

69. The Southern End of the Sea of Galilee

of Galilee (Jn 6:1, etc.) in the NT. It is approximately thirteen miles long and as much as seven miles across, and lies 696 feet below sea level. The Jordan River flows through it from north to south and constantly renews the freshness of its waters, in which are said to be forty different species of fish. The photograph looks from west to east across the southern portion of the lake.

Menahem Talmi, *Lake Kinneret, Sea of Galilee* (Tel-Aviv: E. Lewin-Epstein, 1965); "Galilee and Regionalism," in *Explor*, Winter 1977; Martin Goodman, *State and Society in Roman Galilee, A.D. 132-212*. Oxford Centre for Postgraduate Hebrew Studies (Totowa, N.J.: Rowman and Allanheld Publishers, 1983); James F. Strange, "Galilee," in BI 11, 2 (Winter 1985), pp. 21-26; Willibald Bösen, *Galiläa als Lebensraum und Wirkungsfeld Jesu, Eine zeitgeschichtliche und theologische Untersuchung* (Freiburg, Basel, Wien: Herder, 1985); Sean Freyne, *Galilee from Alexander the Great to Hadrian, 323 B.C.E. to 135 C.E.: A Study of Second Temple Judaism* (Wilmington, Del.: Michael Glazier; and Notre Dame, Ind.: University of Notre Dame Press, 1980); and Sean Freyne, *Galilee, Jesus and the Gospels: Literary Approaches and Historical Investigations* (Philadelphia: Fortress Press, 1988). Photograph: JF.

70. Map of the Sea of Galilee

THIS SKETCH MAP locates the chief places on and near the Sea of Galilee that are mentioned in the following discussion.

Map: JF, cf. Dalman, *Sacred Sites*, pp. 120, 132.

71. Tiberias on the Sea of Galilee

IN 530 THEODOSIUS (Geyer pp. 137-138; LPPTS II-B, p. 8; CCSL CLXXV, p. 115; WJP p. 63) came from Scythopolis, i.e., from the south, to the Sea of Tiberias and visited in succession Tiberias, Magdala (Nos. 73-74), the Seven Springs (et-Tabgha, Nos. 77-84), and Capernaum (Tell Hum, Nos. 87-100). These were the sites of chief importance, enumerated in sequence from south to north, on the west side of the lake.

Tiberias is about five miles north of the outlet of the Jordan, at the south end of the lake. Herod Antipas (4 B.C.-A.D. 39), who had resided at Sepphoris, built the city as a new capital and named it in honor of Tiberius (14-37). Since Josephus (*Ant.* XVIII 2, 3 §36) mentions the building of Tiberias by Herod the tetrach just after recording the coming of Pontius Pilate as procurator

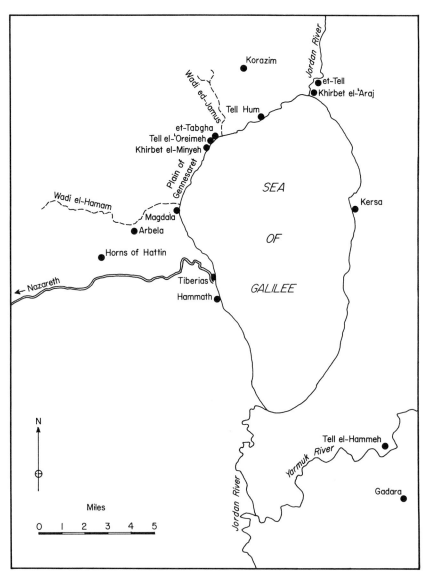

Korazim

Jordan River

et-Tell
Khirbet el-'Araj

Tell Hum

Wadi ed-Jamus

et-Tabgha
Tell el-'Oreimeh
Khirbet el-Minyeh

Plain of Gennesaret

Wadi el-Hamam

Magdala

Arbela

SEA

OF

GALILEE

Kersa

Horns of Hattin

Tiberias

← Nazareth

Hammath

N

Jordan River

Yarmuk River

Tell el-Hammeh

Gadara

Miles

0   1   2   3   4   5

70. Map of the Sea of Galilee

71. Tiberias on the Sea of Galilee

78

(A.D. 15/16 or 26), it has often been held that the city was built about that time. On the basis of coins and other evidence, however, Avi-Yonah (IEJ 1 [1950-51], pp. 160-169) has concluded that the foundation of the city was between the years 17 and 22 of the Christian era, and Spijkerman (LA 13 [1962-63], pp. 303-304) has narrowed the span to A.D. 17-20. Within these years, Avi-Yonah suggests A.D. 18 as the most likely, since the official foundation of Tiberias in that year would coincide with the sixtieth birthday of the emperor in whose honor the city was named.

In the Gospels there is no mention of Sepphoris and mention of Tiberias only in Jn 6:23 ("boats from Tiberias"); thus as far as explicit evidence goes it appears that Jesus did not visit or work in either city—understandably, perhaps, inasmuch as these were the capitals of the king who put John the Baptist to death at Machaerus (No. 14), at which occasion "the leading men of Galilee" were present (Mk 6:21), and the Herodians (presumably followers of Herod Antipas) appear as opponents of Jesus (Mk 3:6; 12:11; Mt 22:16), while Herod Antipas himself was reported as wanting to kill Jesus (Lk 13:31) and later at the trial of Jesus "treated him with contempt" (Lk 23:11). Jesus, however, regarded Herod as crafty and weak ("that fox") and was not driven out of his territory by any threat from Herod, but only moved on toward Jerusalem in accordance with his own time and his own destiny (Lk 13:31). Also it is to be noted that Joanna, the wife of Chuza, Herod's steward (ἐπίτροπος, Mk 8:3, probably financial minister), was one of several Galilean women who were healed by Jesus and afterward provided for him and the Twelve out of their means (Lk 8:3) and were also present at the empty tomb (Lk 24:10).

Josephus says that Herod built a palace for himself in Tiberias, which contained representations of animals and had a roof partly of gold (*Life* 12 §65); also that there was a stadium there which was used for public assemblages (*War* II 21, 6 §618; III 10, 10 §539), and a synagogue (προσευχή, literally "place of prayer," the same word as in Ac 16:13, 16) which was a huge building and capable of accommodating a large crowd (*Life* 54 §277). Josephus also says that Tiberias was built on the site of tombs and was therefore a settlement contrary to the law and tradition of the Jews; hence it was difficult to obtain settlers and the king brought in a heterogeneous population of Galileans and others. While it might be thought that these were all Gentiles, the large synagogue speaks for the presence of many Jews too. In fact Tiberias became a strong center of Jewish life after A.D. 135, and the Sanhedrin or Beth Din, which had been moved from Jerusalem to Jamnia (70-132) and to other places, was at last brought here (cf. No. 282). Also the tombs of the famous Jewish leaders Johanan ben Zakkai, establisher of

the Beth Din at Jamnia, Rabbi Akiba, supporter of Bar Kokhba, Rabbi Meir, second-century scholar whose name means "giver of light," Maimonides, twelfth-century physician and philosopher, and others are at Tiberias. Five miles to the west and a little north are the Horns of Hattin, where the Crusaders were defeated by Saladin in 1187.

In the case of many Hellenistic towns in Palestine the name reverted in due time to an earlier Semitic form; Scythopolis, for example, became known again as Bethshean, Philadelphia as Amman, and so on, but since Tiberias did not displace any earlier Semitic name it has remained the name of the city until today. The photograph shows the city of Tiberias as it lies on the lake shore in what Josephus (*Ant.* XVIII 2, 3 §36) called the best region of Galilee.

M. Avi-Yonah, "The Foundation of Tiberias," in IEJ 1 (1950-1951), pp. 160-169; A. Spijkerman, "Some Rare Jewish Coins," in LA 13 (1962-1963), pp. 303f.; Pearlman and Yannai pp. 60-64; Yizhar Hirschfeld, *Tiberias* (Jerusalem: Yad Ben Zvi, 1987) (Hebrew). For Herod Antipas and the relations of Jesus with him as the ruler of Galilee, see Harold W. Hoehner, *Herod Antipas* (Cambridge: Cambridge University Press, 1972), esp. pp. 154ff., 303ff., 343ff. For Sepphoris, see Bagatti, *Antichi Villaggi*, pp. 112-121; Frédéric Manns, "Un centre Judéo-Chrétien important: Sepphoris," in his *Essais sur le Judéo-Christianisme.* PSBFA 12, 1977, pp. 165-193; Eric M. Meyers, Ehud Netzer, and Carol L. Meyers, "Sepphoris, 'Ornament of All Galilee,' " in BA 49 (1986), pp. 4-19; and "Artistry in Stone, The Mosaics of Ancient Sepphoris," in BA 50 (1987), pp. 223-231. Photograph: JF.

72. Floor Mosaic of the Synagogue at Hammath Tiberias

NOT FAR FROM Tiberias was a hot spring and a village that Josephus (*Ant.* XVIII 2, 3 §36) calls Ammathus ('Αμμαθούς). The name, he says (*War* IV 1, 3 §11), may be interpreted as "warm baths" (θερμά), and the place was probably the Hammath (חמת , "hot spring") of Jos 19:35. The place indicated is undoubtedly to be identified with the hot springs on the lake shore about a mile and one-half south of Tiberias, the place still known as Hammath Tiberias. Excavations were conducted in the mound adjacent to the springs by N. Slousch in 1921 and by Moshe Dothan in 1961-1965. Here there are some remains of the southern gate of Tiberias, and of baths of the Israelite period. Most notable is a series of five superimposed buildings, most or all of which represent the successive buildings of a synagogue. In the lowest level (III) are the remains of a public building that is believed by the recent excavator to date from the first century or first half of the second century A.D., and was perhaps already a synagogue within that period. In level IIB (attributed by the excavator to the third century) the synagogue was a "broadhouse" basilica (13 by 15 meters), with the entrance in the long wall on the side facing Jerusalem. The interior was divided by three rows of three columns each into four areas, a relatively wide nave, an aisle on either side, and an extra aisle on the east side. In the nave there was preserved a fragment of a polychrome mosaic pavement. In level IIA (attributed to the end of the third or early part of the fourth century and in existence throughout the fourth century) the basic plan of the preceding building was still followed, but the entrance was now through the long north wall and there was a permanent place for the Torah against the long south wall. In the debris were fragments of polychrome frescoes that had ornamented the walls, and the floor was covered with a mosaic pavement, done in some thirty colors and still relatively well preserved. The most important part of the mosaic (shown here) is in the nave. At the south in front of the presumed place for the Torah is a depiction of a Torah shrine, with a *menorah* (seven-armed lampstand) on either side, and also a *lulab* (palm branch used in the Feast of Tabernacles), *ethrog* (citron, also a symbol of the Feast of Tabernacles), *shofar* (ram's horn blown at festivals), and incense shovel. In the large middle panel is a circle with the signs of the zodiac and, at the center, is Helios (or Sol Invictus, the "invincible sun," as known by the Romans in the third-fourth centuries, cf. FMM pp. 210f.), riding skyward in his chariot, while outside the zodiac circle, at the four corners of the panel, are the busts of four female figures

representing the four seasons of the year. Of several zodiac mosaics found in ancient synagogues in Palestine, this is one of the earliest.

In the entire mosaic there are inscriptions in Hebrew, Aramaic, and Greek (Dothan, *Hammath Tiberias*, pp. 53-62). In the northern panel, flanked by two lions, are the names of donors and founders of the synagogue. A typical item reads literally, "Maximos vowing fulfilled (it), long may he live!" i.e., this certain Maximos was a donor who made a pledge for a contribution toward the construction of the synagogue and he fulfilled his pledge, therefore may he be blessed. An Aramaic inscription in an aisle panel is translated:

> May peace be upon anyone who has offered charity in this
> holy place and anyone who will offer charity
> may he be blessed. Amen, Amen, Selah, and for myself
> Amen.

The phrase "offer charity" can mean a charitable donation or a donation toward the erection of the building. The phrase "may he be blessed," with slight variations, occurs in many synagogue inscriptions (see No. 57). The doubled Amen is like the same duplication ("verily, verily" or "truly, truly" in English translations) in the Gospel according to John and the Manual of Discipline (Vardaman).

Above, in level IB (sixth century), the synagogue was a larger basilica (24 by 31 meters), with nave, two side aisles, and apse. Finally in level IA (seventh-eighth century) the synagogue was of much the same plan as its predecessor, but the new mosaic floor was mainly of geometric patterns.

The photograph shows the main panels in the mosaic of level IIA. The stonework cutting across the mosaic belongs to the walls of the synagogue of level IA. In the upper left-hand corner there is also a remnant of the mosaic floor of level IIB.

72. Floor Mosaic of the Synagogue at Hammath Tiberias

L.-H. Vincent, "Les fouilles juives d'el-Hamman, a Tibériade," in RB 30 (1921), pp. 438-442; 31 (1922), pp. 115-122; B. Lifshitz, "Die Entdeckung einer alten Synagoge bei Tiberias," in ZDPV 78 (1962), pp. 180-184; M. Dothan in IEJ 12 (1962), pp. 153-154; and in RB 70 (1963), pp. 588-590; and "The Synagogue at Hammath-Tiberias," in *Synagogues Revealed*, pp. 63-69; Rachel Hachlili, "The Zodiac in Ancient Jewish Art: Representation and Significance," in BASOR 228 (Dec 1977), pp. 61-77; Bellarmino Bagatti, "Osservazioni sullo zodiaco e le stagioni nelle sinagoghe e chiese Palestinesi dei sec. V-VI," in *Studia Hierosolymitana* III. SBFCM 30 (Jerusalem: Franciscan Printing Press, 1982), pp. 247-253; Moshe Dothan, *Hammath Tiberias: Early Synagogues and the Hellenistic and Roman Remains* (Israel Exploration Society, University of Haifa, Department of Antiquities and Museums, Jerusalem, 1983); "Synagogue Excavation Reveals Stunning Mosaic of Zodiac and Torah Ark," book review by Hershel Shanks in BAR 10.3 (May/June 1984), pp. 32-44. Photograph: Dothan, *Hammath Tiberias*, pl. 26, courtesy Israel Exploration Society.

73. Magdala

PROCEEDING NORTHWARD from Tiberias along the lake shore, Theodosius (Geyer pp. 137-138; LPPTS II-B, p. 8; CCSL CLXXV, p. 115; WJP p. 63) came next to Magdala, "where the lady Mary was born" (*ubi domna Maria nata est*). He gives the distance as two miles, but repeats the same figure for the distance from Magdala to the Seven Springs and from the Seven Springs to Capernaum, hence we may regard it as a round figure approximation. It is in fact somewhat less than three miles (4.5 km.) along the shore from Tiberias to the present-day village of Migdal (it was known in Arabic as Mejdel), which doubtless preserves the ancient name and probably also preserves substantially the ancient location of Magdala. This site is not only on the road from Tiberias but also at the junction therewith of the ancient road from Nazareth, which came down through the Wadi el-Hamam or Valley of Pigeons and past the great cliffs of Arbela to the lake. At Arbela the Jews fought against the Syrians (1 Macc 9:2), in the grottoes in the mountainside Herod the Great trapped and slaughtered brigands, as Josephus calls them (*Ant.* XIV 15, 5 §§421-430; *War* I 16, 4 §§310-313), and in the war with Rome the village of the Cave of Arbela was one of the places in Lower Galilee, along with other villages and with the cities of Tarichea, Tiberias, and Sepphoris, which were fortified by Josephus (*Life* 37 §188; cf. 60 §311). Magdala itself, occupying this strategic junction, probably derived its name from *migdal*, which is the Hebrew word for "tower" (מגדל), suggesting its place as a guard tower or fortress. As we have seen (No. 44), the name occurs in the Nazareth inscription from Caesarea. In the Talmud Migdal is mentioned as near Tiberias and is also given the fuller name of Migdal Nunaiya or "fish tower" (Pesahim 46a SBT II, 4, p. 219), appropriate to the good fishing here in

the Sea of Galilee. The place that Josephus calls Tarichea, a name evidently derived from Greek τάριχος, meaning salted fish, was probably also the same as Magdala. Josephus (*War* III 9, 7-10, 5 and 9 §§443-502, 522-531) gives a very detailed account of the conquest of Tarichea by Vespasian and Titus, which is not surprising since Tarichea was one of the Galilean cities that he himself had fortified. In the account he describes the Romans as moving up from Scythopolis to Tiberias, then advancing (προελθών) further and pitching camp between Tiberias and Tarichea, and finally taking the city as well as defeating the Jews in a subsequent naval engagement on the lake. The sequence of the places and the description of the topography is entirely in accord with the identification of Tarichea and Magdala. Josephus also speaks of the Taricheans as numbering as many as 40,000—a perhaps exaggerated figure—and makes mention of their hippodrome, an indication of the Hellenistic character of the city (*War* II, 21, 3-4 §§599, 608). In the Gospels Magdala (Μαγδαλά) is mentioned in Mt 15:39 and Mk 8:10 in some manuscripts. Other manuscripts, and in fact the better ones, give Magadan in Mt 15:39 and Dalmanutha in Mk 8:10, while yet other forms of the name also occur. Even so it is probable that most of these are variants of Magdala, related to Hebrew Migdal as explained above, while Dalmanutha may simply be a different name for the same place (cf. Augustine, *The Harmony of the Gospels* 51, 106 NPNF VI, p. 153, who says of Dalmanutha and Magadan [Latin spelling], "There is no reason for questioning the fact that it is the same place that is intended under both names"). For Magdala we have also the witness of the name of Mary Magdalene (Μαρία ἡ Μαγδαληνή), which occurs a number of times in all four Gospels (Mt 27:56, etc.), and which must mean "Mary, the one from Magdala."

Identifying places on the northwest shore of the Sea

73. Magdala

of Galilee, coming down from the north, Epiphanius the Monk (Monachus Hagiopolita, A.D. 750-800) names Heptapegon (No. 77) and then says: "And again about two miles farther is a church (ἐκκλησία) in which is the house of the Magdalene at the place called Magdala. There the Lord healed her. From there one goes to the city of Tiberias" (Herbert Donner in ZDPV 87 [1971], p. 78; WJP p. 120). Likewise Eutychius (940) says of the church: "The Church of Magdala near Tiberias bears witness that Christ here drove out the seven demons which were in Mary Magdalene" (*The Book of the Demonstration*, ed. Watt, CSCO 193, p. 136).

The photograph shows the village of Mejdel and the Plain of Gennesaret behind it.

W. F. Albright, "Contributions to the Historical Geography of Palestine: The Location of Taricheae," in AASOR 2-3 for 1921-22 (1923), pp. 29-46; Joseph Sickenberger, "Dalmanutha (Mk. 8, 10)," in ZDPV 57 (1934), pp. 281-285; Dalman, *Sacred Sites*, pp. 118-119, 126-128; Paul Thielscher, "Εις τα ορια Μαγδαλα," in ZDPV 59 (1936), pp. 128-132; Børge Hjerl-Hansen, "Dalmanutha (Marc, VIII, 10), Énigme géographique et linguistique dans l'Évangile de S. Marc," in RB 53 (1946), pp. 372-384; Clemens Kopp, "Christian Sites around the Sea of Galilee: IV. Magdala," in *Dominican Studies* 3 (1950), pp. 344-350; B. Bagatti, "Magdala, Patria di Maria Maddalene," in Bagatti, *Antichi Villaggi*, pp. 80-83; Frédéric Manns, "Magdala dans les sources litteraires," in *Studia Hierosolymitana*, I (1976), pp. 307-337. Photograph: courtesy École Biblique et Archéologique Française.

74. The Synagogue at Magdala

ARCHEOLOGICAL EXCAVATIONS were conducted at the site of ancient Magdala by Virgilio Corbo in 1971-1977. As thus in part brought to light, Magdala was laid out as a Roman city with a main north-south street (*cardo maximus*) intersected by east-west streets (*decumanus*, from *decumana*, the main entrance of a Roman army camp, farthest from the enemy, named for the tenth cohort of the legion, usually camped there, cf. No. 200) and with regularly laid-out blocks (*insulae*) of buildings (for a general plan, see LA 28 [1978], pl. 71).

At the intersection of an east-west street (Via III on the plan) and the main north-south street (Via II), and surrounded by blocks of buildings, are the ruins of the building (8.16 by 7.25 meters) shown in this picture (for a plan, see LA 24 [1974], p. 24). The rows of columns divide the hall into a nave and two side aisles running the length of the building, and an aisle across the back or south side. On the north side are five rows of stone benches, and the entrance was probably on the east side. From the architecture this was most probably a synagogue, and from its similarity in plan to the synagogues at Herodium (No. 21) and Masada (No. 23), it is probably more or less contemporary with them (Corbo in LA

24 [1974], p. 22; and in *Studia Hierosolymitana*, I [1976], p. 371), a date for which there is confirmation in both coins and pottery of the late Hellenistic and early Roman periods found in the adjacent Block D (*Studia Hierosolymitana*, I, pp. 339, 371). Along with a synagogue of similar style excavated at Gamla, a city east of the Sea of Galilee, destroyed by the Romans in A.D. 67 (Josephus, *War* IV 1, 10 §83) and never resettled (*Synagogues Revealed*, pp. 30-34 [S. Gutman], 35-41 [Z. Ma'oz]), we have, therefore, no less than four excavated synagogues—Masada, Herodium, Magdala, Gamla—which belong very probably to the late Second Temple period, i.e., to the first century of the present era and prior to the year 70 (Meyers and Strange p. 140; *Synagogues Revealed*, p. 26).

To the north of the synagogue, with entrance from the street that runs there (Via III), a large building area with some preserved mosaic (Block C) is identified as a villa; to the west (in Block A) there is a Roman-period masonry water tower (*Studia Hierosolymitana*, I, pp. 357f., 362f.), and to the south with entrance toward the lake there are the ruins of a monastery of Byzantine time (LA 24 [1974], pp. 7ff.), but the church, presumably also of Byzantine date, to which Epiphanius the Monk and Eutychius refer (No. 73) has not been found.

The character of Magdala/Tarichea/Migdal Nunaiya as a center of fishing and the fish industry, and a place where the Jews could try to resist the Romans in their own boats on the lake, has been noted above (No. 73), and in this connection it may be observed that the harbor of Magdala has been located and plotted (Nun, *Ancient Anchorages*, pp. 20f.; IDB-S p. 561). In 1986, when prolonged drought had lowered the level of the Sea of Galilee, the hull of an ancient boat was found in the exposed lakebed offshore about one mile north of Magdala and was dug out of the mud and brought for preservation to the Yigal Allon Museum at Kibbutz Ginnosar, which is on the lake shore, a little farther north. The existing hull is 26.5 feet in length, 7.5 feet in beam, and 4.5 feet in depth. Apparently the boat had a mast and could be sailed as well as rowed, and probably had a large stern platform (cf. Mk 4:38). Carbon-14 dating indicates that the wood from which the boat was built was cut at about 40 B.C. ± 80 years, i.e., between 120 B.C. and A.D. 40. Pottery found in the mud near the boat was typical of the latter part of the first century B.C. and on to after the middle of the first century A.D., or until about A.D. 70. The boat must be, therefore, of the very sort which was available to Jesus and his disciples as well as of the sort used by the Jews of Magdala in their disastrous naval engagement with the Romans.

B. Bagatti, "Magdala, Patria di maria Maddalena," in Bagatti, *Antichi Villaggi*, pp. 80-83; Virgilio C. Corbo, "Scavi archeologici a Magdala (1971-1973)," in LA 24 (1974), pp. 5-37; and "La città

74. The Synagogue at Magdala

romana di Magdala, Rapporto preliminare dopo la quarta campagna del 1975," in *Studia Hierosolymitana*, I 1976), pp. 355-378; and "Piazza e villa urbana a Magdala," in *LA* 28 (1978), pp. 232-240; Stanislao Loffreda, "Alcune osservazioni sulla ceramica di Magdala," in *Studia Hierosolymitana*, I, pp. 338-354; "Gamla: The Masada of the North," in BAR 5.1 (Jan/Feb 1979), pp. 12-19; "The Fall of Gamla," in BAR 5.1 (Jan/Feb 1979), pp. 20-27; S. Gutman, "The Synagogue at Gamla," in *Synagogues Revealed*, pp. 30-34; Z. Ma'oz, "The Synagogue of Gamla and the Typology of Second-Temple Synagogues," in *Synagogues Revealed*, pp. 35-41; Orna Cohen, "The Lifting Operation of the Kinneret Boat, and Some Aspects of the Conservation," in BAIAS 6 (1986-1987), pp. 34f.; Shelley Wachsmann, "The Excavation of the Kinneret Boat," in BAIAS 6 (1986-1987), pp. 50-52; and "The Galilee Boat, 2,000-Year-Old Hull Recovered Intact," in BAR 14.5 (Sept/Oct 1988), pp. 18-33; Mendel Nun, *Ancient Anchorages and Harbours around the Sea of Galilee* (Kibbutz Ein Gev: Kinnereth Sailing Co., 1988). Photograph: Corbo in LA 24 (1974), p. 21, fig. 21, courtesy Studium Biblicum Franciscanum, Jerusalem.

75. The Plain of Gennesaret

FROM THE HILLS near Magdala northward along the lake shore to the hilly promontory on which are the ruins known as Khirbet el-Minyeh, which is a distance of about three miles, and extending inland about a mile and a quarter, is a pleasant and fertile plain. After Vespasian and Titus took Tarichea or Magdala, as noted above No. 73, they prepared rafts to pursue fugitives who had sailed out into the lake for refuge (*War* III 10, 6 §505), and at this point Josephus interrupts his narrative of the warlike events to give some account of the lake

and of the land immediately adjacent to it. The lake, which he calls Gennesar (cf. No. 69), takes its name, he says (*War* III 10, 7 §506), from the adjacent territory, and he describes that territory as follows (*War* III 10, 8 §§516-521):

> Skirting the lake of Gennesar, and also bearing that name, lies a region whose natural properties and beauty are very remarkable. There is not a plant which its fertile soil refuses to produce, and its cultivators in fact grow every species; the air is so well-tempered that it suits the most opposite varieties. The walnut, a tree which delights in the most wintry climate, here grows luxuriantly, beside palm trees, which thrive on heat, and figs and olives, which require a milder atmosphere. One might say that nature had taken pride in thus assembling, by a *tour de force*, the most discordant species in a single spot, and that, by a happy rivalry, each of the seasons wished to claim this region for her own.

After some additional details, he says that this region extends along the border of the lake for a length of thirty stadia and inland to a depth of twenty. These are approximately the dimensions of the plain we have just delimited, and there is no doubt that this is the region that Josephus is describing. Thus we learn that the name of the plain was Gennesar, or Gennesaret as it is found in the Gospels (Mt 14:34, etc.). The photograph shows the Plain of Gennesaret in a view from the north. Toward the right in the distance is the mouth of Wadi el-Hamam, with the heights of Arbela above (cf. No. 73) and, against the horizon, the Horns of Hattin (cf. No. 71).

Photograph: The Matson Photo Service, Alhambra, Calif.

75. The Plain of Gennesaret

76. The Sea of Galilee from the Plain of Gennesaret

76. The Sea of Galilee from the Plain of Gennesaret

AFTER THE FEEDING of the five thousand the disciples of Jesus were to go by boat "to the other side [of the Sea of Galilee]" (Mt 14:22), or "to the other side, to Bethsaida" (Mk 6:45). Bethsaida was most probably at Khirbet el-'Araj at the northern end of the Sea of Galilee and across the Jordan to the east (No. 104). Considering Bethsaida to be thus on the eastern side of the lake, if the disciples were to take boat "to the other side, to Bethsaida," their starting point (and the feeding of the five thousand) must have been somewhere on the western side of the lake (Sherman E. Johnson in IB VII, p. 432). When they were out on the lake they were caught in a storm that lasted from evening until the fourth watch of the night (between 3 and 6 A.M.), and in this storm "the wind was against them" (Mt 14:24; Mk 6:48), i.e., it must have been from the north or northeast. This fact together with the natural current of the Jordan River flowing through the lake from north to south can account for the fact that they were apparently driven back to the south and southwest and landed at Gennesaret or Gennesar (Mt 14:34; Mk 6:53, both spellings being found in the various manuscripts). Thus understood, these references would place the locale of the feeding of the five thousand in the narratives of Matthew and Mark on the west side of the lake and probably somewhere in the vicinity of the Plain of Gennesaret. Likewise in what may be considered a variant parallel, namely, the feeding of the four thousand, the terminal voyage ends at Magadan (Mt 15:39) or Dalmanutha (Mk 8:10), both names probably meaning Magdala (cf. above No. 73, and note that in both cases Magdala is a variant reading in some manuscripts), at the south edge of the same plain, and the same understanding of the probable circumstances can prevail. On the other hand, there is other evidence that points to the east side of the lake for the feeding of the four thousand or even of the five thousand (see below No. 105). At any rate, a place for the feeding of the five thousand on the western shore and in the general vicinity of the Plain of Gennesaret is what is found in the oldest tradition attested by the earliest pilgrims, namely, a location at et-Tabgha, as will be seen in the record of Aetheria (No. 77). This photograph is a view of the Sea of Galilee from the Plain of Gennesaret.

Photograph: JF.

77. Plan of the Church of the Multiplication of the Loaves and Fishes at Tabgha

AT THE NORTHERN edge of the Plain of Gennesaret is the hilly promontory already referred to (No. 55) on which are the ruins called Khirbet el-Minyeh. This is a place visited by Saladin in 1187 and mentioned then under the Arabic name *minyeh*. Excavations begun here in 1932 by A. E. Mader uncovered an Arab palace of the seventh or eighth century, built in a square, with round towers at the corners, and a mosque on the southeastern side with mihrab indicating the direction of prayer toward Mecca. Three hundred yards to the north is a mound which slopes steeply to the lake shore and is known in Arabic as Tell el-'Oreimeh. In 1929 A. Jirku found Late Bronze and Iron II pottery on the tell, and soundings in 1932 by A. E. Mader and R. Köppel confirmed the existence of an important city that flourished notably in the Late Bronze Age. Actual excavation was conducted in 1939 by the Görres Society in cooperation with the German Archaeological Institute in Cairo, and in 1982 and following by the Deutsche Forschungsgemeinschaft, and the history of the city was explored down into the Iron Age. This was probably the city of Kinneret (Kinnereth, Chinnereth, Chinneroth) (Dalman, *Sacred Sites*, p. 130), which is mentioned in a list of Thutmose III (ANET p. 242) and in the OT (Dt 3:17; Jos 11:2; 19:35), and which gave its name to the lake when it was called the Sea of Chinnereth (Num 34:11, etc.; cf. above No. 69). In the Hellenistic period a new city named Gennesaret was established in the plain to the south, and it was from this city that both the plain and the sea took the name of Gennesaret (No. 75).

Before a way was blasted along the shore by Tell el-'Oreimeh, it was not possible to pass on that side and the main road went through a hollow on the western side and was dominated by this mount. This road was the ancient Way of the Sea (דרן הים) mentioned by Is 9:1 (Heb 8:23) as passing through the land of Zebulun and of Naphtali, i.e, through Galilee of the nations (cf. above no. 69): it came from Mesopotamia by way of Damascus, crossed the Jordan, came down through Hazor and on past Capernaum, Seven Springs, and Chinnereth to Magdala, from where it went through Wadi el-Haman (cf. No. 73) and across the Plain of Esdraelon to the pass at Megiddo, then to the coast of the Mediterranean and down this to Egypt. This route, with its branches, was an international highway of immemorial usage, undoubtedly thronged in the time of Jesus, and was the famous Via Maris of the Middle Ages.

Somewhat more than half a mile farther northward along the lake shore from Tell el-'Oreimeh one comes to et-Tabgha, an Arabic corruption of the Greek name Heptapegon (Ἑπτάπηγον [χωρίον]), or place of the Seven Springs. Here there are indeed copious springs in a little plain built up by the silt from Wadi ed-Jamus, which descends to the lake at this point. Josephus probably considered this small plain to be a part of the larger Plain of Gennesaret and, in fact, the spring waters were

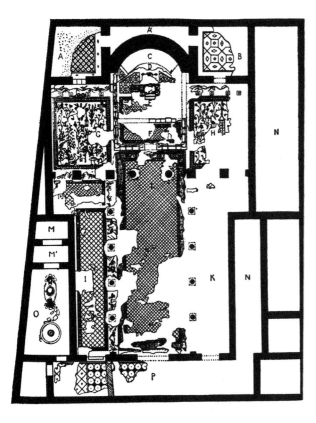

77. Plan of the Church of the Multiplication of the Loaves and Fishes at Tabgha

led around to the vicinity of Khirbet Minyeh by channels. At any rate in his description of the district of Gennesar, Josephus says (*War* III 10, 8 §519) that "the country is watered by a highly fertilizing spring, called by the inhabitants Capharnaum (Καφαρναούμ)," which can hardly be other than one of the chief springs at Heptapegon. The fact that the spring was named after Capernaum is not surprising for the latter was almost certainly at Tell Hum (cf. below No. 87), only a mile and one-quarter farther along the lake shore. The powerful spring was imagined by some, Josephus adds, to be a branch of the Nile; this belief was encouraged by the fact that it produced a fish resembling the *coracin* found in the lake of Alexandria.

Since Capernaum was an important center of the Galilean ministry of Jesus (Mt 4:13, etc.), the nearby plain of the Seven Springs surely also figured in his work, and in fact tradition associated several Gospel events in particular with this region. The pilgrim Aetheria (381-384), as quoted by Peter the Deacon, speaks of the Sea of Tiberias, of Tiberias, and of Capernaum, and then gives this description of the area of the Seven Springs (Geyer p. 113; CCSL CLXXV, p. 99; WET pp. 196, 200):

Not far from there [i.e., from Capernaum] are stone steps (*gradus lapidei*) on which the Lord stood. In the same place by the sea is a grassy field which has sufficient hay and many palm trees and nearby seven springs (*septem fontes*), each of which pours out abundant water, and in this field the Lord fed the people with five loaves and two fishes. Indeed the stone on which the Lord put the bread has been made into an altar, and from this stone those who come now break off pieces for their healing and it benefits all. Near the walls of this church (*ecclesia*) passes the public road where the apostle Matthew had his tax office (*theloneum* = τελώνιον). In the mountain which is nearby is a cave to which the Savior ascended and spoke the Beatitudes. On the other hand, not far from there is the synagogue which the Savior cursed.

The traditional localizations of Gospel events attested in the foregoing passage are to be recognized as the following: (1) the "stone steps on which the Lord stood"—the place where Jesus "stood" on the beach in the resurrection appearance at the Sea of Galilee (Jn 21:4); (2) the grassy field where "the Lord fed the people with five loaves and two fishes"—the feeding of the five thousand (Mt 14:13-21; Mk 6:30-44; Lk 9:10-17; Jn 6:1-13); (3) the "public road where the apostle Matthew had his tax office"—the call of Matthew (Mt 9:9; Mk 2:14; Lk 5:27); (4) the mountain and the cave where the Savior "spoke the Beatitudes"—the "mountain" of the Sermon on the Mount (Mt 5:1); and "the synagogue which the Savior cursed"—in the city of Chorazin (Mt 11:21).

In 1886 Tabgha was acquired by the German (Catholic) Holy Land Association (*Deutscher Verein vom heiligen Lande*) and is held by the Benedictine Societè di Colonia and the Franciscan Custody of the Holy Land in western and eastern zones respectively, these zones having been finally delimited in 1933. In the whole area archeological exploration has uncovered the ruins of three ancient edifices plainly intended to commemorate three of the events in the passage from Aetheria, and now known as the Church of the Multiplication of the Loaves and Fishes, the Chapel of the Beatitudes, and the Chapel of the Primacy of St. Peter. Although Aetheria only explicitly mentions a church (*ecclesia*) at the site of the first event, her knowledge of the sites of the other two events too probably means that they were also already marked by commemorative buildings, i.e., all three were already so marked by her time in the latter part of the fourth century.

Turning first to the remembrance of the feeding of the five thousand, the appropriateness of this locale to various indications in the Gospel records was established in survey and excavation in the Tabgha area in 1968 by Bellarmino Bagatti and Stanislao Loffreda. In general the area is marked not only by the springs already described, but also by outcrops of black basalt and of limestone rock, and is also notable for very good fishing offshore. There are several ruined water towers, which were built of basalt blocks and used to raise the water to flow into irrigation channels and to drive water mills; curiously they have been named *Hammam Ayyub* (Job's Bath), *Tannur Ayyub* (Job's Kiln), and *Birket Ali ed-Daher* (Ali Daher Pool). It was earlier supposed, therefore, that in the time of Jesus Tabgha was a cultivated area and a center of industry for Capernaum. Now, however, it was found that in the early second century (as shown by pottery and a coin from Trajan's time dated in A.D. 108/109) there was an extensive stone quarry here rather than any agriculture or village, that all the masonry constructions are later than Gospel times, that the water towers were only built in the fourth century A.D., and that the water mills only go back to Turkish times. Accordingly, in Gospel times Tabgha was a secluded, unused area, not suited for farming, and not the site of a village, and as such it corresponds well with topographical details in the Gospels. The place was solitary and appropriate for rest (Mk 6:31—"Come away by yourselves to a lonely place [ἔρημον τόπον] and rest a while"). It was close to the lake shore (Mk 6:32—"they went away in the boat to a lonely place by themselves"). There were hills close by (Jn 6:3, 15). While Tabgha was itself secluded, it was close enough to farms and villages that people could run there on foot from the villages and get there before Jesus, coming by boat (Mk 6:33), and the disciples could suggest going to farms and villages round about to buy food (Mk 6:36).

As for the discovery and exploration of the church built in this place to commemorate the feeding of the five thousand, a floor mosaic with loaves and fishes was found by Zepherin Biever at the end of the nineteenth century near the Birket Ali ed-Daher water tower. The site was investigated further by Paul Karge in 1911; then in 1932 excavations were conducted on behalf of the German Catholic Görres Gesellschaft by Andreas E. Mader and Alfons M. Schneider and published by Schneider in German in 1934 and in English translation in 1937 under the title *The Church of the Multiplying of the Loaves and Fishes.*

As brought to light in 1932, the outer walls of the whole complex (Schneider plan I facing p. 80) are in the form of an irregular rectangle (strictly speaking, a trapezoid), oriented to the east, with the north wall at somewhat of an angle, evidently because of an ancient road running close by. In exterior measurements the entire complex is 58 meters long and 24.3 meters wide at the eastern end and 33 meters wide at the western end. The atrium at the western end (not shown in the present plan) is 23 by 13 meters with hospice or other rooms on its west and south sides, such rooms continuing also on either side of the narthex and basilica proper. The narthex (P in the present plan) is 19 by 3.3 meters. The basilica proper (33 meters long) is divided by two rows of

five columns each into nave (L) and two side aisles (I and K) and is crossed by a rectangular transept with a row of columns running across the hall. The enclosed curving apse is 3.5 meters deep (C).

Immediately in front of the apse was the mosaic of the loaves and fishes (D) and in front of the mosaic a rough block of limestone (E) one meter long, over which was once an altar table. Square cavities in the floor at four corners around the stone show the placement of the four small columns that supported the altar; a cavity in the stone shows that a metal cross was once fixed to it (for the relation of the stone and the marks for the altar table to the mosaic, see Schneider pp. 14f., illus. 2, and p. 22, illus. 2 c). Plainly this was a sacred stone, serving in this position as the focus of the church.

A. Jirku, "Durch Palästina und Syrien," in ZDPV 53 (1930), p. 148; A. E. Mader, "Die Ausgrabung eines römischen Kastells auf Chirbet el-Minje an der Via Maris bei et-Tābgha am See Gennesareth," in JPOS 13 (1933), pp. 209-220; Volkmar Fritz, "Kinneret und Ginnosar, Voruntersuchung für eine Ausgrabung auf dem Tell el-'Orēme am See Genezareth," in ZDPV 94 (1978), pp. 32-45; and "Kinneret: A Biblical City on the Sea of Galilee," in *Archaeology* 40.4 (July/Aug 1987), pp. 42-49; Alfons M. Schneider, *The Church of the Multiplying of the Loaves and Fishes at Tabgha on the Lake of Gennesaret and Its Mosaics.* ed. A. A. Gordon, trans. Ernest Graf (London: Alexander Ouseley, Ltd., 1937); Stanislao Loffreda, "The First Season of Excavations at Tabgha (near Capharnaum)," in LA 18 (1968), pp. 238-243; and in "The Rock of the Primacy at Tabgha," in *New Memoirs of Saint Peter by the Sea of Galilee* (Jerusalem: Franciscan Printing Press, n.d.), pp. 43-60; and *Scavi di et-Tabgha.* PSBFCMI 7 (Jerusalem: Franciscan Printing Press, 1970); Ovadiah, *Corpus,* pp. 56-59, no. 46; Bargil Pixner, "The Miracle Church at Tabgha on the Sea of Galilee," in BA 48 (1985), pp. 196-206. For the international coastal highway from Damascus to Egypt, see Barry J. Beitzel in BR 4.5 (Oct 1988), pp. 40f. Plan: Loffreda, *Scavi di et-Tabgha,* p. 39, fig. 10, courtesy Studium Biblicum Franciscanum, Jerusalem.

78. Mosaic of Loaves and Fishes in the Church of the Multiplication of the Loaves and Fishes

THE ALREADY MENTIONED (No. 77) mosaic of the loaves and fishes shows a basket in which four loaves of bread, each marked with a cross, are visible, and on either side a fish. Farther out on either side is also a diamond-shaped mark. While loaves and fishes are often shown in early Christian art, and may be understood variously in connection with the eucharist and/or the heavenly meal, here at Tabgha there is little doubt that it is the miracle of the feeding of the five thousand that is specifically in view, and on the assumption that a fifth loaf of bread is deeper down in the basket the Gospel representation of five loaves and two fishes is followed exactly.

Photograph: JF.

78. Mosaic of Loaves and Fishes in the Church of the Multiplication of the Loaves and Fishes

79. Mosaic of Waterfowl and Marsh Plants in the Church of the Multiplication of the Loaves and Fishes

79. Mosaic of Waterfowl and Marsh Plants in the Church of the Multiplication of the Loaves and Fishes

IN ADDITION to the mosaic of the loaves and fishes (No. 78), the entire floor of the basilica (some 500 square meters) was originally covered with mosaics, and about half has been preserved and was the object of works of restoration by Bernhard Gauer in 1936 and by Dodo Joseph Shenhav in 1970 and thereafter (in the latter case missing portions were also reconstructed and plainly marked as such). On the basis of the average size of the surviving cubes, it is estimated that the whole work originally contained seven million cubes (Gauer in JPOS 18 [1938], p. 238).

The main surviving sections are in the nave (plan No. 77, L) and northern side aisle (I), with geometric and other patterns, and in the northern and southern arms of the transept (G and H), with fauna and flora. The latter are the most remarkable. Beautifully executed in white and black, in violet, red, brown, and yellow, they represent the landscape at the lake, with an abundance of marsh plants and waterfowl. Among lotus, papyrus, oleander, and a thistlelike shrub, we see the duck, dove, heron, goose, cormorant, flamingo, and water snake. Also a few architectural features are included: in the north transept, a tower with a pyramidal top which may be a grave monument like the Tomb of Zechariah (No. 267) in the Kidron valley; a city gate with two towers; and a pavilion; and in the south transept, a tower divided into stories marked with the Greek letters vau, zeta, eta, theta, and iota, corresponding to the numbers 6, 7, 8, 9, and 10, probably a device like a Nilometer to measure the height of the water in the lake.

While the lotus and the Nilometer-like tower can reflect direct or indirect Egyptian influence, all the other plants are native to Galilee and all the birds spend at least part of the year near the lake (Shenhav, in BAR 10.3 [May/June 1984], p. 28). Of the work and the unknown master artist the original excavator wrote: "The well-planned composition, the loving observation of nature and the elegance of the execution . . . give the impression of having been especially conceived and executed for the church by one who was an expert in his craft. . . . No motif is copied twice, each plant and each animal is distinctive and has its own movement and life. With how much love the artist draws the whole of this gaily-coloured flock of birds. . . . Consider . . . the leaf on which a bird stands preening itself. The beautiful curve of its contour and the grace with which it sits on its stem betray a sensitive man endowed with the full knowledge of the aesthetic charm and the stirring beauty of the things of this world. . . . We shall never know either his name or his origin, but in an out-of-the-way corner of the earth we possess a work of his hands which represents

a last flicker of the fast disappearing yet immortal beauty of antiquity" (Schneider pp. 78f.).

In the present photograph we are looking at a small portion of the lower right-hand corner of the mosaic in the north transept (5.5 by 6.5 meters, with a border of lotus blossoms). In this portion we see a heron dipping its beak into a lotus bud and a duck resting upon a lotus flower.

Bernhard Gauer, "Werkbericht über die Instandsetzung der Boden-Mosaiken von 'Heptapegon' (Basilika der Brotvermehrung am See Tiberias)," in JPOS 18 (1938), pp. 233-253; Dodo Joseph Shenhav, "Loaves and Fishes Mosaic Near Sea of Galilee Restored," in BAR 10.3 (May/June 1984), pp. 22-31. Photograph: JF.

80. Mosaic Inscription Beside the Mosaic of the Loaves and Fishes

AS TO THE DATE of the basilica with its mosaic floor, its excavators put its foundation at the end of the fourth century (Schneider p. 80); but it is now generally assigned to the fifth century (e.g., Loffreda, Scavi di et-Tabgha, pp. 40, 42).

To judge from the slightly larger size of its stones the mosaic of the loaves and fishes (No. 78) was probably added somewhat after the original mosaic pavement, and so too were two other nearby mosaic panels containing inscriptions (Schneider p. 55). One inscription is above the mosaic of the left transept; with the abbreviations filled out it reads:

Τῷ] ἁγ (ίῳ) τώπῳ
Μνήσθ(ητ)ι κ(ύρι)ε Σαύρου

In this holy place
Lord remember Sauros

Here we may possibly have the name of the artist himself who made the mosaic of the loaves and fishes and wrote the two inscriptions.

The second inscription (shown here) is immediately adjacent to the loaves and fishes mosaic (for the relationship, see Schneider p. 15, illus. 2); it is transcribed and translated thus:

+ Ὑπὲρ μνήμης [καὶ ἀναπαύσεω]ς τοῦ πρ(οσ)ενένκα[ν-
τ(ος) ὁσ(ίου) πατρ Μ τ

+ To the memory and the repose of the sponsor, the
holy Patriarch . . .

Of the name of the patriarch in the damaged end of the text the initial letter "M" and, after space for two missing letters, the letter "t" survive. Of patriarchs of the

80. Mosaic Inscription Beside the Mosaic of the Loaves and Fishes

Jerusalem church from the fifth to the seventh century the names of three begin with "M"—namely, Martyrios (478-486), Makarios (565-574), and Modestus (631-634)—and of these it is the name of Martyrios that fits with the requirements of the letters "M" and "t" and the space between. Assuming that the word translated "sponsor" in line 3 is from the verb προσενέγκειν, "to found" or "to dedicate," we may believe that we have here the name of the donor of the mosaic floor and possibly of the founder of the fifth-century church itself. Martyrios is otherwise known as the founder of the monastery called by his name east of Bethany, and as a young man he lived in Egypt. It is a reasonable surmise that he might have brought a mosaicist from Egypt to make the mosaic floor, which would account for Egyptian influence in the work (Pixner in BA 48 [1985], p. 202).

Photograph: from Alfons M. Schneider, *The Church of the Multiplying of the Loaves and Fishes at Tabgha* (1937), p. 54, illus. 10.

81. The Modern Church of the Multiplication of the Loaves and Fishes

IN 1936, UNDER FATHER TUPPER as the guardian of the excavated church, Bernhard Gauer was working on restoration of the mosaics (No. 79) and found an earlier chapel underneath (Schneider p. 10 n. 2; Gauer pp. 244f.). This was a rectangular hall with a projecting apse, but a much smaller building than the later basilica, being only 17.3 meters in length including the apse, and

8 meters in width. Compared with the direct eastward orientation of the basilica above, the chapel was inclined 28° to the south. Here also the focus of the chapel was on a large piece of limestone in front of the apse, a piece from which stone was probably taken and moved a little way away to lie under the altar of the later church (Schneider pp. 21f. and illus. 2; Gauer p. 249).

As to the date of this lower chapel, which was the first Church of the Multiplication of the Loaves and Fishes, it was obviously earlier than the fifth-century larger basilica above, and has thus been generally assigned to the fourth century (e.g., Loffreda, *Scavi di et-Tabgha*, p. 40). If the date was around the middle of the century, this would be the church mentioned by Aetheria (No. 77), and it could have been one of the Galilean churches built around that time by the Judeo-Christian Count Joseph of Tiberias (Schneider p. 80; Kroll p. 246; cf. above No. 45). In connection with the work of Count Joseph there is mention of Capernaum (No. 45), but at Capernaum Aetheria says that the original walls of St. Peter's house were still standing "just as they were" until her time (381-384) (No. 99), so a whole new church had not yet been built there; therefore it could be that what Joseph did was to build here at Tabgha, which was not far from Capernaum, rather than in Capernaum proper (Pixner in BA 48 [1985], p. 198). In the work of Paul Karge at the site in 1911 there was found among the paving stones at the western entrance of the atrium of the church a large basalt block (since lost), on which was a badly worn inscription containing the name of a certain

81. The Modern Church of the
Multiplication of the Loaves
and Fishes

"Josepos" (Ἰώσηπος); whether the text is of any connection with Joseph of Tiberias seems doubtful, for it is of funerary character and says of Josepos or of some other person, "he lived 24 years" (ἔζησεν ἔτη κδ′) (Schneider p. 33).

At any rate the description by Aetheria (No. 77) of the location by the public road of the church at Seven Springs, in which was the stone, made into an altar, on which the Lord placed the bread in the feeding of the multitude, is in exact agreement with the finds in the excavations and makes it most probable that the first Church of the Multiplication was there in existence in her time (381-384). It is true that in soundings in 1970 Stanislao Loffreda found in the ruins in the area marked G on the plan (No. 77) a coin of the emperor Honorius, which was minted during the years 395-408, and therefore concluded that the first church was built after 395 (in LA 20 [1970], pp. 378-380). In view of uncertainties otherwise encountered (Nos. 85, 89) with numismatic evidence, this can hardly outweigh the evidence of Aetheria, which still shows more convincingly that the first church was known already in her time, i.e., in the last decades of the fourth century (Kroll p. 443 n. 199).

In A.D. 419 a relatively severe and well-attested earthquake damaged many towns and villages in Palestine (IEJ 1 [1950-51], p. 225; BASOR 260 [1985], pp. 42f.) and may have caused the destruction of this first church and led to the building later in the fifth century of the larger church with the mosaic floor.

In turn the later church was probably very damaged in the earthquake of A.D. 551, which was recorded in the *Chronographia* of Theophanes as "great and terrible" (σεισμὸς μέγας καὶ φοβερός) and affecting all of Palestine and surrounding countries (CSHB 32, p. 352). Restoration was made afterward (Schneider p. 80), then final ruin and abandonment came with the Persian (614) and Arab (638) invasions. When Arculf traveled along the west shore of the Sea of Galilee in 670 he visited the grassy level plain where the Savior fed the five thousand with the five loaves and two fishes, but saw no building, only some columns of stone lying at the edge of the spring from which, it was said, the people drank on that day when they were hungry and the Lord revived them with such a refection (Geyer p. 273; LPPTS III-A, pp. 43f.; CCSL CLXXV, p. 218; WJP p. 108).

Only with the rediscovery of the mosaic of the loaves and fishes and with the subsequent excavations and restorations, as narrated above, did the two successive Churches of the Multiplication of the Loaves and Fishes come to light again. In 1936, following the reconditioning of the mosaics by Bernard Gauer, the whole site was roofed over and enclosed in a simple hall (Schneider p. 10 n. 2); and in 1956 two wings were added to house the Benedictine monastery. In the late 1970s it was decided to build a new church in the same style and on the same ground plan as the Byzantine church of the fifth century. Built of white limestone, the walls rest upon the fifth-century foundations, and the new columns stand in the places of the originals, making again a basilica with nave, side aisles, and transept. Panels of glass allow sight of the foundation wall of the fourth-century church. Only the mosaic of the loaves and fishes (No. 78) was moved from its original position behind the altar to a place in front of the altar, but the sacred stone, seen by the pilgrim Aetheria, is under the altar as before. The new church—the third Church of the Multiplication of the Loaves and Fishes—was completed and dedicated in 1982 and is shown, across the atrium, in the present photograph.

Photograph: JF.

82. Plan of the Chapel and the Monastery of the Beatitudes at Tabgha

ACCORDING TO AETHERIA (No. 77) a public road passed close by the walls of the church that marked the place of the feeding of the five thousand, and in the mountain nearby there was a cave to which Jesus went up when he spoke the Beatitudes, i.e., when he gave the Sermon on the Mount. The site indicated is evidently that which now belongs to the Franciscans, located across the modern road that goes on to Capernaum, on the lower slope of the hill, 300 meters north of the Church of the Multiplication of the Loaves and Fishes. Excavation was conducted at the site in 1935 by Bellarmino Bagatti.

The ruins of a small chapel were uncovered, which the excavator dates to the fourth century. The building is a rectangle, with an atrium or narthex (4.5 by 2.5 meters)

and a main hall (4.4 meters in width, 9.25 meters in length) including an apse (1.75 meters in depth), which projects to the east and is partly hewn from the rock and partly constructed. A small side chapel is also in the rock on the north side of the hall. A colored mosaic floor with geometric and floral patterns was probably added in the fifth century, remnants of which were found in the nave in front of the apse and were taken to Capernaum. Underneath the nave and somewhat in front of the apse is a natural cave (4.5 meters in length, 2.2 meters in width, and 3.5 meters in depth) that opens to the south, and this could well be the cave to which Aetheria refers. On the south and west of the chapel are the remains of a courtyard built out on the slope, as well as remains of buildings, probably the ruins of a monastery. Later in the Byzantine period the chapel was damaged, probably by earthquake or by the Persians (614) and the Arabs (638), then underwent some restoration, until finally in the tenth century all was abandoned.

QDAP 5 (1936), p. 194; B. Bagatti, "La Cappella sul Monte delle Beatitudini: Scavo della Custodia di Terra Santa," in RAC 14 (1937), pp. 43-91; Kopp 1963, p. 206 n. 8; Loffreda, *Scavi di et-Tabgha*, pp. 42f.; Ovadiah, *Corpus*, pp. 59f.; Bagatti, *Antichi Villaggi*, pp. 81-93; Murphy-O'Connor pp. 204f.; Pearlman and Yannai pp. 67f. Plan: Loffreda, *Scavi di et-Tabgha*, p. 43, fig. 12, courtesy Studium Biblicum Franciscanum, Jerusalem.

83. The Modern Church of the Beatitudes

THE HIGHER HILL to the northeast of the Seven Springs and the early Chapel of the Beatitudes (No. 82) is now known as the Mount of the Beatitudes, and near the summit is the modern Church of the Beatitudes, built by the Franciscans in 1938, with A. Barluzzi as the architect. The building is octagonal in commemoration of the eight Beatitudes (Mt 5:3-10), with a great dome above and a gallery all around from which to view the lake and most of the places of Jesus' Galilean ministry.

Photograph: JF.

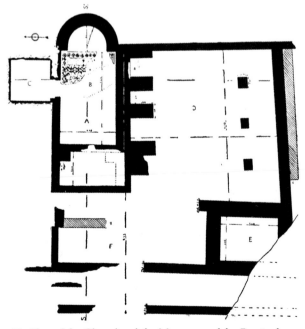

82. Plan of the Chapel and the Monastery of the Beatitudes at Tabgha

83. The Modern Church of the Beatitudes

84. Plan of the Chapel of the Primacy of St. Peter at Tabgha

IT WAS NOTED above (No. 77) that Aetheria's mention of stone steps "on which the Lord stood" is evidently a reference to a traditionally accepted place at Seven Springs where Jesus "stood" (Jn 21:4) on the beach in the resurrection appearance at the Sea of Galilee, and it will be remembered that in the entire account (Jn 21:4-19) Jesus invited the disciples to have breakfast and gave them bread and fish to eat, then afterward engaged in the conversation with Peter that climaxed with the commission to Peter to "feed my sheep." It is plainly this traditional place that is now marked by the small Franciscan chapel (built in 1933) at Tabgha, usually known either as the Chapel of the Table of the Lord in memory of the breakfast meal to which the risen Lord invited the disciples, or as the Chapel of the Primacy of

St. Peter in memory of the commission that conveyed leadership to Peter. In the chapel the latter theme is emphasized in the words of the commission in Latin in an arch over the altar: *Pasce Oves Meas.*

The site of the chapel is 180 meters south of the Church of the Multiplication of the Loaves and Fishes, on a rocky terrace that falls off immediately on the east and south to the shore of the lake. Excavation was conducted on the site in 1968 as a part of the survey of the Tabgha area at that time by Bagatti and Loffreda (No. 77).

Signs of work in the rock indicate that this was a place where limestone was quarried. In a cutting in the rock on the north side of the chapel (near the rock mass H on the plan) a coin of the emperor Trajan, dating to the year 108/109, was found, and this and the Roman pottery that was also found suggest that the quarry was in use from the end of the first century down into the fourth

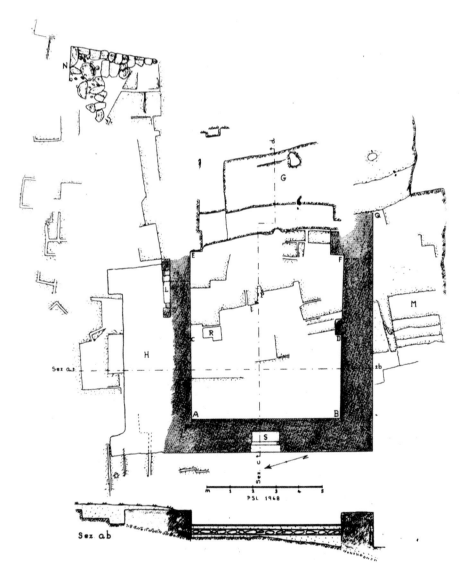

84. Plan of the Chapel of the Primacy of St. Peter at Tabgha

century. At the latter time quarrying work was apparently terminated abruptly, for two rectangular stone blocks were found (near the letter F on the Plan) that had been cut along their sides but not removed from their bed, and in a crack near the stones two iron wedges were still in place. Presumably this was when the Christians were able to move in and build their first chapel, probably at about the same time that the first Church of the Multiplication of the Loaves and Fishes (No. 81) and the Chapel of the Beatitudes (No. 82) were built. That a former quarry site was chosen must have been because of a long-held tradition that this was indeed a place of sacred remembrance.

Of the first evidently very small chapel at this place, attributed thus to the middle or latter part of the fourth century, only a few remains were found, some scattered walls, pieces of white plaster, and pottery (chiefly in the area marked R on the plan). At a date probably in the first half of the fifth century a larger chapel was built, the walls of which the excavators uncovered at the base of the north, south, and west walls of the present chapel. This is the edifice outlined, on the basis of the excavations, in the present plan (Loffreda, *Scavi di et-Tabgha*, p. 54, fig. 17), in substantial agreement with a plan made already some thirty years before by Bagatti (ibid., p. 41, fig. 11). As the walls exist, the internal dimensions are 6.45 meters along the west wall (A-B), and 6.95 meters along the north (A-E) and south (B-F) walls. The east wall and the apse—if there was an apse—are no longer traceable, but the walls that are traceable provided the foundations for all the subsequent buildings on the spot.

Like the Church of the Multiplication of the Loaves and Fishes and the Chapel of the Beatitudes, this chapel was probably destroyed too in the Persian invasion (614) and the Arab conquest (638). From some evidence on the site and from literary references, a third chapel was built at the end of the seventh or in the early eighth century, a fourth chapel existed in the twelfth century, and a fifth and last preceding chapel was built in the thirteenth century only to be destroyed by the Mamluk Sultan Baibars in 1263. The present chapel, built by the Franciscans in 1933 on the same site and according to the same plan, is therefore the sixth edifice to commemorate the traditional events at this place.

The exact place is immediately beside a flight of rock-cut steps, of which five are still to be seen (M on the plan) at the lakeside wall of the present chapel. The rock-cut steps are of indeterminate age, but they must be the "stone steps" (*gradus lapidei*) of which Aetheria speaks. At the top of the steps there is a mass of rock that extends through the wall of the present chapel and comes directly in front of the altar and apse, thus the present chapel and its predecessors were so aligned that

this rock mass has the place of honor and is the focus of the edifice. In the belief that the rock was where Jesus set forth the bread and fish for the disciples, this was known as the Table of the Lord (*mensa Domini*). Close by at the edge of the lake is a row of six heart-shaped flat stones (the typical shape of the base of two joined columns at the corner of a colonnade), and these belonged to the so-called Twelve Thrones (*dodici troni*) of the Apostles. The basis for the two names and the connection of the two is found in the Gospels: Lk 22:29-30, "as my Father appointed a kingdom for me, so do I appoint for you that you may eat and drink at my table in my kingdom, and sit on thrones judging the twelve tribes of Israel"; cf. Mt 19:28, ". . . sit on twelve thrones (δώδεκα θρόνους), judging the twelve tribes of Israel." Both names are found in the *Commemoratorium de casis Dei* (A.D. 808), in which there is mention first of a monastery called Heptapegon near the sea of Tiberias, where the Lord fed five thousand people with five loaves and two fishes, a monastery having ten monks, and then mention of a church named for the Twelve Thrones: "Likewise by the sea there is a church (*ecclesia*) which is called *duodec* [*im thronorum*, where the Lord was present with his disci]ples; here is the Table (*mensa*) where he sat with them; here are (only) one presbyter and two clerics (Tobler and Molinier pp. 303f.; Baldi p. 277, no. 405).

The remaining places that Aetheria mentions in connection with Seven Springs are the tax office of Matthew and the synagogue that the Savior cursed. The tax office is described by Aetheria as on a public road that passed near the walls of the church that commemorated the feeding of the multitude with five loaves and two fishes. The road was presumably the international highway described above (No. 77), and surely a likely place for such an office, and since Jesus came past Matthew's office when he went on from Capernaum (Mt 9:9) the location at Tabgha, not far from Capernaum (No. 87), is also entirely likely. The synagogue that the Savior cursed is said by Aetheria to be not far from Seven Springs and is doubtless the synagogue at Chorazin (No. 85).

Stanislao Loffreda, "The First Season of Excavations at Tabgha (near Capharnaum)," in LA 18 (1968), pp. 240-243; and *Scavi di et-Tabgha*, pp. 48-105; and in *New Memoirs of Saint Peter by the Sea of Galilee* (Jerusalem: Franciscan Printing Press, n.d.), pp. 61-70. In *Scavi di et-Tabgha* see p. 45, fig. 13, for the *mensa Domini*, and p. 66, fig. 22, for the *gradus lapidei* and the *dodici troni*. Plan: Loffreda, *Scavi di et-Tabgha*, p. 54, fig. 17, courtesy Studium Biblicum Franciscanum, Jerusalem.

85. Ruins of the Synagogue at Chorazin

IN THE WOE recorded in Mt 11:21-23 and Lk 10:13-15 Jesus linked two other cities with Capernaum, namely, Chorazin and Bethsaida. When Aetheria (381-384) was at Seven Springs (No. 77) she mentioned but apparently did not visit Chorazin. Her report, according to Peter the Deacon (Geyer p. 113; ccsl clxxv, p. 99; wet pp. 200f.) reads:

> Not far from there is the synagogue which the Savior cursed; for when the Savior passed by and interrogated the Jews who were working on it and said: "What are you doing?" they said: "Nothing." And the Lord said: "Therefore if it is nothing, that you are making, it will always be nothing." So it remains until today. For afterward, whenever the Jews wished to build, what they did in the day fell down at night, and always remained at the same height it was when it was cursed.

In the *Onomasticon* (ed. Klostermann, p. 174) Eusebius locates the place at two miles from Capernaum and describes it as abandoned and desolate (ἔϱημος). Chorazin (or Korazim) is almost certainly to be recognized at the site called Khirbet Karaze (or Kerazeh), which is some two miles up in the hills northwest of Tell Hum (Capernaum) and 900 feet above the Sea of Galilee. The Anglican bishop Pococke, who visited Palestine in 1738, made the identification (cf. William M. Thomson, *The Land and the Book* [New York: Harper, Popular

ed., 1908-1913], vol. 2, p. 421), although it was rejected by Edward Robinson (*Biblical Researches in Palestine*, II, pp. 346f.; cf. Abel's criticism of Robinson on this point in jbl 58 [1939], p. 370). Charles W. Wilson, who conducted the first excavations at Tell Hum in 1865-1866 (cf. No. 89), visited the site of Chorazin and described the main ruins as those of a synagogue built of very hard black basalt, with Corinthian capitals and other ornaments. His description was repeated, and some additional details given, by H. H. Kitchener in *The Survey of Western Palestine* (i, 1881, pp. 400-402). Then a detailed investigation was made (1905) by Kohl and Watzinger, and new excavations were conducted by Ze'ev Yeivin on behalf of the Israel Department of Antiquities between 1962 and 1965, with further excavation and some restoration from 1980 through 1986.

As explored in these excavations the main part of the town of Chorazin was on a flat plateau in the middle of a hill and in all extended over some fifteen acres. In the center and on the main road was the synagogue, facing south toward the lake and toward Jerusalem. Back of the synagogue, to the north, is a public building of considerable extent, and not far from this a ritual bath (*mikvah*) with a large cistern adjacent. East of the synagogue are two large domestic complexes, with a cobblestone court-

85. Ruins of the Synagogue at Chorazin

yard between them. To the west is a residential quarter, yet little explored, and to the south at least two olive oil presses give evidence of an industrial quarter.

Like the other buildings of the town, the synagogue is built of squared blocks of black basalt—the prevailing stone of the surrounding countryside—and is thus in striking contrast with the white limestone of the synagogue down at Capernaum. The basic basilical plan, however, is much the same as at Capernaum, but on a slightly smaller scale. The main hall is 65 feet long and 45 feet wide. Three rows of columns—originally twelve in number—outline a central nave and three aisles, one aisle on either side and one at the back, and in one corner some of the original benches still line the wall. A broad stairway led up to the southern façade, in which were the main central entrance and two side entryways. Inside, on either side of the main entrance, was a platform, presumably intended for the Torah on the one side and for the place of the reader on the other side. Many fragments of carved stonework associated with the synagogue were also found. One piece shows a head with some possibly radiate marks around it, variously identified as Medusa (the queen of the monster Gorgons in Greek mythology) or Helios the Sun, in either case presumably only a conventional decorative motif. Four other fragments may be parts of the lintels over the two side entryways of the synagogue, and they are carved in relief with several examples of the seven-armed *menorah*.

As to the date of the town of Chorazin, the Gospel references (Mt 11:21-23; Lk 10:13-15) attest to the existence of the village in the time of Jesus, but at the present point in reported excavation this village of the first century has not yet been found. The earliest evidence of settlement is in the highest part of town to the north, where an oil press is judged to date not later than the second century A.D.

As to the date of the Chorazin synagogue, the extant ruin was once thought to date from the first century A.D., but has since generally been attributed to the second-third century (N. Avigad in *Synagogues Revealed*, p. 42), perhaps most probably the third century (M. Avi-Yonah in QDAP 14 [1950], p. 55; Fischer in *Levant* 15 [1968], p. 155). The recent excavator (Yeivin in BAR 13.5 [Sept/Oct 1987], p. 35), however, places the initial construction of the synagogue at the end of the third century or the beginning of the fourth, thinks that it and the town were partially destroyed by earthquake in the second half of the fourth century, and that the town and the synagogue were rebuilt in the fifth century, but that the synagogue was no longer in use in the seventh century although the town continued to exist on into the Muslim period (seventh to ninth centuries).

In one archeological particular, it is found that the synagogue was paved with a stone floor in its original construction; when it was rebuilt in the fifth century this was replaced with a plaster floor; then at the end of the fifth century the plaster pavement was destroyed and its place filled with earth, and in the earth filling more than 2,000 coins were discovered (with which may be compared the large number of coins found in the Capernaum synagogue and the debate about the significance of those coins, cf. No. 89). In a published list of 71 identifiable types of the coins (of which many had a good number of examples), a few are from the third century, the majority are from the fourth century, some are from the fifth and sixth centuries, and two coins of Heraclius date to A.D. 612 (Kloetzli in LA 20 [1970], pp. 359-369). Loffreda (in *Synagogues Revealed*, p. 52) holds that the coins show that the synagogue was in use at least until the early seventh century, but Avi-Yonah finds two coins too slim evidence for secure dating (in *Synagogues Revealed*, p. 61). Yeivin (in BAR 13.5 [Sept/Oct 1987], p. 35), holding that the synagogue was no longer in use in the seventh century, suggests a possible explanation for the many coins to the effect that they were thrown here over the centuries by Christian and possibly Jewish pilgrims who visited the site even after its destruction, the Christians perhaps to witness in the ruin the fulfillment of the Gospel prediction of disaster.

With a slight revision in the above reconstructed history, if the synagogue were built in the third century and if the town and synagogue were destroyed in the first part of the fourth century (not in the second half of the century) this could accord with the statement of Eusebius in the *Onomasticon* (probably written in about A.D. 330, not at the end of the fourth century, as Yeivin says) that in his time Chorazin was abandoned and desolate. Further, if attempts at rebuilding were begun but without success already in the latter half of the fourth century this could accord with the legend in the report of Aetheria (A.D. 381-384) of unsuccessful attempts at rebuilding and of the continued state of ruin of the synagogue in her time.

The photograph shows the ruins of the synagogue and the rocky character of the surrounding countryside.

Wilson, *The Recovery of Jerusalem*, pp. 270f., and in *The Survey of Western Palestine*, Special Papers, p. 299; Kohl and Watzinger, *Antike Synagogen in Galilaea*, pp. 41-58; Sukenik, *Ancient Synagogues in Palestine and Greece*, pp. 21-24; Clemens Kopp, "Christian Sites around the Sea of Galilee: III. Chorazin," in *Dominican Studies* 3 (1950), pp. 275-284; Goodenough I, pp. 195-199; Godfrey Kloetzli, "Coins from Chorazin," in LA 20 (1970), pp. 359-369; Saller, *Second Catalogue*, pp. 54f., no. 64; Z. Yeivin in IEJ 12 (1962), pp. 152-153; and in RB 70 (1963), pp. 587-588 and pl. XXIV b; and in PEQ 1963, p. 3; and "Two Lintels with Menorah Reliefs from Chorazin," in *Synagogues Revealed*, pp. 162f.; and "Korazin: a Mishnaic City," in BAIAS 1982-83, pp. 46-48; and "Ancient Chorazin Comes Back to Life," in BAR 13.5 (Sept/Oct 1987), pp. 22-36. Photograph: courtesy École Biblique et Archéologique Française.

86. Seat in the Synagogue at Chorazin

PERHAPS THE MOST interesting single object from the Chorazin synagogue is the large stone seat, found in 1962 near the southern wall of the synagogue and placed in the Palestine Archaeological Museum in Jerusalem. It is 73 centimeters high and, at its maximum, as thick as it is high. On the seat back there is a rosette in a circle, and on the front an inscription in Aramaic in four lines, which is translated:

> Remembered be for good Judah (literally, Judan) ben
>   Ishmael
> who made this stoa
> and its staircase. As his reward may
> he have a share with the righteous.

Instead of "stoa" in this translation the underlying Aramaic word is now believed to mean a platform of some kind, while the "staircase" could better be simply steps. Thus the reference is to the platform or dais on which the chair rested, and to the steps that led up to the chair on its platform. This then was probably the seat occupied by the synagogue official, perhaps "the ruler of the synagogue" (ἀρχισυνάγωγος) of Mk 5:38, etc. (cf. also No. 130), who was the reader of the Torah in the synagogue services. As such the seat was probably the "Chair of Moses" (ἡ Μωυσέως καθέδρα) of Mt 23:2.

J. Ory, "An Inscription Newly Found in the Synagogue of Kerazeh," in PEFQS 1927, pp. 51-52; A. Marmorstein, "About the Inscription of Judah ben Ishmael," in PEFQS 1927, pp. 101-102; Sukenik, *Ancient Synagogues in Palestine and Greece*, pp. 57-61; A. Reifenberg, *Ancient Hebrew Arts* (New York: Schocken Books, 1950), p. 105; Z. Yeivin in BAR 13.5 (Sept/Oct 1987), pp. 32, 35. Photograph: courtesy École Biblique et Archéologique Française.

86. Seat in the Synagogue at Chorazin

87. The Sea of Galilee from Capernaum

A MILE AND a quarter farther along the lake shore from the Seven Springs, and some two miles short of the mouth of the Jordan River as it enters the lake, is the site known as Tell Hum. The location accords with the best indications for the site of Capernaum, the city which was so important a center of the Galilean ministry of Jesus. Mt 4:13 places Capernaum by the sea and in the territory of Zebulun and Naphtali. According to the frontiers of these two tribes as given in Jos 19, Naphtali was immediately west of the Sea of Galilee, and Zebulun was west of that. Josephus suffered an accident near the mouth of the Jordan and was carried to a village called variously in the manuscripts Κεφαρνωκόν or Κεφαρνωμόν (*Life* 72 §403), which is undoubtedly Capernaum. Under the circumstances he would be taken to the nearest place for adequate help, which corresponds with the location of Capernaum at Tell Hum. Likewise, as already noted (no. 71), Theodosius coming from the south passed through Tiberias, Magdala, and the Seven Springs, before reaching Capernaum, and this accords with the same location. The name Capernaum (Καφαρναούμ) is doubtless derived from the Hebrew כפר נחום , Kefar Nahum, meaning Village of Nahum (although which Nahum is meant remains uncertain). The name appears in this form in the Midrash (Midrash Rabbah, Ecclesiastes, I 8; VII 26 SMR VIII, pp. 29, 210) where Capernaum is particularly associated with the *minim*, i.e., "heretics," here and in many other occurrences probably meaning the Judeo-Christians. In one of these same passages (I 8 SMR VIII, p. 27) there is met upon the main street of Sepphoris a man named Jacob (since he is a disciple of Jesus he may be James the son of Alphaeus [Mk 3:18, etc.] or the Less [Mk 15:40]) of Kefar Sekaniah, and his village illustrates the same kind of name. If, then, in the course of time Kefar meaning "village" became Tell referring to the mound of a deserted city, and if Nahum was shortened to Hum, the name of Tell Hum would itself preserve in that form the name of Capernaum. The photograph looks across the Sea of Galilee from the site of Tell Hum, toward Wadi el-Hamam, Arbela, and the Horns of Hattin (cf. Nos. 71, 73).

F.-M. Abel, "Le nom de Capharnaüm," in JPOS 8 (1928), pp. 24-34. Photograph: JF.

88. Private Houses of Ancient Capernaum (*Insula* II)

AS FAR AS the archeological zones of ancient Capernaum are concerned, the western zone belongs to the Franciscan Custody of the Holy Land and the eastern zone belongs to the Greek Orthodox Church of Jerusa-

87. The Sea of Galilee from Capernaum

lem. In the western zone are the synagogue (Nos. 89ff.) and the octagonal church (Nos. 99f.), and between the two is a residential section of the ancient town. In the Franciscan excavations under the direction of Virgiliio Corbo in 1968 and thereafter, the earliest coins discovered are those of Antiochus III (223-187 B.C.) (Spijkerman, *Catalogo delle monete*, p. 26, no. 147) and of Antiochus IV Epiphanes (175-164 B.C.) (ibid., p. 43, no. 342), and the settlement of the town may be placed in about that time, say from the third century B.C. onward (Corbo, *Gli edifici*, p. 215). Likewise numismatic evidence indicates continuation of settlement until in the first half of the seventh century A.D., when this town together with its synagogue and octagonal church came to an end and was never rebuilt (ibid., p. 220; cf. Mt 11:23).

As for the residential area lying between the synagogue and the octagonal church, the excavations uncovered a group of private houses (*Insula* II in the excavation report) between two parallel streets running from east to west and with a broader street in the midst of the group. The houses are themselves arranged around courtyards in which were ovens and grinding stones. The walls are of basalt stones, for the most part held together with mud and pebbles, and the houses were probably of only one story, with stairways leading to flat roofs.

In the eastern zone at Capernaum excavations were conducted in 1978-1982 on behalf of the Israel Depart-

ment of Antiquities with the support of the Greek Orthodox Church of Jerusalem and with participation from several universities in the United States. Here numismatic and ceramic evidence indicated new settlement beginning at about the time the earlier town of the western zone came to its end, i.e., in the seventh century A.D., and continuing until final abandonment during the tenth century (Tzaferis in BA 46 [1983], pp. 198-204). In addition to houses and straight roads, the excavations brought to light a large public building and also a jetty and pier at the water's edge. Whereas the earlier Capernaum uncovered in the western zone was evidently almost entirely Jewish and Judeo-Christian, the later city in the eastern zone was apparently largely Christian, for the nearby synagogue was not rebuilt, and oil lamps and ceramic plates were found decorated with crosses. The octagonal church was also no longer used, but a new church dedicated to St. John the Theologian may have been built, for Epiphanius the Monk says that in his time (ninth century) "the house of [John] the Theologian" was to be seen in Capernaum (WJP p. 120).

Along with Byzantine Christianity, Islam was also represented in this later Capernaum, and it will be remembered that there was an Arab palace of the seventh or eighth century at Khirbet Minyeh not far away (No. 77). In the Capernaum excavations in the eastern zone in 1982, in a house of the early Arab period, which was originally a Byzantine house, a hoard of 218 *dinars* (the

88. Private Houses of Ancient Capernaum (*Insula* II)

chief gold coin of the Muslims in the seventh century and following) was found. The coins bear dates *Anno Hegirae* 77-126 (= A.D. 696/697-743/744) and according to these dates were minted under the Umayyad Caliph of Damascus, 'Abd al-Malik (A.D. 685-705), and his successors. The main inscriptions on the coins are quotations from the Qur'an (9.33; 112.1-3) and are similar in import to the longer Qur'anic inscriptions that the same caliph placed in the contemporary Dome of the Rock in Jerusalem (No. 185). From the point of view of numismatics the coins are of additional interest in that over one-third contain graffiti around or within the main inscriptions in the form of small single letters in Greek, Hebrew, and Arabic, as well as some geometrical signs and monograms. In contrast with the "microletters" cited above in the Table of Archeological and Historical Periods in Palestine, which were imprinted from the die when the coin was struck, these marks were scratched on afterward in the soft gold, but at least they attest the persistence of additional markings on coins. Their specific significance is not clear, but they presumably had some symbolic import (Tzaferis, *Excavation at Capernaum*, I, pp. 145ff. [John F. Wilson], 181-190 [Ariel Berman]; Vardaman telephone May 2, 4, 1990).

The present photograph of the house ruins of *Insula* II looks south from the synagogue and on across the site of the octagonal church and out to the lake.

Stanislao Loffreda, *A Visit to Capharnaum*, 2d ed. The Holy Places of Palestine (Jerusalem: Franciscan Printing Press, 1972), pp. 10-26; *Cafarnao* PSBF 19. I, *Gli edifci della città*, by Virgilio C. Corbo (1975); II, *La ceramica*, by Stanislao Loffreda (1974); III, *Catalogo delle monete della citta*, by Augusto Spijkerman (1975); IV, *I graffiti della casa di S. Pietro*, by Emmanuele Testa (1972); Vassilios Tzaferis, "New Archaeological Evidence on Ancient Capernaum," in BA 46 (1983), pp. 198-204; and *Excavations at Capernaum*, I, 1975-1982 (Winona Lake: Eisenbrauns, 1989). Photograph: JF.

89. Plan of the Synagogue at Capernaum

AT CAPERNAUM JESUS taught in the synagogue (Mk 1:21) and also dealt with a centurion of whom the elders of the city said, "He built us our synagogue" (Lk 7:5). Aetheria (381-384), as quoted by Peter the Deacon (Geyer p. 113; WET p. 196), reports concerning Capernaum: "There is the synagogue in which the Lord healed the demoniac. One goes up to it by many steps. This synagogue is built of quadrangular stones."

In his travels in Palestine in 1838 and 1852 Edward Robinson noted and described the site of Tell Hum and came to the conclusion that the chief ruins were those of a Jewish synagogue, although he did not believe that the place itself was Capernaum. Charles W. Wilson, however, came to the conclusion that Tell Hum was Capernaum and made the first excavations there in 1865-1866. In 1894 the Franciscans acquired the site from the Turks and built a monastery near the synagogue ruins, but because of unsettled conditions covered the site over and planted it to keep it safe. In 1905 the synagogue was excavated by the *Deutsche Orient-Gesellschaft* under Heinrich Kohl and Carl Watzinger, and work was continued

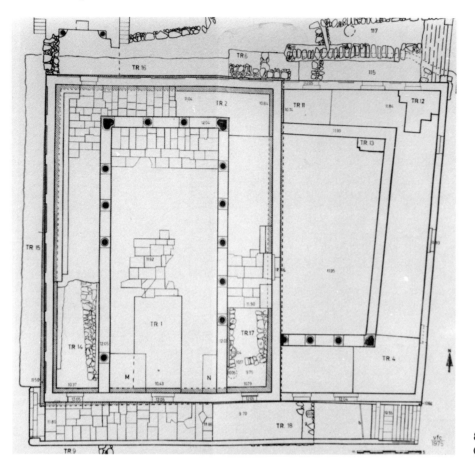

89. Plan of the Synagogue at Capernaum

from 1905 to 1921 under the Franciscan Custody of the Holy Land; the results were published by Gaudence Orfali in the latter year.

Orfali (pp. 74-86) advanced a careful argument for considering the synagogue in its extant ruins to belong to the first century and prior to A.D. 70. The Jerusalem Talmud (Megillah III 1, BA 7 [Feb. 1944], p. 3), however, says that Vespasian destroyed 480 synagogues (an exaggerated figure, perhaps) in the city of Jerusalem, and it has generally been held probable that synagogues were destroyed throughout the land in the wars climaxing in A.D. 70 and 135. Another favorable time for the rebuilding of synagogues may have been after Septimius Severus made a journey through Palestine and Syria in 199: in his reign (193-211) and that of his son Caracalla (211-217) there was a more favorable attitude toward the Jews. These considerations, together with comparative analysis of the architectural and artistic character of the remains, led Kohl and Watzinger (p. 218) to place the extant ruins of the Galilean synagogues, not only that at Capernaum but also others of similar type at Korazim (Chorazin, Nos. 85f.), Kefar Bir'am (Nos. 101ff.), and elsewhere, in the third century (Watzinger II, p. 113), and a date in the late second-early third century has been widely accepted.

New excavations were begun by the Franciscans under Virgilio Corbo in 1969 and continued for many years. In these excavations trenches were cut down into levels underlying the stone pavement of the synagogue and its adjacent courtyard. In what the Franciscan excavators call stratum A (the lowest level) there are the walls of earlier buildings. In stratum B there is a fill to level the ground and make a platform. In stratum C there is a thick layer of white mortar to seal the fill, and on this layer of mortar is laid the stone pavement. In the fill and in the mortar were found both coins and potsherds. For example, at the beginning of the digging, in trench 1 (TR 1 on the plan) extending inward from the central door, a coin was found which is dated to A.D. 352-360; and in trench 4 (TR 4) under a corner of the courtyard, a coin was found of the type issued in honor of Constantine the Great after his death and dated to A.D. 341-346; while all together thousands of coins were found, with dates even into the early fifth century (La Sinagoga, pp. 24, 47, 52, 126, 137, 139; Cafarnao I, pp. 121, 127, 163). Likewise numerous fragments of pottery were found in trench 23 under the courtyard, which are also to be dated in the fourth and fifth centuries (Loffreda in LA 29 [1979], pp. 215-220). Assuming that the date of the building as we know it is after the latest date of the pottery and coins

100

found beneath it, and depending especially upon the coins for their more precise dates, the excavators date the construction from the last decade of the fourth to the middle of the fifth century A.D. (Loffreda in *Synagogues Revealed*, pp. 52-56; cf. Saller, *Second Catalogue*, p. 26, no. 22).

Over against this late date others hold that historical and stylistic considerations still require the second-third century date, perhaps about the middle of the third century (Fischer in *Levant* 18 [1986], p. 142, see below, No. 94), rather than the date in the fourth-fifth century, and that the materials in question as described just above may have come into their place as a result of extensive renovations at a time later than that of the original construction (in *Synagogues Revealed*, p. 10 [Levine], pp. 57-59 [G. Foerster], pp. 60-62 [M. Avi-Yonah]; Tsafrir in *Synagogue in Late Antiquity* [1987], p. 154 n. 2). If the partially restored white limestone synagogue that we still see today at Capernaum was in fact built originally in the second-third century A.D., then it was surely the synagogue that Aetheria saw in her travels in the Holy Land (381-384) and described accurately when she said that one went up to it by many steps and that it was built of quadrangular stones.

The plan of the Capernaum synagogue outlines the basilica and its adjacent courtyard as well as the narrow porch and steps on the south side. The prayer hall is a rectangle 24.4 by 18.5 meters, and the courtyard on the east has a width at the façade of 11.25 meters (*Synagogues Revealed*, p. 13). Indicated in the plan is the location of major trenches of the Franciscan excavations (TR 1 = trincea 1, and so on).

Edward Robinson, *Biblical Researches in Palestine, and in the Adjacent Regions*, 3 vols. (Boston: Crocker and Brewster, II, pp. 406-407; III, p. 346; Charles W. Wilson, *The Recovery of Jerusalem* (New York: D. Appleton & Co., 1872), pp. 266, 292-301; and in *The Survey of Western Palestine*, Special Papers (London: The committee of the Palestine Exploration Fund, 1881), pp. 298-299; Heinrich Kohl and Carl Watzinger, *Antike Synagogen in Galilaea* (Leipzig: J. C. Hinrichs, 1916); Gaudence Orfali, *Capharnaüm et ses ruines d'apres les fouilles accomplis a Tell-Houm par la Custodie Franciscaine de Terre Sainte (1905-1921)* (Paris: Auguste Picard, 1922); Samuel Krauss, *Synagogale Altertümer* (Berlin-Wien: Benjamin Harz, 1922); E. L. Sukenik, *Ancient Synagogues in Palestine and Greece*. Schweich Lectures of the British Academy, 1930 (London: Oxford University Press, 1934); Herbert G. May, "Synagogues in Palestine," in BA 7 (Feb. 1944), pp. 1-20; Goodenough pp. 178-267; Virgilio Corbo, Stanislao Loffreda, and Augusto Spijkerman, *La Sinagoga di Cafarnao dopo gli scavi del 1969*. PSBFCMI 9, reprinted from LA 20 (1970), pp. 7-117 (Jerusalem: Franciscan Printing Press, 1970); Loffreda, *A Visit to Capharnaum*, pp. 48-65; Corbo, *Cafarnao I, Gli edifici della città*, pp. 113-169; James F. Strange, "The Capernaum and Herodium Publications" (review article), in BASOR 226 (April 1977), pp. 65-73; Stanislao Loffreda, "Potsherds from a Sealed Level of the Synagogue at Capharnaum," in LA 29 (1979), pp. 215-220; Shanks, *Judaism in Stone*, pp. 70-72; Lee I. Levine, "Ancient Synagogues—A Historical Introduction," in *Synagogues Revealed*, pp. 1-10; S. Loffreda, "The Late Chronology of the Synagogue of Capernaum," in *Synagogues Revealed*, pp. 52-56; G. Foerster, "Notes on Recent Excavations at Capernaum," in *Synagogues Revealed*, pp. 57-59; and in *Synagogue in Late Antiquity*, pp. 139-146; M. Avi-Yonah, "Some Comments on the Capernaum Excavations," in *Synagogues Revealed*, pp. 60-62; Moshe Dothan, "Research on Ancient Synagogues in the Land of Israel," in *Recent Archaeology*, p. 91; Yoram Tsafrir, "The Byzantine Setting and its Influence on Ancient Synagogues," in *Synagogue in Late Antiquity*, pp. 147-157. Plan: Corbo in *Studia Hierosolymitana*, I (1976), p. 160, courtesy Studium Biblicum Franciscanum, Jerusalem.

90. Model of the Synagogue at Capernaum

AS ILLUSTRATED AT Capernaum, it is not always easy to establish the dates of individual ancient synagogues, and there is increasing evidence that diversity of styles existed at the same time; nevertheless several distinctive architectural styles can be recognized, although the dates mentioned for representative examples may often be tentative. The first of these is commonly spoken of as the Galilean or the basilical type and is represented by the already mentioned synagogues at Capernaum, Korazim, Kefar Bir'am, and the like, while four very early synagogues at Herodium (No. 21), Masada (No. 23), Magdala, and Gamla (No. 74) present a similar basilical style (Moshe Dothan in *Recent Archaeology*, pp. 90f.) in a relatively simple form. The style is essentially that of the Greco-Roman assembly hall called the basilica, which was usually a rectangular building with the interior divided by rows of columns (Watzinger II, p. 108). In the synagogue adaptation of this form the orientation of the short front wall was toward Jerusalem in accordance with the biblical practice of praying toward the holy city (Dan 6:10, etc.). In the Galilean examples this wall is often on the exterior a relatively ornate façade. With the main entrance on the same side, a sacred enclosure for the Torah was probably provided just inside, so that the people within would turn and face in that direction. In the Byzantine period the basilica was also the prevailing type of Christian church building, and it is presumable that there was interrelationship as well as individual development in the architectural forms of the Jewish and the Christian religions. In particular the Christian orientation was toward the east, and there was also a second type of church intended as memorial monuments (*memoria, martyria*) for holy relics or holy places (*loca sancta*) and built with a concentric plan, round, octagonal, or cross-shaped (Tsafrir in *Synagogue in Late Antiquity*, pp. 149-153). In some cases a synagogue was turned into a church, as at Jerash (Gerasa) in Jordan (C. H. Kraeling, *Gerasa*, 1938, pp. 234-241; and below No. 119), or was made into a mosque, as at Eshtemoa nine miles south of Hebron (L. A. Meyer and A. Reifenberg in JPOS 19 [1939-1940], pp. 314-326).

101

90. Model of the Synagogue at Capernaum

A second main architectural type of the synagogue is the broadhouse, in which it is the long walls rather than the short walls that face toward Jerusalem; the place for the Torah is accordingly inside against the long wall on the Jerusalem side; the entrance may be through the long wall on the other side, or through one of the short walls. A number of synagogues of this type are also characterized by the use of mosaic for floors. Examples of the type are the earlier synagogue at Horvat Shema in northern Galilee (third century) (E. M. Meyers, "The Synagogue at Ḥorvat Shemaʾ," in *Synagogues Revealed*, pp. 70-74), and the synagogue already described at Hammath Tiberias with its fourth-century mosaic floor (No. 72).

The third style is characterized by the apse plan. Here the synagogue is a basilica with an apse added in the short wall facing Jerusalem. The apse provides the place for the Torah; the entrance is in the other short wall. Mosaic floors are often a feature. Examples are the synagogue at Hammath Gader (or by Gadara) on the Yarmuk River east of the south end of the Sea of Galilee, built in the late fourth century or first half of the fifth, with a mosaic pavement in which lions stand on either side of a memorial inscription in Aramaic (E. L. Sukenik, *The Ancient Synagogue of el-Hammeh*, 1935); and the synagogue at Beth Alpha west of Scythopolis, where the mosaic floor, with the signs of the zodiac, is attributed to the sixth century but lies over fragments of an older mosaic and is in a building that may be as much as a century older (E. L. Sukenik, *The Ancient Synagogue of Beth Alpha*, 1932).

Returning now to the Capernaum synagogue as an outstanding example of the basilical type, the ruins are located about one hundred yards from the present lake shore. The ground plan has been shown in No. 89, and the model here is intended to represent the probable appearance of the building, viewed from the southeast. The front of the building faces nearly south, toward the lake and toward Jerusalem. Steps lead up from the right to a raised platform or open porch, and the main building is at the left, where three doors give access to the interior. Inside on either side of the central entrance are the foundations of structures, and the worshipers must have faced in this direction, presumably toward the Torah shrine and the reader of the Torah, and toward Jerusalem. Rows of columns outlined the large central nave and formed aisles on the east, west, and north sides. Two benches, one built above the other, ran along the east and west walls. Whether there was an upper gallery, and if so whether this would have been for the women or for other activities, is very uncertain (Loffreda, *Visit to Capharnaum*, pp. 51f.; A. Kloner in *Synagogues Revealed*, p. 12). Adjacent to the prayer hall or synagogue proper, on the east side, is a court of trapezoid shape, which was probably entered by two doorways in front rather than by one as shown in the model. A roofed portico ran around the three walls, and the central part of the court was left open to the sky. The probable use of an arch over the central doorway of the main building and of additional windows in the upper level of the façade are represented in the model, and Nos. 94ff. show more of the rich sculptural decoration of the synagogue.

Shanks, *Judaism in Stone*, pp. 48-53; Meyers and Strange, pp. 142-152; Eric M. Meyers, "Ancient Synagogues in Galilee: Their Religious and Cultural Setting," in BA 43 (1980), pp. 97-168; and

"Synagogues of Galilee," in *Archaeology* 35.3 (May/June 1982), pp. 51-58; and "The Current State of Galilean Synagogue Studies," in *Synagogue in Late Antiquity*, pp. 127-137. Photograph: Kohl and Watzinger, *Antike Synagogen in Galilaea*, pl. v, courtesy J. C. Hinrichs Verlag, Leipzig.

91. Excavation at the West Wall of the Capernaum Synagogue

UNLESS THE CAPERNAUM synagogue as we know it in its white limestone form could be dated before A.D. 70 as Orfali thought (No. 89) it could not be the synagogue that the Roman centurion built and that was in existence in the time of Jesus, and since it is more probably of the second-third or fourth-fifth centuries, it is much later. The Franciscan excavation trenches have penetrated, however, to the lower levels beneath and beside the extant building ruins above ground, and at the present point we are interested in whatever ruins of more ancient edifices have been found there (Corbo in *Studia Hierosolymitana*, I, pp. 159-176).

The excavation in 1974 of trenches 14 and 15 in the western side of the synagogue, and in 1975 of trenches 17 and 18 in the eastern aisle and the porch of the synagogue, unearthed, resting on virgin soil, walls, pavements, habitations, and household pottery of the first century A.D. or earlier, thus revealing a residential section, like *Insula* II (No. 88) of early Roman Capernaum. Above these remains, however, and also traced in other trenches (TR 1, 2, 3, 11), were walls of shaped black

basalt stones, the construction of which evidently involved the destruction of the houses underneath. In turn, above the basalt walls and clearly distinguishable from them are the white limestone walls of the later synagogue. Again in 1981 other trenches were cut, notably trench 24 running east to west across the nave between the stylobates of the two north-south rows of columns of the limestone synagogue, and trench 25 alongside the eastern limestone stylobate, and in both areas the same basalt walls were found under the limestone walls and stylobates above. Associated with the basalt walls was also a section of floor made of black basalt cobbles. All together the outline of the building of the basalt walls was the same as that of the limestone synagogue above, but at the southwest corner the basalt wall was not in exact alignment with the limestone wall above it; therefore the basalt wall was not built as a part of the building above but was a part of an earlier building, the walls of which were used as foundations for the later building.

In the present photograph at the exterior of the west wall of the synagogue the upper tiers are the well-shaped polished blocks of white limestone of the later synagogue, with the lowest course resting upon and slightly offset from the older basalt wall beneath. Adjacent to and below the basalt wall are the yet older corner of a house wall and stretch of pavement, all also of basalt.

As compared with the plan (No. 89) and dimensions (24.4 by 18.5 meters) of the prayer hall of the white limestone synagogue, the dimensions (24.2 by 18.5 meters, BAR 9.6 [Nov/Dec 1983], p. 30) of the building marked out by the black basalt walls beneath the later

91. Excavation at the West Wall of the Capernaum Synagogue

building are almost exactly the same. The basalt walls are nearly four feet thick, which is much thicker than the walls of the private houses otherwise known in the Capernaum excavations, and thicker even than the walls of the limestone synagogue (2.5 feet thick); therefore we must see here the remains of more than a private building. Furthermore, Talmudic references show that it was customary to replace a synagogue by another ("A synagogue should not be demolished before another has been built to take its place," *Baba Bathra* 36 SBT 31, p. 9; *Tractate Megillah* 28b SBT 10, p. 158), and other excavations show that the new synagogue was often built in the very same place as its predecessor. Therefore it is most probable that this building of black basalt walls and cobbled floor was a synagogue and the predecessor of the limestone synagogue above.

The date of this predecessor synagogue (assuming that the edifice was indeed a synagogue) is certainly earlier than that of the limestone synagogue above (second-third or fourth-fifth century), and a more exact date is sought in the ceramic and numismatic evidence. On the cobbled basalt floor associated with the basalt walls were potsherds from the first to the fourth centuries A.D.; in and under the cobbled floor was pottery of the first century A.D. or earlier; and one of the coins found under the same floor is dated to the reign of Ptolemy VIII Euergetes II (146-116 B.C.). All together, therefore, the sequence is (Kroll p. 221, col. 1): (1) remains of houses of the Hellenistic period (say, third century onward), these remains destroyed and lying under (2) walls of the basalt synagogue (probably built in the first half of the first century A.D.), and (3) the white limestone synagogue (second-third or fourth-fifth century).

The excavator (Corbo in *Studia Hierosolymitana*, III, p. 341) says: "After thirteen years of patient labor in excavation and recording, this edifice was found to be exactly under the place of the synagogue of the fourth-fifth centuries. For this reason I think that we are justified in the assumption that the edifice with the basalt walls excavated under the synagogue of the fourth-fifth century is exactly the synagogue which was built in the first decades of the first century by the Roman centurion of whom Jesus said: 'I tell you, not even in Israel have I found such faith' (Lk 7:9)."

Virgilio Corbo, "Edifici antichi sotto la sinagoga di Cafarnao," in *Studia Hierosolymitana*, I, pp. 159-176; and *Cafarnao* I, pp. 158ff., p. 143 foto 81 and color tav. 8 facing p. 208; and "Resti della sinagoga del primo secolo a Cafarnao," in *Studia Hierosolymitana*, III, pp. 313-357; Stanislao Loffreda, "Ceramica Ellenistico-Romana nel sottosuolo della sinagoga di Cafarnao," in *Studia Hierosolymitana*, III, pp. 273-312; James F. Strange and Hershel Shanks, "Synagogue Where Jesus Preached Found at Capernaum," in BAR 9.6 (Nov/Dec 1983), pp. 24-31. Photograph: JF.

92. Main Basilical Hall of the Synagogue at Capernaum

THIS IS A VIEW of the main basilical hall of the white limestone synagogue at Capernaum, partly rebuilt by the Franciscans in 1925, looking northward toward the colonnade at the end and the north wall. The stone of which the building is constructed was probably quarried in Wadi el-Hamam (No. 87).

Photograph: JF.

93. Southeast Corner of the Capernaum Synagogue

HERE WE SEE the steps that lead up the raised platform in front of the synagogue. Kohl and Watzinger (p. 5) found these steps unique among all the synagogues they studied. Presumably they are the "many steps" mentioned by Aetheria, and the wall is also built of "quadrangular stones," just as Aetheria said (cf. above No. 89). At the corner of the wall beneath the white limestone blocks are blocks of black basalt of the earlier synagogue (cf. No. 91).

Photograph: JF.

94. Sculptured Capital at Capernaum

AS SHOWN IN this example, the capitals of the columns in the Capernaum synagogue were elaborately sculptured in the Corinthian order. Comparative analysis of the style of the capitals within the framework of Hellenistic-Roman art tends to confirm a date for the construction of the white limestone synagogue around the middle of the third century or slightly after.

Moshe Fischer, "The Corinthian Capitals of the Capernaum Synagogue: A Revision," in *Levant* 18 (1986), pp. 131-142; H. Bloedhorn in BAIAS 7 (1987-1988), p. 73. Photograph: JF.

95. Ark of the Covenant or Shrine of the Torah at Capernaum

IN THE RICH sculptured ornamentation of the Capernaum synagogue one of the most interesting items is that shown in this photograph. We see a chest with arched roof, double doors at the end, and columns along the side. Beneath also we see wheels, of which there were presumably four in all, on which the chest was transportable. Alternate theories are that this represents the port-

92. Main Basilical Hall of the Synagogue at Capernaum

93. Southeast Corner of the Capernaum Synagogue

94. Sculptured Capital at Capernaum

95. Ark of the Covenant or Shrine of the Torah at Capernaum

able Ark of the Covenant of the wilderness wanderings, or the shrine in which the Torah was rolled into place in the synagogue before a permanent Torah shrine was installed.

Watzinger II, p. 113; Shanks, *Judaism in Stone*, p. 67. Photograph: JF.

96. Menorah at Capernaum

THIS SCULPTURE SHOWS the seven-armed lampstand, at the right the shofar or ram's horn blown at festivals, and at the left the shovel used for incense (cf. Nos. 285-287, 289).

Photograph: JF.

96. Menorah at Capernaum

97. Shield of David at Capernaum

THIS HEXAGRAM, used as a part of the sculptural ornamentation in the synagogue at Capernaum, was later
known as the Shield or Star of David.

Photograph: JF.

97. Shield of David at Capernaum

98. Seal of Solomon at Capernaum

THIS PENTAGRAM, shown here as sculptured at Capernaum, was later known as the Seal or Star of Solomon.

Photograph: JF.

98. Seal of Solomon at Capernaum

99. Plan of the Edifices in the Insula Sacra (Insula I) at Capernaum

IN THE FRANCISCAN excavations at Capernaum the
area nearest the lake is designated *Insula* I and, in view
of the findings, is called the Insula Sacra. When he made
the first excavations at Capernaum in 1865-1866 (No.
89), Charles W. Wilson noted the ruins in this area and
wrote: "Outside the synagogue proper, but connected
with it, we uncovered the remains of a later building,
which may be those of the church which Epiphanius says
was built at Capernaum [cf. above No. 45], and was described by Antonius, A.D. 600 [the reference is to the
Anonymous of Piacenza, see below No. 100], as a Basilica inclosing the house of Peter" (*The Recovery of Jerusalem* [1872], p. 268). Further clearance in 1921 by
Gaudence Orfali brought to light the outlines of this
church as consisting of three concentric rings and with
portions of mosaic still in place. Here in 1968 complete
excavation was conducted by Virgilio Corbo.

At the lowest level (level 1) a group of a dozen or so
closely related dwellings was uncovered, constituting an
insula much like Insula II (No. 88), but with even poorer
houses. The walls are of black basalt rocks and pebbles
without mortar, the floors are of beaten black earth or
basalt pebbles, and a few doorsills were found and traces
of small windows. The walls would hardly have supported heavy roofing, and the roofs were probably made
from tree branches covered with mud and straw. Such a
roof would allow for exactly such a partial and temporary
removal as is described in Mk 2:4 (where the "tiles" of
Lk 5:19 probably reflect a picturization of the scene in
terms of a Roman villa rather than of the Capernaum of
the time). Being close to the shore the dwellings may
well have been those of fishermen. In the ruins were fragments of cooking pots, pans, jars, and lamps. The largest

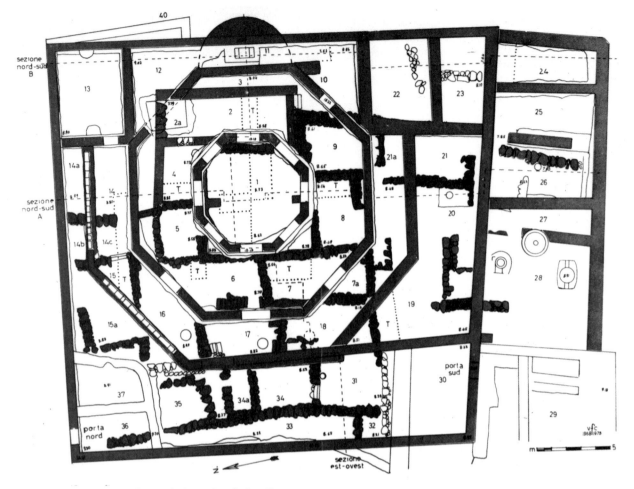

99. Plan of the Edifices in the Insula Sacra (*Insula* 1) at Capernaum

of the houses is on the east side of the *insula* and measures 7 by 6.5 meters. In it were found two practically intact lamps, one Hellenistic and one Herodian (*Cafarnao* 1, p. 91 foto 45), so this house was evidently built at the very end of the Hellenistic period (first century B.C.). Other ceramics and coins too date the private houses of this level 1 from the first century B.C. and the first century A.D. down to the fourth century, and the area itself was inhabited down to the seventh century (Corbo, *New Memoirs*, pp. 23f.; and *House of Saint Peter*, pp. 37-39, 69f.; Loffreda, *Visit to Capharnaum*, pp. 25f., 29-31; Loffreda, *Recovering Capharnaum*. St. Bib. Fran. Guides 1. [Jerusalem: Custodia Terra Santa, 1985]).

Soon this house and its principal and largest room (no. 1 on the plan) became the object of special attention. Whereas the ancient floors of all the other houses in the *insula* are of either the usual beaten earth or basalt pebbles, in this one building, above its earliest floors of dark earth, are several successive floors of crushed limestone. Between these pavements were found fragments of Herodian lamps, so the special attention evidenced by

the limestone floors dates back into the first century A.D. (Corbo, *House of Saint Peter*, pp. 44f., 54f., fig. 14a).

In the following centuries the same room no. 1 was the object of further special attention in that its roughly built walls were plastered at least three times and decorated. Thousands of fragments of this plaster were found with decorations, and many with graffiti, which are assigned to a time from the latter part of the second century to the first half of the fourth century, with the third century as the most important time (Testa, *Graffiti*, pp. 9, 81, 108, 147). The decorations were in many colors and the motifs included flowers, fruits such as the pomegranate, geometrical patterns, and the like. Especially notable are floral crosses, and flowers and fruits probably arranged to symbolize paradise, as in the scene already noticed in the Grotto of Conon at Nazareth (No. 48), a theme thus characteristic of the Judeo-Christians (Testa, *Graffiti*, pp. 21ff., 33ff., 38ff.).

The graffiti include 124 fragments in Greek, 18 in Syriac (Estrangelo), 15 in Hebrew, and one in Latin (Corbo, *House of Saint Peter*, p. 68), and no doubt rep-

108

resent pilgrims from as many linguistic backgrounds. In the following examples the references are to Testa, *Graffiti*. Greek inscriptions include these:

ΠΕΤΡΟ(C *or* Y) ΒΕΡΕΝΙ (ΚΗ)

Peter *or* of Peter Bereni(ce)
(p. 60, no. 47, fig. 9, 47, tav. XIII, 47).

While the name Peter could conceivably be that of a visiting pilgrim, here in Capernaum and in this house it is most probably the apostle who is meant. The name of Berenice was attributed to the woman who suffered from a hemorrhage for twelve years and was said to have been healed at Capernaum (Mt 9:20-22; Mk 5:25-34; Lk 8:43-48; Acts of Pilate VII [HSNTA I, p. 457]; the Coptic *Book of the Resurection of Christ by Bartholomew the Apostle* [JANT p. 183]). Eusebius records that this woman was still venerated in his time and that at her house in Paneas (Caesarea Philippi) bronze images of her and of Jesus commemorated the miracle (*Ch. Hist.* VII 18).

(Ι)ΧΘΥC
(᾿Ι)χθύς

Fish
(pp. 66-67, no. 77, fig. 9, 77, tav. XV, 77).

This can mean the early Christian acrostic based on the Greek word for fish, cf. above No. 30, below p. 350.

(ΧΡΙ)CΤΕ ΕΛΕΗC(ΟΝ)
(Χρι)στέ ἐλέησο(όν)

Christ have mercy
(pp. 71-72, no. 88, fig. 9, 88, color tav. 3, 88c).

(ΚΕ ΙC ΧΕ ΒΟΗΘΙ
Κ(ύρι)ε ᾿Ι(η)σ(οῦ) Χ(ριστ)έ Βοήθι

Lord Jesus Christ help
(pp. 72-76, no. 89, fig. 11, 89, color tav. 3, 89G).

The one Latin inscription is in letter forms also attributed to the second to fourth centuries A.D.

RO M AE BO
PETR US

Romae Bo
Petrus
(p. 174, no. 152, fig. 17, 152, tav. XXXV, 152).

The names "of Rome" and "Peter" are plain, while the letters "Bo" can be an abbreviation or the initial letters of a word. Possible completions of the word could be latin *bo(na)* or *bo(num)*, "good," or Greek βο(ήθι), "help," or βο(ηθός), "helper." If we take the last inter-

pretation, Peter is called the helper of Rome (Loffreda, *Visit to Capharnaum*, p. 36).

The name of Peter may also be recognized in a monogram (p. 169, no. 128, fig. 16, 128, tav. XXXIII, 128, color tav. 3, 128H), where the Latin name is written in Greek letters, Π and ε, then at the right a cross and the final letter C, probably to be completed as ΠΕΤΡΥC plus a cross mark.

There are also various symbols in the graffiti, which are understandable as of Judeo-Christian significance (references in Testa, *Graffiti*). The cross appears in various forms, e.g., a Latin T (pp. 153f., no. 111, tav. XXXII, 111) and an upright cross-mark with a small cross beside it (p. 162, no. 118, tav. XXXII, 118). An upright cross-mark within an enclosure can be a cross-shield (p. 155, no. 112, tav. XXXII, 112). A cross-mark enclosed in a square (pp. 157f., no. 113, tav. XXXII, 113) can suggest the four quarters of the world and the universal efficacy of the cross. A small boat with oars and flying sail (pp. 159f., no. 115, fig. 16, 115, color tav. 3, 115F), like the boats at Nazareth (No. 48), was a symbol of significance not only to Judeo-Christians but also to Gentile Christians (e.g., Justin, *Apology* I 55 ANF I, p. 181, referring to the figure of the cross: "For the sea is not traversed except that trophy which is called a sail abide safe in the ship"; Bagatti, *Church from Circumcision*, pp. 219-221, and cf. below, p. 351).

The above evidences show, therefore, according to a very reasonable interpretation, that this particular room (no. 1) was treated as a venerated hall from the first century onward and was associated with the memory of Peter, i.e., was remembered as the house of the apostle.

In level 2 of the excavations, dated by coins and pottery to the mid-fourth century A.D., it was found that the house in question was provided with a new ceiling supported by a central arch from north to south, and was enlarged with additional rooms on its east and north sides (nos. 2 and 4 in the plan). Beyond this the whole block of dwellings surrounding the venerated hall was surrounded by a quadrilateral wall of finely worked basalt rocks, 27 meters long on three sides, 30 meters long on the east side (the large complete quadrilateral in the plan), with the main entrance on the south side near the lakeshore. This separated the entire small complex from the rest of the town and was evidently intended to form a sacred precinct, centered on the venerated hall. As such, we may recognize here a house-church (*domus ecclesiae*) and from the graffiti and from Jewish references to the *minim* at Capernaum (*Midrash Rabbah Eccl.* 1, 8, 4; 1, 8, 84; SMR VIII, pp. 29, 210; and cf. No. 87) we may recognize that this was the meeting place of the Judeo-Christians of Capernaum. It is well possible, therefore, that it was relatives of Peter who had remained in Capernaum and had transformed Peter's house in this way

(Bagatti, *Church from Circumcision*, p. 131). Confirming the life of fishermen in the place, two fish hooks were found in the flooring of the house-church (Corbo, *New Memoirs of Saint Peter*, fig. on p. 30; and *Cafarnao* I, color tav. 4 facing p. 80).

At any rate there is little doubt that this is the church seen by Aetheria who, in the record of her pilgrimage (A.D. 381-384) quoted by Peter the Deacon (Geyer pp. 112-113; CCSL CLXXV, pp. 98f.; WET pp. 194, 196), not only describes the synagogue (No. 89) but also writes: "In Capernaum, moreover, out of the house of the first of the apostles a church (*ecclesia*) has been made, the walls of which still stand just as they were. Here the Lord cured the paralytic." The first sentence by Aetheria appears to mean that it was the original walls of Peter's house that were still standing; and the reference to the cure of the paralytic recalls the fact that Jesus was "at home" (Mk 2:1) in Capernaum in the house of Peter (Mt 8:14; Mk 1:29; Lk 4:38).

Orfali, *Capharnaum et ses ruines* (1922), pp. 103-109; Virgilio Corbo, "The House at Capernaum," in *New Memoirs of Saint Peter by the Sea of Galilee* (Jerusalem: Franciscan Printing Press, n.d.); and *The House of St. Peter at Capharnaum*. PSBFCMI 5 (Jerusalem: Franciscan Printing Press, 1969); and *Cafarnao* I, 1975, pp. 26-111; Emmanuele Testa, *I Graffiti della Casa di S. Pietro* (*Cafarnao* IV, PSBF 19, 1972); Stanislao Loffreda, *A Visit to Capharnaum* (1972), pp. 28-46; Ernest Saunders, "Christian Synagogues and Jewish Christianity in Galilee," in *Explor* 3 (1977), p. 75; Ovadiah, *Corpus Supplementum* (1981), pp. 209-211, no. 10; James F. Strange and Hershel Shanks, "Has the House Where Jesus Stayed in Capernaum been Found?" in *BAR* 8.6 (Nov/Dec 1982), pp. 26-37. Plan: Corbo, *Cafarnao* I, tav. II, courtesy Studium Biblicum Franciscanum, Jerusalem.

100. The Octagon at Capernaum

FINALLY IN LEVEL 3 of the excavations it was found that all the private houses of the *insula sacra* were destroyed and an octagonal church was erected in the site (*Cafarnao* I, pp. 26-58). As recognized already by Orfali in 1921, as outlined in the plan (No. 99) of the complete excavation by Corbo in 1968, and as seen in the present photograph (taken from the west), the church was arranged in three concentric rings. The walls of the central octagon were placed directly on the foundations of the venerated hall (room 1 in the plan), and the roof was supported by eight columns. The second wall was also a complete octagon, surrounding the central octagon. In turn the third wall was also concentric and provided a portico, but only in five sections from north to west to south, and space was left for subsidiary rooms in the east and south. Probably only a little later an apse containing a baptistery was added on the east side.

Portions of mosaic pavement were still found in the portico, the second octagon, and the central octagon. The section in the central octagon was the best preserved. It features a geometric design and a lotus-flower border as in the Church of the Multiplication of the Loaves and Fishes at Tabgha (No. 79), and the central figure is a peacock, the symbol in early Christianity of immortality (*Cafarnao* I, pp. 50-52).

According to the evidence of coins and ceramics, the construction of the octagonal church was in approximately the middle of the fifth century. There is little doubt that it is the church of which the Anonymous of Piacenza reported in A.D. 570: "We came to Capernaum into the house of St. Peter, which is a basilica" (Geyer p. 163; LPPTS II-D, p. 6; CCSL CLXXV, p. 159; WJP p. 81).

100. The Octagon at Capernaum

The date of construction and the description of it as a basilica make it probable that the octagonal church was built by Gentile Christians who, by that time, had largely succeeded the Judeo-Christians who worshiped in the preceding house-church. The octagonal church appears to have continued in use during the rest of the Byzantine period, and then to have been abandoned at the beginning of the Arab period (A.D. 638).

In terms of architectural styles, the basilical synagogue (No. 90) and the Christian basilica (No. 225) (including the Crusader basilica distinguished by three apses [e.g., Nos. 67, 125, 203]) are marked by their longitudinal plan, intended for worship. In contrast, the octagonal church at Capernaum provides the oldest example found in the Holy Land (*Cafarnao* I, p. 56) of a Christian edifice with a central or concentric plan (polygonal or circular) and plainly intended as a *memoria* church, i.e., a church intended to mark and commemorate a sacred place significant for special event or person. Other examples include the Church of the Ascension on the Mount of Olives (No. 158), the Tomb of the Virgin Mary near Gethsemane (No. 170), the Byzantine Church on Mount Sion (No. 205), and the Anastasis (Rotunda) over the Tomb of Jesus (No. 225).

Photograph: JF.

101. The Synagogue at Bir'am

ALTHOUGH IT IS not a NT site, mention may also be made of Kefar Bir'am, in the hills west of the Huleh valley, because of its very well-preserved synagogue ruins, which have already been mentioned (No. 90) as exhibiting along with Capernaum and Chorazin the typical Galilean or basilical plan of synagogue architecture. In view of such similarity the Bir'am synagogue is presumably of similar date as the Capernaum and Chorazin synagogues and, at least hitherto, has usually been assigned to the second-third century.

The place was visited by Edward Robinson in 1852 (*Biblical Researches* IV, pp. 70f.) and he noted the ruins of two synagogues, as did also Charles W. Wilson who reported on them in *The Survey of Western Palestine* (1881). The smaller of the two has now disappeared completely, its stones no doubt having been carried off for building material. An inscription in square Hebrew characters, which was written in one long line on the lintel of the main entrance, was found in 1861 and is preserved in part in the Louvre. It reads: "May there be peace (שלום) in this place and in all the places of Israel. Jose the Levite, the son of Levi, made this lintel. May blessing come upon his deeds." Lidzbarski (p. 117) assigned the inscription to the second-third century,

which is in harmony with the earlier assignment of the Galilean-type synagogues including those at Capernaum and Chorazin as well as this one at Kefar Bir'am, to that date. The larger of the two synagogues was called by Wilson "the most perfect remain of the kind in Palestine" (*Survey* p. 297), and it still stands amazingly intact as may be seen in the photograph. The façade faces south, i.e., toward Jerusalem, and has a main doorway and two side doors. Before this façade was a porch with six columns in front and one on either end.

Robinson, *Biblical Researches in Palestine* (1852), pp. 70-71; *The Survey of Western Palestine*, Special Papers (1881), p. 297 (Wilson); *Memoirs* I (1881), pp. 230-234 (Kitchener); Mark Lidzbarski, *Handbuch der nordsemitischen Epigraphik nebst ausgewählten Inschriften* (Weimar: Emil Felber, 1898). I. Text, pp. 117, 485 no. 5; II. Tafeln, pl. XLIII no. 4; Kohl and Watzinger, *Antike Synagogen in Galilaea*, pp. 89-100; Goodenough I, pp. 201-203; Saller, *Second Catalogue*, pp. 49-51, No. 54; J. Naveh, "Ancient Synagogue Inscriptions," in *Synagogues Revealed*, p. 137; Pearlman and Yannai, pp. 35-37. Photograph: JF.

102. Arch over the Main Doorway of the Synagogue at Bir'am

THE ROUND DECORATION beneath the lintel is a crown of olive leaves. On the lintel is a grape vine with alternating bunches of grapes and leaves within its convolutions.

Photograph: JF.

103. Interior Hall of the Synagogue at Bir'am

AS THE PHOTOGRAPH shows, the ground plan of the Bir'am synagogue was very much the same as that of the synagogues at Capernaum and Chorazin, i.e., it was essentially a basilica. There was a colonnade around the three sides, east, north, and west, making three aisles around the nave. The corner columns stood on heart-shaped bases. Whether there was a balcony above is uncertain.

Photograph: JF.

104. The Jordan River Flowing into the Sea of Galilee near Bethsaida

IN MT 11:21-23 AND LK 10:13-15 BETHSAIDA is linked with Chorazin and Capernaum in the woe pronounced by Jesus, but Philip was from there (Jn 1:44; 12:21, where it is called Bethsaida in Galilee) and Beth-

101. The Synagogue at Bir'am

102. Arch over the Main Doorway of the Synagogue at Bir'am

103. Interior Hall of the Synagogue at Bir'am

112

104. The Jordan River Flowing into the Sea of Galilee near Bethsaida

saida was also the city of Andrew and Peter (Jn 1:44) and was the place where a blind man was healed (Mk 8:22).

As a place of importance in Gospel history, Bethsaida was on the route of Christian pilgrims and appears in pilgrim records. Theodosius (530) names Tiberias, Magdala, Seven Springs, and Capernaum as located at two-mile intervals along the shore of the Sea of Tiberias, then says that from Capernaum it is six miles to Bethsaida, while from Bethsaida it is fifty miles to Panias where the Jordan rises (Geyer p. 138; LPPTS II-B, p. 8; CCSL CLXXV, p. 115; WJP p. 63). While the mile figures are only approximations (No. 73), the reckoning up the Jordan to its source suggests a location of Bethsaida near where the river enters the lake. Theodosius also says that the sons of Zebedee (i.e., James and John) as well as Peter, Andrew, and Philip were born at Bethsaida.

Josephus (*Ant.* XVIII 2, 1 §28) states that Philip the tetrarch (4 B.C.-A.D. 34) raised the village (χώμη) of

Bethsaida to the status of a city (πόλις) and named it after Julia, the daughter of the emperor Augustus; since Julia was banished in 2 B.C. this must have taken place before that date (SHJP Vermes/Millar II, p. 172). This town of Julias Josephus locates in lower Gaulanitis (*War* II 9, 1 §168), now the Golan Heights, which was Philip's territory east of the Sea of Galilee across from Herod Antipas' territory of Galilee, and Josephus also says that "below the town of Julias" the river Jordan "cuts across the Lake of Gennesar" (*War* III 10, 7 §515). Julias, or Bethsaida-Julias, must therefore have been a little way above where the Jordan enters the Sea of Galilee, and must have been on the east side of the river.

The fact that Jn 12:22 and also Ptolemy (*Geography* v 15, ed. Stevenson, p. 128) speak of Bethsaida as belonging to Galilee, makes a problem. The original village of Bethsaida, however, was probably a fishing village, as suggested by the vocations of Peter and Andrew, James

113

and John (e.g., Mt 4:18, 21) and by the probable derivation of the name from Aramaic with the meaning "house of the fisher," and was therefore probably right on the lake.

Two sites, in fact, come into consideration near where the Jordan enters the Sea of Galilee. The first is Khirbet el-Araj, only fifty yards from the lake shore; the second is a rocky hill above to the northwest about two kilometers from the shore and known only as et-Tell. Since Roman pottery has been found at both sites, settlement of both in the time under question is confirmed. The respective geographical locations of the two sites makes reasonable the supposition that Araj was the place of the original fishing village and et-Tell the location of the citadel of Bethsaida-Julias. The latter is indeed on the east side of the river, which accords with Josephus' placement of the town of Julias in Philip's territory of Gaulanitis. Araj is also now on the east side of the river, but a large lagoon called es-Saki is to the east of Araj and might mark the ancient stretch of the river where it came into the lake. If this surmise is correct, the fishing village of Bethsaida was indeed in Galilee. Otherwise, "Bethsaida in Galilee" could have been a popular if imprecise designation (Raymond E. Brown in AB 29, p. 82 n. 44).

While the sites just described have not been excavated, surface finds in addition to pottery include the remains of a large stone wall at the base of the southern slope of et-Tell and traces of ancient buildings and mosaics at Araj. In the record of the travels of Willibald (725) and his companions it is said that from Capernaum "they went to Bethsaida, where Peter and Andrew were; there is now a church where originally their house was" (Tobler and Milinier p. 261; WJP p. 128). In the absence of excavation no vestiges of such a church have been found, but there is a large unhewn basalt stone at the northern entrance to et-Tell that bears symbols which are evidently Christian: a tree branch is recognized as a Judeo-Christian symbol for the "shoot from the stump of Jesse" (Isa 11:1, 10; Rom 15:12) as a messianic prophecy; a cross with a rainbow over it points to the several divine covenants with humankind (Gen 9;13, etc.); and two eyes, one open and one closed, symbolize the miracle of the healing of the blind man (Mk 8:22).

W. F. Albright in BASOR 29 (1928), pp. 2, 7; Dalman, *Sacred Sites*, pp. 161f.; Clemens Kopp, "Christian Sites around the Sea of Galilee: II, Bethsaida and el-Minyeh," in *Dominican Studies* 3 (1950), pp. 10-40; M. Avi-Yonah in IDB I, pp. 396-397; Bargil Pixner, "Searching for the New Testament Site of Bethsaida," in BA 48 (1985), pp. 207-216. Photograph: The Matson Photo Service, Alhambra, Calif.

105. Looking across the Sea of Galilee to Kursi

IN CONTRAST WITH the localization of the feeding of the five thousand on the west side of the Sea of Galilee and specifically at et-Tabgha (No. 76), in Lk 9:10 Jesus has withdrawn to Bethsaida (No. 104) and the event takes place when the crowds follow him, evidently out from Bethsaida and thus probably somewhere farther along on the east shore of the lake. Likewise in Jn 6:1

105. Looking across the Sea of Galilee to Kursi

Jesus went to the other side of the Sea of Galilee, presumably meaning the east side, and the feeding of the five thousand ensued there; afterward his disciples started across the sea to Capernaum (Jn 6:16), thus were starting back from the east side to the west side. Thus there were pointers in the various Gospel accounts of the feeding of the multitude toward the east side of the lake as well as the west.

Also, although the accounts of a feeding of five thousand and a feeding of four thousand may have originally been simple variants of one narrative (No. 76), already in Mt 16:9-10 and Mk 8:19-20 the two are considered two separate events, and it may not be surprising that at least later these separate events were localized in two separate places. According to Aetheria the feeding of the five thousand was remembered at Seven Springs (Tabgha) on the west shore (No. 77); but according to Eutychius of Alexandria the feeding of the four thousand and also the healing of the Gerasene demoniac were commemorated at Kursi on the east shore. In *The Book of the Demonstration* (ed. Watt, csco 193, p. 137) Eutychius writes:

> The church of Kursi, east of the sea of Tiberias, bears witness that he healed the man possessed who was called Legion because of the many devils in him; Christ commanded them to come out from him, and they asked him to permit them to enter into swine which were pasturing there, and he gave them permission, and they went out of the man, and entered into the swine; and the devils drove the herd of swine into the sea so that they were all drowned, and the man was healed. The church bears witness, too, that he there, from seven loaves and some fish, fed four thousand men, besides the women and children, and they were all satisfied; and the disciples gathered from their superfluity seven baskets full.

From the lake the present view looks eastward to the steep hills that descend to the shore at the probable site of Kursi.

Photograph: JF.

106. Memorial of the Miracle of the Swine at Kursi

WHILE EUTYCHIUS (in the foregoing quotation, No. 105) includes the feeding of the four thousand (Mt 15:32-39; Mk 8:1-10) as localized at Kursi, it is the healing of the demoniac and the destruction of the swine that he speaks of first in connection with that location, and it is evident that it was these events (Mt 8:28-34; Mk 5:1-20; Lk 8:26-39) which were most prominently commemmorated there.

In the Gospel narratives, Mk 5:1 and Lk 8:26 and 37 locate the latter happenings in "the country of the Gerasenes" with "Gadarenes" and "Gergesenes" as textual variants, and Mt 8:28 says it was in "the country of the Gadarenes" with "Gerasenes" and "Gergesenes" as textual variants. The name "Gadarenes" refers to Gadara, which is identified with Umm Qeis five miles southeast of the Sea of Galilee and below the River Yarmuk (see map No. 70). The name "Gerasenes" refers to Gerasa, now called Jerash, which is yet farther south, more than thirty miles from the Sea of Galilee (No. 107). While it is not inconceivable that the "country" of Gadara or even of Gerasa could have been deemed to extend to the shore of the lake, Gerasa is surely too far away to be involved here, and it is not even certain if the territory of Gadara reached to the lake. By the process of elimina-

106. Memorial of the Miracle of the Swine at Kursi

tion the name "Gergesenes" remains, therefore, as the most likely to belong properly to the narrative of the demoniac and the swine. As a matter of fact, Origen, writing his *Commentary on John* (VI 24) in Caesarea, rejected both Gerasa and Gadara as too far away and spoke of the Gergesenes (in the form Γεργεσαῖοι) and of Gergesa (Γέργεσα). Gergesa, he says, is an ancient city (πόλις) by the lake of Tiberias, and there is a cliff there from which, "it is pointed out," the swine were driven down by the demons (Baldi pp. 309f., no. 471; R. G. Clapp in JBL 26 [1907], p. 65; F. C. Burkitt in JBL 27 [1908], p. 130). Eusebius, likewise, in the *Onomasticon* (ed. Klostermann, p. 74) uses the name Gergesa and says that this is a village (κώμη) that "is pointed out" by the lake of Tiberias, into which the swine were thrown down. So also Burchard of Mount Sion, although he uses the name Gerasa, describes the town as on the shore of the Sea of Galilee, "nearly over against Tiberias, but a little to the north of it" (LPPTS XII-A, p. 34).

It is almost surely the case that this name Gergesa is the same as the name Kursi in the quotation from Eutychius (No. 105), and the site to which the name Kursi (or Kersa) still attaches is on the east shore of the Sea of Galilee roughly opposite Tiberias and slightly to the north, exactly as Burchard of Mount Sion described it. The site is at the mouth of the Wadi Samak, which is also known as the Valley of Kursi. The valley is fertile for farming, the hills above are excellent for grazing, especially for hogs; the rocky hill country is said to be the best, and the slope down to the seashore is steep, as is implied in the narrative of the demoniac and the swine.

Excavations were conducted at Kursi by Vassilios Tzaferis for the Israel Department of Antiquities and Museums during the years 1970-1973 and in 1980. On the slopes above the valley are caves; on the top of the ridge along the valley are the evidences of small settlements with Roman and Byzantine pottery on the surface. At the foot of a somewhat isolated hill that slopes steeply down to a narrow beach a large monastic compound was uncovered, surrounded by a rectangular plastered stone wall (145 by 123 meters) with decorative paintings on parts of its interior surface and with a basilical church in the middle of the compound. Between the compound and the lake there are traces of a village of the Roman period, with a small harbor installation for the activities of fishing. Near the shore, 300 meters from the monastic area, Tell Khirbet el-Kursi shows occupation in the Roman, Byzantine, Arab, and Crusader periods.

Three main periods in the archeologically explored later history of Kursi are established. The first phase of the first main period is put in the late fifth or early sixth century A.D. The foundation of the church and the monastery, with a hospice for pilgrims, is assigned to this time. The church was built of local basalt stones. In plan it is a basilica, oriented to the east, with a colonnaded atrium, a narthex, a nave and two side aisles, and an enclosed apse. The columns had Corinthian capitals, the walls were painted plaster, and the floors were of colored mosaics with geometric designs and pictures of the flora and fauna of the area. The prayer hall proper measures 24 by 15 meters. The basic architectural elements are much the same as in the Church of the Multiplication of the Loaves and Fishes at Tabgha, but without the broad transept that gives the church at Tabgha a cruciform plan. An outside chapel on the south side of the church provides an entrance to a crypt that was the burial place of the monastery. The dwellings of the monks were in an area on the north side of the church.

Halfway up the steep slope of the hill overlooking the monastic compound and church are the ruins, locally called Kersa, of another structure, which was probably constructed at the same time as the monastery and basilica. Here a chamber, once surmounted by a tower, enclosed a massive boulder some seven meters in height, while on a terrace above the boulder was a chapel with a mosaic floor and a semicircular apse that extended into a natural rock shelter. The apse was oriented to the east, but was provided with a semicircular bench from which persons seated there would look in the other direction to the enclosed rock on the terrace below, and on down to the monastery and to the lake. It seems most probable that Christians identified the great rock as marking the very site where Jesus healed the demoniac and the swine rushed down into the sea (Mt 8:32; Mk 5:13; Lk 8:33). The present photograph shows the landmark rock and stone-block walls remaining around it, the focal part of the Chapel of the Miracle of the Swine.

The second phase of the first main period at Kursi is assigned to a time from the late sixth century to the Persian invasion in A.D. 614. During this time the Christian population seems to have increased, and some remodeling was done in the main church. In particular a room adjacent to the apse was converted into a baptistery. In a mosaic pavement at the entrance a Greek inscription names a certain Stephanos as the presbyter or priest (πρεσβύτερος) and the ruler or abbot (ἡγούμενος) of the monastery, gives a date of about A.D. 585 in the reign of the Byzantine emperor Maurice (582-602), and calls the baptistery a "photisterion" (φωτιστέριον), i.e., a place of the illumination received in baptism (cf. Justin, Dialogue I 61 ANF I 183, on Christian baptism: "this washing is called illumination [φωτισμός] because they who learn these things are illuminated in their understandings").

The second main period extends from A.D. 614 to the early eighth century. In the Persian invasion (614) severe damage was done. Then with the Arab Muslim conquest (638) Christian pilgrimage was affected, and most of the images of birds and animals in the mosaics were destroyed. By early in the eighth century the settlement was abandoned.

In a third main period from the early to the mid-eighth century the place was resettled for a short time and by a poorer group, and the church was used only for domestic purposes.

Bagatti, *Antichi Villagi*, pp. 74-79; Ovadiah, *Corpus Supplementum*, pp. 238-240; Yoram Tsafrir, "Ancient Churches," in *Recent Archaeology*, p. 102; Vassilios Tzaferis, *The Excavations of Kursi-Gergesa*, '*Atiquot*, English Series, vol. 16, pp. 1-65 (Jerusalem 1983); and "A Pilgrimage to the Site of the Swine Miracle," in BAR 15.2 (Mar/Apr 1989), pp. 44-51. For Gadara, see Ute Wagner-Lux and Karel J. H. Vriezen, "A Preliminary Report on the Excavations at Gadara (Umm Qes) in Jordan from 1976 to 1979," in ADAJ 24 (1980), pp. 157-161; and "Vorläufiger Bericht über die Ausgrabungen in Gadara (Umm Qēs) in Jordanien im Jahre 1980," in ZDPV 75 (1982), pp. 153-162; and "Preliminary Report of the Excavations in Gadara (Umm Qēs) in Jordan, 1980," in ADAJ 28 (1984), pp. 87-90; Mendel Nun, *Ancient Anchorages and Harbours around the Sea of Galilee* (Kibbutz Ein Gev: Kinnereth Sailing Co., 1988), pp. 6-9. Photograph: courtesy of the Israel Antiquities Authority.

DECAPOLIS

107. Plan of Jerash

THE DECAPOLIS (Δεκάπολις) is mentioned only three times in the Gospels (Mt 4:25; Mk 5:20; 7:31) and only the last of these references speaks of Jesus as going there. Even in the last case the language is not unambiguous for ἀνὰ μέσον τῶν ὁρίων Δεκαπόλεως can be translated not only "through the region of the Decapolis" (RSV), but also "through the midst of the borders of Decapolis" (ASV), or even taken to mean "between" the political boundaries of the cities in the Decapolis league (cf. Sherman E. Johnson, Black's NT Commentaries, *Mark*, p. 139). As the name indicates, the Decapolis was a federation of "ten cities," although the actual number varied from time to time. Pliny, in the first century of the Christian era, names the cities in the league as Damascus, Philadelphia, Raphana, Scythopolis, Gadara, Hippo, Dion, Pella, Galasa, and Canatha (*Nat. Hist.* v 16, 74). Scythopolis was on the west side of the Jordan, the other cities on the east, and their territory as a whole, according to this list, formed a triangle from Scythopolis on the west to Damascus on the north and Philadelphia (present-day Amman) on the south. Galasa, in Pliny's list, is probably the same as Gerasa, and this city and Gadara are the two of the ten to which there are allusions in the text of the Gospels, as noted just above (No. 106).

As Hellenistic cities in the Roman Empire, the towns of the Decapolis were characterized by such features as a main colonnaded street, forum, theater, temples, etc. Of the "ten cities" the one where the ruins have been best preserved and most thoroughly excavated is Gerasa or Jerash.

Gerasa is in the mountains of Gilead on a stream called Chrysorhoas, a tributary of the River Jabbok. With many of its ruins still visible above ground, the site attracted the attention of modern travelers from the early nineteenth century onward. J. L. Burckhardt, for example, who was there briefly in 1812, was able to draw a plan showing town wall, temples, theaters, private habitations, colonnaded streets, and forum. The forum he found "enclosed by a magnificent semicircle of columns in a single row" (p. 256). Fifty-seven of these columns were still standing; in the ruins as a whole he enumerated 190 columns, and half again as many broken-off columns, all still standing (pp. 263f.). Guy Le Strange, who went there in 1884, found the ruins "Palmyra perhaps excepted, the most extensive and marvellous remains of the Graeco-Roman rule in Syria," and thought that as they stood out white and glaring in the noontime sun they had "that same appearance of recent desolation which is so striking a characteristic of the freshly cleared streets of Pompeii" (pp. 167f.). After more detailed studies by G. Schumacher who was there repeatedly between 1891 and 1902, and by O. Puchstein who came in 1902 for comparative studies in the course of his work (1898-1905) at Baalbek, repair and conservation work was begun in 1925 by the British School of Archaeology in Jerusalem under George Horsfield. The latter described the situation at that time: "The ruins were unapproachable except on foot; all was choked with earth and fallen stones, and the paved streets were lost under debris and fallen columns. Gardens encroached on monuments and cultivation extended into the theaters. The churches were hardly visible or even known." Large-scale excavation was conducted from 1928 to 1934 by Yale University in conjunction first with the British School of Archaeology and later with the American School of Oriental Research in Jerusalem, and the results were published in 1938 under the editorship of Carl H. Kraeling. In 1953-1956 restoration of the south theater was carried out by Theo Canaan and Diana Kirkbride for the Department of Antiquities of Jordan, and in 1959 chamber tombs of the second century A.D. were excavated for the Department by Farah S. Ma'ayeh. In 1975-1976 a new program was launched by the Jordanian Department of Antiquities together with the University of Jordan, and this was followed in 1981-1983 by the department's Jerash Project for Excavation and Restoration, conducted on an international basis with teams from no less than ten countries participating, and with a volume of preliminary reports published in 1986.

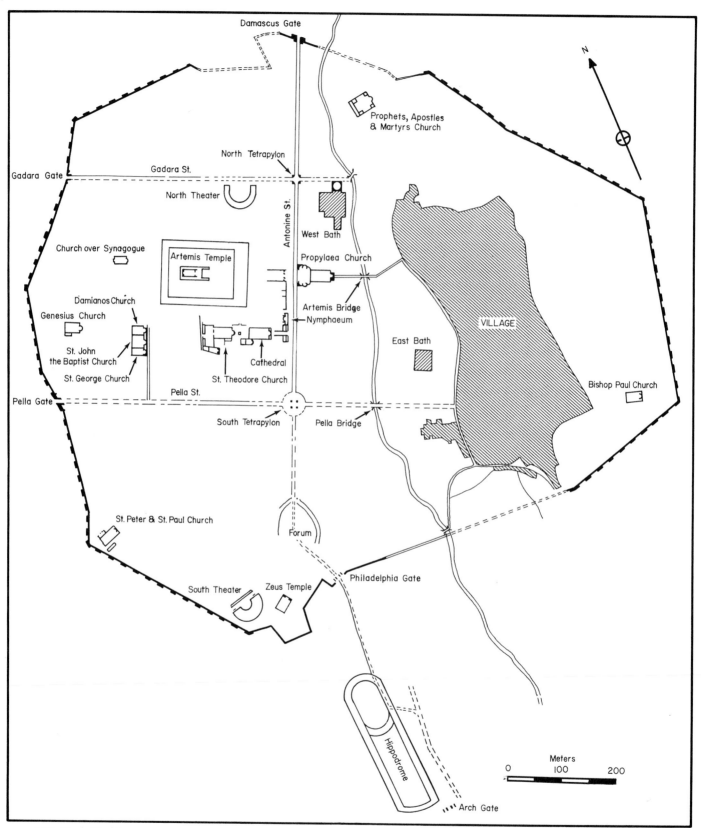

Damascus Gate

Prophets, Apostles
& Martyrs Church

North Tetrapylon

Gadara Gate   Gadara St.

North Theater

West Bath

Church over Synagogue

Artemis Temple   Propylaea Church

Artemis Bridge

Damianos Church   Nymphaeum

Genesius Church

VILLAGE

St. John
the Baptist Church   East Bath

St. George Church   Cathedral

St. Theodore Church   Bishop Paul Church

Pella Gate   Pella St.

South Tetrapylon   Pella Bridge

St. Peter & St. Paul Church

Forum

South Theater   Zeus Temple   Philadelphia Gate

N

Antonine St.

Hippodrome

Meters
0   100   200

Arch Gate

107. Plan of Jerash

118

The plan shows the chief features in the excavated city. The walls, ten feet in thickness and 3,500 meters in circumference, enclosed the slopes of the hills on both sides of the river that flowed through the middle of the city. The main ruins are on the west side, where the major north-south colonnaded street roughly parallels the stream. At the south end of the street is the great elliptical forum of the first century, the ruins of which Burckhardt admired. Not far away on the hill to the west are a temple of Zeus and the south theater. Proceeding north along the colonnaded street, there are tetrapylons at the intersections of two main east-west streets. Between these streets on the hill in the northwest is the chief temple, built in the second century and dedicated to Artemis, and beyond it the north theater. Outside the city walls to the south is the hippodrome, and the triumphal arch with its inscription welcoming the emperor Hadrian on his visit to Gerasa in 130. Like the arch, many of the extant architectural remains belong to the second century rather than the first, yet presumably they preserve much of the plan of the city as it already existed in the first century. Between the fourth and the sixth century the fine Christian churches were built, eleven of which have been found. Many were in the area not far from the Artemis temple, and one replaced a synagogue that had been directly behind the temple (No. 119).

John L. Burckhardt, *Travels in Syria and the Holy Land* (London: John Murray, 1822), pp. 251-264; Guy Le Strange, "Account of a Short Journey East of the Jordan," in PEFQS 1885, pp. 167-168; G. Schumacher, "Dscherasch," in ZDPV 25 (1902), pp. 109-177; Carl H. Kraeling, ed., *Gerasa, City of the Decapolis* (New Haven: American Schools of Oriental Research, 1938); Diana Kirkbride, "A Brief Outline of the Restoration of the South Theatre at Jerash," in ADAJ 4-5 (1960), pp. 123-127; Farah S. Ma'ayeh, "Jerash," in ADAJ 4-5 (1960), pp. 115f.; Rami J. Khouri, "A Jewel in Jordan: The Greco-Roman City of Jerash," in *Archaeology* 38 (1985), pp. 18-25; *Jerash Archaeological Project 1981-1983*, I, Preliminary reports, ed. Fawzi Zayadine (Amman: Department of Antiquities of Jordan, 1986). Plan: courtesy Palestine Institute.

108. The Triumphal Arch at Jerash

THIS PHOTOGRAPH SHOWS the triumpal arch mentioned in the preceding section (No. 107). In the excavation the arch was found preserved to this extent, and additional restoration has since been made. Located about 460 meters south of the ancient city, it is the first major monument seen upon approaching from the south. As excavated, the arch stands upon a rectangular piece of land over 37 meters long and 9 meters wide; the central structure is 25 meters long and, as reconstructed, 21.5 meters high. The arrangement is typical of triumphal arches in that period. In the center is a large arched

108. The Triumphal Arch at Jerash

passageway, 5.7 meters wide and 10.8 meters high; on either side is a smaller arched passage, 2.65 meters wide and 5.2 meters high. Both façades of the arch are decorated with columns and niches. Over the central passageway on the north face was set a panel of some nineteen stones, in all over seven meters long, bearing an inscription that is now in the Palestine Archaeological Museum in Jerusalem. The inscription dedicates the gateway (πύλη) to the emperor Hadrian and mentions among his honors the holding of the tribunician authority for the fourteenth time (δημαρχικῆς ἐξουσίας τὸ ιδ′), which gives the date A.D. 129/130 (Liebenam, *Fasti consulares*, KLT 41-43, p. 107).

Kraeling, *Gerasa*, pp. 73-83, 401-402 no. 58; W. F. Stinespring, "The Inscription of the Triumphal Arch at Jerash," in BASOR 56 (Dec. 1934), pp. 15-16; and in BASOR 57 (Feb. 1935), pp. 3-5 and fig. 2. Photograph: Jerry Vardaman.

109. The Forum at Jerash

ONE ENTERS THIS portion of the forum soon after passing into the area of the city. In extent the forum is over 80 meters wide and 90 meters long. The colonnades curve around it in unequal ellipses, the western one curving in more sharply toward the colonnaded street at the north, the eastern one (shown here) curving more gradually. The heavy paving blocks were laid on lines which follow the curve of the porticoes. The columns stand upon square bases, have Ionic capitals, and carry a continuous architrave. Certain architectural relationships of the forum led the Yale Expedition (Kraeling, *Gerasa*, p. 157) to place its date in the first century.

Photograph: JF.

110. The North-South Colonnaded Street at Jerash

THE MAIN COLONNADED street runs from the forum in the south some 800 meters to the north gate of the city in the north wall. Some of the columns of the porticoes are of the Corinthian order, as in the section shown here; some are of the Ionic order. The Ionic columns are probably of the middle of the first century, the Corinthian of the end of the second century. The heavy paving blocks show the ruts of ancient chariot wheels.

Photograph: JF.

111. Entranceway to the Cathedral at Jerash

IF ONE PROCEEDS northward on the main north-south colonnaded street (No. 110) to the South Tetrapylon and 120 meters beyond, there is on the left the imposing entranceway of which a portion is shown in this photograph. The portico stands on a terrace only a few feet above the street and gives access to a long flight of steps that leads up to a second terrace. On the second terrace are the imposing ruins of a church, which the excavators regard as the cathedral of Gerasa (No. 112). Under the long flight of stairs were found the remains of an older staircase, and under the church the remains of a pagan temple, probably of the first century. While the temple was small (about 25 meters long by 10 meters wide) it was not far from the temple of Artemis and may have been second in importance only to the latter.

J. W. Crowfoot, "Recent Work Round the Fountain Court at Jerash," in PEFQS 1931, pp. 143-154. Photograph: JF.

109. The Forum at Jerash

110. The North-South
Colonnaded Street at Jerash

111. Entranceway to the
Cathedral at Jerash

112. Plan of the Cathedral at Jerash

THE CHURCH STOOD on the second terrace at the top of the long flight of stairs described in the preceding section (No. 111). It was a basilica over forty meters in length, with internal apse, and oriented to the east as usual, so that persons ascending the long staircase from the street approached the apse end of the building. Inside, two rows of twelve columns each, with Corinthian capitals, divided the side aisles from the central nave. The columns were probably all taken from some other building, perhaps from the temple which was previously on the spot. Various considerations analyzed by the excavators lead to the conclusion that the Cathedral was built about 365 (Kraeling, *Gerasa*, p. 219). At the west end the atrium of the church was provided by the so-called Fountain Court (No. 113), twenty meters square and surrounded by colonnades. The portico on the east side of the court had six columns with Corinthian capitals, dating probably at the end of the second century (Kraeling, *Gerasa*, p. 210); the porticoes on the other three sides were lower and of the Ionic order. In the center of the court was a square tank to which water was brought, in a conduit coming in past the Temple of Artemis, from springs two miles away.

Plan: Kraeling, *Gerasa*, plan xxxi, courtesy American Schools of Oriental Research.

121

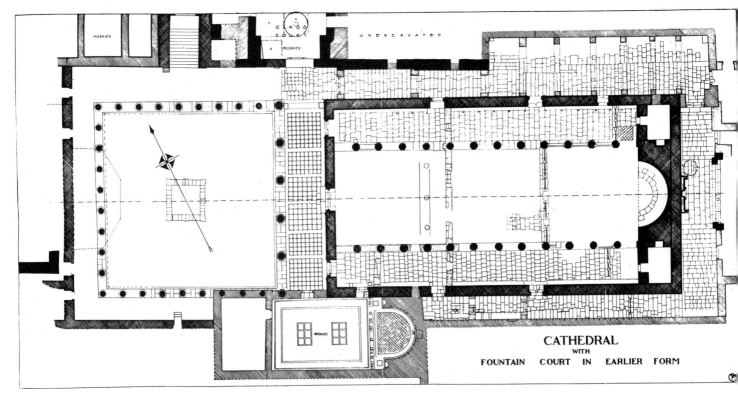

112. Plan of the Cathedral at Jerash

113. The Fountain Court at Jerash

113. The Fountain Court at Jerash

THIS VIEW LOOKS across the Fountain Court to the northwest. Under the paving blocks the excavators found a lead pipe which ran into the fountain from the northwest corner of the court; from the east side of the tank a drain channel ran toward the northeast corner. At the west side of the court a small excavation was made under the apse of St. Theodore's Church (see No. 114) and a small patch of Roman mosaic was found at the level of the court; this probably goes back to the second or third century and the Fountain Court must be that old or older. In 375 Epiphanius (*Pan. haer.* li 30, 1-2 GCS Hall/Dummer ii, p. 301) refers to a martyrium and miraculous fountain in Gerasa, where every year the spring ran with wine on the anniversary of the miracle at Cana, which was also the feast of the Epiphany. It seems most probable that the Cathedral and this adjacent fountain are the very places to which he referred. The fact that some inscriptions found at Jerash mention Dusares,

"the god of Arabia," with whom a similar miracle was associated, suggests the possibility that the church in Gerasa took over a pagan event for its own.

J. W. Crowfoot in PEFQS 1929, pp. 31-35; 1931, pp. 153-154.
Photograph: The Matson Photo Service, Alhambra, Calif.

114. Plan of St. Theodore's Church at Jerash

ON A THIRD terrace (cf. Nos. 111, 112) west of the Cathedral and the Fountain Court was yet another great basilica. As shown in the plan, there was a large atrium on the west end, over 21 meters from west to east and 50 meters from north to south. An entrance hall gave access to an open court surrounded by colonnades on the north, east, and south. The columns had Ionic capitals, and the floor was paved with mosaics. From the east portico of the atrium three doorways led into the basilica, a building about forty meters in length, almost as long as the

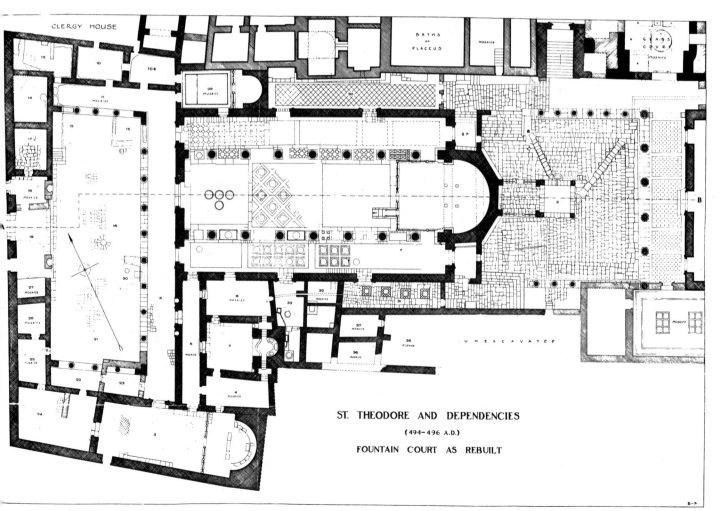

ST. THEODORE AND DEPENDENCIES
(494-496 A.D.)
FOUNTAIN COURT AS REBUILT

114. Plan of St. Theodore's Church at Jerash

Cathedral. The nave and two side aisles were marked off by two rows of seven columns each, with Corinthian capitals, and the floor was laid out in patterns of colored stone and marble. The apse at the east end, polygonal on the exterior and vaulted with stone, was allowed to project into the area of the Fountain Court, where the earlier portico on the western side had been removed. The apse of the church was connected with the square tank of the fountain itself by two arches which supported a vault, and at the same time it appears that some kind of a vault was put up over the fountain tank itself. In addition to the three doors at the west end, the basilica had three doors on the north side, four on the south, and two at the east end of the aisles from which one could go on down into the Fountain Court.

J. W. Crowfoot, "The Church of S. Theodore at Jerash," in PEFQS 1929, pp. 17-36. Plan: Kraeling, *Gerasa*, plan XXXIII, courtesy American Schools of Oriental Research.

115. Broken Blocks with an Inscription from St. Theodore's Church

THE LINTEL OVER the center doorway at the west end of the basilica (No. 114) carried an inscription, in a position to be read from the interior of the church. The lintel was made of four large blocks of stone. These were fallen and broken, and the left end of the first block, with the beginning of each line of the inscription, was missing. The missing piece was found later, and it was then possible to establish the correct reading of the initial portions of the lines (the earlier conjectural restorations were all shown to be incorrect). Altogether the inscription is in four long lines, and in poetically phrased Greek.

As may be seen in the photograph, the first line on the first block is marked with a cross and then starts with the word Ἄχραντο[ς], which means undefiled. This long line continues as follows on the other three blocks, the broken places in the stones being indicated by vertical marks in the transcription: δόμος εἰμὶ ἀεθλοφόρου Θεοδώρου, μάρτυρος ἀθανάτ | ου, θεοειδέος οὗ κλέος ἔ | πτη ἐν χθονὶ κ(αὶ) πόντῳ, and the sentence then concludes

with the first three words of the second line: καὶ τέρμασιν | ὠκεανοῖο. The entire sentence may be translated: "I am the undefiled house of victorious Theodore, immortal and godlike martyr, whose fame has flown abroad over land and sea and the boundaries of the ocean." In a second sentence it is stated that, although the martyr's body is in the earth, his soul is in heaven where it is a defense keeping off evil (ἀλεξίκακο[ο] | ν, the first word in the third line) for the town and its citizens. Toward the latter part of the third line there is another cross, which marks the beginning of a third and final sentence. In the rest of the third line this reads: Χάριτι το | ῦ Θ(εο)ῦ ἐθεμελιώθη, and in the fourth line it continues and concludes: τὸ ἅγιο[ν μα] | ρτύριον μη(νὶ) Δίῳ τῆς [. . .] ή ἰνδ(ικτιῶνος) κ(αὶ) ἀνῆλθεν τὰ ὑπέ[ρ] | θυρα ἐν μη(νὶ) Δίῳ τῆς έ | [ἰν] δ(ικτιῶνος) τοῦ θνφ ἔτ (ους). This may be translated: "By the grace of God the foundation of the holy martyrium was laid in the month Dios in the . . . third indiction and the lintel went up in the month Dios in the fifth indiction in the year 559."

This inscription is of great value as giving both the name of the one to whom the church was dedicated and also the date of its building. The martyr Theodore is described as "victorious" (ἀθλοφόρος, which literally means bearing away the prize of a combat). He may very probably be identified with the young Syrian named Theodorus who was tortured at Antioch by Julian (361-363) and called by Theodoret (*Ch. Hist.* III 11, 3d ed. Parmentier 2d ed. GCS XLIV, p. 187) a "combatant of the truth" (ἀγωνιστὴς τῆς ἀληθείας, a phrase synonymous with ἀθλητὴς τῆς ἀληθείας), "athlete of the truth"). The lintel was raised in the month Dios (Δῖος), i.e., Oct/Nov (FHBC p. 68 table 24), in the year 559 (θνφ′), and the foundation was laid two years before that in the very same month. If the era was that of Pompey, as seems generally to be the case in the inscriptions of Gerasa, with the epoch of that era from which we count falling in 63/62 B.C., then the year 559 given in the inscription as the date of the raising of the lintel would be equivalent to A.D. 496, and the date two years before that when the foundation of the church was laid would be equivalent to A.D. 494.

When excavated, the columns of the basilica and their capitals were all still lying where they had fallen;

115. Broken Blocks with an Inscription from St. Theodore's Church

the basilica was evidently destroyed at an unknown time by an earthquake.

R. P. Germer-Durand, "Exploration épigraphique de Gerasa," in RB (1895), pp. 374-400; F. Bleckmann, "Bericht über griechische und lateinische Epigraphik," in ZDPV 38 (1915), pp. 234-235; A. H. M. Jones, "Some Inscriptions from Jerash," in PEFQS 1928, p. 192; J. W. Crowfoot in PEFQS 1929, pp. 21-23; C. B. Welles in Kraeling, *Gerasa*, pp. 477-478 no. 300. Photograph: PEFQS 1928, pl. II no. 2 facing p. 190, courtesy Palestine Exploration Fund.

116. The Baptistery at St. Theodore's Church

AS THE PLAN (No. 114) of the Church of St. Theodore at Jerash shows, there were a number of additional buildings on both sides of the basilica and its atrium, probably chapels, residences for priests and visitors, etc. The most interesting of these buildings is the baptistery on the south side, which may have been a chapel of some sort before it was made into a baptistery. At the east end of the main room (7 on the plan) was a semicircular apse, where the baptismal font was built. As shown in the photograph, steps led down into the baptismal tank from either end. In the semicircular apse a sort of bench, with three small bins, was installed. One hypothesis is that these may have had something to do with the ceremonies of anointing which accompanied the immersion. The steps descend into the font from very small chambers on either end, and beyond these on either side are large rooms (4 and 8) paved with mosaic floors, perhaps dressing rooms for use before and after the ceremonies. Behind the baptistery was a large cistern and some earthenware piping, which evidently provided for filling the font with water.

Crowfoot in PEFQS 1929, p. 29; Kraeling, *Gerasa*, pp. 224-225. Photograph: Kraeling, *Gerasa*, pl XLI, courtesy American Schools of Oriental Research.

117. A Christian Cross at Jerash

FROM THE NORTH SIDE of the Fountain Court a flight of steps gave access to yet a fourth terrace (cf. Nos. 111, 112, 114), the highest in the entire series. In this area, which was between the Church of St. Theodore and the old court of the Artemis Temple, were public baths and what the excavators judge to have been ecclesiastical residences (not on plan, No. 107). The fragment of sculpture in this photograph was found in this area. It shows a Greek cross inside a wreath together with the alpha and the omega. Considering all the buildings on the four terraces, the first of which were pagan, the later Christian, they form a complex which extends 163 meters from east to west, and the buildings on the highest level at the west are 18 meters above the level of the main colonnaded street where the chief entranceway stood (No. 111). In the arrangement of the masses and the accommodation of the buildings to a site, this great complex may be compared with similar groupings of ecclesiastical structures at the famous pilgrimage centers of St. Simeon Stylites in North Syria, of St. Menas in Egypt, and of the Holy Sepulcher at Jerusalem. Of the Gerasa complex in comparison with that in Jerusalem, J. W. Crowfoot writes the following words (in Kraeling, *Gerasa*, p. 202, quoted courtesy American Schools of Oriental Research), which we quote particularly because we shall later be interested in a consideration of the buildings in Jerusalem:

in disposition the completed group corresponds closely to the original disposition of the buildings round the Holy Sepulchre in Jerusalem. The portico on the street and the great stairway at Gerasa correspond with the propylaea and the eastern atrium at Jerusalem; the Cathedral with the Martyrium of Constantine; the Fountain Court with the second atrium and the Calvary, and St. Theodore's with the Anastasis. Even the baptisteries in the two places occupy approx-

116. The Baptistery at St. Theodore's Church

117. A Christian Cross at Jerash

imately the same position. The configuration of the two sites was, of course, very different. At Jerusalem the ground was more level on the whole and the rock was reduced more radically where it rose at the west end. At Gerasa it sloped gradually and a succession of levels was created with a moderate degree of scarping and terracing. But with this qualification the resemblance between the two dispositions is so close as to leave no doubt that in its final form the Gerasa plan was deliberately modeled on the Jerusalem pattern, and that it now shows better than any other extant group of structures what the buildings in Jerusalem once looked like.

Photograph: JF.

118. Floor Mosaic in the Church of SS. Cosmas and Damianus

ONE HUNDRED AND FIFTY METERS west-north-west of the atrium of St. Theodore's Church is a group of three churches (Kraeling, *Gerasa*, pp. 241-249) all of which open off a common atrium. On the left is a basilica dedicated to St. George in the year 592 = A.D. 529/530 (Inscription no. 309); in the center a round church with a baptistery in a room beside the apse, dedicated to St. John the Baptist and decorated with mosaics in 594 = A.D. 531 (Inscription no. 306); and at the right the basilica dedicated to SS. Cosmas and Damianus. The floor mosaic in this last-named church is shown in the present photograph and is the best preserved of the mosaic pavements in the several Gerasa churches. On the floor immediately below the chancel step is a single line of inscription that gives the dedication to the two famous martyrs and a date in 595 = A.D. 533. There follows below this (at the extreme top of the photograph) an inscription in ten lines. It speaks of the martyrs as victorious in combat (ἀθλοφόρων) (cf. No. 115), mentions a certain Bishop Paul as a shepherd and wise guide, and says that the name of the founder of the church will be learned to preserve the name of the Prodromos (πρόδ-

ρομος), the "forerunner," i.e., John (the Baptist). This is explained by a portrait of the donor, with the name Theodore, immediately at the left of the inscription. The Greek name Theodore, meaning "gift of God," was evidently considered the equivalent of John ('Ιωάνης, Hellenized form of 'Ιωανάν) because this was itself the equivalent not only of the Hebrew Johanan (יוחנן), "Yahweh has been gracious," but also of Jehonathan or Jonathan (יהונתן or יוגתן), "Yahweh has given." In the corresponding position at the right of the inscription, and visible in the photograph, is a portrait of Theodore's wife, Georgia, standing in the attitude of an *orant* (i.e., with arms outstretched in prayer, cf. below p. 351).

The rest of the mosaic covered much of the floor of the nave. As preserved it has a meander border and a field of squares and diamonds. In the first row of diamonds other donors are commemorated, namely, John son of Astricius who is shown in a portrait, the tribune Dagistheus who is named in an inscription (Inscription no. 311), and Calloeonistus who is shown in a portrait. The other diamonds exhibit a great variety of decorative patterns, while the squares contain representations of birds and animals, also in great variety and so arranged that both horizontally and vertically a row of birds alternates with a row of animals and so on.

F. M. Biebel in Kraeling, *Gerasa*, pp. 331-332. Photograph: JF.

119. Floor Mosaic in the Synagogue under the Synagogue Church at Jerash

AS MENTIONED ABOVE (NO. 107) there is a church immediately behind the Artemis temple which was found to have been built over a synagogue that existed there previously. The church is dated by an inscription to A.D. 530/531 and is a basilica with nave, two side aisles, and apse, oriented to the east. Underneath, the synagogue was also of a rectangular, basilical plan and thus lent itself to incorporation in the later church, but orientation was to the west rather than the east, i.e., in the general direction of Jerusalem. The synagogue was approached from the east through a courtyard and entered through a vestibule and three doors. In the interior two rows of columns formed a nave and two side aisles, and some of the columns were reused in their original places in the church. At the western end there was a projecting room, perhaps to be recognized as a rectangular apse. The synagogue was obviously earlier than the church and is thought to have been built in the fifth century A.D. and perhaps abandoned or destroyed in anti-

Jewish persecutions at the beginning of the reign of the emperor Justinian I (A.D. 527-565).

The floors of the synagogue were paved with mosaics that, although preserved only in fragments, are among the fine examples of ancient synagogue mosaic work. The mosaic in the vestibule was devoted to the story of Noah and showed the family leaving the ark after the flood. As seen in the fragment shown here, two heads are recognizable, with identifications in Greek as two of Noah's sons, Shem (CHM) and Japheth (IAΦIA, written Ιαφεθ in the LXX). Above on a branch is a dove with a twig in its beak, bringing the sign that the waters had subsided (Gen 8:11). Around this panel are rows of different animals—no doubt those that were in the ark with

118. Floor Mosaic in the Church of SS. Cosmas and Damianus

119. Floor Mosaic in the Synagogue under the Synagogue Church at Jerash

127

Noah—and also the familiar symbols of the *menorah*, incense shovel, *shofar*, lulab, and *ethrog*. An incomplete Greek inscription reads: "(Peace to this most) holy place. Amen. Selah. Peace to the synagogue." In the northern aisle there is a Hebrew/Aramaic inscription, and it begins with the greeting: "Peace be upon all Israel, Amen, Amen, Selah," then ends with the names of benefactors or artists: "Phinehas son of Baruch, Jose son of Samuel, and Judan son of Hezekiah."

J. W. Crowfoot and R. W. Hamilton, "The Discovery of a Synagogue at Jerash," in PEFQS 9 (1929), pp. 211-219; Kraeling, *Gerasa*, pp. 234-241, 318-324, 473, 483f.; Saller, *Second Catalogue*, pp. 43f.; Shanks, *Judaism in Stone*, pp. 41f., 121. Photograph: Kraeling, *Gerasa*, pl. LXIV.

CAESAREA

120. General Plan of Caesarea

EVEN THOUGH CAESAREA is not mentioned in the Gospels, it was the Roman capital of Palestine and hence of much importance in the time of Jesus. In the days of the early church it is mentioned frequently (Acts 8:40, etc.). A succinct history of the place is given by Pliny (*Nat. Hist.* v 14, 69) when he lists it as "the Tower of Strato, otherwise Caesarea, founded by King Herod, but now the colony called Prima Flavia established by the Emperor Vespasian." Josephus (*Ant.* XIII 11, 2 §§312-313) mentions the place under the name of Straton's Tower (Στράτωνος πύργος) in connection with the reign of Aristobulus (104/103 B.C.), and it may have been founded as a small harbor by the seafaring Phoenicians, for one or more of the last kings of Sidon had the name of Straton (SHJP Vermes/Millar II, pp. 115-118). The 1962 excavation of The Hebrew University–Southern Baptist Seminary (see No. 132 below) was the first to discover this older Phoenician site. Professor Vardaman reports that Strato's Tower was located generally on the northern side of what later was Caesarea's town limit, and stretched at least from the synagogue area to the region around Herod's wall on the north. The Italian excavations uncovered some Hellenistic pottery in the lowest levels of clearing this wall in later seasons of work (see G. Dell'Amore, A. Calderini, L. Crema, A. Frova, *Scavi di Caesarea Maritima* [Rome: "L'Erma" di Bretschneider, 1966], p. 267, illus. 336).

Alexander Jannaeus (103-76 B.C.) took Strato's Tower from a local tyrant named Zoilus (*Ant.* XIII 12, 2 §§324-326), Pompey (63) set the town free and annexed it to the province of Syria (*Ant.* XIV 4, 4 §76), and Augustus gave it to Herod the Great (*Ant.* XV 7, 3 §217).

Herod saw the possibilities in the place and set about building a splendid city there, as Josephus (*Ant* XV 9, 6 §§331-332) tells us: "And when he observed that there was a place near the sea, formerly called Straton's Tower, which was very well suited to be the site of a city, he set about making a magnificent plan and put up buildings all over the city, not of ordinary material but of white stone. He also adorned it with a very costly palace, with civic halls and—what was greatest of all and required the most labor—with a well-protected harbor, of the size of the Piraeus, with landing-places and secondary anchorages inside."

The construction work of Herod at Caesarea occupied either twelve years (*Ant.* XV 9, 6 §341) or ten years (*Ant.* XVI 5, 1 §136) and was completed, according to the latter passage, in the twenty-eighth year of Herod's reign, which fell in the 192d Olympiad. If the twenty-eighth year of Herod's reign is counted from his taking of Jerusalem in the summer or fall of 37 B.C., it was equivalent to 10/9 B.C. and this corresponds with the third year of the 192d Olympiad (FHBC pp. 114, 232), so the date of 10/9 B.C. is the probable date of the completion of the building of the city (against Avi-Yonah in IEJ 1 [1950-1951], p. 169, who counts from 40 B.C. and reaches 13/12 B.C., which was the year before the first year of the 192d Olympiad). The completion of the city was celebrated with a very great festival of dedication (*Ant.* XVI 5, 1 §137) and the institution of quinquennial games (πεν-ταετηρικοὺς ἀγῶνας). In honor of Augustus the city was named Caesarea (Καισάρεια) (*Ant.* XV 9, 6 §339) or Caesarea Sebaste (Καισάρεια Σεβαστή) (*Ant.* XVI 5, 1 §136), and the harbor was also called Sebastos (Σεβασ-τὸς λιμήν). In addition to a palace and harbor, Josephus mentions (*Ant.* XV 9, 6 §§339, 341; *War* I 21, 7 §§414-415) a temple dedicated to Rome and Augustus which stood on an eminence facing the harbor mouth, a theater in the city, and an amphitheater on the south side of the harbor with a view to the sea (here Josephus probably reversed his terms for it is the theater [No. 128] rather than the amphitheater which has been found to the south of the harbor and with a fine view to the sea).

With Judea under Roman rule the procurators established their headquarters at Caesarea. This is indicated by various references in Josephus, e.g., where Pilate brought the Roman army from Caesarea to Jerusalem (*Ant.* XVIII 3, 1 §55), and where the Jews proceeded to Caesarea to present a request to Pilate (*War* II 9, 2 §171). In Caesarea the former palace of Herod the Great was no doubt taken by the procurators for their residence, and must be what is referred to in Ac 23:35 as "Herod's praetorium." The last word (πραιτώριον) is the Latin *praetorium*. It meant originally the tent of a *praetor* or general in an army camp, then the official residence of a governor in a province.

Herod Agrippa I, who ruled most of Palestine A.D. 41-44, governed from Jerusalem but visited Caesarea upon occasion (*Ant.* XIX 7, 4 §332) and, in fact, died there. According to Josephus (*Ant.* XIX 8, 2 §§343-352), he was present in Caesarea to celebrate spectacles in honor of Caesar (probably the quinquennial games instituted by Herod the Great), appeared in the theater in a garment woven completely of silver, was hailed by flatterers as a god, but was smitten by violent pain and died in a few days, probably in the spring or summer of 44 (FHBC pp. 302-303). This is clearly the same event cited in Ac 12:21-23.

At the outbreak of the Jewish War (66) 20,000 Jews were massacred in Caesarea (*War* II 18, 1 §457). In 67 Vespasian led his troops there from Ptolemais and in this connection Josephus remarks (*War* III 9, 1 §409) that the city was one of the largest of Judea, with a population consisting chiefly of Greeks. In the passage just cited Josephus says that Vespasian led his troops "to Caesarea-on-the-sea" (εἰς τὴν παράλιον . . . Καισάρειαν); on another occasion he tells (*War* VII 2, 1 §23) how Titus took his troops off "from Caesarea-on-the-sea" (ἀπὸ τῆς ἐπὶ θαλάττῃ Καισαρείας); and this manner of designation is reflected in the later much-used Latin name, Caesarea Maritima (cf. Leo Kadman, *The Coins of Caesarea Maritima* [1957], p. 9). As not only the foregoing but also many other passages in Josephus show, Vespasian and Titus made Caesarea their headquarters throughout the Jewish War. After the fall of Jerusalem Titus planned

to celebrate the triumph in Rome, but in October A.D. 70 held a victory celebration in Caesarea (on the birthday of his brother, Domitian, then eighteen years of age) with games in which 2,500 Jewish captives perished (*War* VII 3, §§37-38). In the reorganization of the country Caesarea was made the sole capital of the province of Judea, and Tacitus (*Histories* II 78) says that it was the first city of Judea (*hoc Iudaeae caput est*). Vespasian also made Caesarea a Roman colony. As the first city to be honored in this way by the Flavian emperors it was called Colonia Prima Flavia Augusta Caesarea, and we have already noted above the brief reference by Pliny to this title.

With Origen, who lived there 230/231-253/254, and with Eusebius, who was probably born there within ten years of the death of Origen and was bishop from 313 until his death in 339/340, Caesarea became a famous Christian center. The city was overrun by the Persians in A.D. 614, the Arabs took it in 639/640, the Crusaders in 1101, and the Sultan Baibars in 1265. Destroyed by the last named, Caesarea sank beneath the ever-shifting sand dunes of the coast, only to be settled again in the nineteenth century and excavated in the twentieth in long-continuing archeological work first stimulated by the accidental discovery in 1951 by a member of the Jewish settlement of Sedot-Yam (Fields of the Sea, just south of the ancient city) of a statue while plowing a field.

As known from the archeological investigations, the chief sites and monuments of ancient Caesarea are iden-

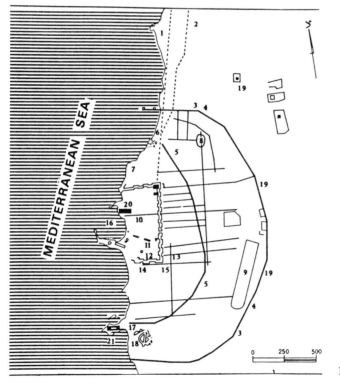

120. General Plan of Caesarea

tified by numbers on the present plan as follows: 1. high-level aqueduct; 2. low-level aqueduct; 3. Byzantine city wall; 4. exploratory trenches attesting to the Byzantine wall; 5. Herodian city wall; 6. one polygonal and two circular towers (a northern gate?); 7. Hellenistic remains and a Byzantine synagogue; 8. amphitheater(?); 9. hippodrome; 10. Crusader city; 11. podium of Herodian temple to Augustus and Rome; 12. Byzantine church; 13. Byzantine street complex; 14. mithraeum; 15. Byzantine archive (library?); 16. port; 17. Byzantine fortress; 18. theater; 19. necropolis; 20. main excavation area, 1975-1979; 21. Promontory Palace.

C. R. Conder, *The Survey of Western Palestine, Memoirs* II (London: The Palestine Exploration Fund, 1882), pp. 13-29; A. Reifenberg, "Caesarea, A Study in the Decline of a Town," in IEJ 1 (1950-51), pp. 20-32; *Archaeology and Caesarea*, a booklet published by the Southern Baptist Theological Seminary (Louisville, Ky., 1963); Vogel, *Bibliography* I, pp. 23f.; and *Bibliography* II, pp. 20f.; Charles T. Fritsch, ed., *Studies in the History of Caesarea Maritima, The Joint Expedition to Caesarea Maritima*, vol. I (1975) and following volumes; Lee I. Levine, *Caesarea under Roman Rule* (SJLA 7) (Leiden: E. J. Brill, 1975); Levine, *Roman Caesarea, An Archaeological-Topographical Study* (Qedem 2, 1975); and Levine, *Excavations at Caesarea Maritima, 1975, 1976, 1979—Final Report* (Qedem 21, 1986); Robert J. Bull, "Caesarea Maritima, The Search for Herod's City," in BAR 8.3 (May/June 1982), pp. 24-40; Kenneth G. Holum, Robert L. Hohlfelder, Robert J. Bull, and Avner Raban, *King Herod's Dream: Caesarea on the Sea* (New York: Norton, 1988). Plan: from *Qedem* 21 (1986), p. 9, plan 1, courtesy The Institute of Archaeology, Hebrew University of Jerusalem.

121. Crusader Moat and Walls at Caesarea

COMING INTO CAESAREA one crosses the line of the Byzantine city wall (3 in plan No. 120) and sees the ancient hippodrome (9) on the left. Although the hippodrome is not yet excavated, the outline of its enclosure, approximately 320 meters long and 80 meters wide, and the line of its *spina*, or central barrier (a low wall dividing the circus longitudinally), are plainly discernible. Along the line of the *spina* are still to be seen, fallen, a mighty obelisk and three conical columns, all of red granite. Also at the side of the running track is an enormous quadrangular block of red granite. In his description of a hippodrome (ἱππόδρομος), Pausanias (*Description of Greece* VI—Elis II 20, 15-19 LCL III, pp. 124-129) says that a racecourse has one side longer than the other and, on the longer side which is a bank, there stands at the passage through the bank the object of fear to the horses which is called the Taraxippus (Ταράξιππος), the "horse frightener." Describing one example of this object as found at Nemea of the Argives, Pausanias writes:

121. Crusader Moat and Walls at Caesarea

"above the turning point of the chariots rose a rock, red in color, and the flash from it terrified the horses, just as though it had been fire." Presumably the purpose of the object was to increase, through fright, the speed of the running horses. The great red granite block, still lying in the Caesarea hippodrome, may be an example (and thus the only one known, certainly in Palestine) of such a Taraxippus. Beyond the hippodrome is a Byzantine ruin of the fifth-sixth centuries, uncovered accidentally in 1954. In it at the foot of a broad staircase are two large Roman seated headless statues, one of white marble and one of red porphyry. In a mosaic floor is a Greek inscription, which states that the mayor Flavius Strategius (sixth century A.D.) built the structure out of public funds (RB 68 [1961], pp. 122f., no. 15). Obviously he brought in the ancient statues from elsewhere for adornment. Although first attributed to the second and third centuries A.D. respectively, it is now thought (Avi-Yonah) that the porphyry statue may represent the emperor Hadrian (A.D. 117-138) and may have come from a temple to Hadrian (Hadrianeum) not far away; that such a temple existed is shown by a Caesarea inscription of the sixth century which marks the successful completion (no doubt in work of restoration) of the mosaic and the steps of "the Hadrianeum" (τὸ Ἀδριανεῖον, RB 4 [1895], pp. 75f.; PEFQS 1896, pp. 87f.). An alternate and probably less likely suggestion (Diplock) sees the statues as representing Claudius (41-54) in the marble statue and Titus (79-81) in the porphyry figure, presented as gifts by Rome to Caesarea in post-Herodian times. At any rate it was probably during the Arab conquest that the heads of both figures were destroyed.

Directly ahead from these ruins is the area of the Crusader city (10 on plan No. 120). The entire Crusaders' fortification system was cleared in 1960 under the direction of Avraham Negev of the Hebrew University. Except for their upper part, the city walls are very well preserved. There are three city gates on the south, east, and north, and near them three postern gates. The main eastern gate is reached by a bridge, protected by a tower on the nearby wall. Here the outer gate gives access to a hall running north and south, from which an inner gate opens at right angles into the city, this angled approach being intended to give the defenders an advantage over attackers. While the Crusader town may have had earlier fortifications, the gate system just described is believed to have come into use in the thirteenth century, and as they exist the fortifications are commonly attributed to Louis IX of France, who is said to have fortified Caesarea in 1251, which was only a few years before the fall of the city to Sultan Baibars. The moat is 30 feet across, and the sloping embankment rises 30 to 45 feet from the bottom. These walls, running around the three landward sides of the Crusader town, enclose an area of 35 acres, but this is only about one-sixth of the known area of the earlier city.

Joachim Jeremias, "Der Taraxippos im Hippodrom von Caesarea Palaestinae," in ZDPV 54 (1931), pp. 279-289; Baruch Lifshitz, "Inscriptions grecques de Césarée en Palestine (Caesarea Palaestinae)," in RB 68 (1961), pp. 121-123 no. 15; M. Avi-Yonah, "The Caesarea Porphyry Statues," in IEJ 20 [1970], p. 203-208; P. Russell Diplock, "The Date of Askalon's Sculptured Panels and an Identification of the Caesarea Statues," in PEQ 1971, pp. 13-16; and Diplock, "Further Commment on 'An Identification of the Caesarea Statues,' " in PEQ 1973, pp. 165-166, retracting his earlier proposal for identification with Augustus and Rome and proposing Claudius and Titus instead. For the clearance of the Crusader fortifications see A. Negev in IEJ 10 (1960), pp. 127, 264f.; and in CNI 11.4, pp. 20f. Photograph: courtesy Government Press Office, State of Israel.

122. Looking Toward the Sea at Caesarea

THE PHOTOGRAPH SHOWS the view from within the Crusader town looking toward the waterfront. In 1884 Muslim refugees from Bosnia established themselves on the ruins of the Crusader city and continued there until 1948; it is the minaret of their mosque that appears at the left side of the picture. On out to sea is the present very small harbor and, under the surface, the remains of Herod's very great harbor (16 on plan No. 120).

In his account of the works of Herod the Great at Caesarea, Josephus lays the greatest emphasis upon the construction of the harbor (Ant. xv 9, 6 §§332-338; War I 21, 5-7 §§409-413). The seacoast, he explains, was without a harbor all the way from Dora (10 miles to the north) to Joppa (35 miles to the south). Even these were only small towns with poor harbors, and the southwest wind beat upon them and drove sand upon the shore. Under the menace of that wind, ships bound coastwise for Egypt had to ride unsteadily at anchor in the open sea. To make a breakwater Herod lowered enormous blocks of stone, 50 feet in length, 10 or 18 feet in breadth, and 9 feet in depth, into 20 fathoms of water; upon this submarine foundation he built above the surface a mole 200 feet broad, of which the outer half broke the surge and the remainder supported a stone wall encircling the harbor. On the wall were towers, the largest named Drusion after Drusus, stepson of Caesar Augustus. The harbor entrance faced to the north, for the north wind was here the most favorable. On either side of the entrance were three colossal statues. These stood on columns and the columns in turn stood on a tower on the left side (as seen from a ship coming into the harbor), and on the other side on two upright blocks of stone which were clamped together and were even higher than the tower.

122. Looking Toward the Sea at Caesarea

The ruins of Herod's splendid harbor are now fifteen or twenty feet beneath the surface of the sea at Caesarea, and were at least partially explored by the Link Marine Expedition to Israel in 1960. Using ship and underwater equipment designed and provided by Edwin A. Link, divers charted the circular breakwater of the ancient harbor and explored the entrance on the northern side. They found gigantic cut stones weighing as much as twenty to thirty tons. Under some of these blocks and beneath the shelter of a large wooden beam was found one intact Roman amphora of the second century. With an earthquake recorded in the Caesarea area about 130 (IEJ 1 [1950-51], p. 225), it is possible that Herod's harbor was at least partially destroyed and these things tumbled into the sea at that time. Among the finds particular interest attaches to a small medal or commemorative coin. On one side is a male figure with beard and dolphin tail. On the other side is the entrance of a port with round stone towers on either side surmounted by statues; two sailing vessels are coming in, and two letters, KA, are presumably the abbreviation for Caesarea (Καισάρεια). Almost certainly this is a contemporary representation, probably of the first or second century, of the ancient harbor.

To continue the work thus begun by the Link Expedition the international Caesarea Ancient Harbour Excavation Project was formed in 1979. As a result of further exploration, it is now known that from the shoreline a southern breakwater extended westward into the sea and then curved to the north for a total distance of over 600 meters, and a northern breakwater extended west for over 200 meters; where the two great moles approached each other at the northwest corner of the harbor was the open entrance from the north, just as Josephus said.

A. Negev in IEJ 11 (1961), pp. 81-82; Immanuel Ben-Dor, "A Marine Expedition to the Holy Land, Summer 1960," in AJA 65 (1961), p. 186; Charles T. Fritsch, "The Link Expedition to Israel, 1960," in BA 24 (1961), pp. 50-56; for a detailed study of the medal described above Vardaman cites Isreal Numismatic Bulletin II; Avner Raban and Robert' L. Hohlfelder, "The Ancient Harbors of Caesarea Maritima," in Archaeology/ 34.2 (Mar/Apr 1981), pp. 56-60; Robert L. Hohlfelder, "Caesarea beneath the Sea," in BAR 8.3 (May/June 1982), pp. 42-47; and Hohlfelder, "Herod the Great's City on the Sea, Caesarea Maritima," in NG 171.2 (Feb 1987), pp. 260-279. Photograph: JF.

123. Harbor Citadel at Caesarea

THIS POINT ON the sea front at Ceasarea is at the south end of the waterfront side of the Crusader town. The ruins of a Crusader port tower stand here, with a later building above, while Roman columns of granite, which were used to buttress the tower, are in the water.

Photograph: The Matson Photo Service, Alhambra, Calif.

124. Sea Front South of the Crusader City at Caesarea

BETWEEN THE PROMONTORY that extends into the sea toward the southern side of the Crusader town (No. 123) and the farther south palace promontory described below (No. 132) there is the relatively large bay a portion of which is seen in this picture. At one time it was thought that Herod's harbor might be sought here, but instead it is now believed that this may have been the location of the main harbor of Byzantine Caesarea after Herod's harbor fell into disrepair and abandonment, as probably happened by the third and fourth centuries, due to earthquakes (cf. No. 122) and neglect.

Levine in *Qedem* 2 (1975), pp. 14f.; Raban and Hohlfelder in *Archaeology* 34.2 (1981), p. 60. Photograph: The Matson Photo Service, Alhambra, Calif.

125. Byzantine Capital and Cross at Caesarea

INSIDE THE CRUSADER WALLS at Caesarea one sees extensive ruins on a low hill facing the water. Here in contrast with the brown limestone of the Crusader masonry are many building blocks of white stone. Since Herod built Caesarea of white stone (Josephus, *Ant.* xv

123. Harbor Citadel at Caesarea

124. Sea Front South of the Crusader City at Caesarea

9, 6 §331) and placed the temple of Caesar, with its statues of Augustus and Rome, on an eminence facing the mouth of the harbor (*Ant.* xv 1, 6 §339; *War* i 21, 7 §414; cf. above No. 120), it is probable that his temple of Rome and Augustus stood in this place. Identification of these ruins with that temple was suggested in the first survey of the remains of the Crusader city by C. R. Conder and H. Kitchener in 1873 for the Palestine Exploration Fund, and excavations in the inner area by A. Negev in 1960-1962 on behalf of the National Parks Authority of Israel found preserved walls as much as seven meters high, with stones dressed in the typical Herodian manner, and with associated pottery not later than the end of the first century B.C. The excavator explains that the remains most probably belong to a large podium (11 in plan No. 120) on which the temple was erected to make it the more conspicuous across the water.

On the southern part and at the eastern end of the just-mentioned podium the Crusaders undertook to build a large cathedral, the ruins of which were cleared in the Negev excavations. The structure was oriented to the east and in its eastern part three well-built apses were found, which evidently terminated a nave about 24 feet wide and two side aisles each about 17 feet wide, while at the west side' were the remains of massive supporting piers. Otherwise nothing remained, and it is surmised that the cathedral was never completed, although a much smaller apse of poorer workmanship was constructed in front of the central apse, so perhaps a much smaller church than the one originally planned was built later.

To the north of the Crusader cathedral are the ruins of a very large Byzantine church, also excavated by Negev. Impressive foundations and meager remains of marble and inlaid stone pavement were uncovered, and also eight capitals, with a cross on the face of each (as shown here).

The Survey of Western Palestine, Memoirs II (1882), pp. 18, 27-28; A. Negev in IEJ 10 (1960), p. 265; 11 (1961), pp. 81-82; and in NAEHL pp. 68-69; EAEHL I pp. 273, 280, 285. Photograph: JF.

126. Statue of the Good Shepherd at Caesarea

IN EXCAVATIONS outside the wall on the south side of the Crusader city in 1960 A. Negev found the ruins of a large network of buildings. Different layers of mosaic pavements were uncovered, thought to indicate use of the buildings from the fourth to the seventh century A.D. On the pavements were a number of Greek inscriptions. One inscription, enclosed in a circle, quotes a part of Rom 13:3 with very slight variations from the standard text (omission of δέ and spelling of φοβίσθαι) as follows:

Inscription	Standard Text	Literal Translation
θέλεις	θέλεις δὲ	(but) do you wish
μὴ φοβίσθαι	μὴ φοβεῖσθαι	not to fear
τὴν ἐξουσίαν	τὴν ἐξουσίαν	the authority
τὸ ἀγαθὸν	τὸ ἀγαθὸν	do
ποίει	ποίει	the good

Above the building was found this marble statue of the Good Shepherd carrying a lamb, a work of perhaps the fifth century. Because of these Christian features it was possible to wonder if there were connections here with the great school and library of Origen and Pamphilus and Eusebius (Negev in CNI 11, 4 [1960], p. 22; and in RB 78 [1971], pp. 257-258; Levine in *Qedem* 2 [1975], p. 46 and pl. 8, 3; and in *Qedem* 21 [1986], p. 11).

As a part of the work at Caesarea beginning in 1971 by the Joint Archaeological Expedition sponsored by the American Schools of Oriental Research and directed by Robert J. Bull, complete excavation was undertaken of the building found by Negev with the Greek inscription quoting Rom 13:3. The building measured 60 feet in

125. Byzantine Capital and Cross at Caesarea

13:3 was in the northeast corner of the building. In one of the southern rooms a mosaic medallion contained the same text, completed with the balance of the sentence (reproduced here), and in exact agreement with the standard Greek text:

Inscription	Standard Text	Literal Translation
καὶ ἕξεις ἔπαινον	καὶ ἕξεις ἔπαινον	and you will have praise
ἐξ αὐτῆς	ἐξ αὐτῆς	from it

Other Greek inscriptions are also of Christian import, such as this one in the central hall of the building: "Christ, help Marinus the President and Ampelios and Musonius." The longest inscription was in the room at the western end of the central hall; it reads: "Christ, help Ampelios, the keeper of the archives and Musonius, the financial secretary, and the other archivists of the same depository." In the light of the last inscription the excavators call this the Archive Building, and in view of the Pauline quotation about proper relationship with the governing authority, suggest that in the time of these inscriptions (fifth-sixth century) the edifice must have served some government function (no. 15 in plan No. 120). The two lower mosaic floors also contain inscriptions, but what these may have to tell is not yet known.

In front of the eastern and main entrance of the building just described, the excavators found three levels of mosaic pavement corresponding with the three mosaic floors inside the building, and rows of white marble column bases together with some fallen column shafts and fragments of Corinthian capitals (no. 13 in plan No. 120). As further surveyed, it was judged that this was nothing less than the main north-south street (*cardo maximus*) of Byzantine Caesarea; between the rows of columns was a roadway eighteen feet wide paved with limestone blocks, and on either side was a mosaic-covered sidewalk of the same width, the whole *cardo* probably extending from the theater (No. 128) in the south to within the site of the Crusader city to the north (plan in BAR 8.3 [May/June 1982], p. 27). Given the probable dates of the mosaics (fifth-sixth, fourth-fifth, and possibly third-fourth centuries), the street as found may be dated to the Byzantine period or the late Roman period at the earliest, but might well have followed the line of the main north-south street of Herod's Caesarea too. Several of the cross streets (*decumanus*, plural *decumani*), which ran from west to east and interested the north-south street at right angles, were also discovered.

A. Negev in CNI 11, 4 (1960), p. 22; in IEJ 11 (1961), p. 82; and in RB 78 (1971), pp. 256-258, nos. 29-32. For other Christian inscriptions from Caesarea, see Baruch Lifshitz, "Inscriptions grecques de Césarée en Palestine (Caesarea Palaestinae)," in RB 68 (1961), pp. 115ff. Photograph: JF.

126. Statue of the Good Shepherd at Caesarea

length and 48 feet in width, and contained eight rooms. A central hall was entered from the east, had three rooms on either side, and an eighth room at the end in the west. A thin layer of ash may indicate that the building was burned by the Persians in A.D. 614, and it was finally destroyed in the Arab conquest of Caesarea in 640. The original plan of the building is thought to have been laid out in the third or fourth century. The uppermost mosaic floor is attributed to the late fifth or early sixth century, and is the pavement in which were found all of the Greek inscriptions mentioned here. Pottery under the second mosaic floor indicated construction in the fourth or fifth century. The third mosaic floor below could belong to the third or fourth century.

The already-cited Greek inscription quoting Rom

127. Marble Medallion of Mithras from the Mithraeum at Caesarea

BETWEEN THE *cardo maximus* just described (No. 126) and the seashore south of the Crusader city a large number of subterranean vaults have been identified and recognized as warehouses for the Herodian harbor at Caesarea. One storehouse (*horreum*) in the series, lying between the Archive Building and the sea (BAR 8.3 [May/June 1982], p. 27 for location plan) and two-thirds filled with sand, was excavated over a two-year period by the Joint Archaeological Expedition. It was a vaulted room 96 feet long, 16.5 feet wide, and 15 feet high. In the lowest floor level, resting on bedrock, were great quantities of fragments of large storage jars (*amphorae*), typical of the sort used in trade with the western Mediterranean between the late first century B.C. and the mid-first century A.D. (Blakely in *Caesarea Maritima* IV, pp. 57f.), so there is no doubt that this and the other vaults on down the shore were part of Herod's harbor installation in that time. Coins of Nero (A.D. 54-68) were also found.

At a later time stone benches were built along the side walls and a stone altar was built at the innermost end of the vault. The benches and altar were covered with plaster; the walls were plastered and filled with frescoes, which are now only very badly preserved but appear to be of Mithraic themes, perhaps initiation scenes; the ceiling was painted blue; and behind the altar was the medallion shown in the present photograph, unmistakably representing Mithra/Mithras. In this phase the vault was therefore a Mithraeum (14 in plan No. 120), a sanctuary for the worship of Mithra/Mithras. Pottery found at the base of the altar and elsewhere in the vault—*amphorae*, cooking vessels, and many lamps and fragments of lamps—together with a coin of Elagabalus dated to 218-222 indicate the use of the Mithraeum from the late first century to the mid to late third century (Blakely, *Caesarea Maritima* IV, pp. 101-103).

The medallion just mentioned is about 3.125 inches in diameter and is carved in bas-relief with the bull-slaying scene that is so characteristic of Mithraism. Mithras, wearing Phrygian cap, cape, and short skirt, bestrides a

127. Marble Medallion of Mithras from the Mithraeum at Caesarea

bull and, looking away as Perseus did in the slaying of Medusa, lifts a dagger against the shoulder of the bull. Serpent and dog are nearby; on the right Cautes lifts his torch upward, on the left Cautopates points his torch downward. Below are, probably, Sol the sun god kneeling before Mithras; the banquet of Sol and Mithras; and Mithras riding a bull toward a reclining figure. Very comparable to many other such known scenes, the representation is probably of astronomical/cosmic import (FMM pp. 207f.).

At the same time that the vault was made into a Mithraeum, a building was erected on top of it which the excavators call the Honorific Portico. The reason for the designation is that it contained inscriptions on short columns that probably once carried sculptures, all in honor of military personnel. These were presumably Roman legionnaires associated with worship in the Mithraeum, which agrees with the fact that in many other places in the Roman empire Mithraic inscriptions are also connected with the military. Related to the Honorific Portico and cut through the ceiling of the vault near its eastern end was an opening that was found to direct a ray of sunlight to fall upon the altar of the Mithraeum precisely at the summer solstice, just after noon on July 21.

Lewis Moore Hopfe and Gary Lease, "The Caesarea Mithraeum: A Preliminary Announcement," in BA 38, 1 (Mar 1975), pp. 1-10; Robert J. Bull in BAR 8.3 (May/June 1982), pp. 34-37; Jeffrey A. Blakely, *The Pottery and Dating of Vault I: Horreum, Mithraeum, and Later Uses* (Joint Expedition to Caesarea Maritima Excavation Reports IV, 1987); M. J. Vermaseren, *Corpus Inscriptionum et Monumentorum Religionis Mithriacae* (The Hague: Martinus Nijhoff, 2 vols., 1956-1960), vol. 2, pp. 351f., no. 2246, fig. 622; David Ulansey, "Mithraic Studies: A Paradigm Shift?" in RSR 13, 2 (Apr 1987), pp. 104-110; and Ulansey, *The Origins of the Mithraic Mysteries: Cosmology and Salvation in the Ancient World* (New York, Oxford: Oxford University Press, 1989). Photograph: courtesy Robert J. Bull.

128. The Theater at Caesarea

AS WE HAVE SEEN (NO. 120), Josephus mentions both a theater and an amphitheater at Caesarea, the amphitheater being said to be on the south side of the harbor with a view to the sea (*Ant.* xv 9, 6 §341; cf. *War* I

128. The Theater at Caesarea

21, 8 §415). In plan No. 120 the theater is at 18 near the southwestern corner of the Roman city and just beyond the more southerly of the two projections into the water. It has a fine view out to sea. It corresponds, therefore, with what Josephus says about the location of the amphitheater; the ruins here, however, are of a theater rather than of an amphitheater, and it may be supposed that Josephus has simply reversed his terms. In 1882 *The Survey of Western Palestine (Memoirs* II, pp. 15-16) described the ruins at this spot as those of a Roman theater. Beginning in 1959 and continuing for a number of years the excavation and restoration of the theater were undertaken by an Italian archeological mission of the Istituto Lombardo of Milan, under the direction of Antonio Frova. As shown in the photograph, the theater was cut out of the cliff in a semicircle of many tiers, and had a magnificent view. There were frescoes on the floor of the orchestra, and oil lamps were found on the stage. The connection of the theater with NT history because of the appearance in it of Herod Agrippa I just before his death (Ac 12:21-23), has already been noted above (No. 120).

For a bibliography on Caesarea covering 1961-1963 and including the publications of the Italian expedition, see 'Atiqot, Supplement to Vol. IV (Jerusalem, 1965), pp. 8-9; and see especially Antonio Frova, *Scavi di Caesarea Maritima* (Rome, 1965). Photograph: courtesy Government Press Office, State of Israel.

129. The Pilate Inscription from Caesarea

DURING THE WORK in the Roman theater (No. 128) in 1961 the Italian expedition found this inscription. The stone had been used to form a landing for a flight of steps at one of the entrances to the seats of the theater and was badly chipped away, probably at that time, on the left side. Originally the stone must have been embedded in the wall of the building for which it provided the dedicatory inscription. Four lines remain legible at least in part, though hard to see in the photograph. With restorations and translation they are as follows:

129. The Pilate Inscription from Caesarea

CAESARAIEN] S (IBUS)	To the people of Caesarea
TIBERIÉVM	Tiberieum
PON] TIVSPILATVS	Pontius Pilate
PRAEF] ECTVSIVDA[EA]E	Prefect of Judea

In the fifth line a diagonal accent mark may be recognizable and, like the one in line 2, may have stood over an "e." Perhaps the word *dedit*, "has given," or *dedicavit*, "has dedicated," once stood there. The entire statement is therefore: "Pontius Pilate the prefect of Judea has dedicated to the people of Caesarea a temple in honor of Tiberius." The name of the dedicated building is written in Latin as Tiberieum. This is a temple to Tiberius with the name formed in the standard way, an example of which we have seen already (No. 121) in the Greek inscription of Caesarea which mentions the Hadrianeion (Ἀδριανεῖον), or temple in honor of Hadrian. As is also standard practice, the Greek ει is reproduced in the Latin by é. The name Pontius Pilate is quite unmistakable and is of much importance as the first epigraphical documentation concerning Pontius Pilate, who governed Judea A.D. 26-36 according to the commonly accepted dates. In mentioning him Tacitus (*Annals* xv 44) and Josephus (*War* II 9, 2 §169) call him "Procurator" (Latin *procurator*, Greek ἐπίτροπος). This inscription uses the title "prefect" (Latin *praefectus*, to which the Greek ἔπαρχος corresponds). The latter term (ἔπαρχος) is used by Josephus for Valerius Gratus (15-26), the predecessor of Pontius Pilate (*Ant.* XVIII 2, 2 §33), and for Cuspius Fadus (44-46), who came after Herod Agrippa I. While the two terms are therefore broadly interchangeable, "prefect" seems to have been more of a military title and "procurator" to have carried more of the connotation of financial administration; also "prefect" seems to have been preferred in the time of Augustus, "procurator" to have become the prevailing title from Claudius (41-54) onward (SHJP Vermes/Millar I, pp. 358-360). Perhaps there is a little evidence in this general development for dating this inscription earlier rather than later in the administration of Pontius Pilate. The Gospels call him only by the general term "governor" (ἡγεμών) (Mt 27:2, etc.).

Antonio Frova, "L'iscrizióne di Ponzio Pilato a Cesarea," in *Rendiconti* (Milano: Istituto Lombardo, Accademia di Scienze e Lettere 95 [1961]), pp. 419-434; Jerry Vardaman, "A New Inscription which Mentions Pilate as 'Prefect,'" in JBL 81 (1962), pp. 70-71. Vardaman cites Carla Brusa Gerra, "Le Iscrizióni," in *Scavi di Caesarea Maritima* (see above, No. 128), especially pp. 217-220. Gerra gives other alternate readings for line 1 as: TIB(erio) CAES(are) AVG. V CONS(ule), and DIS AVGVSTI S. Photograph: courtesy Istituto Lombardo, Milan, and Department of Antiquities, Ministry of Education and Culture, State of Israel.

130. Floor Mosaic in the Promontory Palace, Caesarea

JUST NORTH AND WEST of the theater (No. 128) a rocky promontory extends into the sea. On this promontory a large pool measuring 35 by 18 meters was surveyed in 1973 and at the time thought to be a fishtank (*piscina*) connected with the sea, and at the same time a fine mosaic terrace was accidentally discovered at the eastern end of the tank when heavy rains washed away the top layers of sand (IEJ 26 [1976], pp. 79f.). In 1976 the Institute of Archaeology of the Hebrew University of Jerusalem (Netzer in *Qedem* 21 [1986], pp. 149-160) conducted excavations and uncovered the ruins of what is now described as the Promontory Palace (21 in plan No. 120). At the eastern end of the tank (which may have been a freshwater swimming pool rather than a seawater fishtank) a series of a half-dozen rooms running on a north-south axis was traced, while at the western end of the pool various walls apparently indicate an area also divided into rooms and corridors. The central room at the east (Room P 1 in plans 15, 16 in *Qedem* 21, pp. 151, 155) measures about 11 by 8 meters and is exactly on the east-west axis of the pool. The main feature of this room was the mosaic just mentioned. As shown in the present photograph, which is facing east, the main panel is a "carpet," 5.2 by 2.5 meters in size, made of black, white, pink, and terracotta tesserae, in geometric patterns. As far as recovered, the symmetry of the plan of these buildings, arranged on a central east-west axis, and the very striking location, with Herod's theater immediately behind and the Mediterranean Sea directly in front (Frova, *Scavi di Caesarea*, p. 59, fig. 11), certainly justify the designation of this as a palace and suggest indeed that this was nothing less than Herod's palace at Caesarea. The function of a roughly shaped semicircle at the western extremity of the promontory is unknown, but at least makes one think of the rounded terrace in the upper level of Herod's northern palace at Masada (No. 22).

If this is the correct identification of the buildings just described, this was not only the palace that Herod the Great used at Caesarea, but undoubtedly also that used by Herod Agrippa I when he resided at Caesarea. Likewise when the Roman prefects/procurators (No. 129) ruled Judea their official seat was in Caesarea, and they no doubt took over the same palace for their *praetorium* (originally a general's tent in a camp, then the official residence of a governor, written in Greek as πραιτώριον, cf. No. 215), and we hear of it in Ac 23:35 as the place where the apostle Paul was "guarded in Herod's praetorium."

Alexander Flinder, "A Piscina at Caesarea—A Preliminary Survey," in IEJ 26 (1976), pp. 77-80; E. Netzer, "The Promontory

130. Floor Mosaic in the Promontory Palace, Caesarea

Palace," in *Qedem* 21 (1986), pp. 149-160. Photograph: *Qedem* 21 (1986), p. 154, illus. 135, courtesy The Institute of Archaeology, Hebrew University of Jerusalem.

131. The High-Level Aqueduct at Caesarea

IN PLAN NO. 120 two aqueducts are marked as approaching Caesarea from the north. One (1 in the plan) is a high-level aqueduct, which here is the one nearest the sea; the other is a low-level channel, which is here roughly parallel to the high-level construction. The high-level aqueduct is actually a double structure whose arches carry two parallel channels on top. Of the two parts the eastern channel is the earlier, as shown by the fact that its stones are dressed on both sides, whereas the western channel is faced with dressed stones only on its outer, western side. The earlier, eastern channel brings water from the Shumi springs north of Binyamina at the foot of the Carmel range 6.5 miles northeast of Caesarea. The later, western channel brings water from the Sabbarin and other springs of the Ammiqam area, which is yet 6 miles farther to the northeast. These waters were led at first through an underground tunnel on the side of Mount Carmel (Olami and Peleg in IEJ 27 [1977], pp. 127-132), and as they reached Caesarea they substan-

tially doubled the total capacity of the high-level aqueduct. Along the seashore the aqueduct, although almost 6 meters in height and over 5 meters in breadth, has been almost buried in sand dunes, and about 500 meters before reaching Caesarea it now breaks off (soon after the point of the present photograph), for the action of the sea waves has eroded the coast to the extent of an estimated 50,000 tons of soil and stone, and destroyed the rest of the aqueduct at the same time (Reifenberg in IEJ 1 [1950-1951], pp. 27f., pl. xii, fig. 6).

Josephus does not mention the construction of any aqueduct at Caesarea by Herod the Great, and it has been concluded by some that in Herod's time Caesarea, like many Palestinian towns, must have depended for water only upon rainwater collected in cisterns and upon wells (Reifenberg, in IEJ 1 [1950-1951], p. 26). Remembering, however, Herod's installations for bringing water to Herodium (No. 20) and Masada (No. 22), it can hardly be doubted that he would also have endeavored to supply his great new city with adequate water, and thus the original high-level aqueduct (with its earlier, eastern channel) may most likely be attributed to him (cf. Olami and Peleg in IEJ 27 [1977], p. 136; Bull in BAR 8.3 [May/June 1982], p. 30).

In its entire course there are at least nine Latin inscriptions on the high-level aqueduct, and they all date from the reign of Hadrian (A.D. 117-138) and name several Roman legions: five mention the *legio x Fretensis*, two the *legio vi Ferrata*, one the *legio ii Traiana Fortis*, and one an unidentified legion (Olami and Ringel in IEJ 25 [1975], p. 150). Examples are the following inscriptions, which were found on arches of the aqueduct in a marshy region above Binyamina (Vilnay in PEFQS 1928, pp. 45-47, 108-109). On one stone the inscription is cut into a plain rectangular area surrounded by a raised border. It reads:

IMP(ERATOR) CAESAR	Imperator Caesar
TRAIANVS	Traianus
HADRIANVS	Hadrianus
AVG (VSTVS) FECIT	Augustus has made
	(this aqueduct)
PER VEXILLATIONE(M)	by a detachment
LEG(IONIS) X FR(E)TEN(SIS)	of Legion x Fretensis

On a second stone a wreath is enclosed within an elaborate frame with triangles on either end, with Roman images on pedestals on either side, and the inscription is carved inside the wreath. It reads:

IMP(ERATOR) CAE(SAR)
Imperator Caesar
TR(AIANVS) HAD(RIANVS) AVG(VSTVS)
Traianus Hadrianus Augustus

131. The High-Level Aqueduct at Caesarea

VEXIL(LATIO) LEG(IONIS)
a detachment of Legion
VI FERR(ATAE)
VI Ferrata

Hadrian's title is here the "Imperator Caesar Traianus Hadrianus Augustus" (W. Liebenam, *Fasti Consulares*, KLT 41-43, p. 107). He visited Palestine in 130, suppressed the revolt of Bar-Kokhba a few years later, and during his reign supported various public building works. We have already noted (No. 120) that in Caesarea a temple was built in his honor, and a statue there may be of him. Legion X Fretensis took part in the conquest of Jerusalem by Titus, had its headquarters there afterward (Josephus, *War* VII 1, 3 §17), and had detachments stationed at various places in Palestine. In the southwest corner of the Old City of Jerusalem many fragments of tiles have been found, stamped with the abbreviation or initials of this legion, LEG X FR or LXF (PEFQS 1871, pp.

103-104; PEQ 1966, p. 88). Legion VI Ferrata was brought into Palestine from Syria by Hadrian in the course of his war with Bar-Kokhba (132-135) (PWRE 12:1, col. 1292). At Sebaste a limestone slab has been found, with a carved framework much like that on the Caesarea aqueduct stone but without the wreath, and with the inscription of the same legion:

VEXILLATIO
LEG VI FERR

(G. A. Reisner, C. S. Fisher, and D. G. Lyon, *Harvard Excavations at Samaria* [1924], I, p. 251 no. 1; II, pl. 59, f). At Megiddo there is a village which has been known as el-Lejjun, obviously a corruption of "Legion," nearby are the remains of a Roman camp, and in an adjacent field was found a tile with the stamp LEGVIF, again the abbreviation for Legio VI Ferrata (G. Schumacher, *Tell el-Mutesellim* [1908], I, p. 175).

141

While the inscriptions just noted have sometimes been taken as evidence that these detachments of Hadrian's legions built the high-level aqueduct in the first place (Reifenberg, in IEJ 1 [1950-1951], p. 26), it seems more probable in view of the considerations adduced above that what the legionnaires did was to make repairs and also to add the later western channel of the structure originally built by Herod (cf. Olami and Peleg in IEJ 27 [1977], p. 136; Bull in BAR 8.3 [May/June 1982], p. 30).

As for the low-level aqueduct (2 in plan No. 120), it brought water to Caesarea from numerous springs in the Kabbara marshes about three miles north of Caesarea and one mile inland from the sea. Because these springs are actually lower than Caesarea, two large dams were built to raise the water level, one to impound the waters, the other to keep them from spreading northward. Raised in this manner by several meters, the water was led southward first in an open rock-cut channel, then in a masonry aqueduct, and in the sand dune area the aqueduct was covered by an arched stone roof, once two meters high but now heavily sanded up (Reifenberg, in IEJ 1 [1950-1951], pl. xiv, fig. 9). After somewhat more than one mile the low-level aqueduct crosses under one of the arches of the high-level aqueduct and comes to the city on the east side of the latter. The dams that were necessary for the operation of the low-level aqueduct are believed to be of the fourth century. It is thought that the main purpose of this system was to provide water for agricultural purposes. It was by coming in through this covered aqueduct that the Muslims entered Caesarea and conquered the city from the Byzantines in 639/640 (Reifenberg, in IEJ 1 [1950-1951], p. 29).

The Survey of Western Palestine, Memoirs II (1882), pp. 18-23; Zev Vilnay, "A New Inscription from the Neighbourhood of Caesarea," in PEFQS 1928, pp. 45-47; "Another Roman Inscription from the Neighborhood of Caesarea," ibid., pp. 108-109; A. Reifenberg in IEJ 1 (1950-51), pp. 26-29; A. Negev, "The High Level Aqueduct at Caesarea," in IEJ 14 (1964), pp. 237-249; and Negev, "A New Inscription from the High Level Aqueduct at Caesarea," in IEJ 22 (1972), pp. 52f.; D. Barag, "An Inscription from the High Level Aqueduct of Caesarea—Reconsidered," in IEJ 14 (1964), pp. 250-252; J. Olami and J. Ringel, "New Inscriptions of the Tenth Legion Fretensis from the High Leved Aqueduct of Caesarea," in IEJ 25 (1975), pp. 148-150; Yaakov Olami and Yehudah Peleg, "The Water Supply System of Caesarea Maritima," in IEJ 27 (1977), pp. 127-137; Robert J. Bull in BAR 8.3 (May/June 1982), pp. 29f. Photograph: JF.

132. Marble Capital with Menorah in Relief from the Synagogue at Caesarea

ON THE NORTHERN SIDE of the city where the aqueducts approach, outside the Crusader wall but within the Roman wall and not far from the seashore, synagogue remains were first reported in 1932, partly cleared in 1945, and further excavated in 1956 and 1962 by the Department of Archaeology of Hebrew University under the direction of M. Avi-Yonah with the assistance of A. Negev and, in 1962, of E. Jerry Vardaman. In this area there was a Herodian building, part of which was used later as a plastered pool and then filled with a mixture of earth and debris. Over this filling was laid the pavement of the synagogue. It was a building 18 meters long, from east to west, and 9 meters wide. In it was found the hoard of 3,700 small bronze coins already mentioned (No. 44) in connection with the Nazareth Inscription also found in the general area, but a few hundred feet to the east. Most of the coins date from the time of Constantius II (337-361), there are a few of Julianus Caesar. Since Julian became Caesar in 355 and Augustus in 360 (Liebenam, Fasti Consulares, KLT 41-43, p. 121) the date of 355/356 is suggested for the establishment of the cache. The synagogue may have been built, then, at the end of the third or beginning of the fourth century. Around the date given of 355/356 it may have been destroyed, rebuilt in the early fifth century, and again rebuilt in the sixth-seventh century. Architectural fragments of the fourth- or fifth-century synagogue include marble columns, one of which has a dedicatory inscription reading, "The offering of Theodoros the son of Olympos for the salvation of his daughter Matrona" (Rabinowitz Bulletin III [1960], pp. 44-45); and marble capitals of debased Corinthian type, two of which carry the representation of the menorah, one incised and one in relief (the latter is shown in the photograph). In the later building is a mosaic pavement with an inscription inlaid in Greek, the type of letters suggesting the sixth century. Some of the letters of the first line are damaged, but the whole inscription is probably to be transcribed, restored, and translated as follows (Rabinowitz Bulletin III, p. 47):

```
BH . . ΛΛΟCΑΡΧΙCΥ
ΚΑΙ  ΦΡΟΝΤΙCΤΗC
ΥΟC ΙΟΥΤΟΥ ΕΠΟΙ
ΗCΕ ΤΗΝ ΨΗΦΟ
ΘΕCΙΑΝ ΤΟΥ ΤΡΙ
ΚΛΙΝΟΥ Τω ΙΔΙω
```

Βή[ου]λλος ἀρχισυ(ναγωγὸς) καί φροντιστὴς υ(ἱ)ὸς Ἰού(σ)του ἐποίησε τὴν ψηφοθεσίαν τοῦ τρικλίνου τῷ ἰδίῳ

Beryllos the head of the synagogue and administrator, the son of Iu(s)tus, made the mosaic work of the triclinium from his own means.

If the last word in the first line is restored correctly this is the title which is familiar in the NT (Mk 5:38, etc.) where it is translated "ruler of the synagogue" (RSV) (cf. No. 86).

As Vardaman also reports, the ruins of a large house

132. Marble Capital with Menorah in Relief from the Synagogue at Caesarea

were found near the synogogue. Hellenistic pottery was found (Rhodian jar handles, "fish plates," etc., most of which dated about the middle of the second century B.C.) in one corner of the house. Vast quantities of isolated fragments of "west slope" ware indicated a settlement there certainly before the end of the third century B.C. The area was abandoned in the early first century B.C., perhaps after the conquest of Strato's Tower by Alexander Jannaeus. Thus the original town was doubtless in this area (cf. No. 120). Also a massive wall, which may be a part of the harbor mole of Strato's Tower, can be seen in the sea.

M. Avi-Yonah in IEJ 6 (1956), pp. 260-261; M. Avi-Yonah, "The Synagogue of Caesarea, Preliminary Report," in Louis B. Rabinowitz Fund for the Exploration of Ancient Synagogues, *Bulletin* III (Jerusalem, December 1960), pp. 44-48; M. Avi-Yonah and A. Negev in IEJ 13 (1963), pp. 146-148; M. Avi-Yonah in Vardaman and Garrett, eds., *The Teacher's Yoke* (1964), p. 51 n. 13; Saller, *Second Catalogue*, pp. 25f., no. 21; Levine in *Qedem 2* (1975), pp. 40-45. For other coins of Caesarea, see Leo Kadman, *The Coins of Caesarea Maritima.* Corpus Nummorum Palaestinensium, II (Tel Aviv-Jerusalem: Schocken Publishing House, 1957). Photograph: courtesy Department of Archaeology, The Hebrew University of Jerusalem.

133. Byzantine Church Mosaics at Caesarea

TO THE NORTHEAST outside the city wall of Byzantine Caesarea and adjacent to a cemetery area (19 in plan No. 120) the ruins of a Byzantine church were excavated in 1955 by Sh. Yeivin on behalf of the Israel Department of Antiquities. A narthex and apse were uncovered, with the apse at the north side of the central axis of the church, and remnants of foundations were

found, but there were no traces of columns or column bases, leading to the supposition that this may have been an open or uncovered church (*basilica discoperta*), and the location suggests that it may have had the function of a funerary church. Of most interest is the colored mosaic pavement of the church. In the narthex and aisles there are geometric patterns. In the central mosaic area (about 16 by 13.5 meters), apparently corresponding with the nave, the border depicts many animals such as bear, lion, leopard, elephant, bull, dog, gazelle (above, left), and the main field contains some 120 medallions, in each of which is a bird (above, right), all extant in Palestine, suggesting that the pavement was the work of local artisans. The date of the church is believed to be sixth to seventh century.

Other sites in Caesarea that would be of interest from the point of view of early Christianity are mentioned in pilgrim itineraries, including the following, but the places have not yet been found and identified. When Paula came to Caesarea, as Jerome records (*Letter* 108, A.D. 404, NPNFSS VI, p. 198), "she saw the house of Cornelius now turned into a Christian church; and the humble abode of Philip; and the chambers of his daughters the four virgins 'who prophesied'." Cornelius was the Roman centurion to whom Peter preached at Caesarea (Ac 10-11); Philip was the evangelist and one of the seven (Ac 6:5), with whom Paul stayed in his house in Caesarea, who had "four unmarried daughters, who prophesied" (Ac 21:8-9) (for confusion between Philip the evangelist and Philip the apostle, and between Caesarea and Hierapolis in Asia Minor as the burial place of the evangelist and his daughters, see Eusebius, *Ch. Hist.* III 31). The Anonymous of Piacenza (A.D. 570) (Geyer p.

217; LPPTS II-D, pp. 35f.; CCSL CLXXV, p. 174; WJP p. 89) names Strato's Tower/Caesarea Palaestinae (with which the pilgrim also mistakenly confuses Caesarea Philippi) as the city in which rest St. Pamphilus (the teacher of Eusebius, martyred at Caesarea in A.D. 310, Eusebius, *Mart. Pal.* XI 14 NPNFSS I, p. 353), St. Procopius (the first of the martyrs of Palestine in Eusebius' account, ibid., I 1 NPNFSS I, p. 342, who died under Diocletian A.D. 303/304), and St. Cornelius (Ac 10-11), "from whose tomb (literally *lectus*, couch, funeral bed, bier) we took a blessing (*benedictio*, benediction)."

RB 64 (1957), pp. 259f.; IEJ 8 (1958), p. 61; Sh. Yeivin, *A Decade of Archaeology in Israel 1948-1958* (Istanbul: Nederlands Historisch-Archaeologisch Instituut in het Nabije Oosten, 1960), p. 46 and pl. V, 2; M. Avi-Yonah, *Israel Ancient Mosaics* (New York Graphic Society, UNESCO World Art Series, 1960), p. 17 and pls. XXIX-XXXI; Ovadiah, *Corpus*, pp. 44f., no. 28. Photographs: courtesy of The Israel Antiquities Authority.

Left

133. Byzantine Church Mosaics at Caesarea

Right

144

JERICHO

134. Aerial View of Jericho

THE SYNOPTIC GOSPELS indicate that on his journey to Jerusalem for the last time Jesus passed through Jerico (Mt 20:29; Mk 10:46; Lk 18:35), where he healed one (Mk 10:46-52; Lk 18:35-43) or two (Mt. 20:29-34) blind men and was guest of Zacchaeus (Lk 19:1-10). Jericho was already a prominent city in OT times (Num 22:1, etc.), a city identified with a large mound on the west side of the Jordan Valley know as Tell es-Sultan. This has been excavated by Ernst Sellin and Carl Wat-

zinger (1907ff.), John Garstang (1930ff.), and Kathleen M. Kenyon (1952ff.). According to the findings of the last-named archeologist, Jericho is recognized as the oldest-known city in the world. Settlement began at the location as early as around 8000 B.C. and by around 7000 the city was enclosed in a strong stone wall, with one of its towers still standing to a height of 7.75 meters, with a doorway on the eastern side at the bottom, and an interior staircase to the top, with 22 steps still in place (Kenyon, *Excavations* III plates, pl. 5).

134. Aerial View of Jericho

In the aerial view the *tell* of this most ancient city is in the immediate foreground, modern Jericho is in the distance, and the Dead Sea and the mountains of Moab are in the far distance. Also at the immediate base of the *tell*, about one-third of the way in from the right edge of the picture and adjacent to a small building, is the double pool of the Spring of Elisha.

Kathleen M. Kenyon, *Digging Up Jericho* (New York: Praeger, 1957); and Kenyon, *Excavations at Jericho* (London: British School of Archaeology in Jerusalem, 5 vols. in 6, 1960-1983); Dora Jane Hamblin and the Editors of Time-Life Books, *The First Cities* (New York: Time-Life Books, 1971), pp. 28-41; John R. Bartlett, *Jericho* (Cities of the Biblical World) (Grand Rapids: Eerdmans, 1982); Vogel, *Bibliography* I, pp. 42-44; II, pp. 41f. Photograph: The Matson Photo Service, Alhambra, Calif.

135. Looking from the Site of OT Jericho to Jebel Quarantal

IT IS NOT much more than a mile from Tell es-Sultan to the range of mountains that rises steeply on the west-ern side of the Jordan Valley. These must be "the hills" to which the spies of Joshua fled from the house of Rahab (Jos 2:22). The picture looks westward from the *tell* toward these mountains, and toward the point called Jebel Quarantal, which rises to a height of 1,200 feet above Jericho. The summit was probably the location of "the little stronghold called Dok" mentioned in I Macc 16:15 (cf. Josephus, *Ant.* XIII 7, 4-8, 1 §§228ff.) where Simon, the last of the Maccabees, was treacherously slain by his son-in-law Ptolemy (135 B.C.). Some of the ruins on the top probably belong to that stronghold, and a spring at the foot of the escarpment is still called Ain Duq. On the side of the mountain are numerous caves which attracted Christian hermits, including Chariton (340) and Palladius (386) and their pupils. In the *Life of Chariton* (MPG XCV, col. 912) there is mention of "Luke's Mountain," and in this name the Maccabean Duk is probably still to be recognized (Λουκᾶ as an error for Δουκᾶ). The identification is also confirmed by an unpublished seventh-century Arabic manuscript in which Clermont-Ganneau (II, p. 21) found the name Jebel ed-Duq for the

135. Looking from the Site of OT Jericho to Jebel Quarantal

mountain from under which the Spring of Elisha comes. The center of the Christian hermits was probably where the Greek monastery is now found, halfway up to the summit, and on the summit there are also ruins of a Byzantine church (Dalman, PJ 10 [1914], p. 16). It is possible that the church was connected with the tradition of the temptation of Jesus. At any rate with the Crusaders, who also built on the top, the temptation was located on the mountain and it was called Quarantana in memory of the forty days (*quadraginta diebus*, Mk 1:13, etc.). Today the place of the first temptation is shown at the Greek monastery halfway up the mountain, and of the third temptation (Mt 4:8) on the very summit. From the summit there is indeed a wide-ranging view from the mountains of Moab on the east to the Mount of Olives and the Judean highlands on the west.

Abel, *Géographie* II, p. 307; Dalman, *Sacred Sites*, p. 96; Kopp note 61 on pp. 147-150. Photograph: JF.

136. The Spring of Elisha

AT OT JERICHO there was a spring, the water of which was made wholesome when Elisha threw salt into it (II K 2:19-22). On the east side of Tell es-Sultan (cf. No. 134) and across the present-day road from it, is a copious

spring known as Ain es-Sultan and also as the Spring or the Fountain of Elisha. Although in appearance, as shown here, it is only an unprepossessing double pool, it provides abundant water for a large and pleasant oasis. Already in the OT, Jericho was "the city of palm trees" (Dt 34:3; cf. Jg 1:16).

Photograph: The Matson Photo Service, Alhambra, Calif.

137. A *Tell* of NT Jericho

IN HELLENISTIC AND ROMAN TIMES the city of Jericho was no longer on the original *tell* but was located on the plain and on both sides of Wadi el-Qelt, a mile or so to the south. It was through this wadi (cf. No. 141), that the road to Jerusalem went. In Maccabean times Bacchides, commander of the Syrian army, built a fortress in Jericho (I Macc 9:50), undoubtedly to command this road. In 63 B.C. Pompey destroyed two forts there which were called Threx and Taurus (Strabo, *Geography* XVI 2, 40). When Gabinius, general of Pompey and proconsul of Syria (57-55 B.C.), divided Palestine into five districts he assigned the fourth to Jericho as its capital (*War* I 8, 6 §170; SHJP I i, pp. 372f.; Vermes/Millar I, pp. 268f.). Mark Antony gave the district of Jericho to Cleopatra (Josephus, *War* I 18, 5 §361), but Augustus gave

136. The Spring of Elisha

137. A *Tell* of NT Jericho

it back to Herod the Great (*Ant.* xv 7, 3 §217; *War* I 20, 3 §396). At Jericho Herod did much building, making the city his winter capital, a position for which it was well suited because of its balmy winter climate. Above the town he built a citadel, which he called Cypros after the name of his mother (*Ant.* xvi 5, 2 §143; *War* I 21, 4 and 9 §§407, 417). Other buildings were an amphitheater (*Ant.* xvii 6, 3 §161; 8, 2 §193; *War* I 33, 8 §666), a hippodrome (*Ant.* xvii 6, 5 §175; *War* I 33, 6 §659), and a royal palace. This palace was where Herod died (*War* I 33, 8 §666). After his death it was burned down by one of his former slaves named Simon (*Ant.* xvii 10, 6 §274); then it was splendidly rebuilt by Archelaus (*Ant.* xvii 13, 1 §340). Strabo (*Geography* xvi 2, 41) says that the plain and mountains at Hiericus, as he calls Jericho, gave the city a setting as if in a theater. The plain was watered with streams and full of dwellings, he says, and there were many fruitful trees, mostly palm trees. Pliny (*Nat. Hist.* v 15, 70) also remarks upon the numerous palm groves and springs of water. Josephus (*War* iv 8, 3 §§459-475) calls Jericho a "most favored spot," and describes the region in terms as glowing as those he used for the Plain of Gennesaret (cf. No. 75). The copious spring purified by Elisha irrigates a plain seventy stadia in length and twenty in breadth. Date palms are numerous in their varieties; the richer species, when pressed, emit honey

not much inferior to that of the bees, which are also abundant. The balsam, cypress, and myrobalanus also flourish. Indeed the warm air and wholesome water are beneficial to plants and human beings alike, and "the climate," Josephus concludes, "is so mild that the inhabitants wear linen when snow is falling throughout the rest of Judea."

Photograph: JF.

138. Plan of the Excavations at Tulul Abu el-'Alayiq

THE MOUNDS that represent at least a portion of NT Jericho are found on either side of Wadi el-Qelt where this valley opens out onto the plain, and where it is joined from the north by Wadi Schaqq ed-Debi. The mounds are called Tulul (plural of *tell*) Abu el-'Alayiq. Excavation has been conducted here by the American School of Oriental Research in Jerusalem under James L. Kelso in 1950 and James B. Pritchard in the following year, and by the Jerusalem archeologist E. Netzer beginning in 1973.

The mound to the northwest is marked as Tell A on the plan. It was found to contain the ruins of a palace of Herod the Great (the second of his three winter palaces

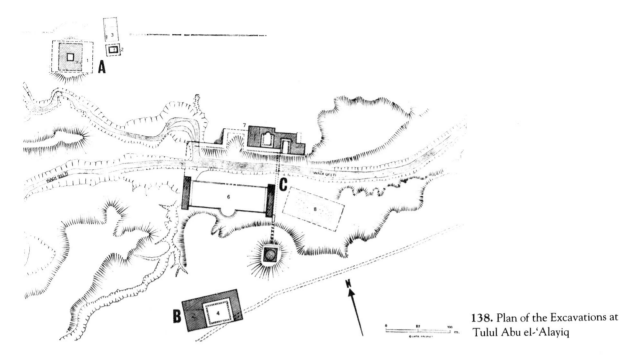

138. Plan of the Excavations at Tulul Abu el-'Alayiq

at Jericho) and the ruins of a palace of the Hasmoneans, the earlier structure at first unnoticed because it was buried beneath the earth thrown there from the construction of the Herodian palace. Identified elements of the Hasmonean palace are a central building 60 by 50 meters in size (no. 1 in the plan), a long colonnade, a large double pool (3) and adjacent pavilion (2), and several ritual baths, the last appropriate to the priestly descent of the Hasmoneans, with a villa (?) superimposed on the Hasmonean building (no. 9 on the plan). The coins that were found cover the time from Antigonus, the last Hasmonean king (40-37 B.C.), back to Alexander Jannaeus (103-76 B.C.), and the latter may be assumed to have been the builder of this as his winter palace in the pleasant winter surroundings of Jericho.

The first of Herod the Great's winter palaces was probably built soon after the beginning (37 B.C.) of his actual rule as king of the Jews, when Jericho still belonged to Cleopatra (d. 30 B.C.), and when Alexandra (d. 28 B.C.), the mother of the Hasmonean princess Mariamme, whom Herod married to strengthen his claim to the kingship, was still occupying the Hasmonean family palace. At any rate Herod located his first Jericho palace at a respectful distance on the far, southern side of Wadi el-Qelt, at B and 4 on the plan. This was essentially an elegant Roman villa, remarkable for only a single entrance. Within the walls were a large inner court, a dining room (*triclinium*), an extensive bathing installation, and a ritual bath.

The central building of Herod's second winter palace at Jericho was on the already-mentioned Tell A. Included in the layout was the large double pool of the Hasmonean palace, now surrounded by gardens, while another large garden was surrounded by columns (*peristyle*), and there was a dining hall (*triclinium*), a basin surrounded by colonnades, a Roman bath installation and, farther away, a ritual bath.

Herod's third winter palace was begun in about the year 15 B.C., and was the most elaborate of all, consisting of structures on both sides of Wadi el-Qelt, facing each other and connected by a bridge across the wadi (at C and 5 in the plan). On the north bank of the wadi a large palace (7) contained a large reception hall, two courts, one with a large apse, and a full-scale Roman bath installation.

Plan: from E. Netzer in IEJ 25 (1975), p. 91, fig. 2, courtesy Israel Exploration Society, Jerusalem.

139. A Façade at NT Jericho

ON THE SOUTH BANK of Wadi el-Qelt were other features of Herod's third winter palace, namely, a large pool (8 in the plan No. 138) and a grand façade directly on the bank of the wadi. The masonry of this façade was lined with small, square-faced, pyramidal stones which give the impression of a net (*reticulum*), producing a type of work known as *opus reticulatum*. An example of this work appears in the photograph. The façade was also provided with semicircular benches and numerous niches. The appearance is somewhat that of an outdoor

139. A Façade at NT Jericho

theater, but the finding of flower pots on the benches makes it perhaps more probable that this was a terraced garden instead (6). It has been suggested that the *opus reticulatum* work at Jericho reflects some of Herod's trips to Rome, where he could have seen Augustus building in this fashion along the Tiber.

Also farther back on the south side of the wadi are the remains of a two-story tower with inner chambers (5), evidently also a part of the entire palace layout, and a place from which a fine view would have been available over the surrounding landscape.

Found in the ruins of the third winter palace were twelve coins of Herod the Great, twenty-two of his son and successor in Judea, Archelaus, three of Roman procurators, and five of Herod Agrippa I (Kroll p. 296, col. 3). This corresponds with the report by Josephus (above, No. 137) that after Herod's death the palace was burned by Simon, then splendidly rebuilt by Archelaus.

James L. Kelso, "The First Campaign of Excavation in New Testament Jericho," in BASOR 120 (Dec 1950), pp. 11-22; Kelso, "New Testament Jericho," in BA 14 (1951), pp. 34-43; and Kelso, in IDB II, pp. 838f.; James M. Pritchard, "The 1951 Campaign at Herodian Jericho," in BASOR 123 (Oct 1951), pp. 8-17; James L. Kelso, *Excavations at New Testament Jericho and Khirbet en-Nitla*, AASOR 29-30 (1949-1951), 1955; James M. Pritchard, *The Excavations at Herodian Jericho, 1951*, AASOR 32-33 (1953-1954), 1958; E. Netzer, "The Hasmonean and Herodian Winter Palaces at Jericho," in IEJ 25 (1975), pp. 80-100; and Netzer, "The Winter Palaces of the Judean Kings at Jericho at the end of the Second Temple period," in BASOR 228 (1977), pp. 1-13. Photograph: JF.

140. A Sycamore Tree at Jericho

WITH RESPECT to the account concerning Jesus and Zacchaeus in Jericho (Lk 19:1-10), J. Wellhausen declared in 1904 (*Das Evangelium Lucae*, p. 103) that the statement in the opening verse that Jesus had entered Jericho and was passing through was contradicted by what followed because Jesus was then still outside the city, not within it, otherwise Zacchaeus would have climbed upon a roof and not up into a tree. Following this lead others have continued to question the localization of the incident in Jericho (e.g., Rudolf Bultmann, *Die Geschichte der synoptischen Tradition* [1931], p. 69; S. MacL. Gilmour in IB VIII, p. 320). But the supposition implicit in Wellhausen's criticism is that Jericho was a city of tight-packed houses where roofs were indeed available for the ascent of Zacchaeus, but not trees. This conception would fit with the tightly-packed buildings found when OT Jericho was excavated in Tell es-Sultan. But it does not accord with the findings at Tulul Abu el-'Alayiq, where the excavators draw their closest comparison with Roman cities such as Rome, Tivoli, and Pompeii. Like such cities NT Jericho undoubtedly had its parks and villas, avenues and public squares, where fine trees grew. The sycamore tree, in particular, grows in Palestine mainly on the coast and in the Jordan Valley. That it was well known in ancient Jericho is shown by the finding of precisely this timber as bonding in one of the Hellenistic forts. As for modern times, the sycamore tree may still be seen in a central square of present-day Jericho and in the surrounding area. In this photograph of the sycamore tree, the low spreading character of its branches may particularly be noted.

In his account of the *Jewish War* (IV 8, 1f. §§449ff.) Josephus dates the arrival of Vespasian at Jericho on the third day of the month Daisios (= May/June) in what is the year 68 of the Christian era. The city itself, he says, the Romans found deserted, for most of the population in the district had fled in fear. From evidence at Qumran seven miles to the south it appears that Vespasian destroyed that place at this time (FLAP p. 275), but with

140. A Sycamore Tree at Jericho

respect to Jericho Josephus (*War* iv 9, 1 §486) says only that he established a camp and placed a garrison there. In the *Onomasticon* (p. 104), however, Eusebius says that Jericho was destroyed at the time of the siege of Jerusalem and a third city built in its place. He does not say when the last city was built, but states that it was to be seen in his time and that traces of its two predecessor cities were still preserved. In the time of Antoninus, son of Severus (193-211), Origen found an OT manuscript in a jar at Jericho (Eusebius, *Ch. Hist.* vi 16, 3) but it is not plain whether this implies a deserted or an inhabited city at the time. The Bordeaux Pilgrim (333) came down from Jerusalem to Jericho, i.e., to the third city described by Eusebius, and saw the sycamore tree, into which Zacchaeus climbed, before entering the city (Geyer p. 24; LPPTS I-B, p. 25; CCSL CLXXV, p. 18; WET p. 160). Paula (386) also came down from Jerusalem to Jericho and was shown both the sycamore tree of Zacchaeus and the place by the wayside where the two blind men sat, who were healed by Jesus, before she entered the city (Jerome, *Letter* 108, 12 NPNFSS VI, p. 201). On the Mad-

aba Mosaic Map (560), as noted above (No. 10), one sees the sanctuary of Saint Elisha, which must mark the famous spring by the OT city, and a stream flowing from it southward to a large city labeled Jericho and set amidst palm trees. This also must be the Byzantine city, and it appears to be in the same place as the present town of Jericho, a mile or so east of the NT city. A little later the Anonymous of Piacenza (570) found the walls of the city destroyed (probably by an earthquake), while not far away, proceeding in the direction of Jerusalem, was the tree of Zacchaeus, enclosed in a chapel with an open roof (Geyer pp. 168-169; LPPTS II-D, pp. 12-13; CCSL CLXXV, pp. 136-137; WJP p. 82). At the time of the visit of Arculf (670) all three successive cities were in ruins (Geyer p. 263; LPPTS III-A, p. 35; CCSL CLXXV, p. 212; WJP p. 106). Under the Arabs, however, *erikha*, as they called Jericho, was again an important place, and a geographer of the ninth century says that it was the capital of the Ghor, i.e., the Lower Jordan Valley. The Crusaders also considered the district to be very valuable, but after their time Jericho became only the small village that it still

151

was at the beginning of the twentieth century. Now, once again, it is a much larger town.

F. J. Bliss in HDB IICE pp. 580-582; Kraeling, *Bible Atlas*, p. 395. Photograph: The Matson Photo Service, Alhambra, Calif.

141. Ruins of the Aqueduct of Herod the Great in Wadi el-Qelt

GOING FOR THE last time from Jericho (Mt 20:29 and parallels) to Jerusalem (Mt 21:1 and parallels), Jesus presumably took the usual main route to which he had doubtless also referred when he spoke in one of his parables about a man who went down from Jerusalem to Jericho (Lk 10:30). In connection with the siege of Jerusalem by Titus, Josephus (*War* v 2, 3 §§69-70) tells how the Roman Tenth Legion came up by the way of Jericho and encamped at the Mount of Olives, and thus they presumably used the same road. In the course of time, perhaps for the most part after the Jewish War and the Second Revolt, the Romans paved the main roads in Palestine and marked them with milestones. The mile-stones, placed at intervals along the road, were normally inscribed with the name of the emperor and of the official who carried out the construction, and with the distance to or from some point of reference. From Jericho to Jerusalem some stretches of the Roman road can be traced and a few of its milestones have been found, thus giving an indication of the route of the older highway which the Roman road no doubt followed. The direct distance is scarcely twenty miles and in that distance the road climbed from Jericho at 770 feet below sea level to Jerusalem at 2,500 feet above sea level. Leaving Jericho, the route ran along the south wall of Wadi el-Qelt for more than three miles, then probably turned off to the southwest. The modern highway swings around farther south for the sake of a less precipitous ascent, but the road up along the wall of the wadi is still usable. In the wadi there were bridges and aqueducts of which ruins still remain, as may be seen in the photograph. By this system the water of three large springs in the wadi was brought down to the pools and palaces of Herodian Jericho and allowed to flow on out to enhance the irrigation of the plain.

141. Ruins of the Aqueduct of Herod the Great in Wadi el-Qelt

The *Survey of Western Palestine, Memoirs* III (1883), p. 188 and map and drawing of aqueducts near Jericho between pp. 222-223; Peter Thomsen, "Die römischen Meilensteine der Provinzen Syria, Arabia und Palaestina," in ZDPV 40 (1917), pp. 1-103, especially pp. 78-79, and map; G. Kuhl, "Römische Strassen and Strassenstationen in der Umgebung von Jerusalem," in PJ 24 (1928), pp. 113-140; M. Avi-yonah, *Map of Roman Palestine* (London: Oxford University Press, 1940), pp. 26-27 and map; Stewart Perowne, *The Life and Times of Herod the Great*, p. 120; Anton Jirku, *Die Welt der Bibel*, 2d ed. (Stuttgart: Gustav Kilpper Verlag, 1957), p. 251 pl. 105. Photograph: Perowne, ibid., pl. facing p. 96 (London: Hodder and Stoughton Ltd., 1956).

142. Traditional Site of the Inn of the Good Samaritan

ON THE ROAD just described (No. 141) running up from Jericho toward Jerusalem, there is a Roman milestone known locally as *dabbus el-'abd*, at a point somewhat more than three miles from Jericho. At a point more than a mile and one-half farther along, or about five miles from Jericho and twelve or thirteen miles short of Jerusalem, there is a pass which is 885 feet above sea level and 1,655 feet above Jericho. The Roman road probably went through here, as does the modern highway, because it is the shortest route between Jericho and Jerusalem. The name of the pass in Arabic is *tal'at ed-damm*, meaning Ascent of Blood. This corresponds with

the Hebrew מעלה אדמים, Ascent of Adummim, in Jos 15:7; 18:17. Actually the Hebrew *adummim* means red objects, in this case probably red rocks, and the original reference was probably to the red marl of the pass. Where he lists the Adummim ('Αδομμίμ) of Jos 15:7 in the *Onomasticon* (p. 24), Eusebius says that the place is called Μαληδομνεῖ, which is a transliteration in Greek of the entire Hebrew phrase, and he declares that there is a castle (φρούριον) there. In his version of the *Onomasticon* (p. 25; cf. *Letter* 108, 12 NPNFSS VI, p. 201) Jerome renders the name as Maledomni, says that it is equivalent to Greek ἀνάβασις πυρρῶν and Latin *ascensus ruforum sive rubrantium*, i.e., Ascent of the Red, and explains that the name was given because of the blood which was repeatedly shed at this place by robbers. Also, Jerome suggests, it was of this blood-stained and sanguinary place that the Lord spoke in the parable of the man who was going down from Jerusalem to Jericho.

The Crusaders, who also had a castle on the hill above the pass, accepted this suggestion and Burchard of Mount Sion (LPPTS XII-A, p. 63) for example, writes: "Four leagues to the west of Jericho, on the road to Jerusalem, to the left of Quarentena, is the Castle of Adummim, the place where the man who went down from Jerusalem to Jericho fell among thieves. This has befallen many on the same spot in modern times, and the place has received its name from the frequent blood

142. Traditional Site of the Inn of the Good Samaritan

shed there. Of a truth it is horrible to behold, and exceeding dangerous, unless one travels with an escort." Because of its strategic location the pass is the site of a police station today and, in line with the opinion of Jerome and the Crusaders, the spot is commonly considered as the location of the Inn of the Good Samaritan. The photograph looks west toward the highlands where Jerusalem is located.

Photograph: JF.

THE MOUNT OF OLIVES

143. Map of the Mount of Olives

AS NOTED ABOVE (NO. 141), when Titus brought the Tenth Legion up to Jerusalem they came by way of Jericho and encamped at the Mount of Olives (Josephus, *War* v 2, 3 §§69-70). Likewise when Jesus came to Jerusalem for the last days of his life we find mention of

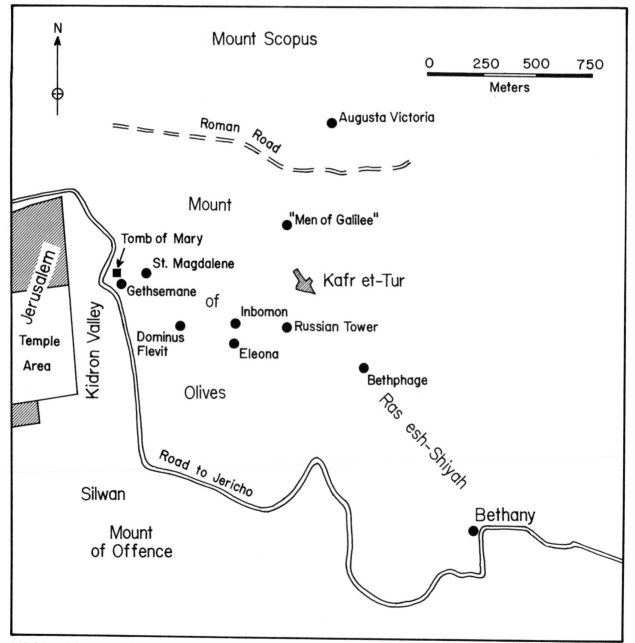

143. Map of the Mount of Olives

arrival at the Mount of Olives (τὸ ὄρος τῶν ἐλαιῶν Mt. 21:1; Mk 11:1, where ἐλαιῶν is the genitive plural of ἐλαία, "olive tree" or "olive," hence literally "the mountain of the olives," i.e., the Mount of Olives; for the slightly different form of the name in the parallel in Lk 19:29 see below under No. 154) and of descent (Lk 19:37) from there to the city. The Mount of Olives is part of a ridge of hills that overlooks Jerusalem across the Kidron Valley from the east, and is therefore encountered first by those approaching the city from the east. The ridge is some two and one-half miles long and has three main summits. The highest summit is at the north, is called Ras el-Mesharif, and is 2,690 feet above sea level. It is almost certainly the Mount Scopus where Titus placed his first camp while he considered the lay of the land and determined how best to proceed with his attack on Jerusalem (PJ 12 [1916], p. 55). In telling of this Josephus (War v 2, 3 §67) explains that the Mount was appropriately so named (σκοπός = "one who looks out") because a person approaching from the north here obtained his first view of Jerusalem "and the grand pile of the temple gleaming afar." The second summit, 2,660 feet above sea level, is directly across the Kidron Valley east from the city and the Temple area, and is the Mount of Olives proper. The location corresponds, for example, with Zec 14:4, which states that the Mount of Olives lies "before" or "opposite" or "facing" Jerusalem on the east. The Arabic name is et-Tur, which means "the Mount," and the village on the top is called Kefar et-Tur. On the summit also are a Russian church and buildings with a high tower that is a prominent landmark from all directions. Running off to the southeast there is also a subsidiary ridge of the Mount with the separate designation of Ras esh-Shiyah. The present-day village of el-'Azariyeh (Bethany) is on the farther downslope of this ridge. The third main summit of the entire chain is farther south and somewhat lower than Mount Scopus and the Mount of Olives. It rises above the village of Silwan and is opposite the oldest part of Jerusalem south of the Temple area. This is probably the Mount of Corruption or Mount of Offence, where Solomon worshiped false gods (II K 23:13). The map shows the places that have just been mentioned and locates sites that are discussed in what follows.

Map: JF, cf. Dalman, Sacred Sites, p. 260.

144. The Mount of Olives and Bethany from the South

ABOUT A MILE WEST of the traditional site of the Inn of the Good Samaritan the road from Jericho to Jerusalem divides into two branches. One branch, which is now the route of the modern road, swings to the southwest and then comes up past el-'Azariyeh (Bethany), continues between the Mount of Offence and the Mount of Olives, and goes up the Kidron Valley and around to the north side of Jerusalem. The other branch, which was the route of the Roman road (cf. No. 141), came up over the ridge between Mount Scopus and the Mount of Olives proper (Dalman, Sacred Rites, p. 260 map). In this area the Empress Augusta Victoria Endowment (a German hospice, hospital, and church established in 1910) stands on the southern slope of Mount Scopus, while the Greek chapel called Viri Galilaei (the name "Men of Galilee" reflects a traditional localization of the event in Ac 1:11 at this spot) is on the northern slope of the Mount of Olives, and the route of the Roman road passes between the two. Some of the paving of this road survived till modern times and one milestone stood not far from the entrance to the Augusta Victoria property, while a branch road running northward (to connect Jerusalem with Neapolis) was traceable through the garden of the same endowment (PJ 12 [.1916], p. 75; ZDPV 40 [1917], p. 78 No. 277). From here the Jericho-Jerusalem road must have proceeded down the western slope of the ridge and brought travelers to the Kidron Valley or allowed them to proceed to a gate on the north side of the city. The photograph is a view of the Mount of Olives from the south. The Russian Tower, mentioned above (No. 143), is visible on the summit. The village of el-'Azariyeh, ancient Bethany, is at the right on the lower slope of the ridge called Ras esh-Shiyah.

Photograph: JF.

145. The Village of Bethany

AS FOR THE VILLAGE of Bethany (Βηθανία), Jn 11 recounts the raising of Lazarus at that place and states that this was a reason for which counsel was taken to put Jesus to death; Jn 12:1 says that Jesus was at Bethany six days before the final Passover, and Mt 21:17-18 and Mk 11:11-12 picture him as going there from Jerusalem for lodging at night. Neh 11:32 mentions Anathoth (which was at Anata three miles north of Jerusalem), Nob (which was on Mount Scopus), and Ananiah in that order and the last place, which could well also have been called Bethananiah, may have been the town which the NT calls Bethany (W. F. Albright in ASOR 4 for 1922-23 [1924], pp. 158-160). Jn 11:18 places Bethany fifteen stadia from Jerusalem, and Eusebius (Onomasticon p. 58) says that it was at the second milestone from Aelia in a steep bank (ἐν κρημνῷ) of the Mount of Olives. The Bordeaux Pilgrim (Geyer p. 23; LPPTS I-B, p. 25; CCSL CLXXV, p. 18; WET p. 160) puts the village of Bethany 1,500

144. The Mount of Olives and Bethany from the South

145. The Village of Bethany

paces eastward from the Mount of Olives and states that the crypt is there in which Lazarus was laid. Aetheria (Geyer pp. 77, 82; LPPTS I-C, pp. 51, 57; CCSL CLXXV, pp. 72, 76; WET pp. 127, 131) gives Lazarium, obviously derived from the name of Lazarus, as the name of Bethany (*Lazarium autem, id est Bethania*), and places it at about 1,500 paces or at the second mile from the city. Theodosius (Geyer p. 147; LPPTS II-B, p. 16; CCSL CLXXV, p. 123; WJP p. 70) says: "As to Lazarus whom the Lord raised, it is known that he was raised, but no one knows about his second death. This happened in Bethany two miles from Jerusalem, and all the people gather in that place at the (feast of the) Raising of Lazarus before Easter day, and services are held." The distance of two Roman miles or fifteen stadia is equivalent to about three kilometers or something less than two English miles. This is the actual distance from Jerusalem to the present village of el-'Azariyeh and, as already stated (Nos. 143, 144), this village is on the lower slope of a ridge (Ras esh-Shi-yah) of the Mount of Olives. It is also possible to see that the ancient name Lazarium, given by Aetheria, developed into the Arabic name, el-'Azariyeh, the initial letter of the Latin name probably being taken as the article (Kopp p. 333). The identification of this village with Bethany is therefore to be accepted.

The photograph shows the village as it appeared earlier in the present century. The hillside beyond the houses from one-third to one-half of the way from the left side of the picture was probably the location of the more ancient village. In this area, two or three hundred meters west of the present village, shaft tombs (cf. Nos. 248f.) were found in 1914 from the Canaanite period and other isolated finds gave evidence of habitation from 1500 B.C. to A.D. 100. In an olive grove owned by the Franciscans west of the ruined medieval tower (standing up prominently a third of the way from the right side of the photograph) and some eighty meters west of the traditional tomb of Lazarus (No. 146) there were new excavations by the Franciscans in 1949-1953. Here the rock was virtually honeycombed with pits, caves, cisterns, and tombs. The objects found showed almost continuous occupation from about the sixth century B.C. to the fourteenth century of the Christian era. There were abundant small finds, including clay lamps and earthen vessels of many kinds, and coins, from the very period of Jesus as well as other periods. Among the coins was one of Herod the Great and another of the time of Pontius Pilate.

Farther west, on the western edge of the ancient village, about 400 meters from the tomb of Lazarus, a remarkable but enigmatical rock grotto was investigated in 1950 by the Dominicans of the École Biblique in Jerusalem. Rock-cut steps with a small center divider lead down to the rock-hewn entrance, itself divided into two openings by a central pillar. The chamber itself is some 5.4 by 4 meters in size, with a height of from 3 to 2.2 meters. The original layer of plaster on the walls is such as was used for many cisterns, and the original usage of the grotto was probably as a cistern. On a second layer of plaster, however, there are many graffiti, judged to have been left by pilgrims from the fourth to the seventh century, in which time this was plainly a sacred shrine of some sort. At the same time the tomb of Lazarus was venerated at the eastern edge of the ancient village, so the grotto was not confused with that grave. Nevertheless Lazarus was remembered here too, for a graffito on the north wall of the grotto reads:

 K̄E O ΘC O ΕΓΙΡΑC ΤΟΝ ΛΑΖΑΡΟΝ ΕΚ ΝΕΚΡΩΝ
ΜΝΗCΘΗΤΙ ΤΟΥ ΔΟΥΛΟΥ COY ΑCΚΛΗΠΙΟΥ ΚΕ
ΧΙΟΝΙΟΥ ΤΗC ΔΟΥΛΗC [CO]Υ

Lord God, who raised Lazarus from the dead, remember your servant Asklepios and Chionion your (feminine) servant

Along with many other pilgrim names and many cross marks, another inscription, for example, reads:

ΘΕΑΙ ΤΩΝ ΧΡΗC
ΤΙΑΝΩΝ ΕΛΕΗCΟΝ
ΑΝΑΜΟΝ ΤΟΝ ΑΜΑΡ
Τ[ΩΛ] ΟΝ ΚΕ ΕΘΑΦΕΡΑΥ
ΤΩ ΤΑC ΑΜΡΤΙΑC [ΑΜ] ΗΝ

God of the Christians, have mercy on Anamos and take away his sins. Amen.

H. Vincent in RB 23 (1914), pp. 438-441; Sylvester J. Saller, *Excavations at Bethany (1949-1953)*. PSBF 12 (Jerusalem: Franciscan Printing Press, 1957), pp. 139-158 and 159ff.; P. Benoit and M. E. Boismard, "Un ancien sanctuaire chrétien à Béthanie," in RB 58 (1951), pp. 200-251, for the two inscriptions see pp. 216f., no. 21, and figs. 3, 5; and pp. 226-228, no. 43, pl. IV, and fig. 6. Photograph: courtesy École Biblique et Archéologique Française.

146. Plan of the Tomb of Lazarus and Adjacent Buildings

AS WE HAVE just seen (No. 145) it was the tomb in which Lazarus was laid that was naturally of greatest interest to Christian pilgrims to Bethany. In the *Onomasticon* (p. 58) Eusebius lists Bethany as the place where Christ raised Lazarus and says, "The place of Lazarus is still pointed out even until now" (δείκνυται εἰς ἔτι καὶ νῦν ὁ Λαζάρου τόπος). As was stated in connection with Origen as well as Eusebius (cf. p. xvi), the characteristic formula, "is pointed out," doubtless attests a tradition of very long standing. The location of the Tomb of Lazarus, as it is still pointed out in Bethany, is shown at 1-2 in the upper left-hand corner of the plan.

Plan: Sylvester J. Saller, *Excavations at Bethany (1949-1953)*, fig. 2 on p. 6, courtesy Terra Santa.

147. Present Entrance to the Tomb of Lazarus

AS SHOWN IN the plan (No. 146) the present entrance to the Tomb of Lazarus is from the street on the north side. The exterior of this entrance is shown in the photograph. Inside this doorway twenty-two steps lead down into the vestibule of the tomb.

Photograph: JF.

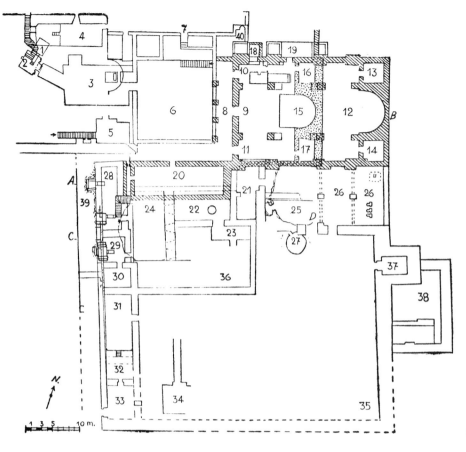

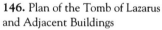

146. Plan of the Tomb of Lazarus
and Adjacent Buildings

147. Present Entrance to the Tomb of Lazarus

148. The Tomb of Lazarus

THIS PHOTOGRAPH SHOWS the vestibule just mentioned (No. 147). From here two steps, as may be seen, descend into a narrow passage and the passaage leads five feet into the vaulted inner chamber, about seven and one-half feet long and eight feet wide, of the tomb. On three sides of this chamber there are niches in the rock which widen out at the bottom to make slightly raised shelves for three burials. Jn 11:38 states that the tomb of Lazarus was a cave, "and a stone lay upon it." As may be seen in the picture, the stone to cover the entrance into this tomb would have been laid horizontally over the entrance steps.

Photograph: courtesy École Biblique et Archéologique Française.

158

148. The Tomb of Lazarus

149. Mosaic Pavement in the First Church at Bethany

AS WE HAVE SEEN (NO. 146) Eusebius said that "the place of Lazarus is still pointed out even until now" at Bethany. When Jerome revised the *Onomasticon* (p. 59) he changed this sentence to read as follows, adding the italicized words: "*a church which has now been erected there* points out his monument." From this it is evident that in the time after 330 when Eusebius composed the *Onomasticon* and before 390 when Jerome translated and revised it, a church was built at Bethany to mark the "monument," i.e., the tomb of Lazarus. While Jerome's word "now" suggests that the church was a relatively recent construction, it was probably built at least prior to the time of Aetheria who visited the Holy Land in 381-384. As we have seen (No. 145) she uses Lazarium as a name equivalent to Bethany. But in the case of Eleona, Aetheria uses this name as both the name of the Mount of Olives and also the name of the important church that stood on it, for she writes both "go up to the Mount of Olives, that is, to Eleona" (*ascendet in monte oliueti, id est in Eleona,* Geyer p. 83; LPPTS I-C, p. 58; CCSL CLXXV, p. 77; WET p. 142), and also "services in Eleona, that is, in the very beautiful church on the Mount of Olives" (*in Eleona, id est in ecclesia, quae est in monte Oliueti, pulchra*

satis . . . celebrantur, Geyer p. 77; LPPTS I-C, p. 51; CCSL CLXXV, p. 72; WET p. 127). By analogy it seems probable, therefore, that Lazarium was the name both of the village and also of the church that was built there. Since Aetheria (Geyer pp. 71ff.; LPPTS I-C, pp. 45ff.; CCSL CLXXV, pp. 67ff.; WET pp. 123ff.) describes elaborate services held at various times of the church year in various churches in and around Jerusalem, such as the Great Church in Golgotha, the Anastasis, and Eleona, and includes along with these "the Lazarium," it certainly seems most probable that this church was already in existence in her time.

In her description of the liturgical celebration by the Jerusalem church at the Lazarium on Saturday before Easter week, Aetheria writes:

> When it begins to be morning, as the Sabbath dawns, the bishop makes an offering and the oblation early on the Sabbath. And when the dismissal is to be given the archdeacon calls out, saying: "Let us all be ready in the Lazarium at the seventh hour (one o'clock in the afternoon) today."
>
> So at the beginning of the seventh hour they all come to the Lazarium. The Lazarium, i.e., Bethany, is about two miles from the city. As they come from Jerusalem to the Lazarium, about 500 paces (half a mile) from the latter place, there is a church in the street at the spot where Mary, the sister of Lazarus, met the Lord. And when the bishop has

159

come here all the monks meet him, and the people enter; one hymn is sung and one antiphon, and they read the passage from the Gospel where the sister of Lazarus meets the Lord (Jn 11:29). So prayer having been made, and all having been blessed, they go from there to the Lazarium with hymns.

When they have come to the Lazarium the whole crowd assembles, so that not only the place itself, but the fields all around, are full of people. Hymns and antiphons are sung appropriate to the day and place, and in like manner readings suitable for the day are read. Before they are dismissed, Easter [*pascha*, meaning both Passover and Easter] is announced. The priest goes up to an elevated place and reads the passage from the Gospel where it is written, "When Jesus had come to Bethany, six days before the Passover" (Jn 12:1), etc. The passage having been read and Easter announced, they are dismissed. These things are done on this day, because it is written in the Gospel that so it was done in Bethany "six days before the Passover"; now from the Sabbath to the fifth day, when, after the supper, the Lord was apprehended at night, is six days. Then they all return to the city straight to the Anastasis. (Geyer pp. 81f.; LPPTS I-C, p. 57; CCSL CLXXV, p. 76; WET pp. 131f.)

In 1949-1953 prior to the erection of the new Church of St. Lazarus in Bethany the Franciscans were able to excavate and study much of the immediate area. This area has already been shown in the plan in No. 146. As seen in this plan the tomb of Lazarus (1-2) was at the west and the church was at the east with a courtyard providing connection between the two. In other words the plan was the same as found in other famous churches of the fourth century, e.g., in the Cathedral (c. 365) at Gerasa (No. 111) where the church was to the east of the celebrated fountain and connected with it. As seen in the plan (No. 146) the oldest Bethany church had nave (9), two side aisles (10 and 11), and apse (15). The foundations of this church were partially uncovered at five different points in the Franciscan excavations, and the mosaic pavements in the nave and side aisles were cleared to a considerable extent. The photograph shows a portion of the mosaic in the nave. The panel at the right is a part of the main field of the mosaic, that at the left is a part of the border. The patterns are geometrical and there is no sign of any living being in them. Numerous small crosses may be noted. The field mosaic has a close parallel in the mosaic pavement of a synagogue at Apamea on the Orontes, which is dated by its inscriptions to the year 391 of the Christian Era (E. L. Sukenik in HUCA XXIII 2 [1950-51], pp. 541-551 and plate VI). From the literary references, the plan, and the mosaics, the first church at Bethany may be dated, therefore, in the fourth century and probably after the middle of the century.

Sylvester J. Saller, *Excavations at Bethany (1949-1953)*. PSBF 12 (1957), pp. 9-33; Ovadiah, *Corpus*, pp. 29-31, no. 18a/b. Photograph: JF.

150. The New Church of St. Lazarus at Bethany

ACCORDING to archeological excavations in Bethany, the first church at the tomb of Lazarus (No. 149) was probably destroyed by an earthquake and then replaced by a second church (Saller, *Second Catalogue*, pp. 35-66). As shown in the plan (No. 146) the apse (12) of the new structure was moved some thirteen meters eastward beyond that of its predecessor, but the basic plan remained the same. The second church also had a mosaic pavement, of which a large part was found intact. It was also geometric in pattern but, in contrast with the pavement of the first church, this mosaic contained no crosses whatever. This may point to a time after the year 427 when the emperor Theodosius prohibited the use of crosses in pavements (Saller, *Second Catalogue*, p. 43). At the same time the continued absence of representations of animals and human beings points to a time prior to the sixth century when such representations became

149. Mosaic Pavement in the First Church at Bethany

150. The New Church of St. Lazarus at Bethany

the olive grove where remains of early Bethany were found are the ruins of the tower (cf. above No. 145) which protected the monastic institution.

William of Tyre (1184) records the events connected with the foundation of the abbey and its protective tower (Babcock and Krey II, pp. 132-135). Queen Melisende, wife of the Crusader king Fulk of Anjou (king of Jerusalem from 1131 to 1143)

conceived the idea of founding a convent for religious women if a place suited to her wishes could be found. She desired in this way to provide for the healing of her own soul and those of her parents as also for the salvation of her husband and children [the eldest son was Baldwin III, king of Jerusalem, 1143-1163]. Her youngest sister Iveta had professed the religious life in the monastery of Saint Anne, the mother of the blessed Mother of our Lord [cf. No. 203]. It was consideration for this sister which led the queen to undertake this enterprise, for she felt that it was unfitting that a king's daughter [Melisende and her sister were daughters of Baldwin II, king of Jerusalem, 1118-1131] should be subject to the authority of a mother superior, like an ordinary person. Accordingly, she mentally surveyed the whole country and made a careful investigation to find a suitable place where she might found a convent. After much deliberation, she finally decided upon Bethany, the home of Mary and Martha and Lazarus their brother, whom Jesus loved—Bethany, the familiar abiding place and home of our Lord and Savior. This village is fifteen furlongs from Jerusalem, and, according to the word of the Gospel, it lies beyond the Mount of Olives, on the eastern slope of the hill. The property belonged to the church of the Sepulcher of the Lord, but the queen gave to the canons Tekoa, the city of prophets, and in exchange received Bethany as her own.

Since the place lay on the edge of the desert and thus might be exposed to the attacks of the enemy, the queen at great expense caused to be built a strongly fortified tower of hewn and polished stone. This was devoted to the necessary purpose of defense, that the maidens dedicated to God might have an impregnable fortress as a protection against the enemy. When the tower was finished and a place prepared, after a fashion, for carrying on the offices of religion, she established consecrated sisters there and placed over them as mother superior a venerable woman full of years and of ripe religious experience. She endowed the church with rich estates, so that in temporal possessions it should not be inferior to any monastery, either of men or women; or rather, as it is said, that it might be richer than any other church. . . .

On the death of the venerable woman to whom she had entrusted the charge of this convent, the queen put her original intention into effect. With the sanction of the patriarch and the willing assent of the holy nuns, she made her sister the superior of the convent. On that occasion, she made many additional gifts, such as chalices, books, and other ornaments pertaining to the service of the church. As long as she lived she continued to enrich the place by her favor, in the interests of her own soul and that of the sister whom she so tenderly loved.

common. A known earthquake of 447, which was very strong at Jerusalem (D. H. Kallner-Amiran in IEJ 1 [1950-51], p. 225), could have damaged the first church and, if so, the second church may have been built about the middle of the fifth century.

In the Crusader period in the twelfth century considerable modifications were made in the second church, leading the excavators to call this now the third church, but the basic plan was still unchanged and the apse (12) remained in the same place. About the same time the western end of the complex (3-5) was transformed into a distinct church, which the excavators call the fourth church (Saller, *Second Catalogue*, pp. 67-97). This church had a crypt that was connected with the tomb of Lazarus. In the Muslim period the crypt was converted into a mosque, however, and the entrance from it into the tomb was sealed off. Then the new entrance into the tomb from the north (No. 147) was constructed. This "fourth church" is still used as a mosque with the name of el-Uzeir. In 1955 it was provided with a new minaret.

South of the churches just described are the ruins of a large monastic establishment or abbey (20-38) (Saller, *Second Catalogue*, pp. 99-130). Here many of the stones bear masons' marks, letters of the alphabet, crosses, etc., characteristic of the Crusaders. Between the abbey and

By the middle of the fourteenth century the churches described above were in ruins (Saller, *Second Catalogue*, p. 97). After the archeological excavations in 1949-

1953 a new Church of St. Lazarus was erected, and dedicated in 1954 (Saller, *Second Catalogue*, pp. 131-137). It was built in the form of a Greek cross above the eastern part of the second and third churches and, where possible, utilized the ancient foundations. The apses of the two earliest churches were left visible within the new church, that of the first church in the western arm, that of the second church behind the altar in the eastern arm. In the western part of the church a portion of the mosaic pavement of the second church also remains visible; in the courtyard west of the church is a portion of the mosaic of the first church (No. 149). The photograph, taken from within the beautiful garden, shows the east side of the new church, with the slender tower at the northeastern corner, and the cupola over the center.

Photograph: JF.

151. The Franciscan Chapel at Bethphage

WHEN JESUS and his disciples drew near to Jerusalem for what is commonly called the "triumphal entry" it is stated in Mt 21:1 that they came to (εἰς) Bethphage to (εἰς Codex Vaticanus) or toward (πρός Codex Sinaiticus) the Mount of Olives. In their parallel accounts Mk 11:1 and Lk 19:29 add to the name of Bethphage also the mention of Bethany and speak of coming to (εἰς) both places along with coming toward (πρός) the Mount of Olives. The instructions that follow immediately in all three Gospels to two disciples to go into "the village opposite" can obviously refer to only one village and therefore agree best with the mention in Mt of only Bethphage. Perhaps Bethany was added in Mk and Lk because it was the better known place and would help to locate Bethphage, and because it was familiar to come up the Jericho-Jerusalem road and turn to one side to Bethphage and Bethany. If, then, the tradition as preserved in Mt is basic to that found in Mk and Lk, the fact that both Mk and Lk speak of going to (εἰς) Bethphage and Bethany along with movement toward (πρός) the Mount of Olives makes it probable that this was also the reading found first in Mt, as is preserved in Codex Sinaiticus where it is said that Jesus and the disciples came both to (εἰς) Bethphage and toward (πρός) the Mount of Olives. Used with the accusative as it is in these passages, the preposition πρός has this literal sense of toward and suggests a location up against. In this sense it well describes the situation of Bethany (el-'Azariyeh, cf. No. 145), located as it is up against the downslope of the

151. The Franciscan Chapel at Bethphage

southeastern ridge (Ras esh-Shiyah) of the Mount of Olives. These facts suggest, therefore, that Bethphage was somewhere between the Roman road and Bethany and probably, like Bethany, somewhere up against the southeastern ridge of the Mount of Olives. If it be supposed, however, that Jesus came up a route something like that of the modern highway, which proceeds directly past Bethany (el-'Azariyeh) and on into Jerusalem, and if the references in Mk 11:1 and Lk 19:29 are taken to mean that on that route he came to Bethphage before Bethany, then a site for Bethphage would have to be sought somewhere east of Bethany. With this in view some have supposed that Bethphage was at the Arab village of Abu Dis, which is still farther down the southeastern ridge, to the southeast and across a ravine from el-'Azariyeh, but this location is much less likely.

At any rate the village of Bethphage (Βηθφαγή) is surely to be identified with the place called Beth Page (בית פאגי) which is mentioned a number of times in the Talmud. The Talmudic references occur particularly in connection with definition of the exact limits within which a sacred thing might be prepared or used. In the tractate *Menahoth* (78b GBT VIII, p. 680; SBT V, 2, pp. 468-469), for example, it is stated in the Mishnah passage that during the slaughtering of the thank offering, the bread of the thank offering must not be found "outside the wall." Then in the Gemara there is discussion of what this stipulation meant. One rabbi said that it meant "outside the wall of the Temple court," but Rabbi Johanan (third century) said it meant "outside the wall of Beth Page." From this we gather that Beth Page or Bethphage was a suburb of Jerusalem and probably located somewhere beyond the main outer wall of the Temple, i.e., the eastern wall, therefore probably somewhere on or over the Mount of Olives, which agrees with the deduction made in the preceding paragraph. Furthermore we learn here that the "wall" of Beth Page, which could have been an actual fortification of the village, or could have been simply a way of designating the extent of its territory, was considered to define the limits of Jerusalem. In the light of this fact it is particularly significant that Jesus now, by special arrangement, obtained a mount from Bethphage and rode on from that point. He who otherwise, as far as we know, had walked all over Palestine, including the long steep ascent from Jericho, chose to ride at last into Jerusalem precisely from the point that marked officially the entry point into the holy city. To this entry he obviously attached a very special significance.

Eusebius lists Bethphage in the *Onomasticon* (p. 58) but gives no more information than is already provided in the Gospels. It is a village, he says, at the Mount of Olives (πρὸς τῷ ὄρει τῶν ἐλαιῶν) to which the Lord Jesus came. Jerome (*Letter* 108, 12 NPNFSS VI, pp. 200-201)

says that Paula visited the tomb of Lazarus (at Bethany) and also Bethphage, and from the latter place "went straight on down the hill to Jericho," presumably going down the Roman road as described above (No. 144). Theodosius (530) (Geyer p. 146; LPPTS II-B, p. 15; CCSL CLXXV, p. 122; WJP p. 69) speaks of the Mount of Olives and goes on to tell of "a church where St. Thecla is. The place is called Bethphage. From there was brought the colt of an ass (*pullum asinae*) on which the Lord sat when he entered Jerusalem by the Gate of Benjamin." Thecla is presumably the famous heroine of the apocryphal *Acts of Paul and Thecla*, and the statement that the Bethphage church is "where St. Thecla is" must intend to say that it marks her burial place. In the apocryphal work, however, Thecla dies at Seleucia or, in some versions, dies at Rome and is buried near the tomb of Paul (JANT p. 281; HSNTA II, p. 331; SWDCB IV, p. 885), and one suggestion is that the Bethphage church was only the place of a memorial observance in honor of Thecla (J. T. Milik in RB 67 [1960], pp. 564f., no. 41). It may be, however, that the name is a mistake for St. Pelagia, the martyr of Antioch (d. c. 306) and that it is she who is said to rest in a grave in this place (Tobler and Molinier p. 67). At any rate Theodosius knows Bethphage on the Mount of Olives as the place where Jesus mounted the colt for his "triumphal entry" into Jerusalem (the Gate of Benjamin through which Jesus entered the city, according to Theodosius, was another name for the Sheep Gate in the city wall on the north side of the Temple area [Nos. 197, 203], since this gate led directly to the territory of the tribe of Benjamin immediately north of Jerusalem [Mackowski p. 51]). The Jerusalem monk Epihanius (750-800) (WJP p. 120) gives distances to locate Bethphage, stating that the place where Christ sat on the colt was about one thousand paces (one mile) from the church marking the Ascension (on the summit of the Mount of Olives, No. 158), and another one thousand paces short of Bethany and the Tomb of Lazarus, but he gives no more details about the place.

For the Crusader acceptance of the site of Bethphage as described in the foregoing and for the Franciscan chapel shown in the present photograph, see further in No. 152.

Photograph: courtesy Terra Santa.

152. Crusader Painting on Bethphage Stone

BERNARD THE FRANKISH monk (870) (Tobler and Molinier p. 317; LPPTS III-D, p. 9), writing before the Crusaders came, tells of Bethany, a mile to the south from the Mount of Olives, with a monastery church that displays the sepulcher of Lazarus (who was said to have

152. Crusader Painting on
Bethphage Stone

afterwards been bishop in Ephesus for forty years), and then says: "As you go down the Mount of Olives on the western side there is shown a block of marble, from which the Lord mounted on the colt of an ass." The German pilgrim Theodericus (1172) (LPPTS V-D, pp. 34f.; WJP p. 152), writing in the time of the Crusaders and before their expulsion from Jerusalem by Saladin in 1187, describes the location of Bethphage and tells of both the stone and the chapel that then enclosed it:

> So on Palm Sunday our dearest Lord Jesus Christ set out from Bethany, came to Bethphage, which place is halfway between Bethany and the Mount of Olives, and where now a fair chapel has been built in his honor, and sent two of his disciples to bring an ass and her colt. He stood upon a great stone which may be seen in the chapel, and sitting upon the ass went over the Mount of Olives to Jerusalem, and was met by a great crowd as he descended the side of the mountain.

In the year 1876 in the area indicated a cubical block of stone (about 5 feet long, 4.5 feet wide, and 3 feet high) was accidentally discovered, on which are Crusader paintings and a broken inscription. The property was acquired by the Franciscans and their Chapel of Bethphage (No. 151) was built in 1883, with the memorial stone preserved within. At the same time, only a little over two yards from the stone, the foundations of the apse of a Crusader church were uncovered.

The paintings with which the Crusaders adorned the stone were of events that were remembered at this place. On the south side, toward Bethany, is the depiction of the resurrection of Lazarus (the present photograph). As the slab of the tomb is removed and a man holds his nose, Jesus, with outstretched hand (at the upper left), commands Lazarus to come forth, while Martha and Mary (their heads at the lower left corner) kneel at his feet. On the north side of the stone are a city wall, a group of men, and an ass and her colt. On the east are people bearing palms, but the place that should show Jesus mounted on the colt is effaced. On the west is a damaged inscription that includes reference to BETH-PHAGE and to the ass that was brought from there (ASINA DUCTVS) (Meistermann p. 285).

Photograph: JF.

153. Tomb with Rolling Stone at Bethphage

ARCHEOLOGICAL STUDY of the shrine of Beth-phage in 1949-1953 by S. Saller and his associates established that the area was occupied from the second century B.C., with numerous coins extending back into the reign of Antiochus IV (175-164) and on down into approximately the eighth century A.D. Ten rock-hewn tombs were found, representing four modes of burial, on a bench, in *kokim*, in trough-like graves, and in shaft-graves, together with a number of ossuaries. As shown in the present photograph, in one trough-like type of tomb (tomb no. 21) a rolling stone for closure is still in place in front of the entrance. In the same tomb are more than a dozen graffiti, which are interpreted as of Judeo-Christian import, with symbols of paradise, signs for the name of Jesus as the Redeemer and the Christ, and an inscription relating to the millennium.

153. Tomb with Rolling Stone at Bethphage

S. Saller and E. Testa, *The Archaeological Setting of the Shrine of Bethphage.* PSBFSS 1 (Jerusalem: Franciscan Printing Press, 1961); Cornfeld p. 308. For a Byzantine tomb with crosses and fragments of mosaic, see A. Barrois in RB 37 (1928), p. 262. Photograph: JF.

154. The Crypt of the Eleona Church

IN HIS LAST DAYS, according to Mt 24:3, Jesus sat on the Mount of Olives when he spoke to the disciples about the end of the world (συντέλεια τοῦ αἰῶνος; cf. τέλος in 24:6), and according to Mk 13:3 the spot was opposite the temple. After his resurrection, according to Lk 24:50 he led the disciples out "until *they were* over against (ἕως πρός) Bethany" (ASV) and parted from them; after he was taken out of their sight (Ac 1:9) they returned to Jerusalem, according to Ac 1:12, "from the mount called Olivet (ἀπὸ ὄρους τοῦ καλουμένου ἐλαιῶνος, where ἐλαιών, olive grove, is a proper noun and the phrase means literally, 'from the mountain called Olive Grove,' i.e., the Mount of Olives; cf. the Latin *mons oliveti*, 'the mountain of the olive grove [*olivetum*],' i.e., the Mount of Olives, whence the English 'Olivet'; so also in Lk 19:29; 21:37), which is near Jerusalem, a sabbath day's journey away." The sabbath day's journey, or distance that one could go without transgressing the commandment of Ex 16:29, was reckoned, on the basis of Num 35:5, at 2,000 cubits (*Erubin* IV 3; V 7 DM pp. 126, 128) or approximately 900 meters. Josephus gives almost exactly the same distance when he says that the Mount of Olives was five stadia (just over 3,000 feet) from the city (*Ant.* XX 8, 6 §169; in *War* V 2, 3 §70 the Tenth Legion encamped at the Mount of Olives at a distance of six stadia from Jerusalem, therefore presumably on the eastern side of the Mount on the way up from Jericho).

As noted above (No. 25), of the churches built in Palestine under the emperor Constantine, the church on the Mount of Olives was one of those the erection of which was particularly credited to Helena Augusta, the mother of the emperor. Eusebius (*Life of Constantine* III 43) says: "The mother of the emperor raised a stately structure on the Mount of Olives also, in memory of his ascent to heaven who is the Savior of mankind, erecting a sacred church and temple on the very summit of the mount. And indeed authentic history informs us that in this very cave the Savior imparted his secret revelations to his disciples."

The rhetorical language of Eusebius is slightly confusing, but from the excavations about to be mentioned it seems evident that Helena and Constantine built only one church on the Mount of Olives. It was over the cave in which Jesus was believed to have taught the disciples about the end (Mt 24 and parallels), and it was near the summit of the mount where the ascension was believed to have taken place (Ac 1:9). That a particular cave on the Mount of Olives was associated with the teaching of Jesus is attested already in the apocryphal *Acts of John* (97, HSNTA II, p. 157), and it was evidently over this cave that the church in question was erected. The Bordeaux Pilgrim, who saw this church in 333, says explicitly that it was at the place "where before the Passion (*ante passionum*), the Lord taught the disciples" (Geyer p. 23; LPPTS I-B, pp. 24-25; CCSL CLXXV, p. 18; WET p. 160). Aetheria (381-384) says with equal explicitness that "the cave in which the Lord used to teach is there" (Geyer p. 83; LPPTS I-C, p. 58; CCSL CLXXV, p. 77; WET p. 139) and, as we have already seen (No. 149), uses Eleona as the name of the church as well as of the mount (Geyer p. 77; LPPTS I-C, p. 51; CCSL CLXXV, p. 72; WET p. 127).

According to Nicephorus (829), the empress Helena had marble stairs built to lead up to her church on the Mount of Olives, and in one of his poetic compositions Sophronius (who became patriarch of Jerusalem in 634) tells of climbing those stairs to the church, and of the beautiful outlook from there to the Holy City to the west (*Anacreontica* 19.8-18; MPG 87, cols. 3811-3812; LPPTS XI-A, p. 28 and n. 1):

> Ascending the steps from the famous valley [the Kidron Valley] I would kiss the Mount of Olives from whence he [Jesus Christ] ascended into the heavens, and after I had magnified the boundless depths of heavenly wisdom, through which he saved me, I would swiftly run thither where he was wont to expound mysteries to his reverend companions, casting light into darksome depths. I would then pass beneath the roof through the greatest gate, and, going out upon the terrace, would admire the beauty of the holy city as it lay towards the west. How sweet to behold thy loveliness from the Mount of Olives, thou city of God!

The ruins of the Eleona church were identified and studied in excavations by L.-H. Vincent and the Dominicans beginning in 1910. The site is 70 meters south and slightly west of the absolute summit of the ridge where the Ascension Mosque (No. 159) stands. The photograph shows the uncovering of the crypt of the church, which was the cave mentioned in the tradition cited above.

Photograph: courtesy École Biblique et Archéologique Française.

154. The Crypt of the Eleona Church

155. Plan and Section of the Eleona Church

FROM THE SCANTY REMAINS of the Eleona church, including its foundation trenches cut in the rock, Vincent made the plan and section shown in this illustration. The entrance is thought to have been a portico of six columns. Three doors gave access to the atrium, under the center of which was a large cistern. Steps led up to the basilica proper which was on a higher level. It was about one hundred feet in length, and had nave, two side aisles, and inscribed apse. The orientation was such that the cave-crypt was beneath the eastern end of the apse. There are also small portions of mosaic pavement which remain in the south aisle and outside the south side of the church, where there may have been a baptistery. The pattern is something like that in the Constantinian church at Bethlehem. Later buildings now obstruct the outlook to the west, but the spot must once have provided the splendid view toward Jerusalem and the Temple praised by Sophronius (cf. Mk 13:3).

Vincent, *Jérusalem nouvelle*, pp. 337-360; Crowfoot, *Early Churches*, pp. 30-34; M. Avi-Yonah in QDAP 2 (1932), pp. 165-166 no. 113; Ovadiah, *Corpus*, pp. 82f., no. 71; Bahat, *Plans*, 114ab. Photograph: Crowfoot, *Early Churches*, p. 33, fig. 5.

156. The Church of the Lord's Prayer

LIKE OTHER CHURCHES on the unprotected Mount of Olives, the Eleona was destroyed by the Neo-Persians in 614, but the tradition that Jesus taught in this vicinity persisted. In the Middle Ages a chapel marked the place where Jesus was supposed to have taught the disciples the Lord's Prayer, and another commemorated the spot where the Apostles were believed to have drawn up the Creed. In 1868 the site was purchased by the Princesse de la Tour d'Auvergne and the present Church of the Pater Noster and Church of the Creed date from that time. The ancient cave crypt and the east end of the Constantinian basilica of Eleona lie under the Pater Noster Church. In 1876 a convent of French Carmelite nuns was also built here. The group of structures is collectively known as the Latin Buildings. The photograph shows the Church of the Lord's Prayer.

Photograph: The Matson Photo Service, Alhambra, Calif.

157. In the Church of the Lord's Prayer

THIS PHOTOGRAPH SHOWS a corridor in the present Church of the Pater Noster. The Lord's Prayer, believed by late tradition to have been taught at this place

(cf. No. 156), is inscribed in panels in the walls of the church in sixty-two different languages (Murphy-O'Connor p. 94).

Photograph: JF.

158. Plan by Arculf of the Church of the Holy Ascension

IN HER DESCRIPTION of the services that were held at Jerusalem on Palm Sunday, Aetheria (Geyer pp. 82-84; LPPTS I-C, pp. 58-59; CCSL CLXXV, pp. 76-78; WET pp. 132-133) says that the people go early to the Great Church at Golgotha, at the seventh hour go up to Eleona (cf. Nos. 149, 154), and then "when it begins to be the ninth hour they go up with hymns to the Inbomon—that is, to the place from which the Lord ascended into heaven." Finally at the eleventh hour "they go down on foot the whole way from the summit of the Mount of Olives" and proceed through the city back to the Cross and the Anastasis (cf. No. 228). The name Inbomon is explicable as a rendering in Latin of the Greek phrase ἐν βωμῷ, which means "upon the height," βωμός being also a regular translation in the LXX of the Hebrew במה or "high place." At least by the time of Aetheria (381-384), then, the ascension was localized at a place of this name on the very summit of the Mount of Olives. Aetheria describes Inbomon simply as a "place" and does not mention a church, which allows question as to whether there was yet a church there (WET p. 51), but in fact a church was probably already in existence and was known as the Holy Ascension. Peter the Iberian (451) is authority for the statement that it was in about 378 that "a very honorable and devout lady named Pomnia (Poemenia) . . . built the Church of the Holy Ascension and surrounded it with buildings" (Richard Raabe *Petrus der Iberer* [Leipzig, 1895], p. 35; Kopp 1959, p. 461), and this is probably the church for which Aetheria only employed a customary topographical designation of Inbomon (Kroll p. 426, col. 1). Likewise when Jerome tells about the travels of Paula (386) in the Holy Land (*Letter* 108, 12, written in 404) he makes her say: "passing through Tekoa the home of Amos, I will look upon the glistening cross of Mount Olivet from which the Savior made his ascension to the Father." This cross was presumably lifted high above the Inbomon church on the uppermost ridge of the Mount of Olives and was hence visible as far away as Tekoa, ten miles south of Jerusalem.

The Inbomon or Holy Ascension church was surveyed by L.-H. Vincent in 1913 and examined again by V. Corbo in 1959. In its original form it appears to have been a centralized memorial church, octagonal in the

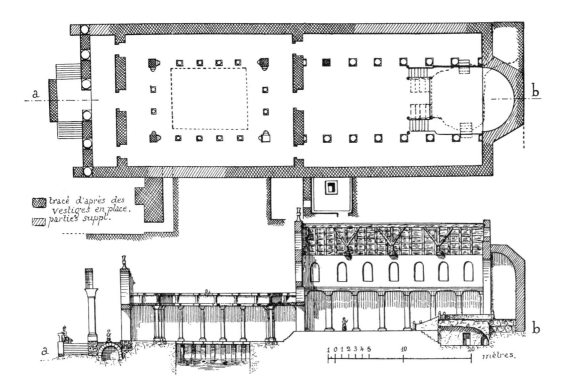

155. Plan and Section of the Eleona Church

156. The Church of the Lord's Prayer

157. In the Church of the Lord's Prayer

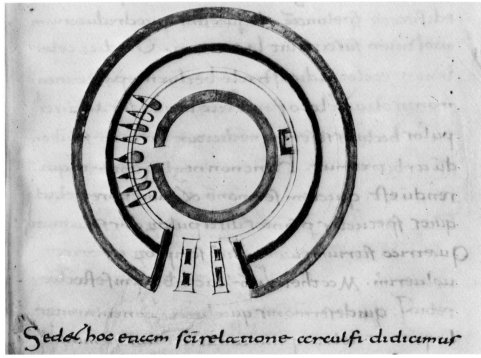

Sedei hoc etiam scirelatione circulfi didicimus

158. Plan by Arculf of the Church of the Holy Ascension

shape of its outer walls and with an interior circular colonnade of sixteen columns that upheld a dome. This church was evidently destroyed by the Persians in 614, but soon rebuilt, for part of a Greek inscription was found in the church area that records reconstruction by Modestus (the patriarch of Jerusalem, d. 634), whose extensive works of rebuilding at the Church of the Holy

Sepulcher are noted below (No. 231). The nearby Eleona church must also have been destroyed by the Persians and too was probably rebuilt by Modestus, for we have seen that Sophronius (634) speaks as if he visited an existent church (see above, No. 154).

As rebuilt, the Inbomon was still a centralized memorial church but now in circular form, according to the description and the drawing that we have of it from Arculf (670). Arculf says (Geyer pp. 246-251; LPPTS III-A, pp. 74-75; CCSL CLXXV, pp. 199-202; WJP pp. 100-101) that there was a large round church (*ecclesia rotunda*) on the summit of the Mount of Olives, with three vaulted porticoes around it which were roofed over. The inner chamber (*interior domus*) of this church was without roof and without vault (*sine tecto et sine camera*) and open under heaven in the free air. In the center the last footprints of the Lord where he ascended were to be seen, and these were illumined by a great lamp which hung on a pulley and burned night and day. To the east of this innermost building was an altar under a narrow roof. In front of the innermost circle on the west side, above its entrance, eight lamps hung by ropes behind glass windows through which their light shone down as far as Jerusalem. The illustration reproduces the drawing with which Arculf accompanied his description, as given in the ninth-century Codex Parisinus Lat. 13048 in the Bibliothèque Nationale in Paris. The drawing clearly shows a main outer entrance that comes in from the south through the three circular porticoes, the inner circular chamber with its entrance on the west, the altar on the east, and the eight lamps on the west.

Vincent, *Jérusalem nouvelle*, pp. 360-373; V. Corbo in LA 10 (1959/60), pp. 205-225; J. T. Milik in RB 67 (1960), pp. 557f.; Ovadiah, *Corpus*, pp. 85-87, no. 72ab; Bahat, *Plans* 111, 112ab, 113ab. Photograph: Arculfus De Locis Sanctis, Codex Parisinus Lat. 13048, courtesy Bibliothèque Nationale, Paris.

159. The Mosque of the Ascension on the Mount of Olives

THE CHURCH of the Holy Ascension, described in the foregoing (No. 158) as it was seen by Arculf (670), was rebuilt by the Crusaders. The plan was the same as before except that the circular structure was now made octagonal. Like the innermost building it replaced, the chapel in the center was left open to the sky. This church was taken by Saladin in 1187 and converted into a mosque, which it remains even today. An octagonal wall encloses a courtyard about one hundred feet in diameter. Near the center stands an octagonal building, twenty-one feet in diameter, surmounted by a cylindrical drum and a dome. This was the Crusader chapel, but the arches on the eight sides have now been walled in and the once-open roof covered with the cupola. Also there is a mihrab or niche showing the Muslim direction of prayer in the interior south wall. The use of this place for a mosque is appropriate from the Muslim point of view, for the statement in the Qur'an (Sura IV 158 cf. III 55 Abdullah Yusuf

Ali, *The Holy Qur-an* [1946], I, p. 230 and note 664 cf. p. 137 and note 394) concerning Jesus that "God raised him up unto himself" provides a basis for Muslim belief in the ascension of Jesus.

Vincent, *Jérusalem nouvelle*, pp. 360-373. Photograph: courtesy École Biblique et Archélogique Française.

159. The Mosque of the Ascension on the Mount of Olives

160. View of Jerusalem from the Summit of the Mount of Olives

FROM THE SUMMIT of the Mount of Olives there is a splendid panorama in all directions. To the east the wilderness of Judea drops down to the Dead Sea, fifteen miles distant and 3,900 feet below, beyond which are the blue mountains of Moab. To the west, as seen in this photograph, one looks across the Kidron Valley and upon the city of Jerusalem with the Dome of the Rock (No. 185) prominently visible in the Temple area.

Photograph: The Matson Photo Service, Alhambra, Calif.

160. View of Jerusalem from the Summit of the Mount of Olives

161. The Franciscan Chapel at Dominus Flevit

IN HIS "TRIUMPHAL" entry into Jerusalem Jesus came from the Mount of Olives (Mt 21:1; Mk 11:1; Lk 19:29), and Lk, who mentions the "descent" of the mount in 19:37, says in 19:41 that "when he drew near and saw the city he wept over it." If Bethphage (No. 151) was indeed on the heights of the Mount of Olives and perhaps about one-half mile east of the summit, then the most direct route to the city would have been right over the summit and straight down the slope to the west. This was a relatively steep descent and provided striking views of the city (cf. No. 166). The Inbomon and the Eleona were on this route at the top of the mount. As we have seen (No. 158), in her description of the Palm Sunday procession in her time (381-384) Aetheria (Geyer pp. 83-84; LPPTS I, pp. 58-59; CCSL CLXXV, pp. 77-78; WET pp. 132-133) says that the people and the bishop go up from the Great Church at Golgotha to the Eleona and to the Inbomon and then, at the eleventh hour, "they go down on foot the whole way from the summit of the Mount of Olives" (*de summo monte oliveti totum pedibus itur*). The people go before the bishop and sing, "Blessed be he who comes in the name of the Lord" (Mt 21:9), and the children hold branches of palm trees and of olive trees (*ramos tenentes alii palmarum, alii olivarum*). Thus

they escort the bishop, singing in response, and thus, slowly and gently (*lente et lente*) lest the people be wearied, they come back to the city and through it to the Cross and the Anastasis (cf. No. 228). Since this was an obvious re-enactment of the triumphal entry it is presumable that what was at that time considered as the traditional route was followed, and since the account emphasizes the going by foot and slowly it is also probable that it was the steep descent down the west face of the Mount of Olives which was used. Whether this steep descent was also the most likely one for Jesus when he rode upon an animal and was accompanied by crowds (Mt 21:7f. and parallels) may perhaps be questioned. If it is questioned, then perhaps a more northerly route along the line of the Roman road (cf. No. 143) might be considered more likely (Kopp 1959, pp. 331-332). But the relatively old tradition attested by Aetheria is surely consonant with the idea of the more direct descent. The paths which go down there now mitigate the steepness by their zigzag course, which may be judged likely for the ancient way too.

About halfway down the direct descent on the west side from the summit of the Mount of Olives is the site known as *Dominus flevit*, the name embodying the tradition that this is the place where "the Lord wept" over Jerusalem (Lk 19:41). It is no doubt the area to which

161. The Franciscan Chapel at Dominus Flevit

many pilgrims of the Middle Ages point, among others the Dominicans, Ricoldus de Monte Crucis (1294) (Kopp 1959, p. 330 n. 92) and Humbert de Dijon (1332) (RB 62 [1955], pp. 534-535). The latter, for example, says that there is a stone halfway up the mount where Jesus wept, and where he also dismounted from the foal, which was young and frisky (*pullus erat iuvenis et lascivus*), and mounted the ass. The last point may in some manner be dependent upon Jerome, who also speaks of the *pullus lasciviens* or frisky foal obtained from Bethphage (*Letter* 108, 12). At this place on the Mount the Franciscans have the striking chapel shown in the photograph and a monastery on the wall of which is a plaque with these words: *Locus, in quo Dominus videns civitatem flevit super illam*, "The place in which the Lord, when he saw the city, wept over it."

Photograph: JF.

162. View from Within the Dominus Flevit Chapel

FROM WITHIN the Dominus flevit chapel and across the altar the view is directly toward the Temple area and the Dome of the Rock, with the Old City beyond.

Photograph: JF.

163. Ossuaries *in situ* at Dominus Flevit

THE FRANCISCANS began excavations in 1953 at Dominus flevit and found a very extensive ancient cemetery with many hundreds of graves. According to the accompanying materials that were discovered, including coins, pottery, and objects of glass and stone, the burials belonged to two distinct periods. The first period was 135 B.C.-A.D. 70 (or possibly 135), and the graves were of the kokim type (cf. No. 255). The second period was that of the third and fourth, especially the fourth, centuries, and the graves were characterized by arcosolia (cf. No. 256). In the graves were seven sarcophagi and 122 ossuaries, or fragments thereof. All of these were from the first period, which is in accordance with the otherwise supported opinion that ossuaries were used at Jerusalem only until A.D. 70 or 135 (cf. below p. 336). In the judgment of some scholars, some of the ossuary inscriptions and marks represent early Jewish Christianity, and they will be discussed in more detail later (Nos. 319ff.). This photograph shows a portion of the excavations, with ossuaries left in place in one of the chambers. Other finds are preserved in the Museum of the Convent of the Flagellation in Jerusalem.

RB 61 (1954), pp. 568-570; P. B. Bagatti and J. T. Milik, *Gli scavi del "Dominus flevit" (Monte Oliveto—Gerusalemme)*, Part I, *La necropoli del periodo romano*. PSBF 13 (Jerusalem: Tipografia dei PP. Francescani, 1958); reviews of the foregoing by J. van der Ploeg in JSS 5 (1960), pp. 81-82, and by M. Avi-Yonah in IEJ 11 (1961), pp. 91-94; Bagatti, *Church from Circumcision*, see index under Dominus Flevit, ossuaries. Photograph: JF.

164. Byzantine Capital at Dominus Flevit

IN 1954 THE FOUNDATIONS of a Byzantine church were found at Dominus flevit, and in 1955 the present

162. View from Within the Dominus Flevit Chapel

163. Ossuaries *in situ* at Dominus Flevit

164. Byzantine Capital at Dominus Flevit

173

Franciscan chapel (No. 161) was built on the same outlines, with the remains of the earlier church and its mosaics still preserved as far as possible (Murphy-O'Connor pp. 90f.). The church was no doubt one of the twenty-four churches that Theodosius (Geyer p. 140; LPPTS II-B, p. 10; CCSL CLXXV, p. 117; WJP p. 65) says were on the Mount of Olives in his time (530).

Photograph: JF.

165. Mosaic at el-Heloueh near Dominus Flevit

OPPOSITE THE DOMINUS flevit chapel there is a ruined mosque known as el-Mansuriya, built perhaps around 1500 (Vincent, *Jérusalem nouvelle*, p. 408). The place is also called el-Heloueh. Here there was found in 1907 an oval basin, 75 by 65 centimeters in size, paved in mosaic. As shown in the photograph, the upper register of the mosaic is a geometrical pattern in large cubes of red and white. In the lower register, surrounded by sprigs, is a large cross. Above the horizontal arms of the cross are the words I($\eta\sigma o\hat{v}$)C X($\rho\iota\sigma\tau\acute{o}$)C, below are the characters A and ω. The Latin form of the cross and the possible unfamiliarity with Greek shown in the strange shaping of the Omega suggest a relatively late date for this Christian inscription, but of course still prior to the building of the mosque.

165. Mosaic at el-Helouah near Dominus Flevit

174

H. Vincent, "Une mosaique chretienne au Mont des Oliviers," in RB 17 (1908), pp. 122-125; M. Avi-Yonah in QDAP 2 (1932), p. 165 no. 110. Photograph: RB 17 (1908), p. 123, courtesy École Biblique et Archéologique Française.

166. Panoramic View of Jerusalem from the Slope of the Mount of Olives

THE CHRISTIAN INTEREST in the area now known as Dominus flevit, evidenced by the possibly Jewish-Christian burials in the cemetery (No. 163), the Byzantine church (No. 164), and the mosaic at el-Heloueh (No. 165), are at least not out of harmony with the traditional identification of this spot as being where Jesus drew near and saw the city and wept over it. Certainly from almost anywhere on the western slope of the Mount of Olives there is a dramatic view of the Old City of Jerusalem. In this panorama in the temple area one can see from left to right the Mosque al-Aqsa, the Dome of the Rock, and the minaret at the northwest corner of the area, and in the background, between the Mosque and the Dome, the tower of the Lutheran Church and the domes of the Church of the Holy Sepulcher.

Photograph: courtesy Government Press Office, State of Israel.

167. The Mount of Olives from the Temple Area

THIS VIEW is from within the temple area near the Dome of the Rock, eastward through an arcade to the Mount of Olives. Through the first arch at the left are seen the domes of the Russian Church of St. Mary Magdalene built by the emperor Alexander III in 1888. Through the second arch is visible the tower at the Russian convent on the summit of the Mount of Olives. More details will be pointed out in the next photograph (No. 168).

Photograph: J.F.

168. The Mount of Olives and the Gethsemane Church

WHEN JESUS and the disciples went to the Mount of Olives after the Last Supper (Mt 26:30; Mk 14:26; Lk 22:39) they went to a place ($\chi\omega\rho\acute{\iota}o\nu$, a piece of land) called Gethsemane (Mt 26:36; Mk 14:32; cf. Lk 22:40) which was across the Kidron Valley where there was a garden ($\varkappa\hat{\eta}\pi o\varsigma$) (Jn 18:1). The name Gethsemane ($\Gamma\epsilon\theta\sigma\eta\mu\alpha\nu\acute{\iota}$) corresponds to the Hebrew גת שמני, which designates an oil-press used for the making of olive oil, a type of installation naturally found at the mount that took its name from the abundant olive trees on its slopes.

Like No. 167 this photograph is taken from the temple area looking toward the Mount of Olives but from a point somewhat farther to the north, near the Golden Gate (No. 193), and at the extreme eastern edge of the area, looking through an aperture in the upper part of the eastern city wall. Again one sees on the summit of the mount the Russian tower. Not far to the right of it and somewhat nearer this way is the minaret at the Mosque of the Ascension (No. 159). Farther to the right and a little farther down the slope of the mount is the tower of the Carmelite convent at the site of the Eleona church (No. 154). In front of this is the large building of a Benedictine convent. Farther down the hill in the midst of many large trees is the Russian Church of St. Mary Magdalene (cf. No. 167). Now in view also, near the foot of the mount and across at the far edge of the Kidron Valley, are the Franciscan Church and Garden of Gethsemane. Plainly visible to the left of the Garden of Gethsemane is the northern path which runs up the Mount of Olives from the Kidron Valley. To the left near the summit of the ridge is the site called Viri Galilaei. Yet farther left, i.e., to the north, was where the Roman road crossed the ridge between Viri Galilaei and the Augusta Victoria buildings (cf. No. 143). The middle and most direct and steepest path up the mount ascends from behind the Garden of Gethsemane, past the Church of St. Mary Magdalene, past Dominus flevit (No. 161), to the sites of the Eleona and the Inbomon. A third and southernmost path swings farther to the right, out of the scope of this picture, to circle around and come to the top of the mount.

The main path, which descends past the north side of the Garden of Gethsemane, joins the automobile road that runs in front of the Church of Gethsemane at a point just to the left, i.e., the north, of what is visible in our picture. Here, north of the path and east of the curve of the highway, is a large mass of rock. In the rock is a cave known as the Grotto of the Betrayal and immediately adjoining this on the west is the Church of the Tomb of Mary (No. 170). From the grotto just mentioned to the Gethsemane Church is a distance of about one hundred yards.

Photograph: JF.

169. Plan of the Gethsemane Area

THIS PLAN SHOWS details in the area just described (No. 168) where the Gethsemane Church and the Grotto of the Betrayal are located. Referring to the num-

bers in this plan, we see the early basilica above which the present Gethsemane Church stands (14), the adjacent garden (16), the Grotto of the Betrayal (21) with the passage leading to it (20), and the Tomb of Mary (22). The route to Jericho is shown which is the present highway (17), and there are olive trees in the area west of it (19) as well as in the garden (16) and in the area between the latter and the Grotto (21). The southern path up the Mount of Olives turns to the right at (10), the middle path is (11), and the northern path is (12). The Russian property is labeled on the plan, and the accompanying legend indicates certain other details.

Under the name Gethsemane (Γεθσιμανῆ) Eusebius says in the Onomasticon (p. 74) that this was the place (χωρίον as in Mt. 26:36 and Mk 14:32) where Christ prayed before the passion. It lies, he says, at the Mount of Olives (πρὸς τῷ ὄρει τῶν ἐλαιῶν), and the preposition πρός, used here with the dative and most simply translatable as "at," carries the sense of up against (cf. No. 151). In this place the faithful were zealous to make their prayers. This language sounds as if at this time (330) the spot indicated had long been identified as the Gethsemane where Jesus prayed, but it does not sound as if it had yet been marked by a church building.

About three years later (333) the Bordeaux Pilgrim (Geyer p. 23; LPPTS I, p. 24; CCSL CLXXV, pp. 17-18; WET p. 159) went out from the city to the gate which is to the eastward (contra oriente) in order to ascend the Mount of Olives. This gate could have been the gate in the eastern city wall just north of the temple area later known as St. Mary's or St. Stephen's Gate (No. 243), or the so-called Golden Gate (No. 193) in the east wall of the temple area itself. Beyond the gate the Pilgrim mentions the "valley which is called Josaphat," which is the Kidron Valley (cf. No. 264). Now the Pilgrim is presumably proceeding southward down the valley and then turning eastward to ascend the main slope of the mount. At this point he says: "On the left, where there are vineyards, is a rock where Judas Iscariot betrayed Christ; on the right is a palm tree from which the children broke off branches and strewed them when Christ came."

In this text the word for "rock" is petra, corresponding to the Greek πέτρα, which means a mass of living rock in distinction from πέτρος which means a detached stone or boulder. The "rock" is therefore probably the very mass of rock in which is found the so-called Grotto of the Betrayal (cf. No. 168). If the Pilgrim was at this point facing up the mount the palm tree on his right would probably have been beside the path descending steeply from the mount. Not far from there, he also says, about a stone's throw away, were the beautiful tombs of Isaiah (this one a monolith) and of Hezekiah. These are quite certainly two of the four large Hellenistic-Roman tombs still seen only a little way farther down the Kidron

166. Panoramic View of Jerusalem from the Slope of the Mount of Olives

167. The Mount of Olives from the Temple Area

176

168. The Mount of Olives and the Gethsemane Church

IV.— SCHÉMA TOPOGRAPHIQUE DE GETHSÉMANI.

Les chiffres se réfèrent à la photogr. pl. XI, t. Ier.

a, *hutte du gardien arabe.* **b,** *hangar (cf phot. fig. 142).*
c, *couloir enserrant la colonne dite de la « Trahison de Judas ».*
d, *entrée du Jardin.* **e,** *oratoire.* **f,** *habitation du gardien.*
g, *rocher dit de la "Ceinture de la Vierge".* **h,** *repos de la Vierge.*
i, *gardien de l'oliveraie des PP. Franciscains.* **j,** *route vers Jérusalem.*
k, *santon musulman anonyme.* **l,** *parvis du tomb. de la Vierge.*

169. Plan of the Gethsemane Area

Valley (Nos. 264ff.), and the tomb of "Isaiah" is probably the tomb that is now called that of "Zechariah" which is indeed a monolith (No. 267). The Bordeaux Pilgrim was therefore quite plainly in the vicinity of what we know as the Grotto of the Betrayal and the Garden of Gethsemane when he saw the place that was considered to be that of the betrayal of Christ, an event (Mt 26:47 and parallels) which followed upon the prayer of Jesus in Gethsemane.

While neither Eusebius nor the Pilgrim from Bordeaux mentions a church at the area which he describes, later in the same century we find that a church existed there. In the account by Aetheria (381-384) of the services at Jerusalem during Holy Week she tells not only of the procession down the Mount of Olives on Palm Sunday (cf. No. 161) but also of the events of the Thursday of that week (Geyer pp. 85-87; LPPTS I, pp. 60-62; CCSL CLXXV, pp. 78-80; WET pp. 135-136). On Thursday evening and night the bishop and people are at the Eleona and the Inbomon churches (Nos. 154, 158). When the cocks begin to crow (but still deep in the night, as the subsequent narrative makes plain), "they descend from the Inbomon with hymns, and come to that place where the Lord prayed, as it is written in the Gospel [Lk 22:41], 'And he withdrew about a stone's throw and prayed, etc.'" "In this place," Aetheria continues, "there is a fine church (*ecclesia elegans*)." After prayers in the church they move on to Gethsemane (*Gessamani*), where more than two hundred church candles give light, and the passage from the Gospel is read where the Lord was apprehended. From Gethsemane they return at last to the city and arrive at the gate at the time when one man begins to be able to recognize another. By the time they are back in front of the Cross it is becoming broad daylight.

From Aetheria we learn, then, that two spots were commemorated, one where Jesus prayed, one where he was taken captive. The spot where he prayed was marked by a fine church, the spot where he was apprehended was called Gethsemane. Coming down the mount the pilgrims reached the church first. Between mention of it and of Gethsemane Aetheria speaks of the weariness of the people from having to descend "so great a mountain," but this probably does not mean that the church was high up on the mountain but only that Aetheria is here making a resumptive reference to the entire nocturnal descent. As for the use of the name Gethsemane for the place of the betrayal and apprehension of Jesus, this is in accord with the Gospel record (Mt 26:36ff. and parallels) where Jesus and the disciples came to Gethsemane, and he went "a little farther" or "withdrew about a stone's throw" to pray, then returned to where the disciples were and was apprehended at that place. That the place a stone's throw away was outside the limits of "Gethsemane" is not, however, necessarily indicated and Eusebius (as cited just above) certainly used this as the name for the place where Jesus prayed.

Revising the *Onomasticon* of Eusebius in 390, Jerome also attests the existence of a church in this time in this area. He reproduces Eusebius' location of Gethsemane "at" the Mount of Olives with the somewhat more exact statement that it was "at the foot" (*ad radices*, literally, at the roots) of the mount, and then he replaces Eusebius' statement about the faithful who pray in the place with the statement, "Now a church (*ecclesia*) has been built over it" (*Onomasticon* p. 75). We conclude, then, that Gethsemane was considered, at least by this time, to include both the place of the betrayal of Jesus and the place of his prayer. The two spots were not far apart and it was the latter on which a church was actually built. These two traditional spots are marked on the plan with the numbers 21 (place of the betrayal) and 14 (place of the prayer and of the church) and, as noted above (No. 168), the distance between them is about one hundred yards.

Bahat, *Plans,* 107a. Photograph: Vincent, *Jérusalem nouvelle,* p. 335 fig. 147, courtesy École Biblique et Archéologique Française.

170. The Tomb of the Virgin

WE HAVE SEEN (NOS. 45-46) that descendants of the family of Jesus lived on in Nazareth at least into the middle of the third century, and that by this time the house believed to be that of Mary the mother of Jesus was a synagogue-church and by the fifth century a Byzantine basilica. As to the death of Mary there are two traditions: one, that she accompanied John to Ephesus and lived, died, and was buried there, where at the Council of 431 she was honored as Theotokos, the Mother of God; the other that she continued to live in Jerusalem, fell asleep on Mount Sion (Nos. 205, 207) or at her house in the Valley of Jehoshaphat (the Anonymous of Piacenza, just below), and was buried in the Valley of Jehoshaphat, with the Byzantine Nea church (No. 196) and the Crusader church Sancta Maria in Sion (No. 210) doing her honor.

Veneration of the tomb of Mary in the Valley of Jehoshaphat is attested in the *Transitus Mariae*, an apocryphal work found in many versions and usually dated around 400 (HSNTA I, p. 429) but considered by Bagatti (*Tomb of Virgin Mary*, pp. 14f., 57f.) to come in its original form from the second-third century and from a Judeo-Christian background. Perhaps it is because of such Judeo-Christian focus upon the tomb that it is not mentioned by such fourth-century writers of the Gentile church as Cyril of Jerusalem, Epiphanius, and Jerome. So the tomb may have been venerated and kept in custody by the Christians of Hebrew origin from the beginning until at least toward the end of the fourth century. By the sixth and seventh centuries, however, the Christians of Gentile origin also venerate the tomb and we learn in the writers cited immediately below of the church that was built above the tomb, which must be a Byzantine church of perhaps the end of the fourth and the fifth centuries.

When Theodosius (530) (Geyer p. 142; LPPTS II-B, p. 11; CCSL CLXXV, p. 119; WJP p. 66) describes the Valley of Jehoshaphat he says that it is where Judas betrayed the Lord and also that there is there a church of St. Mary the mother of the Lord (*ecclesia domnae Mariae matris Domini*). The Anonymous of Piacenza (570) (Geyer p. 170; LPPTS II-DŒ p. 14; CCSL CLXXV, p. 137; WJP p. 83) came

170. The Tomb of the Virgin

down from the Mount of Olives into the Valley of Gethsemane, saw the place where the Lord was betrayed, and found in the same valley "a basilica of St. Mary which, they say, was her house in which she was taken from the body. This valley of Gethsemane is also at this place called Jehoshaphat." Arculf (670) (Geyer p. 240; LPPTS III-A, p. 17; CCSL CLXXV, p. 195; WJP p. 99) describes the Church of St. Mary in the Valley of Jehoshaphat as built in two stories, both round, in the lower of which is "the empty sepulcher of St. Mary in which for a time she rested after her burial." The last reference is of course an allusion to the doctrine of the bodily assumption of the Virgin into heaven (in Rome defined as of faith on November 1, 1950; Benoit, *Jesus and Gospel*, p. 253 n. 1).

When the Crusaders came they found the Byzantine church in ruins, but the tomb of Mary itself was intact. The Russian abbot Daniel (1106/1107) says that there was once a convent at this place, but it was destroyed by the infidels, and then he describes the tomb of Mary as follows (Baldi pp. 763f., no. 1067; LPPTS IV-C, pp. 23-24):

> This tomb, situated in a valley, is a small carve cut in the rock, with an entrance so low that a man stooping can scarcely pass through. At the end of the cave, opposite the entrance, one can see a little bench (*banc*) cut in the rock; and it is upon this bench that the sacred body of our very holy Lady and Mother of God was placed, and from whence it was raised incorruptible into Paradise. This cavern is about the height of a man; it is 4 cubits broad and the same length. The interior of the cavern bears the aspect of a small chapel, faced with beautiful marble slabs.

The Crusaders in turn rebuilt the entire building, again in two stories, one church upon the other, and they also built beside it to the west a large monastery, the Abbey of St. Mary of the Valley of Jehoshaphat. The German pilgrim Theodericus (1172) (LPPTS V-D, pp. 37-38) tells us that the church and abbey were now made into a veritable monastery-fortress: "The church itself and all the conventual building connected with it are strongly fortified with high walls, strong towers, and battlements against the treacherous attacks of the infidels." He also describes the chamber with the tomb of Mary as

> A crypt, in which her holy sepulcher stands, covered with most costly decorations of marble and mosaic work. . . . This sepulcher has around it twenty columns, carrying arches, a border, and a roof above it. On the border itself are inscribed these verses:
>
> > From hence, from Joshaphat's vale, a path leads to the sky!
> > The Virgin here, God's trusting handmaid, once did lie.
> > Spotless, from hence she rose, to her heaven's gate did open.
> > Poor sinners' Light and Way, their Mother and their Hope.
>
> Moreover, the roof has a round dome above it, supported by

six pairs of columns, with a ball and cross above it, and between each pair of these little columns all round the dome there hangs a lamp.

When Saladin defeated the Crusaders at the Horns of Hattin and took Jerusalem (1187), his soldiers destroyed both the abbey and the upper church, using the stones for repairing the city walls, but once again the crypt survived, together with some of the walls of the lower church.

At the now-existing Tomb of Mary (marked 22 in the plan No. 169) studies were carried out by L.-H. Vincent resulting in the publication in 1925 of a plan of the ancient structures (Bahat, *Plans*, 110; a plan of the upper part of the church as octagonal, ibid., 109a, is entirely hypothetical, see Bagatti, *Tomb of Virgin Mary*, pp. 56f.). In 1937 trenches were dug in the area, which uncovered some mosaic floors and an inscription with crosses, reading "Tomb of Kasios and Adios," probably sixth century in date, and also later pavements and masonry of the time of the Crusader reconstruction of the church, as well as some remains of the abbey to the west, where today there is an olive grove. Due to its position in the Kidron Valley the present church was flooded in 1948 and again in 1972, when it was almost entirely covered with earth and mud; then in connection with works of restoration archeological excavations were carried out in 1972-1973. As known on the basis of these studies, the original tomb was a chamber hewn in a rocky area in which were other tombs, the room itself arranged with a sepulchral bench (Bagatti, *Tomb of Virgin*, pl. 13) against one wall. From an archeological perspective, the tomb fits with others in Palestine in the first century A.D. When the Byzantine church was built around the tomb, the purpose was of course to honor Mary, and since the chamber was surrounded by other tombs, it was necessary to isolate the tomb of special interest by destroying the other nearby tombs. Although the upper story of the Byzantine church, which Arculf described as round, was totally destroyed, enough of the walls of the lower level, which Arculf also described as round, were in place to show that it was actually in the form of a cross (see the plan and sections of the church drawn from the measurements of Vincent and those taken during the 1972 excavations, in Bagatti, *Tomb of Virgin Mary*, p. 21, fig. 1, in which the rock cuttings, the work of the fourth-fifth century, and the work of the twelfth century are distinguished). In the Crusader reconstruction of the church great stairs led down to meet the southern arm (E in the plan just cited) of the cross.

An addition to the Crusaders' building is a chapel (F in the plan) off the eastern wall of the church just about opposite the tomb of Mary. This is a chamber with a cupola, which only came to light in 1972. The cupola, done with arches and mouldings, rose as first a square, then an octagon, then a dome. From pilgrim texts from the fourteenth century onwards we learn that the chapel was dedicated to St. Joachim and St. Anna, the parents of Mary the mother of Jesus, but it is now known as the Tomb of Queen Melisende. As noted above (No. 150), this lady was the wife of the Crusader Fulk of Anjou, who was king of Jerusalem from 1131 to 1144, and is known as the founder in 1138 of an abbey in Bethany near the tomb of Lazarus, where her sister Iveta, coming from St. Anne in Jerusalem, became abbess (Saller, *Excavations at Bethany*, pp. 71, 73, 89, 114). Melisende herself died in 1161, was buried somewhere in the Crusader church at the Tomb of Mary, and her body was transferred to the chapel in question probably toward the end of the fourteenth century (Prodomo, *Tomb of Virgin Mary*, pp. 84f., 92).

Exactly opposite the tomb of Mary in the western (stricly speaking, southwestern) wall of the church is an apse or niche (L in the plan). Since the niche does not appear in a plan of the church by G. Zuallart in 1585 (Bagatti, *Tomb of Virgin Mary*, p. 22, fig. 2) but does appear in a plan by B. Amico in 1609 (ibid., p. 35, fig. 9), the niche was probably hewn in the Turkish period in the beginning of the seventeenth century, and was in use by the Muslims as a *mihrab*, pointing the direction of prayer toward Mecca. Thus in that time the church served as a mosque for the Turks, for Muslims as well as Christians honor Mary. The Quran affirms that Mary was "chosen . . . above the women of the world" (3.41, Maulana Muhammad Ali, *The Holy Qur'ān* [Lahore, 1973], p. 141), and Mujir al-Din (fifteenth century) says that on his night journey to Jerusalem Muhammad saw a light over the tomb of his "sister Mary" (Murphy-O'Connor p. 90).

From the facade of the Tomb of the Virgin a narrow passageway leads to the Grotto of the Betrayal (21 in plan No. 169). The latter is the place believed to have been where the disciples rested and slept while Jesus withdrew from them about a stone's throw to pray, and where Judas came to betray Jesus with a kiss (Lk 22:41, 47). The rock cave, about 19 meters long, 10 meters wide, and 3.5 meters high, was once used for an olive oil press and from the fourth century on was a place of Christian devotion. When the Byzantine church of the Tomb of Mary was reconstructed in the Crusader period the Tomb and the Grotto were connected. When Saladin destroyed the church and abbey he also closed the entrance to the Grotto; later a new access was made, which is that of the present. Traces of two levels of mosaic floors, probably Byzantine in date, are near the entrance (Murphy-O'Connor p. 90; Kroll p. 323).

Vincent, *Jérusalem nouvelle*, pp. 805-831; Bagatti, *Tomb of Virgin Mary*. For the alternate Jerusalem and Ephesus traditions concern-

ing Mary, see Clemens Kopp, *Das Mariengrab, Jerusalem?—Ephesus?* (Paderborn: Ferdinand Schöningh, 1955). Photograph: courtesy École Biblique et Archéologique Française.

171. Plan of the Gethsemane Church

AS INDICATED ALREADY (NO. 168), the area of the present Gethsemane Garden and Church (see 16 and 14 in the plan No. 169) belongs to the Franciscans. On behalf of the Studium Biblicum Franciscanum in Jerusalem, excavations were conducted by G. Orfali in 1909 and again in 1919-1920, the latter at the time of the beginning of the construction of the new Franciscan basilica. In these explorations the remains of two earlier churches were uncovered. The spot in question is shown as that of the primitive church (14) in plan No. 169 above. In the present plan we see the superimposition of the two earlier churches. The older church is shown with the darker outline: a basilica 20 meters long and 16 wide. It has a nave and two side aisles, and the aisles as well as the nave end in apses. The orientation is thirteen degrees to the north of east, and the purpose of this was evidently to allow a large mass of rock (marked in the plan with the letter A) to lie immediately in front of the central apse and the altar. Undoubtedly this was held to be the rock where Jesus prayed in Gethsemane. Some capitals, column bases, and portions of geometrical floor mosaics (marked in the plan with the letter m) remained. Since all indications are in harmony with a date in the latter part of the fourth century, this was almost certainly the church to which Jerome referred in 390 when he amended the statement of Eusebius about the place of prayer in Gethsemane to say, "Now a church has been built over it" (*Onomasticon* p. 75, cf. above No. 169). If, as the language may be taken to suggest, the church was built not long before these words were written, a date for the church under Theodosius I the Great (379-395) may be judged possible or probable and in the legend on the plan this structure is labeled the Basilica of Theodosius. It must also have been the *ecclesia elegans* of Aetheria (No. 169).

Like so many Jerusalem churches (cf. No. 156), the Gethsemane church was destroyed by the Persians (A.D. 614) and remained in ruins until the arrival of the Crusaders (Meistermann p. 236). By then its exact lines may have been forgotten; at any rate the church which the Crusaders built in the twelfth century, the outlines of which may also be seen in the plan, was located partly to one side of the earlier church and oriented directly to the east. This was a structure 29.75 meters long and 17.7 meters wide, with three apses at the east end. As marked on the plan, there is a large rock (R) in the central apse and smaller rocks (r and r') in each of the side apses, and the orientation to these three rocks may have been intended to recall the prayer of Jesus that was uttered three times (Mt 26:39, 42, 44).

The new Franciscan basilica, called the Church of All Nations, with A. Barluzzi as the architect, was completed in 1924 and was erected on the foundations of the church of the fourth century, thus the great rock (A in plan No. 171) is preserved in view, and portions of the early mosaic floor may be seen beneath the modern floor.

G. Orfali, *Gethsémani* (Paris: Picard, 1924); Vincent, *Jérusalem nouvelle*, pp. 1007-1013; Avi-Yonah in QDAP 2 (1932), p. 164, no. 108; Ovadiah, *Corpus*, pp. 84f., no. 73; Bahat, *Plans* 108. Plan: Vincent, *Jérusalem nouvelle*, pl. LXXXVIII, 1, courtesy École Biblique et Archéologique Française.

172. In the Garden of Gethsemane

THE PRESENT GARDEN of Gethsemane, immediately adjacent to the Church of All Nations, contains eight large (6-8 meters in circumference) and ancient olive trees, as well as carefully tended plots and pots of flowers. Since the manner of growth of the olive tree does not provide the annual rings upon which dendrochronology depends, it is not easy to judge the age of these trees. We are also told by Josephus (*War* VI 1, 6 §§5-6) that at the siege of Jerusalem by Titus all the trees around Jerusalem were cut down for a distance of 90 furlongs (15 kilometers); therefore the present olive trees can hardly be from the time of Jesus, yet it is not impos-

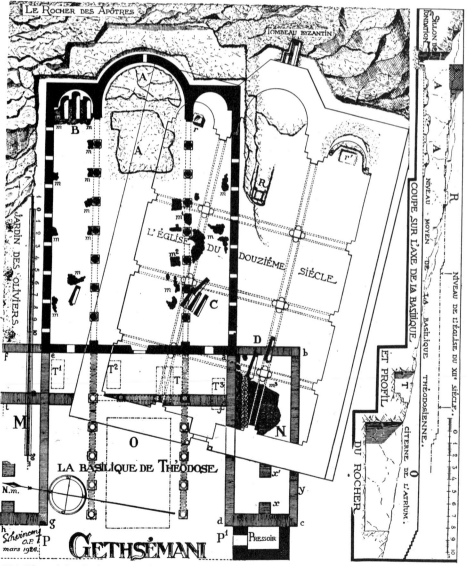

171. Plan of the Gethsemane Church

172. In the Garden of Gethsemane

sible that the oldest may have grown up again from a cut-down stump of such a time (Kroll p. 327, col. 1).

Photograph: JF.

JERUSALEM

173. Plan of Jerusalem in the Time of Jesus

THE SITE of Jerusalem is, as a whole, a rocky quadrilateral plateau, about 2,500 feet above the level of the Mediterranean Sea. The area is bounded on the west and south by what the OT calls variously the valley of Hinnom (Jos 15:8), of the son of Hinnom (Jos 15:8), or of the sons of Hinnom (II K 23:10). In Jos 15:8 and elsewhere this depression is called by the Hebrew word גי , which means a "valley" in the sense of a "gorge" (in dis-

tinction from an עמק , which is a broad level valley or plain) and the entire resultant designation, גי−הנם , Gehinnom, although translatable in Greek as φάραγξ Ὀνόμ (Jos 15:8 LXX), was also rendered Γαίεννα (Jos 18:16 LXX) and hence resulted in the NT name γέεννα, Gehenna (Mt 5:29, etc). From the horrible burning of children in this valley (Jer 7:31, etc.) the name became synonymous with hell (Mt 5:29, etc). Today the valley of Hinnom is called Wadi er-Rababi.

On the east the physical boundary is provided by the Kidron. In the OT the Kidron is always called a נחל (II Sam 15:23, etc.), which means a winter torrent and, by implication, a narrow valley or ravine in which such a stream flows. In the RSV translation the designation is "the book Kidron." The LXX translation of *nahal* is with the word χειμάρρους (from χεῖμα, "winter cold," and ῥέω, "to flow"), which also designates a winter torrent and a ravine. This word is used with the name Kidron in Jn 18:1 and there the RSV translation is "the Kidron valley." That the Kidron Valley was ultimately identified as

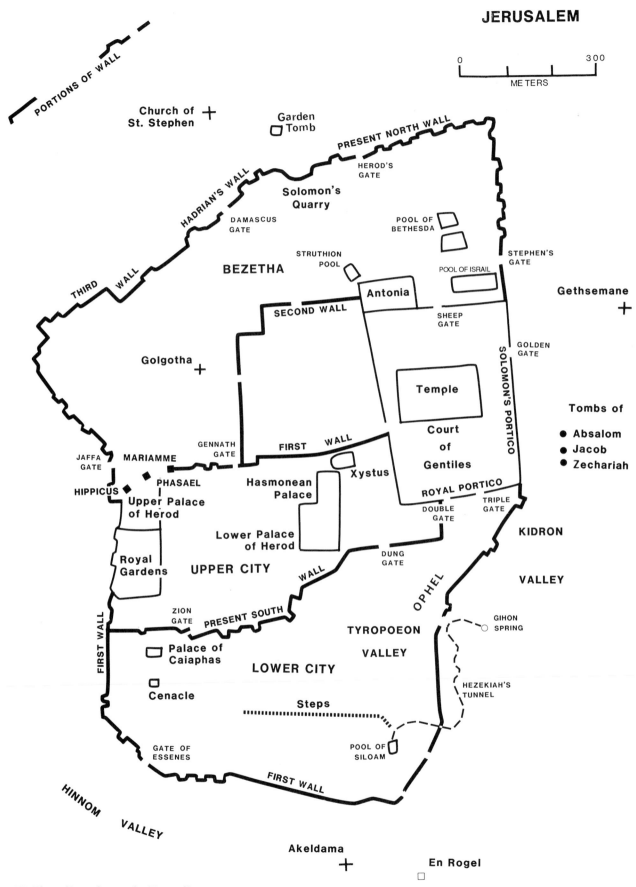

JERUSALEM

0   300
METERS

PORTIONS OF WALL

Church of + St. Stephen

Garden Tomb

PRESENT NORTH WALL

HEROD'S GATE

HADRIAN'S WALL

Solomon's Quarry

DAMASCUS GATE

POOL OF BETHESDA

STEPHEN'S GATE

THIRD WALL

BEZETHA

STRUTHION POOL

POOL OF ISRAIL

Antonia

Gethsemane +

SECOND WALL

SHEEP GATE

Golgotha +

GOLDEN GATE

SOLOMON'S PORTICO

Temple

Court of Gentiles

Tombs of

● Absalom
● Jacob
● Zechariah

GENNATH GATE

FIRST WALL

JAFFA GATE

MARIAMME

Xystus

ROYAL PORTICO

PHASAEL

Hasmonean Palace

DOUBLE GATE

TRIPLE GATE

HIPPICUS

Upper Palace of Herod

KIDRON

Lower Palace of Herod

Royal Gardens

UPPER CITY

WALL

DUNG GATE

OPHEL

VALLEY

ZION GATE

PRESENT SOUTH

TYROPOEON

GIHON SPRING

FIRST WALL

Palace of Caiaphas

LOWER CITY

VALLEY

HEZEKIAH'S TUNNEL

Cenacle

Steps

GATE OF ESSENES

POOL OF SILOAM

HINNOM VALLEY

FIRST WALL

Akeldama +

En Rogel

173. Plan of Jerusalem in the Time of Jesus

184

the valley of Jehoshaphat (Jl 3:2, 12) has already been noted (No. 169). Today it is also called Wadi en-Nar. With the Hinnom gorge on the west and south and the Kidron ravine on the east the whole area described was strongly protected on those three sides. On the north, however, it was relatively open and it was, in fact, from that side that came such a major conquest of Jerusalem as that by the Romans in A.D. 70.

Within the area described there is an eastern ridge and a western ridge with a valley between. The valley, which runs from north to south and is parallel with the Kidron Valley, is called the Valley of the Cheesemakers (ἡ τῶν τυροποιῶν φάραγξ) by Josephus (War v 4, 1 §140), from which designation we derive the name Tyropoeon. The word that Josephus uses for the valley means deep chasm or ravine. Although it presumably merited this designation at that time it has been so filled with debris, like many other low places in the city, that it is now scarcely more than a slight depression, known as el-Wad.

Of the two ridges the western is, as Josephus (War v 4, 1 §137) points out, the higher and straighter. The eastern ridge is lower and convex on each side, a point which Josephus makes by using for it the word (ἀμφίκυρτος) that describes the moon when it is "gibbous," i.e., between half-moon and full.

Each of the two ridges is also cut by one or more transverse valleys. In the case of the western ridge the transverse valley, sometimes called simply the Cross Valley, runs from west to east generally parallel to and on the north side of the present David Street and Street of the Gate of the Chain, and runs into the Tyropoeon Valley at a point nearly opposite the Gate of the Chain in the western side of the Temple area. This divides the western ridge into two parts which, from the point of view of the whole area, may be called the northwestern hill and the southwestern hill. The Church of the Holy Sepulcher is on a part of the northwestern hill. While the hill continues to climb toward the northwest, this particular part amounts to a small promontory by itself and is sometimes designated by the term *ras*, which means top or summit. It is about 755 meters or 2,477 feet above sea level.

The so-called Tomb of David and associated buildings stand on the southwestern hill. Here the plateau is about 771 meters or 2,529 feet above the Mediterranean, the highest part of the main city area. Josephus, accordingly, calls the city on this hill the "upper city" (War v 4, 1 §137). In the same passage Josephus also says that David called this hill the Stronghold (φρούριον), which sounds as if Josephus thought it was included in what David took from the Jebusites (II Sam 5:7). Another passage (Ant. vii 3, 2 §66) states that David enclosed the "upper" city, which gives the same impression, although in this case there is a variant reading that mentions the "lower city" instead. Although the meaning of Josephus is not un-

ambiguous, early Christian tradition certainly considered the southwestern hill to be the Zion or Sion (LXX Σιών) of King David (II Sam 5:7). This is implied by the Bordeaux Pilgrim (Geyer p. 22; LPPTS I-B, p. 22; CCSL CLXXV, p. 16 WET p. 157) who had been at the Temple area and then came out of Jerusalem to go up Mount Sion (*exeuntibus Hierusalem, ut ascendas Sion*) and in doing so had the Pool of Siloam on the left hand. Likewise Eusebius says in the *Onomasticon* (p. 74) that Golgotha was to the north of the mount of Sion (πρὸς τοῖς βορείοις τοῦ Σιὼν ὄρους). No doubt this traditional identification of the southwestern hill with the Sion of David had something to do with the localization of the "tomb of David" in the church of the Last Supper, which became a Muslim mosque of the "prophet David" (Nos. 205ff.). From the southwestern hill a partly separate promontory extended eastward toward the Tyropoeon Valley, and this promontory was the site of the Palace of the Hasmoneans (War II 16, 3 §344; Ant. xx 8, 11 §190).

The eastern ridge may also be recognized as divided into a southeastern hill and a northeastern hill. It has now been established by excavation that the early Canaanite city of Jerusalem was on the southeastern hill above the spring Gihon (No. 176). This was accordingly the place that David took from the Jebusites, which was the stronghold of Zion and the city of David (II Sam 5:7). A portion of the hill was called Ophel (עפל), which means "hump" (Neh 3:26, etc.). This name was reproduced by Josephus (War v 4, 2 §145) in a Hellenized transcription of the Aramaic עפלא as Ὀφλᾶς, Ophlas. In 169/168 B.C. Antiochus IV Epiphanes took treasures from the temple in Jerusalem (I Macc 1:20ff.) and two years later his commander came back with a large force and plundered the city (I Macc 1:29ff.). At that time the Syrians "fortified the city of David with a great strong wall and strong towers, and it became their citadel" (I Macc 1:33). The word used here is ἄκρα, acra, which means highest point and hence citadel. Since this citadel was made by fortifying the city of David it is probable that a whole fortified city-quarter is meant and it is evident that this was on the southeastern hill. Josephus also says that the "lower city" was on the hill that bore the name of Acra (War v 4, 1 §137), or that the lower portion of the town was itself known as Acra (War I 1, 4 §39). For the probable discovery of the foundations of the *acra* fortress itself see below, No. 192.

The northeastern hill is the site of the Temple area. Between the southeastern hill and the northeastern there was once, Josephus says (War v 4, 1 §139; cf. I 2, 2 §50; Ant. XIII 6, 7 §215), a broad ravine which the Hasmoneans filled in when they razed the Syrian Acra. At this time they not only demolished the citadel but also cut down the height of the hill which, according to

Josephus, was once higher than the Temple hill, a supposition which seems actually unlikely. The portion of the northeastern hill occupied by the Temple area itself has an average elevation above the sea of about 737 meters or 2,418 feet. Toward the northeastern corner of what is the present Temple area there was also at one time a small valley which ran diagonally into the Kidron. An upper reach of this valley can be recognized outside the present north city wall to the northeast of Herod's Gate and, inside the wall, to the northeast and east of the Church of St. Anne. The now filled-in reservoir called Birket Israil or Pool of Israel lay in this valley too, and it reached the edge of the Kidron Valley about one hundred meters south of St. Stephen's Gate.

Between St. Anne's Valley (if the valley just described may be so named) and the Kidron Valley on one side, and the Tyropoeon Valley on the other, the ridge of which we have been speaking continues to the north and northwest. This northern part of what we have called all together the northeastern hill, Josephus dignifies by designating as a separate hill. In his enumeration (*War* v 4, 1 §§137-138) the first hill is what we called the southwestern hill with the "upper city"; the second is our southeastern hill with the "lower city" and the Acra; the third is the Temple hill; and the fourth is this northwestern extension of the Temple hill. Of the last and fourth hill Josephus says (*War* v 5, 8 §246) that it was the highest of all the hills. If he means that it is the highest of the summits of the eastern ridge he is correct, but it is not as high as the summits of the western ridge, i.e., the northwestern and southwestern hills. This fourth hill, he also says (*War* v 4, 2 §149; v 5, 8 §246), was called Bezetha (Βεζεθά). The expanding population of Jerusalem made this a "recently built quarter" (*War* v 4, 2 §151) and as a city district it was called not only Bezetha from the hill but also New City (Καινόπολις).

In later centuries, partly due to the gathering of ethnic and religious communities around their sacred centers, but partly due also to economic and political factors, there came to be various "quarters" in Jerusalem. For example, William of Tyre (1184) (Babcock and Krey I, pp. 405-408; cf. Peters, *Jerusalem*, pp. 269-272) gives an account of the so-called Christian Quarter. "From the time the Latins entered Jerusalem, and, indeed, for many years before [William says], the patriarch [whose residence was at the Church of the Holy Sepulcher] had held as his own a fourth part of the city." Then in the year 1063 (thirty-six years before the Crusaders captured Jerusalem) the Egyptian caliph, the Fatimid Mustansir (r. 1035-1094), commanded repairs to the walls of the city, and a fourth of the work was assigned to the Christians, but they were already so ground down by forced labor, tributes, and taxes that it was only by the help of

the Byzantine emperor Constantine I (1059-1067) that they were able to complete the task. William of Tyre continues his account:

> Up to that time the Saracens [as the Christians called the Muslims] and Christians had dwelt together indifferently. Thenceforward, by the order of the prince, the Saracens were forced to remove to other parts of Jerusalem, leaving the quarter named to the faithful without dispute. . . .
> From that day, then, and in the manner just described, this quarter of the city had had no other judge or lord than the patriarch, and the church therefore laid claim to that section as its own in perpetuity.

By the end of the nineteenth century four quarters had taken shape much as they still are in the Old City: (1) the Jewish Quarter is in the southeast and borders on the Western Wall of the Temple area; (2) the Muslim Quarter is to the north and northeast of the Haram esh-Sherif (No. 184); (3) the Christian Quarter is to the northwest, around the Church of the Holy Sepulcher; and (4) the Armenian Quarter (also Christian, but doctrinally separate) is to the southeast.

Simons, *Jerusalem*, pp. 1-23 and especially p. 17, fig. 4, and p. 24, fig. 5, for elevations of rock levels, and pl. VI facing p. 49 for relief map. For rock contours, see also R. Pearce S. Hubbard, "The Topography of Ancient Jerusalem," in PEQ 1966, pp. 130-154, especially p. 134, fig. 1. I. W. J. Hopkins, "The Four Quarters of Jerusalem," in PEQ 1971, pp. 68-84; W. Harold Mare, *The Archaeology of the Jerusalem Area* (Grand Rapids: Baker Book House, 1987); James D. Purvis, *Jerusalem, The Holy City: A Bibliography* (Metuchen, N.H.: Scarecrow Press, 1988). Plan: JF, with Adrienne Morgan, cartographer; cf. Hubbard in PEQ 1966, pp. 148, 150, figs. 7, 8; *The New Jerusalem Bible* (1985), Map of Jerusalem in the Time of Jesus; Kroll p. 102, abb. 81, Jerusalem zur Zeit Jesu. See also the plans in AJPA.

174. Aerial View of Jerusalem

THIS AERIAL VIEW is taken from the east-southeast. Enclosed within the present-day wall is the Old City. Prominent in the foreground is the large rectangle of the Temple area, with the Dome of the Rock near the center. To the left thereof is the site called Ophel on the southeastern ridge. Almost halfway to the top of the picture is the southwestern ridge. The cluster of buildings, one with a high tower, on this ridge, not far from the left margin of the picture and outside the present south wall of the city, is where "Sion" was later localized. At the angle about halfway along the western city wall is the Jaffa Gate and the Citadel with the "Tower of David." About halfway back across the city toward the Temple area is the tall white tower of the Lutheran Church, and a short distance northeast of it are the domes of the

174. Air View of Jerusalem

Church of the Holy Sepulcher. About halfway along the course of the north wall is the Damascus Gate, halfway between it and the northeastern corner is Herod's Gate. In the eastern wall a short distance north of the Temple area is St. Stephen's Gate, and a third of the way along the wall of the Temple area itself is the Golden Gate, walled up. Around the northeastern corner of the city wall curves the road that descends into the Kidron Valley.

Photograph from Gustaf Dalman, *Hundert deutsche Fliegerbilder aus Palästina* (1925), p. 13, fig. 4. Photograph: courtesy C. Bertelsmann Verlag, Gütersloh.

175. The Access to the Gihon Spring

ON THE WEST SIDE of the Kidron Valley at the foot of the southeastern hill and under the part thereof which is probably to be identified as Ophel, is a spring, the passageway leading down to which is shown in this photo-graph. This is undoubtedly the spring Gihon that is mentioned several times in the OT (1 K 1:33, etc.). Its name (גִיחוֹן) is derived from a word (גיח) that means "to gush forth," and this may be connected with the fact that the spring is intermittent in action, gushing forth from its cave once or twice a day in the dry season and four or five times a day in the rainy season. In later times it has been known as Ain Sitti Maryam, the Spring of our Lady Mary, or the Virgin's Spring, or Umm ed-Daraj, "Mother of Steps," the last title referring to the thirty steps that lead down to it. The only other spring in the area is beyond the junction of the Kidron and the Hinnom valleys, 250 yards south of the southern end of the southeastern hill of which we have been speaking, and below the village of Silwan. This latter is almost certainly the spring that the OT calls En-rogel (Jos 15:7, etc.), known today as Bir Ayyub or Job's Well.

Simons, *Jerusalem*, pp. 45ff., 157ff. Photograph: JF.

187

175. The Access to the Gihon Spring

176. The Earliest Wall of Jerusalem above the Gihon Spring

THE GIHON SPRING determined the location of the oldest settlement in the Jerusalem area. This was on the slope of the eastern ridge and the southeastern hill, above the spring. In excavations begun here in 1961 and 1962 Kathleen M. Kenyon found not far above the spring a massive wall, built of rough boulders. The date was established as early in Middle Bronze Age II, c. 1800 B.C., and above it was some rebuilding which the excavator thought might date in the tenth century B.C. The photograph shows a portion of the massive wall, with rebuilding above. The boulder-built wall was evidently the east wall of the earliest town, the town of the Canaanite period. At some time in the history of the settlement on the hill above a tunnel was dug from the spring westward into the hill and connected with a vertical shaft that came up inside the town walls. This gave the inhabitants protected access to the spring water from within the town, although they could also come to the mouth of the spring by a path down the hill and outside the wall.

Since the Egyptian execration texts of the nineteenth-eighteenth centuries (ANET p. 329) and the Amarna Letters of the fourteenth century (ANET pp. 487-489) mention the name of Jerusalem in the form Urushalim or Urusalim, the settlement behind the earliest wall just described may simply be called the earliest town of Jerusalem. In Jos 18:16 a tribal boundary is described which "goes down the valley of Hinnom, south of the shoulder of the Jebusites, and downward to En-rogel." The "shoulder" of the Jebusites must be the southeastern hill with which we have been dealing, and from this passage we learn that the inhabitants at this time were called Jebusites. The identification of the place is confirmed in Jos 15:8 where, after similar mention of "the southern shoulder of the Jebusite," a parenthetical notation adds,

"that is, Jerusalem." From the name of the Jebusites their town was also called Jebus, as in Jg 19:10, "Jebus (that is, Jerusalem)." Similarly in I Ch 11:4 David and Israel went "to Jerusalem, that is Jebus, where the Jebusites were." Both II Sam 5:6-9 and I Ch 11:4-8 record the capture of the Jebusite town by David. At this point the place is also called "the stronghold of Zion," which is the first occurrence of the name Zion (ציון , Σιών) (II Sam 5:7; I Ch 11:5).

Although somewhat comparable water tunnel systems at Megiddo, Hazor, and Gezer may be somewhat later (tenth-ninth centuries B.C.) and may be thought to indicate a later date here too, the water system just described is usually thought to have been the system of the Jebusites from whom David (1000-965 B.C.) took the city, and even to have possibly figured in the conquest (Simons, *Jerusalem*, p. 168; Kroll p. 107, col. 3). In the account of the capture of the Jebusite town by David, the Jebusites are said to have boasted that "the blind and the lame" could protect it (II Sam 5:6), suggesting the strength of the stronghold, and David is reported to have said: "Whoever would smite the Jebusites, let him get up the water shaft to attack the lame and the blind" (II Sam 5:8 RSV). Here the term translated "water shaft" (צנור , *tsinnor*) is subject to not a few different interpretations (Hans Joachim Stoebe, "Die Einnahme Jerusalems und der Ṣinnôr," in ZDPV 73 [1957], pp. 73-99). If "water shaft" is correct, it can suggest that the water tunnel and shaft connected with the Gihon spring gave the attackers their initial access to the town. After the capture of the place by David it was called "the city of David" (II Sam 5:9; I Ch 11:7). He and his successors probably used and reused the old Jebusite wall for several centuries.

Kathleen M. Kenyon, "Excavations in Jerusalem," in PEQ 1962, pp. 72-89, esp. pp. 76, 82; 1963, pp. 7-21, esp. pp. 9-10 and pl. III A; 1964, pp. 7-18; 1965, pp. 11-14; *Jerusalem*, p. 22 and figs. 3-4 on pp. 20-21 (for the Jebusite water tunnel); pp. 24f. and pls.

176. The Earliest Wall of Jerusalem above the Gihon Spring

10-11 (for the Jebusite wall); R. Amiran, "The Water Supply of Israelite Jerusalem," in *Jerusalem Revealed*, pp. 75-78; Bahat, *Plans*, 14, 15ab; Dan Cole, "How Water Tunnels Worked," in BAR 6.2 (Mar/Apr 1980), pp. 8-29; Yigal Shiloh, *Excavations at the City of David, I, 1978-1982. Qedem* 19 (1984), p. 27; and Shiloh, "Underground Water Systems in Eretz-Israel in the Iron Age," in *Archaeology and Biblical Interpretation: Essays in Memory of D. Glenn Rose*, ed. Leo G. Perdue, et al. (Atlanta: John Knox Press, 1987), pp. 203-244, esp. p. 220. Photograph: JF.

177. Plan of the Tunnels Connected with the Gihon Spring

AT THE UPPER right-hand side of this plan are shown the steps that lead down to the Gihon Spring. Referring to the Roman numerals on the plan, Tunnel III leads from the spring westward under Ophel to a basin (the last number III), beside which is the bottom of the shaft that comes down from inside the earliest wall of Jerusalem, as described in the preceding section (No. 176). This was the earliest water system, very possibly attributable to the Jebusites. Tunnels I and II start out from a reservoir that once existed underneath the modern steps to the spring. Tunnel I, the older of the two, has been followed for only a relatively short distance and its ultimate destination is not known. Tunnel II has been followed in most of its sections. This tunnel emerges on the side of the Kidron Valley and continues there as an open-air channel of gentle gradient. Some parts, however, were covered with flat stones and some parts went underground again because of the higher level of the rock. Apertures in the east side-wall of the channel made it possible to draw water from it to irrigate the terraces of the western side of the Kidron. Finally this aqueduct led to the pool below the pool of Siloam now known as Birket el-Hamra, or Red Pool. The canal is probably referred to in Is 8:6 in the words about "the waters of Shi-

loah that flow gently," while the pool to which it led is probably the Pool of Shelah mentioned in Neh 3:15. The root from which these names are derived (שלח) means to send or consign and would be appropriate to an aqueduct in which water was sent to its destination.

Under the threat of the invasion of Sennacherib Hezekiah stopped "the water of the springs that were outside the city" (II Ch 32:3), which may mean that he obstructed the outlets of the aqueduct just mentioned. Also he "closed the upper outlet of the waters of Gihon and directed them down to the west side of the city of David" (II Ch 32:30), and he "made the pool (ברכה) and the conduit and brought water into the city" (II K 20:20). These references almost certainly describe the construction of what is known as "Hezekiah's tunnel." This tunnel turns off from channel III in the plan and proceeds as channel IV. All together it is an underground aqueduct winding through the rock 1,749 feet from the Gihon spring to the Pool of Siloam. In 1880 a Hebrew inscription was found on the wall of the tunnel about six meters in from the Siloam mouth, which told how it was dug by excavators who worked from both ends and finally met in the middle of the mountain. When they finished "the water started flowing from the source to the pool (ברכה), twelve hundred cubits."

H. Vincent, *Jérusalem sous terre* (London: Horace Cox, 1911); Simons, *Jerusalem*, pp. 175-188. Plan: courtesy École Biblique et Archéologique Française.

178. Gihon Spring Cavern and Tunnel Opening

THIS PHOTOGRAPH SHOWS the cavern in which the Gihon spring was contained at a time when the water was diverted to facilitate exploration of the various canals connected with the spring (No. 177). In the far

189

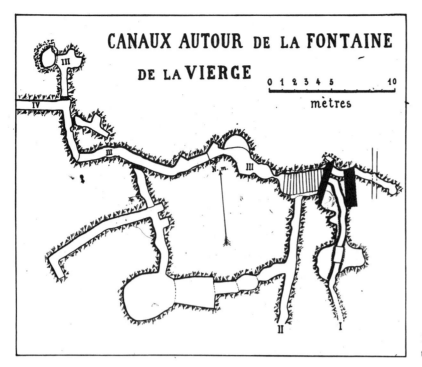

177. Plan of the Tunnels Connected with the Gihon Spring

178. Gihon Spring Cavern and Tunnel Opening

wall is the opening of the tunnel which, after the work of Hezekiah, led all the way to the Pool of Siloam.

Photograph: courtesy École Biblique et Archéologique Française.

179. The Pool of Siloam

THE "POOL" that is mentioned by the same Hebrew word in II K 20:20 and in the inscription found in Hezekiah's tunnel (No. 177) is the reservoir into which this aqueduct empties. When Jn 9:7 refers to the Pool of Siloam (ἡ κολυμβήθρα τοῦ Σιλωάμ) the explanation is added that the name means "Sent." Since Shiloah has this meaning in Hebrew (cf. No. 177) and was transcribed in the LXX as Σιλωάμ (Is 8:6), it seems probable that the name of the earlier water channel on the edge of the Kidron Valley (cf. No. 177) was transferred to the water system of Hezekiah and used for the name of the pool into which the latter conduit emptied. The same name occurs in Latin in the forms Siloae, Silua, etc., and in Arabic as Selwan or Silwan, the latter being the name of the village directly across the Kidron Valley from the Pool of Siloam.

To accord with the purpose of Hezekiah's tunnel and the statement of II K 20:20, the pool into which the water emptied must have been inside the city. When Josephus (War v 4, 2 §145; cf. below, No. 199) speaks of Siloam he says that the city wall on that side of the city was "above (ὑπέρ) the fountain of Siloam," and went on toward the Pool of Solomon, then continued past Ophlas (i.e., Ophel) to the eastern portico of the temple (where it actually ran alongside parallel to the Temple enclosure wall, Mackowski p. 47). This has often been taken to mean that in the time of Josephus the Pool of Siloam was outside the city wall (e.g., Kathleen M. Ken-

179. The Pool of Siloam

yon in PEQ 1966, p. 86, fig. 4; John Wilkinson, "The Pool of Siloam," in *Levant* 10 [1978], pp. 116-125). More probably it is only meant that Siloam was visible from where the wall descended from the Upper City above, while the wall went on around the Pool of Solomon, probably to be identified with Birket el-Hamra (Mackowski p. 46). The fact that Josephus calls Siloam a fountain or spring (πηγή) may mean only that he was thinking of the water pouring out of the mouth of the tunnel, but it might also mean that in his time the Gihon spring itself was covered over and therefore possibly even unknown to many.

In 333 the Pilgrim from Bordeaux (Geyer p. 22; LPPTS I-B, pp. 22-23; CCSL CLXXV, p. 16; WET p. 157; cf. above, No. 173) came out of Jerusalem to go up on Mount Sion (which by then was considered to be the southwestern hill rather than the southeastern) and saw "below in the valley beside the wall" a pool called Siloah (*Silua*). It had a fourfold portico (*quadriporticus*), and there was another large pool outside it. Since Hadrian built a fourfold shrine to the Nymphs (τετρανύμφον) in Aelia Capitolina (*Chronicon Paschale* [631-641] MPG XCII, col. 613), and since a shrine to goddesses especially associated with springs might well have been at this pool, it is probable (Kopp 1959, p. 373) that the fourfold portico was the structure of Hadrian. As for the large pool farther outside, this probably corresponds with the Birket el-Hamra, or Red Pool, which is farther down the valley. A church at the site is attested for the first time in the

year 451 when Peter the Iberian participated in a service "in the church of the so-called Siloah" (Raabe p. 56 in Kopp 1963, p. 317). The Anonymous of Piacenza (570) (Geyer pp. 175-176; LPPTS II-D, pp. 20-21; CCSL CLXXV, p. 166; WJP p. 84) found a domed basilica (*basilica volubilis*) above Siloam (*super Siloa*). Beneath this, the Anonymous says, Siloam rises, with two marble baths, one for men and one for women. In these waters many cures have taken place, and even lepers have been cleansed. In front of the atrium of the church is a large pool, artificially constructed, in which people are constantly bathing. "For at certain hours the fountain (*fons*) of its own accord pours forth many waters (*aquas multas*) which run down through the valley of Gethsemane, which is also called Josaphat, as far as the Jordan." At that time, it is also stated in this record, the fountain of Siloam was included within the city walls because the empress Eudocia (she was the estranged wife of the emperor Theodosius II [408-450], lived at Jerusalem 444-460, and died there) had added the walls at this place to the city. That it was Eudocia who also built the church in question is also likely (Kroll p. 275, col. 1), and this was surely in honor of the miracle of Jesus (Jn 9:1-7). In the Madaba Mosaic Map, which was probably executed only ten years before the coming of the Anonymous of Piacenza, there was shown at the extreme southeast corner of Jerusalem a building with an open dome (damage to the mosaic renders it scarcely recognizable any more, see the photograph in No. 229). The location and the architecture, which would fit a building over a watering place, make it probable that this was a representation of the church which the Anonymous saw.

This church was presumably destroyed by the Persians only a few years later (614), and may not have been rebuilt. In 1897 F. J. Bliss and A. C. Dickie of the Palestine Exploration Fund found and excavated the ruins of a Byzantine church on the hill just above the Pool of Siloam, and this must be the church of which we have been speaking. It was a basilica with nave and two side aisles. The bases of four large piers indicated that it was domed. At the eastern end the apse of the church was directly over the mouth of the water tunnel. In the nave and side aisles some portions of floor mosaic were still preserved. The excavations also uncovered an almost square court about seventy-two feet across, which was surrounded by a probably covered arcade. In the center was the large pool into which the tunnel emptied, and the structure was surely the *quadriporticus* that the Bordeaux Pilgrim mentioned, which may go back, as surmised, to Hadrian. Nearby, on the west slope of the Kidron Valley, are the foundations of a round tower believed to date from the second century B.C., and this could be the "tower in Siloam" mentioned in Lk 13:4 (Kroll p. 277, abb. 226).

After the excavations the people of Silwan erected a small mosque at the northwest corner of the original pool, the minaret of which still rises above the present pool. The photograph shows the mouth of the water tunnel and the Pool of Siloam as they are today. Although the arch of the tunnel exit is more recent, the stumps of ancient columns may be seen. The tank itself, to which one descends by eighteen steps, is about fifty feet long and fifteen feet wide, much smaller than the ancient pool surrounded by the rectangular arcade. Here persons come to do their washing from the southern districts of Jerusalem and from the village of Silwan on the eastern side of the Kidron Valley. As the etymology explained above shows, the village derives its name from the pool and the inhabitants, in the same manner as Josephus (above), call the waters a spring, Ain Silwan.

Frederick J. Bliss and Archibald C. Dickie, *Excavations at Jerusalem, 1894-1897* (London: The Committee of the Palestine Exploration Fund, 1898), pp. 154-159, 178-230; Avi-Yonah in QDAP 2 (1932), p. 164 No. 107; Simons, *Jerusalem*, pp. 189-192; Naseeb Shaheen, "The Siloam End of Hezekiah's Tunnel," in PEQ 1977, pp. 107-112; Ovadiah, *Corpus*, pp. 90-93, no. 78a/b; Bahat, *Plans*, 16ab. For the empress Eudocia, see Kenneth G. Holum, *Theodosian Empresses: Women and Imperial Dominion in Late Antiquity* (Berkeley: University of California Press, 1982), pp. 112ff. Photograph: JF.

180. The Great Rock beneath the Dome of the Rock

AS ESTABLISHED ABOVE (NO. 176), "the city of David" was on the southeastern hill at Jerusalem above the Gihon spring. When the prophet Gad instructed David to make an offering to avert a plague from Israel, he told him to "go up" and erect an altar on the threshing floor of Araunah the Jebusite (by which the destroying angel had been standing), and Araunah saw the king and his servants coming toward him when he "looked down" from where he was (II Sam 24:18ff.). The threshing floor was therefore probably in the relatively free, open land to the north of and higher than the "city of David" on the southeastern hill, i.e., it was on the northeastern hill and in the region which is now recognized as the Temple area (see Nos. 173, 174). Near the center of this area from north to south and to the west of the center from east to west is a large outcropping of natural rock which forms the highest point of the entire hill. The rock (es-Sakhra in Arabic) is about 58 feet long, 51 feet across, and from 4 to 6.5 feet high. It is shown here as now enclosed beneath the Dome of the Rock (Qubbet es-Sakhra) (No. 185) and surrounded immediately by a high wooden screen. As may be seen, there are channels and holes in the surface of the rock; there is also a hole at one side which communicates with a cave underneath. As a high and therefore breezy place the rock itself may have provided the threshing floor for Araunah, and thus the altar of David may have been erected directly upon it (FLAP pp. 179f.).

According to II Ch 3:1 the threshing floor of Ornan (a variant of the name Araunah), which was connected with David in the manner we have just seen, was on Mount Moriah. The name is the same as that of the land of Moriah, on one of the mountains of which Abraham was to offer Isaac but did not (Gen 22:2f.). Whether the three-days' journey of Abraham from Beersheba on that occasion was actually to this site at Jerusalem, or to some other place as some believe (Nelson Glueck, *Rivers in the Desert: A History of the Negev* [New York: Farrar, Straus and Cudahy, 1959], pp. 62-64), the name Mount Moriah, at least from the time of the Chronicler on, was attached to the hill north of the "city of David" and to the area of the great rock which we have just described (cf. below, No. 231). On this mount, we are told in the same passage in II Ch 3:1, Solomon built the house of the Lord. The probability would seem to be that the altar of this Temple, like the altar of David before it (cf. above), was on the sacred rock and, in this case, the sanctuary itself probably rose behind the rock, i.e., to the west (FLAP pp. 180, 326f.). This first temple or Temple of Solomon was burned by the Chaldeans (II K 25:8f.; Jer 52:12f.) in 586 B.C. (Edwin R. Thiele, *A Chronology of the Hebrew Kings* [Grand Rapids: Zondervan, 1977], p. 71).

In 539 Cyrus the Persian took Babylon and decreed the rebuilding of the Temple (II Ch 36:23; Ezr 1:2-3; 6:3-5). At the urging of Haggai (1:2ff.) and Zechariah (4:9f.), and under Zerubbabel, grandson of Jehoiachin (Mt 1:12) and governor of Judah (Hag 1:1), this work was undertaken and, with the support of a fresh decree by Darius (Ezr 6:7-8), finished in the sixth year of the latter king (Ezr 6:15), 515 B.C. (FLAP p. 234). In comparison with the first Temple of Solomon this second temple or Temple of Zerubbabel may have been more modest, for its state, at least during construction, seems to have elicited unfavorable comparisons by those who remembered the first house (Ezr 3:12; Hag 2:3). Also the Talmud (Yoma 21b SBT II 5, p. 94; cf. JE XII, p. 96) says that it lacked five things which were in Solomon's temple, namely, the ark, the fire, the Shekinah or divine manifestation, the Holy Spirit, and the Urim and Thummim.

Josephus tells us that the Temple was also restored (*War* I 21, 1 §401) or reconstructed (*Ant.* xv 11, 1 §380) by Herod the Great. In the two passages just cited contradictory statements are made as to when this work was begun, the former placing it in the fifteenth year of reign of Herod, the latter in the eighteenth year of reign. In both passages Herod's taking of Jerusalem (probably in July in 37 B.C., SHJP Vermes/Millar, I, p. 292 n. 12) is

180. The Great Brook beneath the Dome of the Rock

treated as the beginning of his reign, so the fifteenth year equals 23/22 B.C., the eighteenth year 20/19 B.C. Unless the earlier date refers to preliminary preparations it must be held to be simply an error, for the correct reference is certainly to the eighteenth year, since Dio (54.7.6) provides the corrobative information that the beginning of the work coincided with the arrival of the emperor Augustus in Syria in the spring or summer of 20 B.C. (SHJP Vermes/Millar, ibid.). Professor Vardaman suggests that this date is further supported when it is remembered (see Josephus, *Ant.* xv 10, 4 §365) that the year 20/19 B.C. was a drought year in which the employment of many laborers in this project would have been especially appropriate. Perhaps the wine shipments to Herod from Italy (which are dated to this very year) were sent by Augustus to help alleviate this drought and famine (Y. Yadin, *Masada* [London: Weidenfeld & Nicolson, 1966], p. 189.

On account of Jewish religious sensibilities the temple proper or sanctuary (ναός) was built by the labor of priests only, and it was completed in one year and six months. It so happened that the completion of the work coincided with the anniversary of Herod's accession to rule, so there was a great festival that celebrated both events (*Ant.* xv 11, 6 §423), and this festival is to be dated therefore probably in July and in the year 18 B.C.

In distinction from the priestly work on the temple proper, Herod occupied himself further with the porticos and outer courts (τὰς στοὰς καὶ τοὺς ἔξω περιβόλους), and these were finished in eight years (*Ant.* xv 11, 5-6 §§420-421).

In Jn 2:20 the Jews say to Jesus when he is in Jerusalem at the first Passover which the Fourth Gospel mentions that the temple (ναός) was built (οἰκοδομήθη, aorist denoting completed action) forty-six years, i.e., had then stood for that length of time. From completion in the summer of 18 B.C., forty-six years brings us to A.D. 29/30 and the Passover in question would be that in the spring of the year 30. The date agrees with the probable date of the baptism and the beginning of the ministry of Jesus in the fall of 29 (cf. above, No. 9), and also allows counting ahead three more Passovers in the Fourth Gospel (two of these named and one implied, FHBC pp. 283f., table 134) to crucifixion in A.D. 33, probably on Friday April 3 (Maier in CKC p. 124, table 1). (Nikos Kokkinos dates the completion of the priestly work on the Temple in 19 B.C. and of Herod's work in 12 B.C. and adds forty-six years to the latter date to come to A.D. 34 for Jesus' first Passover, and to crucifixion in 36. Vardaman [in CKC p. 78, table 4, and personal communication, Jan 16, 1990] notes a great earthquake in the spring of 31 B.C., attested by Josephus [*Ant.* xv 5, 2 §§121-122], thinks repair work by Herod on the Temple was necessary at that time, and counts forty-six years from that point to come to the start of Jesus' ministry after midyear A.D. 15 and to crucifixion at Passover A.D. 21.)

In the later history of the Temple, Josephus (*War* v 1, 5 §36) tells us that Herod Agrippa II (who was in charge of the Temple although the various territories over which he reigned did not include Judea, FLAP p. 262 n. 42) brought beams from Lebanon to underprop the sanctuary, and in *Ant.* xx 9, 7 §219 Josephus reports that the whole temple precinct (τὸ ἱερόν) was completed in the time of the procurator Albinus (62-64). In A.D. 70, only a few years later, this Temple of Herod (counting the temple of Zerubbabel separately this is sometimes called the Third Temple, but in Jewish tradition it is still the Second Temple, only restored or reconstructed by Herod, as Josephus says) was burned by the Romans, and both Josephus (*War* VI 4, 5 and 8 §§250, 268) and the Rabbis (FLAP p. 328 n. 4) say that this was done on the very month and day (the ninth day of Ab = July/Aug) when, long before, the First Temple was burned by the Babylonians.

For the Dome of the Rock, see E. T. Richmond, *The Dome of the Rock in Jerusalem* (Oxford: Clarendon Press, 1924); Bahat, *Plans*, 57ab. For differing views on the exact site of the Temple building, see Bellarmino Bagatti, *Recherches sur le site du Temple de Jérusalem*. PSBFCMI 22 (Jerusalem: Franciscan Printing Press, n.d.), p. 30, for the great rock as unsuitable for the threshing floor of Araunah, and pl. XIII for a site for the Temple south of the great rock; Asher S. Kaufman, "Where the Ancient Temple of Jerusalem Stood," in BAR 9.2 (Mar/Apr 1983), pp. 40-59, for a site for the Temple 330 feet/100 meters northwest of the Dome of the Rock, where the Dome of the Tablets now stands. Photograph: The Matson Photo Service, Alhambra, Calif.

181. Plan of the Temple of Herod

WITH RESPECT TO Herod's Temple the chief literary sources of information are Josephus, particularly in *Ant.* xv 11 §§380ff. and *War* v 5 §§184ff., and the tractate *Middoth* ("Measurements") in the Mishna (SBT v 6; DM pp. 589-598), a work written probably in the middle of the second century. There is also a "Temple Scroll" from Qumran that came through an antiquities dealer in Bethlehem in 1960 and into Israeli hands in 1967, but the temple it describes appears to be an ideal structure and not to be taken as fully the same as the Temple of Herod (Yigael Yadin, *The Temple Scroll*, 3 vols. [Jerusalem: Israel Exploration Society, 1977, 1983].

As far as archaeological exploration is concerned, no excavation has been possible within the Temple area proper for it has long been a sacred area of the Muslim

religion. Outside, on the four sides, however, Charles Warren was able in 1867-1870 to make some excavations and reach some of the substructures of the walls by shafts and tunnels (Charles Warren, *The Recovery of Jerusalem* [New York: Appleton, 1872], pp. 42ff.). Then beginning in 1968 and continued throughout the year for twelve years excavations were conducted adjacent to the enclosure walls of the Temple area on the south side and in the southern section of the west side under the direction of Benjamin Mazar of the Hebrew University, with Meir Ben-Dov as the field director.

Josephus (*War* v 5, 1 §§184ff.) says that the level area on the summit of the Temple hill was originally barely large enough for shrine and altar, but was gradually enlarged by additions to the embankment through the ages. By erecting new foundation walls Herod himself enlarged the area to double its former extent (*War* I 21, 1 §401). Each side of the enclosure was now the length of a stade (*Ant.* xv 11, 3 §400), i.e., approximately 600 feet. The tractate *Middoth* (II 1) states that the "Temple Mount" (which is the name used in this work for the entire enclosed area) measured 500 cubits, which would make at least 750 feet on each side. Today the outside measurements of the Temple area are reckoned at 912 feet on the south side, 1,035 feet on the north, 1,536 feet on the east, and 1,590 feet on the west. The level of the courtyard is 2,418 feet above sea level, and the total area is some thirty-five acres.

Entry into the Temple area was by gates on all four sides. Some information concerning them is given by Josephus and by *Middoth* and will be analyzed below, together with discussion of archeological vestiges of them (Nos. 190, 191, 193). Within the Temple area and evidently running around it on all four sides were great "stoas" or porticoes (μεγάλαι στοαὶ περὶ τὸ ἱερόν) which, Josephus (*War* I 21, 1 §401) says, were reconstructed by Herod from the foundations. For the most part these consisted of double rows of monolithic marble columns, twenty-five cubits high, with ceilings of cedar panels (*War* v 5, 2 §190). On the south side the colonnade known as the Royal Portico was more elaborate still (No. 188). On the east side the colonnade bore the name of Solomon (No. 193). These porticoes enclosed the "first court" (*Ant.* xv 11, 5 §417), and this large area was entirely paved with varicolored stones (*War* v 5, 2 §192). The court was freely open even to Gentiles, but at the edge of the next court a stone balustrade (δρύφακτος) three cubits high carried slabs giving warning, some in Greek and some in Latin, that no foreigner might go farther under threat of the penalty of death (*Ant.* xv 11, 5 §417; *War* v 5, 2 §194). The "second court" (*Ant.* xv 11, 5 §417) beyond this balustrade was a quadrangular area screened by a wall of its own, forty cubits in height

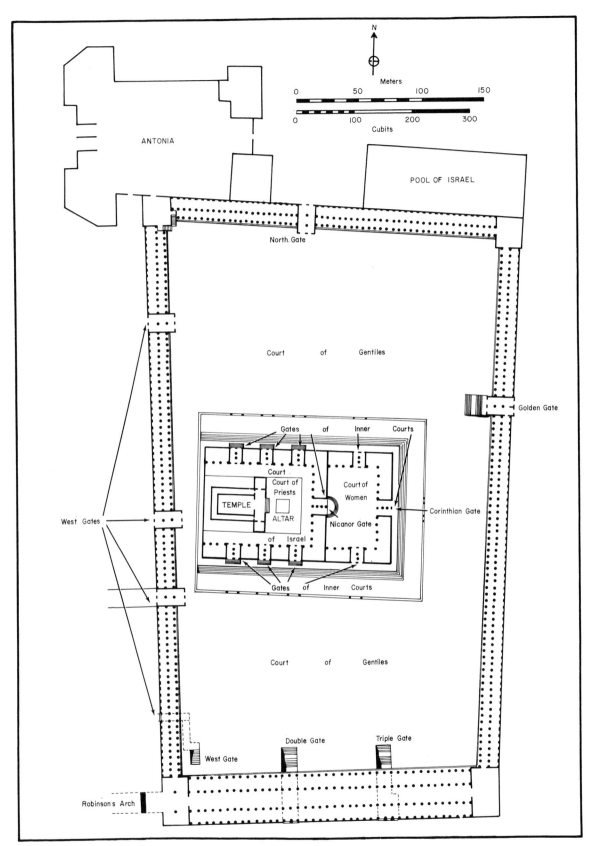

N

Meters
0   50   100   150
0   100   200   300
Cubits

ANTONIA

POOL OF ISRAEL

North. Gate

Court   of   Gentiles

Gates   of   Inner   Courts

Golden Gate

Court

Court of
Priests

Court of
Women

TEMPLE

ALTAR

West Gates

Corinthian Gate

Nicanor Gate

of   Israel

Gates   of   Inner   Courts

Court   of   Gentiles

West Gate

Double Gate

Triple Gate

Robinson's Arch

181. Plan of the Temple of Herod

195

(*War* v 5, 2 §196). Fourteen steps led up to a terrace around the wall and five more steps ascended to the gates in the wall. The first part of this entire second court was walled off to make a special place into which all Jewish women, whether natives of the country or visitors from abroad, were allowed to go. Access was through a gate on the north side, a gate on the south, and a gate on the east. Opposite the last gate another gate allowed access to the second part of the second court, namely, the part into which only Israelite men might go (*Ant.* xv 11, 5 §418), for which there were also three gates on the north side and three gates on the south. Of the ten gates now accounted for, nine were overlaid with gold and silver, but one was of Corinthian bronze and far exceeded in value the ones that were plated with silver and set in gold (*War* v 5, 2-3 §§198, 201). This bronze gate may have been the famous Nicanor Gate, but whether it was the east gate leading from the court of the Gentiles into the court of the women, or the one leading from the court of the women into the court of the men, is debated, the latter position being perhaps the more probable (cf. No. 193). Still farther within was the "third court" (*Ant.* xv 11, 5 §419), which only the priests were allowed to enter. Here was the great altar (standing, we think, on the sacred rock, cf. No. 180) on which whole burnt-offerings were sacrificed (*Ant.* xv 11, 5 §419). Behind it to the west, and approached by its own flight of twelve steps, was the temple edifice proper (ὁ ναός) (*War* v 5, 4-5 §§207ff.). The façade of its porch was of equal height and breadth, each being 100 cubits. The interior of the building itself was 60 cubits high, 60 cubits long, and 20 cubits wide. The first room, 40 cubits long, contained the seven-armed lampstand (cf. Ex 25:31-40), the table for the bread of presence (cf. Ex 25:23-30), and the altar of incense (cf. Ex 30:1-10, 27). Of these objects the table and the lampstand were among the spoils carried off by the Romans and exhibited in the triumphal procession of Vespasian and Titus in Rome in the year after the fall of Jerusalem (*War* vii 5, 5 §148). The representation of them may still be seen sculptured on the inner side of the Arch of Titus (A.D. 81) in the Roman Forum (FLAP p. 329 and fig. 120). The second room of the temple edifice was 20 cubits long and screened from the first room by a veil. In it was no furniture whatsoever. "Unapproachable, inviolable, invisible to all, it was called the Holy of Holy" (*War* v 5, 5 §219).

It was probably on the rocky ridge at the northwest corner of the Temple area that the Tower of Hananel stood, mentioned in Jer 31:38 and Zec 14:10 as apparently marking the northern extremity of the city. Neh 3:1 and 12:39 mention the same tower along with the Tower of the Hundred, both perhaps part of "the fortress (בירה) of the temple" mentioned in Neh 2:8 (Simons, *Jerusalem*, pp. 231, 327, 429 and n. 2). This tower or fortress probably became the citadel that Josephus (*Ant.* xv 11, 4 §403) says the Hasmoneans built and called Baris (βᾶρις), a name perhaps derived from the Hebrew word for "fortress" seen in Neh 2:8. Herod, in turn, made the Baris stronger for the safety and protection of the Temple and, to please his friend Mark Antony, called it Antonia (*Ant.* xv 11, 4 §409). Josephus (*War* v 5, 8 §§238ff.) says the Antonia, the work of King Herod, was built upon a rock 50 cubits high, precipitous on all sides, and covered with smooth flagstones to make it unclimbable. The edifice itself rose to a height of 40 cubits and had towers at its four corners, three of these 50 cubits high, the one at the southeast angle 70 cubits high to command a view of the whole area of the Temple. Inside the Antonia resembled a palace in spaciousness and appointments. Broad courtyards provided accommodation for troops, and a Roman cohort was quartered there permanently. Particularly at festivals the soldiers kept watch on the people in the Temple area to repress any insurrectionary movement. Stairs led down at the point where the fortress impinged on the Temple area porticoes, so that the soldiers could descend rapidly. The tribune and his soldiers and centurions ran down these steps to apprehend Paul (Ac 21:32) and from them Paul addressed the people (Ac 21:35). Also there was a secret underground passage from the Antonia to the eastern gate of the inner sacred court (*Ant.* xv 11, 7 §424). Including the Antonia and the porticoes, the entire circuit of the Temple precinct was six stades (*War* v 5, 2 §192).

The plan corresponds with the preceding description of the Temple of Herod. In addition to the features that are labeled, note the porticoes that surround the entire area: on the east is the Portico of Solomon, on the south the Royal Portico. At the northwest corner is the Antonia, at the northeast is a one-time pool known as the Pool of Israel (Birket Israil, now filled in for a parking lot near St. Stephen's Gate). Note also that the scale for measurements indicates cubits as well as meters.

F. J. Hollis, *The Archaeology of Herod's Temple, with a Commentary on the Tractate "Middoth"* (1934); Watzinger II, pp. 35-45; Galling, *Reallexikon*, cols. 518-519; André Parrot, *The Temple of Jerusalem* (Studies in Biblical Archaeology 5) (New York: Philosophical Library, 1955); Vincent, *Jérusalem*, pp. 711-713; Joan Comay, *The Temple of Jerusalem* (New York: Holt, Rinehart and Winston, 1975); Bahat, *Plans*, 42, 43, 44abc; Benjamin Mazar, *The Mountain of the Lord* (New York: Doubleday, 1975); and Mazar, "Excavations Near Temple Mount Reveal Splendors of Herodian Jerusalem," in BAR 6.4 (July/Aug 1980), pp. 44-59; Meir Ben-Dov, *In the Shadow of the Temple* (New York: Harper and Row, 1985); and Ben-Dov, "Herod's Mighty Temple Mount," in BAR 12.6 (Nov/Dec 1986), pp. 40-49; Hershel Shanks, "Excavating in the Shadow of the Temple Mount," in BAR 12.6 (Nov/Dec 1986), pp. 20-38; Joseph Patrich, "Reconstructing the Magnificent Temple Herod Built" (with Drawings by Leen Ritmeyer), in BAR 4.5 (Oct 1988), pp. 16-29; Kathleen Ritmeyer and Leen Ritmeyer, "Reconstructing Herod's Temple Mount in Jerusalem," in

BAR 15.6 (Nov/Dec 1989), pp. 23-42; Leen Ritmeyer, "Quarrying and Transporting Stones for Herod's Temple Mount," in BAR 15.6 (Nov/Dec 1989), pp. 46-48. Plan: Vincent, *Jérusalem*, pl. *CII*, courtesy École Biblique et Archéologique Française.

182. Fragment of a Warning Inscription from Herod's Temple

AS WE HAVE just seen (No. 181), Josephus says that there were warning inscriptions in Greek and in Latin on the balustrade between the court of the Gentiles and the next more inward court of the temple area, "prohibiting the entrance of a foreigner (ἀλλοεθνῆ) under threat of the penalty of death" (*Ant.* xv 11, 5 §417). One of these stones slabs with a complete inscription in Greek was found by Clermont-Ganneau and published in 1871 (FLAP p. 325 and fig. 118). The text reads:

ΜΗΘΕΝΑΑΛΛΟΓΕΝΗΕΙΣΠΟ
ΡΕΥΕΣΘΑΙΕΝΤΟΣΤΟΥΠΕ
ΡΙΤΟΙΕΡΟΝΤΡΥΦΑΚΤΟΥΚΑΙ
ΠΕΡΙΒΟΛΟΥΟΣΔΑΝΛΗ
ΦΘΗΕΑΥΤΩΑΙΤΙΟΣΕΣ
ΤΑΙΔΙΑΤΟΕΞΑΚΟΛΟΥ
ΘΕΙΝΘΑΝΑΤΟΝ

μηθένα ἀλλογενῆ εἰσπο-
ρεύεσθαι ἐντὸς τοῦ πε-
ρὶ τὸ ἱερὸν τρυφάκτου καὶ
περιβόλου. ὃς δ' ἂν λη-
φθῇ ἑαυτῷ αἴτιος ἔσ-
ται διὰ τὸ ἐξακολου-
θεῖν θάνατον.

No foreigner is to enter within the balustrade and enclosure around the temple area. Whoever is caught will have himself to blame for his death which will follow.

The fragment of a second stone with a portion of the same Greek inscription was found outside St. Stephen's Gate (No. 243) and published in 1938. This stone is shown in the illustration. In this case the inscription was arranged in six lines rather than seven. The words at least partly preserved are the following, and from them it would appear that the wording of the entire inscription was identical (except for αὐτ) instead of ἑαυτῷ with the complete example above:

ΜΗ]ΘΕΝΑΑΛΛ[ΟΓΕΝΗ
ΕΝ]ΤΟΣΤΟΥΠ[ΕΡΙ . . . . . . ΤΡΥ
ΦΑΚ]ΤΟΥΚΑΙ[
Λ]ΗΦΘΗΑΥ[ΤΩΙ
Δ]ΙΑΤΟΕΞ[ΑΚΟΛΟΥΘΕΙΝ
ΘΑΝΑΤΟΝ

μη]θένα ἀλλ[ογενῆ
ἐν]τὸς τοῦ π[ερὶ . . . . . . τρυ-

182. Fragment of a Warning Inscription from Herod's Temple

φάκ]του καὶ[
λ]ηφθη αὐ[τῷ
δ]ιὰ τὸ ἐξ[ακολουθεῖν
θάνατ[ον.

Interestingly enough, in this case at least, the letters of the inscription were painted red, and when the stone was found, the incised marks still retained much of the red paint with which they were filled.

Charles Clermont-Ganneau in PEQ 1871, p. 132; *Une stèle du temple de Jérusalem* (Paris, 1872); L.-H. Vincent in RB 30 (1921), p. 263 and n. 1 and pl. IV; J. H. Iliffe, "The ΘΑΝΑΤΟΣ Inscription from Herod's Temple, Fragment of a Second Copy," in QDAP 6 (1938), pp. 1-3 and pl. I. Photograph: Palestine Archaeological Museum.

183. Latin Inscription of Hadrian on Stone Built into Southern Temple Enclosure Wall

WHEN JERUSALEM was captured by the Romans in A.D. 70 the Temple and almost the whole city were razed

183. Latin Inscription of Hadrian on Stone Built into Southern Temple Enclosure Wall

to the ground. Afterward, to have custody of Jerusalem, the tenth legion (Fretensis) was left as a local garrison (*War* VII 1, 1-3 §§1-17). In A.D. 130 (SHJP Vermes/Millar, I, p. 541 n. 120) Hadrian traveled in the East, went from Syria to Egypt and back again, and visited Jerusalem twice. In his *Weights and Measures* (14 [54c], ed. Dean, p. 30) Epiphanius gives an account of what must be this journey even though he dates it erroneously only forty-seven years after the destruction of Jerusalem, i.e., in 117. He calls Hadrian "a man who loved to see places," and writes:

And he went up to Jerusalem, the famous and illustrious city which Titus, the son of Vespasian, overthrew in the second year of his reign [the second year of Vespasian's reign began on July 1, A.D. 70]. And he found the temple of God trodden down and the whole city devastated save for a few houses and the church of God, which was small, where the disciples, when they had returned after the Savior had ascended from the Mount of Olives, went to the upper room. For there it had been built, that is, in that portion of Zion which escaped destruction, together with blocks of houses in the neighborhood of Zion and the seven synagogues which alone remained standing in Zion, like solitary huts, one of which remained until the time of Maximona the bishop and Constantine the king, "like a booth in a vineyard," as it is written [Is 1: 8]. Therefore Hadrian made up his mind to (re)-build the city, but not the temple. . . . And he gave to the city that was being built his own name and the appellation of the royal title. For as he was named Aelius Hadrian, so he named the city Aelia.

Dio (A.D. 229) gives an account of the same journey of Hadrian in his *Roman History* (LXIX 12), and writes: "At Jerusalem he founded a city in place of the one which had been razed to the ground, naming it Aelia Capitolina, and on the site of the temple of the god he raised a new temple to Jupiter." Dio continues to explain that this brought on a war, because the Jews felt it was intolerable for foreign races to be settled in their city and foreign religious rites planted there. As long as Hadrian was still close by in Egypt and again in Syria they remained quiet, but when he went farther away they revolted openly. This was of course the uprising which was led by Bar Kokhba and lasted from 132 to 135.

From Epiphanius we derive a vivid picture of the desolation of Jerusalem and the Temple area after the destruction by Titus. From Dio we understand that it was Hadrian's projected building of a new pagan city and a new pagan temple which provoked the revolt of Bar Kokhba. Presumably only after that revolt was quelled was the full project carried out. The two sources appear to differ, however, as to whether Hadrian built a temple at Jerusalem. But perhaps Epiphanius only means to say that Hadrian did not propose to rebuild the Jewish temple. If that is his meaning it would not necessarily exclude the building of a pagan temple, which Dio says Hadrian did. That a pagan sanctuary was actually established on the former site of the Jewish temple is confirmed by other writers including Jerome, who says

(*Commentary on Isaiah* I ii 9 CCSL LXXIII, p. 33): "Where once were the temple and the religion of God, there a statue of Hadrian and an idol of Jupiter are set up together." The fact that the Bordeaux Pilgrim (Geyer p. 22; LPPTS I-B, p. 22; CCSL CLXXV, p. 16; WET p. 157) mentions two statues of Hadrian in the Temple area probably can be explained by supposing that the statues were so similar in appearance that he mistakenly took the statue of Jupiter to be a second statue of the emperor.

Interestingly enough there is now built into the south enclosure wall of the Temple area, just east of the Double Gate (No. 190), a block of stone which must have been the base of this statue of Hadrian. Although the stone is built into the wall with the inscription upside down, we have inverted the drawing of it in the illustration and the text is easily read, as follows:

TITO AEL HADRIANO
ANTONINO AUG PIO
P P PONTIF AUGUR
D D

In the inscription PP abbreviates *pater patriae*, and DD abbreviates *decreto decurionum*, the *decuriones* being the members of the senate of a Roman colony. The whole text is:

To Titus Aelius Hadrianus
Antoninus Augustus Pius,
the father of his country, pontifex, augur.
By decree of the decurions.

Other archeological witness to the history recounted above is provided by the coins of Aelia. They give the official name of the city as *Col(onia) Ael(ia) Cap(itolina)*, and sometimes show the figure of Jupiter (SHJP Vermes/ Millar, I pp. 553-555 and n. 186 on p. 554). From Jerome in his Latin version of the *Chronicle of Eusebius* (ed. Helm, 2d ed. 1956, p. 201) we learn that as a final sign of the subjection of the Jews to the Roman power a swine was sculptured in the marble of the gate through which one went out of Aelia toward Bethlehem. Such a sculptured stone has not, however, been found.

Simons, *Jerusalem*, pp. 358-359 and fig. 51; Vincent, *Jérusalem*, pp. 753-782; Vincent, *Jérusalem nouvelle*, pp. 1-39; Leo Kadman, *The Coins of Aelia Capitolina*. Corpus Nummorum Palaestinensium, I (Jerusalem: Universitas Publishers, 1956); Bahat, *Plans*, 5. Photograph: courtesy Palestine Archaeological Museum.

184. General View of the Temple Area from the Air

AFTER MENTIONING the two statues in the Temple area supposed to be of Hadrian (No. 183), the Bordeaux

Pilgrim also mentions the custom of annual lamentation for the destroyed Temple by the Jews at the "perforated stone" (probably the sacred rock under the present Dome of the Rock, cf. the List of Bishops of the Jerusalem Church), thus the Temple area certainly appears to have been included in the pilgrim's itinerary. Nevertheless the place seems to have remained for the most part in ruins ever since the Roman destruction. Eusebius (*Demonstratio Evangelica* VIII 3, 12 ed. Heikel p. 393) says that it is a sad spectacle to see with the eyes the stones of the Temple area and even of the formerly inaccessible sanctuary taken away to be used for the temple precincts of idols, or for the erection of places for public pageants. He also comments (*Theophany* IV 18 ed. Gressmann p. 193), with only slight exaggeration, that in his time the desolation of the Temple had already lasted more than four times as long as the seventy years of ruin in the time of the Babylonians. This long-continued desolation was nothing other, Eusebius declares, than a fulfillment of the words of Jesus, for when Jesus said, "Behold, your house is left unto you desolate" (Mt 23:38), he meant by "house" nothing other than the Temple, and when the disciples were impressed by the mighty buildings of the Temple area he spoke plainly of this area and said, "There shall not be left here one stone upon another, that shall not be thrown down" (Mt 24:2). The example of the Bordeaux Pilgrim shows that Christians continued to visit the site of the Temple, and the fact that the statues of Hadrian and Jupiter are no longer mentioned after Jerome (cf. No. 183) may mean that these evidences of paganism were removed from the site because of Christian influence. But Eutychius (940), who quotes the same two Gospel passages as Eusebius (Mt 23:38; 24:2), makes it evident that the Christians considered these words as a curse upon the Temple area and says explicitly: "On this account the Christians left it desolate, and built no church upon it" (*Annales* II; MPG 111, cols. 1099-1100; LPPTS XI-A, p. 67).

Such was evidently the desolate state of the Temple area when the Muslims came. In A.H. 17 = A.D. 638 Jerusalem fell to the conqueror 'Umar (634-644), second successor (*khalifah*) of Muhammad. According to Eutychius in the record just cited 'Umar himself cleared the sacred stone (No. 180) in the Temple area of much accumulated filth. Some then proposed to build a temple and use the stone to mark the direction of prayer (*qibla*). 'Umar, however, said that the temple should be built so that the stone was in the back of it. The Byzantine chronographer Theophanes (751-818) says that 'Umar began to build the temple in Jerusalem in the year of the world 6135 which would correspond, in the Alexandrian system, to A.D. 643 = A.H. 22/23 (MPG 108, col. 700; Vincent, *Jérusalem nouvelle*, p. 413), but other sources would make the date a few years earlier (CEMA I, p. 25).

184. General View of the Temple Area from the Air

Theophanes also says in the same passage that when 'Umar experienced difficulty in the collapse of his building, the Jews persuaded him that he could not succeed unless he took down the cross which was above on the summit of the Mount of Olives (on the Church of the Ascension, No. 158), and 'Umar did remove the cross. Although Eutychius and Theophanes speak of 'Umar as erecting a "temple," it may be assumed that any building which he put up in the Temple area, and in the orientation of which the *qibla* or direction of prayer was a factor, was in fact a mosque. This is confirmed by Arculf (670), who was in Jerusalem within thirty years of the date of 'Umar's work, for he explicitly uses for the building he describes in the Temple area the term "house of prayer," which corresponds to the Arabic *masjid* or "mosque," meaning literally a place of prostration (FAWR p. 508). Arculf's record reads as follows (Geyer pp. 226-227; LPPTS III-A, pp. 4-5; CCSL CLXXV, p. 186):

> But in that renowned place where once the temple had been magnificently constructed, placed in the neighborhood of the wall from the east (*in vicinia muri ab oriente locatum*), the Saracens now frequent a quadrangular house of prayer (*quadrangulam orationis domum*), which they have built rudely, constructing it by raising planks and great beams on some remains of ruins (*super quasdam ruinarum reliquias*); which house, it is said, can hold three thousand men at once.

If the "wall from the east" may be taken to mean the enclosure wall running from the southeastern angle along the south side of the Temple area, then the "remains of ruins" on which the planks and beams of the new structure were placed may have been what remained at that time of the colonnades of the famous Royal Por-

tico (No. 188). If the mosque was placed thus at the southern side of the Temple area it would indeed leave the sacred stone to the back of it, i.e., to the north, as 'Umar said. This would also place the building in more or less the same position as the present al-Aqsa Mosque (No. 186). In the latter building the mihrab, or niche marking the direction of prayer (No. 187), is in the south wall, and a line drawn from it and perpendicular to the wall will pass directly through the center of the sacred stone (CEMA I, p. 25).

From this time on, the Temple area was in the hands of the Muslims. As such it has been known as the Haram esh-Sherif or Noble Sanctuary. This photograph is a general view of the area from the air.

Vincent, *Jérusalem nouvelle*, pp. 875-1006. Photograph: courtesy Palestine Archaeological Museum.

185. Windows in the Dome of the Rock

IT WAS THE UMAYYAD CALIPH of Damascus, 'Abd al-Malik (685-705), who erected a building over the sacred rock (No. 180) itself. This was not a mosque but a shrine or "place or witness" (*mashhad*) and is known today simply as the Dome of the Rock (Qubbet es-Sakhra) (FAWR pp. 511-513). In architecture it is essentially a circle of four masonry piers and twelve marble columns around the rock, upholding a drum and dome, and around this circle an octagonal colonnade and outer octagonal wall. In each face of the wall are five windows and in the drum above sixteen windows. A Kufic inscription in the interior of the building still shows the date,

200

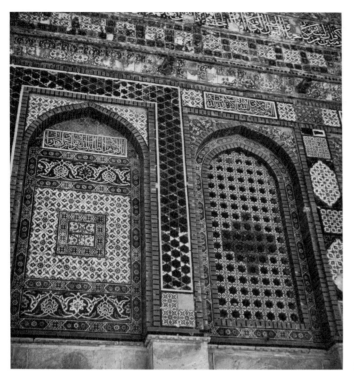

185. Windows in the Dome of the Rock

"in the year two and seventy" (A.H. 72 = A.D. 691), which falls in the reign of 'Abd al-Malik and substantiates the attribution of the building to that Caliph. It is thus the oldest existing monument of Muslim architecture. Extensive mosaic decorations still remaining in the interior enhance the beauty of the building; they derive also in large part from the seventh century. In the inscription just mentioned the name of the 'Abbasid Caliph al-Ma'mun (813-833) has been inserted–he probably made restorations on the structure. In A.H. 407 = A.D. 1016 the wooden dome fell and was reconstructed soon after, to be replaced eventually by the modern aluminum dome. In 1189 Saladin put slabs of marble on the walls of the building. On the lower windows is the name of Suleiman the Magnificent, sultan of Turkey, and the date A.H. 935 = A.D. 1528; the beautiful tile work in blue and white and green around the windows was added by this ruler in 1561. The windows have perforations filled with colored glass in a variety of designs. Above are passages from the Qur'an, in beautifully interwoven characters, running around the building like a frieze. The photograph looks up at a pair of the windows from the outside, and also shows a portion of the inscription above.

CEMA I, pp. 42-94, and pp. 147-228 (by Marguerite van Berchem on the mosaics); Bahat, *Plans*, 57ab. Photograph: JF.

186. The Mosque al-Aqsa

AS WE HAVE SEEN (NO. 184), the first Muslim mosque in the Jerusalem Temple area was probably built by the Caliph 'Umar soon after the taking of Jerusalem in A.H. 17 = A.D. 638. From the description by Arculf (670), we think that it was built in the ruins of the former Royal Portico on the south side of the area, and we learn that it was "rudely" constructed. This first mosque was replaced by a second and no doubt better structure, erected by the Umayyad Caliph al-Walid (705-715), son of 'Abd al-Malik, builder of the Dome of the Rock; he himself was also the builder of the Great Mosque at Damascus (FAWR pp. 513-514). Confirmation of the enterprise at this time is found in the dated contemporary Aphrodito papyri (CEMA II p. 119), which record the sending of laborers from Egypt to work on "the mosque of Jerusalem" (μασγιδα Ἱεροσολύμων). In the course of time the mosque was frequently damaged by earthquakes and there is evidence for repeated rebuildings by several more caliphs: the third mosque was built by al-Mansur perhaps in A.H. 154 = A.D. 771, the fourth by al-Mahdi perhaps in A.H. 163 = A.D. 780, and the fifth by az-Zahir in A.H. 426 = A.D. 1035. While there is also work by the Crusaders to the east and west of the nave, in quite large part the mosque as it still stands is the work of az-Zahir, and his plan was probably much the same as that of al-Mahdi. From the description of the mosque of al-Mahdi by Muqaddasi (985) (LPPTS III-C, pp. 41-42)

186. The Mosque al-Aqsa

and the portions of masonry which remain probably from the mosque of az-Zahir and earlier ones (CEMA II, p. 123 fig. 119), it appears that the plan of that time had a central nave and seven aisles on either side (four more on each side than in the present mosque). On the north end of the building was the great central doorway, opposite the mihrab, with seven doors to the right of it and seven to the left. Inside the aisles were marked out with rows of columns and of round piers. Over the central part of the building was a mighty gable roof with a magnificent dome rising behind it.

In the Qur'an (Sura XVII 1 tr. A. Yusuf Ali p. 693) it is related that Muhammad was taken for "a journey by night" (the famous Mi'raj on which he went on through the seven heavens) from the Sacred Mosque, i.e., the Ka'bah at Mecca, to the Farthest Mosque. This name, Masjid al-Aqsa or the Farthest Mosque, designated the Temple site in Jerusalem as the farthest west place of worship known to the Arabs in that time. Thus it became the name of the mosque built in the Temple area and is so used, for example, by Muqaddasi in his description (cited above) of the mosque which stood there in his time.

Today the Aqsa Mosque stands perpendicularly against the south wall of the Temple enclosure and occupies an area eighty-eight yards long and sixty yards wide not including the various annexes on either side.

On the north the entrance is through a porch consisting of seven arcades. The porch was constructed by Melik el-Mu'azzam 'Isa (who died in 1227) and has been restored since. The photograph shows this north end of the mosque, with the seven arcades of the porch.

CEMA II, pp. 119-126; Bahat, *Plans*, 58-61. For the importance of Jerusalem in Islam, see Isaac Hasson, "Muslim Literature in Praise of Jerusalem," in *The Jerusalem Cathedra* I (1981), pp. 169f. Photograph: JF.

187. Minbar and Corner of Mihrab in the Aqsa Mosque

AT THE SOUTH END of the Aqsa Mosque, marking the direction of prayer toward Mecca, is the niche known as the mihrab and, beside it, the minbar or pulpit. The pulpit, carved in wood and inlaid with ivory and mother-of-pearl, was made in A.H. 564 = A.D. 1168 by an artist of Aleppo. The prayer niche, flanked by marble columns, is a part of a restoration in this end of the mosque by Saladin in A.H. 583 = A.D. 1187. The photograph shows the upper side of the mihrab and most of the minbar.

Photograph: JF.

187. Minbar and Corner of Mihrab in the al-Aqsa Mosque

188. The Pinnacle of the Temple

AS JOSEPHUS SAID (*War* I 21, 1 §401; cf. above No. 181), in order to enlarge the Temple area Herod had to erect new foundation walls. In another passage (*War* v 5, 1 §188) the same author says that where the foundations were lowest the walls were built up from a depth of three hundred cubits or even more, a depth which was not fully apparent, however, since the ravines were in considerable part filled up. It is evident that these foundation walls must have been set well down the slopes of the Kidron Valley on the east and the Tyropoeon on the west, and that is where the present walls of the temple area are found. At the southeastern corner the level of the Temple area is now about forty feet above the ground outside but the slope of the valley has been built up a great deal in the course of time. Warren (*Recovery of Jerusalem*, p. 117) sank a shaft here outside the wall and then drove a gallery in until he struck the enclosure wall at a point thirty-two feet to the north of the southeastern angle; at this point he was at a level of 2,312 feet above the sea, or 106 feet below the average level of the Temple area above (cf. No. 181). Inside the walls it was then necessary to build up a level area. This was probably done not only by the filling of the former ravines to which Josephus referred (above) but also by the building

of extensive substructures. At any rate Josephus says (*War* v 3, 1 §102) that during the siege of Jerusalem by the Romans people took refuge in the temple vaults (εἰς τοὺς ὑπονόμους τοῦ ἱεροῦ), i.e., in underground passages beneath the Temple area, and (*War* VI 9, 3 §§429-430) that when the city fell the victors found more than two thousand dead down there (ἐν τοῖς ὑπονόμοις). Actually the south side of the Temple area rests almost entirely upon massive and vaulted substructures. Those under the southwest corner are inaccessible, but those in the middle are reached by a flight of eighteen steps which descends east of the entrance of the al-Aqsa Mosque, and those in the southeast corner are similarly accessible from that part of the area. These last are known as Solomon's Stables, a name used by the Crusaders who probably rebuilt this structure and used it for their horses and camels. Here there are thirteen rows of vaults 30 feet high with eighty-eight piers, and the floor of the hall is over 40 feet below the surface of the Temple area above. From the angle of the enclosure the structure extends more than 260 feet to the west and 200 feet to the north. Herodian masonry may still be seen in the lower part of some of the piers; the upper part represents the rebuilding of the Crusader period.

Above ground here on the south end of the Temple area there was, according to Josephus (*Ant.* xv 11, 4

188. The Pinnacle of the Temple

§§411ff.), a Royal Portico (ἡ βασίλειος στοά) of four rows of columns and three aisles, stretching from the eastern to the western ravine, i.e., from the Kidron to the Tyropoeon. Josephus says that if one went up on the high rooftop of this portico and looked down into the ravine, doubtless meaning the Kidron Valley on the east, "he would become dizzy and his vision would be unable to reach the end of so measureless a depth." In Mt 4:5 and Lk 4:9 there is mention of "the pinnacle of the temple" (τὸ πτερύγιον τοῦ ἱεροῦ). Here the word used for "temple" is that which refers to the entire area, and the word "pinnacle" is literally a "little wing," a term used for the tip or extremity of anything, hence the edge or the summit. It is a probable supposition, therefore, that the point referred to was precisely that described by Josephus at the southeastern corner of the Temple area, high above the Kidron. The photograph looks up from the south toward the southeastern angle of the Temple enclosure wall which, according to the reasoning just presented, was the "pinnacle" of the temple. At this cor-

ner, Herodian masonry survives to within about twenty feet of the top of the wall.

Charles Warren, *The Recovery of Jerusalem* (New York: D. Appleton and Company, 1872); Warren, *Underground Jerusalem* (London: Richard Bentley and Son, 1876); Charles Warren and C. L. Conder, *The Survey of Western Palestine*, v, *Jerusalem* (London, 1884); Kenyon, *Jerusalem*, pls. 60-62, 64; Bahat, *Plans*, 47abc, 50; Benjamin Mazar, "The Royal Stoa in the Southern Part of the Temple Mount," in Hershel Shanks, *Recent Archaeology in the Land of Israel* (Washington, D.C.: Biblical Archaeology Society; Jerusalem: Israel Exploration Society, 1984), pp. 141-147. Photograph: JF.

189. The Western Wall

IN THE SOUTHERN SECTION of the east wall of the Temple enclosure (cf. No. 188), in the south wall, and in the west wall the lower courses of stone are all of the same style. When Edward Robinson observed this stonework in 1838 he spoke of the stones as beveled and described them as having the whole face first hewn and squared, then a narrow strip cut along the edge one-quarter or one-half inch lower than the rest of the surface. In some cases the stone has a depressed plane surface of this sort around the margin and a plane surface in the center too, in other cases there are rough projections in the center and these blocks may perhaps have been intended to be hidden underground. Such a rectangular building stone with its surfaces trimmed at right angles to fit smoothly against the adjacent stone is now called an *ashlar*, and the term drafted or bordered describes the stone in terms of the treatment of the margin. Masonry of the sort just described is found not only here in lower courses of the Temple area enclosure wall but also in lower courses of the so-called Tower of David in the Citadel in Jerusalem (QDAP 14 [1950], pp. 140ff., plate XLVII, 3), and in the great enclosure wall known as the Haram el-Khalil at the traditional Cave of Machpelah in Hebron (L. H. Vincent and E. J. H. Mackay, *Hébron, le Ḥaram el-Khalil* (1923), pp. 99f., 102f., 108f.; Ovadiah, *Corpus*, pp. 131-133, no. 135). In the Tower of David we undoubtedly have the surviving base of Herod's tower called Phasael (No. 198), the masonry of Hebron is most probably Herodian even though Josephus does not speak of building work there by Herod, and the masonry just described in the east, south, and west walls of the Temple enclosure at Jerusalem is surely Herodian too (Simons, *Jerusalem*, pp. 270, 324 n. 1, 384-391, 412, 422f.). In the eastern enclosure wall at a point 32 meters/105 feet north of the south end of the wall there is, however, a vertical seam known as the "straight joint," north of which the masonry is of a different type and is surely older than that of Herod the Great, but whether Hellenistic, Persian, or even Solomonic in date is debatable (No. 193).

At the southwest angle of the Temple enclosure the Tyropoeon Valley runs diagonally under the corner of the Temple area. Along the present plaza to the north seven courses of Herodian masonry may be seen, while underground there are no less than nineteen Herodian courses, reaching down to bedrock 69 feet below (Mazar, *Mountain of the Lord*, p. 131). We have already quoted (No. 184) the statement of the Bordeaux Pilgrim (Geyer p. 22; LPPTS I-B, p. 22; CCSL CLXXV, p. 16; WET p. 157) concerning the "perforated stone" near the statues of Hadrian, to which the Jews came every year to make lamentation for the destroyed temple, and have judged that this stone was none other than the great sacred rock itself (No. 180). In the course of time, however, the place of Jewish lamentation came to be on the outside of the stretch of wall on the west side of the Temple enclosure just described. For this reason this used to be called the Wailing Wall, now it is simply the Western Wall. A small portion of this wall is shown in the photograph. In speaking of the foundation walls of the temple enclosure Josephus (*War* v 5, 1 §189) mentions stones that measured forty cubits. Elsewhere he speaks of the temple building proper as built of stones twenty-five (*Ant.* xv 11, 1 §392) or even forty-five (*War* v 5, 6 §224) cubits in length. In fact the stones before us in the first seven courses in the Western Wall are very large: many are 15 feet long and 3-4 feet high; at the southwestern corner there are stones 40 feet long, 3 feet high, and 8 feet thick, estimated to weigh about 50 tons apiece. These are smooth-faced marginally drafted blocks typical of the work of Herod the Great, and they are fitted together with such precision that no cement or mortar of any kind is used. Above the Herodian levels are four courses of smooth undrafted stones, which are probably of the Roman and Byzantine period, and above these are smaller stones representing Arabic and Turkish work.

189. The Western Wall

190. The Double Gate

Edward Robinson, *Biblical Researches in Palestine, Mount Sinai and Arabia Petraea: A Journal of Travels in the Year 1838*, 3 vols. (Boston: Crocker and Brewster, 1841), I, p. 423; Simons, *Jerusalem*, p. 361; Mazar, *Mountain of the Lord*, pp. 131ff.; Ben-Dov, *Shadow of Temple*, pp. 88ff., 101-103. Photograph: JF.

190. The Double Gate

IN THE ENCLOSURE WALL of the Temple area, as described by Josephus and *Middoth*, there were a number of gates. Josephus describes four gates on the west side (*Ant.* xv 11, 5 §410), says that there were "gates in the middle" on the south side (ibid.) and, in telling about the Roman attack, speaks of a gate on the north side of the Temple area (*War* II 19, 5 §537; VI 4, 1 §222). The fact that he does not mention a gate on the east side is probably only an inadvertent omission, for in his basic description he speaks of the north side of the Temple

area (*Ant.* xv 11, 4 §403) and of the west side (xv §411) without having accounted for a third side at all. *Middoth* (I 1 and 3) states that there were five gates to the temple mount, two Huldah Gates on the south, "serving for entry and exit," the Kiponus Gate on the west, the Tadi Gate on the north, and the Eastern Gate on which was portrayed the Palace of Shushan.

On the south side of the Temple enclosure may be seen two gates, which are about seventy meters apart and now walled up. They are known as the Double Gate and the Triple Gate. They are usually identified with the gates in the middle on the south side mentioned by Josephus, and with the two Huldah Gates mentioned in *Middoth*, and they are sometimes called the Western and Eastern Huldah Gates, with the supposition that pilgrims entered the Temple area by the western gate and departed by the eastern gate. An alternate theory supposes that the Double Gate itself provided for entry and exit of pilgrims and was thus itself the two Huldah Gates, while the Triple Gate (No. 191) was used by the priests. The photograph shows what is visible of the Double Gate in its present state. The building that encroaches on the left is a Crusader structure built to protect the Double Gate in that period. The ornamental arch above the opening dates from the Muslim Umayyad period (seventh century). Behind and above, however, may be seen part of an enormous lintel stone, five and one-half meters long and nearly two meters thick, with drafted margins. This and other large stones notably visible in the lower right-hand corner are surely Herodian. Inside this double gate is a double-vaulted vestibule and a tunnel-like passage which rises in inclines to an opening on the main level of the Temple area above. Presumably it became necessary to construct this subterranean connection when the Temple area was filled in above and when Herod's Royal Portico (cf. No. 188) was built. In the vestibule and passageway Herodian masonry is still extant. Today the passage runs under the al-Aqsa Mosque, a little to the east of its central aisle, and comes out in front of the mosque.

Watzinger II, pp. 35-38; Spencer Corbett, "Some Observations on the Gateways to the Herodian Temple in Jerusalem," in PEQ 1952, pp. 7-14 and especially pl. I; Mazar, *Mountain of the Lord*, pp. 140ff.; Ben-Dov, *Shadow of Temple*, pp. 135ff.; Bahat, *Plans*, 46abc; Kathleen Ritmeyer and Leen Ritmeyer, "Reconstructing Herod's Temple Mount," in BAR 15.6 (Nov/Dec 1989), pp. 35f.; and "Reconstructing the Triple Gate," ibid., pp. 49-53. Photograph: courtesy Palestine Archaeological Museum.

191. The Triple Gate

THE TRIPLE GATE is 70 meters west of the Double Gate. As seen now the three blocked-up arches are of Umayyad construction, but the width is probably the same as that of the original Herodian gate. In the photograph there can still be seen near the lower left-hand corner a portion of an immense jamb stone that is surely from the Herodian structure.

As for the name Huldah (whether applicable to both the Double and the Triple Gates, or only to the former), a prophetess by the name of Huldah is mentioned in II K 22:14; II Ch 34:22, but the connection between this personage and these gates is not known. In view of the tunnel-like passages leading up from the gates into the Temple area, one hypothesis (C. Schick in ZDPV 22 [1899], pp. 94-97) explains the name from the Hebrew word חלדד, which means "mole" as well as "weasel" (in Lev 11:29 the related חלד is translated "weasel" in RSV, but

191. The Triple Gate

"mole" in the New Translation of the Torah by the Jewish Publication Society of America [1962]). Whether the name of the prophetess was from the same root is also not known.

For bibliography see under No. 190. Photograph: courtesy École Biblique et Archéologique Française.

192. Excavated Area South of the Temple Mount

ON THE SOUTH SIDE of the Temple area and in front of the Double and Triple Gates the Israeli excavations beginning in 1968 (No. 181) have revealed a large formal square with a monumental staircase leading up to the two gates. In the late Byzantine period (early seventh century) fine Byzantine houses were built in this area; in the Umayyad period (later seventh to first half of the eighth century) magnificent palaces of the Muslims were built over the ruins of the Byzantine houses. With the establishment of an archeological garden in the area, the monumental staircase can be seen in considerable part of its original extent. This was plainly the main approach to the Temple, with the Double and Triple Gates opening to the passages to the level above. In front of the Double Gate a small fragment of a stone utensil was found, with the Hebrew word *corban* (cf. Mk 7:11 Greek κοϱβάν for Hebrew קרבן), meaning offering or sacrifice, which makes it probable that this was an actual instrument used in the Herodian temple and, if so, the first such ever found (for the ossuaries found in the same excavations, see No. 309). In the same area, about forty meters south of the Double Gate, under the later buildings, foundations were found that are very possibly those of the *acra*, the fortress built by Antiochus IV Epiphanes to overlook the Temple, and occupied by the Syrians until finally captured and destroyed by Simon the Hasmonean in 141 B.C. (cf. above, No. 173). The present photograph shows (in a telephoto view from the Mount of Olives) the south end of the temple area (with the dome

192. Excavated Area South of the Temple Mount

of the al-Aqsa Mosque) and the whole adjacent excavated area as just described.

B. Mazar, *Excavations in the Old City of Jerusalem: Preliminary Report of the First Season, 1968* (Jerusalem: Israel Exploration Society, 1969), pp. 15f.; and Mazar, *Mountain of the Lord*, pp. 70, 143, 216, 256f., 267f.; M. Ben-Dov, *Excavations in the Old City of Jerusalem near the Temple Mount: The Omayyad Structures near the Temple Mount* (Jerusalem: Israel Exploration Society, 1971), pp. 37-44; and Ben-Dov, *Shadow of Temple*, pp. 66-71, 108ff.; Bahat, *Plans*, 55abc. Photograph: JF.

193. The Golden Gate

AS FAR AS the east side of the Temple area is concerned, Josephus (*Ant.* xx 9, 7 §§220-221) mentions an east portico (στοά) which he attributes to Solomon (cf. No. 181, no doubt the Solomon's Portico of Jn 10: 23; Ac 3:11; 5:12) but (probably by inadvertence, as we think, cf. No. 190) does not mention any gate. *Middoth* I 3, however, speaks of "the Eastern Gate on which was portrayed the Palace of Shushan" (cf. No. 190). Shushan, or Susa, was a capital of the Persian Empire (Est 1:2; Dan 8:2, etc.) and representation of the Shushan palace on the Jerusalem gate was intended, according to a Rabbinical tradition (*Menahoth* 98a SBT v 2, p. 599),

to make the people "ever mindful whence they came," and presumably therewith to commemorate the permission granted by the kings of Persia for the rebuilding of the Temple (cf. No. 180). We may therefore call the east gate of the Temple area the Shushan Gate.

In Ac 3:2, 10 there is mention of the Beautiful Gate (ἡ θύρα ἡ ὡραία and ἡ ὡραία πύλη) of the temple. In the narrative a lame man was laid at this gate so that he would be in position to ask alms "of those who entered the temple" (Ac 3:2). Here he also saw Peter and John when they were "about to go into the temple" (Ac 3:3) and, being made able to walk, he "entered the temple with them" (Ac 3:8). The word used for "temple" in all three of these statements is not the word that designates the sanctuary or temple building proper (ναός) but is the word normally used to designate the entire temple area (ἱερόν).[*] Therefore the gate at which the man was laid was probably a gate in the outer enclosure wall through which people came into the temple area. After his healing the man went on with Peter and John into the temple area. At this point "all the people ran together to them in the portico called Solomon's" (Ac 3:11). Since this was the portico on the east side, as Josephus tells us (above), the gate from which the apostles and the formerly lame man had just come must also have been on the east side. If this is correct, the Beautiful Gate of Ac

193. The Golden Gate

3:2, 10 must have been the Shushan Gate. It is true that in Ac 3:11 there is a reading in Codex Bezae (D) different from that of the other major manuscripts from which we have just quoted a portion of this verse. The reading in Codex Bezae describes the action of the healed man and of the people at the point of verse 11 as follows: "But when Peter and John were going out he went with them holding on to them, and they [the people], astonished, stood in the portico called Solomon's." This can simply mean that the man who was healed at the eastern gate and then went on into the Temple area with the apostles was now going back out with them and was the object of this excited attention in Solomon's portico. But it can mean that the healing had taken place at a different gate farther within the Temple area, from which the apostles and the man were now returning. In this case the guess frequently accepted is that the Beautiful Gate was the Nicanor Gate. Josephus (*War* II 17, 3 §411) refers to "the bronze gate—that of the inner temple (τοῦ ἔνδον ἱεροῦ) facing eastward," and (*War* v 5, 3 §201) says that it was of Corinthian bronze and exceeded in value the other gates that were plated with silver and set in gold (cf. No. 181). *Middoth* II 3 gives the name Nicanor Gate (cf. No. 309) for what is probably the same gate of bronze. As to the location of this gate, it has commonly been held that the references in Josephus imply that it gave access from the east from the court of the Gentiles to the court of the women (the Corinthian Gate in plan No. 181), but that the Mishna puts it between the court of the women and the court of the men (the Nicanor Gate in the plan); it is quite possible, however, that both sources are actually in agreement and that this gate gave access from the east from the court of the women to the court of the men (E. Stauffer in ZNW 44 [1952-53], pp. 44-66). So, it is held, Ac 3:11 in Codex Bezae supposes that the healing took place at the Nicanor Gate, the apostles and the lame man went on within and then, when they "were going out," and had reached Solomon's portico at the east side of the temple area the crowd stood there astonished. In fact, however, the reading of Ac 3:11 in Codex Bezae seems less likely than the reading in the other major manuscripts. Both readings agree that there was intense excitement (ἔκθαμβοι in B etc.; θαμβήθεντες in D) over the healing of the lame man. Surely it is more likely that this excitement arose immediately. This agrees with the supposition that the healing took place at the Shushan Gate and the crowd gathered around in their astonishment as soon as the lame man had stood up and walked on with Peter and John into the immediately adjacent portico called Solomon's.

At least in the course of time it was the Shushan Gate (Golden Gate) that Christian pilgrims saw as the Beautiful Gate of Ac 3:2, 10 and also as the gate of the Palm Sunday entry of Jesus into Jerusalem. The Anonymous of Piacenza (Geyer pp. 170-171; LPPTS II-D, pp. 14-15; CCSL CLXXV, p. 163; WJP p. 83) tells of ascending by many steps from Gethsemane to the Gate of Jerusalem, and says: "This is the gate of the city which is connected with what was once the Beautiful Gate of the temple (*porta civitatis, quae cohaerit portae speciosae, quae fuit templi*), of which the threshold and floor still stand." Likewise Peter the Deacon (Geyer p. 108; WET p. 182) says that below the temple to the east was the Beautiful Gate where Peter healed the lame man, and where the Lord entered, seated upon the colt of the ass.

The references just given surely point to the part of the eastern Temple area enclosure wall opposite the Garden of Gethsemane, where the so-called Golden Gate now stands. While the name of the Beautiful Gate is rendered correctly in the Latin text of Ac 3:2, 10 and also in the Anonymous of Piacenza and Peter the Deacon as Porta Speciosa, in the course of time the Greek word ὡραία ("beautiful") evidently suggested the Latin word *aurea* and gave rise to the name Porta Aurea or Golden Gate.

In Herod's Temple this eastern gate was probably of the same plan as the two Huldah Gates (Nos. 190, 191), i.e., twin doorways led into a double vaulted vestibule from which there was access into the temple area. The original gate was no doubt largely destroyed in the destruction of the Temple in A.D. 70, then is believed to have been rebuilt by the empress Eudocia (in Jerusalem 444-460). Of the Byzantine structure the Anonymous of Piacenza (570, as quoted just above) saw only threshold and floor, but the gate must have been soon restored for in the year 628 the emperor Heraclius entered here when he came bearing the "true cross" recovered from the Persians. As noted just above, Peter the Deacon (1137) understood the same gate to be the place of the triumphal entry of Jesus as well as of the healing of the lame man, and in the twelfth and thirteenth centuries the Crusaders restored the gate again, but only opened it twice in the year, on Palm Sunday and on the feast of the Exaltation of the Holy Cross. Finally in 1538, when Suleiman the Magnificent was building the present walls of Jerusalem, he caused the Golden Gate to be walled up as it is until today (Kroll p. 309, col. 1). The explanation is supposed to be in the expectation, based on Ezk 44:1-3, that the gate will only be opened when Christ comes again.

As it exists the Golden Gate is a massive structure, 24.6 meters long and 17.25 meters wide. On either side of the great double gateway there are still in place two immense jamb stones, which probably remain from the building of Herod. In the Muslim cemetery immediately outside the present Golden Gate an accidental discovery in 1969 revealed an earlier "lower gate" and earlier wall, the wall of masonry like that of the eastern temple enclosure wall north of the "straight joint" (No. 189); therefore this gate and wall are at least prior to the Herodian period and possibly very early. The photograph is taken from within the Temple area and shows the vaulted vestibule (probably of Byzantine date) inside the present gate.

C. Schick, "Durch welches Thor ist Jesus Palmsonntag in Jerusalem eingezogen?" in zdpv 22 (1899), pp. 94-101; Spencer Corbett, "Some Observations on the Gateways to the Herodian Temple in Jerusalem," in peq 1952, pp. 7-14 and especially fig. 2 on p. 10; Bahat, *Plans*, 53; James Fleming, "The Undiscovered Gate beneath Jerusalem's Golden Gate," in bar 9.1 (Jan/Feb 1983), pp. 24-37. Photograph: JF.

• Yet, as Professor Vardaman points out, the use of ἱερόν is also to be noted at the Nabatean temple at Si'a in Syria. There the term is equivalent to the Aramaic *hirtha* (בירתא), both of which terms refer to the sanctuary (to Baal Shamayin) proper. This Nabatean temple at Si'a was in the territory of Herod and the temple was constructed at the same time Herod's Temple at Jerusalem was built. See M. de Vogüé, *Syria Centrale*, p. 38; cil ii, no. 163; Enno Littmann, *Princeton Expedition to Syria, Semitic Inscriptions*, pp. 85-90, for a fuller form of the Nabatean text. See also, for ἱερόν, Gerhard Kittel, *Theologisches Wörterbuch zum Neuen Testament*, vol. Θ-Κ, 232ff. (Eng. ed.).

194. Robinson's Arch

CONCERNING THE WESTERN SIDE of the Temple area Josephus writes (*Ant.* xv 11, 5 §410): "In the western part of the court there were four gates. The first led to the palace by a passage over the intervening ravine, two others led to the suburb, and the last led to the other part of the city, from which it was separated by many steps going down to the ravine and from here up again to the hill."

Middoth (ı 3) mentions only one gate on the west side, presumably the most important of the four specified by Josephus, and says that it was called Kiponus, a name which some think could have been derived from the name of Coponius, the first Roman procurator of Judea (Simons, *Jerusalem*, p. 405 n. 3; for other explanations see Mackowski pp. 131f.). The passage that led over the ravine and to the palace, according to the quotation from Josephus just given, is presumably the same as the bridge that connected the temple area with the Xystus (probably the gymnasium built by Jason, ıı Macc 4:9), later converted into a colonnaded promenade), and the same as the bridge that connected the Temple area with the upper city, which the same author mentions in *War* ıı 16, 3 §344 and vı 6, 2 §325. In two other passages (*Ant.* xıv 4, 2 §58; *War* ı 7, 2 §143) Josephus mentions the bridge that connected the Temple area with the city as in existence in the time of Pompey; therefore some such bridge was a feature of the approach to the Temple even before the rebuilding by Herod.

The gate from which this bridge led was no doubt the most important on the west side of the Temple area, and therefore probably the same as the Kiponus gate of *Middoth*. As the most important gate, Josephus (in the passage quoted above) mentions it first. The two other gates, which "led to the suburb," would have been farther north in the western enclosure wall to give access to the new northern suburb. The last gate, Josephus says, led to "the other part of the city." In distinction from the northern suburb and the western area with the royal palace, this must have been the southwestern region of the city, and this last gate was therefore somewhere to the south of the main gate (Simons, *Jerusalem*, p. 424; other hypothetical locations of the four gates are marked on the plan No. 181).

In 1838 Edward Robinson found several courses of stone projecting from the western Temple enclosure wall at a point twelve meters north of the southwestern angle. As shown in the photograph, these appear to be part of an ancient arch and they have been known ever since as Robinson's Arch. The stones are twenty or more feet in length and about five feet in thickness. They are an in-

194. Robinson's Arch

tegral part of the ancient wall, in contrast with the later stonework above. Measured along the wall the arch was over 15 meters long. From the curve of the arch its span, if complete, has been estimated at 12.8 meters. Robinson supposed the arch to have belonged to the bridge of which Josephus speaks in the passages cited above. Charles Warren dug shafts and galleries in a line west of the fragment and found a pier at the point to which the calculated span of the arch would reach, but beyond that found no evidence of further arches. Now from the modern Israeli excavations (No. 181) it is established that Robinson's Arch supported a large staircase that came from the Royal Portico, led across the street below, and turned at right angles to descend into the Tyropoeon Valley, where the Herodian shopping street ran through that valley alongside the temple area.

At the foot of the same southwestern corner of the Temple area an eight-foot-long broken stone was found, dressed on two sides and the top, to be the topmost stone of that corner, with an inscription in Hebrew which, as far as preserved, reads, "To the house of trumpeting. . . ." The reference is understood to be to the place on top of the Temple enclosure wall where a priest would stand to blow a trumpet to announce the beginning and the end of the Sabbath day.

Edward Robinson, *Biblical Researches in Palestine* (1856), I, pp. 287-289; Charles Warren, *Underground Jerusalem* (1876), pp. 310-316; Simons, *Jerusalem*, pp. 362-364, 424-425; Bahat, *Plans*, 48ab; Mazar, *Mountain of the Lord*, pp. 132, 135, 138; Ben-Dov, *Shadow of Temple*, pp. 95f., 121ff.; Aaron Demsky, "When the Priests Trumpeted the Onset of the Sabbath," in BAR 12.6 (Nov/Dec 1986), pp. 50-52. Photograph: courtesy Palestine Archaeological Museum.

195. Wilson's Arch

IN THE WESTERN Temple area enclosure wall 82 meters north of the southwestern angle is Barclay's Gate, named after the American who discovered it in 1848. Here there is an enormous lintel 7.5 meters in length and over two meters in height (Simons, *Jerusalem*, p. 364). The gateway of which it was a part is now walled in and extends deep underground. Behind it is a passage, only partly accessible, which undoubtedly once led up into the Temple area. A part of this passage has been made into a mosque called al-Buraq, the name coming from the traditional belief that here Muhammad tethered the horse al-Buraq on which he made his "night journey" (cf. No. 186) through the heavens (A. J. Wensinck, *A Handbook of Early Muhammadan Tradition* [1960], p. 40). From the same connections the gate is also called the Gate of the Prophet. Above it is a present-day portal in the enclosure wall of the Haram esh-

Sherif, called Bab el-Mugharibeh or Gate of the Moors. In location and relationships it would seem as if Barclay's Gate could well have been the fourth gate mentioned by Josephus in the quotation above (No. 194), namely, the gate which gave access to "the other part of the city," i.e., probably the southwestern region, and from which many steps went down into the Tyropoeon, and from there up again to the hill (Simons, *Jerusalem*, p. 424).

Just north of Barclay's Gate is the stretch of ancient Temple enclosure wall formerly called the Wailing Wall (No. 189) and beyond that, at a total distance of 100 meters from the southwestern angle of the Temple enclosure, is Wilson's Arch. At this point on the ground level above is the main entrance to the Temple area from the west, a double gate called Bab es-Salam or the Gate of Peace, and Bab es-Silsileh or the Gate of the Chain, the latter providing also the name of the main west-east street that reaches the Temple enclosure here, namely, the Street of the Gate of the Chain. Below ground under the Gate of the Chain is the ancient arch that has been called by his name ever since it was found in 1864 by Charles Wilson. In 1867 and later Charles Warren explored the arch and other subterranean vaults, passages, and chambers associated with it. He found that the bedrock of the Tyropoeon Valley was here at a depth of 80 feet beneath the present level of the Street of the Gate of the Chain, and the top of Wilson's Arch is itself about 10 feet beneath the street level. The arch is 13.4 meters or 43 feet wide and has a span of 12.8 meters or 42 feet, the same span calculated for Robinson's Arch (No. 194). Wilson (*The Recovery of Jerusalem*, p. 13) judged the arch to be of the same age as the wall at the Wailing Place, which would mean that it was a part of the Herodian Temple area. Probably because the arch is so perfectly preserved, Warren (ibid., p. 64) was inclined to attribute it to the fifth or sixth century. One large chamber associated with the arch which Warren, himself a member of the Masonic order, called the Masonic Hall, he thought (ibid., p. 68) to be perhaps as old as the Temple enclosure walls. This chamber is built of well-joined, square stones and at each corner there were pilasters with capitals, the one at the northeast angle being fairly well preserved.

The first scientific investigation of Wilson's Arch since Warren's work was conducted by William F. Stinespring in 1963, 1965, and 1966. He found that the arch, built entirely of undrafted stones, was an integral part of the ancient enclosure wall of the temple area. Therefore it was probably built by Herod and was a part of the bridge that Josephus (cf. above No. 194) describes as connecting the Temple area with the upper city including the Xystus and the palace. Since Josephus also mentions a bridge here in the time of Pompey, Herod's bridge probably replaced a smaller Maccabean bridge at this same location. As for the so-called Masonic Hall, the preliminary opinion is that this large chamber existed as far back as the Hellenistic period, perhaps in the time of Antiochus IV.

In the photograph the underside of the arch is shown, looking toward the north. In the curve of the arch at the right are rectangular indentations, which may have held timber supports when the arch was being built. The far end is blocked by the wall of a cistern, so that only 27 feet of the total width of 43 feet can be seen. At the right is the opening of a shaft dug by Warren. In current opinion, the Wilson's Arch of the Herodian period was destroyed and then rebuilt, probably by the Muslims (BAR 12.6 [Nov/Dec 1986], p. 31). Today, cleared out in its entirety the great arch provides a place for a simple Jewish prayer hall. Two shafts in the floor make it possible to look far down upon the foundations of the Temple enclosure wall.

Wilson and Warren, *The Recovery of Jerusalem* (1872), pp. 13, 58-72; William F. Stinespring, "Wilson's Arch Revisited," in BA 29 (1966), pp. 27-36; "Wilson's Arch and the Masonic Hall, Summer 1966," in BA 30 (1967), pp. 27-31; Bahat, *Plans*, 45; Mazar, *Mountain of the Lord*, pp. 217-222; Ben-Dov, *Shadow of Temple*, pp. 121f., 169-178. Photograph: courtesy Palestine Archaeological Museum.

196. In the Ruins of the Burnt House

IN ISRAELI EXCAVATIONS in 1969 and thereafter under Nahman Avigad and Meir Ben-Dov in the Jewish Quarter in the southeast of the Old City across the Tyropoeon Valley from the Western Wall of the Temple area, traces of many ruined houses were found from the time of the Second Temple before and during the destruction of Jerusalem (A.D. 70). Of these the most important are known as the Herodian Residence, and the Palatial Mansion (No. 215), as well as the Burnt House. The ruins of the Burnt House, shown in the present photograph, represent the basement level of the house, with an entrance hall, four rooms, a kitchen, and a pool. The house belonged to a member of the Kathros family, from which family the high priests were chosen. Plain evidences of the fire that destroyed the building in the Roman conquest are still to be seen.

In the extreme south of the Jewish Quarter Avigad and Ben-Dov found the scanty but massive remains of a very large basilica, the southeastern corner of which projects outside the present Turkish south wall of the Old City. The probable plan of the church was with nave and two side aisles and three apses to the east. With a length of about 116 meters in all, portions of two walls at the west mark the narthex and entrance almost back on the line of the *cardo maximus*. Plainly the church corresponds with the large basilica shown in exactly the same position in the Madaba Mosaic of Jerusalem (No. 229). In all there was a complex of associated buildings, and subterranean vaults supported a section where the hill sloped off. A Greek inscription affixed in the vaults, accompanied by a large cross, stated that this was the work of the emperor Justinian and gave a date for the vaults probably equivalent to A.D. 549/550. There is no doubt that this is the church of Justinian that was dedicated six years before (543) and written about at length by Procopius (560) with these words at the beginning of his description (*Buildings* V 6): "And in Jerusalem he [Justinian] dedicated to the Mother of God (*Theotokos*) a shrine with which no other can be compared. This is called by the natives the 'New Church.' "

Known in full, therefore, as the New Church of St. Mary, Mother of God, the name was commonly abbreviated as the "Nea" (Greek for "New"). The church was

195. Wilson's Arch

196. In the Ruins of the Burnt House

burned by the Persians in A.D. 614 (see below, No. 231) and destroyed by earthquake in the eighth century (Ovadiah, *Corpus Supplementum*, p. 222, no. 24).

Bahat, *Plans*, 37c, 39a; Avigad, *Discovering Jerusalem*, pp. 120ff. for the Burnt House, and pp. 229-246 for the Nea Church; also Avigad, "Jerusalem in Flames—The Burnt House Captures a Moment in Time," in BAR 9.6 (Nov/Dec 1983), pp. 66-72; for the Nea Church also Ben-Dov, *Shadow of Temple*, pp. 233-241. Photograph: JF.

197. Looking toward the Northwestern Corner of the Temple Area

AS FOR THE NORTH SIDE of the Temple area, we have seen (No. 190) that Josephus (*War* II 19, 5 §537; VI 4, 1 §222) says that there was a gate there, and that *Middoth* (I 3) gives the name of the portal on the north side as the Tadi Gate, a name the meaning of which is unknown. In the absence of any ancient architectural remains which can be identified with such a gate, other evidence must be sought. Other than Josephus it is Nehemiah who gives the most detailed information on the topography of Jerusalem. Nehemiah came to Jerusalem to rebuild the walls in the twentieth year of Artaxerxes (Neh 2:1) and, assuming that this was Artaxerxes I (FLAP p. 238), the date was 445/444 B.C. The account of the rebuilding in Neh 3 begins and ends with the Sheep Gate. As we near the end of the circuit with Nehemiah we are obviously coming north from Ophel (3:27) and we encounter the East Gate (3:29), then the Hammiph-

kad Gate, translated Muster Gate in the RSV, and then "the upper chamber of the corner" (3:31). The "corner" mentioned in this sequence must be the northeast corner of the city wall. After that the next point specified is the Sheep Gate (3:32). Beyond the Sheep Gate, i.e., farther westward, in Nehemiah's description we come "as far as the Tower of the Hundred, as far as the Tower of Hananel" (3:1), after which we come to the Fish Gate (3:3). Likewise in Neh 12:39 the reverse sequence, i.e., from west to east, is the Fish Gate, the Tower of Hananel, the Tower of the Hundred, and the Sheep Gate. The sequence makes it most probable that the Fish Gate was in the north wall and this is at least in harmony with the fact that the fish merchants in Jerusalem at the time were men of Tyre (Neh 13:16), a city to the north. So the Sheep Gate was between the northeastern angle of the city wall and certain points farther west along the northern city wall, accordingly it was probably only a little way west of the northeastern angle. Perhaps, then, there was some correspondence between the Tadi Gate on the north side of the Temple enclosure and this Sheep Gate. At any rate the persistence of tradition is such that the Jerusalem sheep market is still held at the northeastern corner of the Old City (Mackowski pp. 54f.).

By the same reasoning the Tower of the Hundred and the Tower of Hananel could well have been somewhere in the vicinity of the northwestern corner of the Temple area. At least the first of these names has a probable military connotation, and it is a reasonable surmise (Simons, *Jerusalem*, p. 429 n. 2) that the two towers were the eastern and western towers of a fortification over-

197. Looking Toward the Northwestern Corner of the Temple Area

looking the Temple which Neh 2:8 calls "the castle (בירה) which appertaineth to the house" (ASV), i.e., "the fortress of the temple" (RSV). As we have already observed (No. 181), this fortress was evidently replaced by the Hasmonean citadel called Baris (from the Hebrew *birah*) and then by the famous Antonia of Herod (Josephus, *Ant.* xv 11, 4 §§403, 409).

In the northwestern corner of the Temple area there is still evidence of how the terrain rose in that direction toward the hill on which the Antonia stood. The photograph looks toward that corner of the area and shows the minaret (el-Gawanimeh) at the extreme northwestern angle and the large building of the Muslim Omariyyah School (on the site of earlier Turkish barracks) to the east of it. In that area the native rock rises to the surface and slopes upward toward the angle, while vertical scarps are cut in it both to the east and to the south of the minaret. Concerning the Antonia more will be said later (Nos. 215ff.).

Simons, *Jerusalem*, pp. 342f., 347, 429ff. Photograph: JF.

198. The Tower of David

AS WE HAVE SEEN (NO. 173), the southwestern hill of Jerusalem is the highest of the city's hills and is separated by a cross valley from the northwestern hill. The point at the northwestern corner of the southwestern hill, which commands the saddle made by the cross valley between the southwestern hill and the northwestern hill, was obviously of great strategic importance. It is undoubtedly to this commanding high point that Josephus refers when he speaks (*War* v 4, 4 §173) of the crest of a lofty hill on which Herod the Great erected three mighty towers (*War* v 4, 3 §§161-171). One tower was called Hippicus after a friend of Herod who is otherwise unmentioned but was evidently deceased by this time. This tower had a quadrangular base that measured 25 cubits on each side and was solid throughout to a height of 30 cubits. Above this were a reservoir, a double-roofed chamber, and turrets and battlements, making the total height of the tower 80 cubits. The second tower was named for Herod's brother Phasael, who fell prisoner to the Parthians and took his own life (*War* I 13, 10 §271). This tower was 40 cubits in length and breadth, and 40 cubits also in the height of its solid base. Above this were sumptuous apartments, and the tower as a whole had the appearance of a palace. Its total height was about 90 cubits, and Josephus even compared it with the Pharos tower at Alexandria (cf. *War* IV 10, 5 §613). The third tower bore the name of Mariamme, a loved wife whom Herod put to death (*War* I 22, 5 §§443-444; *Ant.* xv 7, 4ff. §§218ff.). This tower was only 20 cubits in length and breadth and 55 cubits in height, but in its residential quarters was the most luxuriously appointed of all. The

215

198. The Tower of David

stones of these towers, Josephus says (*War* v 4, 4 §§174-175), were cut of white marble, each block 20 cubits long, 10 cubits broad, and 5 cubits deep, all so well joined together that each tower seemed like one natural rock.

Josephus came to his description of the three towers, from which we have excerpted the preceding information, from mention (*War* v 4, 3 §159) of a tower called Psephinus, which was at the northwestern angle of the "third wall" (cf. No. 201), therefore he probably lists the towers from west to east, Hippicus, Phasael, and Mariamme. He also says (*War* v §§161, 173) that they were all three built into what he calls "the old wall." To the south of the towers Herod built his palace (*War* v 4, 4 §§176-183). This was enclosed within a wall of its own, had banquet halls and guest chambers, cloisters and gardens. So Herod secured his control of Jerusalem by the two palace-fortresses which we have now described, his palace with the adjacent three great towers here on the hill dominating the city, and the Antonia overlooking and commanding the Temple area (*War* v 5, 8 §245; *Ant.* xv 8, 5 §292). When Titus took Jerusalem (A.D.

70) he razed Antonia (*War* vi 2, 1 §93) but left standing the loftiest of the towers, Phasael, Hippicus, and Mariamme (which Josephus names here in the order of their height), as well as the portion of the wall enclosing the city on the west (*War* vii 1, 1 §§1-2). The towers were to show to posterity the kind of formidable defenses the Romans had overcome, the wall was to provide an encampment for the garrison that was to remain, namely, the Tenth Legion, called Fretensis (cf. No. 131).

Not only the Romans but also the Arabs, the Crusaders, and the Mamluke and Turkish governors continued to use the site of Herod's palace as the seat of government in Jerusalem, and the place is still known today as the Citadel of the city. Excavations in the Citadel were conducted from 1934 to 1948 by C. N. Johns. As it stands the present castle is mainly Mamluke work of the fourteenth century, but its plan follows that of the Crusader castle of the twelfth century. Among the several towers of this castle the most imposing is the one in the northeastern angle which has been known, at least since the time of the Crusaders, as the Tower of David. In fact, Arculf (670) already calls the adjacent gate the Gate of

David (Geyer pp. 224, 242; LPPTS III-A, pp. 2, 19; CCSL CLXXV, pp. 185, 197; WJP pp. 95, 100), so the identification probably goes back that far or farther. The photograph shows the northwestern angle of this tower. The lower courses of stonework, which have been followed further underground by excavation, are of large drafted blocks like the stones in the ancient enclosure wall of the Temple area (No. 189) and, like those, are almost surely of Herodian origin. The material is limestone, which was white when it was cut and could easily have been called white marble by Josephus. The jointing is very close, which also accords with the statement of Josephus. The figures given by Josephus for the size of the stones in the towers are equivalent to approximately 9 by 4 by 2 meters, but the largest of the presently visible stones are only about half that size; yet they are not small, for the largest ones wiegh 10 tons and the average weight is 5 tons. As revealed by excavation the substructure of the Tower of David consists of sixteen courses in all. The total height of these courses is 19.7 meters, which is only a little less than the 40 cubits or 21 meters which Josephus gives as the height of the solid base of the Phasael tower. The base measurement of the Tower of David, 22 by 17 meters, is also not far from the same figure of 40 cubits given by Josephus for the length and breadth of Phasael. From these correspondences it is probable that the substructure of the Tower of David is actually the remaining base of Phasael. Hippicus, then, stood to the west of it, probably close to the present Jaffa Gate, and Mariamme must have been to the east. In the excavations Johns found that the base of the Tower of David was set into a more ancient wall of Hasmonean date, which agrees with the statement of Josephus that all three towers were built into "the old wall."

C. N. Johns in PEQ 1940, pp. 36-56; and in QDAP 5 (1936), pp. 127-131; 6 (1938), p. 214; 9 (1942), pp. 207-209; 13 (1948), pp. 170-171; 14 (1950), pp. 121-190; Simons, *Jerusalem*, pp. 265-271; R. Pearce S. Hubbard in PEQ 1966, p. 133; Mazar, *Mountain of the Lord*, p. 30; Bahat, *Plans*, 17 (Jaffa Gate), 18ab and 20a (Citadel), 19 (David's Tower). Photograph: courtesy École Biblique et Archéologique Française.

199. Plan of Western and Southern Sections of the First Wall of Jerusalem

THE FOREGOING DISCUSSION (NOS. 180ff.) has provided positive information concerning the temple area and the adjacent Antonia, and the palace of Herod with the three great towers nearby: Hippicus, Phasael, and Mariamme. Of temple, Antonia, and palace Josephus wrote (*War* v 5,8 §245): "If the temple lay as a fortress over the city, Antonia dominated the temple, and the occupants of that post were the guards of all

three; the upper town had its own fortress–Herod's palace." These points also provide the reference points from which to understand what Josephus says (*War* v 4, 1-3 §§136ff.) about the walls of the city.

There were, in the time of Josephus, three walls. Of the three, the most ancient (ἀρχαῖον), Josephus says (*War* v 4, 2 §§142-145), was built by David and Solomon and the kings after them. The first stretch of this First Wall, as it is now commonly called, is described thus by Josephus: "Beginning on the north at the tower called Hippicus, it extended to the Xystus, and then joining the council-chamber terminated at the western portico of the temple."

We have already seen (No. 198) that the tower of Hippicus probably stood near the present Jaffa Gate, and that the adjacent tower of Phasael is probably the present Tower of David. Also we have noted the statement of Josephus (*War* v 4, 3 §§161, 173) that the three towers, Hippicus, Phasael, and Mariamme, were built by King Herod into "the old wall," which must be this same "first wall," and that portions of a wall of Hasmonean date have in fact been found at the base of the Tower of David. This gives virtually positive identification, therefore, for the beginning point of the first wall as described by Josephus. The Xystus was the gymnasium and later promenade connected by bridge with the Temple area (*War* II 16, 3 §344), therefore it lay somewhere westward across the Tyropoeon from the main west gate of the Temple area, and the latter was probably about at the present Gate of the Chain (cf. Nos. 194f.). The council-chamber (βουλή), not encountered previously, was a meeting place of the Sanhedrin, called in the Mishna by a name usually translated as the Chamber of Hewn Stone, but perhaps rather to be rendered the Chamber beside the Xystus (SHJP Vermes/Millar II, pp. 223f.). *Middoth* v 4 places the chamber to the south in the Temple court, but the description by Josephus sounds more as if it were between the Xystus and the Temple area enclosure wall. The western portico of the Temple is, of course, the colonnaded porch along the western side of the Temple area. Therewith we are given a reasonably plain indication of the route of the first wall. It began at Hippicus, i.e., in the vicinity of the present Jaffa Gate, ran eastward along the north edge of the southwestern hill, parallel to the cross valley and probably parallel to and not far south of the present David Street and Street of the Gate of the Chain (*Tariq Bab es-Silsila*), passed and enclosed the Xystus and the council-chamber, and reached the western enclosure wall and western portico of the Temple area at Wilson's Arch and the present Gate of the Chain, a total length of wall of approximately 500 meters.

Actual remains of this east-west stretch of the first wall on the northern side of Jerusalem have been found in the excavations by Nahman Avigad (No. 196) in the Jewish Quarter of the Old City (Avigad, *Discovering Jerusalem*, pp. 50-54, 70f., map 8 on pp. 32f. and plan 30 on p. 50). The place is about 275 meters west of the Western Wall of the temple area, at a spot (marked W on map 8) some 35 meters south of the Street of the Gate of the Chain and a short distance prior to the Jewish Quarter street (more precisely at the corner of Shonei Halakhah and Pelugat Hakotal Streets). Uncovered here, and preserved in an underground area some 15 meters below the present street level, are two massive stone block structures. One is a 9-meter-square tower dated to the Hasmonean period, and it is built against the northeast corner of an Israelite tower of the eighth-seventh century

B.C., its walls 4-5 meters thick and standing to a height of 8 meters. At the foot of this latter tower were charred wood and ashes, as well as four iron arrowheads of the type common in this country in Israelite times, and one bronze arrowhead of the type used by foreign armies from the late seventh century onward, evidence no doubt of the conquest of Jerusalem in 586 B.C. by the Babylonians, who burned the city and broke down the walls (II K 25:9-10). Thus a city wall on this line was indeed "ancient," as Josephus said, and was rebuilt on the same line four hundred years later by the Hasmoneans.

This then was the line of the First Wall from the Western Wall of the Temple in the east to the Towers of Herod in the west, a wall built to protect Jerusalem on

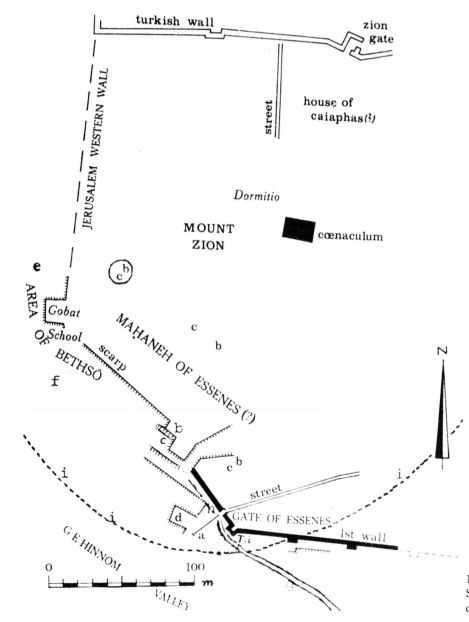

199. Plan of Western and Southern Sections of the First Wall of Jerusalem

its northern side. Now we continue with Josephus at the point of the Hippicus tower in his description of the further course of the First Wall:

> Beginning at the same point [the Hippicus tower] in the other direction, westward (πρὸς δύσιν, i.e., facing west), it descended past the place called Bethso (Βηθσώ) to the gate of the Essenes (τὴν Ἐσσηνῶν πύλην), then turned southwards (πρὸς νότον, i.e., facing south) above (ὑπέρ) the fountain of Siloam; thence it again inclined to the east (πρὸς ἀνατολήν, i.e., facing east) towards Solomon's pool, and after passing a spot which they call Ophlas [Ophel, cf. No. 173], finally joined the eastern portico of the temple.

In general this description means that where the wall was facing west it ran southward along the edge of the Hinnom Valley on the west side of Jerusalem, and where it was facing south it continued to follow the same valley as that valley swung eastward on the south side of the city. As for the first north-south stretch, portions of the wall were found along this line in 1934-1948 by C. N. Johns and in 1968-1969 by Ruth Amiran and A. Eitan in the courtyard of the Citadel near the Jaffa Gate, with building phases recognized in the Early Hellenistic period, the Hasmonean period, and in the time of Herod the Great (Amiran and Eitan in *Jerusalem Revealed*, pp. 52-54); and in 1971 and 1975-1976 by Dan Bahat and Magen Broshi in the Armenian Garden south of the Citadel, where long continuous segments of the same wall were uncovered, attributable likewise to the Hasmonean period, and running directly alongside the present west wall of the Old City as built by Suleiman the Magnificent in the sixteenth century (Bahat and Broshi in *Jerusalem Revealed*, pp. 55f.; Broshi, "Along Jerusalem's Walls," in BA 40 [1977], pp. 11-17; Bahat, *Plans*, 20bc, 21b; AJPA 2-5, 2-6). As for the last stretch of the wall described by Josephus in relation to the pools of Siloam and of Solomon, that has been discussed above (No. 179). In the present context we are interested in the connection of the wall with Bethso and the Gate of the Essenes.

As explained already (No. 173), at least from early Christian times the entire southwestern hill of Jerusalem has been considered to be the location of Mount Zion/Sion (which was originally the southeastern hill), although at present the name is sometimes applied in particular only to that part of the hill which lies outside the present city wall in the area of the Zion Gate (Bahat, *Plans*, 27, 28, 35b), with the Hinnom Valley on the west and south and the Tyropoeon Valley to the east. In Josephus' description the first wall is evidently enclosing this area, and this is now archeologically confirmed. Points of reference of immediate concern are the Institute of Holy Land Studies, formerly the Bishop Gobat School, on the southwest side and the Protestant ceme-

tery on the south side of the area. Exploring the area in 1874 on behalf of the newly formed Palestine Exploration Fund, Henry Maudsley uncovered a long scarp of perpendicularly cut rock and a quantity of large dressed stones (now preserved in a retaining wall near the Institute of Holy Land Studies), all probably from the first wall as described by Josephus. In continuation of this work F. J. Bliss reported in 1895 the finding of a longer stretch of wall, a tower (still to be seen beside the new road Hativat Yerushalayim), a gate eight feet wide, with four layers of superimposed sills showing use for a long time, and a paved street leading to the northeast (AJPA 2-7). Although these materials found in 1895 became covered afterward with debris, the gate has been located and excavated again by Bargil Pixner; the place is only a few yards to the southeast of the grave of the famous Egyptologist W. R. Flinders Petrie in the Protestant cemetery (Mackowski pp. 46, 62f.). This must be the Gate of the Essenes, and with the name of such a gate in the city wall there is little doubt that there was a "camp" (מחנה , *maḥaneh*) of the Essenes here within the wall. By way of comparison for a gate taking its name from a group settlement to which it led, the present Dung Gate near the Temple area was formerly called the Bab el Magribeh from the Muslims from Maghreb in West Africa who were settled there (Meistermann p. 213; Bahat, *Plans*, 37b). As for Bethso, the word is recognized as a Greek rendering of a Hebrew term (בית צואה , *bethso'ah*) meaning "house of excrement" (for the latter word see Ezk 4:12, and for the requirement that the place of excrement be outside the camp see Dt 23:12-14), and must designate a latrine area of the Essenes outside the wall (G. Dalman, *Jerusalem und sein Gelände* [Gütersloh: Bertelsmann, 1930], pp. 86f.). In the Temple Scroll from Qumran (Yadin, *The Temple Scroll*, 1, pp. 294-304; 2, pp. 199f.; 3, pl. 61, col. XLVI, lines 13-16) there is reference to an area of the same purpose as the Bethso of Josephus, an area which the Temple Scroll requires to be outside the city (Yadin, *The Temple Scroll*, 1, pp. 294-304). Also in the Copper Scroll from Qumran there is mention of an area called by the similar name of So' (שוא), and this was probably somewhere close to the southwest corner of Jerusalem and outside the wall (John Marco Allegro, *The Treasure of the Copper Scroll* [Garden City, N.Y.: Doubleday, 1960], pp. 46f., col. VIII, 37-38; p. 92; pp. 155f. n. 178; p. 177, fig. 9). Both inside and outside the wall in the area of the Gate of the Essenes there are also ritual baths (*mikvaoth*) and cisterns. In the present plan the chief features are named and in addition there are these references by letter: (a) drain and outlet; (b) baths; (c) cisterns; (d) scarp and counterscarp before gate; (e) fallow part of So'; (f) irrigated part of So'; (g) Essene path leading to Gehinnom Valley; (h) path to Bethso in northwesterly direction; (i) aqueduct; (T.i) tower I. In the plan in AJPA, Nos. 2-7 mark the wall, tower, and gate of the present discussion.

Claude R. Conder, "The Rock Scarp of Zion," in PEFQS January 1875, pp. 7-11, 81-89; F. J. Bliss, "Third Report on Excavations of Jerusalem," in PEFQS 1895, pp. 9-13; Y. Yadin, "The Gate of the Essenes and the Temple Scroll," in *Jerusalem Revealed*, pp. 90f.; Bargil Pixner, "An Essene Quarter on Mount Zion?" in *Studia Hierosolymitana* I (1976), pp. 245-285. Plan: from Pixner in *Studia Hierosolymitana* I (1976), p. 240, courtesy Studium Biblicum Franciscanum, Jerusalem.

200. The Cardo Maximus of Jerusalem

OF THE THREE WALLS of Jerusalem Josephus describes the second in a single sentence (*War* v 4, 2 §146): "The second wall started from the gate in the first wall which they called Gennath, and, enclosing only the northern district of the town, went up as far as Antonia."

A little later (*War* v 4, 3 §158) he states that this "middle wall" (as he here calls it) had fourteen towers, which compares with sixty in the old wall and ninety in the third wall. Both the mention of "only" one district of Jerusalem as enclosed by the second wall, and the enumeration of a relatively small number of towers in it, suggest that the second wall was of relatively short length. Although Josephus does not say who built the second wall, it was obviously later than the first one since it began from a gate in that wall. It was also obviously earlier than the third wall, which was built by King Agrippa c.

A.D. 41 (see No. 201) and, like the First Wall in its later form may perhaps be attributed to the Hasmoneans (M. Avi-Yonah in *Jerusalem Revealed*, p. 11). Probably both this wall and the first wall constituted the fortifications for the restoration of which Julius Caesar issued a decree of permission in 44 B.C. (*Ant.* XIV 10, 5 §200); at any rate both walls must have been in existence in the time of Jesus.

The gate called Gennath is not mentioned elsewhere by Josephus, but since he says plainly that it was in the first wall, and that the second wall which started from it went on up to Antonia, it must have been somewhere in the east-west stretch of the first wall on the north side of the city, i.e., somewhere in the wall's more or less direct line between Hippicus and the temple area. Since Josephus otherwise describes both the first wall and the third wall as beginning at the tower Hippicus, it is not likely that the second wall began at or near Hippicus or Phasael or Mariamme; in that case he would surely have been more likely again to use one of the great and frequently mentioned towers as the point of reference. Therefore the gate in question must have been a considerable distance east of the towers.

In the attempt to find the probable location of the Gennath Gate more precisely, and also the line of the Second Wall which extended from it, archeological investigations have provided clues. Above (No. 199) we have described the remains of the First Wall found by Avigad in the Jewish Quarter of the Old City. In the continuation of that archeological work between 1975

200. The Cardo Maximus

and 1978 further segments of the same wall were found on the same line some 50 meters to the west. The spot is between parallel Jewish Quarter Street and Habad Street, near their northern ends and a little ways south of David Street.

Here the excavation was intended in the first place as a part of a project for tracing the *cardo maximus* of Jerusalem (Avigad, *Discovering Jerusalem*, pp. 213-229). As explained already (No. 74), in a Roman and Byzantine city the *cardo maximus* was the main north-south street and was intersected by the main west-east street, known from the customary position of the tenth cohort (*decumanus*) of a Roman legion at the main gate (*decumana*) of a Roman military camp as the *decumanus maximus*. In the Madaba Mosaic Map depiction of Byzantine Jerusalem (No. 229) the *cardo* is a colonnaded street extending from a place inside what is now the Damascus Gate in the north, past the Holy Sepulcher Church, to the Nea Church (No. 196) in the south, while the *decumanus* is a street running eastward from what is now the Jaffa Gate. In terms of modern streets the course of the *cardo* was from the Damascus Gate southward through the Suq Khan ez-Zeit (Bahat, *Plans*, 90d), down three parallel market streets and, below David Street, on down between the two parallel streets called Jewish Quarter Street and Habad Street; while the course of the *decumanus* was eastward along David Street and the Street of the Gate of the Chain, with a tetrapylon in the quarter known as al-Bashurah, possibly at the present Qahwe el-'Umdan, the Coffeehouse of the Columns (Mackowski p. 67).

Corresponding with the preceding description and the Madaba Map depiction, extensive sections of the *cardo* were found in the Avigad excavations in the Jewish Quarter on the line between Jewish Quarter Street and Habad Street from south of David Street on down to opposite the Hurvah and Ramban Synagogues (Avigad, *Discovering Jerusalem*, map p. 32; Murphy-O'Connor pp. 53-55 and fig. 17; AJPA 3-12). Here the *cardo* is about 22.5 meters wide, bordered on the west by a wall of dressed stones and on the east by an arcade with arches resting on square pillars. Two rows of columns (some shown in the present photograph) line the central street, 12 meters wide, and there was a roofed portico on either side. With only Byzantine pottery found beneath pavement, it was the conclusion of the excavators that this whole southern stretch of the *cardo* dated only from Byzantine rather than Roman times, the suggestion being that the builder may have been Justinian (A.D. 527-565), the builder of the Nea church, one purpose being to connect the new church with the Church of the Holy Sepulcher at the middle of the northern section of the *cardo*.

We return now to the Jewish Quarter and Habad Streets at a point a short distance south of David Street,

where the northernmost portion of this whole southern stretch of the *cardo* was found (Avigad, *Discovering Jerusalem*, pp. 67-69, plans 30, 38). Here beneath the Byzantine pavement four sections of ancient walls were brought to light. One (no. 3 in Avigad, ibid., p. 50, plan 30) is from the Israelite period, like the Israelite tower in the section of the First Wall 50 meters to the east, three others (nos. 5-7 in the plan) are ascribed to the late Hellenistic or Hasmonean period, like the Hasmonean tower in the same spot 50 meters to the east. Here also, then, are remains of the First Wall spanning time from the Israelite to the Hasmonean period. At this point the combined sections nos. 5-6 and section no. 7 are separated by a gap, from which the excavator concludes that this was a gate and suggests that it may in fact be identified with the Gennath Gate (ibid., p. 69).

That the Gennath Gate, according to this identification, is directly under the later *cardo maximus* is especially significant because the *cardo* and the *decumanus* were most probably laid out on the lines of already existing streets of older Jerusalem (Wilkinson in *Levant* 7 [1975], pp. 118ff.), and we may thus picture a street leading up to this gate along the line of the *cardo* already in the time of Jesus. From the gate the Second Wall, to accord with Josephus' description, would have led on northward and then at some point have bent off to extend to the Antonia. Specifically the south-north line could have been that of the present bazaar streets, Suq el-'Attarin and Suq Khan ez-Zeit, up to the traditional site of the Seventh Station of the Cross, and the west-east line from that point along the Via Dolorosa (No. 222) to the Fifth Station at el-Wad Street (Mackowski p. 49), and this is substantially the course of the Second Wall in our Plan (No, 173). Such a course would indeed enclose a "northern district" of the city, as Josephus says, and would also be reasonable from the point of view of topographical and defense considerations (C. T. Norris in PEQ 1946, pp. 19-37, against N. P. Clarke in PEQ 1944, pp. 199-212).

On this course the Second Wall would have run in its south-north section past the east side of the present Muristan and Church of the Holy Sepulcher. The Muristan is a large relatively open area, north of David Street and south of the Church of the Holy Sepulcher, about 170 yards long and 150 yards wide (Bahat, *Plans*, 62, 63). In the Middle Ages there were pilgrim inns and hospitals in this space, particularly institutions of the Knights of St. John (Hospitalers). Later under the Muslims one hospital was called by the Arabic-Persian name Muristan, and this name was later applied to the whole plot of ground. In the northeast corner of the area was the Church of Santa Maria Latina, built in 1030. This was replaced in 1898 by the German Lutheran *Erlöserkirche* or Church of the Redeemer, built along the lines of the original church, with a high tower which is a prominent landmark in present-day Jerusalem (cf. No. 174). Outside of the Muristan but not very far to the north and east of the Church of the Redeemer is the Russian Alexander Hospice, and north and west of it is an Ethiopian monastery. The Russian hospice is just to the east of the Church of the Holy Sepulcher and the Ethiopian monastery is to the northeast of the church (Murphy-O'Connor p. 36, fig. 9, A, B, D; Kroll p. 375, abb. 300).

In 1961 and later Kathleen M. Kenyon excavated in a small area in the Muristan (her Site C), belonging to the Order of St. John, due south of the Church of the Holy Sepulcher and north of David Street (which presumably approximates the line of the First Wall). A deep pit was dug here which reached bedrock at a depth of fifteen meters. At the bottom of the pit there was a rock quarry, with pottery of the seventh century B.C. Above this was a large fill containing pottery, most of which was of the first century of the Christian era, with a little which was probably later, i.e., of the beginning of the second century. This fill can well be explained as a part of the work of Hadrian leveling up the area in the course of building Aelia Capitolina. Since a quarry would naturally not be inside a city, this site must have been outside the seventh century B.C. town. Since there are no buildings or occupation layers between the pottery and the large fill, the area must have remained vacant until the construction of Aelia Capitolina (Kenyon in PEQ 1964, pp. 14-16; 1966, p. 86, fig. 4; and her Jerusalem, pp. 151-154 with pls. 70-72). Likewise excavation in 1970-1971 by Ute Lux in the Muristan beneath the Church of the Redeemer confirmed that this area was a quarry outside the walled city in Second Temple times (Lux in ZDPV 88 [1972], pp. 185-201). Since the area explored by Kathleen Kenyon and Ute Lux is directly south of the Church of the Holy Sepulcher, the site of the church must also have been outside the city in those times. In addition Charles Coüasnon, in his work at the Church of the Holy Sepulcher (No. 225), excavated a section just south of the place of the tomb of Jesus in the church above and there too found that this area was used as a stone quarry, with pottery dating to the seventh century B.C. (Bruce E. Schein in BA 44 [1981], p. 24).

Further evidence that the area in question was outside the city is in rock-hewn tombs under the Church of the Holy Sepulcher and others which were found already in 1885 under the Ethiopian monastery to the northwest of the Russian Alexander Hospice (C. Schick in PEFQS 1887, pp. 154f. and accompanying plans; and in PEFQS 1893, p. 192). When the third wall of Herod Agrippa I (A.D. 41-44) was built (No. 201) this area was enclosed within the city, but prior to that time it is plain that it was first a quarry and later a place of tombs cut in the

rock walls. That the area also became a place of plants and trees is shown by the fact that the gate through which one went out to it was called the Gennath Gate. This name (Γεννάθ), which Josephus gives us, is evidently derived from the Hebrew word for "garden," which appears, for example, in the form גנת in Est 1:5, etc., hence this was the Garden Gate.

> John Wilkinson, "The Streets of Jerusalem," in *Levant* 7 (1975), pp. 118-136; Rivka Gonen, "Keeping Jerusalem's Past Alive," in BAR 7.4 (July/Aug 1981), pp. 16-18 (about the *cardo*); Kathleen M. Kenyon, "Excavations in Jerusalem," in PEQ 1962, pp. 72-89; 1963, pp. 7-21; 1964, pp. 7-18; 1965, pp. 9-20; 1966, pp. 73-88; Ute Lux, "Vorläufiger Bericht Über die Ausgrabung unter der Erlöserkirche im Muristan in der Altstadt von Jerusalem in den Jahren 1970 und 1971," in ZDPV 88 (1972), pp. 185-201; Karel J. H. Vriezen, "Zweiter vorläufiger Bericht über die Ausgrabung unter der Erlöserkirche im Muristan in der Altstadt von Jerusalem (1972-74)," in ZDPV 94 (1978), pp. 76-81; Bruce E. Schein, "The Second Wall of Jerusalem," in BA 44 (1981), pp. 21-26. Photograph: JF.

201. Ancient Wall and Arch beside the Damascus Gate

THE THIRD WALL of Jerusalem is described thus by Josephus (*War* v 4, 2 §§147-148):

> The third began at the tower Hippicus, whence it stretched northwards to the tower Psephinus, and then descending opposite (ἀντικρύ) the monuments of Helena (queen of Adiabene and daughter of king Izates), and proceeding through the royal caverns (διὰ σπηλαίων βασιλικῶν) it bent round a corner tower over against the so-called Fuller's tomb and joining the ancient rampart terminated at the valley called Kedron. This wall was built by Agrippa to enclose the later additions to the city, which were quite unprotected; for the town, overflowing with inhabitants, had gradually crept beyond the ramparts.

The Agrippa mentioned is Herod Agrippa I (A.D. 41-44), and Josephus also states (*War* v 4, 2 §152) that after the king had laid only the foundations of the wall he desisted from the project because he feared that the emperor Claudius (A.D. 41-54) might suspect that he had revolutionary designs. Another passage (*Ant.* XIX 7, 2 §§326-327) states that Claudius, for the same reason, ordered him to stop. Still another passage (*War* II 11, 6 §219) says that Agrippa died at Caesarea (A.D. 44) before his work reached its projected height. In the first passage cited Josephus goes on (*War* v 4, 2 §155) to say that the Jews subsequently completed the work which Agrippa had not finished. Since he says that at that time the wall was "hurriedly erected by the Jews," it seems likely that this was not done until the great war with the

201. Ancient Wall and Arch beside the Damascus Gate

Romans was imminent and under the pressure of that emergency. As thus completed the wall rose to a height of twenty cubits with battlements of two cubits and bulwarks of three cubits, making a total height of twenty-five cubits. When Titus attacked Jerusalem, coming from the north, he therefore confronted a series of three walls. At this point, in his narrative of how Titus selected a spot against which to direct his attack, Josephus (*War* v 6 §§259-260) mentions all three walls, but speaks of them now in reverse order—the first, second, and third from the point of view of Titus: "Baffled at all other points, the ravines rendering access impossible, while beyond them the first wall seemed too solid for his engines, he decided to make the assault opposite the tomb of John the high priest; for here the first line of ramparts was on the lower ground, and the second was disconnected with it, the builders having neglected to fortify the sparsely populated portions of the new town, while there was an easy approach to the third wall, through which his intention was to capture the upper town and so, by way of Antonia, the temple."

Of the points mentioned in Josephus' formal description of the third wall from which we may hope to get an idea of its course, the tower of Hippicus at one end and the Kidron Valley at the other are of course well known. Proceeding from Hippicus the next point mentioned is the tower Psephinus. According to another reference in Josephus (*War* v 4, 3 §§159-160) this tower was at the northwest angle of the third wall and Titus placed his camp opposite it; the tower was octagonal in form, seventy cubits high, and from it one could see both Arabia

and the utmost limits of Hebrew territory as far as the sea. The northwest corner of the present north wall of Jerusalem is indeed on the high point of the northwestern hill and at a likely place for a high tower with a far-reaching view, even if this view were not quite as extensive as that described by Josephus. At this place just inside the wall there are the remains of a tower, built of very large stones. The tower is known as Qasr Jalud or the Castle of Goliath because of the tradition that it was here that David slew Goliath, and it is also called Tancred's Tower because it was here that the Crusader Tancred broke through the wall in the capture of Jerusalem in 1099. As studied in excavations in 1971-1972 (D. Bahat and M. Ben-Ari in *Jerusalem Revealed*, pp. 109f.; Bahat, *Plans*, 85b) the tower was about 35 by 35 meters in size, built throughout of reused ashlars from the Herodian period, but only itself constructed in the early twelfth century. It is therefore not itself the Psephinus tower, but the latter could still have been in somewhat the same area (Vincent in RB 22 [1913], pp. 88-96; 36 [1927], pp. 525-532; Simons, *Jerusalem*, pp. 486-491; M. Avi-Yonah in IEJ 18 [1968], pp. 103-105).

The last point mentioned before the third wall reached the Kidron Valley was a corner tower which was over against the so-called Fuller's tomb. On the Fuller's tomb we have no other information, but if the third wall "bent around" a corner tower at about the place where the present wall turns south on the edge of the Kidron Valley to run down to the northeast angle of the Temple area, the monument in question could have been on the knoll called Karm esh-Sheikh where the Palestine Archaeological Museum now is (Vincent in RB 36 [1927], p. 547 n. 1; Simons, *Jerusalem*, p. 482 n. 1).

Between the points thus far provisionally identified there are mentioned the monuments of Queen Helena of Adiabene and the royal caverns: the wall descended opposite the monuments of Helena and proceeded through the royal caverns. The monuments of Helena are quite certainly identified with the so-called Tombs of the Kings (Nos. 275ff.) which are on the Nablus Road about 700 meters in a direct line north of the present north wall of Jerusalem. The royal caverns are likewise quite certainly the so-called Solomon's Quarry, the entrance to which is 100 yards east of the Damascus Gate. These are subterranean caverns, 100 by 200 meters in extent, from which much of the building stone of ancient Jerusalem was probably obtained. Across the road to the north is another quarry known as the Grotto of Jeremiah. This was probably connected originally with the Quarry of Solomon but the connecting portion has been cut away. The statement that the third wall was "opposite" (ἀντικρύ) the monuments of Helena can allow a considerable intervening distance, for the camp of Titus, for example, was "opposite" Psephinus but also about two stadia from the ramparts (*War* v 3, 5 §133). In fact Josephus elsewhere (*Ant.* xx 4, 3 §95) states that the tomb of Helena was three stadia from the city. If the north wall of the time of Josephus, i.e., the third wall which we are discussing, ran on the line of the present north wall of the city, Josephus has estimated the distance from it to the monuments of Queen Helena at not much less than the actual measurement of about 700 meters between the two points today. Although the statement about the third wall in relation to the royal caverns is sometimes translated to say that the wall ran "past" the caverns (LCL), the phrase is διὰ σπηλαίων βασιλικῶν and should strictly be translated, "through the royal caverns." This is exactly true of a wall on the line of the present north wall of Jerusalem, for this wall has broken into the roof of Solomon's Quarry and runs between that cavern and the Grotto of Jeremiah on the north side of the road, the latter once having been part of the same set of caverns (Simons, *Jerusalem*, pp. 461-463, 478-481).

As for the tomb of John the high priest, mentioned in *War* v 6, 2 §259 (see above), it is mentioned again (*War* v 7, 3 §304; cf. v 9, 2 §356) in the fighting after Titus had shifted his camp within the outer wall. This monument, which was probably that of John Hyrcanus (135-105 B.C.), was therefore probably somewhere inside the third wall but outside the second wall and outside the first wall, and one suggestion places it at the site of the Byzantine and medieval Church of St. John the Baptist at the southwest corner of the Muristan (Simons, *Jerusalem*, pp. 299 n. 5; AJPA 3-29).

The line of the third wall thus described by Josephus (*War* v 4, 2 §147) running from Hippicus to Psephinus, opposite the monuments of Helena and through the royal caverns, around a corner tower, and to the Kidron Valley, appears then to correspond very closely with the line of the present north wall of Jerusalem (cf. Vincent in RB 36 [1927], p. 523 fig. 1).

In 1937-1938 R. W. Hamilton made soundings at the Damascus Gate in the present north wall, and in 1966 J. B. Hennessy excavated much more fully, and a new bridge was built to carry foot traffic to the gate above the level of the earlier remains. As shown in the photograph, to the east side of the present Damascus Gate and at a lower level there is the base of a massive wall and the arch of a gate. Here the stones of the wall are of Herodian style (which was used both before and after the time of Herod the Great himself [37-4 B.C.]). In the immediate area the most ancient remains were of the first half of the first century of the Christian era. Some burials, including an infant burial in a jar of the beginning of the first century, showed that at that time this area was outside the city. Other pottery, of the end of the first century B.C. and the beginning of the first century of the Christian era, and coins of the procurators were found. After that, the massive wall was built, and it may therefore in all probability be considered to be the work of Herod Agrippa I in about A.D. 41-42. To the west side of the Damascus Gate and at a similar lower level there are also some massive blocks which probably belong to this same period (QDAP 10 [1940], p. 6). The lower part of the arch associated with the wall to the east of the Damascus Gate is also probably the work of Herod Agrippa. The upper part of the arch is of different masonry, and in the first course of stones above it there is a stone on which, although most of its face has been chiseled away, a few letters of an inscription still remain. In the second line from the bottom one letter remains, and in the bottom line are these letters; CO AEL CAP D D, i.e., Colonia Aelia Capitolina Decurionum Decreto. Thus the inscription refers to a decree of the decurions (cf. No. 183), and gives the name of Jerusalem as the Colony Aelia Capitolina. The date of the inscription is probably in the time of Hadrian (QDAP ibid., pp. 22-23 and fig. 12). As seen in our illustration, then, the archway probably represents the rebuilding or the completion by Hadrian of the earlier arch of Herod Agrippa, to serve as part of the main north gateway of Aelia Capitolina. That entire gateway was presumably triple-arched, like the other great gateways of Hadrian (Nos. 217, 224, cf. 108), and this arch was the eastern passageway for foot traffic alongside the higher, central passageway. In further excavations by Menahem Magen in 1979 and 1982 the towers and vaults on either side of the arches were also explored, and nearly 100 feet of the large paving stones

(4 by 5 feet and 5 by 7 feet) of the great plaza immediately inside Hadrian's gate were uncovered and are now enclosed within the Damascus Gate museum.

The Islamic rulers of Jerusalem, including the Mamlukes and the Turks, also did work on the walls of the city. The major restoration was carried out in A.D. 1537-1541 by Suleiman I the Magnificent, sultan of Turkey (r. 1520-1566). While even later repairs may be seen on upper parts of the walls, the main lower parts of the existing walls in almost their entire circuit of the Old City are his masonry, and the present Damascus Gate appears much as it did in his day. The work of Suleiman is attested by no less than eleven inscriptions still in place on the walls; one of these is at the Damascus Gate and gives a date for the gate corresponding to A.D. 1537. Since there is evidence (Kenyon, *Jerusalem*, p. 197) that the wall of Suleiman corresponds at key points with the walls of Hadrian, the present outlines of the Old City may be seen to reflect the configuration of Aelia Capitolina. Only on the south the city extended earlier in the Herodian period and also later in the Byzantine period farther down toward the Hinnom Valley (cf. Nos. 179, 229).

Vincent, "La troisième enceinte de Jérusalem," in RB 36 (1927), pp. 516-548; 37 (1928), pp. 80-100; R. W. Hamilton, "Excavations against the North Wall of Jerusalem, 1937-8," in QDAP 10 (1940), pp. 1-54; Vincent, "Encore la troisième enceinte de Jérusalem," RB 54 (1947), pp. 90-126; Simons, *Jerusalem*, pp. 459-503; Kenyon, *Jerusalem*, pp. 162-163, 188, 196-197, Pls. 76-78; J. B. Hennessy in RB 75 (1968), pp. 250-253; and Hennessy, "Preliminary Report on Excavations at the Damascus Gate, 1964-6," in *Levant* II (1970), p. 22; Menahem Magen, "Recovering Roman Jerusalem—The Entryway Beneath Damascus Gate," in BAR 15.3 (May/June 1988), pp. 48-56. Photograph: courtesy École Biblique et Archéologique Française.

202. South Face of a Wall North of the Old City of Jerusalem

ONE OTHER LINE of wall is represented by considerable remains on the north side of the Old City of Jerusalem. These were first noted by Edward Robinson in 1838 (*Biblical Researches*, I, pp. 465-467) and thought to represent Josephus' third wall. In more recent time in the course of street repair at the intersection of Nablus Road and Richard Coeur de Lion Street a large block of drafted stone was found which was similar to the stones in the Temple enclosure wall (cf. No. 189), and in 1925-1928 E. L. Sukenik and L. A. Mayer undertook excavations. They found other portions of wall or traces thereof from as far west as the Swedish Girls' School (where they thought it could be seen that a wall had rested) to Saladin Road in front of the American School of Oriental Research, and in 1940 they found two other portions east of the same school. Because they found remains of towers projecting from the north face of the wall they believed that it faced north, and in publication they presented these finds as parts of the "third wall" of Jerusalem, built by Herod Agrippa I. In order not to prejudge a debatable question the wall is best called simply the Sukenik-Mayer wall.

202. South Face of a Wall North of the Old City of Jerusalem

As now known the entire line of the wall, 1,500 feet north of the Old City and parallel to the present north wall of Suleiman the Magnificent (No. 201), runs from west to east for a distance of about 2,500 feet (Bahat, Plans, 96-97). In all about 14 feet thick, the wall contains carefully drafted stones like the large block mentioned above, other ashlars only roughly finished, and large field stones as well as pebbles and mortar.

Further excavation of a portion of the wall between Nablus Road and Saladin Street was done in 1965 by Kathleen M. Kenyon, with E. W. Hamrick as site supervisor. In view of their findings it was the opinion of Kenyon that the wall "certainly faced south and not north," and therefore certainly could not be the north wall of Herod Agrippa's city (PEQ 1966, p. 87), but it was the opinion of Hamrick that the wall faced north. In view of "the incredibly poor and haphazard masonry," however, Hamrick agreed that the wall would not be from Agrippa (BASOR 183 [Oct 1966], pp. 24-25; 192 [Dec 1968], pp. 23f.). In association with the wall two coins of Roman procurators were found, one of the fourteenth year of Claudius (A.D. 54), one of the fifth year of Nero (A.D. 58/59), and this also indicates that the wall is of later date than Agrippa. Kenyon, therefore, suggested that this was part of the circumvallation wall which, according to Josephus (War v 12, 1-2 §§499-511), Titus put around the city in the siege, while Hamrick suggested that this was part of an outwork put up by the Jews early in the war and set far enough out to keep Roman catapults from reaching the city. Another theory mentioned at the time was that the wall was associated with the headquarters of the Tenth Legion Fretensis, which Titus left to guard Jerusalem after the war was over (cf. Nos. 131 and 183), but this is unlikely, since these headquarters were evidently in the southwestern corner of the city where many tiles bearing the stamp LEG.X.FR. or a variant thereof have been found (Kenyon in PEQ 1966, p. 88; and her Jerusalem, p. 168).

Again between 1972 and 1974 the Israeli archeologists Sara Ben-Arieh and Ehud Netzer dug along the wall and, with the full excavation of two more of the north-facing towers, felt it was proved that the wall faced north and could not have been an offensive wall built by Titus; rather they concurred with the original opinion of Sukenik and Mayer that the excavated portions were to be ascribed to Josephus' third wall.

On the other hand, the line of the Sukenik-Mayer wall does not correspond with what Josephus describes (No. 201), for this wall is only about 250 meters from the tomb of Queen Helena of Adiabene and Josephus says (Ant. xx 4, 3 §95) that the distance from that monument to the city was three stadia (a much greater distance), nor does the line go "through" any known "royal caverns." Also Josephus (War v 4, 2 §153) says that

Agrippa began the wall with stones "twenty cubits long and ten broad, so closely joined that they could scarcely have been undermined with tools of iron or shaken by engines." Here, however, the portions of wall which have been uncovered were not well built but, as described above, were indeed a "haphazard" construction. As such this can therefore more convincingly be understood as a forward defense put up by the Jews in about A.D. 66 (Benoit in Studia Hierosolymitana I [1976], p. 125), and it remains probable that the "third wall" of Herod Agrippa I was not here but rather on the line followed afterward by the north wall of Hadrian's Aelia Capitolina and by what is the present north wall of the Old City as constructed by Suleiman the Magnificent (Mackowski p. 69). The photograph shows the south face of one portion of the Sukenik-Mayer wall.

E. L. Sukenik and L. A. Mayer, The Third Wall of Jerusalem: An Account of Excavations (Jerusalem, 1930); and "A New Section of the Third Wall, Jerusalem," in PEQ 1944, pp. 145-151; Simons, Jerusalem, pp. 470-481; Kathleen M. Kenyon, "Excavations in Jerusalem, 1965," in PEQ 1966, pp. 87-88; E. W. Hamrick, "New Excavations at Sukenik's 'Third Wall,'" in BASOR 183 (Oct. 1966), pp. 19-26. Kenyon, Jerusalem, pp. 162, 166-168, pl. 86; M. Avi-Yonah, "The Third and Second Walls of Jerusalem," in IEJ 18 (1968), pp. 98-125; Pierre Benoit, "Ou en est la question du 'troisieme mur'?" in Studia Hierosolymitana I (1976), pp. 111-126; Sara Ben-Arieh and Ehud Netzer, "Excavations along the 'Third Wall' of Jerusalem, 1972-1974," in IEJ 4 (1974), pp. 97-107; Ben-Arieh, "The 'Third Wall' of Jerusalem," in Jerusalem Revealed (1975), pp. 60-62; and Ben-Arieh and Netzer, "Where Is the Third Wall of Agrippa I?" in BA 42 (1979), p. 140; Emmett Willard Hamrick, "The Third Wall of Agrippa I," in BA 40 (1977), pp. 18-23; and Hamrick, "The Northern Barrier Wall in Site T," in A. D. Tushingham, Excavations in Jerusalem 1961-1967, I (Toronto: Royal Ontario Museum, 1985), pp. 215-232. Photograph: courtesy École Biblique et Archéologique Française.

203. The Church of St. Anne

AN EVENT of interest in the earlier ministry of Jesus in Jerusalem, connected with a specific place in the city, is recorded in the fifth chapter of the Gospel according to John. This was the healing of the man ill for thirty-eight years to whom Jesus said, "Rise, take up your pallet, and walk" (5:8). Because it was the sabbath the objection was raised that it was not lawful for the man to carry his pallet, and the event became one in a series of circumstances which led finally to the death of Jesus in the same city.

The place where the healing of this man took place is described in Jn 5:2 in a Greek sentence which appears in different forms in different manuscripts. All agree that the sentence begins, "Now there is in Jerusalem." After that it is a question of how to connect and interpret the Greek word, probatike, which is an adjective meaning "of sheep." The oldest manuscript presently available which

203. The Church of St. Anne

contains this text is P[66] or Papyrus Bodmer II, about A.D. 200 in date. On numbered Page 25 (KE) of this codex and in Lines 18-19 (ed. Victor Martin and J. W. B. Barns, 1962) the words are: ΕΙΙΙ ΤΗ ΠΡΟΒΑΤΙΚΗ · ΚΟΛΥΜΒΗΘΡΑ ·. The same Greek text, but not necessarily with the same punctuation marks, is found also in P[75] (Papyrus Bodmer XV, early third century), Codex Vaticanus, and many manuscripts of the Koine text, and also in D and other Western manuscripts except that in the latter ἐπί is replaced by ἐν without any real change of meaning. The fact that the word *probatike* is here preceded by the preposition ἐπί meaning "at" or "by" or "near" (or by ἐν, "in"), indicates that it must be taken as a dative, ἐπὶῇ (ἐν) τῇ προβατικῇ, "at the sheep. . . ." In and of itself the last word in the sequence from Papyrus Bodmer II, which means "pool," could also be taken as a dative, but that would complicate the grammar with respect to the continuation of the sentence, so it probably is to be taken as a nominative, κολυμβήθρα. This also appears to have been the understanding of the scribe who wrote P[66] for, as shown above, the word is set off in this manuscript between punctuation dots. Accordingly we have, literally, "at the *probatike* a pool." What the *probatike* was must be surmised, and it is at least a reasonable guess that the reference is to a sheep market or a

sheep gate. Both of these meanings could of course be related, for the holding of a sheep market outside a certain gate would lead naturally to the designation of that portal as a sheep gate. If this is correct, then a suitable English translation can be, "Now there is at Jerusalem by the sheep market a pool" (KJV), or "Now there is in Jerusalem by the sheep *gate* a pool" (ASV), or "Now there is in Jerusalem by the sheep gate a pool" (RSV).

Codex Sinaiticus, however, reads simply, "Now there is in Jerusalem a sheep pool" (προβατικὴ κολυμβήθρα). Since this does simplify the text as compared with the preceding reading, it may be judged to be secondary. At the same time, whether because of the existence of this reading or simply because of the proximity of the pool to the sheep market and/or the sheep gate, it would appear that the pool was, at least in due time, known as the sheep pool. In the *Onomasticon* (pp. 58-59) Eusebius speaks of "a pool in Jerusalem which is the Probatike," and Jerome repeats and adds, "a pool in Jerusalem which is called Probatike, which can be interpreted by us as 'belonging to cattle' " (*piscina in Ierusalem quae vocabatur* προβατική, *et a nobis interpretari potest pecualis*).

We have reference, then, to a pool which was near a certain place associated with sheep, probably a sheep market and/or a sheep gate, a pool which was itself, at

227

least later, also naturally enough called the sheep pool. Now we have already noted (No. 197) that there was in fact a Sheep Gate which is mentioned by Nehemiah (3:1; 12:39) and that, according to his references, this was probably in the north city wall on the north side of the Temple area, between the "corner" on the northeast and the Tower of the Hundred and Tower of Hananel, the latter probably predecessors of the Antonia, on the northwest. The fact that this gate was built by Eliashib the high priest and his brethren the priests (Neh 3:1) confirms its close association with the Temple area, and it may have been the same as the Tadi Gate mentioned by Middoth I 3 as the portal on the north side of the Temple area (cf. No. 190). Since the pool in question was "by" this gate we have thereby established its approximate location.

The text in Jn 5:2 continues, "Now there is in Jerusalem by the sheep gate a pool, in Hebrew called. . . ." At this point the name of the pool is given, but again there is a problem for different manuscripts give different names. The manuscripts which were found probably the most accurate in the earlier part of the sentence now give, with some variation in spelling, the name Bethsaida. P⁶⁶ reads Βηδσαϊδά and P⁷⁵, Codex Vaticanus, and other manuscripts have Βηθσαϊδά. Jerome also changes the Onomasticon (p. 59) at this point to read Bethsaida. As we have seen (No. 104) this name probably means House of the Fisher and is the name of a town on the Sea of Galilee. With reference to this place, which was the city of Andrew and Peter as well as of Philip, the name has already occurred in Jn 1:44. Appropriate as the name is to a fishing village, it seems that it would be less appropriate to a pool in the city of Jerusalem. Therefore in spite of the early and wide attestation of the name in sources just cited, it may be judged probable that this name is due to a scribe who wrongly wrote here what was really the name of a well-known town.

In Codex Alexandrinus and Codex Ephraemi rescriptus, both of the fifth century, and in other manuscripts including the majority of the Byzantine manuscripts, the name Bethesda (Βηθεσδά) is found, and this is the reading adopted in the KJV and ASV. In Hebrew בית means "house" and אשד means "pour," and the related form in Aramaic, בית אשדא, can lie back of the Greek name, thus giving some such meaning as House of Outpouring or House of Poured-out Water. Interestingly enough this can recall the statement in the fourth-century parchment from Oxyrhynchus (OP 840 lines 25, 32-33; FHRJ §262) about the Pharisee who said that he had washed in the pool of David (ἐν τῇ λίμνῃ τοῦ Δ(αυεί)δ), to whom the Savior said that he had washed "in these poured-out waters" (τοῖς χεομένοις ὕ[δ]ασιν). Perhaps this last expression, which otherwise appears lacking in any particular significance, is actually a reference to the pool of Bethesda. In this case the pool of David of the Oxyrhynchus parchment, which is otherwise unidentified, can be identified with the pool of Bethesda.

In the Old Syriac version, found as early as the fifth-century Curetonian manuscript, the name is given as Byt ḥsd', i.e., Bethesda. Back of this form must be the Hebrew בית "house" and אשד "mercy," and the related Aramaic בית חסדא, giving the meaning. House of Mercy. This name was certainly appropriate in view of the healing performed by Jesus, but probably appropriate earlier, in view of the healings which were evidently already associated with the pool.

That there was a place called Bethesda, with a pool or pools, in Jerusalem is now confirmed in the Hebrew text of the Copper Scroll from Qumran (3Q 15 DJD III p. 297, cf. pp. 271-272; J. T. Milik in RB 66 [1959], pp. 328, 345, 347-348; J. M. Allegro, The Treasure of the Copper Scroll, 2d ed. [1964], p. 84), a work written probably between A.D. 25 and 68 (F. M. Cross, Jr. in DJD III pp. 217, 219). Here in column XI lines 12-13 and in a list of places at Jerusalem we read: "At Beth Eshdathayin (בית אשדתין]), in the pool where you enter its small(er) reservoir. . . ." This is a writing of the name Bethesda which agrees with the etymology suggested in the second paragraph above, but with two interesting additional features. The first is the simple fact that the initial aleph in the second word has been written twice, no doubt the result of a familiar type of error in the copying of manuscripts known as dittography. The second is the important fact that the word is written with the Hebrew dual ending. In view of the latter fact and if we may now take the phrase "poured-out water," which was explained above, in the broad sense of "pool," we may understand the name, as written here, to mean the House of the Twin Pools.

At this point we may note the remaining significant variant in the name, which is the reading Bethzatha (Βηθζαθά). This reading is found in Codex Sinaiticus. Also in the Onomasticon (p. 58) Eusebius omits one letter of the same name and writes Βηζαθά. The Western text in Codex Bezae and several manuscripts of the Itala has Βελζεθά, and this is also no doubt only an orthographic variation. We have then simply to account for the name Bethzatha. In the Copper Scroll we have seen the Hebrew dual form, Beth Eshdathayin. If we suppose that this name was reproduced in Aramaic, we have to remember that in Palestinian Aramaic the dual ending was largely lost (Franz Rosenthal, A Grammar of Biblical Aramaic [1961], p. 24 no. 45). If in this case the Hebrew dual was replaced by the feminine plural, the Aramaic form of the name would have been בית אשדתא, Beth Eshdatha. Then we can explain the name Bethzatha as a Greek transcription of the Aramaic which does not reproduce the aleph, and which represents the shin and the daleth together by zeta, as may be paralleled for example in the Greek Ἄζωτος which renders the Hebrew אשדוד, Ashdod.

We have just observed that in writing the name Beth-zatha in Greek the first theta could be omitted and the name be given as Bezatha (Βηζαθά) as Eusebius did. In this form the name is very similar to the name Bezetha (Βεζεθά), which is found in Josephus. In his description of the "third wall" of Jerusalem, built by King Herod Agrippa I (No. 201), Josephus says (War v 4, 2 §§148-151) that this wall was built to enclose later additions to the city which were in a district north of the Temple. Here there was a hill, opposite Antonia, called Bezetha; the recently built quarter was also called in the vernacular Bezetha which, Josephus says, might be translated into Greek as New City (cf. No. 173). New City is not actually a translation of Bezetha, and in another passage (War II 19, 4 §530) Josephus says more accurately that the district was known as Bezetha and also as New City (τὴν τε Βεζεθὰν . . . τὴν καὶ Καινόπολιν). The name Bezetha is then in all probability the same as the name Bethzatha, and the area to which it applies as the name of a city district, namely, the area north of the Temple, is the area within which we have already suggested that the Bethesda/Bethzatha pool was located. Accordingly it is a reasonable surmise that the pool gave its name to the expanded city district.

From this survey of the most important variants in the manuscript evidence we conclude that the name Beth-saida is a scribal alteration which erroneously introduces the name of a well-known town, but that otherwise the tradition is essentially consistent and homogenous, i.e., Bethesda and Bethzatha (and the variant spellings of these two names) represent respectively the Hebrew and the Aramaic forms of the name of the pool. Furthermore, comparing the tradition with the item in the Copper Scroll from Qumran, we have evidence (in a Hebrew dual ending) that the pool was in fact a twin or double pool.

Eusebius, we have noted, uses the name Bezatha in the Onomasticon (p. 58), where he gives the oldest description of the pool after the NT. Eusebius writes: "Bezatha. A pool in Jerusalem, which is the Sheep Pool (ἡ προβατική), which formerly had five porticoes (ἐστοάς). And now it is shown in the twin pools which are there, each of which is filled by the yearly rains, but one of which paradoxically exhibits water colored purple-red (πεφοινιγμένον), a trace, it is said, of the sacrificial animals formerly washed in it. That is also why it is called Sheep Pool (προβατική), on account of the sacrifices." From this we learn that the place was pointed out in Jerusalem, and we are told explicitly that it had twin pools. The tradition of connection with sacrifices implies proximity to the Temple area.

In a description of Jerusalem in the vicinity of the Temple the Bordeaux Pilgrim (Geyer p. 21; LPPTS I-B, p. 20; CCSL CLXXV, p. 15; WET p. 156) mentions the same double pool: "Farther in the city are twin pools (piscinae gemellares), having five porticoes, which are called Beth-saida. There those who have been sick for many years are cured. The pools contain water which is red when it is disturbed (in modum coccini turbatam)." Here the additional item is the reference to the disturbance of the water which evidently took place from time to time (cf. Jn 5:7).

In a sermon on the healing of the ill man at the pool, Cyril of Jerusalem says (MPG 33, col. 1133): "For in Jerusalem there was a Sheep Pool (προβατικὴ κολυμβήθρα), having five porticoes, four of which ran around it, but the fifth ran through the middle, in which [i.e., in the portico in the middle] lay a multitude of the sick." Knowing from the other references that the pool was in fact a twin pool, i.e., really two pools, we can picture the four porticoes as surrounding both, and the fifth portico as running between the two pools.

Next we learn that a church was built here. Peter the Iberian (Raabe p. 94 in Kopp 1963, p. 309), who came to Jerusalem in 451, on his way from the Church of the Holy Sepulcher to Gethsemane, went "into the (Church) of the Lame Man." Eutychius of Alexandria (ed. Watt CSCO 193, p. 139) also speaks of "the church which is called the Place of the Sheep in Jerusalem" and describes it as bearing witness to the healing by Christ of the man paralyzed for thirty-eight years. The church was therefore evidently known as the Church of the Lame Man, or the Church of the Sheep Place (Probatike).

Interestingly enough the place of the pool was also associated with commemoration of the birth of Mary the mother of Jesus. First we learn that there was a Church of St. Mary at the pool. Theodosius mentions it in 530, saying only that it was near the pool. Speaking of the Sheep Pool, he writes (Geyer p. 142; LPPTS II-B, p. 11; CCSL CLXXV, pp. 118-119; WJP p. 156): "There the Lord Christ healed the paralytic, whose bed is still there. There near the Sheep Pool is the church of St. Mary (iuxta piscinam probaticam ibi est ecclesia domnae Mariae)." And the Anonymous of Piacenza (570) locates the church in relation to the pool more precisely in the statement (Geyer p. 177; LPPTS II-D, p. 22; CCSL CLXXV, p. 143; WJP p. 84): "Returning to the city we came to a swimming pool (piscina natatioia) which has five porticoes, one of which has the basilica of St. Mary." From this we gather that the church was built right into a stoa of the pool, therefore it was probably the same as, or a replacement of, the Church of the Lame Man which was presumably also closely related to the pool. The pool itself was now choked with filth, according to the Anonymous, and the relic to be seen there was no longer the bed of the healed man but rather the iron chain with which Judas had hanged himself.

From these references we still do not know the particular connection of the church here with the name of Mary, but we learn the answer when we find that the place was believed to have been the place of the birth of Mary. Concerning "the church which is called the Place of the Sheep in Jerusalem," Eutychius of Alexandria not only says, as noted just above, that it marked the place where Christ healed the man, but he also writes (ed. Watt csco 193, p. 139): "That church also bears witness that the birth of Mary, the mother of Christ, took place there, her father being Joachim son of Binthir of the sons of David of the tribe of Judah, the tribe of the king, and her mother being Anne of the daughters of Aaron of the tribe of Levi, the tribe of the priesthood" (also cf. William of Tyre, above, No. 150). Eutychius then continues with a brief account not only of the birth of Mary but also of how Joachim and Anne, in accordance with a vow, placed Mary in the temple in the charge of Zacharias, where she also received food from the hands of an angel. This account corresponds generally with the fuller narrative in the apocryphal work of the middle of the second century known as The Protevangelium of James (HSNTA I, pp. 374ff.), and with the brief summary in the Qur'an (Surah III, 35-37). In the Protevangelium the connection of events with the Temple could lead one to the surmise that Joachim and Anne were living in the vicinity; also Joachim is represented as a shepherd, and therefore it could be appropriate to suppose that his residence was near the Sheep Gate. These factors were perhaps influential in fixing upon the place at the Sheep Pool for the home of Joachim and Anne and the birthplace of Mary.

When the Persians took Jerusalem in May 614 the church at the pool was no doubt among the buildings they destroyed, but afterward a small chapel was built there in its place. When the Crusaders took Jerusalem on July 15, 1099, the chapel was probably in ruins. They built a new basilica of St. Anne, the existence of which is attested by Saewulf in 1102. He writes (LPPTS IV, p. 17; Vincent, Jérusalem nouvelle, p. 681): "From the temple of the Lord you go towards the north to the Church of St. Anne, the mother of blessed Mary, where she lived with her husband, and where she brought forth her most beloved daughter Mary, the savior of all the faithful. Near there is the Probatica Pool which is called in Hebrew Bethsayda, having five porches." An account of the Crusader conquest called Deeds of the Franconians Conquering Jerusalem (1108) states that the Crusaders found "in front of" the church the vestiges of the old pool with five porticoes (Jeremias, The Rediscovery of Bethesda, p. 22), therefore the new Church of St. Anne must have been to the east of the Pool of Bethesda where the present-day church stands. Underneath is a grotto which was taken to be the very place where Mary was born. In addition to this church, however, the Crusaders also built a chapel over the ruins of the chapel and the Byzantine church at the pool. This is mentioned by the French pilgrim Ernoul in 1231, who calls it a moutier, literally a monastery (Vincent, Jérusalem nouvelle, p. 681).

In 1192 Saladin turned the Church of St. Anne into a Muslim college. The ancient double pool had evidently long since been filled with debris, and even the Crusader chapel disappeared below the rising level of the ground. At the end of the Crimean War in 1856 the Sultan of Turkey gave the basilica of St. Anne to Napoleon III of France. In 1871 the French architect C. Mauss, restoring the church, found thirty meters to the northwest a vaulted cistern and surmised that this was a part of the ancient pool. Five years later heavy rain removed more of the debris and over the cistern was found a structure which was part of the Byzantine church of the fifth century, with ruins of the Crusader chapel over it. Finally in 1878 the French government gave the property of St. Anne's Church to the White Fathers, and modern excavations became possible (see No. 204).

The photograph shows the Church of St. Anne as it still stands today (Bahat, Plans, 75), the finest existing example of the Romanesque church architecture of the Crusaders in the Holy Land. The church measures 112 by 66 feet, is entered through the western façade, and is divided in the interior into nave and two side aisles, each ending in an apse at the eastern end. In the middle of the southern aisle a staircase leads down to a subterranean grotto (about 24 feet in length from east to west and 20 feet in width from north to south), which forms the crypt of the church and is believed to have been the modest dwelling, partly built and partly cut in the rock, of Joachim and Anne, the parents of the Virgin Mary (Meistermann pp. 215-218).

Vincent, Jérusalem nouvelle, pp. 669-742; Joachim Jeremias, The Rediscovery of Bethesda, NTAM 1 (1966); D. J. Wieand, "John V.2 and the Pool of Bethesda," in NTS 12 (1966), pp. 392-404. Photograph: courtesy École Biblique et Archéologique Française.

204. Excavations at the Pool of Bethesda

EARLY EXCAVATIONS at the Pool of Bethesda by the White Fathers were carried out with assistance from the Dominicans of the École Biblique, while further work on behalf of the White Fathers was done by J.-M. Rousée and R. de Vaux in 1957-1962. It is now known that the cistern already mentioned (No. 203) and another cistern found later, occupied only a small part of the south side of the entire area of the northern of two very large pools.

These pools were in the small valley running off diagonally from the Kidron, which has already been mentioned and called St. Anne's Valley (No. 173). In part the pools were cut in the rock and in part they were built of large well-dressed blocks of stone. The two pools were separated by a dike of stone over six meters in width. Since the pools extend far underground and in part under heavily built-up sections of the city it has not yet been possible to trace them fully. They appear to have been generally rectangular in shape, but of irregular proportions. Provisional estimates make the northern pool 174 feet on its south side, 131 feet on the east and west sides, and 164 feet on the north side, and the southern pool 189 feet on its north side, 162 feet and 157 feet on the east side and west sides respectively, and 215 feet on the south side. Such dimensions would mean a water surface in the two pools in excess of 5,000 square yards.

The first cistern mentioned above, in the southeast corner of the northern pool, is a vaulted chamber about 16 meters in length from east to west, and 6 meters in breadth from north to south. As early as 1888 it was observed (C. Schick in PEFQS 1888, pp. 115-124, especially p. 119) that while this cistern was cut out of the rock on its west, south, and east sides, its north side was a built-up wall. The lowest part of this wall is now recognized as Roman work, so it as a possible guess that the cistern was part of their effort to preserve drinkable water, free from contamination by the rest of the pool. As to the source

of water for the two large pools, their location in the valley as already mentioned undoubtedly meant that they were in a good place for the collection of rainwater. Perhaps there was also a spring in the valley, at least in ancient times. It may be surmised that some feature of the connecting channels for the water, or even the existence of an intermittent spring like the Gihon spring (No. 175), accounted for the occasional troubling of the water mentioned by Jn 5:7 and the Bordeaux Pilgrim (cf. No. 203).

As to the date of the original construction of the two large pools, there is a statement in the Wisdom of Jesus ben Sirach (Ecclus. 50:1-3) in connection with the reign of the high priest Simon II (220-195 B.C.) which reads: "In his days the cistern for water was quarried out, a reservoir like the sea in circumference," and it is thought possible that this refers to the pools here in question (Mackowski p. 79). As to what the five porticoes were like or where they were located, the present state of the archeological work does not provide an answer (WJJK p. 103).

In further excavations just to the east of the twin pools a natural grotto was found and around it a series of rock-cut vaulted chambers with various basins and canals, the whole evidently related to similar installations under the nearby Church of St. Anne. Steps led down into these grottoes and in some there was evidence of paintings and mosaics. Already in 1866 a broken marble foot was found

204. Excavations at the Pool of Bethesda

in the debris in the vaults of the Church of St. Anne. On the top was this inscription in Greek:

ΠΟΝΠΗ
ΙΑ ΛΟΥΚΙ
ΛΙΑ ΑΝΕΘΗ
ΚΕΝ

i.e., Πονπηῖα Λουκιλῖα ἀνέθηκεν, "Pompeia Lucilia dedicated (this as a votive gift)" (Vincent, *Jérusalem nouvelle*, pp. 694-695). The donor, a Roman lady to judge from her name, had evidently visited the place and left this sign of her visit, the foot presumably commemorating the healing which she had experienced. Paleographically the inscription may be from the second century A.D., and other votive offerings and objects of related import, likewise dating probably in the second and third centuries, have also been found. The evidence, therefore, points to this as a pagan healing sanctuary of the Roman period, and it may be supposed that, like the Asclepieia at Epidaurus in Greece and Pergamum in Asia Minor, it was dedicated to the healing god Asclepius. For the Jews it was simply the House of Mercy (Aramaic, Bethesda), and for the lame man it became that simply at the command of Jesus.

In the Curetonian Syriac version of Jn 5:2, where the Aramaic form of the name Bethesda is so plainly recognizable (cf. No. 203), the text runs, ". . . there was in Jerusalem a baptistery. . . ." This makes it likely that in some periods the Bethesda pools were used as a place of Christian baptism, a fact likely enough in and of itself in view of the paucity of places of abundant water in Jerusalem (Jeremias, *The Rediscovery of Bethesda*, pp. 33-34).

That when it became possible the Christians also built a church here was no doubt both to commemorate the healing by Christ of the ill man and also to supplant the pagan sanctuary. As we have seen (No. 203), Peter the Iberian in 451 refers to a Church of the Lame Man, and this was undoubtedly the church at this location, the ruins of which have been uncovered in the excavations. In its western part the center of this church and its main entrance were on the rock dike between the two pools, while the north side was supported on the Roman structure of the cistern and the south side was carried by a system of arches. This was a basilica with three halls, each ending at the east end in an identical semicircular apse. The central hall was of the same width (6 meters) as the rock dike upon which it rested in its western part, and the halls on either side were of the same width, making a total width of the basilica of 18 meters, while the length was 45 meters. To the east of the two pools the underground Roman sanctuary was filled in, and the eastern part of the basilica, with its three apses, was built out on this ground. From fragmentary remains the nar-

thex at the west end appears to have had a mosaic floor, and the rest of the church to have been paved with slabs of marble. Since this is presumably the church to which Peter the Iberian refers it must have been built prior to his time (451), and since there are crosses on the surviving portions of the mosaic floor it must have been prior to 427 (when Theodosius II forbade crosses in church pavements, see No. 30); therefore the probable date of the church is early in the fifth century.

The Byzantine basilica just described was probably destroyed by the Persians (614) and then replaced by a small chapel erected above the north aisle of the church, but this also suffered from the devastations of the caliph Hakim (1009) and was in ruins when the Crusaders came. The Crusaders in turn built only a chapel over the Roman cistern in the southeast corner of the north pool, a chapel which, as we have seen (No. 203), was known as the Moutier. A stairway running under a Byzantine vault was constructed to give pilgrims access to a corner of the cistern as the presumed place of the miracle of Jn 5, and it is this stairway that still gives access there today.

Nearby the Crusaders built their beautiful still-standing Church of St. Anne, to enshrine the traditional home of the Virgin Mary (No. 203), and for its construction they took most of the stones of the Byzantine basilica just described. In excavation under the Church of St. Anne in 1896 Van der Vliet partly uncovered a rock-hewn room about one meter below the floor of the church, with some plaster and mosaic floor remaining, attributed to the second century. At first this was interpreted as a chapel and the original Church of the Birthplace of Mary, later replaced by a pagan sanctuary (Vincent, *Jérusalem nouvelle*, pp. 717-718), but there are no graffiti and signs to attest early pilgrim veneration of the site, as there are at such places as Nazareth and Capernaum, and the grotto is more probably only to be understood as a part of the installations of the healing sanctuary described above (Bagatti, *Church from Gentiles*, pp. 162f.).

J.-M. Rousée and R. de Vaux in RB 64 (1957), pp. 226-228; J.-M. Rousée in RB 69 (1962), pp. 107-109; Mackowski pp. 79-83; Ovadiah, *Corpus Supplementum*, pp. 223f., no. 26 (Church of the Lame Man); pp. 224f., no. 27 (Church of St. Anne); Bahat, *Plans*, 73-74. Photograph: JF.

205. Plan of the Church on Mount Sion According to Arculf

ACCORDING TO MK 14:15 AND LK 22:12 the last supper of Jesus with his disciples was in an "upper room" (ἀνάγαιον). According to Ac 1:13 the disciples were staying, after the ascension, in an "upper room" (ὑπερῷον). Although two different Greek words are used in these passages they both designate a room upstairs, and in his Latin translation Jerome rendered both by the same word, *cenaculum*. This word, also spelled *coenaculum*, English cenacle, means a dining room, and since such a room was usually in an upper story, it means also an upper room. No doubt the use of *cenaculum* for the upper room of the last supper and also for the upper room of the time after the ascension furthered the supposition that one and the same room was in question. Although that supposition is not fully demonstrable it is not impossible. That the same room was still the center of the disciples on the day of Pentecost (Ac 2:1) is also well possible. Still later, many of the disciples were gathered together in the house of Mary, the mother of John Mark (Ac 12:12), and the further supposition that this was the house of the "upper room" is likewise not impossible although not fully demonstrable from the NT texts alone. The several combinations were affirmed, however, in early tradition, as will be seen in what follows.

It will be remembered (No. 173) that the southwestern hill of Jerusalem was the highest hill in the city and came to be called Zion or Sion. It will also be remembered (No. 183) that this portion of the city was the least destroyed by the Romans in A.D. 70 and that, as Epiphanius tells us (*Weights and Measures* 14 [54c], ed. Dean, p. 30), when Hadrian came in 130 he found in Zion "the church of God, which was small, where the

disciples, when they had returned after the Savior had ascended from the Mount of Olives, went to the upper room," and also "the seven synagogues which alone remained standing in Zion, like solitary huts, one of which remained until the time of Maximona the bishop and Constantine the king, 'like a booth in a vineyard,' as it is written [Is 1:8]." From what Epiphanius (himself born in Palestine c. 315) records we learn that the small church which Hadrian saw was at the place where the disciples stayed after the ascension of Christ (Ac 1:13), therefore we may suppose that the private home with that "upper room" had been converted into this church, a conversion of such sort as is also attested at Nazareth (No. 46), at Capernaum (No. 99), and at other places (Mackowski p. 145). We know from Eusebius (*Dem. Evang.* III 5, 103 GCS Eusebius VI, p. 131, cf. above, List of Bishops of the Jerusalem Church) that until the time of Hadrian the Jerusalem church was headed by a line of "bishops of the circumcision," beginning with James, the brother of Jesus; therefore we may assume that this church was a church of the Judeo-Christians.

Since the seven synagogues that Hadrian also found in Zion were like solitary huts they were probably unused; at any rate after Hadrian excluded the Jews from Aelia Capitolina they certainly could no longer have been used for Jewish services. One synagogue remained, however, until in the first half of the fourth century (the time of the bishop Maximona or Maximus [c. 335-347/348] and

205. Plan of the Church on Mount Sion
According to Arculf

the emperor Constantine), a fact the significance of which Epiphanius does not clarify. The specific mention of Maximona may provide a clue. It was Maximona (Maximus) who transferred the central seat of the Jerusalem church from Mount Zion to the Holy Sepulcher, therefore the "synagogue" that remained until his time may have been the church of the Judeo-Christians, who preferred to call their churches by that name (συναγωγή, Jas 2:2). With this explanation it becomes possible to think that Epiphanius has called the primitive church of Sion one time a church and another time a synagogue (Bagatti, *Church from Circumcision*, p. 118; and Bagatti, *Church from Gentiles*, p. 26).

The Bordeaux Pilgrim (333) ascended Sion and confirms what Epiphanius reported about the synagogues, saying that of the seven which were once there only one remained and the rest were " 'ploughed over and sown upon,' as Isaiah the prophet [Is 1:8, cf. Mic 3:12] said" (Geyer p. 22; LPPTS I-B, p. 23; CCSL CLXXV, p. 16; WET pp. 157f.). Of a church on Sion the Bordeaux Pilgrim says nothing, but the inclusion of Sion in the itinerary shows the importance of Sion to a Christian pilgrim, and the mention of the one "synagogue" may again be a reference to the synagogue/church which was the assembly place of the Judeo-Christians, about which the Gentile pilgrim will not otherwise speak (Bagatti, *Church from Gentiles*, p. 26; Cornfeld p. 294).

As to the significance of the place occupied by the primitive synagogue church on Sion, we have learned from Epiphanius that the "small church" which Hadrian saw was where the disciples went to the upper room when they came back from the Mount of Olives after the ascension of Christ (Ac 1:13). From Origen (who lived in Palestine from c. 230 on for over twenty years) we gain another indication of the significance of the place, namely, that this was the place of the Last Supper. In his *Commentary on Matthew* (MPG 13, cols. 1736-1737; Bagatti, *Church from Gentiles*, p. 25) Origen writes:

> If then we wish to receive the bread of benediction from Jesus, who is wont to give it, let us go in the city to the house of that person where Jesus celebrated the Pascha with his disciples. . . . Let us go up to the upper part of the house. . . . After they had celebrated the feast with the master, had taken the bread of benediction and eaten the body of the Word and drunk the chalice of the action of grace, Jesus taught them to say a hymn to the Father, and from one high place pass to another high place, and since there are things that the faithful do not do in the valley, so they ascended, to the Mount of Olives.

The two high places to which Origen refers in this poetic way are unmistakably Mount Zion, which is the southwestern hill and highest point in the city (No. 173), and the Mount of Olives, with the Kidron Valley between. On the former height, in the upper part of a house (by then a "small church") the Last Supper was remembered.

Eusebius (bishop of Caesarea 313-340) speaks of Sion and says that the Gospel, the Law of Christ, spread through Christ and his apostles to all the nations from Mount Sion in Jerusalem, where Jesus stayed a long time and taught his disciples many things (*Dem. Evang.* I 4 MPG 22, col. 43; Baldi pp. 473f., no. 728), a statement which can also be reminiscent of the event of Pentecost and the preaching of Peter on that day to "devout men from every nation under heaven" (Ac 2:5). It was probably also on Mount Sion that there was the library founded by Bishop Alexander (212-250), in which Eusebius himself worked (*Ch. Hist.* VI 20, 1; Kroll p. 315, col. 1); and on Mount Sion where the episcopal chair (θρόνος) of James the brother of the Lord was preserved and honored, as Eusebius also records (*Ch. Hist.* VII 19).

In the Easter season of the year 348 Cyril, the bishop of Jerusalem, delivered catechetical lectures in the Church of the Holy Sepulcher and devoted Lecture XVI to the subject of the Holy Spirit. Here he remarked (XVI, 4 NPNFSS VII, p. 116) that, just as it was appropriate to discourse concerning Christ and Golgotha in the church right there at Golgotha, so it would be appropriate to speak concerning the Holy Spirit "in the Upper Church" (ἐν τῇ ἀνωτέρᾳ ᾽εκκλησίᾳ). But, he reflected further, the One who descended there (i.e., the Holy Spirit) partakes jointly of the glory of him who was crucified here (i.e., Jesus Christ), therefore it was in fact not inappropriate to speak here (i.e., at Golgotha) also of him who descended there (i.e., at the site of the Upper Church). The "upper church" that marked the place where the Holy Spirit came upon the disciples must have been the church on Sion, and by this time it was probably a larger and more splendid structure than the church which Hadrian saw, "which was small," now probably a Byzantine basilica (Mackowski p. 142).

Aetheria (381-384) (Geyer pp. 91-94; LPPTS I-C, pp. 67-69; CCSL CLXXV, pp. 83-86; WET pp. 140-141) also knows "the church of Sion," as she calls it, and tells of several times when services were held there. On Easter Sunday (*dominica die per pascha*) the people go in the evening with the bishop from the Anastasis (the Church of the Holy Sepulcher) to Sion, and there in addition to hymns and prayer they have the Gospel reading that tells how the Lord came to this place on this day, "when the doors were shut" (Jn 20:19-25), and this was "in the same place where the church now is in Sion." Again on Sunday eight days later the service at Sion includes the reading about the Lord coming on that day and rebuking Thomas for his unbelief (Jn 20:26-29). From Easter till Pentecost (the Fiftieth Day after Easter) the people assemble on Sion on Wednesday and Friday mornings. Finally on Pentecost Sunday, after early service in the Great Church, the Martyrium (at the Church of the Holy Sepulcher), the ensuing service is at nine o'clock (cf. Ac 2:15) at Sion and includes the reading of the passage in the Acts of the Apostles (Ac 2:1ff.) about the descent of the Spirit and the speaking in tongues. "For the presbyters read this passage because the place is in Sion (which has been altered into a church [alia modo ecclesia est]), where once after the Lord's passion a multitude was gathered with the apostles, when that happened of which we spoke above." Like Cyril, Aetheria emphasizes Sion as the place of the climactic event of Pentecost, and with her statement that Sion had by then "been altered into a church" she must be referring to the Byzantine basilica, the existence of which has just been inferred.

In Rome the Church of Santa Pudenziana (believed built over the house of the senator Pudens, whose guest the apostle Peter was) is attributed in its original construction to Pope Pius I in the middle of the second century, and was rebuilt by Pope Siricius (384-399), while its great apse mosaic probably belongs to the time of the latter (FLAP p. 524), thus the mosaic is approximately contemporary with Aetheria. Across the entire mosaic runs an arcade with tile roof. Above and behind the arcade are two sets of buildings. Those at the viewer's left are almost certainly a representation of the Church of the Holy Sepulcher (No. 228) and those at the right are now believed to represent the Church of Sion (the pointed-roof building, probably octagonal in the form of a memorial church) and beside it the Cenacle (with the Eleona on the Mount of Olives above and behind, and the southern city wall and gate at the extreme right) (Mackowski p. 143, pl. 125; p. 146. fig. 24 B; Pixner in BAR 16.3 May/June 1990, p. 29).

Theodosius (530) calls the church Holy Sion (sancta Sion), describes it as "the mother of all churches" (mater omnium ecclesiarum), says that it was the house of St. Mark the Evangelist, and locates it at 200 paces from Golgotha (Geyer p. 141; LPPTS II-B, p. 10; CCSL CLXXV, p. 118; WJP p. 66). Also Eutychius of Alexandria (940), drawing upon the source from which his information about the sanctuaries in Jerusalem came, writes (ed. Watt, CSCO 193, p. 142): "The church of the holy Mount Zion bears witness that Christ ate the passover of the Law in the upper room there on the day of the passover of the Jews."

These references indicate that all of the connections rendered possible by the scripture passages cited at the beginning of this section were brought into play. The church on Mount Sion commemorated the upper room of the Last Supper and the upper room of the early dis-

ciples after the ascension and their gathering place at Pentecost, being in fact a room in the house of Mary, the mother of John Mark the writer of the Second Gospel.

In the Madaba Mosaic Map (560) (see No. 229) what must be the Holy Sion church, "the mother of all churches," as Theodosius calls it, appears in the Sion area as a very large basilica, even larger than the Church of the Holy Sepulcher, with a red roof and yellow doors. Attached to the main basilica is another building with red roof, and this is presumably the Cenacle as also noted in the Santa Pudenziana mosaic.

Along with many other Jerusalem churches, Holy Sion was destroyed by the Persians (614) but rebuilt, apparently on the lines of its predecessor, twenty years later (Ovadiah, Corpus, pp. 89f., no. 77a/b). Writing at that time Sophronius (made patriarch of Jerusalem in 634) saluted the Sion church in one of his poems as the place of the descent of the Holy Spirit, the place of the Last Supper with the footwashing (Jn 13:4ff.), and the place of the death of Mary the mother of Jesus (Anacreontica 20 MPG 87, 3, col. 3821; LPPTS XI-A, p. 31). Departing from the Church of the Holy Sepulcher, Sophronius says:

> Thence would I ply my steps until I came to Sion, to the place where the grace of God came down in the likeness of tongues of fire; where the Lord of all celebrated the mystic supper and washed his disciples' feet, to teach them not to be high-minded. It is Mary who pours forth salvation for all men, like rivers, running from that stone whereon the Mother of God was laid. Hail to thee, Sion, splendid sun of the world, for whom I yearn with groans day and night. And when he had burst the bonds of hell and had brought up the dead rescued from thence, it was here that he graciously manifested himself.

Arculf (670) also spoke of the church on Mount Sion as a "great basilica" (Geyer p. 243; LPPTS III-A, p. 20; CCSL CLXXV, p. 197; WJP p. 100) and accompanied his reference to it with a drawing. The legends in the drawing not only identify this as the place of the Last Supper, the Day of Pentecost, and the death of Mary, the mother of Jesus (as Sophronius also said), but show that the column where Jesus was scourged was not believed to be preserved here too. Arculf's drawing is reproduced here from a page of the ninth-century manuscript of De locis sanctis known as Codex Parisinus (Latin 13048), preserved in the Bibliothèque Nationale. From the lower left and around to the lower right the legends in the drawing read: Entrance, Site of the Lord's Supper, Here the column to which the Lord was bound when he was scourged, Here the Holy Spirit descended on the apostles, and Here St. Mary died.

Vincent, *Jérusalem nouvelle*, pp. 421-459, 472-481; E. Power, "Cénacle," in DB Supplement I, cols. 1064-1084. Photograph: Arculfus De Locis Sanctis, Codex Parisinus Lat. 13048, courtesy Bibliothèque Nationale, Paris.

206. Door of the Syrian Orthodox Church of St. Mark

WITH RESPECT TO the house of Mary the mother of John Mark, the tradition of the Syrian Orthodox community in Jerusalem should also be noted. Their Church of St. Mark stands on St. Mark Street in the Old City, and the door of the church is shown in this photograph. In this community Syriac is still a living language, and in 1940 a sixth-century Syrian inscription was discovered and is preserved on the wall of the church, which affirms that this is the house of Mary, the mother of John, called Mark, and that it was proclaimed a church by the apostles after the ascension of Christ, and renewed after the destruction of Jerusalem by Titus in the year 73. In all, according to the Syrian tradition, this

206. Door of the Syrian Orthodox Church of St. Mark

was the place of the Upper Room and the Last Supper, the place of the Pentecost event, and the place to which Peter came when released from prison (Ac 12:12). A picture on leather of the Virgin Mary and Child, believed to have been painted by St. Luke, is also in the possession of the church.

Murphy-O'Connor pp. 64f.; Mackowski p. 195 n. 12. Photograph: JF.

207. Mount Sion as Seen from Abu Tur

AS DESCRIBED ABOVE (NO. 199), the site of Mount Sion in the restricted sense is today, outside the south wall of the Old City of Jerusalem (Bahat, *Plans*, 30a, 31). A whole complex of buildings is now located there, namely, the Dormition Church, the supposed place of the falling asleep in death of St. Mary (*dormitio sanctae Mariae*), with the Monastery of the Benedictines from Beuron adjacent; the traditional Tomb of David, which has also been used as the Mosque of the Prophet David; and, in the second story of the Tomb of David building, the supposed hall of the Last Supper. The photograph is taken from the south, from the village of Abu Tur, which was, until 1967, divided by the line of partition between Jordan and Israel. The large buildings at the left are those of the Dormition, and the small dome not far to the right of them is above the Tomb of David and the Hall of the Last Supper. The dome at the extreme right is that of the Dome of the Rock in the Temple area.

Photograph: JF.

208. The Tomb of David on Mount Sion

HERE, IN A closer view, the Tomb of David is the building under the black dome. The minaret of the adjacent mosque rises at the right.

Photograph: The Matson Photo Service, Alhambra, Calif.

209. The South Wall of the Tomb of David on Mount Sion

ACCORDING TO I K 2:10 AND NEH 3:16 David was buried in the City of David, presumably meaning the southeastern hill of Jerusalem. Josephus (*Ant.* XVI 7, 1 §§179ff.) records an attempt of Herod the Great to plunder the tomb, but does not tell where the tomb was located. As the birthplace of David, Bethlehem was also called the city of David (Lk 2:4, 11), and according to

207. Mount Sion as Seen from Abu Tur

208. The Tomb of David on Mount Sion

237

Eusebius (*Onomasticon*, ed. Klostermann, p. 42) the tomb of David was pointed out there, while Jerome (*Letter* 46.13 NPNFSS VI, p. 65) also mentions a "mausoleum" of David in Bethlehem, and the Anonymous of Piacenza (Geyer p. 209; LPPTS II-D, p. 23; CCSL CLXXV, pp. 143-144; WJP p. 85) says that the tomb of David was half a mile from Bethlehem and a basilica called At Saint David was built over it. Peter, however, speaking on the day of Pentecost on Mount Sion, said of David that "his tomb is with us to this day" (Ac 2:29), which could have given rise to the tradition but perhaps more probably means that a tradition existed already in the first century or earlier placing David's tomb there on the southwestern hill of Jerusalem. According to the Jerusalem Calendar (before 638) the feast of David and the feast of St. James were celebrated together on Sion on December 26 (Baldi p. 490, no. 748), a collocation of feasts that was not inappropriate inasmuch as the bishop James was a descendant of David. The tradition that placed the tomb of David on the Zion hill was accepted by the Muslims as well as by the Jews and Christians, and in the late Middle Ages the building containing the supposed tomb was made into the Mosque of the Prophet David, while the Zion Gate is also known as the Gate of the Prophet David (Arabic Bab Nebi Daoud). Today the Tomb of David is a Jewish sanctuary.

The building containing the Tomb of David is a two-story structure. On the ground floor there is a long rectangular hall, extending from west to east and now divided into two rooms. The large stone cenotaph, which is the focus of interest, stands in the eastern room in front of an apse in the north wall (Bahat, *Plans*, 35ac). In 1951 J. Pinkerfeld removed the plaster in this apse and found a well-built wall of squared stones (ashlars), which he judged to belong to the late Roman period. The same large blocks were found in the eastern part of the north wall of the building, in the east wall, and in the eastern part of the south wall, thus outlining to that extent the original shape of the building. Within these walls the width of the building is 10.5 meters; the length to the western wall is 20 meters, but that wall is later so the figure is not necessarily correct for the original building. The photograph shows the south wall from the outside, and the large squared stones may be seen at the right and in the lower part of the picture.

According to the study just mentioned, the apse in the eastern room faces several degrees to the east of north and thus exactly toward the Temple Mount, and Pinkerfeld concluded that this was a Jewish synagogue from the first centuries after the destruction of the Temple (A.D. 70). Further examination, however, finds the orientation of the apse slightly more to the west and quite exactly toward the present location of the Church of the Holy Sepulcher, i.e., toward the site of Jesus' crucifixion and tomb, and if this was the intention of the direction it accords well with the supposition for which there is other evidence (below) that this was in fact a synagogue church of the Judeo-Christians (Mackowski p. 195 n. 16; Pixner in BAR 16.3 [May/June 1990], p. 24).

In the floor there are several levels, in descending order, marble slabs from the Turkish period, a plastered floor of the Crusader period, a mosaic floor of the early Byzantine or late Roman period, and a stone pavement, and probably also a mosaic, which must have belonged to an original first-century building (Mackowski p. 145). The large ashlars in the walls would be too large to have belonged to a private house, but the building of which they are a part could have been built to mark the site of an earlier house, and if in that house Peter could address 120 persons it was itself probably a spacious dwelling with courts and many rooms.

On the earliest floor several fragments of plaster were found which must have come from the original walls of the building. These bore graffiti that were copied by Pinkerfeld but only interpreted by Testa and published by Bagatti in 1971 (*Church from Circumcision*, pp. 120f., fig. 25). One graffito has Greek characters that can be understood as initials of words translatable as "Conquer, O Savior, mercy." Another is seen as reading, "O Jesus, that I may live, O Lord of the autocrat," the last word possibly embodying an allusion to David, mentioned in Peter's sermon (Ac 2:29). In all, then, this was probably the synagogue/church that Hadrian saw (No. 205), and the place of worship of the early Judeo-Christians of Sion (Bagatti, see in the bibliography below; Pixner in BAR 16.3 [May/June 1990], p. 25).

As to other parts of the ground floor hall of the present building, the west wall appears to have been built in the Arab period, and the dividing wall between the two rooms in the late Turkish period. Opposite the apse in the north wall of the eastern room a small niche was made by the Muslims in the south wall to serve as a *mihrab* and indicate the direction of prayer toward Mecca. The large plain cenotaph in the hall, adorned on the front with a rosette of acanthus leaves, is Crusader work. The upper level of the building is described below (No. 211).

J. Pinkerfeld, " 'David's Tomb,' Notes on the History of the Building," in the Hebrew University Department of Archaeology, Louis M. Rabinowitz Fund for the Exploration of Ancient Synagogues, *Bulletin* III (1960), pp. 41-43; B. Bagatti, S. *Giacomo il Minore* (Jerusalem, 1962), p. 16; cf. H. Z. Hierschberg, "The Remains of Ancient Synagogues in Jerusalem," in *Qadmoniot* I, 1-2 (1968), pp. 56-62, all cited in Saller, *Second Catalogue*, p. 45; Emile Puech, "La synagogue judéo-chrétienne du Mont Sion," *Le Monde de la Bible* (Jan./Feb. 1989), pp. 18-19. Photograph: courtesy École Biblique et Archéologique Française.

209. The South Wall of the Tomb of David on Mount Sion

210. Column from the Ancient Church on Mount Sion

IN 966 THE GREAT Byzantine church of Sancta Sion/ Hagia Sion (No. 205) was looted and burned by the Arabs (Ovadiah, *Corpus*, pp. 89f., no. 77a/b), then in 1099 the Crusaders came and built upon the ruins their own new church, still often called Holy Sion, but now dedicated to Mary the mother of Jesus and known as Sancta Maria in Sion. Of the church in this time we have descriptions by Daniel (1106), John of Würzburg (1170), Theodericus (1172), and Phocas (1185).

Daniel writes (LPPTS IV-C, pp. 36f.): "In the present day Mount Sion is outside the walls of the city, to the south of Jerusalem. On this mount Sion was the house of St. John the Evangelist; and a large church with a wooden roof was erected there; it is as far as one can throw a small stone from the wall of the city to the holy Church of Sion." He goes on to describe the chamber in which Christ washed the feet of his disciples as on the ground floor, and the room of the Last Supper as on the upper floor. Also on the lower floor was the chamber in which the Virgin Mary died.

John of Würzburg (LPPTS V-B, pp. 25f.) likewise finds the chamber (*coenaculum*) of the Last Supper in the upper story of the house and the place of the washing of the disciples' feet in the lower part of the house. Marking the two events there was in the Church of Sion, he says, a painting of the Supper in the upper story and in the lower, i.e., in the crypt, a representation of the foot washing.

Theodericus (LPPTS V-D, pp. 36f.) speaks of the church as dedicated to St. Mary and well fortified with walls, towers, and battlements against the assaults of the infidels. In an upper chamber is the table where the Lord supped with his disciples and in the same upper chamber at a distance of some thirty feet to the southward an altar marks the place of the descent upon the apostles of the Holy Spirit, while in a lower chapel is the place of the foot washing.

Phocas (LPPTS V-C, pp. 17f.) describes "the Holy Sion, the mother of the churches," as of great size, with a vaulted roof. Entering the beautiful gates, there is on the left side the house of St. John the Evangelist, where the Virgin Mary dwelt after the Resurrection, and where she fell asleep. In the upper chamber are the places of the Last Supper and of the descent of the Holy Spirit upon the apostles; in the lower chamber is the place of the washing of the apostles' feet.

The Crusader church too was soon destroyed. In 1219 the Sultan of Damascus, Melek el Mouadhem, ordered most of the Christian sanctuaries in Jerusalem razed, and Sancta Maria in Sion was largely brought down, although the Cenacle with the Chapel of the Holy Spirit (and also the Church of the Holy Sepulcher) were spared (Meistermann pp. 172f.).

Only scanty remains (such as the column in the present photograph), therefore, of the Crusaders' Sancta Maria in Sion and of its predecessor the Byzantine Hagia Sion survived for future investigation. In 1898 the German emperor Wilhelm II obtained and presented to the German Catholic Society of the Holy Land the plot of ground northwest of the Tomb of David building, where the two earlier churches had stood and where the new Church of the Dormition, also known as the Marien-Kirche or Church of the Virgin, was built in Romanesque style in 1901-1910 by the architect Heinrich Renard.

In 1899, prior to building, Renard conducted a small excavation and brought to light the remains of a Byzantine church, afterward also investigated by Vincent, which was certainly the Hagia Sion of the fourth century, known as "the mother of all churches" (No. 205). Much of its materials had evidently been used in the construction of the Crusaders' church of Sancta Maria in Sion, but from the remnants Renard and Vincent were

able to estimate the length of the Byzantine church at approximately 55 meters and its width at half of its length, thus extending over a large area north and northwest of the Tomb of David. The provisional reconstruction of its plan makes it a basilica with a nave and two aisles on either side, marked out by four rows of columns supported on stylobates, and with three apses at the east end, a large central apse and a small apse at the end of each of the inner aisles (Ovadiah, *Corpus*, pp. 89f., no. 77a/b, pl. 38, plan No. 77; Bahat, *Plans*, 33b; Kroll p. 317, abb. 262). The Crusader church was of much the same plan, provisionally seen as a basilica 55.5 meters in length (about the same as the Byzantine basilica), with nave, two side aisles, and a single apse at the east. But opinions differ as to the main axis: Renard locates the main line enough to the north that the church lies to the north of the "tomb of David" and the Cenacle; Vincent moves the line to the south so that the synagogal building comes within the corner of the Crusader church (Bahat, *Plans*, 33a; Kroll p. 317, abb. 262).

The assumption that the words *sancta Sion* in Theodosius (No. 205) were the name of the Byzantine basilica, the predecessor of the Crusader church, as just described, is confirmed by finding the same name, in Greek, in inscriptions in a number of rock-hewn tombs in the nearby Valley of Hinnom (Wadi er-Rababi). Beside the road that leads southward from the Tomb of David there is a tomb with three chambers (PEFQS 1900, pp. 226-227). Over the entrance to the tomb, and accompanied by two crosses which have been defaced, is this inscription:

ΤΗϹ ΑΓΙΑϹ
ϹΙѠΝ

Over the doorway that leads from the first chamber in the tomb to the second, and also accompanied by the sign of the cross, is this inscription:

ΜΝΗ[ΜΑ] ΤΗϹ
ΑΓ[ΙΑϹ Ϲ]ΙѠΝ

Similar inscriptions are found in a number of other tombs in the area. What we have, then, are readings, τῆς ἁγίας Σιών, "of Holy Sion," μνῆμα τῆς ἁγίας Σιών, "tomb of Holy Sion," and the like. In other words these burial places were in the possession of the church on the hill above, and the name of that church was Hagia Sion, the Church of Holy Sion.

R. A. Stewart Macalister, "The Rock-Cut Tombs in Wâdy er-Rababi, Jerusalem," in PEFQS 1900, pp. 225-248; 1901, pp. 145-158, 215-226; Vincent, *Jérusalem nouvelle*, pp. 421-481, especially pp. 431-440; Kopp, p. 386 n. 45. Photograph: JF.

210. Column from the Ancient Church on Mount Sion

211. The Cenacle in the Franciscan Restoration of the Fourteenth Century

AS FOR THE CENACLE, which escaped the general destruction by the Sultan of Damascus in 1219 (No. 210), in 1228 the Franciscans established themselves in Jerusalem, and in 1335 Margaret, a noble Sicilian lady devoted to the pilgrims of Jerusalem, bought a small estate which contained the Cenacle and gave it in part to the Franciscans, after which Robert of Anjou, king of Sicily, and Sanchia, his queen, purchased more ground in the area and presented the same to Pope Clement VI (1342-1352) on the condition that the Franciscans should be its perpetual guardians, and in about 1342 the pope in agreement with the Muslims confirmed the grants and rights of the Franciscans and their guardianship of many sacred sites in Palestine, thus establishing their Custody of the Holy Land (*Custodia Terrae Sanctae*). With the Cenacle as the last surviving part of the Crusader church, the Franciscans repaired and restored

this room, and it is in the form which they gave it that it is seen at the present day.

As the belief spread that the burial place of David—a prophet to the Muslims (Qur'an 4.163, Maulana Muhammad Ali, *The Holy Qur'ān* [Lahore: 1973], p. 233 n. 651) as well as to Jews and Christians (Ac 2:30)—was in fact in the lower part of the same building, Suleiman the Magnificent issued an edict in 1523 that commanded "the expulsion of the infidels from the convent and church of the Cenacle" (Meistermann p. 173), and the building housing the "tomb of David" was converted into the Mosque of the Prophet David (No. 209), a mosque which continued in use as such until recent times.

The upper level of the "tomb of David" building is of substantially the same horizontal dimensions as the lower level (No. 209). The minaret of the Muslim mosque rises at the southwest corner; a large dome is over the northeast corner, below which is the cenotaph of David. The Cenacle, the room of the Last Supper, is

211. The Cenacle in the Franciscan Restoration of the Fourteenth Century

to the west, a hall 14 meters long, 9 meters wide, and 6 meters high (Bahat, *Plans*, 32, 34). As shown in the present photograph, there are two columns in the middle of the room, and half-pillars are built into the wall, and these carry a pointed vaulting of Gothic type. In the southeast corner of the hall a stairway leads up to a small room, which is considered the place of the descent of the Holy Spirit. So the hall that commemorates the holding of the Last Supper and the coming of the Holy Spirit exists even today in the form of a Gothic chapel.

Summary of the History of the Church of Sion

	A.D.
The "church of God which was small," seen by Hadrian	130
The "Upper Church," named by Cyril	348
Sancta Sion/Hagia Sion, the "mother of all churches"	
named by Theodosius	530
destroyed by the Persians	614
burned by the Arabs	966
Sancta Maria in Sion, built by the Crusaders	1099
destroyed by the Sultan of Damascus	1219
The Cenacle, under the Franciscan Custody of the Holy Land	c. 1342
Church of the Dormition	1901-1910

As seen in the foregoing sections, both literary and archeological evidence make it probable that an Essene center (No. 199) and the place of the Last Supper and the center of the early Judeo-Christian church (Nos. 205ff.) were not far from each other on Mount Zion, a proximity which could have meant interrelationship and which may help to explain and illuminate the striking similarities in organization, worship, and social structure of the Essene communities and of the early Christians as seen in the Qumran texts on the one hand and the New Testament records on the other (cf. above, No. 5), all questions calling for further study.

For various dates in relation to the Custody of the Holy Land and the history of the Franciscans in Palestine, see Meistermann p. 173; Raphael M. Huber, *A Documented History of the Franciscan Order* (Milwaukee: Nowiny Publishing Apostolate, 1944), pp. 754f.; Herbert Holzapfel, *The History of the Franciscan Order* (Teutopolis, Ill.: St. Joseph Seminary, 1948), pp. 210f.; Mackowski p. 141. For relations between the Essenes and the early Christians, see FLAP pp. 288-293 with references; Pixner in *Studia Hierosolymitana* I (1976), pp. 276-284; David Beck, "The Composition of the Epistles of James" (Ph.D. diss., Princeton Theological Seminary, 1973). For critical evaluation of the hypothesis of Annie Jaubert (*The Date of the Last Supper* [Staten Island: Alba House, 1965]) that the Last Supper of Jesus and his disciples was observed on the Passover date of the calendar of the Essenes (FHBC pp. 44ff.), therefore on a Tuesday evening, rather than a Thursday evening as the sequence of days in the Gospels appears to make likely, see Josef Blinzler, "Qumran-Kalender und

Passionschronologie," in ZNW 49 (1958), pp. 238-251. For the whole history of the Church on Mount Sion, see Bargil Pixner, "Church of the Apostles Found on Mt. Zion," in BAR 16.3 (May/June 1990), pp. 16-35, 60. Photograph: The Matson Photo Service, Alhambra, Calif.

212. The Church of St. Peter in Gallicantu

AFTER JESUS was apprehended in Gethsemane (Nos. 168ff.) he was taken to Annas (Jn 18:13) and to Caliaphas (Jn 18:24). Annas had been high priest A.D. 6-15 and his son-in-law Caiaphas held the office A.D. 18-36. The scribes and elders gathered with Caiaphas (Mt 26:57; Mk 14:53), i.e., in the high priest's house (Lk 22:54), and there ensued the trial and condemnation of Jesus and the denial of Peter.

In A.D. 66, as Josephus tells us (*War* II 17, 6 §426), revolutionists went into the upper city and burned the house of Ananias the high priest (appointed by Herod of Chalcis [d. in the eighth year of Claudius = A.D. 48], predecessor of Herod Agrippa II [*Ant.* XX 5, 2 §§103-104], Ananias figures in Ac 23:2 and 24:1 and was slain by the brigands in 66 [*War* II 17, 9 §441]) as well as the palaces of Agrippa and Bernice. The palaces were probably additions of Agrippa II to the former palace of the Hasmoneans (*Ant.* XX 8, 11 §189) on the western slope of the Tyropoeon, and the house of Ananias must also have been somewhere on the southwestern hill which was the site of the upper city (cf. No. 173). If the house of the high priest went with the office this house which Ananias occupied could have been that formerly used by Caiaphas (and perhaps Annas, his father-in-law, at the same time). Even if this was not the case, it probably gives a clue as to the area in which the high priest would be likely to reside.

When the Bordeaux Pilgrim came (333) it was in fact up on Mount Sion that he was shown "where the house of Caiaphas the priest was" (*ubi fuit domus Caifae sacerdotis*) Geyer p. 22; LPPTS-B p. 23; CCSL CLXXV, p. 16; WET p. 137. The perfect tense suggests that the house was in ruins, although still well known, and this is confirmed some years later by Cyril who also knew it well and describes it as ruined and desolate. "The house of Caiaphas will arraign thee," says Cyril (*Catechetical Lectures* XIII, 38 NPNFSS VII, p. 92), "showing by its present desolation the power of him who was formerly judged there." Evidently in the Christian thought of the time it was deemed appropriate that the place be left lying in its ruins as a visible sign of judgment.

Theodosius (530) gives at least a rough indication of how far the house was from the Cenacle (but not, unfortunately, in what direction), and also gives the information that it had by then been converted into a church

212. The Church of St. Peter in Gallicantu

named after Peter. Having just referred to the Church of Holy Sion as the mother of all churches (cf. No. 205), Theodosius says (Geyer p. 141; LPPTS II, p. 10; CCSL CLXXV, p. 118; WJP p. 66): "From holy Sion to the house of Caiphas, now the Church of St. Peter, it is 50 paces more or less" (*De sancta Sion ad domum Caiphae, quae est modo ecclesia sancti Petri, sunt plus minus passi numero L*).

Fifty meters north of the Cenacle and across a narrow street from the Dormition is the present Armenian Monastery of St. Savior, held to be built around the house of Caiaphas. The monastery dates from the fifteenth century, but excavations show that there was a church here in the sixth century. A piece of Byzantine mosaic pavement 4-5 meters long and 2.5 meters wide has been found, and a threshold farther west; taken together, these remains may indicate a church some 30-35 meters in length (Vincent, *Jérusalem nouvelle*, p. 489). This was presumably the Church of St. Peter, named by Theodosius. In the courtyard of the Armenian Monastery excavations in 1971-1972 by M. Broshi, E. Netzer, and Mrs. Yael Yisraeli, on behalf of the Armenian Patriarchate and the Israel Department of Antiquities and Museums,

have revealed the remains of luxurious houses of the Herodian period. Especially remarkable are the fresco fragments found in them, for the first time in Israel containing animal motifs: birds on a stylized architectural-floral background. The excavators remark that the presumably wealthy residents evidently allowed themselves to be lax in respect of the prohibition against graven images.

The monk Epiphanius (780-800) also refers to the place of the Last Supper as the place where the disciples gathered after the ascension at Hagia Sion (MPG CXX col. 209), and puts the house of Caiaphas and thus the place where Peter denied Jesus nearby (MPG CXX col. 261). But with respect to the statement in the Gospels that after his denial Peter "went out and wept bitterly" (Mt 26:75; cf. Mk 14:72; Lk 22:62), Epiphanius indicates a different place for this event and points to another church which marked it. The description he gives seems to be written from the standpoint of one on Mount Sion, inside the city wall, and facing northward. He says: "To the right outside the city and near the wall there is a church where Peter, when he went out, wept bitterly; and to the right from the church, approximately three bowshots distant, is the Pool of Siloah" (MPG CXX col. 264 Kopp 1959 pp. 406-407). In distinction, then, from the Church of Peter which was at the house of Caiaphas and near Hagia Sion, the location of this church is eastward down the slope of Mount Sion and perhaps halfway to the Pool of Siloam, and while the former was really a Church of the Denial of Peter this one was a Church of the Repentance or of the Tears of Peter.

Also the monk Bernard (870), having visited Hagia Sion, says: "Directly to the east is a church built in honor of St. Peter, in the place where he denied the Lord" (Tobler-Molinier, *Itinera Hierosolymitana* I 2, p. 316; RB 23 [1914], p. 78; *Biblica* 9 [1928], p. 172). The church must be the one indicated by Epiphanius but here the distinction is not drawn between one place of denial and another place of repentance.

In the time of the Crusaders the church commemorating the Repentance is mentioned repeatedly and in particular connection with the Gospel statement (Mt 26: 74 and parallels) that it was when "the cock crowed" (*gallus cantavit*) that Peter remembered the prediction by Jesus of his denial and went out and wept bitterly. Saewulf (1102) speaks of Hagia Sion, which he calls the Church of the Holy Spirit and locates on Mount Sion outside the city wall a bowshot to the south, and a little later writes (LPPTS IV-B, pp. 19, 21; Vincent, *Jérusalem nouvelle*, p. 494): "Under the wall of the city outside, on the declivity of Mount Sion, is the Church of St. Peter which is called Gallicantus (*ecclesia sancti Petri quae Gallicanus* [sic] *vocatur*), where he hid himself in a very deep cave, which may still be seen, after his denial of our Lord, and there wept over his crime most bitterly." Daniel (1106), having mentioned Mount Sion, writes (LPPTS IV-C, p. 37): "Not far off, on the eastern slope of the mountain, there is a deep cavern to which one descends by thirty-two steps. It is there that Peter wept bitterly (after) his denial. A church is built above this cave and named after the holy Apostle Peter." And Anonymous VII (1145), to cite one more witness where the church is brought into connection with the Latin phrase about the cock-crowing, writes (LPPTS VI-A, p. 73): "Beyond Mount Sion is a church where Peter fled when he denied the Lord at the crowing of the cock (*in galli cantu*)."

On the eastern slope of Mount Sion, 250 meters east of the Cenacle, is an area which corresponds to the place indicated in the foregoing quotations and which belongs to the Assumptionist Fathers. Excavations were begun here in 1888, and in 1911 the ruins of an ancient church were found, with further excavation on behalf of the Assumptionist Fathers by J. Germer-Durand in 1914. Original construction toward the end of the fifth century was indicated by coins from Theodosius II (408-450) to Leo I (457-474), and restoration on a smaller scale (no doubt

after destruction by the Persians in 614) in the first half of the seventh century by coins of Phocas (602-610) and Heraclius I (610-642). According to the excavator's plan this was a rectangular church with three halls, oriented west-east. There is no sign of a circular apse, but the eastern part is the most damaged because of the slope of the hill, and little remains there (Ovadiah, *Corpus Supplementum*, pp. 225f., no. 28). To judge from the citations given above, this was the Church of St. Peter in Gallicantu, marking the supposed place to which the apostle went to weep in repentance after the cock crowed. In 1931 a new church of the same name was dedicated here by the Assumptionists.

The situation of the church just described appears plainly in the photograph. This is a telephoto view, looking westward from above Siloam. At the upper right is a portion of the present south wall of the Old City. Outside the wall, on the summit of Mount Sion, are the buildings and high tower of the Dormition Church and Monastery. To the right of the high tower is the small black dome over the Cenacle and the Tomb of David. Coming down the hill, the large, domed building nearest the camera is the present Church of St. Peter in Gallicantu.

Under this church there are certain rock-hewn chambers (Bahat, *Plans*, 36). One was probably originally a tomb chamber. Steps lead down into it on the east side but stop abruptly halfway down, showing that it was artificially deepened at a later time. In this room there are galleries surrounding a central court, and rings high up on the walls. On the south side there is a step from which one can look through an aperture in the stone wall and down into the other chamber which is itself a very deep pit. On the inner walls and roof of this pit are fourteen Byzantine cross marks, eleven painted on the walls and three incised in the roof.

On the basis of these finds the theory has been advanced that the house of Caiaphas was actually here rather than near the Cenacle, and that the rock-hewn chambers were the prison associated with that palace. The upper chamber, it is suggested, was a guard chamber and the rings in the walls were used to tie prisoners for flagellation; the lower pit was the place of incarceration and the aperture in the wall allowed the guards to watch those below. That Christ himself was confined here during the night of his trial before Caiaphas is then also surmised.

One other line of argument is also held to favor the location of the house of Caiaphas here at St. Peter's in Gallicantu. If the Cenacle is indeed the place where the disciples gathered after the ascension, it would seem strange that they would so soon meet in a place as close to the residence of Caiaphas as would be the case if that house was at the Armenian site as described above. But if the house of Caiaphas was far down the slope of the hill at this latter place the difficulty would not arise.

On the other hand the most natural reading of the earlier witnesses, as followed above, would seem to locate the house of Caiaphas in proximity to Hagia Sion, and this makes it most natural to recognize here, farther down the hill, only the church marking the supposed place of Peter's repentance. As for the rock-hewn chambers under the church, some simpler explanation may account for them and some hold, in fact, that the deep pit is only an ancient cistern.

J. Germer-Durand, "La maison de Caiphe et l'église Saint-Pierre a Jérusalem," in RB 23 (1914), pp. 71-94, 222-246; E. Power, "The Church of St. Peter at Jerusalem, Its Relation to the House of Caiaphas and Sancta Sion," in *Biblica* 9 (1928), pp. 167-186; 10 (1929), pp. 116-125, 275-303, 394-416; Vincent, *Jérusalem nouvelle*, pp. 482-515; and "Saint-Pierre en Gallicante," in RB 39 (1930), pp. 226-256; Kopp 1959, pp. 405-408; M. Broshi, "Excavations in the House of Caiaphas, Mount Zion," in *Jerusalem Revealed*, pp. 57-60. Photograph: The Matson Photo Service, Alhambra, Calif.

213. Ancient Walk with Steps by the Church of St. Peter in Gallicantu

IN THE VICINITY of the Church of St. Peter in Gallicantu are the clear traces of a number of paths or streets, probably representing routes through the city in Jewish and Roman as well as Byzantine times. One of these runs from the vicinity of the Cenacle to the Pool of Siloam and passes directly beside the Church of St. Peter in Gallicantu. A portion of this way beside the church is shown in the photograph, with stone steps to mitigate the steepness of the descent. This path is believed to be from the Jewish period and if, when Jesus went from the Last Supper to Gethsemane (Jn 18:1), he went from Mount Sion to the Kidron, he could have walked upon these very steps.

Germer-Durand in RB 23 (1914), pp. 244-245 and pl. I and III; Lagrange pl. XXVII facing p. 584. Photograph: JF.

214. The Traditional Site of Akeldama in the Valley of Hinnom

ACCORDING TO MT 27:3-10 when Judas returned to the chief priests the money he had received for betraying Jesus, they purchased with the money the potter's field to buy strangers in. Therefore the field was called the Field of Blood (ἀγρὸς αἵματος, v. 8). Ac 1:19 explains that in the language of Jerusalem this name (χωρίον αἵματος) is Ἀκελδαμάχ, Akeldama (RSV), probably corresponding to Aramaic חקל דמא .

In the *Onomasticon* (p. 38) Eusebius gives this listing for the place: "Akeldama. 'Field of Blood.' In the Gospels. It is shown until now in Aelia north of Mount Sion (ἐν βορείοις τοῦ Σιὼν ὄρους)." Jerome (ibid., p. 39) corrects this statement to read "south" (*ad australem*) rather than north.

Akeldama is also mentioned in the *Onomasticon* p. 102) in connection with the listing of Topheth. According to Jer 7:31f. the high place of Topheth was in the valley of the son of Hinnom, and was where sons and daughters were burned in the fire (cf. No. 173). Eusebius writes: "Topheth. Altar of Topheth in Jeremiah. The

213. Ancient Walk with Steps by the Church of St. Peter in Gallicantu

214. The Traditional Site of Akeldama in the Valley of Hinnom

place thus called is shown until now in the suburbs of Aelia. The Pool of the Fuller and the Field Akeldama lie beside it." According to this, Akeldama was in the Valley of Hinnom and in the vicinity of the Pool of the Fuller. The Pool of the Fuller is probably the same as Enrogel, the Spring of the Fuller, which in Jos 15:7 and 18:16 appears to be located near the junction of the valley of the son of Hinnom with the valley of the Kidron. This location makes it probable that the spring is to be identified with what is today called Bir Ayyub or Job's Well, which is below the village of Silwan on the left bank of the Wadi en-Nar, or Kidron Valley, shortly after its junction with the Wadi er-Rababi, or Valley of Hinnom. Accordingly Akeldama should be sought somewhere toward the east end of the Valley of Hinnom.

The Anonymous of Piacenza (570 (Geyer p. 177; LPPTS II-D, p. 22; CCSL CLXXV, p. 167ᵛ) went from Siloam; WJP p. 84 to Akeldama; Arculf (670) (Geyer pp. 243, 245; LPPTS III-A, p. 21; CCSL CLXXV, p. 198ᵛ), who visited Akeldama; WJP p. 100 often, said that it was situated toward the southern region of Mount Sion (*ad australem montis Sion plagam situm*).

The traditional site, which corresponds with the above indications, is on the south slope of the Valley of Hinnom toward its eastern end. A view of the region is shown in the photograph. Looking across to the south side of the valley, we see at the left the enclosure and buildings of the Greek Monastery of St. Onuphrius. To the west and above, the ruins mark the traditional site of Akeldama.

Kopp 1959 pp. 408-411. Photograph: courtesy École Biblique et Archéologique Française.

215. Plan Showing the Site of the Antonia

THE TRIAL of Jesus before the Roman governor Pilate, procurator of Judea probably in A.D. 26-36 (cf. No. 129), was held at a building, or palace (αὐλή, literally "courtyard" and hence "palace," Mk 15:16), in Jerusalem which is called the praetorium (the Greek πραιτώριον is a loan word from the Latin *praetorium*) in Mt 27:27, Mk 15:16, and Jn 18:28, 33; 19:9. Here Pilate sat on the judgment seat (βῆμα) (Mt 27:19; Jn 19:13) which, as the last reference states, was at a place called Lithostroton, i.e., the Pavement and, in Hebrew, Gabbatha (Λιθόστρωτον, Ἑβραϊστὶ δὲ Γαββαθά). The adjective λιθόστρωτος is derived from λίθος, "stone," and στρώννυμι, "spread," hence means "paved with blocks of stone," and the substantive τὸ λιθόστρωτον means a "stone pavement." As for the equivalent word Γαββαθά, this is the Greek transliteration of an Aramaic word, but one of which the etymological derivation is still uncertain.

At Caesarea in the time of the governor Felix (for his date see FHBC pp. 322f.) we hear of "Herod's praetorium" (Ac 23:35) and surmise, as mentioned above (No. 120), that this was the former palace of Herod the Great, which the procurators had taken over for their official residence. In Jerusalem also it may be assumed that the Roman governors appropriated the buildings of Herod for their own use.

From Josephus we know that in Jerusalem Herod the Great had three major buildings at his disposal. In the first place, when Rome made him king of the Jews (40 B.C. and he returned, captured Jerusalem, turned Antigonus, the last of the Hasmonean rulers, over to the Romans to be beheaded, and began to reign in fact (37 B.C.), the palace of the Hasmoneans naturally fell into his hands. From then on it must have provided his official residence for some fourteen years until he built his own new palace on the western hill (see immediately be-

low), and in comparison with the latter the Hasmonean palace may be called Herod's own Lower Palace. It was presumably here where the trial and condemnation to death of his wife Mariamme took place (29 B.C., SHJP Vermes Millar, I, p. 302), and likewise the same palace which Alexandra, Mariamme's mother, had tried to possess in the absence of Herod, and experienced the same fate (28 B.C., SHJP Vermes/Millar, I, p. 303).

The Hasmonean palace (αὐλή) is described by Josephus (War II 16, 3 §344; Ant. xx 8, 11 §190; cf. above, No. 173) as above the bridge that connected the Upper City with the Temple enclosure (at Wilson's Arch, No. 195). We also learn that in his time Herod Agrippa II (who did not reign in Jerusalem but had the oversight of the Temple [Ant. xx 9, 7 §222] and lived in the Hasmonean palace during his visits to the city) built a chamber in this palace where he could recline at meals and look down into the inner court of the Temple, which distressed the priests and led them to erect a wall that would obstruct his view (Ant. xx 8, 11 §§180ff.).

The Hasmonean palace was, therefore, at some relatively high point on the west bank of the Tyropoeon Valley, across from the southwestern part of the Temple en-

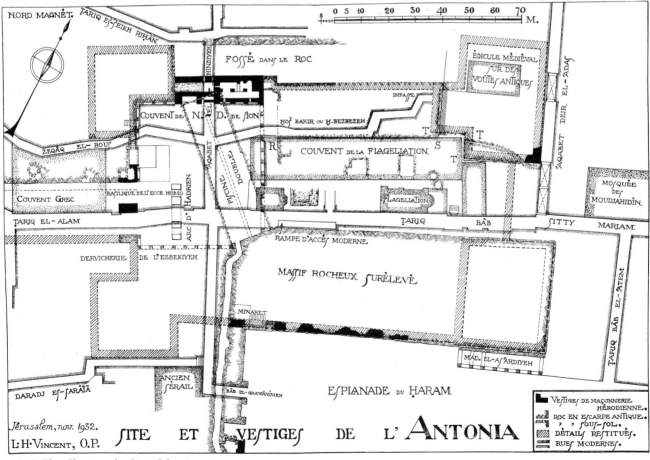

215. Plan Showing the Site of the Antonia

closure wall, i.e., in what is now the Jewish Quarter of the Old City. In the Israeli excavations in this quarter the Hasmonean palace was one object of search, but no remains were found which the excavators could ascribe to it. The remains were uncovered, however, of several elegant houses of the Herodian period (37 B.C.-A.D. 70), built with mosaic floors and ornamented with frescoes and stucco work (Avigad in *Jerusalem Revealed*, pp. 41-51; and *Discovering Jerusalem*, pp. 88-137; cf. above. No. 196). According to the finds of coins, one large Herodian residence was definitely in use during the reign of Herod the Great, but intentionally destroyed toward the end of Herod's reign or shortly thereafter when a new street pavement was laid down directly over the ruins, a very broad street (13 meters in width at one point) of very large flagstones (up to 2-2.5 meters in length), which was uncovered for a stretch of 50 meters, running from east to west. Another dwelling was a palatial mansion, the scale of which would even justify calling it a palace. In addition to painted walls, some of the interior walls are modeled in stucco to imitate ashlar masonry as at Masada and Herodium. Although destroyed in A.D. 70, luxury items were still found in the house: a stone table with a floral pattern on its edge, an ornamented blown-glass pitcher, a ribbed bowl of glass, a ribbed bronze bowl, and fine pottery. The location of the house at the eastern edge of the Jewish Quarter (on the east side of Misgav Ladakh Street and south of the new flight of stairs leading down to the plaza in front of the Western Wall) provides a splendid view to the Temple area and across it to the Mount of Olives. Another residence, not far away, is the Burnt House, described above (No. 196) as evidently belonging to a high-priestly family. In all, this would appear to have been a quarter dwelt in by Jerusalemite nobility and therefore appropriately found in the probable vicinity of the Hasmonean palace; perhaps the palatial mansion was even a Herodian annex of that palace (Jaroš in *Bibel und Liturgie* 53 [1980], p. 14).

In the second place (as noted above, No. 181), Herod the Great rebuilt the Hasmonean fortress called Baris at the northwestern corner of the Temple area and named it in honor of his friend Mark Antony (*Ant.* xv 11, 4 §409). This must surely have been done before Antony was defeated (September 2, 31 B.C.) and Herod transferred his loyalty to Octavian (*Ant.* xv 6, 6 §§187-193; Plutarch, *Antony* 71). Named thus the Antonia, Josephus designates the building as a fortress (φρούριον, *Ant.* xv 8, 5 §292) and a tower (πύργος, πυργοειδής, *War* v 5, 8 §§240, 242), and also describes the splendid arrangements of the interior (*War* v 5, 8 §241):

> The interior resembled a palace (βασιλείων) in its spaciousness and appointments, being divided into apartments of ev-

ery description and for every purpose, including cloisters, baths, and broad courtyards for the accommodation of troops (στρατοπέδων αὐλαῖς πλατείαις cf. the "barracks," παρεμβολή, Ac 21:34, 37 RSV); so that from its possession of all conveniences it seemed a town (πόλις), from its magnificence a palace (βασίλειον) [cf. *War* I 21, 10 §421 for a similar description of Herodium].

Although Josephus describes the Antonia thus as fitted out appropriately for royalty, he does not employ for it the word properly meaning a palace (αὐλή), which he uses for both the Hasmonean palace and Herod's palace on the western hill, and in one passage (*Ant.* xv 8, 5 §292) in which he mentions both the palace of Herod and the fortress Antonia it is only of the former of which he speaks explicitly as "the palace in which he lived." So, although upon occasion Herod could have stayed in the Antonia in considerable comfort, it was the other two buildings, the former Hasmonean palace and his own structure on the western hill, which must have been his true palaces. With two palaces at his disposal, perhaps the palace on the western hill provided the luxury of a private dwelling, while the Lower Palace continued as the residence of official administration, i.e., as the praetorium, a usage which might have been continued as well by the procurators of the time of Jesus (Pixner in ZDPV 95 [1979], p. 86).

In the third place, Herod the Great built his own new palace with the already described (No. 198) adjacent towers, Hippicus, Phasael, and Mariamme, on the "lofty" (*War* v 4, 4 §173) western hill (more precisely stated, the northwestern corner of the southwestern hill) of the city. As explained above (Nos. 173, 198, 199), the entire southwestern hill was later called Mount Sion, one of Herod's towers is the present Tower of David, and the site of Herod's palace is in part the Citadel of the Old City of Jerusalem (Meistermann pp. 165f.). Located as it was in the "upper city" (*War* v 5, 8 §245), and in distinction from his Lower Palace, here was Herod's Upper Palace.

As to the time of this project, in the thirteenth year of Herod's reign (*Ant.* xv 9, 1 §299), i.e., 25/24 (FHBC p. 232), there was a famine, and around that time he sent some forces to reinforce the expedition of Aelius Gallus in Arabia (*Ant.* xv 9, 3 §317), then when Herod's affairs were in good order and prosperous he built the palace in the upper city (*Ant.* xv 9, 3 §318); after that Herod built the Herodium (*Ant.* xv 9, 4 §323) and then started the construction of Caesarea (*Ant.* xv 9, 6 §331), probably in 22/21 since it was probably completed in 10/9 after twelve years of work (cf. No. 120). Within this sequence of dates (for which cf. SHJP I i, pp. 406-408 and SHJP Vermes/Millar, I, pp. 290-291), the building of the

Upper Palace would appear to fall in approximately 24 or 23 B.C.

It is after telling about the three towers—Hippicus, Phasael, and Mariamme—that Josephus continues with a description of the adjacent palace (*War* v, 4, 4 §§176-181):

> Adjoining and on the inner side of these towers, which lay to the north of it, was the king's palace (αὐλή), baffling all description: indeed, in extravagance and equipment no building surpassed it. It was completely enclosed within a wall thirty cubits high, broken at equal distances by ornamental towers, and contained immense banqueting-halls and bed-chambers for a hundred guests. The interior fittings are indescribable. . . . All around were many circular cloisters . . . and their open courts all of greensward; there were groves of various trees intersected by long walks, which were bordered by deep canals, and ponds everywhere.

In Jerusalem, therefore, Herod's Lower Palace, his Antonia, and his Upper Palace were no doubt all available for the use of the Romans and the Roman procurators when they took over the control of Jerusalem, and the analogy has been noted just above of the use by the procurator Felix of "Herod's praetorium" (Ac 23:35) in Caesarea, which must have been the former palace of Herod in that place. Since in Greco-Roman usage a praetorium is properly the official residence of a governor (Benoit, *Jesus and Gospel*, pp. 168-172), and since an official residence would presumably be in a palace rather than in a fortress, and since it is the Lower Palace and the Upper Palace of Herod each of which is called by Josephus by the word proper to a palace (αὐλή), while the Antonia is a "fortress" (φρούριον), the praetorium of Pilate in Jerusalem would most likely be in one or the other of these two palaces.

In fact the oldest Jerusalem tradition, attested by the pilgrims down into the seventh century, points to the praetorium of Pilate as being on the west bank of the Tyropoeon Valley, which was the area of the Hasmonean palace which became Herod's Lower Palace, and the area of other fine residences, as described above.

The first testimony comes from the Bordeaux Pilgrim (333) (Geyer pp. 22-23; LPPTS I-B, p. 23; CCSL CLXXV, pp. 16-17; WET pp. 157-158). From the Temple area the pilgrim came past the Pool of Siloam, went up on Mount Sion, saw the place of the house of Caiaphas (which was about 50 paces from the Holy Sion church, according to Theodosius [WJP p. 66]), and mentions the one of the seven ancient synagogues that was still left in Sion (No. 205). Mount Sion was at the time outside the city wall, and the record now reads:

> As you leave there and pass through the wall of Sion towards the Gate of Neapolis (*ad portam Neapolitanam*), to-

wards the right (*ad partem dextram*), below in the valley, are walls, where was the house or praetorium of Pontius Pilate (*ubi domus fuit sive praetorium Pontii Pilati*); here the Lord was tried before he suffered. On the left hand is the little hill of Golgotha where the Lord was crucified. . . . There by the command of the Emperor Constantine a basilica has been built.

The Bordeaux Pilgrim has come inside the city wall probably at a place near the present Sion Gate and is facing north toward the gate through which one would go out north toward Neapolis (now Nablus, cf. No. 62), i.e., the equivalent of the present Damascus Gate (Meistermann p. 219). Below to the right in the valley, which must be the Tyropoeon, is the place of the praetorium. Proceeding, the pilgrim also passes on the left the hill of Golgotha and the newly built Church of the Holy Sepulcher.

In 451 Peter the Iberian (Baldi p. 553, no. 888; Raabe p. 99 in Kopp 1959, p. 419) came from the north. He came first to the martyrium of St. Stephen. This was the site north of the Damascus Gate, earlier called St. Stephen's Gate, where the empress Eudocia (444-460) built a basilica in honor of the martyr (Ac 7:60), and where the present St. Stephen's Church now stands with the Dominican Monastery and the École Biblique et Archéologique Française (see No. 239). From there Peter came to Golgotha. From there he descended to the church which is called after Pilate, then went on to the Church of the Paralytic (i.e., at the Pool of Bethesda) and to Gethsemane. From its name the Church of Pilate, of which Peter speaks, presumably marked the place believed to have been that of Pilate's praetorium. The place was evidently down in the Tyropoeon Valley, as also previously pointed to by the Bordeaux Pilgrim.

Theodosius (530) put the house of Caiaphas at 50 paces more or less from Hagia Sion as we have seen (No. 212), and then he says (Geyer pp. 141-142; LPPTS II-B, pp. 10-11; CCSL CLXXV, pp. 118-119; WJP p. 66): "From the house of Caiaphas to the praetorium of Pilate (*De domo Caiphae ad praetorium Pilati*) it is 100 paces more or less. There is the Church of Holy Wisdom (*ecclesia sanctae Sophiae*). . . . From the house of Pilate to the Sheep Pool (*De domo Pilati usque ad piscinam probaticam*) is 100 paces more or less." The praetorium of Pilate and the house of Pilate are presumably one and the same, and the Church of St. Sophia (Holy Wisdom) by which the place is marked must be the same as the church called after Pilate, mentioned by Peter the Iberian. That a church first designated by its location at a place connected with Pilate would not keep permanently the name of the Church of Pilate but would be given a different name—the name of the Holy Wisdom which stood before Pilate in the trial of Jesus—is very understandable. It seems evident that the distances given by Theodosius are somewhat arbitrary and approximate, but a point about halfway along a line from the house of Caiaphas on Mount Sion to the Sheep Pool (No. 203) would fall somewhere in the Tyropoeon Valley.

The Anonymous of Piacenza (570) (Geyer pp. 174-175; LPPTS II-D, pp. 19-20; CCSL CLXXV, p. 141; WJP p. 84) gives the longest (and in part the most credulous) account of the praetorium and of its location of any in this series of relatively early pilgrims. The Anonymous was on Mount Sion and went down to the Pool of Siloam, with the following narrative falling in between:

> From Sion we went to the basilica of St. Mary, where there is a great congregation of monks, and also guest houses for men and women, and on behalf of travelers they have innumerable tables, and more than three thousand beds for the sick. And we prayed in the Praetorium where the Lord was tried, where is now the basilica of St. Sophia in front of the ruins of the temple of Solomon, below the street which runs down to the fountain of Siloam outside the portico of Solomon. In this basilica is the seat where Pilate sat when he heard the Lord's case. There is also a quadrangular stone which used to stand in the center of the Praetorium, upon which the accused person was placed during his trial so that every one could hear and see him, upon which the Lord was placed when he was heard by Pilate, and his footprints (vestigia) are still on it. The portrait, which was painted during his lifetime and placed in the Praetorium, shows a beautiful small, delicate foot, a person of ordinary height, a handsome face, hair inclined to curl, and a finely formed hand with long fingers. From this stone where he stood come many blessings. People take measures from the footprints, and wear them for their various diseases, and are healed. The stone itself is adorned with gold and silver.

Between Sion and Siloam it is plain that the "basilica of St. Mary," with its large numbers of resident and visiting persons, is the Nea, the New Church of St. Mary, Mother of God, now found archeologically at the south Turkish wall in the Jewish Quarter of the Old City (No. 196). Likewise the basilica of St. Sophia (Holy Wisdom) is the same church we met in the itinerary of Theodosius (just above), which church in both Theodosius and the Anonymous of Piacenza marks the place of Pilate's praetorium. Here in the Anonymous the location of St. Sophia is more exactly indicated with respect to definitely known points: it is between the Nea and the Temple area, and below the street running to the Pool of Siloam (see AJPA Byzantine Period). In the Madaba Mosaic (560) a small church not far to the left of the Nea is probably St. Sophia: two unusual columns at the west wall of the church may be intended to mark the judgment seat (bema) of Pilate; in the main façade a now-lost red stone may have been the place where the accused stood. In general the location of St. Sophia is not far from the excavated fine houses in the Jewish Quarter

(No. 196) and the hypothetical place of the Hasmonean palace, which became Herod's Lower Palace (Kroll p. 339, col. 2; p. 340, col. 3).

Sophronius (634) writes in the Anacreontica (MPG 87-3, cols. 3821-3822; Baldi p. 585, no. 892; LPPTS XI-A, p. 31): "Now, leaving Sion and the heights . . . I would go into the house and weep with sighs over the stone that marks the spot where the Chief of all Wisdom heard his own sentence, and I would bow myself to the ground and kiss it. I would enter the place of the holy sheep-pool." Sophronius' route, "leaving Sion and the heights" and going to the sheep pool would necessarily be down across the Tyropoeon Valley, and the mention of the place where the "Chief of Wisdom" heard his sentence is surely an allusion to the Church of St. Sophia, so the poem of Sophronius evidently reflects the same tradition noted in the foregoing sources.

The Armenian Description of Holy Places (660) contains the statement (Baldi p. 585, no. 894; PEFQS 1896, p. 348): "To the right of Sion is the Palace of Pilate, called Kappata, and the stone on which Christ stood before Pilate. On it are seen his footprints to this day." The direction "to the right of Sion" would be down into the Tyropoeon Valley, and the reference to the footprints of Christ corresponds with what the Anonymous of Piacenza said in connection with the Church of St. Sophia, so the Armenian Description is evidently also a witness to the same oldest Jerusalem tradition about the location of the praetorium.

The consistency and antiquity of the tradition just traced require that it be taken seriously, and it appears probable that the praetorium of Pilate is indeed to be sought at the Hasmonean palace, which became the Lower Palace of Herod the Great, at or near the site of the Byzantine Church of St. Sophia.

> References for the Praetorium at St. Sophia: B. Bagatti, "La Tradizione della Chiesa di Gerusalemme sul Pretorio," in RIVB 21 (1973), pp. 429-432; Bargil Pixner, "Noch einmal das Prätorium, Versuch einer neuen Lösung," in ZDPV 95 (1979), pp. 56-86; Karl Jaroš, "Ein neuer Lokalisierungsversuch des Praetoriums," in Bibel und Liturgie 53 (1980), pp. 13-22, see esp. no. 15 on abb. 1, and also abb. 2 and 3.

The St. Sophia Church, as well as the Nea Church (No. 196), was no doubt destroyed in the Sasanian Persian invasion in A.D. 614, and the name of St. Sophia does not appear any more after that (J. Rhétoré, "La prise de Jerusalem par les perses," in RB 6 [1897], p. 480). Then after the conquest of Byzantine Jerusalem by the Muslims in A.D. 638 there was new building activity in the Temple area (the Dome of the Rock under Caliph 'Abd al-Malik, 685-705, and the al-Aqsa Mosque under Caliph al-Walid, 705-715, cf. Nos. 185, 186) and also much building work on the periphery of the Temple enclosure (No. 192). It may not be surprising, therefore, that the site of the St. Sophia church was lost sight of, and the early localization of the praetorium at this place in the Tyropoeon Valley is not further attested. Instead, references from the eighth century and onward even into the Crusader period point to a place for the praetorium on Mount Sion.

The Jerusalem monk Epiphanius Hagiopolita (780-800) gives an involved series of references (Donner in ZDPV 57 [1971], pp. 69f., 83f.; WJP p. 117):

> And at the west gate of the Holy City is the Tower of David, in which the king sat in the dust (σπόδος, the word means either dust or ashes) and wrote the Psalter. On the right of the Tower is the Pavement (λιθόστρωτον, a small church where Judas betrayed the Lord. But to the right of the Pavement is the Holy Sion (ἡ ἁγία σιών), the House of God. And at the great door on the left is the place where the holy Apostles carried the body of the most holy Mother of God after her departure. And . . . (nearby) is set up the stone at which they scourged Christ our God. And at the holy doors of the sanctuary are the footprints of Christ. There he stood when he was judged by Pilate. To the right side of the altar is the Upper Room, where Christ had the Supper with his disciples. . . . And in the apse of the Holy Sion, that is to say, of the Praetorium (καὶ εἰς τὴν κόγχην τῆς ἁγίας σιὼν ἤγουν τοῦ πραιτορίου), there is a small structure with four columns containing the coal-brazier. In this place St. Peter was questioned by the little maid. . . . And in the same place is the palace of Pilate, and also of Annas and Caiaphas and of Caesar.

While the Tower of David to which Epiphanius Hagiopolita refers in the beginning of the foregoing passage is near the present Jaffa Gate, the pilgrim known as Anonymous I (1096) mentions a different gate and makes a statement which, although it needs to be noted, does not fit into the present series completely (LPPTS VI-A, p. 1): "Near the Gate of Neapolis is Pilate's judgment hall (*praetorium Pilati*), where Christ was judged by the chief priests. Not far from thence is Golgotha, or the place of Calvary." As noted just above in connection with the Bordeaux Pilgrim, the Neapolis Gate corresponds with the present Damascus Gate, so the area indicated is to the north of Mount Sion proper.

The pilgrim known as Anonymous VII (1145) cites the church built on Mount Sion in honor of Mary, and says (Baldi p. 587, no. 902; LPPTS VI-A, p. 72): "On the left-hand side of this church there is a chapel on the place where was the judgment hall (*praetorium*) and judgment of Christ."

John of Würzburg (1170) says that for his trial before Pilate Jesus was "brought to Mount Sion, where at that time was the Praetorium of Pilate (*praetorium Pilati*), called the Pavement (*lithostrotos*), in Hebrew Gabbatha (Baldi p. 588, no. 903; LPPTS V-B, pp. 28-29).

Theodericus (1172) too recalls the trial of Jesus before Pilate, and writes (Baldi p. 589, no. 904; LPPTS V-D, p. 41):

> After he had asked him many questions, Pilate caused him to be led to the judgment hall, and sat down, by way of a judgment-seat, in the place which is called the Pavement (*lithostrotos*), which place is situated in front of the Church of St. Mary on Mount Sion. . . . In front of the church, on a stone cut in the likeness of a cross, these words are inscribed: "This place is called the 'Pavement,' and here the Lord was judged."

Likewise the Anonymous Pilgrim VIII (1185) (LPPTS VI-A, p. 76) speaks of coming to Jerusalem from Nazareth, i.e., from the north. Outside the walls, he says, you will find the place where St. Stephen was stoned. In the midst of the city you will come to the Church of the Holy Sepulcher. Then he writes: "After this we come to Mount Sion, where is St. Savior's Chapel, which is called the judgment hall of Pilate. Here our Lord was crowned, bound, spat upon, and judged by Pilate."

Beyond that he speaks of the place where the Virgin Mary passed away, and the place of the Lord's Supper, and the place where the Holy Spirit descended on the Day of Pentecost, etc., i.e., of Hagia Sion, and beyond that of the place where Peter hid himself when he had denied Christ, and of the fountain of Siloam. The routing is plain and the praetorium, commemorated by a church named St. Savior's, is on Mount Sion a little short, coming from the north, of Hagia Sion. We have already learned (above, No. 212) that the vestiges of an ancient (sixth-century) church have been found at the site here indicated, at the Armenian Monastery of St. Savior. Whereas Theodosius (530) knew this as the Church of St. Peter, commemorating the house of Caiaphas where Peter denied his Lord, we learn from Anonymous VIII (1185) that the name has been changed to St. Savior and the place held to be that of the praetorium. The name of St. Savior persists in the name of the monastery (Meistermann p. 293); the present fifteenth-century chapel, however, is still held to be the house of Caiaphas (Kopp 1963, p. 356).

For the most part, then, the foregoing references put the praetorium on Mount Sion at or near the Sancta Maria/Hagia Sophia church, and may be understood as simply a part of the increasing tendency to localize many traditional events in that area. As for the Upper Palace of Herod the Great, which was farther north on Mount Sion (adjacent to the Tower of David, which Epiphanius Hagiopolita does mention), at the outset of the Jewish war against the Romans (September A.D. 66) the palace, then occupied by a Roman garrison, was burned by the revolutionists, leaving Josephus only a "harrowing memory" of the building that he had described as so splendid

(*War* v 4, 4 §§182-183; cf. II 17, 9 §§430-440); therefore it may be not surprising that it is no longer mentioned in these later references.

As for intrinsic probability, however, although the oldest Jerusalem tradition makes Herod's Lower Palace the more probable place for Pilate's praetorium, serious consideration can also be given to the Upper Palace. The fact is that most if not all of the available evidence as to the residence of the Roman procurators when they were in Jerusalem points to their use of the palace of Herod, and this presumably means the Upper Palace, which was Herod's own construction and no doubt his main residence in his later years (Benoit, *Jesus and Gospel*, pp. 175-179). Examples are these: Philo (*The Embassy to Gaius* XXXVIII 299; XXXIX 306; LCL X, pp. 150f., 154f.) relates that on one occasion Pilate, to the annoyance of the Jews, put up golden shields in the palace of Herod; in this connection Philo specifically calls Herod's palace the residence of the procurators (οἰκία τῶν ἐπιτρόπων, using the same word ἐπίτροπος by which Josephus [*War* II 9, 2 §169] designates Pilate as procurator). Josephus (*War* II 14, 8-9 §§301-308) tells how the procurator Gessius Florus (64-66) came from Caesarea and lodged at the palace (ἐν τοῖς βασιλείοις), and this palace is later (*War* II 16, 5 §328) clearly distinguished from the fortress Antonia. In the course of events Florus had his judgment seat (βῆμα) placed in front of the building, and took his seat upon it to receive the chief priests and others who came before him. An uprising was involved, and Florus was no doubt seated on the same judgment seat when prisoners were brought before him and he condemned them to be scourged and crucified, a scene all too reminiscent of the trial of Jesus before Pilate.

As to archeology, the modern excavations in the area of Herod's palace, i.e., in the courtyard of the Citadel near the Tower of David and the Jaffa Gate and in the Armenian Garden south of the Citadel, have chiefly uncovered only a network of massive stone walls, filled with enormous quantities of earth and stones, to make a huge podium. Spreading from the Citadel on the north, along the Turkish wall on the west, and to the south, but with its eastern limits undetermined beneath present-day buildings, this great platform is estimated to extend over an area of about 300-350 meters from north to south, and at least 60 meters from west to east. But of the superstructures of Herod's great palace complex little remains, although small finds within the fill include bits of Herodian pottery to guarantee the date and to distinguish these remains from the walls of the much smaller Crusader palace built on the same site (after 1118).

If this palace of Herod was the praetorium of Pilate (SHJP Vermes/Millar, I, p. 361), the place of the *lithostroton* and the *bema* could have been in the city square of the Upper City, which Josephus (*War* II 15, 1-2 §§305, 315) calls "the agora known as the 'upper market'" and speaks of as next to the royal palace, therefore could have been across the Street of the Armenian Orthodox Patriarchate to the east in the Armenian Orthodox compound of St. James Cathedral (Mackowski pp. 107f.)

> References for the praetorium at Herod's Upper Palace: Pierre Benoit, "Prétoire, Lithostroton et Gabbatha," in RB 59 (1952), pp. 531-550, and in *Jesus and Gospel*, pp. 167-188; Eduard Lohse, "Die römischen Statthalter in Jerusalem," in ZDPV 74 (1958), pp. 69-78; Josef Blinzler, *The Trial of Jesus* (Cork: The Mercier Press Ltd., 1959), pp. 173-176. References for Herod's palace at the Citadel: Ruth Amiran and A. Eitan, "Excavations in the Courtyard of the Citadel, Jerusalem, 1968-1969 (Preliminary Report)," in IEJ 20 (1970), pp. 9-17; "Herod's Palace," in IEJ 22 (1972), pp. 50f.; and "Excavations in the Jerusalem Citadel," in *Jerusalem Revealed*, pp. 52-64; D. Bahat and M. Broshi, "Jerusalem, Old City, the Armenian Garden," in IEJ 22 (1972), pp. 171f.; and "Excavations in the Armenian Garden," in *Jerusalem Revealed*, pp. 55f.; A. D. Tushingham, *Excavations in Jerusalem 1961-1967*, I (Toronto: Royal Ontario Museum, 1985), pp. 25-32, "The Palace Complex of Herod the Great."

Although the site of the praetorium was still being pointed out on Mount Sion when the Crusaders came, within the Crusader period (1099-1291) yet a third site came to be indicated and indeed became the prevailing view for a long time thereafter. In this case it was also in one of Herod's great buildings that the site was sought, namely, in the Antonia, but the Antonia, as we have seen, was primarily a fortress rather than a residential palace of Herod, and we will see in what follows that this localization is not now considered likely, although it was earlier argued seriously and indeed involves attention to very interesting archeological items.

Reference to the praetorium as apparently in the Antonia appears already in the record of the Russian abbot Daniel, who came to the Holy Land in 1106/1107. Daniel tells of the place of the crucifixion and of the place where St. Helena found the Holy Cross (i.e., at the Church of the Holy Sepulcher), and then writes (Baldi p. 587, no. 900; LPPTS IV-C p. 18): "A short distance thence, towards the east, is the Praetorium, where the soldiers brought Jesus to Pilate. . . . There, too, is the Jewish prison, from which an angel freed the holy Apostle Peter in the night."

The account of the imprisonment of Peter by Herod Agrippa I in Ac 12:2-11 does not say where Peter's prison was, but in v. 10 where Peter and the angel have passed through the iron gate leading into the city and are going out, the Western text (D) adds that "they descended the seven steps" and, like the stairs from which Paul later addressed the people (Ac 21:40), these may most probably have been steps leading down from the lofty Antonia (although hardly the same stairs, since the steps on which Paul stood led into the Temple and these led to a city street). Since Peter's prison and Pilate's praetorium are in the same place, according to Daniel, both are most probably thought of as being in the Antonia.

In the quotation (above) from Theodosius (530) the praetorium of Pilate and the house of Pilate appear to be the same, but when we come to Theodericus (1172) we find that he separates the two. In the passage quoted just above he says that Pilate's judgment hall where he sat down at the pavement was on Mount Sion; in another passage he speaks separately of the house of Pilate and places it in the Antonia (Baldi pp. 588f., no. 904; LPPTS v-D, p. 7):

> Of the other buildings [in Jerusalem], whether public or private, we have scarcely been able to find any traces, or at least very few, with the exception of the house of Pilate, near the Church of St. Anne, the mother of our Lady, which stands near the sheep-pool (*piscina probatica*). Of all the work which Josephus tells us was built by Herod, and which now is utterly ruined, nothing remains save one side, which is still standing, of the palace which was called Antonia, with a gate beside the outer courtyard.

The *piscina probatica* is the Pool of Bethesda (No. 203), the gate beside the outer courtyard must be the Ecce Homo Arch (No. 217), and the house of Pilate is evidently in the Antonia.

It is of course not impossible that Pilate was at the Antonia at the time of the trial of Jesus and conducted the affair at that place. An argument for Pilate's presence there at this time lies in the fact that it was Passover, a time when often there were disturbances at the Temple and the procurator might wish to be close by in person. A possible illustration is in an account by Josephus (*War* II 12, 1 §§224-227; *Ant.* xx 5, 3 §§105-113) of a time when Passover was at hand and a large multitude was assembled for it. In the first version of the account, the procurator Ventidius Cumanus (48-52), fearing an uprising, ordered his troops to stand watch on the roof of the portico of the temple, a practice of previous procurators as well. When one soldier gave crude offence to the people, they began to throw stones, and Cumanus, "fearing a general attack upon himself, sent for reinforcements" (*War* II §226). This sounds as if Cumanus were immediately at hand. In the second version (*Ant.* xx §109) Josephus says that when Cumanus was informed (ἀκούσας) he admonished the people and then ordered more troops. This can be interpreted to mean that when Cumanus was told about the matter at his usual place at his palace, he came to take charge in person (Benoit, *Jesus and Gospel*, p. 176). At any rate, there is nothing to suggest that the regular residence of the procurators was in

the Antonia; rather we can understand that the Roman cohort, which was permanently quartered in the Antonia (*War* v 5, 8 §244, cf. No. 181), was normally there under its own commanding officer, as illustrated in the rescue of Paul from mob violence at the temple, when it was the tribune of the cohort (ὁ χιλίαρχος τῆς σπείρης) who "took soldiers and centurions, and ran down to them" (Ac 21:32).

Archeological considerations in connection with the Antonia have also been thought to agree with details in the Gospel accounts of the trial of Jesus and to confirm that Antonia was Pilate's praetorium at the time, but more recent investigation does not support that conclusion.

> References for the praetorium at the Antonia: Vincent, *Jérusalem nouvelle*, pp. 562-586; and Vincent, "L'Antonia, palais primitif d'Hérode," in RB 61 (1951), pp. 87-107; Soeur Marie Aline de Sion, *La forterésse Antonia à Jérusalem et la question du prétoire* (Ex Typis PP. Franciscalium, 1955). Plan: courtesy École Biblique et Archéologique Française.

216. View from the Courtyard of the Convent of the Flagellation

LOOKING NOW to the probable site of the Antonia, it will be remembered (No. 197) that the minaret el-Gawanimeh and the Muslim school Omariyyah are landmarks at the northwestern corner of the Temple area. In the plan No. 215 the minaret is marked and the large rectangular mass of rock is where the Omariyyah school now stands. It is this mass of rock, measuring some 120 by 45 meters, that is the probable location of the Antonia (Benoit in *Jerusalem Revealed*, p. 89), although it is possible that the fortress extended over a yet larger area (Mackowski pp. 99f.). Running along the north side of the rock mass is the Tariq Bab Sitty Mariam (Street of the Gate of St. Mary), so called because it runs into the city from the east gate in the Turkish wall, which was earlier called St. Mary's Gate (cf. Nos. 169, 243), now St. Stephen's Gate or the Lions' Gate (Bahat, *Plans*, 72). On the north side of this street are, from east to west, the Franciscan Convent of the Flagellation, the Convent of Our Lady of Sion also called the Ecce Homo Orphanage, with the Ecce Homo Basilica, and the Greek Orthodox Convent. Under these buildings exploration and excavations have been possible, chiefly the excavations of M. Godeleine and L.-H. Vincent in 1931-1937 under the Convent of Our Lady of Sion, of the Franciscans in 1955 under the Convent of the Flagellation, and of the people of the Convent of Our Lady of Sion in 1966 in the Ecce Homo Basilica. The illustration is a view from the courtyard of the Convent of the

216. View from the Courtyard of the Convent of the Flagellation

Flagellation looking up toward the el-Gawanimeh minaret.

L.-H. Vincent, "L'Antonia et le prétoire," in RB 42 (1933), pp. 83-113; "Autour du prétoire," in RB 46 (1937), pp. 563-570; Jérusalem, I (1954), pp. 193-221. Photograph: JF.

217. The Ecce Homo Arch

IN THE NARROW street in front of the Convent of Our Lady of Sion (Ecce homo Orphanage) is to be seen this arch, a portion of the central arch of a great Roman gateway (Bahat, *Plans*, 79b). The rest of the main arch seen here extends on northward within the walls of the Basilica of the Ecce Homo, which is a part of the Convent of Our Lady of Sion, while the northern side arch of the same gateway stands behind the altar in the same basilica. The southern side arch of the gateway has been lost on the other side of the street.

Josephus tells us that when Titus took Jerusalem and destroyed the Temple (cf. No. 183) he razed the foundations of the Antonia (*War* VI 2, 1 §93), and Josephus also speaks explicitly of "the demolition of Antonia" (τὴν καθαίρεσιν τῆς Ἀντωνίας) (*War* VI 5, 4 §311). Af-

ter that we know that Hadrian built the new city of Aelia Capitolina, and we recognize, in the arch preserved in the Russian Alexander Hospice (No. 224), what is probably the remains of a great gateway leading into the western forum of Hadrian's city. The most probable reconstruction of that gateway is a monumental structure with three passages, a larger arch in the center and two smaller ones on the sides. Here we have preserved more extensive portions of another gateway of exactly the same type (see the reconstructions of the two gateways in Vincent, *Jérusalem nouvelle*, p. 31 fig. 13 for the gateway in the Russian Alexander Hospice; p. 25 fig. 6 for the gateway here at the Ecce Homo Basilica). Still another gateway of the same type, which is even better preserved and of which the date is certainly known, is the triumphal arch at the southern approach to the city of Gerasa, dating from the time of the visit of Hadrian (129/130) (No. 108). It is generally accepted, therefore, that the Jerusalem arch here discussed is also an arch of Hadrian and that it stood in a forum in the eastern part of Aelia Capitolina. Other fragments of columns, capitals, and the like, found in the area appear to be in part from the time of the Herods, in part from that of Hadrian, and it is not always possible to decide clearly between the two periods (ZDPV 80 [1964], p. 148). A fur-

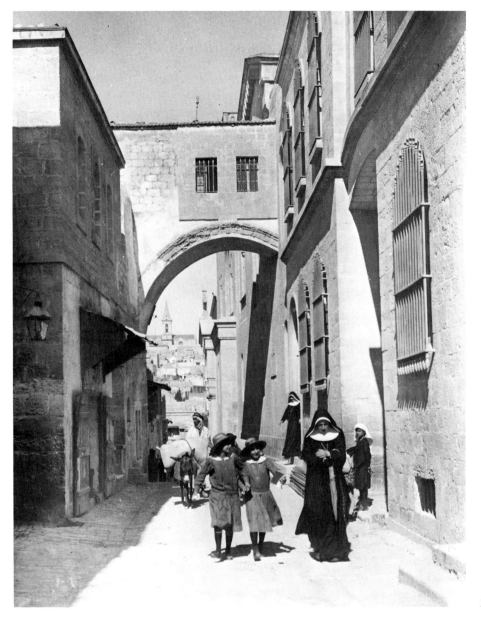

217. The Ecce Homo Arch

ther theory supposes that the arch was originally the east gate of the city in its enlargement to the north by Herod Agrippa I (No. 201), was destroyed in A.D. 70, and was rebuilt by Hadrian (Kroll p. 353 and p. 446 n. 278; cf. Murphy-O'Connor pp. 24f.).

The arch and the mass of ruins to the north of it were acquired in 1857 for the Convent of Our Lady of Sion, and when the Ecce Homo Basilica was built in 1865 the northern side-arch was incorporated in it. At that time the arch was supposed to have been the place where Pilate said, "Behold the man!" ('Ιδοὺ ὁ ἄνθρωπος, Jn 19:5; in Latin, which the Roman procurator might well have spoken in the legal proceeding, *Ecce homo*), and the popular designation has continued to be the Ecce Homo Arch.

Vincent, *Jérusalem nouvelle*, pp. 24-31; Aline, *La forterésse Antonia*, pp. 36-38. Photograph: The Matson Photo Service, Alhambra, Calif.

218. Plan of Stone Pavement Formerly Called the Lithostroton

THIS PLAN SHOWS the large stone pavement, extensive sections of which have been found under the Convent of the Flagellation, the Convent of Our Lady of Sion, and the Greek Orthodox Convent. The pavement extended over an area some 32 meters from west to east, and 48 meters from north to south, thus covering an area of over 1,500 square meters. Architectural remains

255

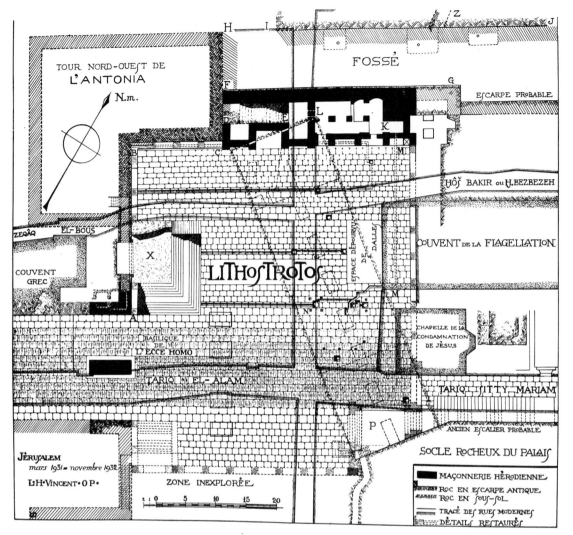

218. Plan of Stone Pavement Formerly Called the Lithostroton

around the area show that this was an impressive court-yard surrounded by galleries. The paving stones are slabs of limestone, some square and some rectangular, as much as a meter on a side, sometimes as much as two meters or more. Some channels are cut out into the stones for the drainage of rainwater.

L.-H. Vincent, "Le Lithostrotos évangélique," in RB 59 (1952), pp. 513-530; *Jérusalem*, pp. 207-214, 216-221; Aline, *La forterésse Antonia*, pp. 88-94, 107-118; W. F. Albright in *The Background of the New Testament and Its Eschatology*, edited by W. D. Davies and D. Daube in honor of Charles Harold Dodd (Cambridge: University Press, 1956), pp. 158-159. Photograph: courtesy École Biblique et Archéologique Française.

219. Striated Paving Stones

TOWARD THE SOUTH SIDE of the pavement just described (No. 218) there is a transverse zone of the paving stones running from east to west, where the slabs are grooved or striated. The striations run from north to south. Thus it seems that there was a roadway here running across the court from east to west, and the stones were grooved to prevent the horses' hoofs from slipping. Some of the striated stones appear in the photograph.

Aline, *La forterésse Antonia*, pp. 95-106. Photograph: JF.

220. A Game Board on a Paving Stone

ON SOME of the stones of the pavement there were also patterns incised, such as appear in this picture. Such a pattern is thought to be a playing board (*lusoria tabula*), intended for games.

With the Crusader-period view that the praetorium of Pilate was at the Antonia it was easy to believe not only that the arch (No. 217) was where Pilate said *Ecce homo*

219. Striated Paving Stones

220. A Game Board on a Paving Stone

(Jn 19:5), but also that the pavement (No. 218) was the *lithostroton* (λιθόστρωτον) on which was Pilate's judgment seat (Jn 19:13), and that the game board was used by Roman soldiers quartered in the Antonia. When the arch was recognized as of later date it was still thought that it rested on the pavement, therefore the pavement

was earlier and could be of the time of Jesus. In the 1966 excavations, however, it was found that the northern pier of the arch rested upon bedrock; moreover the rock was so hewn that the adjacent pavement slab was set against the lower edge of the lowest course of the pier, thus both arch and pavement were constructed at the

257

same time, therefore both were later than the time of Jesus.

Aline, *La forterésse Antonia*, pp. 119-142; B. Bagatti, "Resti romani nell area della Flagellazione in Gerusalemme," in LA 8 (1957-58), pp. 309-352; Benoit in *Jerusalem Revealed*, p. 88. Photograph; The Matson Photo Service, Alhambra, Calif.

221. Cistern under the Stone Pavement

UNDERGROUND IN THE AREA just dealt with (Nos. 215-220) is a very large basin extending from northwest to southeast, 52 meters long, 14 meters wide, and as much as 10 meters deep. This is vaulted in such fashion that it looks much like a great double tunnel, and in the plan (No. 215) it is labeled "piscine double." The construction is integral with that of the paved courtyard above, formerly called the *lithostroton*.

In his description of the attack of Titus upon Jerusalem Josephus tells of four earthwork embankments which the Romans erected. Of these one was at the Antonia, and concerning it Josephus writes (*War* v 11, 4 §467): "Of the first two, that at Antonia was thrown up by the fifth legion over against the middle of the pool called Struthion (κατὰ μέσον τῆς Στρουθίου καλουμένης κολυμβήθρας)." The Greek κατὰ μέσον, here translated "over against the middle," probably has the actual meaning of "right through the middle." The Struthion pool (the name is the diminutive of στρουθός, "sparrow," sug-

221. Cistern under the Stone Pavement

gesting small) here in question cannot be the Pool of Bethesda (Nos. 203-204) or the Pool of Israel (No. 181), which are too far away to have hindered the attack on Antonia; it must be what is now represented by the vaulted cistern under the pavement. But in A.D. 70 this was not a covered reservoir beneath a paved courtyard, rather it was an open pool through which the Romans had to build their embankment in order to get at the Antonia. So again, the pavement as well as the Ecce Homo Arch must be later than the time of Jesus.

Therefore, with the exclusion of the Antonia, it remains probable that the praetorium where Jesus stood before Pilate was either at what had been the Upper Palace of Herod the Great at the present Citadel of Old Jerusalem, or very possibly as per the oldest Jerusalem pilgrim records at what had been Herod's Lower Palace, marked in the time of those pilgrims by the Church of the Holy Wisdom (St. Sophia) in the Tyropoeon Valley.

Vincent in RB 42 (1933), pp. 96-102; Vincent, *Jérusalem*, pp. 203-207; Aline, *La forterésse Antonia*, pp. 64-87; Christian Maurer, "Der Struthionteich und die Burg Antonia," in ZDPV 80 (1964), pp. 137-149; P. Benoit, "L'Antonia d'Hérode le Grand et le Forum Oriental d'Aelia Capitolina," in HTR 64 (1971), pp. 135-167; and Benoit, in *Jerusalem Revealed*, pp. 87-89. Photograph: JF.

222. On the Via Dolorosa Today

THE WAY OF JESUS from the place of his judgment by Pilate to the place of his execution at Golgotha (the present Church of the Holy Sepulcher, Nos. 225ff.) is known by the Christian world as the Via Dolorosa, the Way of Sorrows. If the praetorium of Pilate was at Herod's Lower Palace marked by the St. Sophia Church in the Tyropoeon Valley, then the way would probably have been from there northward to what is now the line of the Street of the Gate of the Chain and David Street, then westward to the crossing of what became the *cardo maximus* (Tetrapylon), and from there through the Gennath Gate to Golgotha (Pixner in ZDPV 95 [1979], pp. 67f.). If the praetorium was at Herod's Upper Palace at the Citadel, the way could have been eastward along the line of David Street (Benoit) or along the line of the Street of the Armenians (Mackowski), and in either case to the line of the *cardo maximus* and northward through the Gennath Gate to Golgotha (Mackowski p. 111 and p. 191 n. 7).

With the Crusader-period location of the praetorium at the Antonia, however, the now traditional Way of the Cross was traced out from there to the Church of the Holy Sepulcher, and gradually elaborated into Fourteen Stations. As followed by the faithful in annual Good Friday processions even now, the stations commemorate

222. On the Via Dolorosa Today

nine events in the Gospels and five derived from legend (Jesus falling three times, meeting his mother, meeting Veronica). They are: (1) at the former Turkish Barracks/present Omariyyeh School at the site of the Antonia and place of the trial; (2) at the *lithostroton* where Jesus was ordered to carry the cross; (3) under the Ecce Homo Arch and to where he fell the first time; (4) where he met his mother; (5) where Simon of Cyrene took the cross (and where the street climbs toward Golgotha, in the present photograph); (6) where Veronica wiped his face with a linen cloth dipped in cold water; (7) where he fell a second time; (8) where he said to the women of Jerusalem to weep not for him but for themselves; (9) where he fell a third time; and the last five stations in the Church of the Holy Sepulcher, (10) where he was stripped of his clothes, (11) was nailed to the cross, (12)

died upon the cross; (13) was taken down, and (14) was laid in the tomb.

Baldi pp. 593, nos. 910-923; Meistermann pp. 143-163, 728-731; wjjk p. 145, fig. 100. Photograph: JF.

223. Ancient Walls in the Russian Alexander Hospice

IT HAS BEEN SEEN above (No. 200 and plan No. 173) that in the time of Jesus the Second Wall of Jerusalem most probably ran from south to north along the east side of the area in which is the present Church of the Holy Sepulcher, and that that area had anciently been a rock quarry and was in that time a place of gardens and tombs, one of which tombs became the sepulcher of Jesus as me-

223. Ancient Walls in the Russian Alexander Hospice

morialized in the Church of the Holy Sepulcher. Later Herod Agrippa I (A.D. 41-44) started a Third Wall (only finished c. 66) which swung out around to the north, thus enclosing that area within the city. Yet later, as Eusebius tells us (*Life of Constantine* III 26 NPNFSS I, p. 527), Hadrian (A.D. 135) buried the holy sepulcher of Christ and covered the whole area with a large quantity of earth, then laid a stone pavement over everything, upon which he erected a shrine of Venus. Like Hadrian's forum at the eastern edge of Aelia Capitolina (still marked by the Ecce Homo Arch and the *lithostroton*, Nos. 217, 218), this was evidently a new forum at the western side of his city (Simons, *Jerusalem*, p. 318; Vincent, *Jérusalem nouvelle*, planches II, pl. I).

In 1844 excavation at the Russian Alexander Hospice (on Suq Khan ez-Zeit, east of the Church of the Holy Sepulcher, No. 200) brought to light ancient remains, two walls, the threshold of a gateway, and a part of an arch, all carefully preserved now in their original position inside the hospice. The walls are built of large stone blocks (Bahat, *Plans*, 71). One wall runs north and south, the other east and west, and as seen in this photograph (No. 223) the two meet at a little more than a right angle. In the line of an eastward continuation of the east-west wall are two stone slabs worn as if from many footsteps and with depressions which could have had to do with the support of a gate (Vincent, *Jérusalem*

nouvelle, p. 63, fig. 32). At one time it was thought this might be a part of the Second Wall of Jerusalem (which we believe ran along the line of the Suq Khan ez-Zeit, No. 200), and the gate even that through which Jesus went out to Golgotha. Now, however, it is believed that many of the stone blocks, some with narrow margins and flat central bosses, are actually old Herodian ashlars, probably left after the Roman destruction of the Temple in A.D. 70 and used by Hadrian for the enclosure wall of his forum and Venus shrine in this place (Wilkinson in *Levant* 7 [1975], p. 135), although the purpose of the well-worn doorsill in Hadrian's plan is not evident.

Vincent, *Jérusalem nouvelle*, pp. 40-88; and in DB Supplément 4, cols. 926-935; Simons, *Jerusalem*, pp. 319-324; *The Threshold of the Judgment Gate on the Place of the Russian Excavations in Jerusalem*, compiled upon works of Archimandrite Antonine, B. P. Mansourov and V. N. Khitrovo (Jerusalem: Greek Convent Press, 1959); Meistermann pp. 138-140. Photograph: courtesy École Biblique et Archéologique Française.

224. Ancient Arch in the Russian Alexander Hospice

ASSOCIATED WITH THE WALLS just described in the Russian Alexander Hospice (No. 223) and standing a short distance southward on the line of the north-south wall is a portion of an arch with a Corinthian capital

224. Ancient Arch in the Russian Alexander Hospice

built into it, as shown in the photograph. Altered though it is, it is believed to be part of a triumphal arch that once stood here at Hadrian's forum.

Murphy-O'Connor pp. 51f. Photograph: JF.

225. Plan of the Constantinian Church of the Holy Sepulcher

THE PLACE WHERE JESUS was crucified was called Golgotha. Where they use this name Mt 27:33 and Mk 15:22 explain parenthetically that it means the place of a skull (κρανίου τόπος), and Lk 23:33, omitting the Semitic name, simply calls the place the Skull (Κρανίον). Jn 19:17 also calls the place the place of a skull, and explains that Ἑβραϊστί, i.e., "in Hebrew," as the word means literally and as it probably means actually in Rev 9:11 and perhaps also in Rev 16:16, or "in Aramaic," as the word probably means actually here and elsewhere in Jn, the name is Golgotha. This name is in fact Aramaic, גלגלתא, corresponding to Hebrew, גלגלתא, which is translated by κρανίον in Jg 9:53 LXX, etc. In Latin the word for skull is *calva*, and in Jerome's Latin translation of the NT the name of the place is *Calvariae locus* in Mt 27:33, Mk 15:22, and Jn 19:17, and *Calvariae* in Lk

23:33, hence Calvary in English. The most probable explanation of the name is simply that a skull stands for death, and this was a place of execution. The place was "near the city" according to Jn 19:20, and "outside the gate" according to Heb 13:12, a place outside the city certainly being normal for execution as well as for burial in both Jewish and Roman custom. In the place there was a garden, and in the garden a new tomb (Jn 19:41), which became the tomb of Jesus.

The remembrance of the place of Golgotha and of the tomb of Jesus on the part of the early Christians in Jerusalem is highly probable. Even when the Jewish Christians fled to Pella on the eve of the Jewish War (Eusebius, *Ch. Hist.* III 5, 3) they were only fifty miles away, and when Jews were forbidden entry into Jerusalem by Hadrian there were Gentile Christians in Jerusalem under a series of bishops, of whom Marcus was the first (Eusebius, *Ch. Hist.* IV 6), to continue the tradition (cf. above, List of Bishops of the Jerusalem Church).

As we have seen (No. 183), both Dio and Jerome tell us that Hadrian put a pagan sanctuary of Jupiter on the site of the former Jewish temple. Likewise Jerome (see No. 32) compares the pollution of the birthplace of Jesus in Bethlehem with the fact that from Hadrian onward there was a marble statue of Venus (cf. No. 3) on the rock where the cross had stood, and a figure of Jupiter at

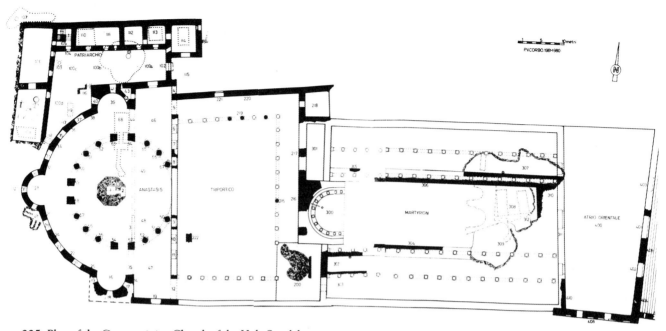

225. Plan of the Constantinian Church of the Holy Sepulcher

the place of the resurrection; and Eusebius tells us, as we have just seen (No. 223), that Hadrian covered and paved the whole area and built a shrine of Venus there. So it seems evident that Hadrian deliberately chose places sacred to both Jews and Christians (and also Samaritans, for he built a temple of Jupiter on Mount Gerizim, No. 60), on which to erect Roman shrines. So he must have selected the place of Calvary for such treatment on the basis of a traditional identification that long antedated his own time and thus reached back into the earliest periods of the Christian movement. (With respect to Hadrian's sacred enclosure, note that Corbo calls it the Capitolium on the doubtful supposition that it was dedicated to the Capitoline Jupiter; see Bahat in BAR 12.3 [May/June 1986], pp. 34f.)

When we continue with the report of Eusebius concerning these events in *The Life of Constantine* (written after the death of Constantine in 337 [IV 64] and before the death of Eusebius in 340), we learn (III 26ff.) that the emperor ordered the clearing away of the Venus shrine and, while this was being done (326/327), "contrary to all expectation" a tomb came to light in a manner which was a similitude of Christ's own return to life. Thereupon Constantine instructed Bishop Macarius to build a church (the term used in the emperor's letter [III 31] is βασιλική, "basilica," and this word appears here for the first time in literature in reference to a Christian church [FLAP pp. 506, 527]) upon the site and this was done. Constantine's architect was Zenobius (the name is given by Theophanes under A.M. 5828 = A.D. 328,

Crowfoot, *Early Churches*, p. 21 n. 1) and the dedication of the church was in 335 (which was also the thirtieth year [*tricennalia*] of the reign of Constantine), when a large synod of bishops was convened in Jerusalem for the services of consecration (Socrates, *Ch. Hist.* I 28; Sozomen, *Ch. Hist.* II 26). Eusebius was present at the occasion and soon afterward in the same year in Constantinople delivered an oration on the sepulcher of the Savior (ἀμφὶ τοῦ σωτηρίου μνήματος λόγος), as well as an oration in praise of Constantine. He proposed to append both orations to his *Life of Constantine* (IV 33, 40); the latter is found in this position (NPNFSS I, pp. 581ff.) but the former is no longer extant.

While in the foregoing context Eusebius speaks only of the tomb, i.e., of the place of the resurrection, in the *Onomasticon* (p. 74) he lists Golgotha with the notation: " 'Place of a skull,' where Christ was crucified. It is pointed out in Aelia to the north of Mount Sion." This general statement of location is in agreement with what we hear from the Bordeaux Pilgrim (333). As we have already seen (No. 215), he came from Mount Sion and went toward the Neapolis Gate in the north wall of Jerusalem, and the hill of Golgotha was on his left hand. The passage in the itinerary of the Pilgrim from Bordeaux, beginning with the statement just alluded to and continuing with a brief description of the basilica of Constantine which was at that time not yet finished, reads (Geyer pp. 22-23; LPPTS I-B, pp. 23-24; CCSL CLXXV, p. 17; WET p. 158): "On the left hand is the little hill of Golgotha (*a sinistra autem parte est monticulus Gol-*

gotha) where the Lord was crucified. About a stone's throw from thence is a crypt where his body was laid and the third day was raised (*Inde quasi ad lapidem missum est cripta, ubi corpus eius positum fuit et tertia die resurrexit*). There by the command of the Emperor Constantine a basilica has been built, that is, a church (*basilica . . . id est dominicum*), of wonderful beauty, having at the side reservoirs (*excepturia*) from which water is raised, and a bath behind in which infants are washed [i.e., baptized] (*balneum a tergo, ubi infantes lavantur*)."

The location of Golgotha and the tomb of Christ thus indicated by Eusebius and the Bordeaux Pilgrim, north of Mount Sion and on the left hand as one proceeds toward the Neapolis Gate in the north wall of Jerusalem, corresponds with the location of the present Church of the Holy Sepulcher. Although it was inside the third wall of Jerusalem, which corresponded with Hadrian's wall and the present wall of the city on the north side, it was outside the second wall, i.e., the wall of the time of Jesus, according to the evidence presented above (Nos. 198ff.), and in the area of an old quarry that had been utilized as a cemetery and a garden (Nos. 198, 200, 226); thus it may be accepted as the correct site in accordance with the earliest Christian tradition.

When Eusebius wrote *The Life of Constantine* between 337 and 340 the church had been dedicated (335) but a short time before, and Eusebius gives a description of it in some detail (III 33-40). As for modern investigation, by 1913 studies by L.-H. Vincent outlined a relatively complete plan of the church in its Constantinian form (see No. 181 in the first edition of the present book). In 1927 the existing church suffered severe earthquake damage, and a structural survey by William Harvey revealed such great dilapidation of the building that in 1938 the administration of the British Mandate of Palestine provided for the installation of supportive iron constructions to prevent complete collapse. The church is shared by six ecclesiastical communities: Latin Catholic, Greek Orthodox, Armenian Orthodox, Syrian Orthodox, Copts, and Ethiopians. In 1960 the major occupants, the Latins, Greeks, and Armenians agreed upon thoroughgoing works of restoration (for some reservations about some Greek Orthodox additions, see Murphy-O'Connor pp. 40f.). In the course of the restoration extensive archeological investigations and excavations were possible and have been reported on most fully by Charles Coüasnon and Virgilio C. Corbo (see the bibliography at the end of this section). Together, the literary sources and the archeological study provide the basis for the present plan and the following discussion. In the plan, walls still remaining today from the original church are shown in solid black. We now take the description by Eusebius in reverse order and move

through the plan from right to left, i.e., from east to west, and see the church as consisting of four main parts.

(1) The First Atrium (called the Eastern Atrium on the plan). This was an open court to which steps led up from the main street on the east (the *cardo maximus*). In the façade of the atrium Constantine's builders used the wall of Hadrian's forum enclosure and cut three doors in it, one wide main portal and two smaller ones on the side (Corbo, *Santo Sepolcro* 2, pl. 68, nos. 404-408). It is the south one of these three doorways the remains of which are seen in the Russian Alexander Hospice (Nos. 223-224); the inner surface and the jambs of the massive central door are in the storeroom of the Zalatimo Bakery just to the north in Suq Khan ez-Zeit. In the Constantinian phase the well-worn doorsill noted in the Russian hospice gave access to a cloister running along the south side of the church (Coüasnon p. 45; Murphy-O'Connor fig. 9, c and pp. 42f.; Mackowski p. 150). The three doorways appear on the present plan as nos. 401, 402, 403. The atrium was probably surrounded by colonnades, was crossed to enter the next main part of the entire complex, namely, the basilica, and was of about the same width as the basilica, i.e., approximately 39 meters wide with a depth of some 15 meters.

(2) The Basilica. From the first atrium the basilica (called the Martyrion on the plan) was entered through three doors, and some stretches of the foundations have been brought to light in the recent excavations (Corbo, *Santo Sepolcro* 1, p. 226 III). The basilica was 58 meters long and 38.5-40 meters wide, and was divided into a wide nave and two side aisles on either side, with a central apse facing west. The foundations of this apse (no. 300 on the plan) were uncovered in excavation in 1968 and presented to the public in 1971 by Athanase Ekonomopoulos, thus the location of the apse and the orientation of the entire basilica are definitely established. As thus known, the east-west axis of the basilica is offset to the south in comparison with the axis of the Rotunda over the tomb, and the apse is thereby brought contiguous to the Rock of Calvary, which stands in line with the first southern side aisle. The placement of the apse at the west end of the basilica (rather than at the east as most often usual in Christian basilicas) must be due to the practical fact that the façade of the Constantinian complex as well as a wall of its Hadrianic predecessor was at the east on the *cardo maximus*, and also due to a theological consideration of a focus upon the Rock of Calvary and the Tomb (Coüasnon pp. 37, 41, and pl. xx; Corbo, *Santo Sepolcro* 2, pl. 3; cf. also the similar disposition of the Christian complex at Gerasa, noted above, No. 117).

In his description Eusebius calls the basilica the μαρτύριον, as do later pilgrims (Aetheria, No. 228; Arculf,

No. 231). While the English word "martyr" is derived from the same Greek root, the original thought of the term is that of witnessing and a *martyrion* is a place which bears witness, thus this basilica bears witness to the death and resurrection of Jesus Christ. According to Eusebius the building was floored with marble slabs of various colors and roofed with lead on the outside for protection against the winter rains. At the west end, he says, was a hemisphere (ἡμισφαίριον), which must be his way of referring to the apse with its half-dome. Here there were twelve columns, with their capitals adorned with large silver bowls presented by the emperor.

(3) The Second Atrium. Beyond the basilica to the west was the second atrium, a large open court, paved with highly polished stone slabs, some of which were found in Trench XIII of the excavations. Also uncovered in the excavations was a stretch of about 35 meters of Constantinian wall (no. 220 in the plan), marking the north flank of the atrium. Around three sides of the courtyard were long porticoes (according to Eusebius; according to Corbo [Santo Sepolcro 1, p. 225 II] these were on the north, east, and south sides, and the atrium may be called the Triportico).

Although Eusebius does not mention it at this point, in the southeast corner of this court was the Rock of Calvary (no. 200 on the plan). Recalling evidence cited above, the probable history of the site was this: From the seventh century B.C. onward an extensive area in this region was used as a quarry. After the quarry was abandoned, probably in the first century B.C., much of the area was filled in with soil and became a garden or orchard and was also used for rock-hewn tombs. This was the configuration when Jesus was crucified on a rocky spur known as Golgotha/Calvary, and was buried in a nearby, as yet unoccupied tomb (Jn 19:41). When Hadrian filled in the area to make a level platform for his shrine of Venus the rocky spur was presumably buried. When Constantine cleared the area for the construction of his church, the rocky slopes were cut back to isolate both the tomb and the rock of Calvary, the latter left standing to a height of 4.8 meters, as it still is. Around the rock was probably only a railing and on it a cross (Corbo, Santo Sepolcro 2, pl. 67).

(4) The Anastasis. Finally at the west end was the holy sepulcher itself. The tomb was evidently cut free from the hill and "as the chief part of the whole" it was "beautified with rare columns, and profusely enriched with the most splendid decorations of every kind" (Eusebius, *Life of Constantine* III 34). Around the tomb was built an imposing Rotunda, the whole known as the Anastasis (ἀνάστασις, the Greek word for "resurrection," used by Aetheria, no. 228). Here a wall 46 meters long, pierced by twelve doorways, separated the Rotunda from the Second Atrium; of the doorways four (nos. 5,

8, 9, 12 in the plan) are still sufficiently preserved as to be recognized in their original Constantinian shape. Inside this wall (i.e., in the direction of the tomb), there was a transept about 8 meters wide. In the northern area (no. 46 in the plan) recent excavation down to bedrock has uncovered not only portions of the Constantinian walls but also foundations of a Hadrianic wall and rock cuttings of the earlier quarry (Corbo, *Santo Sepolcro 2*, pl. 10). In the central part of the transept a sounding traced the foundation of a Constantinian stylobate running north and south in front of the tomb, which probably supported the grill or screen (*cancellus*, literally "lattice") of which Aetheria speaks (No. 228; Corbo, *Santo Sepolcro 2*, pl. 19). Around the tomb in a large circle (with the tomb set slightly to the west to give room for the long transept just described) were twelve columns (mentioned by Arculf, No. 231) in four sets of three units each, intercalated by three pairs of pilasters. Of this circle two of the original columns are still preserved (nos. 65 and 66 in the plan). They are of a large size (113 to 118 centimeters in diameter) unusual in Christian churches, and it is believed that they are the two halves of what was once a single, tall column, and that in fact all twelve columns of the rotunda were originally six high columns that had belonged to the Hadrianic shrine in this place (Corbo, *Santo Sepolcro 2*, pl. 21, 3). Starting from the line of the stylobate mentioned just above, and leaving an ambulatory around the circle of columns, an outside wall made a semicircle to the west, and was marked by an apse at the north, the west, and the south. Together with the wall at the east side of the transept, this formed a D-shape and supported a great dome above. Fifteen windows in the wall and an "oculus" in the dome gave light within. Architecturally the whole is known as the Rotunda; theologically it is the Anastasis, a witness to the resurrection.

Immediately to the northwest of the Rotunda were found the walls of various rooms and a courtyard (called the Patriarchion on the plan). These evidently constituted the dwelling of the bishop, later known as the Patriarchate (Coüasnon p. 46; Corbo, *Santo Sepolcro 1*, p. 227 V). The area immediately on the southwest side of the Rotunda has not been explored, but this was most probably the location of the baptistery, which the Bordeaux Pilgrim, as quoted above, puts behind (*a tergo*) the church (Coüasnon p. 48). At Jerash the baptistery (No. 116) adjoining the church of St. Theodore is in an analogous position, and we have already noted (No. 117) that the entire cathedral complex at Gerasa was probably a reflection of the arrangement of buildings in the complex at the holy sepulcher in Jerusalem. As for a precedent, it may be added that the Constantinian Martyrion is much like the Severan basilica at Leptis Magna in Tripolitania (Conant p. 8).

As for the centrally important Tomb itself, it was presumably surmounted in Constantine's rotunda by an edicule ("little house, small shrine") of some sort, at any rate silver flasks (*ampullae*) preserved in Monza, Italy, in which pilgrims carried away oil from the lamps which burned at the Tomb, have representations of what is presumably the Constantinian edicule as it was still standing at the end of the sixth century, some twenty years before the Persian invasion. Shown is a structure which is apparently either square or polygonal, with side columns supporting a steep pyramidal roof (Grabar, *Ampoules*, nos. 3, 5, 6, 9, 12, 14; Corbo, *Santo Sepolcro 3*, photos 81-86).

Vincent, *Jérusalem nouvelle*, pp. 89-300 and specially pl. XXXIII; Joachim Jeremias, *Golgotha*. ΑΓΓΕΛΟΣ, Archiv für neutestamentliche Zeitgeschichte und Kulturkunde, Beiheft 1 (1926); Crowfoot, *Early Churches*, pp. 9-21; J. G. Davies, "Eusebius' Description of the Martyrium at Jerusalem," in *AJA* 61 (1957), pp. 171-173; André Parrot, *Golgotha and the Church of the Holy Sepulchre*. Studies in Biblical Archaeology 6 (New York: Philosophical Library, 1957); Kenneth J. Conant and Glanville Downey, "The Original Buildings at the Holy Sepulchre in Jerusalem," in *Speculum* 31 (1956), pp. 11-48 (this article is cited in the present context as Conant); P. Testini, "L'Anastasis alla luce delle recenti indagini," in *Oriens Antiquus* 3 (1964), pp. 263-292; Robert H. Smith, "The Tomb of Jesus," in *BA* 30 (1967), pp. 74-90; William Harvey, *Church of the Holy Sepulchre, Jerusalem: Structural Survey, Final Report* (London: Oxford University Press, 1935); Andre Grabar, *Ampoules de Terre Sainte (Monza-Bobbio)* (Paris: C. Klincksieck, 1958); Charles Coüasnon, *The Church of the Holy Sepulchre in Jerusalem*, The Schweich Lectures of the British Academy 1972 (London: Oxford University Press, 1974); R. W. Hamilton, Review of Coüasnon, *Church of the Holy Sepulchre*, in *PEQ* 107 (1975), pp. 78f.; J.-P. B. Ross, "The Evolution of a Church—Jerusalem's Holy Sepulchre," in *BAR* 2.3 (Sept 1976), pp. 3-8, 11; C. Katsimbinis, "The Uncovering of the eastern side of the Hill of Calvary and its base," in *LA* 27 (1977), pp. 197-208; Virgilio C. Corbo, *Il Santo Sepolcro di Gerusalemme*, 3 vols. SBFCM 29 (Jerusalem: Franciscan Printing Press, 1981); Dan Bahat, "Does the Holy Sepulchre Church Mark the Burial of Jesus?" in *BAR* 12.3 (May/June 1986), pp. 26-45; Ovadiah, *Corpus*, pp. 75f., no. 65a; Bahat, *Plans*, 66-69. For the decree of the Sultan Uthman III in 1757 which determined the disposition of the Christian ecclesiastical groups within the Church of the Holy Sepulcher much as it continues until today, see Peters, *Jerusalem*, p. 540 and pp. 618f. n. 9. Plan: from Corbo, *Santo Sepolcro 2*, pl. 3, courtesy Studium Biblicum Franciscanum, Jerusalem.

226. Ancient Masonry under the Church of the Holy Sepulcher

IN WHAT THE BORDEAUX PILGRIM (333) says about Golgotha (quoted in No. 225) there is mention of the burial crypt of Jesus and of the Constantinian basilica but no reference to the Rotunda/Anastasis as such. Likewise in the extended description of the Constantinian structures in *The Life of Constantine* written between 337 and 340, Eusebius tells of the beautiful columns and other decorations that the emperor put at the tomb of Jesus, but he does not make it plain whether an actual building (the Rotunda) was erected over the sepulcher or not. On these grounds it has been theorized (Coüasnon pp. 14-16) that the building of the Basilica was begun immediately after the disinterment of the Tomb in 326/327 and completed for the dedication in 335, but that the work of disengaging the Tomb from the hill in which it had been buried, while retaining the mass of rock surrounding it, was a much longer process, so that the Rotunda was not erected before the year 380 (long after the death of Constantine, A.D. 337). After that, Aetheria (381-384) can describe the daily services held in what is plainly a building: "All the doors of the Anastasis are opened before cock-crow each day" (Geyer p. 71; LPPTS I-C, p. 45; CCSL CLXXV, p. 67; WET p. 123). On the other hand, in his *Oration in Praise of Constantine*, delivered in 335, Eusebius speaks of "the hallowed edifices and consecrated temples which you have raised as trophies (τρόπαια) of his victory over death; and those lofty and noble structures, imperial monuments of an imperial spirit, which you have erected in honor of the everlasting memory of the Savior's tomb" (XI 2). Here the plural certainly sounds as if more than just the Martyrion basilica were referred to, and one interpretation would make the "consecrated temples" the buildings of the Martyrion and the baptistery, and the "hallowed edifices" those of the tomb and its porticoes (Conant p. 44). If this is correct, Constantine had probably already built an actual building around the tomb. In fact, in addition to the literary evidence, examination of the preserved remains by Corbo also leads to the conclusion that the Rotunda/Anastasis was not only part of the original plan of the Constantinian complex but was completed under Constantine (*Santo Sepolcro* 1, p. 223 I; Bahat in BAR 12.3 [May/June 1986], p. 40). Furthermore, such a building surely existed only a few years later, when Cyril gave lectures in it (see below, No. 227).

Far underground, beneath the Rotunda/Anastasis and accessible from the Chapel of the Syrians at the back of the Rotunda, is a central rock chamber surrounded on three sides by *kokim*, the long, narrow, horizontal recesses which were a main form of tombs in the first century A.D. and for a time before and after (see below Nos. 255f., 258) here cut into the vertical rock face of the ancient quarry. Of these, two are traditionally attributed to Joseph of Arimathea and Nicodemus (Mt 27:57-60; Mk 15:43-46; Lk 23:50-53; Jn 19:38-42), but without known justification. In the limestone floor of the same area there are also shaft graves cut down vertically, and still under the church not far away are the remains of an arcosolium chamber tomb. Seen in the present photograph, opposite the *kokim* named for Joseph of Arimathea and Nicodemus, are some of the huge blocks that

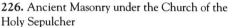
226. Ancient Masonry under the Church of the Holy Sepulcher

are part of a curving wall, the building of which destroyed some of the other *kokim* and which belonged to the Constantinian foundations of the Rotunda/Anastasis above (Meistermann pp. 125f.; Mackowski p. 158, pl. 135; Bahat in BAR 12.3 [May/June 1986], pp. 30f.; Kroll p. 378, abb. 302).

Photograph: JF.

227. Hypothetical Reconstruction of the Tomb of Jesus

IN THE YEAR 348 in the season leading up to Easter (Quadragesima, see Outline of Festivals of the Early Church), Cyril of Jerusalem gave his famous series of *Catechetical Lectures* (NPNFSS VII, pp. 1-157) in the church of the Holy Sepulcher. We can discern that the introductory lecture was delivered in the basilica proper, i.e., the Martyrion, before the whole congregation, with the catechumens present, because we hear Cyril ask them (*Procatechesis* 4 NPNFSS VII, p. 2) if they behold the venerable constitution of the church, and if they view her order and discipline, the reading of Scriptures, etc. For the third lecture, which dealt with baptism, it is possible that the catechumens were assembled in front of the baptistery, for Cyril says (*Catechetical Lectures* III 2) to them that they are now meanwhile standing outside the door. In several later lectures mention is made of looking at the rock of Calvary. The Martyrion may have been so arranged that a view of the rock was possible for at least some of the congregation from inside the basilica. But it is also very possible that for these lectures the group was assembled in the second atrium. There Cyril could have lectured in one of the porticoes, as the Greek philosophers did in the stoas, and the rock would have been visible to all. That this was the case is the more probable because in *Lecture* IV 10 he speaks of "this

blessed Golgotha, in which we are now assembled," and goes on to say that Jesus was crucified "on Golgotha here" (IV 14) and "in Golgotha" (XIII 23). Again he speaks of Golgotha as "the holy hill standing above us here" (X 19) and uses such phrases as "here is Golgotha" (XIII 4), "this most holy Golgotha" (XIII 22), "in this Golgotha" (XIII 26), and "this holy Golgotha, which stands high above us" (XIII 39). On one occasion he even asks his hearers if they see the spot of Golgotha, and they answer with a shout of praise (XIII 23).

In Lecture XVIII Cyril speaks to the catechumens when they have been "wearied by the prolongation of the fast of the Preparation [i.e., Friday], and by the watchings" (XVIII 17), and when they are about, on Easter eve, to receive baptism (XVIII 32 cf. NPNFSS VII p. xlv). After baptism and after celebration of the church service on Easter Sunday, the newly initiated ones are to come on the second day of the week (i.e., on Monday) and for four more days to hear of the "spiritual and heavenly mysteries" (XIX 1), i.e., the doctrines which may be taught only to fully admitted church members, doctrines which are set forth by Cyril in his so-called Mystagogical Lectures (XIX-XXIII). As he instructs his hearers about attendance at these post-Easter lectures Cyril says that they are to come "into the holy place of the resurrection" (ἅγιον τῆς ἀναστάσεως τόπον). This must assuredly mean that there was a building around and over the tomb, and a building of proportions sufficient for such a meeting as Cyril was announcing. At a later date the same thing is attested when Epiphanius Bishop of Salamis visited Jerusalem in 394 and delivered an address to clergy and people in the presence of John the Bishop "in front of the Lord's tomb," as Jerome reports (*To Pammachius against John of Jerusalem* 11 NPNFSS VI, p. 430, cf. VII p. 142 n. 3).

In the *Catechetical Lectures* Cyril not only appeals to Golgotha and the Holy Sepulcher as bearing witness to

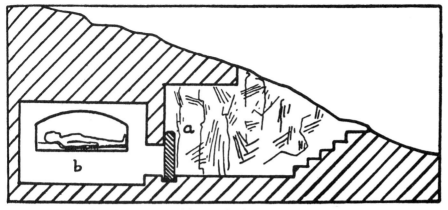

227. Hypothetical Reconstruction of the Tomb of Jesus

Christ, but also speaks of the wooden Cross in the same way. He says, for example (x 19 cf. IV 10; XIII 4): "The holy wood of the Cross bears witness, seen among us to this day, and from this place now almost filling the whole world, by means of those who in faith take portions from it." Here there must be an allusion to the discovery of what was believed to be the cross on which Jesus was put to death, a discovery made, according to Socrates (*Ch. Hist.* I 17) and Sozomen (*Ch. Hist.* II 1), by Helena the mother of Constantine. According to the narrative of these fifth-century church historians, three crosses were found and the cross of Jesus was identified by a miracle. Eusebius himself, however, although he tells of the visit of Helena to Palestine (*The Life of Constantine* III 41-47) does not mention her finding of the cross. In the sixth century the Jerusalem Breviary (Geyer p. 153; LPPTS II-A, p. 13; CCSL CLXXV, p. 109; WJP p. 59; Conant p. 11) states that when one enters the church of Constantine there is at the west (*ab occidente*) a vault where the three crosses were found and, above (*desuper*) this vault a place at a higher level with an altar supported by nine columns. These places will appear in the church of Constantine IX Monomachus and in the Crusader church as the Chapel of the Finding of the Cross and the Chapel of St. Helena (No. 232).

Most interesting of all, perhaps, in the *Lectures* of Cyril is what he has to say about the original tomb itself. In this connection it may be remembered that Cyril was probably born in Jerusalem c. 315 and therefore could very well have seen the tomb as it was before the changes made by Contantine's workmen, as well as after. As to the location of the tomb, it was stated in Jn 19:41 to be in a garden, and Cyril says (XIV 5) that, although the place had by then been so much adorned with royal gifts, "yet formerly it was a garden, and the signs and the remnants of this remain." As to the type of construction of the original tomb and the nature of the changes made in the course of Constantine's constructions, Cyril says (XIV 9) that there was formerly a cave before the door of

the Savior's sepulcher, but this outer cave was cut away for the sake of the present adornment. Presumably this means that the cutting away of the outer cave was to make room for the "rare columns" and "splendid decorations" which, as we have seen (No. 225), Eusebius (*Life of Constantine* III 34) says were put around the tomb, as well as for such building as was erected above it. There was also a stone which closed the door of the tomb, and Cyril says that this was rolled away and was still "lying there to this day" (XIII 39; XIV 22).

What Cyril says suggests that this tomb was a normal Jewish tomb as known from other examples in the Herodian period (cf. Nos. 255-256). In its simplest form and as shown in the drawing (No. 227), such a tomb consisted of an antechamber (a) which was cut out of the rock and entered perhaps by some steps, then a low doorway closed by a stone door or by a rolling stone (cf. Nos. 153, 274, 281), and a passageway leading into a generally rectangular tomb chamber (b). In the tomb chamber the graves were usually of either the kokim or the arcosolia type. The kok was a horizontal shaft driven back into the vertical rock face, into which the body was placed lengthwise. The arcosolium provided a ledge cut laterally into the rock with a vaulted arch over it. In either case the body, wrapped in a winding-sheet, was usually laid on the bare rock. Occasionally a sarcophagus was used. The drawing is intended to represent a rolling stone at the doorway and an arcosolium grave in the tomb chamber. That the arcosolium is shown as recessed into a side wall is only a matter of simplicity in the drawing; it might as well have been in the back wall. The antechamber or vestibule in front with its projecting ledge of rock for a partial roof would constitute what Constantine's workmen cut away to isolate and beautify the tomb proper.

The reconstruction corresponds not only with the allusions by Cyril but also with the details of the Gospel narratives. The tomb of Joseph of Arimathea was hewn in the rock (Mt 27:60; Mk 15:46; Lk 23:53), and was closed by a rolling stone (Mt 28:2; Mk 16:4, Lk 24:2; cf. Jn 20:1). There was probably an antechamber into which one could go without entering the tomb chamber proper; standing in this vestibule one had to stoop down to look into the tomb chamber itself (Jn 20:5). The actual burial place was probably a shelf or ledge, no doubt with an arch above, i.e., it was an arcosolium rather than a kok, for there was place to sit where the body was (Mk 16:5; Jn 20:12).

> Vincent, *Jérusalem nouvelle*, pp. 93-96, with fig. 53 giving the reconstruction of a tomb essentially the same as we have shown but slightly more elaborate; Conant p. 3; Parrot, *Golgotha and the Church of the Holy Sepulchre*, pp. 43-48. Drawing: Parrot, ibid., p. 45, fig. IX, courtesy Philosophical Library, New York.

228. Apse Mosaic in Santa Pudenziana

AS THE PILGRIM AETHERIA (381-384) TELLS of the church services held at Jerusalem (as well as at Bethlehem, No. 25) (see above, Outline of Festivals of the Early Church), she speaks of many of these as held in "the Great Church on Golgotha," and in particular in the Martyrium and in the Anastasis. In addition to services there on an ordinary Sunday and on every day of the pre-Easter season and the like (Geyer pp. 76-78; LPPTS I-C, p. 53; CCSL CLXXV, p. 73; WET pp. 127-128), Aetheria also refers to an eight-day festival called the "days of dedication" (*dies enceniarum* = Greek τὰ ἐγκαίνια), which we recognize to be the same as the festival of the same length described by Sozomen (*Ch. Hist.* II 26) in which the anniversary of the consecration of the "temple" (as she calls it) at Golgotha was celebrated by the church of Jerusalem, the length of the festival being the same as the length of the ceremonies in the dedication of Solomon's temple (II Ch 7:8-9). The record of Aetheria is (Geyer p. 100; LPPTS I-C, p. 76; CCSL CLXXV, p. 89; WET p. 146): "Those days are called the days of dedication, on which the holy church in Golgotha, called the Martyrium (Latin *martyrium* = Greek μαρτύριον), and the holy church at the Anastasis (Latin *anastase* = Greek ἀνάστασις), where the Lord rose again after his passion, were on that day (*ea die*) consecrated to God," and Aetheria goes on to say that this feast ranks with Easter or Epiphany. From the most natural reading of this statement we gather that both the Basilica and the Rotunda had been dedicated in a double ceremony on a single day, hence had been built at the same time, i.e., both by Constantine, as we have already thought probable (No. 226).

In the account by Aetheria we also read with interest of the services held on the Friday of the Easter week, particularly those which extended from the sixth to the ninth hour of that day. At this point Aetheria speaks of what we have called the second atrium of the Constantinian complex, namely, the "atrium, very large and beautiful, situated between the Cross and the Anastasis," and says that in this place "a chair (*cathedra*) is placed for the bishop in front of the cross" and there readings take place during the solemn hours just mentioned (Geyer p. 89; LPPTS I-C, p. 64; CCSL CLXXV, p. 81; WET p. 137).

This passage is of particular interest because it is practically a description of much of the scene in the apse mosaic of the Church of Santa Pudenziana in Rome. This mosaic, shown in the illustration, has already been cited in No. 205 where it was explained that it probably dates from Pope Siricius (384-399), and is therefore approximately contemporary with Aetheria 381-384. Central in the background in the mosaic is what is surely the rock of Calvary, and this is surmounted by a jeweled cross. The arcade with tiled roof which runs across the picture may be intended to represent the porticoes of the second atrium in the complex of Constantinian buildings at Jerusalem. In front of the rock Christ is seated upon a throne, and on either side of him are the apostles. These were once twelve in number but the outermost figure on each side has been lost in later alterations of the apse. As was customary in Roman tradition at that time (FLAP p. 522 and p. 524 n. 47) Peter stands at the viewer's right at the left hand of Christ, and Paul at the viewer's left. Over the heads of these two men two women probably representing the Jewish Church and the Gentile Church, hold wreaths of laurel, the symbols of victory for the two great martyrs. Above in the sky, partly destroyed, are the winged symbols of the four evangelists, the man, lion, ox, and eagle from Ezk 1:10; 10:14; Rev 4:7, standing for Matthew, Mark, Luke, and John respectively (FLAP p. 525). The buildings behind the arcade at the right have been explained above (No. 205) as chiefly those on Mount Sion; the buildings at the left are recognized as those of Constantine at the rock of Calvary and the tomb of Jesus, and the round, domed building is presumably to be identified as the Anastasis.

> Photograph: courtesy of the University Prints, Boston, cf. FLAP fig. 187.

229. Jerusalem on the Madaba Mosaic Map

ON THE MADABA MOSAIC MAP (560) we have a representation of Jerusalem at the height of the Byzantine period and the most prominent of all the city's monuments is unmistakably recognizable as the Church of the Holy Sepulcher. The Madaba Mosaic pictures the

Church of
Holy Sepulcher

Church of
Sion

228. Apse Mosaic in Santa Pudenziana

229. Jerusalem on the Madaba Mosaic Map

269

city as enclosed in an oval wall. Above at the left is the label, ἡ ἁγία πόλις Ιερουσα[λημ], "the holy city Jerusalem." Through the city from north to south runs a great colonnaded street which, in a Roman/Byzantine city such as Aelia Capitolina, is the *cardo maximus*. At the north end of this street is an oval place, with a large column, and in the wall an important gate. As the principal gate on the north this will be the Gate of Neapolis (*porta Neapolitana*) of the Bordeaux Pilgrim (333) (Geyer p. 22; LPPTS I-B, p. 23; CCSL CLXXV, p. 16; WET p. 158; cf. Nos. 215, 225). Theodosius (530) (Geyer pp. 141-142; LPPTS II-B, p. 11; CCSL CLXXV, p. 118; WJP p. 66) calls the gate on the north the Galilean Gate (*porta Galilaeae*) and says that outside it was the church built by Eudocia (444-460) in memory of the stoning of Stephen. Because of this connection the gate was also known as St. Stephen's Gate (*porta sancti Stephani*), as it is called by Arculf (670) (Geyer p. 224; LPPTS III-I, p. 2; CCSL CLXXV, p. 185; WJP p. 95). Today it is the Damascus Gate, and the Arabic name for it is Bab el 'Amud or Gate of the Column, an obvious reference to the great column which once stood in the plaza and is shown on the Mosaic Map.

At the south end the main colonnaded street ends at a small gate that is beside the Nea Church (Nos. 196, 200), thus may be called the Nea Gate and is not to be confused with the Zion Gate some 120 meters farther west (Avigad, *Discovering Jerusalem*, pp. 227-229). Farther west the south wall of the city surrounds the area of Mount Sion where we have already recognized (No. 205) that the large building (indeed even larger than the Church of the Holy Sepulcher) represents the basilica of Hagia Sion. The same south wall evidently continues on eastward to enclose the Pool of Siloam. We have already seen (No. 178) that the Anonymous of Piacenza (570) (Geyer p. 176; LPPTS II-D, p. 21; CCSL CLXXV, p. 166; WJP p. 84) says that Eudocia (444-460) added to the city those walls which enclosed Siloam, so this entire southern city wall of this time is probably the work of that empress. In this connection it may be recalled that the Bordeaux Pilgrim found Sion outside the wall (No. 215), but the monk Epiphanius (750-800) spoke of Sion as inside the wall (No. 212), while Saewulf (1102) again found Sion outside, as it is today (No. 212).

Another colonnaded street runs from the southeastern corner of the plaza and more or less parallels the *cardo maximus* to the east. This probably follows the course of the Tyropoeon Valley, between the Temple area and the upper city, and corresponds to the street called Tariq el-Wad in modern times. At about the middle of this street, a shorter street runs eastward to a gate. These correspond to the street called Tariq Bab Sitty Mariam and the gate known as St. Stephen's Gate in the east wall of the city (cf. No. 216).

In the west city wall about one-third of the way from the Church of the Holy Sepulcher to the southwest corner of the city is a gate with a tower behind it and a street running eastward from it. The gate corresponds to the modern Jaffa Gate, and the tower must be the Tower of David. The street would be the *decumanus*, the street running through the city from west to east. Although there was not room on the mosaic to show its continuation, it probably continued across the *cardo* to the temple area and thus was equivalent to the modern David Street and Street of the Gate of the Chain.

Now we come to the Church of the Holy Sepulcher. In the middle of the *cardo* the colonnade on the west side is broken by four steps which lead up to three doors. These give access to a basilica which has a triangular pediment and a red sloping roof indicated by criss-cross lines. This must be the Martyrion. Beyond, i.e., west of this is a court shown in black cubes, which must be the second atrium of the Calvary. And further west is a great dome, which must be the Anastasis.

South of the church in line with the three doors is an open area which is probably the forum of Aelia Capitolina, where the Russian Alexander Hospice, Lutheran Church, and Muristan are now (cf. Nos. 200, 223-224). On the west side of this area and on the south side of the basilica is another building with a red roof, the criss-cross lines of which are probably intended to represent a dome. This will probably be the baptistery attached to the Church of the Holy Sepulcher.

Vincent, *Jérusalem nouvelle*, pp. 922-925; Peter Thomsen, "Das Stadtbild Jerusalems auf der Mosaikkarte von Madeba," in ZDPV 52 (1929), pp. 149-174; 192-219 and especially pl. 6 facing p. 184; Avi-Yonah, *Madaba Mosaic*, pp. 50-60; R. T. O'Callaghan in DB Supplément V, cols. 656-666. Photograph: courtesy Victor R. Gold.

230. Archimandrite Guregh Kapikian Standing on Excavated Byzantine Street

LEADING FROM THE SQUARE beside the Church of the Holy Sepulcher, the Madaba Map (No. 229) also shows a rather wide street, parallel to the *cardo maximus* on the west side, which must have been intended to connect the Holy Sepulcher Church and the Sion Church. It is exactly this Byzantine street, the paving blocks of which have been found in excavations in the Armenian cemetery by M. Broshi (in *Jerusalem Revealed*, p. 59). Standing on this ancient street in the present photograph is Archimandrite Guregh Kapikian of the Armenian community.

Photograph: JF.

230. Archimandrite Guregh Kapikian Standing on Excavated Byzantine Street

231. Plan of the Church of the Holy Sepulcher According to Arculf

IN THE MONTH of May in the year 614 the Persians broke into the city of Jerusalem, burned the Christian sanctuaries, massacred many persons who had taken refuge in them, and carried others off captive, including Zacharias the patriarch. An account of the events is found in the *Annals* of Eutychius (940) (*Annales* MPG 111, cols. 1082-1084, 1091; LPPTS XI-A, pp. 36-39; trans. Breydy, CSCO 472, pp. 98-101) as follows: In a time of temporary peace between the Byzantine empire and the Persian (Sasanian) empire, the Persian king Chosroes II (r. 590-628) and the Byzantine emperor Maurice (r. 582-602) were allies, but when Phocas (r. 602-610) obtained the throne in Constantinople and Maurice and his sons were executed, Chosroes, impelled by his wife Marian, who was a daughter of Maurice, and advised by his ministers and officers, undertook a wide-reaching war of revenge. Declaring that the Christians are not faithful to a covenant and have no true religion, otherwise they would not have killed their king, the councillors proposed to the king a deed which would break their hearts and reduce their religion to naught. Eutychius tells what

the councillors said: "There is a house in the Holy City which they venerate. Send there and destroy it. When you have destroyed this house, their strength will be shattered and their empire will pass away."

Accordingly Chosroes' general proceeded to Palestine, where he was joined by many Jews who had suffered much from the Byzantines, and they helped the Persians destroy churches and murder Christians. When the Persian general came to Jerusalem, as Eutychius continues the account,

> the first which he destroyed were the churches of Gethsemane and the Nea [trans. Breydy, CSCO 472, p. 99, "al-Nea," presumably the church built by Justinian little more than half a century before, see No. 196; MPG 111, col. 1083 and LPPTS XI-A, p. 36 read "the church of Helena," presumably the Eleona, see No. 155, cf. Kroll p. 420, col. 1], both of which remain in ruins to this day. He also destroyed the church of Constantine and the Kranion (Golgotha) and the Sepulcher. He set the Sepulcher and the Kranion on fire, and destroyed the greater part of the city as well. Together with the Persians the Jews killed innumerable Christians. . . . After the Persians had destroyed, burned, killed, and taken the people into captivity, they went away. Among those taken away was Zacharias the patriarch of the Holy City, with a group of his own. (The Persians) also took with them to Persia the wood of the Cross, which Helena had left there. . . . Mariam, the daughter of King Maurice, asked for the wood of the Cross, together with the patriarch Zacharias and many of the other captives, and took them into her own house. . . .
>
> After the Persians had laid waste the churches of the Holy City and had burned them with fire and then had gone away, a monk by the name of Modestus, who was the abbot of the Monastery of Dawakes [the Monastery of St. Theodosius in the Judean desert southeast of Bethlehem], journeyed to Ramla and Tiberias and Damascus and begged the Christians for gifts and help, whereby he could rebuild the holy places, which the Persians had destroyed. They contributed, and he collected the monies and returned to the Holy City. He built the churches of the Resurrection, the Sepulcher, the Kranion, and of Constantine, the building which stands to this day.

In 614 while the Persians were attacking Jerusalem some Arab bands came from east of the Dead Sea and sacked the Monastery of St. Sabas (Arabic Mar Saba, southeast of Jerusalem, Meistermann pp. 410f.) and killed forty-four of the monks, and Modestus also went there and helped to reestablish the life of the monastery. A certain Antiochus was the abbot of the monastery, and in an introductory letter prefixed to his Pandect of the Holy Scriptures (NPG 89, cols. 1427-1428) Antiochus tells of all these events and, in tribute to Modestus' works of reconstruction, says that Modestus was like "a second Bezaleel (Ex 31:2-5) or a second Zerubbabel (Ezr 3:2ff.)."

In the same records the Byzantine emperor Heraclius (r. 610-641), successor to Phocas, is said to have ap-

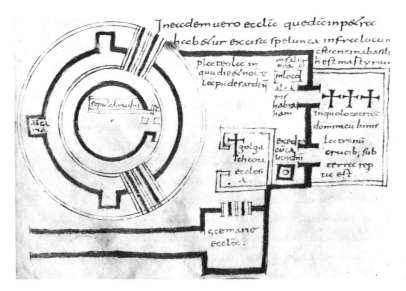

231. Plan of the Church of the Holy Sepulcher According to Arculf

pointed Modestus vicar of the captive bishop Zacharias and to have provided funds for the rebuilding of the Church of the Holy Sepulcher. In 622 Heraclius took the field agains the Persians and by 628 recovered the "true cross" from the Persian capital of Ctesiphon and brought it back in triumph to Jerusalem. The patriarch Zacharias also returned to his post, to serve until his death in 633, when Modestus succeeded him as patriarch for nine months (633-634) until his own death (swDCB IV, p. 929).

By the time Zacharias returned to his post (628) the repairs by Modestus on the Church of the Holy Sepulcher must have been at least partly completed (Coüasnon p. 17). The Persians had destroyed the roofing, the decorations, and the furnishings of the church, and notable as was the work of reconstruction by Modestus, the restored church must have been much less splendid than the original church of Constantine. On the whole the basic outlines remained (Vincent, *Jérusalem nouvelle*, p. 218), but with changes sufficient to justify calling this the second church in the long history of the Holy Sepulcher. By way of comparison the roughly contemporary Church of St. Demetrius in Thessalonica was probably built on much the same lines (Conant p. 8).

In the church as restored by Modestus, the Rotunda (Anastasis) was built out into a complete round church; the Second Atrium between the Rotunda and the Basilica (Martyrion) was named the "Holy Garden," and in the middle of this court was the "omphalos" which marked "the center of the world." The Rock of Calvary, previously standing free in the southwest corner of the same court was enclosed in a two-story chapel, and a Chapel of Adam was built at the base of the rock on the west side; and nearby was an installation marking the altar of Abraham (Kroll p. 388, col. 3-p. 390, col. 1; cf.

descriptions by the Armenian pilgrim and by Arculf, just below).

In the several items just mentioned we recognize the transferral of tradition from the Jewish Temple to Calvary and the Holy Sepulcher (Jeremias, *Golgotha*, pp. 34-50). The Jewish tradition that put the center of the world at the Sacred Rock (No. 180) at the Temple is set forth in Midrash Tanhuma (Jeremias, ibid., p. 44):

> The land of Israel lies in the center of the world;
> Jerusalem lies in the center of the land of Israel;
> the holy precinct lies in the center of Jerusalem;
> the Temple building lies in the center of the holy precinct;
> the ark of the covenant lies in the center of the Temple building;
> the Sacred Rock, however, lies before the ark of the covenant,
> for from it the world was founded.

The Christian adaptation of the idea is seen when Cyril of Jerusalem says of Jesus in the crucifixion (*Catechetical Lecture* XIII, 28): "He stretched out his hands on the cross, that he might embrace the ends of the world; for this place Golgotha is the very center of the earth."

The Chapel of Adam at the foot of the Rock of Calvary obviously has to do with tradition about Adam. Jewish tradition about the connection of Adam with the Temple is found in Rabbinical and Pseudepigraphical sources, in which the chiefly relevant points are these: The rabbis taught that "Adam was created from the dust of the place where the sanctuary [the Temple in Jerusalem] was to rise for the atonement of all human sin" (JE I, p. 177). The *Book of Jubilees* relates that when Adam and Eve went forth from the Garden of Eden "they dwelt in the land of Elda [a corruption of 'land of nativity'] in the land of their creation" (3:33), and when Adam died "all his sons buried him in the land of his creation" (4:29) (CAP II, pp. 17, 19). Likewise the *Books of Adam and Eve* tell of the burial of Adam together with Abel and state that "both were buried, according to the commandment of God, in the spot where God found the dust" (*Apocalypsis Mosis* 40.6; cf. *Vita Adae et Evae* 45.2-3; 48.5-6 CAP II, pp. 149, 151 [with note], 152). So Adam was buried at the spot where God got the dust to make him in the first place, and this was where the Temple was later built. (Another Jewish tradition that puts Adam's grave at Hebron is probably later and due to the feeling that the sacred Temple should not be thought of as a place of burial, and was supported by taking the "greatest man" in Jos 14:15 to be Adam, since in Hebrew "man" and "Adam" are the same word [Jerome, *Letter* 108.11 NPNFSS VI, p. 200]. Yet another variant occurs in Muslim tradition, in which Adam's creation, dwelling place, and grave were all at Mecca [Jeremias, *Golgotha*, p. 40 and n. 3; cf. A. J. Wensinck, *A Handbook of Early Muhammadan Tradition* (Leiden: E. J. Brill, 1960), p. 11]).

The Christian transfer of the tradition of the burial place of Adam to Calvary is attested in Origen (*Origenis in Matthaeum Commentariorum Series*, sec. 126 on Mt 27:32, 89, MPG 13, cols. 1777-1778): "Concerning the place of a skull it has come to us that the Hebrews [doubtless meaning the Christians of Hebrew descent, the Judeo-Christians] give the tradition that the body of Adam has been buried there, so that as in Adam all die, on the other hand in Christ all shall be made alive" (I Cor 15:22; cf. Rom 5:12, 15). Epiphanius (*Pan. haer.* 45.5 Williams NHS 35, pp. 351f.) explains the same matter at some length, and also thinks to find herein an explanation of the name Golgotha, although what he says is hardly the original connotation of the name (No. 225, cf. K. W. Clark in IDB II, p. 439). Jesus Christ, Epiphanius says, was crucified on the very place where Adam's body was buried. After Adam left Paradise, he lived opposite it for a long time and grew old. Later he came and died in Jerusalem and was buried on the site of Golgotha; hence the name "skull" or "place of a skull," because the remains of the first-formed man were laid to rest there. By being crucified just above, the water and blood from the pierced side of Christ (Jn 20:34) sprinkled the one who lay buried on the site, to give hope also to us his descendants. In fact in front of the apse of the Chapel of Adam at the base of the Rock of Calvary there was a fissure in the rock (visible today through a glass plate). This was supposedly caused by the earthquake of Mt 27:51, and Cyril of Jerusalem (*Catechetical Lecture* XIII, 39) refers to it when he describes "this holy Golgotha, which stands high above us, and shows itself to this day, and displays even yet how because of Christ the rocks are

then riven." Thus the fissure in the rock was congruent with the mystical idea that the blood of Christ descended to fall upon the skull of Adam.

A complex form of the same tradition is found in a Syriac work of probably the sixth century called *The Book of the Cave of Treasures* (trans. Budge, see esp. pp. 21, 34f.) and related texts (Battista and Bagatti, *La Caverna dei Tesori*, see esp. pp. 19, 51, 59-63). Here we are told that after expulsion from Paradise Adam and Eve lived not far away in the so-called Cave of Treasures, in which Adam collected gold, frankincense, and myrrh, thus symbolizing the cave in Bethlehem in which the Magi presented their gifts to Christ. When Adam died he was buried in the Cave of Treasures, as were also several of his sons and descendants. In time Noah took Adam's body from the Cave and transported it in the Ark to Jerusalem, where it was deposited in an opening in the earth. There it remained until the Cross was set up above it on Golgotha, and when the soldier (called Longinus) pierced the side of Jesus with a spear, the blood and water flowed down upon Adam. The blood gave him life, and he was baptized by the water.

As for thinking of the altar of Abraham at the Rock of Calvary, this was also a transfer of Jewish tradition from the Temple. According to Gen 22:2 the place where Abraham was about to sacrifice his son Isaac was in the land of Moriah, the location of which land is not otherwise specified, but according to II Ch 3:1 Mount Moriah was in Jerusalem and was the place where the Temple was built, therefore it was at the later Temple site that the earlier event of Abraham and Isaac took place, and Jewish tradition continued to accept this localization (also placing at the same site an altar upon which Melchizedek offered bread and wine [Gen 14:18; JE VIII, p. 450]; while in Muslim tradition Ishmael took the place of Isaac, and the place of the intended sacrifice was transferred to Mina near Mecca [JE I, p. 89]). For the continuing Jewish tradition putting the sacrifice of Isaac at the Temple site in Jerusalem see, for example, the following: in the *Book of Jubilees* (in which the original suggestion to test Abraham in this way is made by "the prince Mastema," as *Jubilees* calls Satan, 17.16), the place is on Mount Sion (18.13 CAP II, pp. 39, 40); in Josephus (*Ant.* I, ix, 7 §226; VII, xiii, 4 §333) it is said that the threshing floor of Araunah, which David purchased as the site for the Temple (No. 180), was "the very place" to which Abraham brought Isaac on that occasion.

The transfer of this tradition to Calvary was in line with the very early attested idea that the intended offering of Isaac was a type of the sacrificial death of Jesus Christ (e.g., *Epistle of Barnabas* [A.D. c. 100], VII, 3 ANF I, p. 141). So Theodosius (530) (Geyer pp. 140f.; LPPTS

II-B, p. 10; CCSL CLXXV, pp. 117f.; WJP p. 65) tells us: "In the city of Jerusalem at the sepulcher of the Lord is the place of Calvary; there Abraham offered his son as a whole burnt-offering (holocaustum), and because the hill (mons, literally "mountain") is rocky (mons petreus) Abraham made the altar in the hill itself, i.e., at the foot of the hill itself. Above the altar the hill stands out, and the hill is climbed by steps (per grados scalatur): there the Lord was crucified." The Anonymous of Piacenza (570) (Geyer p. 204; LPPTS II-D, p. 16; CCSL CLXXV, pp. 138f.; WJP p. 83) gives a similar description, mentions Melchizedek as well as Abraham, and mentions the fissure in the rock: "From the Tomb it is eighty paces to Golgotha. One side is ascended by steps (ascenditur per gradus), up which the Lord ascended to be crucified. In the place where he was crucified drops of blood appear. At one side of the rock is the altar of Abraham, where he went to offer Isaac when God tempted him. And here Melchizedek offered sacrifice to Abraham. . . . Next to the altar itself is an aperture (cripta) [in the rock] where, if you place your ear, you will hear the rushing of waters."

Returning to the work of Modestus, it was the church as he restored it that was seen by the Muslim Arabs when they came only a few years later. Following upon the death of Muhammad in A.D. 632 his first successor the Caliph Abu Bakr (532-634) sent Arab forces into Syria, where Heraclius withdrew and carried off to Constantinople the remains of the "true cross" which he had brought back from Persian Ctesiphon (Coüasnon p. 18). Under the second caliph, 'Umar (634-644), Damascus was taken (635), the Byzantine army was defeated at the Battle of the Yarmuk River (636), and at Jerusalem the patriarch Sophronius (634-638) surrendered the city to the invaders (February 638), while Caesarea the capital was taken after siege two years later (640). Eutychius tells us what happened when the Muslims took Jerusalem (MPG 111, col. 1099; LPPTS XI-A, pp. 65-66; Breydy pp. 118-119; CEMA I, pp. 25-26). The conquering caliph came to the Church of the Holy Sepulcher and sat down in the sahn (court) of the Ἀνάστασις, i.e., probably in the Second Atrium in front of the Rotunda. When the time of prayer was at hand 'Umar said to Sophronius, "I wish to pray." The patriarch responded, "O Commander of the Faithful, pray where you are," but 'Umar replied, "I will not pray here." The patriarch then took the caliph to the basilica of Constantine, i.e., the Martyrion, but 'Umar said, "I will not pray here either." Then the caliph went out to the steps which are at the door of Constantine's church, at the east end, and prayed there alone upon the steps. He explained that if he had prayed within the church the Muslims would have considered that a ground for seizing the church, and he gave Sophronius a charter forbidding Muslims to be called together in that place for prayers by the voice of the mu-

ezzin. While this was a happier outcome for the church of the Holy Sepulcher than when the Persians had come and burned it, in the long run it might have been better if the church had been made a mosque for then it would presumably have been spared the complete destruction visited upon it by the Fatimid Caliph al-Hakim in 1099 (Coüasnon pp. 18f.; and see below, No. 232).

For the Church of the Holy Sepulcher as restored by Modestus after it was destroyed by the Persians, and after it was thereafter left intact by the Muslims, the earliest description we have is that given by an unnamed Armenian pilgrim of A.D. 660 (PEFQS 1896, p. 347), and his account also contains the first mention by a visiting pilgrim of the Chapel of Adam at the foot of the rock of Calvary. In the account the pilgrim speaks of "the rock-hewn tomb (grave) of the life-giving Jesus"; of the "colonnaded cupola-shaped church," with twelve columns below and twelve columns above (presumbly the ἀνάστασις, with an upper gallery; and of the "chief church," with sixty-five (or seventy-five according to another manuscript) columns, this being the μαρτύριον and also called the Katholikon (καθολικόν), this name having the meaning of "cathedral" and signifying the principal church in the city and the residence of the patriarch (E. A. Sophocles, Greek Lexicon of the Roman and Byzantine Periods, 2 vols. [New York: Frederick Ungar, 1887], 2, p. 613). Ten steps distant from the Resurrection (the ἀνάστασις) was the Church of Holy Golgotha (which must be the chapel enclosing the rock of Calvary), "called also the tomb of Adam" (i.e., the Chapel of Adam at the foot of the rock).

Arculf came not many years later (670) and tells us at some length how this "very great church" appeared to him (Geyer pp. 227ff.; LPPTS III-A, pp. 5ff.; CCSL CLXXV, pp. 186ff.; WJP 95ff.). Also he made the drawing of the church that is reproduced here, from the ninth-century manuscript of his De locis sanctis known as Codex Parisinus (Latin 13048) (cf. Testini in Oriens Antiquus 3 [1964], pp. 272f.). Reading his description and looking at his drawing, we find that he describes a large, round church over the sepulcher, supported by twelve stone columns (not shown in his drawing), with entrances from the northeast and southeast, and with altars in recesses in the walls on the north, west, and south. Next, moving eastward, there is a four-sided church on the site of Golgotha. Opposite this, on the north side of the court, is an area in which, the legend on the plan says, by day and night lamps burn. Beside this is another place where, also according to the legend, Abraham built an altar, namely, the altar on which it was proposed to sacrifice Isaac. On to the east is the basilica known as the Martyrium. Under this was found the cross of Christ, with the two crosses of the robbers. Between the basilica of Golgotha and the Martyrium is an exedra, i.e., a small chamber or chapel, in which, it was said, was the cup which the Lord gave to the apostles at the Last Supper. Finally, adjoining the four-sided Church of Golgotha on the south side is the four-sided Church of St. Mary, the mother of the Lord, a building evidently somewhat to the east of the baptistery in the Constantinian complex (No. 225).

Vincent, *Jérusalem nouvelle*, pp. 218-247; Ovadiah, *Corpus*, pp. 76f., no. 65b; Joachim Jeremias, *Golgotha*. AΓΓΕΛΟΣ, *Archiv für neutestamentliche Zeitgeschichte und Kulturkunde*. Beiheft 1 (Leipzig: Eduard Pfeiffer, 1926); E. A. Wallis Budge, trans., *The Book of the Cave of Treasures* (London: Religious Tract Society, 1927); A. Battista and B. Bagatti, *La Caverna dei Tesori*. SBFCMI 26 (Jerusalem: Franciscan Printing Press, 1979); Joan E. Taylor, "A Critical Investigation of Archaeological Material Assigned to Palestinian Judeo-Christians of the Roman and Byzantine Periods" (Ph.D. diss., University of Edinburgh, 1989). Plan: Arculfus De Locis Sanctis, Codex Parisinus Lat. 13048, courtesy Bibliothèque Nationale, Paris.

232. Bell Tower at the Church of the Holy Sepulcher

IN 1009 THE FATIMID CALIPH AL-HAKIM (996-1021) ordered the demolition of the Church of the Holy Sepulcher, and destruction spread to many other churches and also synagogues. The Fatimids, who traced their ancestry to Fatima, the daughter of Muhammad and wife of 'Ali, the fourth successor of Muhammad, conquered Egypt in 969 and spread their rule over Mecca, Medina, Syria, and Palestine. In Palestine in 716 the Umayyad Caliph Suleiman (715-717), second son of 'Abd al-Malik (685-705, builder of the Dome of the Rock), had established the Arab/Muslim capital at Ramla (10 miles northeast of Lod/Lydda, probably ancient Arimathea [Meistermann pp. 74-80; Kroll p. 368, col. 2]), and under al-Hakim his governor at Ramla was named Yarukh.

Yahya ibn Sa'id, an eleventh-century Arab Christian historian of Antioch, records what happened (PO 23, pp. 491f.; cf. Peters, *Jerusalem*, p. 260):

[After the demolition of churches in Cairo, al-Hakim] likewise sent to Syria, to Yarukh, governor of Ramla, written orders to destroy the Church of the Holy Resurrection, to make the Christian emblems disappear, and to take away the holy relics. [Yarukh sent several representatives to Jerusalem and] they seized all the furnishings which they found there, after which they pulled down the church to its foundations, with the exception of the parts which it was impossible to destroy or too difficult to carry off. Then the Skull (Golgotha), the Church of St. Constantine, and all the other edifices found in the precinct were destroyed, and the sacred relics were completely annihilated. [One of those sent to do the work] attempted to clear away the Holy Sepulcher and to make every trace of it disappear, and he broke and demolished the greater part of it [but evidently not all]. In the

232. Bell Tower at the Church of the Holy Sepulcher

neighborhood there was a convent of women, known as as-Sari, which was likewise destroyed. The demolition began on [the date equivalent to] 28 September 1009. All the property and all the pious bequests were seized, as well as all the vessels and sacred objects and pieces of gold work.

Ibn al-Qalanisi (d. 1160), a Syrian historian who wrote in Arabic (Canard in *Byzantion* 35 [1965], pp. 20-24; cf. Peters, *Jerusalem*, pp. 258-260) also records the destruction and includes a curious story about what caused al-Hakim to do this, namely, that the caliph was offended by a report he was given of how the Christians believed that at Passover holy fire descended from heaven to light the lamps at the Sepulcher.

When the Christians come there on the day of their Passover (Easter), and their metropolitan appears in public and they raise their crosses and perform their prayers and ceremonies, all that makes a great impression on their spirits and introduces confusion in their hearts. They suspend their lamps over the altar, and then by a contrivance they cause fire to appear in the balsam oil in their lamps, since this oil has the property of igniting with the oil of jasmine, and it produces a flame of brilliant whiteness. . . . Those who see it imagine that the fire has come down from heaven and lit the lamps.

When al-Hakim was so told, he sent to Ramla the order to destroy the church and to send back an official report that it was done. The Christians in Egypt learned of the order and informed the patriarch in Jerusalem, and some of the church's valuables were removed.

> The representatives of al-Hakim came, surrounded the church, gave orders to loot it, and carried away whatever was left, which was of considerable value. Then the building was destroyed and demolished stone by stone. A report was prepared, signed as he had ordered, and sent to al-Hakim. News of the event spread in Egypt; the Muslims rejoiced and performed acts of gratitude to thank al-Hakim for what he had done. His information agents reported on the public sentiment in that regard. Al-Hakim was pleased, and ordered the destruction of the churches and the synagogues in the various provinces.

Bar Hebraeus (1286) records the same complete destruction of the Church of the Holy Sepulcher by al-Hakim and is the first Christian writer to report the same story as that given by Ibn al-Qalanisi about what offended the Caliph (*Chronography*, trans. Budge, p. 184):

> And at this time, the *khalifah* of Egypt, commanded and the Temple of the Resurrection which is in Jerusalem was dug up from its roots, and all its furniture was looted. . . .
>
> This persecution began through a certain man who hated the Christians. He told Hakim the *khalifah* a story (to the effect that) "the Christians, when they assemble in the temple of Jerusalem to celebrate the festival of Easter, deal cunningly with the overseers of the church, and they anoint with oil of balsam the iron wire on which hangs the lamp over the tomb. And when the governor of the Arabs seals the door of the tomb [in a further arrangement drawn up in the thirteenth century, because of differences of the Christian denominations as to rights in the church, and continuing until today, an Arab/Muslim family, Nusseibeh, holds the keys for opening and closing the church, FDI p. 86], the Christians from the roof light a fire at the top of the iron wire, and the fire runs down to the wick of the lamp and kindles it. And then they cry out 'Kurie layson' [Κύριε ἐλέησον, 'Lord have mercy'] and weep, pretending that they see the light which descends from heaven upon the tomb, and they are confirmed in their faith.

The first mention of the descent of the "holy fire" in the Church of the Holy Sepulcher is by the French pilgrim Bernard (870), who reports: "they go on singing the *Kyrie eleison* till an angel comes in and kindles light in the lamps which hang above the aforementioned sepulcher. The patriarch passes some of this fire to the bishops and the rest of the people, that each may light his home

with it" (Tobler and Molinier p. 315). The Russian pilgrim Daniel (1106) gives a full account (LPPTS IV-C, pp. 74-81), and the event continues annually until the present day (see Peters, *Jerusalem*, index under "Holy Fire, Descent of").

William of Tyre (1184) (Babcock and Krey I, pp. 66ff.) summarizes the destruction by al-Hakim: "Yarukh, the governor of Ramla, one of Hakim's officers, took it upon himself to carry out the imperial command and immediately razed the edifice to the very ground." The great Constantinian church of the fourth century and its successor, the restored church of Modestus of the seventh century, were at a virtual end. William of Tyre tells also of the severe persecution of the Christians which followed.

In 1012, however, as Yahya ibn Sa'id (PO 23, p. 505) tells us, by permission and with the help of a Bedouin of the Djarrah family, named Mufarridj (d. 1013), who was for a time in control of Ramla and Palestine, the Christians were able to begin some rebuilding (EI II, 1965, p. 483). In 1021 al-Hakim died and was succeeded by his son, the Caliph al-Zahir (r. 1021-1036). The latter, as William of Tyre records (Babcock and Krey I, pp. 69f.), entered into an alliance of friendship with the Byzantine emperor Romanus (III, r. 1028-1034), and at the request of Romanus, al-Zahir granted the Christians the privilege of restoring the church. The work was broken off, however, and only finally, with a treaty concluded in 1038 at the beginning of the reign of the Caliph al-Mustansir, was there a period of continuing friendly relations between the Fatimids and the Byzantines, in which the work could go on. The Christians at Jerusalem, however, William of Tyre continues, knew that their own means were not adequate for the restoration of so important an edifice, and therefore sent an embassy to the emperor Constantine IX Monomachus (1042-1055), under whom friendly relations between Byzantium and the Fatimids were continuing.

> In charge of this embassy was a certain John, surnamed Carianis. He was a native of Constantinople, noble according to the flesh but still more noble in character. He had laid aside the honors of the world to follow Christ and put on the habit of religion and was then living at Jerusalem, a poor man for Christ's sake. He was sent on this mission and, with all due persistence and energy, faithfully presented the matter to the lord emperor, beloved of God. He succeeded in obtaining from Constantine the promise that sufficient money to carry on the work of restoration should be taken from the emperor's own fiscal purse. John then went back to Jerusalem, rejoicing that he had obtained the promise which the faithful so eagerly desired. When the news was received that his journey had been successful and his petition granted, the spirits of the clergy and people revived; they were like those who are recovering from serious illness. At this time the Patriarch Nicephorus was presiding over the church.

Since permission had been granted and the expenses were assured from the imperial treasury, they built the church of the Holy Resurrection, the same which is now at Jerusalem. This was in the year 1048 of the Incarnation of the Lord. . . . When the building was completed, the people were comforted for the many deadly perils and imminent danger to which they were exposed.

Even with the support of Constantine IX Monomachus for its rebuilding, the church which arose again in this its third form in 1048 was much less than what had been before (Coüasnon pp. 54-56; Corbo, *Santo Sepolcro* 1, p. 229; 2, pls. 4, 5). The entryway on the *cardo* together with the First Atrium and the whole great basilica (Martyrion) lay in ruins and were permanently abandoned. The circular wall on the west side of the Rotunda (Anastasis) still stood to some height, and this building was reconstructed in substantially its original Constantinian form. To balance the three apses already found in the Constantinian plan, a new fourth apse was introduced on the east side in front of the Tomb (pl. 4, nos. 70-71). A new octagonal edicule was built over the Tomb, and the surface of the rock bench was covered with marble (pl. 4, nos. 1-2). Partly counterbalancing the disappearance of the Martyrion, several new chapels were built: to the north of the Anastasis the Chapel of St. Mary (pl. 4, nos. 126-129), and to the south of the Anastasis three chapels (pl. 4, nos. 501-503), the central one used as a baptistery. Underground to the east an old Roman cistern was remodeled into a chapel, reached by a western staircase, and was thus honored as the place of "The Finding of the Cross" (pl. 4, no. 309).

The Muslim pilgrim Nasir-i Khusraw was in Jerusalem in A.D. 1047 and visited the Church of the Holy Sepulcher when its rebuilding under Constantine IX Monomachus must have been nearly complete (1048). The portion of his diary which recounts his journey through Syria and Palestine contains this description of the church (LPPTS IV-A, pp. 60-61; cf. Peters, *Jerusalem*, pp. 267f.):

Hakim at one time ordered the church to be given over to plunder which was so done, and it was laid in ruins. Some time it remained thus; but afterwards the Caesar of Byzantium sent ambassadors with presents and promises of service, and concluded a treaty in which he stipulated for permission to defray the expenses of rebuilding the church, and this was ultimately accomplished.

At the present day the church is a most spacious building, and is capable of containing eight thousand persons. The edifice is built, with the utmost skill, of colored marbles, with ornamentation and sculptures. Inside, the church is everywhere adorned with Byzantine brocade, worked in gold with pictures. [The account goes on to name pictures of Jesus, Abraham, Ishmael, Isaac, and Jacob with his sons—"peace be upon them all"—these pictures being varnished with oil of juniper and the face of each portrait covered with a plate

of thin glass, and there was also a double picture of heaven and hell.]

There are seated in this church great numbers of priests and monks who read the Gospel and say prayers, for both by day and by night they are occupied in this manner.

The church of Constantine IX Monomachus was that which the Crusaders saw when, on July 15, 1099, they entered Jerusalem. Two pilgrims, the Scandinavian Saewulf (1102) and the Russian Daniel (1106), came soon afterward and wrote descriptions of the church as it still existed at that time, which was before the Crusaders carried out their own changes, which gave the church most of its present form.

Saewulf (LPPTS IV-B, pp. 9-14) says that the Church of the Holy Sepulcher is called the Martyrium and is more celebrated than all the other churches in Jerusalem. In the middle of the church is the sepulcher of Christ, surrounded by a strong wall and covered over for protection from rain, since the church above is open without a roof. In front of the sepulcher is an atrium. Then, with multiple allusions to items already elucidated (see No. 231), Saewulf continues his account:

Afterwards you go up to Mount Calvary, where formerly the patriarch Abraham built an altar, and at the command of God was ready to sacrifice to him his own son. In the same place, afterwards, the Son of God, whom [Isaac] prefigured, was sacrificed to God the Father as the victim for the redemption of the world. The rock of that same mountain is a witness of our Lord's passion, being rent close to the hole in which the Cross of our Lord was fixed, because it could not bear without rending the slaying of its Creator, as we read in the Passion: "And the rocks were rent" (Mt 27:51). Underneath is the place which is called Golgotha, where Adam is said to have been raised from the dead by the stream of our Lord's blood falling upon him, as we read in our Lord's Passion: "And many bodies of the saints that slept arose" (Mt 27:52). . . . At the head of the Church of the Holy Sepulcher in the wall outside, not far from the place of Calvary, is a spot which is called Compas, where the same our Lord Jesus Christ himself, with his own hand, assigned and marked out the middle of the world, as the Psalmist testifies: "But God, our King before the ages, wrought salvation in the midst of the earth" (Ps 74:12, LXX 73:12).

Daniel (LPPTS IV-C, pp. 11-17) gives a description on the whole very similar to that of Saewulf, but supplies many measurements (stated in the unit *sagene*, equivalent to 7 English feet, 2.1 meters) and also says much about the mosaics with which the church was decorated.

The Church of the Resurrection is of circular form; it contains twelve monolithic columns and six pillars, and is paved with very beautiful marble slabs. There are six entrances, and galleries with sixteen columns. Under the ceiling, above the galleries, the holy prophets are represented in mosaic as if they were alive; the altar is surmounted by a figure of Christ in mosaic. At the high altar there is an "Exaltation of Adam" in mosaic; and the mosaic of the arch above represents the Ascension of our Lord. There is an "Annunciation" in mosaic on the pillars on either side of the altar. The dome of the church is not closed by a stone vault, but is formed of a framework of wooden beams, so that the church is open at the top. The Holy Sepulcher is beneath this open dome.

Here is the description of the Holy Sepulcher: it is a small cave hewn in the rock, having an entrance so low that a man can scarcely get through by going on bended knees; its height is inconsiderable, and its dimensions, equal in length and breadth, do not amount to more than 4 cubits. When one has entered the grotto by the little entrance, one sees on the right hand a sort of bench, cut in the rock of the cavern, upon which the body of our Lord Jesus Christ was laid; it is now covered by marble slabs. This sacred rock, which all Christians kiss, can be seen through three small round openings on one side. There are five large oil-lamps burning night and day suspended in the Sepulcher of our Lord. The holy bench upon which the body of Christ rested is 4 cubits in length, 2 in width, and 1 1/2 in height. Three feet in front of the entrance to the cavern there is the stone upon which the angel sat who appeared to the women and announced to them the resurrection of Christ. The holy grotto is cased externally with beautiful marble, like a raised platform and is surrounded by twelve columns of similar marble. It is surmounted by a beautiful turret resting on pillars, and terminating in a cupola, covered with silver-gilt plates, which bears on its summit a figure of Christ in silver, above the ordinary height; this was made by the Franks. This turret, which is exactly under the open dome, has three doors skillfully executed in trellis-work; it is by these doors that one enters the Holy Sepulcher. It is this grotto, then, which served as the Lord's Sepulcher; and I have described it according to the testimony of the oldest inhabitants, who thoroughly know the holy places.

The Church of the Resurrection is round in form [Daniel repeats], and measures 30 sagenes each way. It contains spacious apartments in the upper part, in which the Patriarch lives. They count 12 sagenes from the entrance of the tomb to the wall of the high altar. Behind the altar, outside the wall, is the "Navel of the earth," which is covered by a small building on (the vault of) which Christ is represented in mosaic, with this inscription: "The sole of my foot serves as a measure for the heaven and for the earth."

It is 12 sagenes from the "Navel of the earth" to the place of the crucifixion of our Lord and to Calvary. The place of crucifixion is towards the east, upon a rounded rock, like a little hill, higher than a lance. On the summit of it, in the middle, a socket-hole is excavated, one cubit deep, and less than a foot in circumference; it is here that the cross of our Lord was erected.

Beneath this rock lies the skull of the first man, Adam. At the time of our Lord's crucifixion, when he gave up the ghost on the cross, the veil of the Temple rent, and the rock clave asunder, and the rock above Adam's skull opened, and the blood and water which flowed from Christ's side ran down through the fissure upon the skull, thus washing away the sins of men. The fissure exists to this day, and this holy token is to be seen to the right of the place of crucifixion.

The holy rock and the place of crucifixion are enclosed by a wall, and they are covered by a building ornamented with marvelous mosaics. On the eastern wall there is a wonderful life-like representation of the crucified Christ, but larger and higher than nature; and on the south side an equally marvelous representation of the Descent from the Cross. There are two doors; one mounts seven steps to the doors, and as many after. The floor is paved with beautiful marble. Beneath the place of crucifixion, where the skull lies, there is a small chapel, beautifully decorated with mosaic, and paved with fine marble, which is called "Calvary," signifying the place of the skull. The upper part, the place of the crucifixion, is called "Golgotha." The distance between the "Crucifixion" and the place of the descent from the cross is 5 sagenes. In the neighborhood of the place of the crucifixion, on the north side, is the place where the garments of our Lord were parted; and close to it there is the spot where they placed the crown of thorns on his head, and laid on him, in mockery, the garment of purple.

Close to this place is Abraham's altar, upon which he offered his sacrifice to God, and slew a ram instead of Isaac. At this same place, to which Isaac was led, Christ was brought as a sacrifice and crucified for the salvation of us sinners.

When the Crusaders came in 1099, if they were to rebuild the Church of the Holy Sepulcher for themselves, they faced a choice of whether to attempt to reconstitute the entire fourth-century complex of Constantine, which was almost entirely destroyed, or to limit themselves to a renovation of the more modest building of the emperor Constantine IX Monomachus, which was then only about fifty years old. Instead of either alternative, they chose a middle way, but a way which required another fifty years of work, leading to dedication of their church, the fourth in the long series, on July 15, 1149 (Corbo, *Santo Sepolcro* 2, pl. 6).

The Constantinian complex, made up of four units, the First Atrium, the Martyrion, the Second Atrium in front of the Anastasis, and the Anastasis, was already reduced to two units (Anastasis and Second Atrium) by Monomachus. By the Crusaders the Anatasis was left substantially unchanged, except that the eastern apse, by which Monomachus had stressed the centrality of the Tomb (pl. 4, nos. 70-71), was removed and replaced by a great triumphal arch (pl. 6, no. 511). The edicule of the Tomb itself was also remodelled, the octagonal shape being replaced by a polygonal structure, and the old vestibule being changed in to the Chapel of the Angel (pl. 6, no. 510). In front of the Anastasis in the spacious area which was formerly the Second Atrium or the "Garden" (the Triportico in pl. 4) the Crusaders built an entire Romanesque church, closely linked to the Anastasis by the triumphal arch just mentioned and consisting of the so-called Chorus Dominorum (later the Choir of the Greeks), a southern (pl. 6, nos. 514-515 and 538-539) and a northern (pl. 6, nos. 521-522 and 523-525) transept, and an ambulatory with radiating chapels (pl. 6, nos. 527, 529, 533). Now the Rock of Calvary no longer stood in an isolated chapel but was included, together with the Chapel of Adam at its western base (pl. 6, no.

537), within the perimeter of the sacred buildings. In the vestibule of the Chapel of Adam the first two Crusader kings were buried, Godfrey de Bouillon (d. 1100) and Baldwin I (d. 1118) (pl. 6, A and B). Beside the central chapel at the east end of the church (pl. 6, no. 529), steps led down to an underground church known as the Chapel of St. Helena, which the Crusaders built in close relation to the eleventh-century chapel of the Finding of the Cross (pl. 6, no. 309). On the south side of the church, at the south end of the southern transept, the Crusaders built an entirely new façade with the two great entryway doors (pl. 6, nos. 541, 542) through which the church is still entered today, and with two windows high above. On one side was an imposing bell tower (campanile, pl. 6, no. 540, and pl. 51), added after the south façade had already been completed, and built by the Crusaders on what was one of the chapels (pl. 4, no. 501) in the church of Monomachus. On the other side of the entrance was the Crusader entrance to Calvary (pl. 6, no. 543; Peters, *Jerusalem*, illus. after p. 274) (now the steps and edicule of the Chapel of the Franks), although the more ancient staircase, starting from the northern spur of the Rock (pl. 6, no. 536; pl. 40, no. 3b), was also still preserved. As for the façade, it was built on Constantinian foundations, following the line of the enclosure wall of the original platform of Hadrian (Corbo, *Santo Sepolcro* 1, p. 233; for the sculptures of the façade see 3, photos 194-202).

Two carved marble lintels that stood over the eastern and western doors of the Crusader church are preserved in the Rockefeller Museum in Jerusalem. The eastern lintel was above the door which led through the Chapel of Adam into the Chorus Dominorum (Choir of the Greeks). It depicts human and animal figures in the midst of trees, branches, fruit, and flowers. The gestures of naked men and the presence of birds of prey, a Harpy, a centaur, and two dragons, suggest that this is a representation of the world of sin and evil, appropriately enough to be recalled when going by the tomb of Adam. The western lintel, on the other hand, which was above the door opening into the place of the burial and resurrection of Christ, shows scenes from his life, from his presence at Bethany to the Last Supper; thus the believer is invited to follow on the way of redemption. Together these lintels and the Crusader capitals at Nazareth (No. 45) are the finest examples of Crusader sculpture found in the country.

A gold ring found in 1974 in the excavations to the south of the Temple area carries on top a representation in gold of a building that is a square with a large round vault on each side and with a cone-shaped cupola on top. A similar structure is represented on a marble screen from a lintel in the façade of the Crusader church, and it is thought probable that the building in question is intended to depict the edicule over the tomb of Jesus in the Church of the Holy Sepulcher as it was seen during the Crusader period.

The Crusader church endured substantially intact until in 1808 a devastating fire almost destroyed the Rotunda, burned the wooden roof of the church, and did much other damage (G. Dalman, "Die Grabeskirche in Jerusalem," in PJ 3 [1907], pp. 34f.). Repairs were carried out in the next two years by the Greek Orthodox, and the restored structure, dedicated anew in 1810, may be accounted the fifth church in the long sequence marked by the earlier names of Constantine, Modestus, Constantine Monomachus, and the Crusaders. In 1865-1869 the edicule over the grave was rebuilt in its present form, but preserving some ancient columns. As it stands, a small door opens into a tiny vestibule, which is supposedly where the angel sat upon the stone that he had rolled away (Mt 28:2; Mk 16:4-5), and a supposed fragment of that stone is inserted in the pedestal in the center. An even smaller door opens into the sepulcher proper, where the rock remains around the chamber to a height of four feet, but the rock is covered by a marble slab over the rock couch where the body presumably was laid (Meistermann pp. 123f.; Mackowski p. 159, pl. 136). A small portion of the rock of the tomb may also be seen at the base of the Chapel of the Copts immediately behind the present edicule (Murphy-O'Connor p. 41).

That the church was also so severely damaged by an earthquake in 1927 as to require the support of iron constructions, and that recent restoration was inaugurated in 1960 has been noted above (No. 225). As it stands today, then, the Church of the Holy Sepulcher is essentially the church of the Crusaders, but within its walls are the marks of a very long history all together.

Summary of History of the Church of the Holy Sepulcher
1. Built by Constantine the Great, dedicated 335
   Burned by Persians, 614
2. Restored by Modestus, c. 628
   Spared by Muslim Arabs, 638
   Destroyed by al-Hakim, 1009
3. Rebuilt by Constantine IX Monomachus, 1048
4. Rebuilt by Crusaders, dedicated 1149
   Burned, 1808
5. Repaired by Greek Orthodox, dedicated 1810
   Damaged by earthquake, 1927
   Recent restoration and archeological study, 1960-present

The photograph is taken from the court on the south side of the church and shows the Crusaders' bell tower at the left of the main entrance. As explained just above, the tower was by this time held together with iron bands, and some of the iron scaffolding supporting the walls of the church is visible at the right. Behind the bell tower the dome of the Rotunda may be glimpsed.

Vincent, *Jérusalem nouvelle*, pp. 248-300; Marius Canard, "La destruction de l'Eglise de la Résurrection," in *Byzantion* 35 (1965), pp. 16-43; Shlomo D. Goitein, "Jerusalem in the Arab Period (638-1099)," in *The Jerusalem Cathedra* II (1982), pp. 184f. For the Fatimid dynasty, see Clifford Edmund Bosworth, *The Islamic Dynasties, A Chronological and Genealogical Handbook* (Edinburgh: University Press, 1967), pp. 46-48. For the rulers of the Byzantine empire, see A. A. Vasiliev, *History of the Byzantine Empire, 324-1453*, 2 vols. with pages numbered consecutively (Madison: University of Wisconsin Press, 1958); for Romanus III, Constantine IX Monomachus, and the restoration of the Church of the Holy Sepulcher, see pp. 302, 312f., 392. For the Crusader lintels, see J. Prawer, "The Lintels of the Holy Sepulchre," in *Jerusalem Revealed*, pp. 111-113; L. Y. Rahmani, "The Eastern Lintel of the Holy Sepulchre," in IEJ 26 (1976), pp. 120-129. For the gold ring, see Yaakov Meshorer, "Ancient Gold Ring Depicts the Holy Sepulchre," in BAR 12.3 (May/June 1986), pp. 46-48; Cornfeld p. 273. Photograph: JF.

233. The Church of the Holy Sepulcher from the Tower of the Lutheran Church

THIS VIEW of the church of the Holy Sepulcher is taken, looking northwest, from the high tower of the German Lutheran Church of the Redeemer at the northeast corner of the Muristan. At the left is the bell tower (No. 232), and beside it the portal of the church. The large dome rises over the tomb. The small dome is above the Choir of the Greeks, at the east side of which steps lead down into the Chapel of St. Helena. The small terrace on this side of the domes is over the rock of Golgotha.

Photograph: JF.

234. Looking East from the Tower of the Lutheran Church

THIS ADDITIONAL VIEW, also taken from the tower of the Lutheran Church, helps to bring out the relationship of the Muristan and Holy Sepulcher area to the rest of Jerusalem. Looking across the rooftops of the city we see at a distance the Dome of the Rock in the temple area and, beyond that, the Mount of Olives with the Russian Tower on the high summit.

Photograph: JF.

235. Ship and *Domine ivimus* Inscription

UNDERGROUND IN THE CHURCH of the Holy Sepulcher, the Chapel of St. Helena and the Chapel of

233. The Church of the Holy Sepulcher from the Tower of the Lutheran Church

234. Looking East from the Tower of the Lutheran Church

235. Ship and *Domine ivimus* Inscription

the Finding of the Cross (No. 232) are in the possession of the Armenians. Under the direction of the Armenian Archimandrite Guregh Kapikian (No. 230) and with supervision by Magen Broshi, curator of the Israeli Shrine of the Book, excavation was conducted in 1975 behind (to the east of) the apses of the Chapel of St. Helena (called the Chapel of St. Krikor, i.e., Gregory, by the Armenians) and to the north of the Chapel of the Find-

ing of the Cross. A space was found here which had been blocked up in antiquity and was now cleared and fitted out as a new Chapel of St. Vartan and the Armenian Martyrs. Like other areas under the Church of the Holy Sepulcher, this area was a rock quarry in the seventh century B.C. (as also seen at the Muristan, No. 200), and also contained walls which were probably those of a system of vaults supporting the pavement of the complex of

281

Hadrian's temple of Venus (No. 223). One of these walls (see IEJ 35 [1985], p. 120, fig. 5, w1, and pp. 124f.), which is probably a part of this vaulting system (or possibly even pre-Hadrianic, Kroll p. 385, col. 3, abb. 308, no. 4), is of special interest. Set into this wall is a carefully polished block of stone, 83 cm. long and 45 cm. high, on which are the drawing and inscription shown in the present photograph. The drawing, executed in black and red, depicts a sailing ship of a type well known in the Roman world. The stern is adorned with a goose-headed ornament (*cheniscus*), and there are two steering rudders. The mast is lowered (some think broken), and the mainsail is apparently furled, while a foresail is at the bow. The inscription below reads, *Domine ivimus*, "Lord, we shall go." The two words are found in the Latin text of Jn 6:68 (*Domine, ad quem ibimus* [in Latin *b* and *v* are interchangeable]), "Lord, to whom shall we go?" The allusion, however, is probably to Ps 122:1, "Let us go to the house of the Lord," which reads in the Latin version, *In domum Domini ibimus*. Like several other related Psalms, this Psalm has the superscription, "A Song of Ascents" (RSV), apparently meaning that it was for pilgrims going up to Jerusalem (IB 4, pp. 638f.).

The Latin language and the pilgrimage allusion of the inscription and the Roman style of the ship suggest as the most likely interpretation that we have here the record of pilgrims who have come from the West to a sacred place and are expressing their happiness at arrival. The script is assigned to a time from the last half of the third century to the first half of the fourth century (Testa p. 221), and the record may be supposed to have been placed here around the time of the erection of the Con-

stantinian basilica, say c. 330. Coming from such a date, these are the earliest known inscription and drawing by any Christian pilgrim to Palestine (Broshi, IEJ 35 [1985], pp. 124, 128), and as such their sentiment is expressive of the thought of many a pilgrim to the Holy Land and to the place of the Church of the Holy Sepulcher from then until now.

Lionel Casson, *Ships and Seamanship in the Ancient World* (Princeton: Princeton University Press, 1971), esp. pp. 174, 347f. and n. 15, figs. 147 (the ships to left and right for the goose-headed ornament) and 191; E. Testa, "Il Golgota, porte delle quiete," in *Studia Hierosolymitana in onore di P. Bellarmino Bagatti,* I, *Studi archeologici,* SBFCM 22 (Jerusalem: Franciscan Printing Press, 1976), pp. 197-244; M. Broshi, "Evidence of Earliest Christian Pilgrimage to the Holy Land comes to light in Holy Sepulchre Church," in BAR 3.4 (Dec 1977), pp. 42-44; and Broshi, "Excavations in the Chapel of St. Vartan in the Holy Sepulchre," in IEJ 35 (1985), pp. 108-128 (see pp. 127f. for criticism of Testa's allegorical interpretation of the ship as sailing on a mystical sea). Photograph: JF.

236. The Rocky Hill Known as Gordon's Calvary

FROM THE FOREGOING (NOS. 225ff.) it is abundantly evident that the appearance of the site of Golgotha and the Holy Sepulcher is very different now from what it was in the time of Jesus. At that time, if the above analysis is correct, the area was a garden area outside the city wall, and now the area is within the city wall and densely packed with buildings. Also the modifications introduced by Hadrian in the building of the forum of Aelia Capitolina, and by the workmen of Con-

236. The Rocky Hill Known as Gordon's Calvary

stantine as they cut away large parts of the rock of Calvary and of the tomb, have very largely altered the appearance of what does remain of the natural and ancient features of the first century, while the church of the Crusaders is different in many ways from the Martyrion and Anastasis of the fourth century. For this reason a rocky hill and adjacent garden tomb outside the present north wall of Jerusalem have seemed to some visitors a better place in which to try to visualize Golgotha and the tomb of Christ.

It has already been noted (No. 201) that there is an ancient quarry under the present north wall of Jerusalem some one hundred yards east of the Damascus Gate, known as Solomon's Quarry; another quarry, known as the Grotto of Jeremiah, lies across the road to the north, and the two have probably been separated by a cutting away of the rock between. The rocky hill above the Grotto of Jeremiah is called *el-heidemiyeh*, and in 1842 Otto Thenius (in ZHT 1842, pp. 16ff.) suggested that this was the real hill of Golgotha. In 1867 a rock-hewn tomb was found in the northwestern slope of this hill. In 1883-1884 Charles G. Gordon visited Jerusalem and accepted the view originally proposed by Thenius (Gordon in PEFQS 1885, pp. 79f.). After that the hill became known as Gordon's Calvary. In 1894 the tomb below the hill and the surrounding garden were purchased by the Garden Tomb Association in England, and the tomb is known as the Garden Tomb (No. 237).

The rocky hill in question is shown in this photograph, which is a view taken from the north wall of the Old City. On the top of the hill is a Muslim cemetery.

Gustaf Dalman, "Golgotha und das Grab Christi," in PJ 9 (1913), pp. 98-123; L.-H. Vincent, "Garden Tomb, Histoire d'un mythe," in RB 34 (1925), pp. 401-431; Simons, *Jerusalem*, pp. 287-290; C. C. Dobson, *The Garden Tomb, Jerusalem, and the Resurrection* (London: George Pulman and Sons Ltd., 1958); W. S. McBirnie, *The Search for the Authentic Tomb of Jesus* (Montrose, Calif.: Acclaimed Books, 1975); Gabriel Barkay, "The Garden Tomb, Was Jesus Buried Here?" in BAR 12.2 (Mar/April 1986), pp. 40-53, 56-57. For General Gordon's own letter about Golgotha, see WJJK pp. 198-200. Photograph: The Matson Photo Service, Alhambra, Calif.

237. The Garden Tomb

THIS PHOTOGRAPH SHOWS the tomb just mentioned (No. 236) cut into the rock in the lower slope of the hill which some have believed to be the hill of Calvary. From the entrance one descends one step into an antechamber, then turns right to enter the tomb chamber proper. The small window above and to the right of the entrance admits light to this chamber, in which are ledges on three sides, of which the one on the left hand, i.e., on the north side, is the best finished. Like a number of geographically related tombs within the grounds of the nearby Monastery of St. Stephen (No. 242), it is now believed that the Garden Tomb dates originally from the eighth and seventh centuries B.C., in the time of the First Temple. Between then and the fifth and sixth centuries A.D. (in the Byzantine period) usage is not indicated, and the tomb was probably recut in the Byzantine period to attain its present shape. When the tomb

237. The Garden Tomb

was first discovered in 1867 there were two Byzantine crosses painted in red on the east wall of the tomb chamber.

L. Y. Rahmani, "Ancient Jerusalem's Funerary Customs and Tombs," in BA 44 (1981), p. 234; Gabriel Barkay and Amos Kloner, "Jerusalem Tombs from the Days of the First Temple," in BAR 12.2 (Mar/Apr 1988), pp. 22-39.

238. At the Entrance to the Garden Tomb

HERE THE ENTRANCE doorway of the Garden Tomb (No. 237) appears at the right and we also see the rock-cut trough which runs along the whole front of the tomb at ground level. The trough does not appear adequate to provide for a rolling stone closure of the tomb such as may be seen in certain other Jerusalem tombs (Nos. 274, 281), and probably its purpose was simply to carry away rainwater from the cliff above (Dobson, *The Garden Tomb*, p. 20).

Photograph: JF.

238. At the Entrance to the Garden Tomb

239. Excavations at the Basilica of St. Stephen

IT WILL BE remembered that in 451 Peter the Iberian came to Jerusalem from the north and saw the martyrium of St. Stephen before he came on into the city and to Golgotha (No. 215); that in 530 Theodosius says that outside the north gate of the city, which he calls the Galilean Gate, was the church which was built in memory of the stoning of Stephen by Eudocia (No. 229); and that Arculf calls the north gate St. Stephen's Gate (No. 229). The Anonymous of Piacenza (570) (Geyer p. 176; LPPTS II-D, p. 21; CCSL CLXXV, p. 166; WJP p. 84) also tells us that Eudocia (444-460), who extended the southern walls of Jerusalem so that they enclosed the fountain of Siloam (Nos. 179, 229), herself built the basilica and tomb of St. Stephen, and placed her own tomb next to the tomb of St. Stephen. For help in the identification of the traditional site and in the work of building, Eudocia was no doubt assisted by Juvenal, then the bishop of Jerusalem (422-458).

The site that best corresponds to these indications is about 320 meters north of the Damascus Gate on the Nablus Road, and about 150 meters northwest of the Garden Tomb, the latter being reached from a side street off from the Nablus Road. Certain ancient ruins were found here in 1881, and in the next year the site was acquired by the French Dominicans. In 1885 the latter inaugurated serious excavations, which were continued for many years.

In these excavations were found the remains of a basilica of the fifth century, which is doubtless that built by Eudocia. Under the atrium was a large cistern. The basilica had nave, two side aisles, and apse, oriented to the east (Vincent, *Jérusalem nouvelle*, pl. LXXVII). Many fragments of columns and capitals were found, and considerable portions of mosaic pavement, also of the fifth century (QDAP 2 [1932], pp. 176-177). The photograph shows these excavations while they were still in progress. The view is from the north-northwest and looks toward the hill of Bezetha in the distance. The cistern in the atrium and debris of the basilica are to be seen.

Vincent, *Jérusalem nouvelle*, pp. 766-804; Ovadiah, *Corpus*, pp. 77f., no. 66; "BAR Interviews Pere Benoit," in BAR 12.2 (Mar/Apr 1986), pp. 58-66. Photograph: courtesy École Biblique et Archéologique Française.

240. The Basilica of St. Stephen

IN ITS EXPOSED position on the north side of Jerusalem the basilica of Eudocia (No. 239) was no doubt quickly destroyed by the Persians in 614. At the end of the century a new chapel was built in the atrium of the former basilica, and this chapel was restored by the Cru-

239. Excavations at the Basilica of St. Stephen

240. The Basilica of St. Stephen

saders. The remains of these building operations were also uncovered in the excavations (No. 239). In 1900 the modern Basilica of St. Stephen, built upon the foundations of the church of Eudocia, was consecrated, and this photograph shows its façade. Adjacent to the basilica are the Dominican Monastery and the École Biblique et Archéologique Française, the latter founded in 1890.

Photograph: JF.

285

241. In the Atrium of the Basilica of St. Stephen

THIS PICTURE SHOWS the atrium of the modern basilica, which is built over the atrium of the church of the fifth century. In the center stands a portion of a column of the ancient church.

Photograph: JF.

241. In the Atrium of the Basilica of St. Stephen

242. Inscription of the Deacon Nonnus

IN THE GROUNDS of the Basilica of St. Stephen a number of rock-hewn tombs have been found, extending in the direction of the Garden Tomb (No. 237) not far away (cf. No. 239), all it is now believed dating originally from the time of the First Temple (eighth and seventh centuries B.C.) and used again in the Byzantine period (fifth and sixth centuries A.D.) (cf. No. 237). In the north portico of the atrium of the basilica a stone slab was found in excavations in 1889, which covered the steps leading down to a Byzantine-type tomb of about the middle of the fifth century A.D. On the stone a Greek inscription begins with a cross, and reads as follows:

> ΘΗΚΔΙΑ
> ΦΕΡΝΟΝ
> ΝΟΥΔΙΑ
> ΚΟΝΙϹ

> ΤΗϹΑΓΤ
> ΟΥΧΥΑϹΚ
> ΤΗϹΜΑΥΤΗ
> Ϲ

Θήκ(η) διαφέρ(ουσα) Νοννοῦ διακ(όνου) Ὀνισ(ίμου) τῆς ἁγ(ίας) τοῦ Χ(ριστο)ῦ Ἀ(ναστάσεω)ς κ(αὶ) τῆς μο(μῆς) αὐτῆς

Private tomb of the deacon Nonnus Onesimus, of the Holy Anastasis of Christ, and of this monastery.

This says, then, that this particular monk, Nonnus Onesimus, had been attached during his lifetime to the Anastasis, i.e., to the Church of the Holy Sepulcher, and had been a member of the monastery of St. Stephen's, where he was buried.

Considering all the foregoing, the inscription just quoted of course does not mean that the Anastasis of Constantine was to be found at the site of the Basilica of St. Stephen, which would place it near to the Garden Tomb. Rather the existence of these various tombs of First Temple and of Byzantine date near the Basilica of St. Stephen suggests that the Garden Tomb, not far away, may well have been another of the same group and of the same date (cf. No. 237).

242. Inscription of the Deacon Nonnus

Vincent in RB 34 (1925), pp. 408-409; and Vincent, *Jérusalem nouvelle*, p. 802; Simons, *Jerusalem*, pp. 288-289; Jerome Murphy-O'Connor, "The Garden Tomb and the Misfortunes of an Inscription," in BAR 12.2 (Mar/Apr 1986), pp. 54f. Photograph: courtesy École Biblique et Archéologique Française.

243. St. Stephen's Gate

AS WE HAVE just seen (No. 239), the earliest tradition places the place of death (Ac 7:60) and the martyrium of Stephen outside the north gate of Jerusalem, this gate being called St. Stephen's Gate by Arculf and corresponding to the Damascus Gate today. By the ninth century another tradition began to speak of a chapel dedicated to St. Stephen in the Valley of Josaphat, i.e., the Valley of the Kidron (No. 169), doubtless in line with the tendency to associate a number of martyrs with that valley (Vincent, *Jérusalem nouvelle*, p. 758). In the same way the place of the stoning of Stephen was later thought by some to have been outside an east gate of Jerusalem, and thus the name, Gate of St. Stephen, was attached to the gate in the east wall not far north of the Temple area. Earlier, however, this was known as the Gate of St. Mary, with reference to her tomb in the Kidron Valley below (No. 170), and the street leading into the city from the gate was called the Tariq Bab Sitty

243. St. Stephen's Gate

Mariam (No. 216), which means the Street of the Gate of St. Mary. The photograph shows St. Stephen's Gate, as it is now called. Like the Damascus Gate, it was restored by Suleiman in the sixteenth century (cf. No. 201). The lions on either side of the arch were heraldic emblems of the Mamluke Sultan Baibars, reused by Suleiman (Murphy-O'Connor p. 17).

Photograph: JF.

EMMAUS

244. Aerial View of el-Qubeibeh, A Possible Site of Emmaus

WITH RESPECT TO the resurrection appearances of Christ, the specific place that is mentioned in addition to Jerusalem and its environs and Galilee is on the road to Emmaus (Lk 24:13-35). Here (Lk 24:13) Emmaus (Ἐμμαοῦς) is said to be at a distance of 60 stadia (σταδίους ἑξήκοντα) (about "seven miles" RSV) from Jerusalem, according to Papyrus Bodmer XIV (P75 of the early third century), Codex Vaticanus, and many other manuscripts, but 160 stadia (ἕκατον ἑξήκοντα) (about eighteen miles) according to Codex Sinaiticus and some other manuscripts, including the Palestinian Syriac.

Corresponding to the two distances given in these variant readings, there are two main sites which have been thought to represent the ancient Emmaus, namely, el-Qubeibeh and ʿAmwas. The modern village of el-Qubeibeh is beyond Nebi Samwil on the road that runs northwest from Jerusalem and is at a distance of seven or eight miles from the city, which agrees with the sixty stadia of Papyrus Bodmer XIV, Codex Vaticanus, and the other manuscripts. The ancient name of the place is unknown, however, for the Arabic name means only "a little dome," possibly referring to a small Muslim shrine, and appears first in the time of the Crusades. Only at the end of the fifteenth century is the name explicitly given as that of the Emmaus of Lk 24. In 1485 the Franciscan friar Francesco Suriano writes (*Il Trattato della Terra Santa*, 19, Baldi pp. 717-718, No. 985).

> On the main road from Rome to Jerusalem, at a distance of fifteen Roman miles (*quindece miglia*, an estimate which is not much more than the sixty stadia already stated), is located the castle of Emmaus, which is called Chubebe [Qubeibeh] in Arabic. In it stands the church of Cleopas, where he and St. Luke had supper with Christ (after the resurrection), in the breaking of the bread.

244. Air View of el-Qubeibeh, A Possible Site of Emmaus

In 1852 the Franciscans noted church ruins, in 1861 purchased the site, and in 1902 erected above the ruins of the older church the church that still stands. According to their excavations the older church, which was used as a foundation for the new building, was a basilica of the Crusaders. Within its enclosure were the remains of a more ancient structure, which might have been a Byzantine church, but which some think was a house of the Roman period, and even the very house of Cleopas. Additional excavation in 1943 confirmed the existence of a village of the time of Christ very near the church. Identification of the place with the NT Emmaus remains doubtful, however, because of the lateness of any tradition to that effect. The aerial view looks eastward in the direction of Jerusalem, shows the village of el-Quebeibeh, and just beyond it the Franciscan church and monastery on the site just described.

At about the same distance as el-Qubeibeh of some seven or eight miles from Jerusalem, to the west-northwest, is the village of Abu Ghosh. Although it takes its name from a brigand chief of the Turkish period, the earlier Arabic name was Qaryet el-Enab, a version of Qiryat Yearim or Kiriath-jearim, the OT city where the ark of the covenant was for twenty years (1 S 7:2). An identification of this site with NT Emmaus was first made by the Crusaders, who built a church there (excavated in

1944), and this was probably just on the basis of the correspondence of the distance with the sixty stadia of Lk 24:13, therefore Abu Ghosh is also probably not the NT Emmaus.

Eugene Hoade, *Guide to the Holy Land* (Jerusalem: Franciscan Press, 1946), pp. 387-391; Bellarmino Bagatti, *I monumenti di Emmaus el-Qubeibeh e dei dintorni, resultato degli scavi e sporalluoghi negli anni 1873, 1900-2, 1940-44*, PSBF 4 (Jerusalem: Franciscan Printing Press, 1947); Kopp 1959, pp. 449-450; V. R. Gold in IDB III, pp. 37f.; Murphy-O'Connor, pp. 133f., 320f. Photograph: The Matson Photo Service, Alhambra, Calif.

245. Mosaic of the Roman Villa at 'Amwas, Ancient Emmaus

THE SITE of the Arab village of 'Amwas, now Canada Park, with the Cistercian Abbey of Latrun nearby, is on the main ancient road that ran west-northwest from Jerusalem to Jaffa. The place is about eighteen miles from Jerusalem, which is about the 160 stadia mentioned in Lk 24: 13 according to Codex Sinaiticus and the Palestinian Syriac. Preserving as it does in Arabic form the very name of Emmaus, there is little doubt that this was the ancient town of that name which is mentioned frequently in 1 Macc (1 Macc 3:40, etc.) and in Josephus

(*War* II 5,1 §71 Ἀμμαοῦς; *Ant.* XVII 10, 7 §282 Ἐμμαοῦς, etc.).

Concerning this Emmaus Josephus relates that the place was burned down by Varus, Roman governor of Syria (6–4 B.C.). Sozomen (*Ch. Hist.* V 21), in turn, reports that after the conquest of Jerusalem by the Romans, Emmaus was given the name of Nicopolis. Finally Eusebius identifies this well-known Emmaus as the Emmaus of Lk 24:13, for in the *Onomasticon* (p. 90) he says that Emmaus "is now Nicopolis, a famous city of Palestine." Likewise the Bordeaux Pilgrim (Geyer p. 25; LPPTS I-B, p. 28; CCSL CLXXV, p. 20; WET p. 163 n. 2) mentions a city by the name of Nicopolis, and places it at twenty-two Roman miles from Jerusalem. While this distance of ʿAmwas from Jerusalem has often been urged as an argument against the identification of the place with the Emmaus of Lk 24:13, it agrees well, as we have noted, with the 160 stadia of the text in Codex Sinaiticus and the Palestinian Syriac (probably representing Palestinian tradition), and F.-M. Abel and J. W. Crowfoot (PEFQS 1935, p. 43) agree that no one who is acquainted with the country and the habits of the people of Palestine will have any difficulty in believing that Cleopas and his companion could have walked from Jerusalem to ʿAmwas and back on the same day.

At ʿAmwas excavations were begun in 1875 and completed in 1924–1930 by the Dominicans of the École Biblique in Jerusalem. On the main site five buildings of considerable magnitude were distinguished. The first was a small church which L.-H. Vincent assigns to the first half of the twelfth century, i.e., to the period of the Crusaders. Under this was an earlier and much larger church, a basilica with nave and two aisles, and with three apses, oriented toward the southeast. The floor of this basilica was 70 centimeters below the floor of the Crusaders' church. In turn, under the northwest corner of the basilica were the remains of a house which was partially destroyed when the basilica was built. Part of the west wall of the basilica coincided with one of the house walls, and some of the floor mosaics of the house were reused as floor mosaics of the church. The house had extended farther to the north and there, against one of its walls, and separated from the larger basilica by a small court, was built another and smaller basilica. At the southeast end of the latter basilica was a baptistery. These are the five buildings, the Crusaders' church, the larger and the smaller basilicas, the baptistery, and the house.

Vincent (*Emmaüs*, pl. VIII) attributed the mosaics of the house, presumably part of a fine Roman villa, to the Severan epoch, i.e., the late second and early third century, and put the large basilica, in which the mosaics were reused, in the third century. The smaller basilica was only built in the sixth century, he thought, after the

245. Mosaic of the Roman Villa at ʿAmwas, Ancient Emmaus

great church had fallen. Watzinger (II, p. 126) thinks the house was built in the third or fourth century, and the large basilica after that. Crowfoot (PEFQS 1935, pp. 45-47) puts the house not earlier than the end of the fifth century and the larger basilica not earlier than the middle of the sixth century. The smaller basilica could possibly have been in existence, he thinks, while the house with the mosaics was still standing. A section of the house mosaics, re-used in the large basilica, featuring birds and plants, is shown in this photograph.

L.-H. Vincent and F.-M. Abel, *Emmaüs, sa basilique et son histoire* (Paris: Ernest Leroux, 1932); Review by J. W. Crowfoot in PEFQS 1935, pp. 40-47; Vincent in RB 35 (1926), pp. 117-121; and "Autour du groupe monumental d'Amwas," in RB 45 (1936), pp. 403-415; Kopp 1959, pp. 445-449; *Bible et Terre Sainte* (Mar 1961), pp. 1-13; Ovadiah, *Corpus*, pp. 63-65, nos. 53-54; Murphy-O'Connor, pp. 270-275. Photograph: courtesy École Biblique et Archéologique Française.

246. Plan of the Basilica at 'Amwas

THE PLAN and restoration show the large basilica with its nave, two aisles, and three apses, as described above (No. 245). The dimensions of the church are 46 meters in length and 24 meters in width.

Plan: courtesy École Biblique et Archéologique Française.

247. The Baptistery at 'Amwas

WITH ABOUT SIX METERS between their respective walls, the smaller basilica was located parallel to the larger basilica on the north side. At its southeast end, directly in line with the three apses of principle basilica, was a small enclosure with the baptismal basin. This view is taken from the southwest side in the angle of the

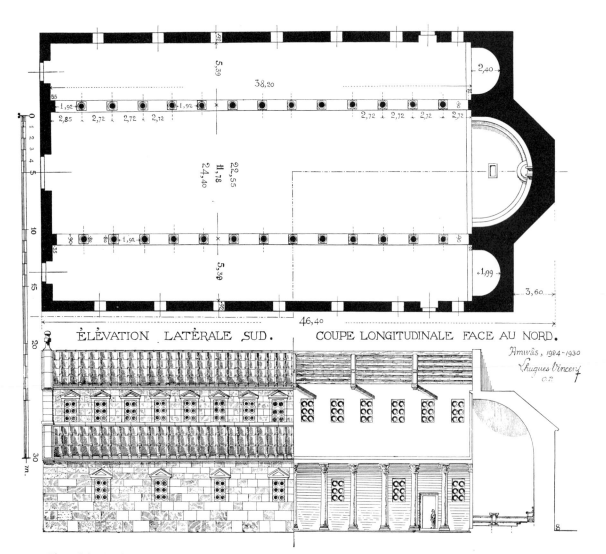

246. Plan of the Basilica at 'Amwas

247. The Baptistery at 'Amwas

modern shelter which is over the baptistery. In the left wall near the corner are the openings of the canals which brought water to the baptistery from an adjacent reservoir. The baptismal basin itself is in the shape of a quatrefoil, like a flower with four leaves.

Yet a fourth site comes into consideration and is thought by some to be the NT Emmaus rather than any one of the preceding three (Nos. 244ff.). In just one instance Josephus (*War* VII 6, 6 §217) mentions an Emmaus which cannot be identified with 'Amwas for it was, he says, only thirty stadia (about three and one-half miles) from Jerusalem. At this place, so near to Jerusalem, Vespasian in A.D. 75 settled 800 army veterans. Since there is a place called Qaloniyeh, probably derived from Latin Colonia, which is near the Israeli settlement of Motza-Illit about four miles west of Jerusalem, beside the main road down to Jaffa, this can be the site of the Emmaus mentioned by Josephus in the one instance. Excavation of the ruins in 1942 and 1964-1965 revealed

remains of a Christian church and monastery of the Byzantine period (fifth to sixth centuries). Early literary support for this place in pilgrim records is lacking, however, and the distance of 30 stadia from Jerusalem does not agree with the much larger figures of 60 or 160 stadia in Lk 24:13.

As to places associated with the Ascension of Christ, these have been dealt with in connection with earlier consideration of sites on the Mount of Olives (Nos. 154ff.).

Richard M. Mackowski, "Where is Biblical Emmaus?" in *Science et Esprit* 32 (1980), pp. 93-103; and Mackowski, *Jerusalem, City of Jesus*, p. 184 n. 19; Ovadiah, *Corpus*, pp. 139-140, no. 142. Photograph: courtesy École Biblique et Archéologique Française.

TOMBS

IN A PRECEDING section a hypothetical reconstruction of the tomb of Jesus has been presented (No. 227), based upon knowledge of contemporary Jewish tombs and comparison with references in the Gospels. In order to substantiate what was said there briefly about the tombs of that time, a survey will now be made of the evolution of Jewish tombs, and this will also prepare for what follows when we look at some marks and signs that have been found in burial places, some of which are possibly and some certainly connected with early Christianity.

It may be presumed that from the earliest times the great mass of burials in Palestine were simple interments in the earth, which have long since been irrevocably lost. In pre-pottery Neolithic Jericho burials were made in pits under the floors of the houses. At Teleilat Ghassul in the Chalcolithic period there is a child burial in a house in a pottery jar surrounded by stones. Where the burial pit is lined and covered with stones, as is often the case, it is customary to speak of a cist burial (from Greek κίστη and Latin *cista*, "box"). Natural caves as well as excavated pits also served as burial places, and could also of course be more or less modified for this purpose.

More elaborate tombs were cut in the rock. Because they were more elaborate and more difficult to make it may be assumed that these were usually the property of the minority better able to afford them. At Jerusalem there are approximately 500 ancient rock tombs known and, it has been estimated, these would have provided for less than 5 percent of the burials that must be assumed for a city of that size during the period in which those tombs were used. The historical development of the chief types of rock-hewn tombs will be illustrated (Nos. 248-258) and then some specific tombs of the NT period (Nos. 259-281).

Kathleen M. Kenyon, *Digging Up Jericho* (New York: Frederick A. Praeger, 1957, pp. 63f.); Alexis Mallon, Robert Koeppel, and René Neuville, *Teleilat Ghassul*, I, *Compte rendu des fouilles de l'Institut Biblique Pontifical 1929-1932*. Scripta Pontificii Instituti Biblici (Rome: Piazza della Pilotta, 35, 1934), p. 49 and pl. 24, fig. 5; *Tell en-Nasbeh* I, pp. 68-76, 77-83; Galling, "Nekropole," p. 80; Joseph A. Callaway, "Burials in Ancient Palestine: From the Stone Age to Abraham," in BA 26 (Sept. 1963), pp. 74-91; L. Y. Rahmani, "Ancient Jerusalem's Funerary Customs and Tombs," in BA 44 (1981), pp. 171-177, 229-235; 45 (1982), pp. 43-53; 109-119; Gabriel Barkay and Amos Kloner, "Jerusalem Tombs from the Days of the First Temple," in BAR 12.2 (Mar/Apr 1986), pp. 22-39; NAEHL "Burial," pp. 60-65; IDB-S "Tomb," pp. 905-909. For Jewish regulations and customs in relation to funerals and mourning, see the tractate '*Ebel rabbati* or Major Mourning, probably meaning the Major (Tractate) on Mourning, and generally called by the euphemistic title *Semaḥot* or Rejoicings, a work probably written down at the end of the third century A.D. but preserving knowledge of rulings and practices in Jerusalem before A.D. 70 (Dov Zlotnick, *The Tractate "Mourning" (Šěmaḥot) (Regulations Relating to Death, Burial, and Mourning)*, YJS 17 (New Haven: Yale University Press, 1966).

DEVELOPMENT OF EARLY TOMBS

Shaft Tombs

248. Section and Plan of Tomb A 111 at Jericho

AT JERICHO from the second half of the fourth millennium down into the Iron Age hundreds of tombs were cut into the rock in the area north and northwest of the *tell* of the ancient city. Except for the Iron Age burials, which were made in the side of a steep slope with an almost horizontal approach, most of these tombs consisted of a vertical shaft at the bottom of which a small opening, closed by a stone or stones, gave access to the burial chamber. The arrangement of such a shaft tomb is shown in this section and plan. In the excavations at Jericho this grave was designated as Tomb A 111. It belongs to the Intermediate Early Bronze—Middle Bronze period.

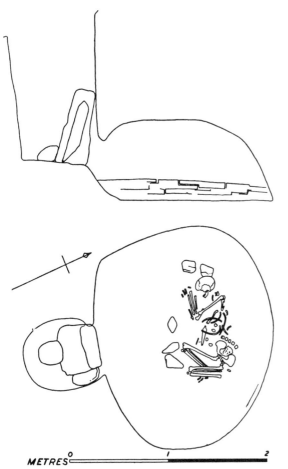

248. Section and Plan of Tomb A 111 at Jericho

Kenyon, *Digging Up Jericho*, p. 196, fig. 10; Kenyon, *Excavations at Jericho*, I, *The Tombs Excavated in 1952-54* (Jerusalem: The British School of Archaeology, 1960), p. 188, fig. 69. Photograph: courtesy Jericho Excavation Fund.

249. The Shaft of Tomb A 3 at Jericho

THIS SHAFT TOMB is also of the Intermediate Early Bronze—Middle Bronze period. The view looks down into the shaft and shows the large stone that closes the entrance into the burial chamber.

Kenyon, *Digging Up Jericho*, pl. 38, fig. B; Kenyon, *Excavations at Jericho*, I, pl. XI, fig. 3. Photograph: courtesy Jericho Excavation Fund.

250. Burial in Tomb A 23 at Jericho

THIS BURIAL was found intact in the inner chamber of another shaft tomb at Jericho, known as Tomb A 23. The body was placed in a contracted position at the back

of the chamber, with the head to the west, and a dagger laid between the arms and the chest. The date is in the Intermediate Early Bronze—Middle Bronze period. Shaft tombs are found at many other places besides Jericho.

Interestingly enough, a quite similar type of burial was still in use at the end of the pre-Christian and the beginning of the Christian era at the famous site of Qumran, not many miles from Jericho. Here there is an extensive cemetery to the east of the main settlement, with two smaller cemeteries to the north and south of the larger one, containing in all perhaps 1,200 graves. One of these tombs was excavated by Charles Clermont-Ganneau in 1873, more than forty by R. de Vaux between 1949 and 1955, and one more by S. H. Steckoll in 1966. These consisted of a shaft some four to six feet deep, at the bottom of which was a recess in the side wall for the burial place proper. On the side of the recess toward the bottom of the shaft was a slight ledge and, supported by this ledge, sun-dried bricks were piled above the body. The opening of the recess was closed by flat stones, and finally the shaft was filled with soil. Thus Qumran seems to have maintained the use of an early type of tomb when elsewhere in Palestine different types, to be noticed below (§§255-256), were in vogue.

Kenyon, *Excavatons at Jericho*, I, pl. IX, fig. 1; Clermont-Ganneau II pp. 15-16; de Vaux in RB 60 (1953), pp. 95, 102-103; 61 (1954), p. 207; 63 (1956), pp. 569-572; Steckoll in *Revue de Qumran* 23 (1968), pp. 323-336. Photograph: courtesy Jericho Excavation Fund.

Chamber Tombs

251. The Entrance to Tomb 77 at Megiddo

IN THE CASE of a normal shaft tomb the distinctive feature of design is the vertical shaft, which ordinarily leads to a burial chamber or chambers. Where the emphasis falls upon the inner room or rooms, more or less carefully hewn out of the rock, and access is by any one of several ways other than a vertical shaft, such as a direct doorway, or horizontal or sloping passageway, or stairs, we may speak of a chamber tomb. At Megiddo in the many Bronze Age burials which have been explored the predominant form is still that of the normal shaft tomb (some, such as Tomb 84, with numerous chambers), but in the Late Bronze Age we find examples of the chamber tomb. The entrance to one of these tombs is shown in this photograph.

P. L. O. Guy, *Megiddo Tombs.* OIP XXXIII (Chicago: University of Chicago Press, 1938), p. 83, fig. 96. Photograph: courtesy The Oriental Institute, University of Chicago.

249. The Shaft of Tomb A 3 at Jericho

250. Burial in Tomb A 23 at Jericho

252. Plan of Tomb 77 at Megiddo

THIS IS THE PLAN of the Late Bronze Age tomb of which the entrance was shown in No. 251. The tomb consists of a short passageway and an inner rock-hewn chamber. Within, on the southwest side, there is a recess, separated by a raised place from the main chamber, which is large enough for a full-length adult burial and was probably used for such, although the bones and pottery which remained in the tomb were, when found, all on the floor of the main chamber. Chamber tombs are found at many other places besides Megiddo.

Guy, *Megiddo Tombs*, p. 84, fig. 98. Photograph: courtesy The Oriental Institute, University of Chicago.

251. The Entrance to Tomb 77 at Megiddo

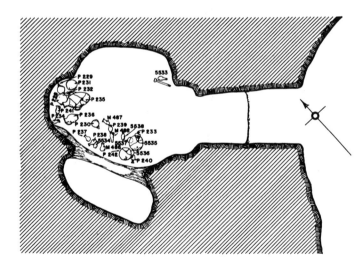

252. Plan of Tomb 77 at Megiddo

Chamber Tombs with Ledges

253. Plan and Section of Tomb 5 at Tell en-Nasbeh

A DISTINCTIVE FORM of chamber tomb was developed when, instead of placing the burial on the floor or even in a recess, as in the preceding plan, place was provided for the body on a rock ledge, shelf, bench, or divan, as the arrangement is variously called. This plan and section represent an excellent example of such an arrangement as found in Tomb 5 in the north cemetery at Tell en-Nasbeh. According to the pottery found in it, the tomb was in use in Iron I and Iron II, probably begin-

295

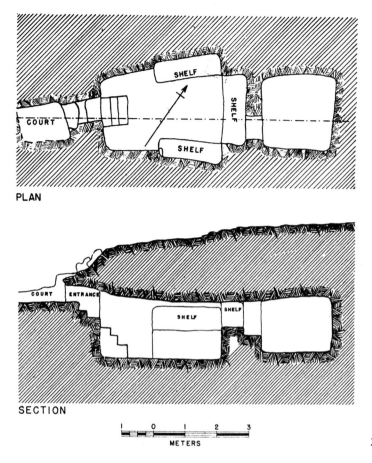

PLAN

SECTION

253. Plan and Section of Tomb 5 at Tell en-Nasbeh

ning in the tenth century and continuing through the eighth century. In Palestine in general this type of tomb is known from the Late Bronze Age, is predominant in the ninth century and later, is gradually replaced by new styles in the Hellenistic period, but is still found in some examples in Roman times.

Galling, *Reallexikon* I, col. 244, no. 8; Nötscher, p. 100; *Tell en-Nasbeh* I, p. 84, fig. 8. Photograph: courtesy Palestine Institute.

254. Model of Tomb 5 at Tell en-Nasbeh

IN ADDITION TO the plan and section in No. 253, this "exploded" model makes it possible to visualize Tomb 5 at Tell en-Nasbeh. There was an exterior court, then a small square entrance, and then five steps that led down into a rectangular room. In the rear half of this room on each side and against the back wall a stone ledge or shelf had been left in the excavation. At the right end of the back shelf there was another small square entranceway, with one broad step down, which gave access to a plain inner chamber almost cubical in dimensions. Like most tombs this one had been plundered long

ago and what was left in it, meager skeletal remains and much pottery, was thrown together into the large chamber. It seems evident, however, that originally the bodies of the deceased were placed on the ledges in the large chamber; when room was needed on these ledges for new burials, the bones of the older ones were probably collected in the smaller chamber at the back. From numerous examples we learn that this type of chamber tomb with burial ledges was in use in Palestine throughout the time of the Israelite kings and into the Persian period.

Badè, *Tombs*, pp. 18-33, 48-63; *Tell en-Nasbeh* I, pp. 83f., 99. Photograph: courtesy Palestine Institute.

Chamber Tombs with Kokim

255. Plan and Section of Tomb 4 at Tell en-Nasbeh

ANOTHER DEVELOPMENT of the chamber tomb was that in which the burial places in the inner chamber or chambers consisted of horizontal shafts or niches driven

254. Model of Tomb 5 at Tell en-Nasbeh

straight back into the walls. Such a shaft was ordinarily quadrangular or perhaps vaulted, and of such dimensions as to accommodate a body put into it lengthwise and probably head first. A good example of a tomb of this type is found in Tomb 4 in the north cemetery at Tell en-Nasbeh, the plan and section of which are shown here. There was a large sunken forecourt with a covered vestibule and a small entrance, no doubt once closed with a movable stone. The main chamber was roughly square, with a squarish pit in the center of the floor, presumably a place for the collection of skeletal remains. The broad floor space which remained around the four sides of this pit provided a passageway adjacent to the walls of the chamber. On this floor level and into the walls of the chamber were cut horizontal burial shafts, three on the north side, three on the east, and two on the south. One shaft on the south side was bordered on three sides by a broad ledge, and was probably intended for a person of special importance such as the head of the family. The pottery in the tomb was Hellenistic-Roman, and one bronze coin of Herod Archelaus was found which probably dates the tomb to his reign (4 B.C.-A. D. 6).

The type of tomb illustrated here may have originated in Egypt and become known in Palestine through Phoenician influence. The underground room or hall, with rows of horizontal burial shafts extending off from it, is especially common in the neocropolis of Alexandria and is known in the cities of Phoenicia as well as elsewhere in the Hellenistic world. In Palestine it is already found at Marissa (Nos. 259ff.), a Phoenician colony in exis-

tence around 200 B.C. At Jerusalem the great majority of ancient tombs are of this type, and date approximately from 150 B.C. to A.D. 150. It may fairly be said that this type of tomb virtually became the canonical form of the Jewish family grave.

With respect to such tombs in the Hellenistic world it is customary to designate the horizontal burial shafts or niches of which we have been speaking as *loculi*, singular *loculus*, literally "a little place." In Palestine, however, it is customary to use the late Hebrew word by which the Rabbis called the burial shafts, namely, כוכים, *kokim*, singular *kok*. Using this term for the niches and employing the customary Hebrew designations of length where 6 handbreadths = 1 cubit = approximately 18 inches, the Mishna (Baba Bathra VI 8 fol. 100b-101a GBT VI 1211f. SBT IV 3, 421ff. DM 375) explains the construction of a family tomb: "The central space of the grotto must have [an area of] four cubits by six, and eight burial niches (*kokim*) are to open out into it, three on this side, three on that side, and two opposite [the doorway]. The niches (*kokim*) must be four cubits long, seven handbreadths high, and six wide." Varying opinions of various Rabbis follow, and in the accompanying Gemara different plans and dimensions are discussed in detail.

Badè, *Tombs*, pp. 33-38; *Tell en-Nasbeh* I, pp. 103-104 and fig. 12; Galling, "Nekropole," p. 76; Nötscher p. 100. Photograph: courtesy Palestine Institute.

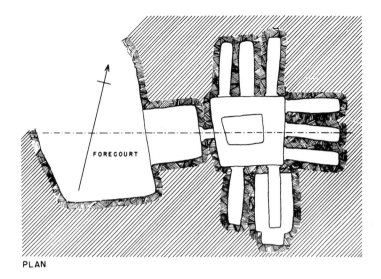

PLAN

FORECOURT

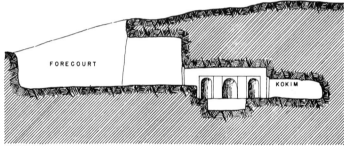

FORECOURT

KOKIM

SECTION

1 0 1 2 3
METERS

255. Plan and Section of Tomb 4 at Tell en-Nasbeh

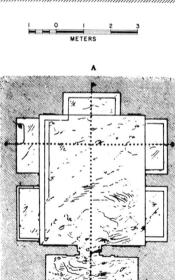

A

B

C.

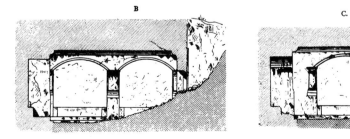

256. Plan and Sections of a Tomb at Tell ez-Zakariyeh

298

Chamber Tombs with Arcosolia

256. Plan and Sections of a Tomb at Tell ez-Zakariyeh

AS WAS ILLUSTRATED in the example of Tomb 5 at Tell en-Nasbeh (Nos. 253-254), a familiar type of tomb in Palestine from the Iron Age onward was that of the chamber in which a ledge or shelf was left in the process of excavation as a place on which to lay the body. When the ledge was hewn sideways into the rock wall and a sort of overhanging arch or vault was formed above it we have a distinctive kind of burial place which it is customary to call by the term *arcosolium*. The Latin term (*arco*, "arch" + *solium*, "sarcophagus") is used particularly for an arched niche in the Roman catacombs, where often a sarcophagus was placed. The form itself may have come to Palestine from Greece and Asia Minor through Syria, but was the more readily acceptable because the ledge burial was already so widely used. A relatively elaborate example of this type of tomb construction, with five arcosolia, is represented in the plan and sections shown here. This tomb is at Tell ez-Zakariyeh, probably biblical Azekah, in the Shephealah. The date is probably in the Late Hellenistic period. In the illustration A is the plan of the entire tomb, B is a section on the long axis in A, and C a section on the short axis. As the example in the next illustration (No. 257) shows, the arcosolium type tomb was still being used in Palestine in the fourth century of the Christian era.

Clermont-Ganneau II, pp. 353-355; Watzinger II, p. 71. Photograph: courtesy Palestine Exploration Fund.

Chamber Tombs with Sunk Graves

257. Arcosolium and Sunk Grave in Tomb 33 at Tell en-Nasbeh

THE BURIAL LEDGE beneath an arcosolium (cf. No. 256) might be a simple shelf, or it might be provided with a raised margin at the front edge and a raised place at the head end, or be deepened into a whole trough or sunk grave to receive the body. Tomb 33 in the west cemetery at Tell en-Nasbeh provides an example of the combination of the arcosolium and the sunk grave. In this tomb an oblong shaft leads to a small square en-

trance, closed with a stone of unusual shape, which gives access to a rectangular chamber. On the wall to the left of the entrance are three kokim, on the back wall three more, but on the wall to the right is an arcosolium with a grave sunk in its shelf, as shown in the illustration. This grave had a profusion of glass beads, bracelets, and other objects. In the tomb were numerous lamps, some decorated with pillars and arches and with as many as seven holes for wicks. Half a dozen lamps were decorated with crosses, so the tomb was ultimately, even if not originally, used by Christians. A date in the early part of the Byzantine period, perhaps in the fourth century, is probable.

Tell en-Nasbeh I, pp. 112-116, pl. 23 no. 5; Galling, "Nekropole," p. 90. Photograph: courtesy Palestine Institute.

258. Plan and Section of Tomb 19 at Tell en-Nasbeh

TOMB 19 IS IN THE WEST cemetery at Tell en-Nasbeh. The original tomb was probably a simple chamber, perhaps provided with rock shelves for the burial places as in Tomb 5 (No. 254), and other tombs at Tell en-Nasbeh. The original tomb was probably as old as the period of the Exile, since the famous seal of Jaazaniah (cf. II K 25:23; Jer 40:8; FLAP pp. 176-177) was found in it. Later, however, the tomb was enlarged with large barrel-vaulted recesses containing sunk graves as shown in this plan and section. While a little of the pottery in the tomb, and the Jaazaniah seal, belong to the Middle Iron Age, the rest of the pottery, especially numerous lamps, belongs to the fourth to the sixth centuries of the Christian era. Indeed more than one-third of the lamps are explicitly Christian, since they are ornamented with crosses and one has, in a garbled form, the inscription φῶς Χριστοῦ, "light of Christ." Many other examples also show that the period of wide use of the vaulted chamber tomb with sunk or trough graves was from the fourth to the sixth centuries, and this type has been called the essentially Christian form of tomb in the Byzantine period.

Tell en-Nasbeh I, pp. 118-122, fig. 18; Galling, "Nekropole," pp. 79, 90. Photograph: courtesy Palestine Institute.

In summary of the main forms: The shaft tomb, with a deep vertical shaft leading down to the burial chamber, prevailed throughout the Bronze Age and was also in use in some places much later. The chamber tomb with burial ledges is found already in the Late Bronze Age and prevails in the Iron Age (the time of the Israelite kings and into the Persian period, the time of the First Temple). The chamber tomb with the horizontal niches

257. Arcosolium and Sunk Grave in Tomb 33 at Tell en-Nasbeh

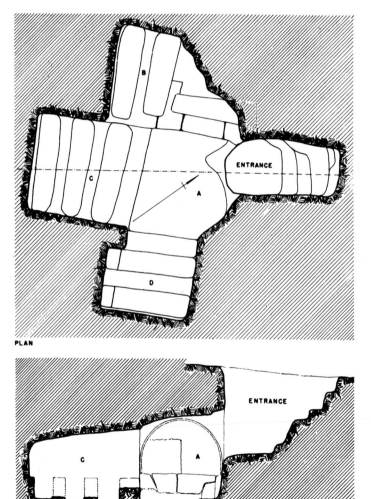

PLAN

SECTION

0   1   METERS   2   3

258. Plan and Section of Tomb 19 at Tell en-Nasbeh

called *kokim* (singular *kok*) appears in the Hellenistic period (first in Palestine at Marissa in the second century B.C., Nos. 259ff.) and continues as the main form to the end of the Second Temple period. The chamber tomb with *arcosolia* (singular *arcosolium*), where the roof over the burial ledge is made into an arch, is a more elaborate type, also found in the period of the Second Temple (BAR 12.2 [Mar/Apr 1986], p. 36). Sarcophagi (Nos. 296ff.) or full-sized burial chests, usually of stone and often highly decorated, are also found in the Hellenistic and Roman periods. Ossuaries (Nos. 302ff.) or smaller stone chests for the secondary collection of the bones of a burial, were in use chiefly from the reign of King Herod and into the earlier part of the third century A.D. In the Byzantine period the chamber tomb is the usual form, is often vaulted, and the burial ledge or bench is often deepened into a trough or sunk grave and sometimes provided with a raised place at the head end. As for the closure of the opening into a tomb: in a vertical shaft tomb, which was still used for private burial even in NT time, the shaft was closed with a stone laid across the access (cf. Jn 11:38 AB 29, p. 426); in a chamber tomb with horizontal access the entrance might be closed by a boulder but in more elegant examples of the first century B.C./first century A.D. (Nos. 274, 281) a stone in the shape of a disk is rolled in a channel in front of the doorway and is "rolled away" (Lk 24:2; cf. Mk 16:3 AB 29A, p. 982) to open the tomb.

DECORATED HELLENISTIC-PERIOD TOMBS AT MARISSA

259. Plan of the Uppermost City at Tell Sandahannah

TELL SANDAHANNAH is two kilometers south of Beit Guvrin (Eleutheropolis) in the Shephelah. The Arabic name is a corruption from the nearby Church of St. Anna, a twelfth-century Crusader building over a Byzantine basilica. The *tell* is probably to be identified with the OT city of Mareshah, known as Marissa in Greek. This was originally a Canaanite city (Jos 15:44 LXX Μαρησά); it was fortified by Rehoboam (II Ch 11:8 LXX Μαρεισάν), captured from the Idumeans by John Hyrcanus c. 110 B.C. (Josephus, *Ant.* XII 9, 1 §257 Μάρισα; Μάρισσα according to some manuscript evidence in *Ant.* XII 8, 6 §353), and destroyed by the Parthians in 40 B.C. (*Ant.* XIV 13, 9 §364). The ancient town on top of the *tell* was excavated by the Palestine Exploration Fund in 1900, and examined again by Eliezer Oren in 1961-1963. The town area, roughly five hundred feet square in maximum dimensions, was surrounded by an inner wall on the edge of the *tell* or slightly down the slope, and by an outer wall farther down the slope. Within the

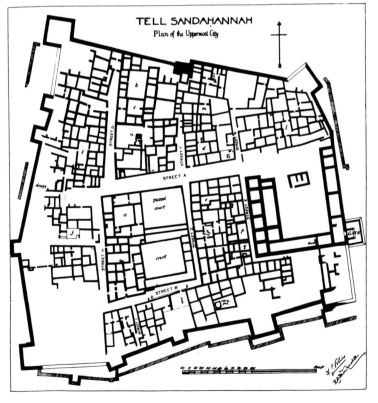

259. Plan of the Uppermost City at Tell Sandahannah

301

inner wall the town is roughly divided into blocks by streets, and the houses and buildings are built on the streets and around open courts within the blocks. The relatively regular plan and also the objects found, including pottery, coins, and Greek inscriptions, indicate a town of the Hellenistic period. The middle stratum of the excavations may be assigned to the third and second centuries B.C., the upper stratum to the first century B.C. and later.

Clermont-Ganneau II, pp. 445-447; F. J. Bliss, "Report on the Excavations at Tell Sandahannah," in PEFQS 1900, pp. 319-338; R. A. Stewart Macalister, "Preliminary Observations on the Rock-Cuttings of Tell Sandahannah," in PEFQS 1900, pp. 338-341; and Macalister, " 'Es-Suk,' Tell Sandahannah," in PEFQS 1901, pp. 11-19; John P. Peters and Hermann Thiersch, "The Necropolis of Mareshah," in PEFQS 1902, pp. 393-397; and Peters and Thiersch, *Painted Tombs in the Necropolis of Marissa (Marêshah)* (London: Palestine Exploration Fund, 1905); RB 11 (1902), pp. 438f.; Eliezer Oren, "The Caves of the Palestinian Shephelah," in *Archaeology 18* (1965), pp. 218-224. Photograph: PEFQS 1900, plan facing p. 326, courtesy Palestine Exploration Fund.

260. Burial Loculi and Niches in Tomb D at Marissa

IN 1873-1874 CLERMONT-GANNEAU STUDIED the Church of St. Anna at Sandahannah/Marissa (Ovadiah, *Corpus*, pp. 135-137, no. 138), and in the same vicinity examined a tomb with nineteen triangular-topped loculi and noticed a second tomb of the same type. In 1902 Peters and Thiersch investigated four more tombs of this type one-quarter of a mile to the south. In 1961-1963 Oren examined no less than fifty-two tombs,

including those already known, in the region around Tell Sandahannah. All the tombs were cut into the rock in the same way, with the same basic plan. On top there are remnants of structures which were probably pyramids. Steps lead through a stone door to an entrance hall. From the entrance hall there is access to a central burial hall, with burial chambers branching off from it. In the latter are the loculi or kokim with triangular tops. These were sealed with stone slabs and clay. Above the recess the name of the deceased and sometimes the date of his or her death are written with red paint, clay, or charcoal. The inscriptions are in Greek, Nabatean, and Aramaic, and extend in date from the beginning of the third century to the first century B.C. In the ledge beneath the kokim are smaller niches, which may have been used for the keeping of bones from previous burials. The illustration shows Tomb D, as it is designated by Oren, with its gabled loculi and small niches below.

Eliezer Oren in *Archaeology 18* (1965), pp. 218-224. Photograph: courtesy E. Oren, Beit-Jibrin Survey.

261. Plan and Sections of Tomb I at Marissa

OF THE TOMBS at Marissa, that which Peters and Thiersch designated as Tomb I is the best known and in many ways still the most interesting. As seen in plan and sections in the present illustration, the entrance of the tomb gives access to a flat-roofed antechamber (A). On either side is an oblong barrel-vaulted chamber (B and C), while ahead is the flat-roofed main chamber (D),

260. Burial Loculi and Niches in Tomb D at Marissa

with a niche-like extension (E). There is a ledge or shelf around the edges of the chambers and above it, cut at right angles into the walls, are the triangular-topped loculi, forty-one in number. Opening out of the extension (E) at the east end of the main chamber are three burial chambers probably meant for sarcophagi and intended for the chief persons buried in the tomb.

Photograph: Peters and Thiersch, *Painted Tombs in the Necropolis of Marissa*, pp. 16–17, figs. 1, 2, courtesy Palestine Exploration Fund.

262. Hunting Scene in Tomb I at Marissa

TOMB I AT MARISSA is most remarkable for the paintings of its main chamber (D in No. 261). On either side of the entrance to this chamber is a painted cock, and on the right-hand jamb a three-headed jackal-like dog, the Cerberus of Greek and Roman mythology who guards the lower regions. Inside on the wall just over the kokim is an animal frieze which begins in the southwest corner and ends near the opposite northwest corner. The first portion of this frieze is shown here. While a man blows a long trumpet, a hunter on horseback, assisted by hunting dogs, raises his lance against a leopard. The identity of this animal, as well as of those that follow in the frieze, is indicated by the name written above in Greek, in this case ΠΑΡΔΑΛΟΣ, "leopard."

Photograph: Peters and Thiersch, *Painted Tombs in the Necropolis of Marissa*, pl. VI, courtesy Palestine Exploration Fund.

263. Portion of the Animal Frieze in Tomb I at Marissa

IN THE ENTIRE frieze in Tomb I, as far as the inscriptions are legible or the drawings unmistakable, we find the following animals: leopard, panther, bull, giraffe, boar, griffin, oryx, rhinoceros, elephant, crocodile, ibis, hippopotamus, wild ass, porcupine, and lynx. The illustration shows the last portion of the frieze on the south side. The animals are bulky rhinoceros (ΡΙΝΟΚΕΡѠϹ) painted reddish-brown, and a grayish-black elephant (ΕΛΕΦΑϹ).

In addition to the inscriptions above the animals which give their identity and were presumably written at the time the paintings were made, there are also graffiti in more or less similar script just over the entrances to many of the loculi. In the photograph, for example, we see at the right in the triangular area between the sloping line of the right top of the entrance to the loculus and the base of the animal frieze the inscription.

ΔΗΜΗΤΡΙΟΥ ΤΟΥ
ΜΕΕΡΒΑΛΟΥ

which means, "(Grave) of Demetrios, son of Meerbal." Demetrios is a common Hellenistic name; Meerbal is a Greek form of the common Phoenician name, Maherbaal, "gift of Baal." In similar script there is a long graffito over the entrance to the sarcophagus chamber on the south side of the extension (E) (see the plan in No. 261) of the main chamber of the tomb. It reads:

Ἀπολλοφάνης Σεσμαίου ἄρξας τῶν ἐν Μαρίοη Σιδωνίων ἔτη τριάκοντα καὶ τρία καὶ νομισθεὶς | πάντων τῶν καθ' αὑτὸν χρηστότατος καὶ φιλοικειότατος ἀπέθανεν δὲ βιώσας ἔτη | ἑβδομήκοντα καὶ τέσσαρα ἔτ.

"Apollophanes, son of Sesmaios, was the ruler of the Sidonians in Marise for thirty-three years, and he was recognized as the kindest and most household-loving of all those of his time, and he died having lived seventy-four years."

At the end the writer started to repeat the word ἔτη again and then, recognizing his mistake, desisted. The importance of this inscription is evident, for it confirms the name Marissa (in the spelling Μαρίοη) for this place, shows that a colony of Phoenicians from Sidon was settled here, and gives the name of the ruler who was their chief for one-third of a century.

Still other burial inscriptions are painted above the loculi, usually in the animal frieze itself, and since they are sometimes written across the animal figures and damage them in that way they are evidently later in date. An example of these painted superscriptions also shows in the photograph. It begins with the angular sign for a year and the letter beta corresponding to the numeral two, and reads:

LB ΔΥϹΤΡΟΥ
ϹΑΒΟΥϹ   ΤΗϹ
ΚΟϹΝΑΤΑΝΟΥ

In the second year in the month Dystros. (Grave) of Sabo, the daughter of Kosnastanos.

Kosnatanos is an Idulmean name, meaning "Kos has given." It may be compared with the name of the Idumean Kostobaros (or Kosgobaros), whom Josephus mentions (*Ant.* xv 7, 9 §§253–254) as married to Salome, the sister of Herod the Great. In the same connection Josephus says that the ancestors of Kostobaros had been priests of the Idumean god Koze (Κωζέ). Dystros is a month-name (usually corresponding to February/March) in the Macedonian calendar which was used in varying forms throughout the ancient Middle East (FHBC §§117ff.).

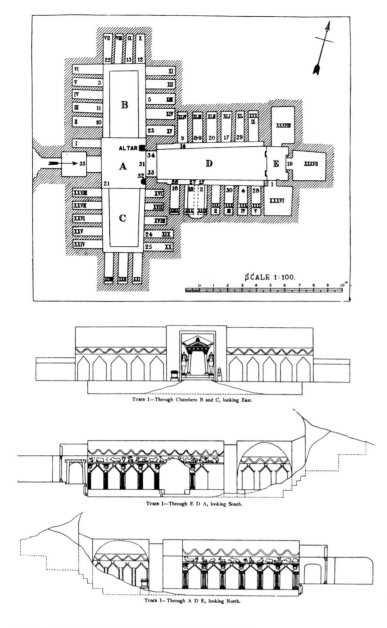

TOMB I—Through Chambers B and C, looking East.

TOMB I—Through E D A, looking South.

TOMB I—Through A D E, looking North.

261. Plan and Sections of Tomb I at Marissa

262. Hunting Scene in Tomb I at Marissa

In comparison with the date "in the second year" (beta) in the foregoing inscription there may be noted also the date "in the first year" (alpha) in another painted superscription and the date "in the fifth year" (epsilon) in a graffito which paleographically is one of the latest inscriptions in the tomb. These three dates are presumably stated in terms of some era that had only recently been established and come into use at Marissa. Since there is inscriptional evidence for a local era of the nearby city of Eleutheropolis (RB 11 [1902], pp. 438f.), an era which perhaps began about the birth of Christ or earlier, the dates may be in terms of this era. Otherwise the rather numerous dates in Tomb I and in the other three tombs of this necropolis comprise a consistent series extending from the 117th to 194th year. If these dates are stated in terms of the widely used Seleucid era, according to the Macedonian calendar (FHBC §193), they correspond to dates extending from 196/195 to 119/118 B.C.

The other tombs in this necropolis at Marissa need be mentioned only briefly. Tomb II was constructed on a plan much the same as that of Tomb I. In general it was simpler in its arrangements and contained fewer inscriptions and paintings. Of the paintings the best preserved represents two musicians, a man and a woman, both in colorful striped garments. Likewise Tombs III and IV were of the same general arrangement. In all, then, this necropolis at Marissa represents a community of the Hellenistic period. It was in Idumean territory, and an Idumean divine name appears in personal names in the inscriptions. The region was under the Ptolemies until 198 B.C., and the fauna of the animal frieze are primarily Egyptian. After 198 B.C. the area was under the Seleucids, and the majority of the dates are Seleucidan. At Marissa a Sidonian colony was settled, and its chief,

Apollophanes, and others of his family were evidently buried here.

Photograph: Peters and Thiersch, *Painted Tombs in the Necropolis of Marissa*, pl. x, courtesy Palestine Exploration Fund.

HELLENISTIC AND ROMAN TOMBS IN THE KIDRON VALLEY

264. Plan of the Tomb of James and the Tomb of Zechariah

IT HAS BEEN NOTED (NO. 176) that the ancient or Jebusite city of Jerusalem was on the west side of the Kidron Valley above the Gihon spring. Across the valley on the west slope of the Mount of Olives and in the area of the present Dominus flevit (Nos. 161ff., 319ff.) was the Jebusite burial place, a necropolis that was in use from the end of the Middle Bronze Age into the Late Bronze Age or approximately from the sixteenth to the thirteenth century. Jl 3:2 speaks of the valley of Jehoshaphat ("Yaweh judges") as the place where the Lord will hold judgment on the nations, and it is located by the Bordeaux Pilgrim (cf. No. 169) and by Eusebius and Jerome (*Onomasticon* pp. 118-119) as lying between Jerusalem and the Mount of Olives, i.e., as being identical with the ravine of the Kidron. So the fact that there were burials on the slopes of this valley from an early time and the fact that the prophet's words were taken as pointing to the valley as the place of the last judgment worked

263. Portion of the Animal Frieze in Tomb I at Marissa

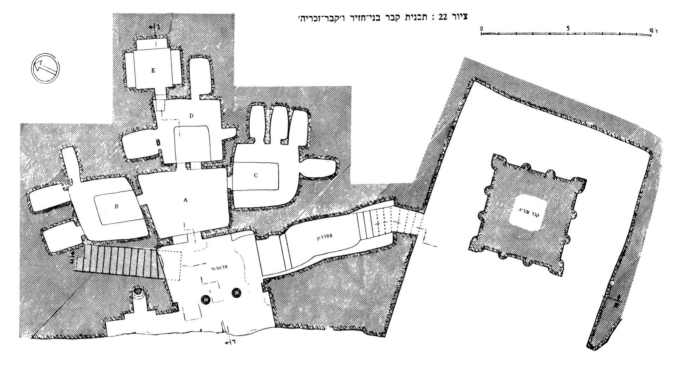

ציור 22 : תבנית קבר בני־חזיר ו'קבר־זכריה'

264. Plan of the Tomb of James and the Tomb of Zechariah

together to make it a much-used burial place through many centuries, for Jews, possibly for Christians (No. 326), and for Muslims. Of the great number of tombs in the valley four which are particularly notable and belong to Hellenistic and Roman times (according to recent opinion between the reign of Herod the Great and A.D. 70, Rahmani in BA 45 [1981], p. 47) will be discussed, namely, the tombs popularly known as those of James, of Zechariah, of Absalom, and of Jehosphaphat.

In the plan the Tomb of James is at the left and the Tomb of Zechariah at the right. The portico of the Tomb of James is actually high up on the side of a cliff (see No. 265), and the porch behind is entered by two passages, the one on the north coming from the open, the one on the south connecting with the enclosure around the Tomb of Zechariah. Through the porch there is access to a large chamber (A), which in turn connects with a number of tomb chambers (B, C, D, E) in which are both kokim and arcosolia.

Sylvester J. Saller, *The Excavations at Dominus Flevit (Mount Olivet, Jerusalem)*, II, *The Jesbusite Burial Place.* PSBF 13 (Jerusalem: The Franciscan Press, 1964); Theodore Reinach, "Les fouilles de M. Nahoum Schlouszch dans la Vallée du Cedron," in CRAI 1924, pp. 144-146; Watzinger II, pp. 63-64; Simons, *Jerusalem*, pp. 10, 14; Vincent, *Jérusalem*, 1:1, pp. 331-342; N. Avigad, *Ancient Monuments in the Kidron Valley* (in Hebrew, with summary in English) (Jerusalem: Bialik Institute, 1954); Howard E. Stutchbury, "Excavations in the Kidron Valley," in PEQ 1961, pp. 101-113. Photograph: Avigad, ibid., p. 37, fig. 22, courtesy The Bialik Institute, Jerusalem.

265. General View of the Tomb of James and the Tomb of Zechariah

THE TOMB of James is again at the left and the Tomb of Zechariah at the right. The portico of the Tomb of James is marked by two Doric columns and two corner pilasters supporting an entablature above. At the left is a smooth face of rock with an open doorway, which leads only a short distance into the rock. This portion of the façade may once have carried a higher superstructure, perhaps in the form of a pyramid. The hypothesis that this was so is strengthened by comparison with examples of funerary structures in Egypt which combine colonnade with pyramid. On the basis of its architecture the tomb is judged to belong to the latter half of the second century B.C.

Photograph: courtesy Palestine Archaeological Museum.

266. Inscription on the Tomb of James

THIS INSCRIPTION is found on the architrave immediately above the two Doric columns of the porch of the Tomb of James. It is written in square Hebrew characters judged paleographically to belong to the first half of the first century of the Christian era, i.e., perhaps two generations after the tomb was first prepared. It is transcribed and translated as follows:

265. General View of the Tomb of James and the Tomb of Zechariah

266. Incription on the Tomb of James

זה קבר והנפש
שלאלעזר חניה יועזר יהודה שמעון יוחנן | בני יוסף בן
עובד יוסף ואלעזר בני חניה | כהנים מבני הזיר·

This is the tomb and the *nephesh* of Eleazar, Haniah, Jo'azar, Iehudah, Shime'on, Iohannan, (the) sons of Joseph son of 'Obed (and also) of Joseph and Eleazar (the) sons of Haniah, priests (of the family) of the sons of Hezir.

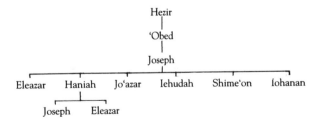

The tomb was, accordingly, the burial place of family of priests, the Bene Hezir (בני חזיר) or the "sons of Hezir." The genealogical table implied by the inscription is:

In the OT the name Hezir appears as that of the head of a priestly house in 1 Ch 24:15, and of a person associated with Nehemiah in Neh 10:20.

At the beginning of the inscription the monument which it identifies is described as "the tomb and the *nephesh*" (קבד והנפש) of the person buried there. The

307

word *nephesh* ordinarily means "life," "soul," or "self,"
but is used on occasion to refer to a tomb or to a sepulchral monument. Here, since the word is used in addition to the word "tomb," it must mean a "sepulchral
monument." Accordingly some feature of the entire arrangement must be the "monument" in distinction from
the tomb proper. If there was in fact originally a pyramidal superstructure at the left that was probably the
"monument" or *nephesh.* Another possibility is to identify the *nephesh* of the burial place of the Bene Hezir with
the Tomb of Zechariah (No. 267). The latter is not far
away and a passage leads from the porch of the Tomb of
James to the enclosure around it.

While the burial place just described was that of the
Bene Hezir, as the inscription shows, tradition has called
it the Tomb of James. The head of the early Christian
church in Jerusalem was James the brother of the Lord
(Gal 1:19). Hegesippus relates (according to Eusebius,
Ch. Hist. II 23) that he was martyred by being cast down
from the pinnacle (πτερύγιον) of the temple, and that he
was buried on the spot, by the temple, where his monument still remains. If the "pinnacle" (cf. Mt. 4:5; Lk 4:9)
of the temple was the southeast corner of the enclosure
wall which was so high above the Kidron ravine that
"one who looked down grew dizzy" (Josephus, *Ant.* xv
11, 5 §412) (cf. No. 188), then James might have fallen
into the valley at a point approximately opposite the
tomb of the Bene Hezir. Later it would not have been
difficult to imagine that that tomb was the monument to
James.

Frey II, pp. 324–325 no. 1394. Photograph: Avigad, *Ancient Monuments in the Kidron Valley,* p. 60 fig. 35, courtesy The Bialik Institute, Jerusalem.

267. The Tomb of Zechariah

THE PLAN IN NO. 264 and the photograph in No. 265
have already shown the relationship of the Tomb of
Zechariah to the Tomb of James; this is another view of
the western front of the Tomb of Zechariah. The monument is cut out of the cliff as a monolith 9 meters high
and 5.2 meters wide. The sides are adorned with pilasters
and columns with Ionic capitals, and the top is a large
pyramid. Architecturally a date is suggested in the second half of the first century B.C. Since no opening is to
be found anywhere this is probably a sepulchral monument (*nephesh*) rather than a tomb. The passage leading
from the porch of the Tomb of James to the enclosure
around the Tomb of Zechariah makes it possible to think
that the latter monument is the *nephesh* associated with
the tomb of the Bene Hezir. If that *nephesh* was, however, a pyramidal superstructure once existing immediately beside the tomb of the Bene Hezir (cf. No. 266),
then the Tomb of Zechariah is presumably the *nephesh* of
another burial complex and the tombs associated with it
may be hidden somewhere in the adjacent hill.

The traditional attribution of this monument to Zechariah presumably refers to Zechariah the son of Jehoiada
the priest, who was stoned under King Joash in the court

267. The Tomb of Zechariah

of the house of the Lord (II Ch 24:20-22). In Mt 23:35 most manuscripts mention Zechariah the son of Barachiah, presumably thinking of the well-known prophet whose father was Berechiah (Zec 1:1), but there is no other information about such a murder of this prophet. Actually Codex Sinaiticus mentions only Zechariah here, without any father's name, and the Gospel according to the Hebrews reads "son of Joiada." Therefore the original reference in Mt 23:35 was undoubtedly to the martyr of II Ch 24:20-22. Since he was slain "between the sanctuary and the altar," it was natural to look for his monument not too far away from the temple.

Vincent, *Jérusalem*, 1:1, pp. 335-337; 1:2, pl. LXXIX. Photograph: JF.

268. Plan of the Tomb of Absalom and the Tomb of Jehoshaphat

THIS PLAN SHOWS the arrangement and relationship of the Tomb of Absalom and the Tomb of Jehoshaphat.

Vincent, *Jérusalem*, 1:1, pp. 332-335. Photograph: ibid., p. 333, fig. 90, courtesy École Biblique et Archéologique Française.

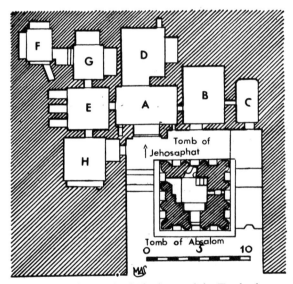

268. Plan of the Tomb of Absalom and the Tomb of Jehoshaphat

269. The Tomb of Absalom

LIKE THE TOMB of Zechariah (No. 267), the Tomb of Absalom is also, in its lower part, a monolith cut out of the side of the cliff. This part of the monument is 6 meters wide and 6.5 meters high. It is adorned with corner pilasters and Ionic columns, which support an entabla-

ture with architrave, frieze, and cornice. On this is a square structure of large stone blocks. On the south side above the cornice is the opening of a staircase which leads down to a small interior burial chamber with two arcosolia. Thus far the monument was therefore a tomb. Above the square structure there is a superstructure with a cylindrical body and a conical tower, which brings the total height of the monument to 16.5 meters. Architecturally this is like the *tholos* found in Hellenistic and Roman sepulchral monuments, except that the columns which there lift the conical portion above the cylindrical part and provide a place for statues of the dead are here, understandably in a Jewish environment, omitted. In effect, then, the superstructure constitutes a *nephesh* (cf. No. 266) for the tomb below. The date of the tomb may be at the beginning of the first century of the Christian era. As for the connection of the monument with Absalom, this tradition undoubtedly embodies the idea that this is the pillar (LXX στήλη) which Absalom set up for himself in the King's Valley (II Sam 18:18), a name which probably designates the Kidron.

Vincent, *Jérusalem*, 1:2, pl. LXXII. Photograph: JF.

270. The Pediment of the Tomb of Jehoshaphat

THE TOMB of Jehoshaphat is behind the Tomb of Absalom (see plan No. 268) and is reached by a flight of steps and through a doorway eight feet wide. The illustration shows the triangular pediment over this doorway. It is ornamented with an acanthus and with oranges, lemons, grapes, and olive branches. Through the doorway one enters a large, oblong chamber and from it, in turn, there is access to a complex of tomb chambers (A to H in the plan). One tomb chamber (E) has kokim graves, several of the others have arcosolia. The connection of this burial complex with the Tomb of Absalom suggests that both are of the same date, i.e., at the beginning of the first century of the Christian era. The Tomb of Absalom may also be a burial monument to mark the entire burial place behind it. Since this relatively large burial place and its prominent *nephesh* (if the Tomb of Absalom may be considered as such) were located in the Valley of Jehoshaphat, it may have been natural enough for tradition to identify it as the Tomb of Jehoshaphat.

If the dates given above for the four "tombs" which have just been described are correct, all of these monuments existed in the Kidron Valley in the time of Jesus. When he crossed that valley (Jn 18:1) he would have seen them; when he spoke of those who hypocritically "build the tombs of the prophets and adorn the monuments of the righteous" (Mt 23:29) he could have had these very objects in mind.

269. The Tomb of Absalom

270. The Pediment of the Tomb of Jehoshaphat

310

Vincent, *Jérusalem*, 1:2, pl. LXXVI upper; Parrot, *Golgotha and the Church of the Holy Sepulchre*, pp. 94-95. Photograph: courtesy École Biblique et Archéologique Française.

THE SANHEDRIYYA TOMBS

271. Plan and Sections of Tomb XIV of the Sanhedriyya Tombs

THE SO-CALLED SANHEDRIYYA Tombs, also previously known as the Tombs of the Judges, are located in a northern suburb of Jerusalem, off Samuel Street (Rehov Shemuel Hannavi). When the tombs were discovered at the beginning of the seventeenth century it was reckoned that there were seventy burial places. Like the seventy elders appointed by Moses (Num 11:24), the Sanhedrin had seventy members (*Sanhedrin* I 6 DM 383) with the high priest as president (Mt 26:57 and parallels; Josephus, *Ant.* xx 9, 1 §200), so the idea arose that this was the burial place of those seventy personages. There is no reason to suppose, however, that the members of the Sanhedrin were buried otherwise than in their own family tombs. This is the normal Jewish custom, attested by the OT phrases, "was gathered to his people" (Gen 25:8, etc.) "lie with my fathers" (Gen 47:30, etc.), and

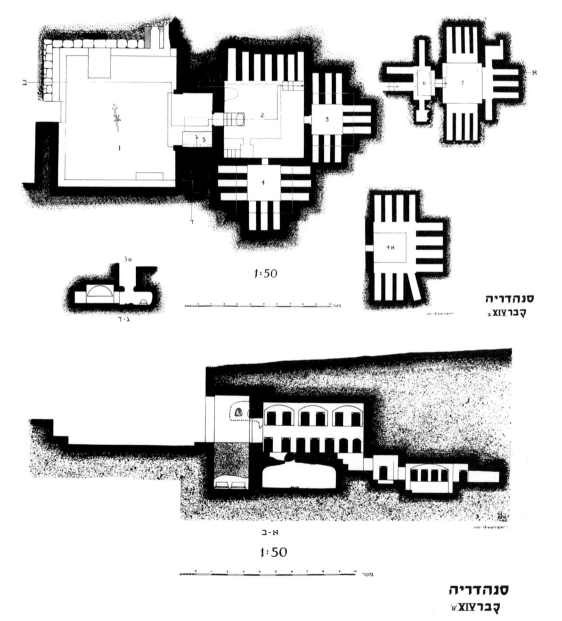

271. Plan and Sections of Tomb XIV of the Sanhedriyya Tombs

"sleep with your fathers" (Dt 31:16), and by the passage in *Sanhedrin* VI (DM 391; SBT IV 5, 305) where "buried in their proper place" can hardly mean anything but in the family burying-place. Also when Julius Jotham-Rothschild counted the tombs carefully he found only fifty-five known *kokim*, four *arcosolia*, and two caves used to contain ossuaries, rather than the supposed seventy. The tombs are indeed large and fine and must have belonged to wealthy families, so individual members of the Sanhedrin might have been buried in some of them, but as a whole this is not to be considered the mass burial ground of the Sanhedrin. In date the tombs are attributed to the time between Herod the Great and A.D. 70 (Rahmani in BA 45 [1981], p. 49). In plan the Sanhedriyya Tombs consist of a forecourt, a vestibule, and a main chamber with adjoining side chambers. The burial places are kokim, arcosolia, and rock benches or shelves. Also nearly all of the tombs have separate small chambers which may be for the collection of bones or the reception of ossuaries. The one known as Tomb XIV is outstanding architecturally, and it is shown here in plan and sections.

Julius Jotham-Rothschild, "The Tombs of Sanhedria," in PEQ 1952, pp. 23-38; L. Y. Rahmani, "Jewish Rock-Cut Tombs in Jerusalem," in 'Atiqot 3 (1961), pp. 93-104, and fig. 4. Photograph: courtesy Department of Antiquities, State of Israel.

272. Entrance to Tomb XIV of the Sanhedriyya Tombs

THE FORECOURT of Tomb XIV of the Sanhedriyya Tombs, shown here, is 9.9 meters in breadth and 9.3 meters in length, second in size only to the forecourt of the Tombs of the Kings (No. 277). On three sides are almost perfectly preserved benches, cut from the rock, on which the people would presumably sit during the last rites. At the entrance to the vestibule of the tomb is a fine façade, and the pediment is carved with acanthus leaves, pomegranates, and citrons. The tomb chambers within are arranged in three descending stories, as seen in the sections (No. 271).

The pottery found in the Sanhedriyya Tombs is important for the establishment of their date. Numerous jars are of a type common between the middle of the first century B.C. and the year 70 of the Christian era. Pyriform or pear-shaped bottles, used to contain costly oils or wine, are like those found in Herodian Jericho. Lamps are of the round, closed type with the nozzle shaped like a spatula, such as are also found in Jericho together with coins belonging to the early years of the reign of Herod. So the use of these tombs evidently extended from about 37 B.C. when Herod began his reign in fact (FHBC §363), to the time of the fall of Jerusalem in A.D. 70. Other important objects found from this period were fragments of sarcophagi and possibly of ossuaries. Some later material including fragments of glazed ware and glass indicates use of the tombs, probably as dwellings, in the thirteenth to fifteenth centuries, when the Arabs probably had a caravanserai in the forecourt of Tomb XIV.

Jotham-Rothschild in PEQ 1952, pl. IX, fig. 2. Photograph: courtesy Government Press Office, State of Israel.

272. Entrance to Tomb XIV of the Sanhedriyya Tombs

THE HERODIAN FAMILY TOMB

273. Plan and Sections of the Herodian Family Tomb

ONE OF THE LANDMARKS at Jerusalem to which Josephus refers in his account of the Jewish War (*War* v 12, 2 §507) is the memorial monument or tomb of Herod (τὸ Ἡρώδου μνημεῖον). In one passage (*War* v 3, 2 §108), using the plural, he speaks of the tombs of Herod as near the Serpent's Pool. West of the Old City of Jerusalem, near the King David Hotel and off from King David Road, is the subterranean burial place of which the plan and sections are shown here. This tomb is cut out of the solid rock, and its corridors and chambers are also walled with fine, large blocks of limestone. There are no kokim or arcosolia in the tomb-chambers, and the manner of burial was presumably by the use of sarcophagi. Two sarcophagi were, in fact, still in the longest tomb-chamber (F) (see No. 296). The impressive architecture of this tomb, which probably also had a superstructure now lost, agrees well with its identification as the tomb of Herod mentioned by Josephus. If the identification is correct, then the Serpent's Pool which Josephus described as near the tomb of Herod may perhaps be identified with the nearby Mamilla Pool, which goes back at least to Roman times. Herod the Great himself, however, was not buried in this tomb, but at the Herodium four miles southeast of Bethlehem (No. 19). His oldest son, Antipater, was buried at Hyrcania, probably to be identified with Khirbet Mird five miles southwest of Qumran (FLAP p. 280), and two other sons, Alexander and Aristobulus, in the Alexandrium seventeen miles north of Jericho. It remains possible that other members of the family rested in the tomb at Jerusalem.

F.-M. Abel, "Exils et tombeaux des Herodes," in RB 53 (1946), pp. 56-74; Vincent, *Jérusalem*, 1:1, pp. 342-346; Smith, *Jerusalem*, I, p. 114; Dalman, *Jerusalem*, pp. 202f. Photograph: Vincent, *Jérusalem*, 1:2, pl. LXXXII, courtesy École Biblique et Archéologique Française.

274. Rolling Stone in the Herodian Family Tomb

THE HERODIAN FAMILY TOMB is notable for one of the two examples (the other is in the Tomb of Queen Helena of Adiabene, No. 281) still to be seen at Jerusalem of a "rolling stone" used to close the entrance of a place of burial. On the plan of the Herodian family tomb (No. 273) the main entrance is at the point labeled A. Here there is a side channel in which the great stone stands on its edge and from which it can be rolled forward to close the doorway. This photograph shows that the stone is an enormous disk like a millstone, 1.6 meters in diameter and 0.8 meters in thickness, and almost perfectly preserved.

F.-M. Abel in RB 34 (1925), pp. 278-279. Photograph: courtesy École Biblique et Archéologique Française de Jerusalem.

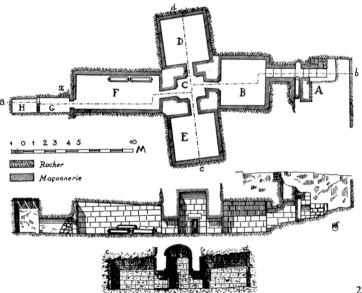

273. Plan and Sections of the Herodian Family Tomb

274. Rolling Stone in the Herodian Family Tomb

THE TOMB OF QUEEN HELENA OF ADIABENE

275. Restoration in Perspective of the Tomb of Queen Helena of Adiabene

THIS TOMB is north of the Old City of Jerusalem in the Nablus Road, a short distance beyond St. George's Cathedral and just beyond the intersection of Saladin Road with Nablus Road. When L. F. Caignart de Saulcy excavated at the spot in 1863 he believed that these were the tombs of the kings of Judah, and they have continued to be known popularly as the Tombs of the Kings. There is reason to believe, however, that the tombs are the burial place established by Queen Helena of Adiabene, which was a district on the upper Tigris (Pliny, *Nat. Hist.* v 13, 66; vi 16, 41-42). Josephus relates (*Ant.* xx 2-5 §§17-117) that Helena and her son Izates were both converted to Judaism. She made a journey to Jerusalem in order to worship in the temple there, and she also procured food from Alexandria and Cyprus for the people, since there was a great famine. This famine took place when Tiberius Alexander was procurator (A.D. 46-48) and is probably the same as that mentioned in Ac 11:28 as coming to pass in the days of Claudius (A.D. 41-54). Upon his death Izates was succeeded by his older brother, Monobazus ii. Helena died soon after, and Josephus (*Ant.* xx 4, 3 §95) reports: "But Monobazus sent her bones and those of his brother to Jerusalem and ordered that they should be buried at the pyramids, three in number, which the mother had erected three stadia from the city of Jerusalem" (cf. above No. 201). Elsewhere Josephus also makes mention of the monuments or tomb of Helena (τῶν Ἑλένης μνημείων) as a well-known landmark at Jerusalem (*War* v 2, 2 §55; 3, 3 §119; 4, 2 §147). Pausanias (viii 16, 4-5) compares this grave in Jerusalem with the tomb of Mausolus at Halicarnassus; and Eusebius (*Ch. Hist.* ii 12, 3) says that the splendid monuments (στῆλαι διαφανεῖς) of Queen Helena were still shown in his time in the suburbs of Aelia, as Jerusalem was then called. The three pyramids mentioned by Josephus no longer exist. They may have had somewhat the appearance of the Tomb of Absalom (No. 269), and are included in the hypothetical restoration in this drawing.

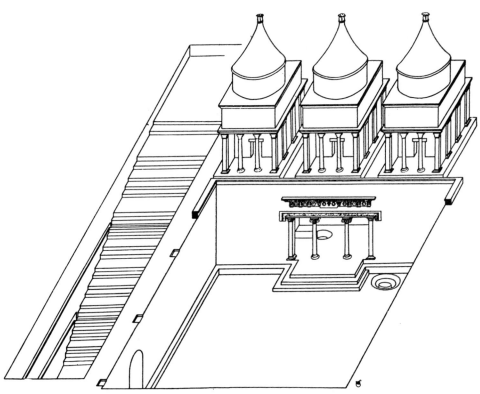

275. Restoration in Perspective of the Tomb of Queen Helena of Adiabene

L. F. Caignart de Saulcy, *Carnets de voyage en Orient (1845-1869), publiés avec une introduction, des notes critiques et des appendices par Fernande Bassan* (Paris: Presses Universitaires de France, 1955), pp. 29, 167f., 185; Vincent, *Jérusalem*, 1:1, pp. 346-363. Photograph: ibid., 1:2, pl. xcvii, courtesy École Biblique et Archéologique Française.

276. Steps, Water Channels, and Cisterns at the Tomb of Queen Helena of Adiabene

THIS PHOTOGRAPH SHOWS the bottom of the monumental stairway seen in the preceding drawing (No. 275). It leads down to the sunken courtyard of the tomb. Water was collected from the stairs and conducted through channels in the rock side-wall to two large cisterns near the foot of the steps, an arrangement which evidently provided water for the ablutions connected with burial ceremonies.

Photograph: JF.

277. In the Courtyard of the Tomb of Queen Helena of Adiabene

THE COURTYARD of the tomb, to which the steps shown in the preceding illustration (No. 276) lead, is sunk to a depth of eight or nine meters below the top of

the rock cliff and is about 26.5 meters square. This photograph looks toward the vestibule at the west side of the court, through which one passes to the burial chambers.

Photograph: JF.

278. The Entablature of the Tomb of Queen Helena of Adiabene

THE DOORWAY to the vestibule of the tomb, shown in the preceding photograph (No. 277), is twelve meters wide. Two columns, now missing, supported the entablature, the center and right-hand portions of which are shown here. On the architrave is a bas-relief with thick foliage, pomegranates, and pine cones. The frieze above has triglyphs and circular ornaments, and in the center is a bunch of grapes with a crown and triple palm on either side of it. The cornice consists of projecting ledges.

Photograph: courtesy of École Biblique et Archéologique Française.

279. Plan of the Tomb of Queen Helena of Adiabene

FROM THE VESTIBULE of the tomb a passage at the left leads to a large antechamber (A) about six meters

276. Steps, Water Channels, and Cisterns at the Tomb of Queen Helena of Adiabene

277. In the Courtyard of the Tomb of Queen Helena of Adiabene

square. From this, other passages lead to the tomb chambers with their kokim and arcosolia. Also sarcophagi were used for some of the burials. The tomb chambers were closed with stone doors which turned on hinges.

Photograph: Vincent, *Jérusalem*, 1:2, pl. LXXXIX, courtesy École Biblique et Archéologique Française.

280. Sections of the Tomb of Queen Helena of Adiabene

THE RAMIFICATIONS of the tomb chambers suggest that the preparation of them continued over quite a long period of time. Also two chambers (c and E in the plan and sections) were placed on a lower level. In one lower

278. The Entablature of the Tomb of Queen Helena of Adiabene

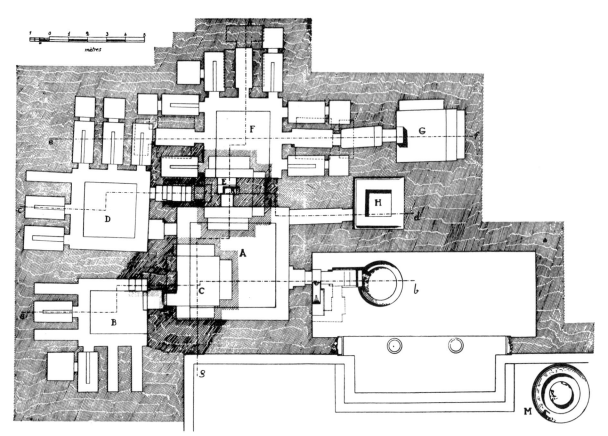

279. Plan of the Tomb of Queen Helena of Adiabene

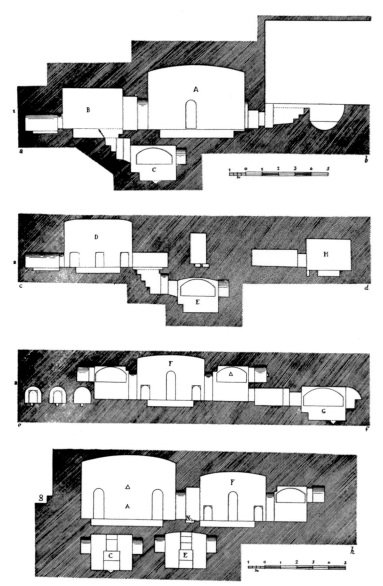

280. Sections of the Tomb of Queen Helena of Adiabene

chamber, which had not been plundered, a sarcophagus still contained the dust of the deceased (see No. 298).

Photograph: Vincent, *Jérusalem,* 1:2, pl. xc, courtesy Ecole Biblique et Archéologique Française.

281. Rolling Stone at the Entrance of the Tomb of Queen Helena of Adiabene

THE ENTRANCE to all the subterranean chambers of the tomb is through a passageway at the left end of the vestibule (cf. plan No. 279). This photograph shows the arrangement for closing that entrance, consisting of a large rolling stone set in a deep transverse channel. Behind the stone is a small chamber just large enough to admit the men who would push the stone forward across

the doorway. In his account of this tomb, and probably referring to this stone, Pausanias (VIII 16, 5) reports that at a fixed time on one certain day of the year a mechanism would, unaided, open the door and then, after a short interval, shut it. While this is obviously only a legend which was believed in the second century, the great rolling stone itself is very tangible. It and the similar stone at the Herodian family tomb (No. 274) are the two examples still to be seen at Jerusalem of the type of tomb closure referred to in the Gospels (Mt 27:60, etc.) in connection with the burial place of Jesus. Such stones are also at Bethphage (No. 153), Nazareth (No. 43, Kroll p. 369, abb. 297, 3), and Abu Ghosh (No. 244, Kroll p. 369, abb. 297, 1). Judging by the known examples, this manner of tomb closure with a rolling stone seems to have been characteristic of Jewish practice only in the Roman period up to A.D. 70 (NAEHL p. 63).

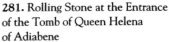

281. Rolling Stone at the Entrance
of the Tomb of Queen Helena
of Adiabene

Vincent, *Jérusalem*, 1:1, p. 349, fig. 97. Photograph: The Matson
Photo Service, Alhambra, Calif.

CATACOMBS

BETH SHE'ARIM

282. General View of Beth She'arim

UNDER CERTAIN CIRCUMSTANCES Jewish tombs
were expanded into the form known as catacombs (cf.
FLAP pp. 469f.). These are subterranean cemeteries consisting of galleries and rooms (*cubicula*) in the walls of
which are burial niches in the form of simple loculi or
more elaborate arched arcosolia. In Palestine the most
remarkable Jewish catacomb is at Beth She'arim.

As we have noted (No. 199), the Jewish law court
known as the Sanhedrin (סנהדרין , συνέδριον) met in
Jerusalem in a place the name of which is usually translated as Chamber of Hewn Stone, but which may actually have meant Chamber beside the Xystus. After the
destruction of Jerusalem (A.D. 70) the court of course
had to move elsewhere. In the Talmud (Rosh Hashanah
31a-b SBT II, 7, p. 149) Rabbi Johanan (d. 279) reports
the tradition that "the Sanhedrin wandered to ten places
of banishment." We list the original location of the Sanhedrin and the ten places to which it moved, with a few
explanatory notes: Chamber of Hewn Stone (or, Cham-

ber beside the Xystus; in or near the temple area); (1)
Hanuth (perhaps the chamber of the sons of Hanan, a
priestly family, Jer 35:4; the place to which the Sanhedrin moved when it ceased to judge capital cases); (2) Jerusalem (since the two preceding locations were in Jerusalem it is not clear what is meant here); (3) Jabneh (also
called Jabneel or Jamnia, a town on the western border
of Judea, nine miles northeast of Ashdod and only four
miles from the Mediterranean; when Jerusalem fell
Rabbi Johanan ben Zakkai took the court here and it,
now called the Beth-Din, remained at Jamnia until the
beginning of the Second Revolt in 132); (4) Usha (a
town in Galilee; this was in the time of Rabban Gamaliel
II); (5) Jabneh (back there from Usha, according to Johanan); (6) Usha (back there again from Jabneh); (7)
Shefar'am (also a town in Galilee; the last three were in
the time of Rabbi Simeon ben Gamaliel); (8) Beth
She'arim; (9) Sepphoris; (10) Tiberias ("and Tiberias is
the lowest-lying of them all," a figurative way of saying
that at Tiberias [the city itself being on the shore of the
Sea of Galilee, 696 feet below the level of the Mediterranean, cf. No. 71] the authority of the Sanhedrin was
reduced to its lowest level).

With respect to Beth She'arim, in which we are presently interested, it is known from many references in the
Talmud (cf. JE VII, pp. 333-337) that it was the Patriarch
Judah I, usually called Rabbi Judah ha-Nasi (i.e., "the
Prince"), who moved the court and the center of Jewish
studies to this place. Judah is famed as the great redactor
of the Mishnah, in which are many of his own statements, introduced by the words, "Rabbi says," and with
respect to his time it was said that to follow justice meant
to follow Rabbi to Beth She'arim (Sanhedrin 32b SBT IV

282. General View of Beth She'arim

5, p. 205). Along with his Hebrew studies Judah also took a liberal attitude toward Hellenistic culture, and was the author of the saying (Sotah 49b SBT III 6, p. 269): "Why use the Syrian language (i.e., Aramaic, spoken generally by the unlearned) in the land of Israel? Either use the holy tongue (i.e., Hebrew) or Greek!" After illness during which he moved to Sepphoris for its higher ground and more salubrious air, the patriarch died at the age of eighty-five in about the year 220 and was buried in a place reserved for him at Beth She'arim (Kethuboth 103b SBT III 4, p. 663). Before his death he distributed his various functions with the sentence (Kethuboth 103b SBT II 4, p. 658): "My son Simeon is Hakam (i.e., 'wise'), my son Gamaliel Nasi (i.e., the "prince" in succession to his father), and Hanina ben Hama shall preside (i.e., over the Sanhedrin)."

In Hebrew the name of Beth She'arim means House of Gates. In Josephus the name appears in Greek in the form Βησάρα, Besara (*Life* 24 §§118-119). In view of the great prominence of Beth She'arim, as shown in the foregoing references and particularly those of the Talmud, it

is surprising that the place was utterly lost. This was the case, however, and later it was even supposed (IEJ 5 [1955], p. 237) that the tomb of Rabbi Judah ha-Nasi was at Sepphoris, the town where he did in fact die but not where he was actually buried. Then in 1936 the accidental discovery of a tomb let to the explorations and excavations which have brought to light a town and a number of very large catacombs, which almost certainly represent the long lost Beth She'arim.

The site was in the vicinity of an Arab village called Sheikh Abreiq after a local holy man whose white domed tomb is on a small hill. In 1936 a Jewish youth group settled here and made the initial discoveries; these were followed by the excavations of the Israel Exploration Society under Benjamin Maisler (Mazar) in 1936-1940 and Nahman Avigad and others from 1953 onward.

Josephus said that Besara was twenty stadia from Gaba (*Life* 24 §118). The latter was the Gaba Hippeum (Γάβα, πόλις ἱππέων) or "city of cavalry" where Herod the Great settled his discharged cavalrymen, and was adjacent to Carmel (*War* III 3, §§35-36). The indicated location of Besara agrees with the location of Sheik Abreiq, which is beside the high road between Haifa and Nazareth. Furthermore, in the early excavations, the very name Βεσάρα was found in a Greek inscription on a marble slab at Sheikh Abreiq (Maisler, *Beth She'arim*, p. 3).

According to the excavators, the city on the mound at Beth She'arim was probably built originally in the second century B.C., was at its height in the third and early fourth centuries of the Christian era, and was destroyed in the fourth century, probably in A.D. 351 when Gallus, the brother-in-law of Constantius II, suppressed a Jewish revolt in Galilee (IEJ 10 [1960], p. 264). Excavations have uncovered a large synagogue (something like the one at Capernaum), a basilica, public buildings, dwelling houses, a glass factory with a slab of glass weighing nearly nine tons still in place (IEJ 15 [1965], pp. 261-262; *Archaeology* 20 [1967], pp. 88-95), an olive press and, of course, the catacombs, of which more than twenty have been found so far, with a variety of methods of burial.

In this general view of Beth She'arim, the entrances of Catacombs no. 20 and no. 14 may be seen at the left and the right, respectively, just above the center of the picture. Above each catacomb may be recognized an open-air structure also cut back into the hillside and obviously planned as an integral part of the structure (see also No. 284). These are provided with stone benches and evidently were a place of assembly for mourning and anniversary services (IEJ 9 [1960], pp. 212-214).

N. Avigad, "Excavations at Beth She'arim," in IEJ 4 (1954), pp. 88-107; 5 (1955), pp. 205-239; 7 (1957), pp. 73–92, 239-255; 9 (1959) pp. 205-220; 10 (1960), p. 264; Benjamin Maisler, *Beth She'arim, Report on the Excavations during 1936-1940.* Jerusalem: Israel Exploration Society, Vol. I, *English Summary*, 1950; Benjamin Mazar (Maisler), *Beth She'arim, Report on the Excavations during 1936-40* (in Hebrew). Jerusalem: Israel Exploration Society, Vol. I, *The Catacombs I-IV* (with English summary), 2d ed. 1957; Vol. II, *The Greek Inscriptions* (with French summary), 1967; cf. Norman Bentwich, *The New-Old Land of Israel* (London: George Allan and Unwin Ltd., 1960), pp. 109-114; Robert Payne, *The Splendor of Israel* (New York: Harper and Row, 1963), pp. 111-117; Moshe Pearlman and Yaacov Yannai, *Historical Sites in Israel* (Tel Aviv: Massadah—P.E.C. Press Ltd., 1964), pp. 86-93. Photograph: courtesy Government Press Office, State of Israel.

283. Burial Chambers in the Beth She'arim Catacombs

IN GENERAL, each of the Beth She'arim catacombs is approached through an open courtyard cut into the hill, with entrances on the three sides of the court. These entrances are closed with large stone doors, which move on hinges and are decorated with panels and knobs, to make

them look like wooden doors. Within, as seen in this photograph, are long halls with arched openings into the burial chambers.

Photograph: courtesy Government Press Office, State of Israel.

283. Burial Chambers in the Beth She'arim Catacombs

284. Entrance of Catacomb No. 14

OF ALL THE CATACOMBS at Beth She'arim, perhaps the greatest interest has attached to no. 14, with its triple-arched main façade, and the open-air stone benches of the assembly place above (cf. above No. 282). This catacomb was judged to be one of the oldest at Beth She'arim and to date from the end of the second century of the Christian era, although its façade was perhaps added only in the first half of the third century (IEJ 4 [1954], p. 106; 5 [1955], pp. 225-226).

Inside, there are two large rooms, with connecting corridors. As usual there are various tombs cut in the walls, and smaller niches perhaps for the collection of bones, but in the farther large room there is also one built tomb. In a long burial niche at the end of the left-hand wall of the first large room part of a vertical slab is still in place (IEJ 4 [1954], Pl. 9 c). On it, painted in large red letters, is the name רבי שמעון , Rabbi Simeon (ibid., p. 104 fig. 6). Above the first loculus on the right side of the passage which leads to the room with the built tomb there is a bilingual inscription written in black letters. It reads in Hebrew: זו של רבי גמליאל מ , "This is (the tomb) of Rabbi Gamaiel M"; and in Greek: ΡΑΒΙ ΓΑΜΑΛΙΗΛ, "Rabbi Gamaliel" (ibid., p. 104 fig. 7). Not far from the Tomb of Simeon there is another grave cut in the wall at ground-level, and above the opening there is an inscription in Hebrew which reads: אנינא הקטן , "Anina ha-Qatan," i.e., "Anina the Little" (IEJ 5 [1955], p. 222 fig. 9).

Interestingly enough, the names in the inscriptions just cited are precisely those of the two sons of Rabbi Judah ha-Nasi, namely, Simeon and Gamaliel, while Anina is equivalent to Hanina, the name of the man whom Judah designated to preside over the Sanhedrin after his own death (cf. No. 282). While identification is of course not guaranteed, it is at least possible that these were the same persons and that this was none other than the family tomb of Rabbi Judah ha-Nasi. As for the obviously most important tomb in the whole catacomb, namely, the built grave, the question has naturally been raised as to whether this may be the tomb of the patriarch himself. But the grave carries no inscription whatsoever, and the identification remains uncertain.

IEJ 4 (1954), pp. 99-107; 5 (1955), pp. 218-226, 236-239. Photograph: courtesy Government Press Office, State of Israel.

285. Plan of Catacomb No. 20

CATACOMB NO. 20 at Beth She'arim has also been of much interest. Its façade is visible in the general view (No. 282), and this sketch plan shows the entire complex. The entrance gives access to a long central hall which runs north and south, with rooms and chambers branching off on either side. At the far end, collapse of the rock has destroyed several rooms. In most of the rooms there were arcosolia in the walls, and also small niches closed with perpendicular stone slabs, the latter perhaps for the collection of bones (IEJ 7 [1957], p. 81), as in Catacomb no. 14 (No. 284). In some rooms graves were also cut in the floor.

In most of the Beth She'arim tombs burial was without any coffin, but particularly in this catacomb, in addition to scanty remains of burials in coffins of wood, lead, and pottery, there were many sarcophagi of stone and marble. Sometimes these were placed in recesses in the walls, but in most cases they stood inside the rooms as shown in numerous examples in the plan. Among these burial chests those that were found intact or partly intact were all of limestone and numbered approximately 130. Most were made smooth and without ornamentation, but not a few were adorned with various reliefs in patterns taken from animal or still-life. Among the representations are lions (No. 300), bulls' heads, an eagle, a

284. Entrance of Catacomb No. 14

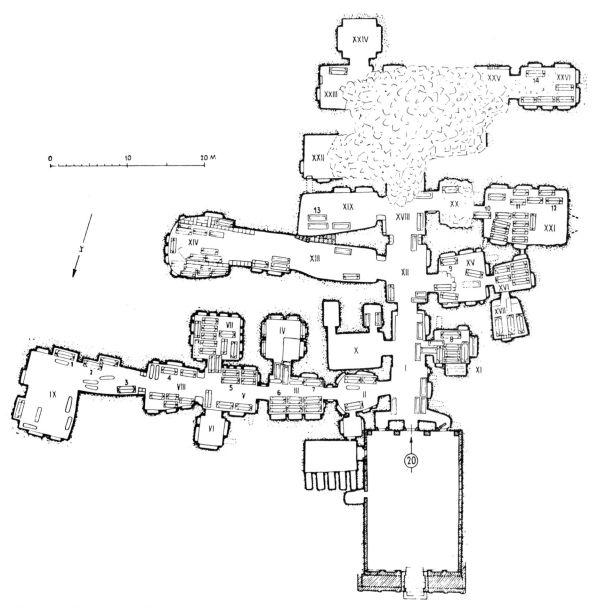

285. Plan of Catacomb No. 20

lion in pursuit of a gazelle, and the head or mask of a bearded man, as well as rosettes, shells, acanthus, a gate with flanking columns, and a menorah or seven-branched lampstand (cf. No. 286).

IEJ 7 (1957), pp. 77-92. Photograph: ibid., fig. 4 facing p. 81, courtesy Israel Exploration Society.

286. Menorah in Catacomb No. 3

IN ADDITION to the menorah on a sarcophagus (cf. above No. 285), this symbol is also carved on the wall of one room (no. XXIII) in Catacomb no. 20. In other cat-

acombs at Beth She'arim the menorah is found very frequently on the walls. The fine example shown in this photograph is in Hall E in Catacomb no. 3.

As is well known, the menorah or seven-armed lampstand goes back to Ex 25:31-39; 37:17-24, and was found not only in the temple at Jerusalem (FLAP p. 329) but also in synagogues and homes everywhere. It was thus a symbol of Judaism (FLAP p. 455) and, in a funerary context, it may have been thought of as a provision for the afterlife and thus have been especially associated with the thought of immortality.

W. Wirgin, "The Menorah as Symbol of After-Life," in IEJ 14 (1964), pp. 102-104. Photograph: Benjamin Maisler, Beth She'arim (1950), pl. XXVI, courtesy Israel Exploration Society.

286. Menorah in Catacomb No. 3

287. Epitaph of Marinos and His Wife in Catacomb No. 13

IT WILL BE REMEMBERED (NO. 282) that Rabbi Judah ha-Nasi commended the use of the Hebrew and Greek languages rather than Aramaic. In most of the catacombs at Beth She'arim the language of the inscriptions is predominantly Greek, but in nos. 14 and 20 it is predominantly Hebrew, which accords well with the supposition that these two catacombs in particular are for the burial of rabbinical families. In the examples already given (No. 284) from Catacomb no. 14 we saw inscriptions in Hebrew and, bilingually, in Hebrew and Greek.

This photograph shows a Greek inscription on a marble slab found in Catacomb no. 13 at Beth She'arim (see *The Greek Inscriptions*, by Schwabe and Lifshitz, p. 64 no. 149). The slab measures 18 by 37 centimeters. It is carved with a menorah (cf. No. 286), *shofar* (ram's horn blown at festivals [cf. Ps 81:3], especially at the New Year [*Mishnah Rosh ha-Shanah* 3.2-5; 4.7-9 DM pp. 191, 193f.]), *lulab* (palm branch used in the Feast of Taber-

nacles [cf. Lev 23:40]), and shovel (used at the altar for incense [cf. Ex 27:3; 38:3; Num 4:14], especially at Yom Kippur [*Mishnah Yoma* 4.3-4; 5.1–2 DM pp. 166f.]).

The inscription is in seven lines and reads: Τόπος Μαρινου καὶ Ειουσστας γυνεκὸς αὐτοῦ. Place (i.e., Tomb) of Marinos and his wife Justa.

In addition to identifying the person or persons buried in a given tomb, as in the foregoing example, the inscriptions sometimes express a malediction upon anyone who might molest the burial, this being a common means of attempting to prevent tomb robberies. For example in Catacomb no. 12, which dates probably in the second half of the third century, there is this inscription above Arcosolium no. 3 in Room no. III: "Anyone who shall open this burial upon whoever is inside shall die of an evil end" (IEJ 4 [1954], p. 95). But in spite of the maledictions all of the tombs found at Beth She'arim were plundered long ago.

Another interesting inscription is one of the six in Greek found in Catacomb no. 20. It is a graffito written in three lines, as follows (IEJ 7 [1957], p. 247):

287. Epitaph of Marinos and His Wife in Catacomb No. 13

ΕΥΤΥΧΩС
ΤΗ ΥΜΩΝ
ΑΝΑСΤΑСΙ

εὐτυχῶς
τῇ ὑμῶν
ἀνάστασι

Good fortune
in your
resurrection

Thus along with the idea of immortality (if the menorah stands for that), belief in resurrection is also attested at Beth She'arim.

IEJ 5 (1955), p. 217; 7 (1957), pp. 239-255. Photograph: IEJ 5 (1955), pl 26 c, courtesy Israel Exploration Society.

ROME

SINCE THE MOST NUMEROUS and earliest Jewish catacombs are those found at Rome, it is necessary, in order to complete the survey of Jewish burial places more or less contemporary with the life of Jesus and the early church, to consider them also. At Rome the underlying volcanic tufa lent itself particularly well to the construction of this type of burial place, and no less than six Jewish catacombs have been found there. The first was discovered in 1602 by Antonio Bosio. It was on the Via Portuensis in Monteverde about a mile outside the Porta Portese on the west side of the Tiber. It was afterward lost again, then accidentally rediscovered in 1904, at which time Nikolaus Müller began its partial excavation. Inscriptions taken from the catacomb at that time and others obtained in 1913 were placed in a Sala Giudaica in the Museo Cristiano Lateranense in Rome. The second Jewish catacomb was found in 1859 in the Vigna Randanini, on the Via Appia outside the Porta San Sebastiano and near the side road called the Via Appia Pignatelli. This catacomb was explored, and many of its inscriptions published, by Raffaele Garrucci. The third was discovered in 1867 by Giovanni Battista de Rossi in the Vigna Cimarra, which was also on the Via Appia outside the Porta San Sebastiano. The fourth was found accidentally in 1882 in the Vigna Apolloni, on the Via Labicana over a mile outside the Porta Maggiore, and was explored by Orazio Marucchi. The fifth was found in 1885 by Nikolaus Müller on the Via Appia Pignatelli near the cemetery already mentioned in the Vigna Randanini. Finally, the sixth Jewish catacomb was discovered accidentally in 1919 in the Villa Torlonia on the Via Nomentana, about a half mile outside the Porta Pia. It was excavated by Agostino Valente, and investigated by Roberto Paribeni and later by Hermann W. Beyer and Hans Lietzmann.

In location the Jewish catacomb in Monteverde corresponds with the statement of Philo (*The Embassy to Gaius* XXIII 155) that the Jews inhabited a great section of Rome on the other side of the Tiber; and the three catacombs on the Via Appia agree with the mention by Juvenal (*Satire* III 10-15) of Jews in the vicinity of the old Porta Capena, which was on the Appian Way. Many stamped bricks are found in the catacombs with formulas which provide indications of date. The bricks found in Monteverde show that its first burial galleries could have been dug in the first century before the Christian era, that it was certainly in use in the first century of the Christian era and most widely employed in the second and third centuries, but was abandoned in the fourth century. In the catacomb of the Villa Torlonia the bricks belong to the first and second centuries of the Christian era and show that the catacomb was established not later than the second and third centuries. In the catacomb in the Vigna Randanini the stamped bricks belong to the second century of the Christian era. The inscriptions in the Jewish catacombs therefore probably extend over a period of two or three hundred years. In all approximately 500 inscriptions are known. They contain mention of nearly a dozen synagogues in Rome and confirm the existence of a relatively large Jewish population at that time, estimates of which have run from 20,000 to 60,000. A count of the inscriptions with respect to language shows 366 or 74 percent in Greek, 120 or 24.4 percent in Latin, and 8 or 1.6 percent in Hebrew or Aramaic. The Jews of Rome were therefore predominantly Greek-speaking, while the more Romanized ones used Latin too, but the Semitic languages were relatively little known. In the personal names of over 500 individuals named in the inscriptions, however, 40 percent are purely Latin names, 32 percent are Greek, 13 percent are Hebrew names, and the rest are combinations of Latin and Greek or Latin and Hebrew. The largest proportion of Hebrew names (17 percent) is found in the catacomb in Monteverde; in the catacomb in Villa Torlonia there are more Greek names (43 percent) than Latin names (37 percent); and in the three catacombs on the Via Appia there is the largest proportion of Latin names (50 percent). Accordingly, if any distinction is to be made, it may be supposed that the most conservative community was on the other side of the Tiber; the most Hellenized in the northeast (Villa Torlonia); and the most Romanized on the Via Appia. And, in fact, the painted catacomb rooms found on the Via Appia reveal such allegorical symbols of paganism as a winged Victory, the goddess Fortuna with a cornucopia, and the genii of the seasons; the paintings in the rooms at the Villa Torlonia are Hellenistic in style but emphasize symbols of the Jewish faith; but the catacomb in Monteverde, as far as is known, has no such paintings.

Harry J. Leon, "The Jewish Catacombs and Inscriptions of Rome: An Account of Their Discovery and Subsequent History," in HUCA 5 (1928), pp. 299-314; "New Material about the Jews of Ancient Rome," in JQR 20 (1929-30), pp. 301-312; *The Jews of Ancient Rome* (Philadelphia: The Jewish Publication Society of America, 1960), *passim*; and in *The Teacher's Yoke: Studies in Memory of Henry Trantham*, ed. E. Jerry Vardaman and James L. Garrett, Jr. (Waco, Tex: Baylor University Press, 1964), pp. 154-165.

288. An Aramaic Inscription from the Jewish Catacomb in Monteverde

ALTHOUGH THE JEWISH CATACOMB in Monteverde has long since fallen again into ruins, many inscriptions from it are preserved in the Museo Cristiano Lateranese in Rome. In that Museum the marble plaque shown here is no. 21 in the Sala Giudaica. The first word in the text is probably the personal name Annia, comparable to the Hebrew חניה, Hania or Ḥanniya, and perhaps influenced in form by the Greek ᾽Αννία. After that, interpretations of the text vary, but the second word in the first line can contain the Aramaic possessive pronoun and mean "the wife of him." The second line then repeats "of" (ד) and gives the name of the husband. This name employs the Aramaic *bar*, equivalent of Hebrew *ben*, meaning "son" or "son of," and apparently uses the man's country of origin, Calabria in South Italy, as a part of his name. If these interpretations are correct, the translation is literally, "Annia, the wife of him, of Bar-Calabria," or more simply, "Annia, wife of Bar-Calabria." Accordingly, as usual in grave inscriptions, the name of the deceased is given, and some indication of the family relationship.

Nikolaus Müller, *Die Jüdische Katakombe am Monteverde zu Rom, der älteste bisher bekannt gewordene jüdische Friedhof des Abendlandes*. Schriften herausgegeben von der Gesellschaft zur Förderung der Wissenschaft des Judentums (Leipzig: Gustav Fock, 1912); Giorgio Graziosi, "La nuova Sala Giudaica nel Museo cristiano Lateranense," in NBAC 21 (1915), pp. 13-56 and pl. II no. 3; Umberto Cassuto, "Un 'iscrizione giudeo-aramaica conservata nel Museo cristiano Lateranense," in NBAC 22 (1916), pp. 193-198; Müller-Bees pp. 129-131 no. 142; DACL 8:2, col. 1872 no. 7; Frey I, pp. 228-229 no. 290. Photograph: courtesy Museo Cristiano Lateranense.

289. A Greek Inscription from the Jewish Catacomb in Monteverde

THIS MARBLE PLAQUE from the catacomb is no. 28 in the Jewish Hall in the Lateran Museum. While the spellings employed are frequent enough in that time, it would more normally be written as follows: ἐνθάδε κεῖται ᾽Ιούδας ἱερεύς. The translation is: Here lies Judas, a priest. The first two words, "here lies," are a standard formula in the grave inscriptions.

Along with the text are shown three objects. In the center is a menorah or seven-armed lampstand (cf. No. 286). At the left is a vase, probably thought of as containing olive oil necessary for the lamps on the lampstand (Ex 27:20; 35:14). At the right is probably an ivy leaf, of the sort usually identified with the genus of vines known as Hedera. Such an ivy leaf is used in Latin inscriptions, and is also taken over in Greek inscriptions, to separate words, mark abbreviations, etc. (Cagnat p. 28; Avi-Yonah, *Abbreviations*, p. 38). Here it is presumably used, therefore, simply as a conventional decoration accompanying an inscription. Insofar as the leaf was recognized as belonging to a type of vine, however, one wonders if its use with a Jewish inscription could have anything to do with the conception of Israel as a vine (e.g., Ps 80:8). It must be said also that it is not always possible to distinguish the drawing of the ivy leaf from the drawing of the *ethrog*. The latter at any rate is a specifically Jewish symbol. It is the citron which was used along with the *lulab* or palm branch (cf. No. 287) in the Feast of Tabernacles (Lev 23:40), and *ethrog* and *lulab* are often shown together as symbols. Other fruits also are shown, e.g., the pomegranate, and exact identification is sometimes not easy.

Schneider Graziosi in NBAC 21 (1915), p. 15 no. 2; Müller-Bees p. 88 no. 98; DACL 8:2, col. 1871 no. 2; Frey I, p. 271 no. 346; Goodenough II, pp. 6–7, III, no. 713; cf. J. B. Frey, "Inscriptions inedites des catacombes juives de Rome," in RAC 5 (1928), pp. 281-282 for the most frequent formulas, and 7 (1930), pp. 248–250, 259-260 for the most usual symbols. Photograph: courtesy Museo Cristiano Lateranense.

290. A Latin Inscription from the Jewish Catacomb in Monteverde

THIS MARBLE PLAQUE, NO. 32 in the Jewish Hall of the Lateran Museum, is broken into three pieces, with a portion completely missing. The menorah is in the upper left-hand corner, and the last letter in the first line has been traced in double outline. To judge from the available space, the first word in the fourth line may have been abbreviated and is to be read, *an(nos)*. In the last line the first part of the word [*die*]*s* was probably in the space now broken away. The translation is therefore: "Flavius Constantius, who lived 23 years, 14 days."

288. An Aramaic Inscription from the Jewish Catacomb in Monteverde

289. A Greek Inscription from the Jewish Catacomb in Monteverde

Schneider Graziosi in NBAC 21 (1915), p. 47 no. 107; Müller-Bees, p. 117 no. 128; Frey I, pp. 341-342 no. 463. Photograph: courtesy Museo Cristiano Lateranense.

Orazio Marucchi, *Le catacombe romane* (Rome: La Libreria dello Stato, 1932), pp. 676–678; Frey I, p. 97 no. 138. Photograph: courtesy Pontificio Istituto di Archeologia Cristiana.

291. A Greek Inscription in the Jewish Catacomb in the Vigna Randanini

THIS MARBLE PLAQUE, which is still in the catacomb, contains a text in four lines and a representation of the menorah. It would now be written: Ἐνθάδε κεῖται νήπιος Μαρκέλλος. Ἐν εἰρήνη ἡ κοίμησις σου.

The text uses a standard phrase with which we are already familiar (above No. 289) in the first line, and another phrase also very customary in Jewish burial inscriptions (cf. Ps 4:8) in the last two lines, and reads: Here lies a child, Marcellus. May your sleep be in peace.

292. A Latin Inscription in the Jewish Catacomb in the Vigna Randanini

THIS MARBLE PLAQUE is also still in the catacomb. The text reads: *Deutero gramateo bene merenti dulcis(simo)*. Deuteros is a Greek name corresponding to the Latin name Secundus; *dulcis* is a frequently found abbreviation of the superlative adjective, *dulcissimo*. The inscription may be translated: To Deuteros, a scribe well meriting it, most sweet.

Beneath the text, in the center, is the menorah. To the left is the *ethrog*. Along with the *ethrog* the *lulab* is

290. A Latin Inscription from the Jewish Catacomb in Monteverde

291. A Greek Inscription in the Jewish Catacomb in the Vigna Randanini

also often shown, but if the latter was once on this plaque it is no longer visible. To the right are a scroll of the law and an ivy leaf (cf. No. 289).

Frey I, pp. 160-161 no. 225; Leon, *The Jews of Ancient Rome*, p. 296 no. 225. Photograph: courtesy Pontificio Istituto di Archeologia Cristiana.

293. Plan of the Jewish Catacomb in the Villa Torlonia

THE GALLERIES of this catacomb lie on two levels, and in the plan the outlines of the higher level are drawn in solid lines, those of the lower level in dotted lines. Points of reference are marked with capitals letters, the more important *cubicula* and arcosolia with Roman numerals, and the inscriptions with Arabic numbers. Entrance to the lower level is at the west at the point marked A. At the crossing marked M it is possible to climb up to the higher level. Originally, however, there must have been separate access to the higher level, perhaps at the east beyond the present end of the corridor marked P. The higher and the lower catacombs were actually, therefore, separate complexes. The stamped bricks already mentioned (above p. 763) belong to the northern area of the lower level and suggest that this may have been laid out in the second century or beginning of the third, while the separate higher level will not be later than the third century. As the legends on the plan show, it is in the northern area of the lower level that most of the inscriptions have been preserved; in the larger *cubicula* of the higher level are the paintings.

Hermann W. Beyer and Hans Lietzmann, *Die jüdische Katakombe der Villa Torlonia in Rom.* Studien zur spätantiken Kunstgeschichte 4, Jüdische Denkmäler I (Berlin and Leipzig: Walter de Gruyter

and Co., 1930), pl. 31. Photograph: courtesy Walter de Gruyter and Co., Berlin.

294. A Painting in the Jewish Catacomb in the Villa Torlonia

CUBICULUM II, as it is labeled in the plan (No. 293), is the most fully decorated chamber in the catacomb. This photograph shows the painting in the arch of the arcosolium on the north side. In the center is the seven-armed lampstand, painted in green-blue with daubs of black, and with flames in red, set within two concentric circles, one of red and one of blue-green. At the left is a horn, the shofar (cf. No. 287). At the right is a round red fruit which looks much like a pomegranate.

Beyer and Lietzmann, *Die jüdische Katakombe der Villa Torlonia in Rom*, pp. 10f., pl. 6; Goodenough II, p. 37. Photograph: courtesy Walter de Gruyter and Co., Berlin.

295. Another Painting in the Jewish Catacomb in the Villa Torlonia

THIS PAINTING is in the arch of the arcosolium on the east side in Cubiculum II. Again the seven-armed lampstand, with its red flames, is in the center, and on the left is the red fruit. On the right, however, is a scroll of the Torah or Law. Both ends of the scroll are shown at the same time, and it is represented as rolled around a rod, whose knobs are indicated by heavy points. At the upper end there is a small triangular tab; this would have been glued to the roll and would have carried the title.

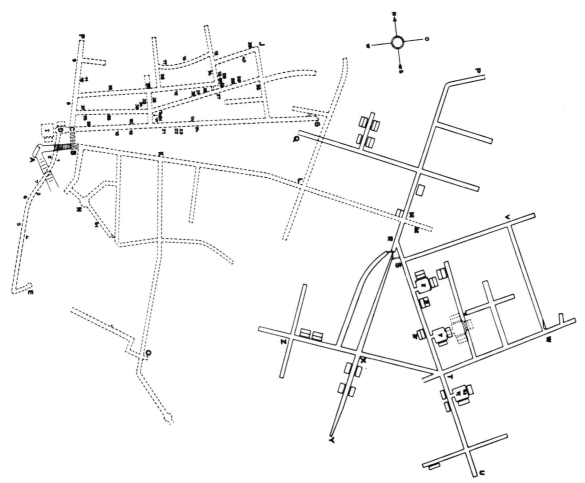

293. Plan of the Jewish Catacomb in the Villa Torlonia

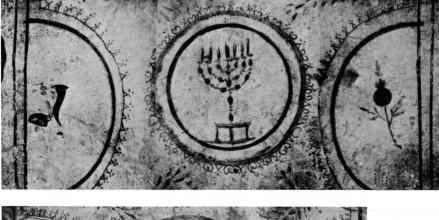

294. A Painting in the Jewish Catacomb in the Villa Torlonia

295. Another Painting in the Jewish Catacomb in the Villa Torlonia

Beyer and Lietzmann, *Die jüdische Katakombe der Villa Torlonia in Rom*, pp. 12, 21, pl. 4: FLAP p. 455, fig. 155; Goodenough p. 38. Photograph: courtesy Walter de Gruyter and Co., Berlin.

SARCOPHAGI

296. Sarcophagi in the Herodian Family Tomb

IN THE PRECEDING survey of representative types of tombs (Nos. 248ff.) we have seen that the body of the deceased was often placed in the tomb in a simple way such as being laid on a ledge or pushed into a loculus. In these cases the earlier custom was probably to wrap the corpse in the garment which the person wore when alive, as is reflected when the medium at En-dor sees Samuel coming up as an old man "covered with a mantle" (I Sam 28:14); and the later custom was to wrap the body in a linen shroud, as is stated in respect to the burial of Jesus (Mt 27:59 and parallels) (cf. above No. 227). The latter custom is also evidently reflected when the Talmud says of Rabban Gamaliel II (fl. A.D. c. 140-165) that "they carried him out in garments of linen, and

[then] all the people followed his example and carried out [the dead for burial] in garments of linen" (Kethuboth 8b SBT, III 3, 43; cf. Moed Katan 27b SBT II 8, 178). The use of a chest or coffin for the reception of the corpse was also familiar, however, among the Egyptians, Greeks, and Romans, and so also in due time among the Jews. The first of these burial chests were probably made of wood, and a Rabbinic source (Pal. M. K. 1, 5, 80c ap. Rahmani in *'Atiqot* 3 [1961], p. 102 n. 48) refers to the bodies or bones of the deceased and says, "They were buried in cedars," i.e., in boxes of cedar wood. When such a coffin is made of stone, particularly of limestone, it is called a sarcophagus. In Greek and Latin the words σαρκοφάγος and *sarcophagus* mean "flesh-eating" and were used adjectivally to describe a kind of limestone which, because it quickly consumed the flesh of corpses, was widely used for coffins (Pliny, *Nat. Hist.* XXXVI 27). Used substantively the same words denoted a coffin, and hence passed into English as "sarcophagus." Since these great stone chests, often elaborately carved, must have been not inexpensive, they usually occur in tombs which also otherwise appear to have belonged to the wealthy. Thus in the Herodian family tomb, in the longest tombchamber (F in the plan in no. 273), there were still two sarcophagi, as shown here.

296. Sarcophagi in the Herodian Family Tomb

Vincent, *Jérusalem*, pl. LXXXIV, 1. Photograph: courtesy École Biblique et Archéologique Française.

297. Ornamentation of a Sarcophagus in the Herodian Family Tomb

THIS PHOTOGRAPH SHOWS the front of the two sarcophagi just mentioned (No. 296) in the Herodian family tomb. In the center an acanthus rises above a vase-shaped object, and scrolls with leaves extend on either side, while rosettes are placed in the curves of the scroll.

The rosette, which is a frequent symbol in funerary art, looks like a conventionalized drawing derived ultimately from the representation of a star with several points, and star and rosette are very widespread symbols in the ancient Middle East, from early Mesopotamia onward. In Sumerian pictographs a star is the sign for "heaven" and "god." Thus the rosette could come to symbolize God as the source of light and life, and could express the hope for life in him and in heaven. But in particular the rosette could well be derived from the star of the goddess Inanna or Ishtar, who was often identified with the planet Venus. This star, shown with eight points, appears, for example, on boundary stones of the Kassite period soon after Hammurabi (ANEP no. 518) and on a stela of Bel-harran-bel-usur, a chamberlain under Tiglath-pileser III (744-727 B.C.) (ANEP no. 453), where Inanna is called "shining goddess of the stars" (ARAB I, §824). Also it may be noted that in later Jewish thought stars represent angels (e.g., II En 30:14) and angels carry the deceased to heaven (Lk 16:22) and are there in charge of their souls, as Enoch saw on his visit to the sixth heaven (II En 19:5). Along this line of thought the rosette would be a very appropriate symbol in a funerary context.

Vincent, *Jérusalem*, 1:2, pl. LXXXIV, 2; Goodenough VII, pp. 179-198. Photograph: courtesy École Biblique et Archéologique Française.

298. Sarcophagus of Queen Saddan

THIS SARCOPHAGUS, now in the Louvre Museum, was found in an arcosolium in an unopened lower chamber of the Tomb of Queen Helena of Adiabene at Jerusalem (cf. No. 280). When the cover was removed the contents had long since been reduced to dust. The inscription on the front side reads in Aramaic זדן מלכתא , *Saddan malakta'*, and in Hebrew זדה מלכתה, *Ṣaddah malaktah*, i.e., the Queen Saddan or Saddah. In accordance with the widespread custom among the Jews in the Hellenistic era of using both a Semitic and a Greek name, it is quite possible that the famous Queen of Adiabene was known by this Semitic name as well as the Greek name Helena (Ἑλένη), which Josephus uses regularly. If this is correct, this is the sarcophagus of Queen Helena of Adiabene to whom the entire tomb is attributed.

Vincent, *Jérusalem*, 1:1, p. 351, fig. 98, pp. 352f., 355f.; Frey II, p. 320 no. 1388; André Parrot, *Le Musée du Louvre et la Bible* (Neuchatel and Paris: Delachaux and Niestlé S. A., 1957), pp. 139-140. Photograph: Cliché du Service de Documentation Photographique des Musées Nationaux.

297. Ornamentation of a Sarcophagus in the Herodian Family Tomb

298. Sarcophagus of Queen Saddan

299. Sarcophagus from the Tomb
of Queen Helena of Adiabene

299. Sarcophagus from the Tomb of Queen Helena of Adiabene

THIS LARGE SARCOPHAGUS, also in the Louvre
Museum, probably also comes from the Tomb of Queen
Helena of Adiabene at Jerusalem. It is adorned with flo-
ral designs in the form of large rosettes (cf. No. 297).

Vincent, *Jérusalem*, 1:2, pl. xciii, 2; Parrot, *Le Musée du Louvre et
la Bible*, p. 140. Photograph: Cliché du Service de Documentation
Photographique des Musées Nationaux.

300. The Lion Sarcophagus at Beth She'arim

SARCOPHAGI WERE ALSO USED, we have noted
(No. 285), at Beth She'arim and in particularly large
numbers in Catacomb no. 20 (iej 7 [1957], pp. 82-92).
The sarcophagus shown in this photograph was found
still in its recess in the wall in this catacomb. In the relief
carvings of the front panel we see a twisted column at
either end, and a sort of twisted cord decoration across
the top. A lion on the left and a lioness on the right face
each other with a vessel between, from which they are
perhaps about to drink. Primitive as is the execution, the

300. The Lion Sarcophagus at Beth She'arim

impression of strength and fierceness is unmistakable. Elsewhere in the Palestinian tombs and synagogues of the Hellenistic and Roman periods the lion is not uncommon in the decorations (cf. Goodenough I, pp. 68, 95, 185, 195, 199, 207, etc.).

IEJ 7 (1957), pp. 82-84. Photograph: courtesy Government Press Office, State of Israel.

301. A Lead Coffin from Beth She'arim

ON THE SLOPE of the hill above Catacomb no. 20 (cf. above No. 282) at Beth She'arim was a group of surface graves. Burials may have been made here after the town was destroyed in the middle of the fourth century and the digging of catacombs stopped. In one of these graves was the lead coffin of which one end is shown in this picture. The coffin is 1.94 meters long and about 0.3 meters wide and high, with a cover which had been welded on at eight points around the edges. While the dimensions are sufficient for this to have been a container for a complete body, the excavators believe that only the bones of the deceased were interred in it (IEJ 9 [1959], pp. 215, 217), as in the case of ossuaries next to be discussed (see below pp. 335ff.). In decoration, the lead coffin is ornamented on the cover and long sides with vines, birds drinking from a bowl, human heads, and small *menorot*. On the narrow sides, the other end is plain, but on this end is an arch supported by two columns with Corinthian capitals, and in the archway a menorah. The lampstand has three legs, and the central leg has three prongs. On the right are a shofar and an incense shovel, on the left are a *lulab* and *ethrog* (cf. No. 287). Interestingly enough, the coffin is virtually identical with another lead coffin discovered in the nineteenth century at Sidon in Phoenicia, save that in the latter there is an arch on either end and, in

the archway, on one end the standing figure of a man, presumably the deceased, and on the other end a Christ-monogram (cf. p. 253f.) with the letters of the word ΙΧΘΥC, "Fish" (cf. No. 30) written around it in the interstices of the monogram (Goodenough V, p. 56 and fig. 59). Thus on similar coffins the symbols of Judaism and of Christianity respectively were employed in accordance with the faith of the deceased. That the coffin at Beth She'arim belonged to a Jew from Sidon is probable, for the epitaphs show that many Sidonian Jews were buried in this place.

IEJ 8 (1958), p. 276; 9 (1959), pp. 214-218. Photograph: IEJ 9 (1959), pl. 24 A, courtesy Israel Exploration Society.

301. A Lead Coffin from Beth She'arim

OSSUARIES

THE OSSUARY is a small chest, usually of wood or stone, and usually 50-80 centimeters (20-32 inches) in length, 28-50 centimeters (11-20 inches) in width, and 25-40 centimeters (10-16 inches) in height, i.e., just of the size to contain the bones of a burial. When such a container is made of stone, and particularly of limestone as is usually the case, the Greek word ὀστοφάγος, meaning "bone-eating" (cf. Strabo XVI 4, 17), is applied to it in analogy with the word "sarcophagus" (cf. No. 296). In Latin it is called an *ossuarium* (from *os, ossis*, "a bone"), and from this we have the English word "ossuary."

The ossuary is used for a secondary disposition of the bones. While sometimes a sarcophagus was employed for burial (cf. No. 296) and presumably served as the permanent resting place of the remains, in a great many cases the body was simply placed on a ledge or in a loculus or kok. It could be possible, then, that the same place would later be needed for another deposition. To make room, the dry bones which finally remained could be collected and put in some available place or in some receptacle. In Tomb 5 at Tell en-Nasbeh (Nos. 253-254), with its ledge burials, there was a small chamber at the back which is thought to have been used for such a collection of bones. In Tomb 4 at Tell en-Nasbeh (No. 255), with its kokim burials, there was a pit in the floor of the main chamber which is supposed to have been used in the same way. In the tombs at Marissa (No. 260) there are niches beneath the burial loculi, and these probably served in the same fashion. From this custom doubtless came the practice of using ossuaries, as described above. In the Sanhedriyya tombs certain small chambers may have been places for such receptacles, and some of the stone fragments found in these tombs are probably fragments of ossuaries as well as of sarcophagi (No. 271). At Beth She'arim there were a few skeletons without coffins, and sarcophagi of wood and stone were used, but there were smaller niches probably used for the collection of bones. The lead coffin described above (No. 301) was probably employed just for bones, and there were many fragments found, the excavators report, of stone and wooden ossuaries. They say that the practice of secondary burial was evidently the rule, i.e., the bones were transported to Beth She'arim, or they were gathered there, in ossuaries which were placed in the arcosolia and the kokim (*Beth She'arim*, Vol. I by Mazar [Maisler], English summary, 1st ed. p. 7, 2d ed. p. viii). In fact one Greek inscription has this very interesting reading (*Beth She'arim*, Vol. II by Schwabe and Lifshitz, p. 25 no. 78):

ΜΑΓΝΑ
ΓΛΟΟΟ
ΚΟΜΩ ΚΙΤΕ

i.e., Μαγνα γλοοοκόμῳ χῖτε. In Greek the word γλωσσόκομος or γλωσσόκομον properly designates "a case for the mouthpiece" of a flute, and then is used generally for a casket, and also for a coffin or sarcophagus. In this case there seems to be no doubt that the word means an ossuary, and the excavators translate: "Magna lies in the ossuary."

This practice of secondary burial is also attested in the Mishnah. One passage which has already been cited (No. 271) for the fact that "proper place" means the family burying-place, reads: "When the flesh was completely decomposed, the bones were gathered and buried in their proper place" (Sanhedrin VI 6 DM p. 391 SBT IV 5, p. 305). In a discussion of activities which were deemed permissible during the middle days of the Feasts of Passover and of Tabernacles, Rabbi Meir (fl. A.D. c. 140-165) said: "A man may gather together the bones of his father or his mother, since this is to him an occasion for rejoicing" (Moed Katan I 5 DM p. 208; cf. Pesahim VIII 8 DM p. 148). Likewise the Tractate on Mourning quotes Rabbi Eleazar bar Zadok (first century A.D., JE V, p. 120) as saying at the time of his death to his son: "My son bury me at first in a fosse. In the course of time, collect my bones and put them in an ossuary" (*Semahot* 13, Zlotnick p. 82). A reason why the gathering of the bones was deemed an occasion for rejoicing may lie in the fact that the process of decay of the flesh was considered to be a means of expiation, and only when this was complete was atonement accomplished. In the Talmudic discussion of the first Mishnaic passage quoted just above, it is stated that in the case of a criminal both death by execution and burial in the criminal's graveyard are necessary for forgiveness, but even more than that is required, it is said, for "the decay of the flesh too is necessary" (Sanhedrin 47b SBT IV 5, p. 314). Yet the righteous also are in need of the same expiation, for "there is not a righteous man on earth who does good and never sins" (Ec 7:20) (Sanhedrin 46b SBT IV 5, p. 308).

It may also be supposed that where belief in the resurrection was held, this could be favorable to the use of the ossuaries. While such belief was denied by the Sadducees who held that "souls die with the bodies" (Josephus, *Ant.* XVIII 1, 4 §16; cf. Mt 22:23 and parallels), it was affirmed by the Pharisees (Ac 23:8) and was held by many to be as much a fundamental of the Jewish faith as belief in the Law (Sanhedrin X 1 DM p. 397). In Ezk 37 the figure of resurrection applied to the return of the community of Israel to Palestine involved a picture of dry bones which came together again, were clothed with flesh, and made to live. While the nation was referred to here in a symbolic way, in Is 26:19 there was almost certainly thought of a literal resurrection of individuals and, where this passage says that their bodies shall rise, the Targum adds, "the bones of their dead bodies." Given such conceptions, it is possible that the gathering and keeping of the bones in an ossuary would seem especially appropriate.

It is true that some aspects of Jewish thought might seem to militate against any practice which went beyond the original burial procedure. There was, for example, a very strong feeling in Judaism against coming into any kind of contact with the remains of the dead. Num 19:16 states that to touch a dead body, or a bone of a man, or a grave, makes a person unclean (cf. Num 6:6). Mt 23:27 describes the "whitewashed tombs" which were "full of dead men's bones and all uncleanness," and Lk 11:44 makes it likely that the plain marking of the tombs was to prevent coming upon them inadvertently. Such markings of graves is confirmed in the Mishnah, where it is said that a grave must be marked "by whiting mingled with water and poured over the grave" (Maaser Sheni v 1 DM p. 80), and it is stated that this is done, evidently annually, on the 15th of Adar (Shekalim I 1 DM p. 152; cf. Moed Katan I 2 DM p. 208). We have also noted (No. 287) a concrete example of the kind of malediction which was expressed against any disturbance of a completed burial. Again, we have a case where it was desired to exhume a body to ascertain age by a *post mortem*, and Rabbi Akiba refused to permit this act of dishonor (Baba Bathra 154a SBT IV 4, p. 669). Nevertheless these considerations were evidently not powerful enough to preclude the practice of secondary burial and the use of ossuaries, for which there is abundant evidence as indicated above.

It also seems quite possible that early Christians, as well as Jews, could have made use of ossuaries. Among at least many of the early Christians there was a less strict regard for all the details of the Law, and there was also an increased emphasis upon the resurrection. At any rate we have various references to the preservation of the bones of the deceased by the early Christians. After Ignatius was thrown to the beasts in Rome (A.D. c. 110), "only the harder portions of his holy remains were left," and these were carried back to be kept by his home church at Antioch (The Martyrdom of Ignatius 6 ANF I, p. 131). Likewise when Polycarp was burned to death at Smyrna (A.D. 156), his companions "took up his bones, as being more valuable than jewels and more precious than gold, and deposited them in a suitable place, to gather together there every year on the anniversary [literally, the birthday] of his death" (The Martyrdom of Polycarp 18 ANF I, 43). If then we actually find on the ossuaries signs, markings, names, etc., which can with some probability be connected with early Christianity,

there is no real reason for denying the possibility of such a connection and perhaps even real reason for affirming it.

As to the date of the ossuaries, fragments of them were found in the Sanhedriyya Tombs (No. 271), and these tombs are quite definitely dated by other contents to the period from the beginning of the reign of Herod (37 B.C.) to the fall of Jerusalem (A.D. 70). In many other tombs at Jerusalem the situation is much the same, and the use of ossuaries is indicated for a period beginning not much earlier than 50 B.C. and continuing up to the year 70 of the Christian era (Rahmani in 'Atiqot 3 [1961], p. 116 and n. 4). Many ossuaries have also been found in the cemetery at Dominus flevit (Nos. 319ff.), in tombs which were in use up to A.D. 70 and possibly to A.D. 135 (W. F. Albright in BASOR 159 [Oct. 1960], p. 37). That the use of ossuaries at Jerusalem ceased with the fall of the city in A.D. 70, or at any rate with the exclusion of Jews (and Jewish Christians) from the area by Hadrian in A.D. 135, is understandable. Elsewhere, however, there is evidence that they were in use over a much longer period of time. Many ossuaries were found in the "Maccabean" cemetery at Gezer (R. A. S. Macalister in PEFQS 1904, pp. 340-343), so they must have come into use in Hellenistic times, say around 150 B.C. (Goodenough I, pp. 114-115) or 200 B.C. (Vincent in RB 43 [1934], pp. 564-567). While Goodenough and Vincent also think that the custom continued to around A.D. 150 or 200, the evidence from Beth She'arim cited above shows that ossuaries were still in use there into the third and fourth centuries, and the Greek inscription quoted with explicit mention of an ossuary must belong to the first half of the fourth century (BASOR 189 Feb. 1968, p. 54). For Jerusalem, however, the most probable dates are from about 50 B.C. to A.D. 70 or 135 (cf. above No. 163).

On the ossuaries the most common decoration is the rosette (see e.g., No. 302), a symbol of which we have already spoken (No. 297). In many cases the ossuaries have inscriptions, scratched, carved, drawn with charcoal, or painted. These are usually names, and it may be presumed that these were normally the names of those whose bones were contained within.

Samuel Krauss, "La double inhumation chez les Juifs," in REJ 97 (1934), pp. 1-34; L.-H. Vincent, "Sur la date des ossuaires juifs," in RB 43 (1934), pp. 564-567; P. B. Bagatti, "Resti Cristiani in Palestina anteriori a Constantino?" in RAC 25 (1949), pp. 117-131; L. Y. Rahmani, in 'Atiqot 3 (1961), pp. 116-117; and Rahmani, in BA 45 (1982), pp. 109-117; Testa pp. 446-474; R. A. Mastin, "Chalcolithic Ossuaries and 'Houses of the Dead,' " in PEQ 1965, pp. 153-160; Saul Lieberman, "Some Aspects of After Life in Early Rabbinic Literature," in Harry Austryn Wolfson Jubilee Volume (Jerusalem: American Academy for Jewish Research, 1965), English Section, II, pp. 495-532; Arthur D. Nock, "The Synagogue Murals of Dura-Europos," ibid., pp. 638f.

302. Ossuary from Tomb 14 at Tell en-Nasbeh

THIS OSSUARY was found in Tomb 14 in the west cemetery at Tell en-Nasbeh, a tomb which was probably in use from the Iron Age and into the Roman period, as late as the third century. The chest is 71 centimeters (23.5 inches) long, 28 centimeters (11.25 inches) wide, and 34 centimeters (13.5 inches) high. The lid on the top is shaped like a barrel vault, with a projecting beveled edge. The front of the chest is ornamented with two large rosettes, between which is a short pillar set on a three-staged plinth and supporting a large capital. The back is carved to look like a wall of regularly laid blocks, and three rosettes are drawn thereon. Another rosette is still to be seen on the left end of the chest, and similar decoration may once have existed on the other end as well as on the lid. The significance of the rosette has already been spoken of (No. 297). As for the carving of the back side to look like a wall of stone blocks, this also is a familiar decoration of the ossuaries. Since this appears to represent the wall of a house, it may be taken as symbolic of the בית עלם, οἶκος αἰῶνος, *domus aeterna*, or house of eternity (Ec 12:5), the last resting place of mortal man.

Tell en-Nasbeh, I, p. 124 and pl. 43; Goodenough, I, pp. 75, 116. Photograph: courtesy Palestine Institue.

303. Ossuary Inscriptions from a Tomb in the Kidron Valley

IN 1934 A SIMPLE TOMB was found by the Archaeological Department of the Hebrew University in the Kidron Valley near Beit Sahur el-'Atiqa. It consisted of a single chamber, partly cut out of the rock and partly built of layers of stone. The few pottery fragments suggested the Herodian period. Five ossuaries were in the chamber, most of them broken by the collapse of the roof of the tomb. Three had inscriptions, as shown in the illustration. The first inscribed ossuary was 67 centimeters in length, 30 centimeters in width, and 39 centimeters high. It stood on four small feet, and was covered with a flat lid. On the back, cut in the soft stone with a sharp tool, was the inscription numbered 1. It may be transcribed as follows, and recognized as Aramaic: חניה א בר אלכשה . The first word is doubtless one possible spelling of the name Onias ('Ονιας), a name which is familiar in the books of the Maccabees and in Josephus. The single letter, aleph, which follows, was probably written by mistake as the initial letter of the last name, and then it was recalled that *bar*, "son (of)," should be inserted first. In the last name the characters kaph and shin can transliterate the Greek letter xi, and the name can be a hypocoristic form of Alexander ('Αλέξανδρος), or a slightly shortened form of Alexas ('Αλεξᾶς), both of which names are well known in Josephus (e.g., *Ant.* XVIII 5, 4 §138). In this case the inscription may be translated: Onias, son of Alexa.

The second inscribed ossuary was of unknown length, since it had been broken, but was 26 centimeters wide and 29 centimeters high, and had a rounded lid. On the fragments of a long side was an inscription in Greek, of which this much can be read (3 in the illustration): ΑΠ-ΦΙΑС ΑΘ.

Scratched somewhat more hastily on an end of the same chest, but preserved completely, is a Hebrew graffito which may be recognized as a transcription of the foregoing Greek. It reads (2 in the illustration): אפיחם בת אתנגרש. The first name is the same as the 'Απφία in Phm 2, but written here in the genitive case, meaning the ossuary "of Apphia." Although not actually necessary in the Hebrew, the Sigma of the Greek genitive has been reproduced by what is probably a Samekh

302. Ossuary from Tomb 14 at Tell en-Nasbeh

in the Hebrew transcription. The Hebrew also supplies next the word *bath*, "daughter (of)," making it plain that the first name is that of the daughter of the person identified by the second name. The complete Hebrew of the second name makes it possible also to recognize that this was probably the Greek name Ἀθηναγόρας in the genitive form, Ἀθηναγόρου. The translation of this inscription is, therefore: (Of) Apphia, daughter of Anthenagoras.

The third inscribed ossuary was a plain chest, but scratched on its back side was this graffito (4 in the illustration): ΟϹΤΟΦΑΓΟϹ ΟϹ[Τ]ΟΦΑΓΟϹ. This, twice repeated, is the word ὀστοφάγος, ostophagus, "bone-eat-

ing," which, as already explained (p. 335), was the term for an ossuary, analogous to the term *sarcophagus*, or "flesh-eating."

Other ossuaries will be dealt with in what follows (Nos. 309ff.), where we will note some marks and names which may possibly be connected with early Christianity and may involve reference back to Jesus. It is chiefly with the mark of the cross that we shall be concerned.

E. L. Sukenik, "A Jewish Tomb in the Kedron Valley," in PEFQS 1937-38, pp. 126-130 and pl. v. Photograph: courtesy Palestine Exploration Fund.

303. Ossuary Inscriptions from a Tomb in the Kidron Valley

THE CROSS

HISTORY OF
THE CROSS MARK

304. Painted Pebbles with Cross Marks from Tell Abu Matar

IN THE SENSE of a figure formed by the intersection of two more or less straight lines, a cross is one of the most elemental marks which it is possible to make, and may of course be used as a purely secular mark for any number of purposes. At Tell Abu Matar, 1.5 kilometers southeast of Beersheba, a small settlement of the Chalcolithic Age was excavated in 1952-1954. The two lowest levels consisted of underground houses, connected in groups by tunnels, a type of dwelling useful for protection from sun and sandstorms and still employed by Bedouin in the Central Negev. Here in the lowest level and on the earliest floor of House 127 was a group of "painted pebbles." Fourteen in number, these flat stones were arranged in a crescent shape and each was marked with red ocher

which had been applied with the fingers after the pebbles were in place. Most of the marks are in the form of a cross. Since these pebbles were found in their original place and were connected stratigraphically with the setting up of the dwelling, the guess may be hazarded that the cruciform mark was intended as a sign to avert evil and give protection. Similar marks are indeed found widely in the whole history of religions, and a similar protective significance may often be surmised for them. The photograph shows these crossmarked pebbles as they are displayed in their original arrangement in the Negev Museum in Beersheba.

> J. Perrot, "The Excavations at Tell Abu Matar, near Beersheba," in IEJ 5 (1955), 17-40, 73-84, 167-189, and specially p. 168 fig. 17 and pl. 21 A. Photograph: JF.

304. Painted Pebbles with Cross Marks from Tell Abu Matar

THE CROSS MARK AS A CHARACTER OF THE SEMITIC ALPHABET

THE SIMPLE MARK of a cross also became a character of the alphabet in Semitic languages including Canaanite, Phoenician, Hebrew, and Aramaic. In 1905 W. M. Flinders Petrie discovered at Serabit el-Khadem in the Peninsula of Sinai the so-called proto-Sinaitic inscriptions. As he recognized at the time, these date about 1500 B.C. The inscriptions were composed of characters which appeared to depict or at least represent specific objects. An oxhead, for example, was quite plainly recognizable, and there was a rectangle, sometimes with an opening into it, which could be the drawing of the plan of a house. Several times there occurred a certain sequence of characters, and these appeared to be, in sequence, a house, an eye, an oxgoad, and a cross. The order in which these signs were to be read was established by the fact that they sometimes occurred in vertical columns which were no doubt to be read from top to bottom, while in horizontal lines they gave the same order when read from left to right. In 1915 Alan Gardiner suggested that these characters were acrophonic in nature, which means that a given character stands for the initial sound of the name of the object which it depicts, and he identified the sequence of characters just mentioned as corresponding to the Semitic letters which are called in Hebrew beth, 'ayin, lamedh, and taw. Therewith he read the sequence of characters as giving the name Ba'alat, which means "the female Ba'al." Since the Canaanite goddess, Ba'alat, was called Hathor by the Egyptians, as is shown by an inscription (No. 305) which will be mentioned shortly, and since Hathor was recognized as the goddess of the turquoise mines at Serabit el-Khadem, as the inscription also shows, this identification made very good sense. Accepting this explanation of the signs as correct, we have in the proto-Sinaitic inscriptions an early form of the Semitic alphabet. This early alphabetic writing contains an oxhead, and in Hebrew the first letter of the alphabet is 'aleph, which is a word (אלף, occurring in the OT only in the plural, אלפים , e.g., Pr 14:4) which means ox. Another character is a house, and in Hebrew the second letter is beth, which is a word (בית, e.g., Ex 12:30) which means house. In the course of time the drawing of the characters was increasingly conventionalized and so we have finally in Hebrew for the oxhead the letter א and for the house the letter ב. Yet another character is a simple cross mark, and in Hebrew the twenty-second and last letter of the alphabet is taw, which is a word (תו, e.g., Ezk 9:4) which means mark or sign. Inasmuch as the characters we have been discussing are essentially little pictures they remind us of the picture writing of Egyptian hieroglyphics and suggest that this manner of writing arose under Egyptian influence, either directly or indirectly. Inasmuch as the pictographs are employed according to the acrophonic principle, however, they are the characters of a true alphabet and thus, in that respect, they represent a new invention. In view of the area in which this alphabet was widely used, as examples to be given shortly will show, it may be supposed that its origins are to be sought somewhere in Syria-Palestine. Indeed it is now considered that the language of the proto-Sinaitic inscriptions is Canaanite and that the script is the normal alphabetic Canaanite of its period, i.e., of the early fifteenth century B.C. (FLAP pp. 148-149).

305. Sandstone Statue from Serabit el-Khadem with proto-Sinaitic Inscription

THIS STATUE is now in the Egyptian Museum in Cairo. The squatting figure of a man is a familiar Egyptian type. The inscription (no. 346 in the series) is in proto-Sinaitic, and the main line of writing, running from left to right and sloping somewhat downward across the front of the statue, consists of a sequence of characters which, according to Gardiner's explanation, correspond to lamedh, beth, 'ayin, lamedh, and taw. This, then, means 'belonging to Ba'alat." As for the character with which we are presently concerned, it is the last one at the right, namely, a cross mark, serving as a letter of the alphabet and corresponding to the Hebrew taw. Of the several other examples where the same sequence of characters, spelling "Ba'alat," occurs, it will suffice to mention the inscription on the left side of the base of a sandstone sphinx from Serabit el-Khadem which is now in the British Museum (no. 41748). This is of special interest because on the right shoulder of the sphinx is a hieroglyphic inscription reading, "Beloved of Hathor, [lady of] the turquoise" (no. 345 in the series), thus confirming the identification of Ba'alat and Hathor. The character in which we are particularly interested, namely, the simple mark of the cross, is, in fact, the most common sign in the proto-Sinaitic inscriptions, occurring more than thirty-five times.

W. M. Flinders Petrie, *Researches in Sinai* (London: John Murray, 1906), 129 and figs. 138, 139, 141; Alan H. Gardiner, "The Egyptian Origin of the Semitic Alphabet" in JEA 3 (1916), 1-16 and pl. III, no. 345, pl. IV, no. 346; Romain F. Butin, "The Protosinaitic Inscriptions," in HTR 25 (1932), 130-203 and pl. X, no. 345, pl. XI, No. 346; W. F. Albright, "The Early Alphabetic Inscriptions from Sinai and Their Decipherment," in BASOR 110 (Apr. 1948), 6-22; *The Inscriptions of Sinai* by Alan H. Gardiner and T. Eric Peet, 2d ed. rev. by Jaroslav Černý (London: Egypt Exploration Society, pt. I, 1952, pt. II, 1955), I, 202, no. 345; II, pl. LXXXII, no. 345; Frank M. Cross, Jr., "The Evolution of the Proto-Canaanite Alphabet," in BASOR 134 (1954), 15-24. Photograph: HTR 25 (1932), pl. XI, no. 346 front, courtesy Egyptian Museum, Cairo.

There are many more inscriptions and texts that illustrate the evolution of the alphabet in which the Semitic languages are written. In these, for a millennium and a half, we continue to find the cross mark as an alphabetic character. As examples, this mark may be seen in the following. In Canaanite, in the inscriptions on the bronze javelin heads which come from el-Khadr, five kilometers west of Bethlehem, dating about 1100 B.C. (the last character in each inscription, reading from top to bottom). In Phoenician, in the temple inscription of

King Yehimilk (see below No. 306) which was found at Byblos (no. 1141), dating c. 950 B.C. (the second character in the first line, reading from right to left, and a number of other occurrences in the balance of the text). In Aramaic, in the Bir-Hadad stela, a votive stone set up c. 850 B.C. by Ben-Hadad I of Damascus in honor of, and with a carved representation of, the god Melqart (the first character, reading from right to left, in line 4). In Hebrew (reading from right to left), in the Gezer Calendar in what has been called "perfect classical Hebrew," c. 925 B.C. (at the end of line 3); in the Lachish ostraca, c. 588 B.C. (e.g., in Letter II, in the second line, the sixth letter); and in several parchment manuscripts from Qumran, namely, in a large scroll with much of the Book of Exodus from Cave 4 (4QEx^a), c. 225-175 B.C. (e.g., on the page containing Ex 32:10-30, in the seventh line, the eighth character); in a fragment of the Book of Genesis from Cave 6 (6Q1), probably from the second half of the second century B.C. (the second character in the second readily legible line, and a number of other instances); and in fragments of the Book of Leviticus from Caves 1 and 2 (1Q3 and 2Q5), c. 125-75 B.C. (in 1Q3,

fragment 2, line 5, the second character; in 2Q5, line 3, the fifth character, and line 5, the fourth character).

El-Khadr: J. T. Milik and Frank M. Cross, Jr., "Inscribed Javelin-Heads from the Period of the Judges: A Recent Discovery in Palestine," in BASOR 134 (Apr. 1954), 5-15 and fig. 1 on p. 7. Yehimilk: Maurice Dunand, "Nouvelle inscription Phénicienne archaïque," in RB 39 (1930), 321-331 and pl. XV; and Fouilles de Byblos (Paris: Paul Geuthner), I, Atlas (1937), pl. XXXI, 2; Texte (1939), 30, no. 1141; W. F. Albright, "The Phoenician Inscriptions of the Tenth Century B.C. from Byblus," in JAOS 67 (1947), 153-160. Bir-Hadad: W. F. Albright, "A Votive Stele Erected by Ben-Hadad I of Damascus to the God Melcarth," in BASOR 87 (Oct. 1942), 23-29, figs. 1, 2; Frank M. Cross, Jr. and David N. Freedman, Early Hebrew Orthography (New Haven: American Oriental Society, 1952), 23-24. Gezer Calendar: W. F. Albright, "The Gezer Calendar," in BASOR 92 (1943), 16-26; Sabatino Moscati, L'Epigrafia ebraica antica 1935-1950 (Rome: Pontificio Istituto Biblico, 1951), 8-26, pl. VII, 1. Lachish Ostraca: Harry Torczyner, Lachish I (Tell ed Duweir), The Lachish Letters (London: Oxford University Press, 1938), 34ff. 4QEx^a: Patrick W. Skehan, "Exodus in the Samaritan Recension from Qumran," in JBL 74 (1955) 182-187 and fig. fac. p. 185. 6Q1: DJD III Textes 105-106 no. 1, Planches XX no. 1. 1Q3: DJD I, 51-53 and pl. VIII, no. 3. 2Q5: DJD III Textes 56f. no. 5, Planches XII no. 5. Solomon A. Birnbaum, "The Leviticus Fragments from the Cave," in BASOR

305. Sandstone Statue from Serabit el-Khadem with proto-Sinaitic Inscription

118 (Apr. 1950), 20-27, fig. 1; S. Yeivin, "The Date and Attribution of the Leviticus Fragments from the Cache in the Judaean Desert," in BASOR 118 (Apr. 1950), 28-30. Richard S. Hanson, "Paleo-Hebrew Scripts in the Hasmonean Age," in BASOR 175 (Oct. 1964), 26-42.

306. The Inscription of Yehimilk, King of Byblos

FROM THE INSCRIPTIONS carved on the rocks of Serabit el-Khadem in the fifteenth century B.C. to the texts penned on the parchments at Qumran in the second and first centuries B.C., the documents which have just been cited extend over a period of nearly 1,500 years. They also extend from the lapidary script with which inscriptions were cut into stone to the cursive script with which texts were written on ostraca and parchment. But the alphabetic character we are discussing continued to be formed essentially as a simple cross mark. The major difference in the way in which it is written consists in whether it stands erect with a vertical and a horizontal bar or whether it is shifted sideways to produce an X form. In the inscriptions from Serabit el-Khadem (c. 1500 B.C.) in the example on the squatting figure (Inscription no. 346, our illustration No. 305), except for the slanting of the entire line of text, the character stands quite erect and symmetrical; in the text on the sphinx (Inscription no. 345), however, the vertical line of the character is shifted considerably sideways. In the el-Khadr inscriptions (c. 1100 B.C.) the cross is quite firmly upright and symmetrical, although in one case the horizontal bar slopes considerably; but in the Yehimilk inscription from Byblos (c. 950 B.C.), which we illustrate here, the character is shifted fully sideways to the X position. In this last text the sign may be seen frequently, beginning with the second character (reading from right to left) in the first line, where it is the second letter in the word בת, beth, "house," in this case meaning temple. In Albright's translation, and in lines corresponding to those on the stone, the text reads:

> The temple which Yehimilk, king of Byblus, built—
> it was he who restored the ruins of these temples.
> May Baal-shamem and Baal(ath)-Gebal
> and the assembly of the holy gods of Byblus
> prolong the days of Yehimilk and his years
> over Byblus as a rightful king and a true
> king before the h[oly] gods of Byblus!

Dunand in RB 39 (1930), pl. xv fac. p. 322; and Fouilles de Byblos, I, Atlas, pl. XXXI, 2; Albright in JAOS 67 (1947), 156-157. Photograph: RB 39 (1930), pl. xv fac. p. 322, courtesy École Biblique et Archéologique Française.

In addition to the major difference as to whether the cross mark is formed in an upright position or shifted

306. The Inscription of Yehimilk, King of Byblos

sideways, there are also other differences. These include the lengthening of the horizontal stroke in the Gezer Calendar, the lengthening of the vertical stroke in the Bir-Hadad stela, the thickening of the main stroke in the Lachish ostraca, and the thickening and curving of the main stroke in the Qumran fragments.

As far as texts in the Hebrew language are concerned, the script we have been discussing is commonly called Phoenician Hebrew, Paleo-Hebrew, or Old Hebrew. The conclusion at this point may be stated simply. In Old Hebrew script the letter taw was written as a cross mark. This stood erect like what we ordinarily mean by a "cross," or it tilted sideways like an X, or it was formed with intermediate variations, but it was still essentially a cross mark. The examples we have noted of the use of this mark extend from the inscriptions at Serabit el-Khadem in the fifteenth century B.C. to the fragments at Qumran dating in the second and first centuries B.C. In fact Jerome (*In Hiezechielem* III 9, 4 CCSL LXXV 106) states that the ancient Hebrew letters, including the taw which was similar to a cross, were still in use in his day among the Samaritans.

In the pen-and-ink texts of the ostraca from Lachish and the fragments cited from Qumran there is a decided tendency to curve the main stroke of the character, and in other manuscripts written on parchment or papyrus there was developing, meanwhile, a cursive script which was considerably modified from the lapidary script of the old stone inscriptions. This development may be seen in the Aramaic papyri of the fifth century from Elephantine, in the Nash Papyrus, a Hebrew document of c. 165-37 B.C., and in the majority of the Dead Sea Scrolls. The final result is the so-called square character which is still considered the standard script in Hebrew. Here the taw is less and less obviously a cross mark and is ultimately transformed into the character as we know it today (ת).

Frank M. Cross, Jr., "Epigraphic Notes on Hebrew Documents of the Eighth-Sixth Centuries B.C.," in BASOR 163 (Oct. 1961), 12-14; 165 (Feb. 1962), 34-46; 168 (Dec. 1962), 18-23; and "The Development of the Jewish Scripts," in *The Bible and the Ancient Near East, Essays in honor of William Foxwell Albright*, ed. by G. Ernest Wright (Garden City: Doubleday, 1961, Anchor Books edition, 1965), 170-264.

THE HEBREW TAW AND ITS EQUIVALENTS

IN HEBREW, then, the word *taw* both signified a "mark" and was also the name of the last letter of the alphabet, a letter which, in the Old Hebrew script, was still written in the elemental form of a cross down at least to the eve of the NT period, or even into that period. In the further evolution of the alphabet the Semitic taw became the tau (ταῦ) of the Greek alphabet and the t of the Latin. The Greek letter chi (χῖ) was also recognized as an equivalent of the taw. This was the more readily possible because, on the one hand, in early Greek the chi was often written as an erect cross mark, and because, on the other hand, the taw itself was often written in the sideways position, so that it was already like the later more usual form of the chi (χ) and like the Latin x. However, since the Taw was the last letter of the Hebrew alphabet, it was sometimes considered that the last letter of the Greek alphabet, the omega (ὦ μέγα), was also its equivalent. Examples of all of these equivalences will appear in what follows.

Leonard Whibley, *A Companion to Greek Studies*, 3d. ed. (Cambridge: University Press, 1916), p. 690, Epigraphy: Table of Phoenician and early Greek local alphabets.

THE SIGN OF PROTECTION AND DELIVERANCE

IN THE OT the word *taw* is used in three passages in all of which it can very well mean "mark" not only in a general sense, but also in the specific sense of the cross mark which was also the alphabetic character. In 1 S 21:14, when David was much afraid of Achish the king of Gath, he feigned madness and, using the word *taw* in a verbal form, the text says that David "made marks on the doors of the gate" (RSV) (reference by Rabbi Ivan Caine and Richard Hirsh, both of the Reconstructionist Rabbinical College, Philadelphia, in BAR 6.2 [Mar/Apr 1980], p. 51). Here the marks were most probably of the same form and of the same apotropaic significance as the cross marks on the painted pebbles at Tell Abu Matar long before (No. 304), i.e., they were intended to ward off danger and provide protection.

In Jb 31:35, where Job makes a passionate plea for a hearing before the Almighty, he says, "Here is my signature!" (RSV), and the Hebrew is literally, "Here is my *taw*!" (i.e., "Here is my mark!"). Thus Job probably made his mark, at least figuratively, in the form of a cross mark, erect or like an x, just as a person may make an x as a legal signature today.

In Ezk 9:4-6 the word occurs again. In 9:4 the man clothed in linen is instructed to go through the city of Jerusalem and put a mark (*taw*) upon the foreheads of the men who sigh and groan over the abominations that are committed in the city. In 9:5-6 we learn that destroyers are to come and pass through the city after the angel and smite and slay old men and young men and maidens, and little children and women, but those who are to come on this grim mission are also strictly told to "touch no one upon whom is the mark." Here again the mark is of protective significance and can still be reminiscent of the cross marks on the painted pebbles from Tell Abu Matar and the marks made by David on the doors of the gate. Now, however, what is envisioned is nothing less than a time of ultimate judgment commanded by the Lord. In that time destruction will fall upon all those guilty of abominations in the land. Only those who lament the sins of the city, and thus manifest their faithfulness to the Lord, will be spared, and it is the mark bestowed by the man clothed in linen which will signify who they are when the decisive time comes. As for the mark being on the forehead, this was often a preferred place for ritual marks as the history of religions abundantly shows. And as to the form of the mark in this case, it is probable that it was nothing other than the cross mark which was also the alphabetic character, taw, and this will be substantiated by the evidence which follows in the next two paragraphs.

In the Cairo Document of the Damascus Covenanters (CD), known more briefly as the Damascus Document or also as the Zadokite Document, a work which doubtless represents in general the same movement as that of the Qumran community, there is a significant reference to the passage in Ezekiel. At this point in the text there is an introductory reference to the prophecy of Zechariah about the smiting of the shepherd and the scattering of the sheep (Zec 13:7), and then the passage in which we are interested continues, including an allusion to Zec 11:11 and an explicit quotation of Ezk 9:4, as follows (Manuscript B, VII [XIX] 9-12 Rabin 30): "And 'they that give heed unto Him' are 'the poor of the flock.' These shall escape in the time of the visitation, but they that hesitate shall be given over to the sword when the Messiah of Aaron and Israel shall come. As it happened in the epoch of the visitation of the forefathers, which He said by the hand of Ezekiel: 'to set the mark upon the foreheads of such as sigh and groan.' "

The argument of this passage is extremely interesting. As other statements in the Damascus Document (VII 9; VIII 2-3 Rabin 28, 32) make plain, the time of visitation is the Last Judgment. When that time comes and the Messiah appears, the circumstances of the destruction of Jerusalem as described by Ezekiel will be repeated, i.e., only those marked with the taw on their foreheads will be saved. While the statement may be only figurative, it is at least possible that the taw mark was literally put upon the foreheads of the members of this community,

perhaps at the time of their initiatory baptism, as a sign to guarantee their salvation in the final Judgment. It may also be noticed that in the Masoretic text of Ezk 9:4 we have the simple word תו, taw, "a mark," but in the quotation here in the Damascus Document we have the same word written with the definite article, התיו, "the taw." Therefore, as we have already surmised, the form of the mark in Ezk 9:4 was almost certainly that of the cross mark which was the alphabetic character, taw.

This understanding of the taw in Ezk 9:4 as the alphabetic character in the form of the cross mark is also represented by some of the Greek translations of the passage. The LXX indeed simply translates the Hebrew taw here with σημεῖον, meaning "mark" or "sign," but Origen (Selecta in Ezechielem 9 MPG XIII 800) states that Aquila and Theodotion translated the passage to read that the mark of the tau (τοῦ Θαῦ) was to be put upon the foreheads of the faithful, and the use of the name with the definite article surely points to the alphabetic character we are discussing. Tertullian (Against Marcion III 22 ANF III 340) also was familiar with a similar form of the text, for he quotes it thus: "Go through the gate, through the midst of Jerusalem, and set the mark Tau upon the foreheads of the men." In all probability, then, in its original meaning, and certainly in the understanding of these Greek translations and of the Damascus Document, Ezk 9:4 refers to a mark (taw) which is nothing other than the alphabetic character, taw, a mark in the form of a cross, standing for protection, deliverance, and salvation.

The influence of the passage in Ezekiel may also be noted in the Psalms of Solomon, a work of the middle of the first century B.C., now found in Greek and Syriac but doubtless originally written in Hebrew. In this work in 15:8, 10 it is said that "the mark of God is upon the righteous that they may be saved," but concerning the sinners it is declared that "the mark of destruction is upon their forehead." The allusion to Ezk 9:4-6 is unmistakable, but now the sinners are marked for destruction and the righteous for salvation. For "mark" the Greek has in both statements the word σημεῖον. For the righteous the mark is undoubtedly the taw, meaning deliverance; for the sinners it may even be the same mark, but if so it is certainly with the opposite connotation of destruction. In explicit connection with Ezk 9:4 the Talmud (Shabbath 55a SBT II 1, 253-254) also tells of two taws, and distinguishes between them as "a taw of ink upon the foreheads of the righteous," and "a taw of blood upon the foreheads of the wicked." In the same context Rab (third century) is quoted in the explanation: "Taw [stands for] תהיה [thou shalt live], taw [stands for] תמות [thou shalt die]."

It may also be mentioned here that in the discussion of Ezekiel to which we have referred above, Origen (Se-

lecta in Ezechielem 9 MPG XIII 800-801) tells how he asked among the Jews about the teachings which had been handed down on the subject of the taw. The answers which he received are included in the following passage, which may be quoted in its entirety because some of the opinions stated are relevant to the further course of our investigation.

> Upon inquiring of the Jews whether they can relate any traditional teaching regarding the Taw (τοῦ Θαῦ), I heard the following. One of them said that in the order of the Hebrew letters the Taw is the last of the twenty-two consonantal sounds. The last consonant is therefore taken as proof of the perfection of those who, because of their virtue, moan and groan over the sinners among the people and suffer together with the transgressors. Another said that the Taw symbolizes the observers of the Law. Since the Law, which is called Tora by the Jews, begins [its name] with the consonant Taw, it is a symbol of those who live according to the Law. A third [Jew], one of those who believe in Christ, said the form of the Taw in the old [Hebrew], script resembles the cross (τοῦ σταυροῦ), and it predicts the mark which is to be placed on the foreheads of the Christians.

Saul Liebermann, *Greek in Jewish Palestine* (New York: The Jewish Theological Seminary of America, 1942), 185-191; Erich Dinkler, "Zur Geschichte des Kreuzsymbols," in ZTK 48 (1951), pp. 148-272 (trans. "Comments on the History of the Symbol of the Cross," in JTC 1 [1965], pp. 124-146); and Dinkler, "Kreuzzeichen und Kreuz," in JAC 5 (1962), pp. 93-112.

THE PHYLACTERIES AND THE SIGN OF THE NAME OF GOD

IT HAS BEEN NOTED thus far that the wearing of a ritual sign on the forehead is a custom widely attested in the history of religions, and that in the particular case in Ezk 9:4 the taw on the foreheads of the faithful signified that they belonged to the Lord and were under his protection for salvation. We have even thought that the literal placing of such a mark upon the forehead could possibly have been a practice of the people of the Qumran community and its related groups. Another adaptation of the basic idea of a ritual sign on the forehead is to be seen in the wearing of phylacteries, as they are called in Mt 23:5. With respect to the feast of unleavened bread Ex 13:9 and 16 state that "it shall be to you as a sign on your hand and as a memorial between your eyes"; and with respect to the commandments of the Lord Dt 6:8 and 11:18 say, "you shall bind them as a sign upon your hand, and they shall be as frontlets between your eyes." Whether these statements were meant in the first instance figuratively or literally, they became the basis of a

literal practice. A small box containing portions of Scripture was tied upon the forehead. and another such upon the hand or arm. Such a box was called a תפלה, *tefillah*, "a prayer," in Hebrew and a φυλακτήριον, phylactery, "a safeguard," in Greek. In the Talmud there are numerous references to the *tefillin*, with a particularly extended description in *Menahoth* 34a-37b (SBT V 2, 215-232). The hand *tefillah* was worn on the left hand and more exactly on the left forearm or, according to one authority, on the biceps muscle; for the head *tefillah* the Scriptural place "between your eyes" was interpreted to mean not between the eyebrows but upon the brow of the head (*Menahoth* 37a-37b SBT V 2, 228-230). To wear the head phylactery too low down, or the other one on the palm of the hand, was in the manner of heresy (*Megillah* 24b SBT II 8, 148). The *tefillah* worn on the forehead has the letter shin (שׁ) on each side, while the strap holding it is tied in a knot in the shape of the letter daleth (ד). Also the *tefillah* worn on the arm is tied on with a knot in the shape of the letter yodh (י). Together these letters form the divine name שדי, Shaddai (*Menahoth* 35b V 2, 222 note 3), a word which was often rendered παντοκράτωρ in the LXX (e.g., Jb 5:17, etc.) and hence is now usually translated "Almighty." So the faithful Jew wore the divine name upon his forehead in the form of an abbreviation consisting of the first letter (shin) of that name or, if the knot be counted as making a daleth, an abbreviation consisting of the first two letters of the name, while the knot on the arm could be considered as completing the spelling of the name.

Since the shin on the box on the forehead stood for the name of the Almighty and signified that the bearer belonged to him, we wonder if the taw which signified that its bearer was faithful to the Lord and under his protection, as we have already established, did not itself also stand for the very name of the Lord. In the quotation from Origen given above, it was stated that one opinion in Jewish tradition was that the taw, as the twenty-second and last letter of the Hebrew alphabet, stood for perfection. As the last letter of the alphabet it could also be connected with the statement of the Lord in Is 44:6 and 48:12, "I am the first and I am the last." This statement might indeed suggest that both aleph, the first character, and taw, the last, could stand together for the name of the Lord. Indeed in the Midrash *Rabbah* on Genesis (81, 2 SMR II 747) it is stated, with explicit citation of Is 44:6, that the seal of God consists of the three letters, aleph, mem, and taw. the first. the middle, and the last of the alphabet, which together form the word אמת, *'emeth*, meaning "truth." Of these letters special importance attaches to the last and final one, and the Talmud (*Shabbath* 55a SBT II 1, 254) says with respect to the same seal of God, *"Taw* is the end of the seal of the Holy One." Taken together, the Hebrew aleph and taw correspond

345

to the Greek alpha and omega, and in the collocation of the two characters we probably have the Hebrew expression upon which is based the statement of God in Rev 1:8 and 21:6, and of Christ in Rev 22:13, "I am the Alpha and the Omega." Furthermore in the Book of Revelation, even as in the Psalms of Solomon (15:8, 10) cited above, both the righteous and the sinners are marked. The followers of the beast are marked on the right hand or the forehead (Rev 13:16) or, more probably, on both (Rev 20:4). The position of these marks reflects the Jewish phylacteries, which we have described above, but the manner of the followers of the beast is a travesty of the Jewish custom, for here the one mark is on the right hand, not the left, and the other mark is on (ἐπί) the brow, not over the brow. The one hundred and forty-four thousand servants of God are sealed on their foreheads (Rev 7:3; 9:4; 14:1), and this plainly reflects Ezk 9:4. In Ezk 9:4 the mark on the foreheads of the faithful showed that they belonged to the Lord. Here what presumably was the very same mark is plainly stated in Rev 14:1 and 22:4 to represent the name of God. Therefore it is a reasonable conclusion that already in Jewish thought, as well as certainly here in Christian application, the taw stood for the name of God as well as marking the one upon whom it was placed, literally or figuratively, for protection and salvation.

THE SIGN OF
THE ANOINTED ONE

THE *TAW*-SIGN STOOD for deliverance and for the name of God. Since, however, the name of God stood for the manifestation of God in the world (see, e.g., Dt 12:11, where his name is made to dwell in the temple), it was easy for the early Christians to think of the divine name as manifest in Jesus Christ (see, e.g., Jn 17:6, where Christ has manifested the name of the Father). That this mode of thought was prevalent already in Jewish Christian circles, and that the Name was there a designation of Christ, is made most probable by Jas 2:7, where "the honorable name which was called upon you" (ASV margin; cf. Ac 15:17) is probably the name of Christ, or includes the name of Christ; and by the *Gospel of Truth* (cf. No. 338), a Gnostic work of the second century with strong elements of Jewish Christian theology, which says flatly, "But the Name of the Father is the Son" (ed. Malinine, Puech, and Quispel, *Evangelium Veritatis*, folio XIX *verso*, p. 38, lines 6-7; cf. Daniélou, *The Theology of Jewish Christianity*, pp. 147-163; *Primitive Christian Symbols*, pp. 141-142). Therefore the *taw*-sign,

which stood for the name of God in Jewish thought, probably also stood for the name of Christ in Jewish Christian thought. In fact in Rev. 22:4, where it is said that "his name shall be on their foreheads," it may be noted that the reference in the immediately preceding verse was not only to God but also to the Lamb.

Where the Greek language was known it was almost inevitable, for another reason, that the taw would come to stand for the name of Christ. Particularly when it was written in its sideways position, the taw was immediately identifiable with the Greek chi, and chi is the first letter of the Greek word χριστός, *Christos*, Christ. This word is, of course, the usual translation in the LXX and elsewhere of the Hebrew word "anointed," or Messiah, and it is of interest to find that in connection with the "anointed one" there was also a characteristic application of a mark to the forehead. In the OT both the king (I Sam 10:1) and the high priest were anointed in consecration to office. The pattern for the anointing of the high priest was set when Moses anointed Aaron, as is recorded in Lev 8:12, "And he poured some of the anointing oil on Aaron's head, and anointed him, to consecrate him." In the Talmud (*Horayoth* 12a SBT IV 7, 86; cf. *Kerithoth* 5b SBT V 6, 36) this passage is taken to imply two acts corresponding to the two words "poured" and "anointed." In practice the pouring evidently consisted of pouring oil upon the head, and the anointing was the application of some oil on the forehead and specifically between the eyelids. The discussion here turns upon which should be done first and is not of consequence to us, but in the same connection there is a very interesting statement as to the shape in which the oil was traced upon the forehead in the anointing. "Our Rabbis taught: How were the kings anointed?—In the shape of a wreath. And the priests?—In the shape of a Chi. What is meant by 'the shape of a Chi'? R. Menashya b. Gadda replied: In the shape of a Greek χ."

The oil mark on the forehead of the anointed priest must, therefore, have been the old letter taw, probably written with the sideways orientation which made it immediately identifiable with the Greek chi, and so the initial letter of Greek *Christos*, "anointed."

307. Column XXXV of the Isaiah Scroll from Cave 1 at Qumran

ANOTHER EXAMPLE of the use of the taw mark with reference to the "anointed," the Messiah, is possibly to be recognized in the Qumran literature. In the Isaiah Scroll from Cave 1 (1QIsᵃ) there is a whole series of signs marked in the margins of the manuscript. One of these is a cross mark which can be the taw, written sideways

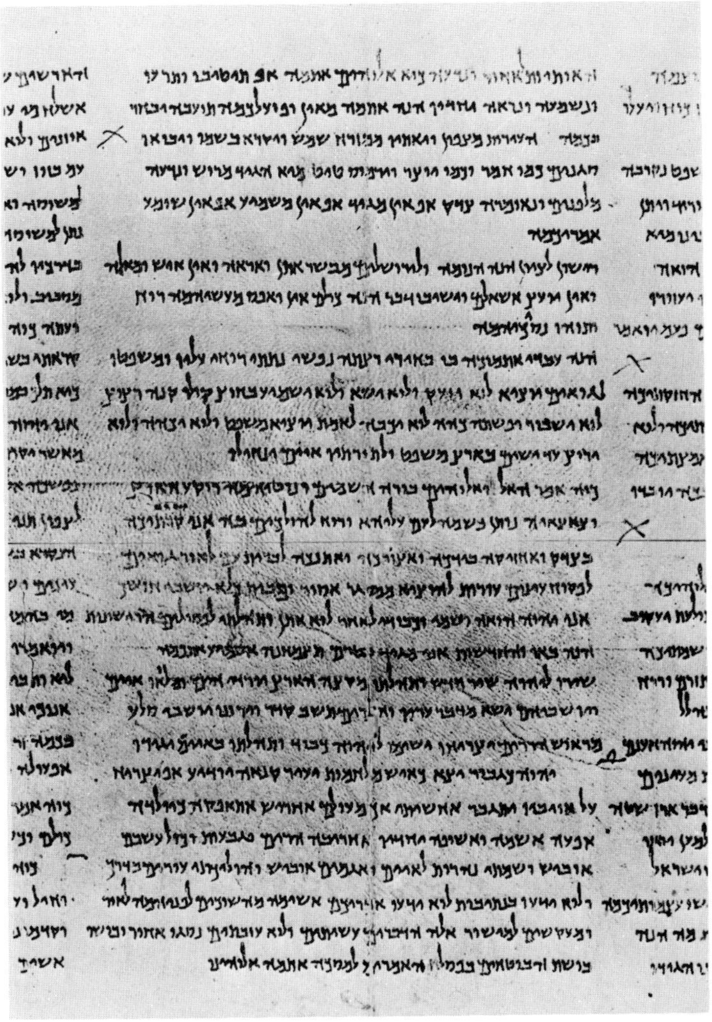

307. Column xxxv of the Isaiah Scroll from Cave 1 at Qumran

like a chi, and it appears eleven times, namely, in columns xxviœ xxxv twice, xxxvi, xxxviii, xli, xlv, xlvi twice, xlviii, and liii. In each case it looks as if it were intended to mark the passage to its left, with the exception of the example on column xlv where the placement of the mark may more probably relate it to the text on its right. If this is correct, the passages to which attention is called by the cross marks are Is 32: 1ff.; 42:1ff. and 42:5ff.; 42:19ff.; 44:28; 49:5-7; 55:3-4; 56:1-2 and 56:3ff.; 58:13ff.; 66:5ff. In general these may be recognized as passages having to do in one way or another with messianic expectation, an expectation which we know otherwise was a subject of much interest in the Qumran community. In column xxvi the mark stands to the left of a seam in the parchment and there seems no question but that it must refer to the passage at its left. This passage is the beginning of chapter 32 in the Book of Isaiah, "Behold, a king will reign in righteousness. . . ." In column xxxv, illustrated here, the mark is seen twice in the right-hand margin. The text to the left of the first mark

is the beginning of chapter 42, "Behold, my servant, whom I uphold . . ."; the text to the left of the second mark is 42:5ff., where the Lord is continuing to address his "servant." The same mark in the left-hand margin near the top of the column doubtless refers to the passage at its left, in column xxxvi, and here in the first three lines, in 42:19ff., the Lord is also speaking about the "servant." It may also be noted that in the lower part of the right-hand margin there is another sign, this one consisting essentially of a loop which is on top of a straight line and which tends to extend in a single stroke below that line. In fact if the vertical stroke extended farther downward we would have something very much like the ankh sign of ancient Egypt which became a form of the cross among the Coptic Christians, as we will illustrate below (Nos. 339ff.). In this case the sign may appear to be more closely related to the text at its right, in column xxxiv, which consists of Is 41:17ff., an eschatological passage about the transformation of nature in the end time.

347

With these signs in the Isaiah Scroll we may compare a list of signs given by Epiphanius in *On Weights and Measures*, a work written in A.D. 392, the first part of which is extant in late Greek manuscripts, and the whole in Syriac translation in two manuscripts of the seventh and ninth centuries. Near the beginning of this work Epiphanius lists a number of signs which are employed, he says, in the prophetic writings. One of these signs appears in the Greek manuscripts (MPG 43, 237) as an upright, symmetrical cross mark, and in the Syriac manuscripts (ed. Dean, 15) as a cross mark written in the sideways position, in other words it is precisely the taw in the two positions with which we are familiar. This sign, Epiphanius says, is for the Messiah or the Christ, i.e., it is used to mark passages of messianic import. It is precisely this sign, in form like a chi, which marks messianic passages in the Isaiah Scroll of the Qumran community. Therefore the later custom of Christian scribes, attested by Epiphanius, may have had its antecedent in the markings used by Jewish scribes, as illustrated here in the Jewish sectarian community. In this Jewish and later Christian tradition of markings, the taw = chi was a mark for passages which had to do with the Messiah. The continuity of tradition in the signs in the Isaiah Scroll and in Epiphanius appears to be confirmed also in the case of the other sign we have noticed in the Isaiah manuscript, namely, the one which bears some resemblance to the ankh. In the Isaiah manuscript this sign appears in columns XXVIII, XXXII, XXXIV, XXXVIII, XLIII, and XLIX, and seems to refer to Is 36:1ff.; 40:1ff.; 41:17ff.; 45:1ff.; 52:7ff.; 60:1ff. Like the example we see here in column XXXIV, which refers to Is 41:17ff., all of these passages may be considered eschatological. Turning again to Epiphanius, we find that the last of the several signs he lists was one probably very similar to this ankh-like one. In the Greek manuscripts, indeed, it is not recognizable as such, but the sign that is reproduced in these manuscripts at this point is virtually the same as another sign which occurs earlier in the list, therefore is probably not correctly reproduced at all. In the Syriac manuscripts, however, we find at this point a sign which, except that the loop is formed in a rectangular manner, is probably the same as the one we see in the Isaiah manuscript. As to the significance of this sign, the text of Epiphanius says in both the Greek and the Syriac that it is for the foretelling of future events . This is precisely the nature of the passages marked by this sign in the Isaiah Scroll. Almost all are obviously eschatological in character, and even the first one which appears to be purely historical may be supposed to have had some eschatological interpretation. The congruity of what Epiphanius says with the evidence in the Isaiah Scroll, therefore, justifies us in taking the Christian signs as a heritage from Jewish

scribes, and in recognizing the cross marks in the Isaiah manuscript as the taw = chi alphabetic character which was used to single out passages of messianic import, just as the other sign, possibly related to the ankh-cross, marked those of eschatological character.

John C. Trever, "Preliminary Observations on the Jerusalem Scrolls," in BASOR 111 (Oct. 1948), 8f., cf. 12, 14; Millar Burrows, *The Dead Sea Scrolls of St. Mark's Monastery*, I, *The Isaiah Manuscript and the Habakkuk Commentary* (New Haven: The American Schools of Oriental Research, 1950); J. L. Teicher, "Material Evidence of the Christian Origin of the Dead Sea Scrolls," in JJS 3 (1952), 128-130; Isaiah Sonne, "The X-Sign in the Isaiah Scroll," in VT 4 (1954), 90-94; J. L. Teicher, "The Christian Interpretation of the Sign X in the Isaiah Scroll," in VT 5 (1955), 189-198; Jack Finegan, "Crosses in the Dead Sea Scrolls," in BAR 5.6 (Nov/Dec 1979), pp. 41-49 (criticisms in BAR 6.2 [Mar/Apr 1980], pp. 50-52). Photograph: Burrows, *The Dead Sea Scrolls of St. Mark's Monastery*, I, pl. XXXV, courtesy American Schools of Oriental Research.

The evidence cited above shows that the cross mark which was called *taw*, and the alphabetic character which consisted of that mark and was named the taw, already stood in Jewish thought for protection, deliverance and eschatological salvation, and probably also for the name of God and for the Messiah. The sign was written either + or ×, and the one who, literally or figuratively, bore this sign was distinguished as belonging to the Lord and was marked for deliverance at the end time.

THE CROSS MARK IN JEWISH CHRISTIANITY

IT COULD HAVE BEEN from this background that the cross mark passed into use in early Christianity. We must speak first of Jewish Christianity, including the eschatological community in Palestine prior to A.D. 70 and the Jewish Christianity known in Syria and elsewhere after that date. Writers and written sources in which Christianity is expressed in the thought forms of later Judaism, which are therefore witnesses to the Jewish Christianity of which we speak, include the following. The Shepherd of Hermas was probably written at Rome between A.D. 90 and 140 and shows strong influence of Jewish apocalyptic. Ignatius, bishop of Antioch, died in Rome under Trajan about A.D. 110; although his name is Latin, as was common enough, his style is very Semitic and his thought is an expression of Syrian Christianity. The Letter of Barnabas was written between A.D. 70 and 132, perhaps about 120, and perhaps in Egypt; it employs ty-pological and allegorical exegesis of Scripture. The Odes of Solomon were probably written in Greek in Syria about the middle of the second century and are extant in Syriac. The Acts of John may have been written in Syria or Asia Minor, perhaps in the latter part of the second century. The Acts of Thomas were probably written in Syria in the early part of the third century. The Sibylline Oracles are of various dates, some are Jewish, some Jew-ish Christian. All of these sources will be cited in what follows.

In the quotation given above from Origen (*Selecta in Ezechielem* 9 MPG XIII 801) we saw that one of the Jews who was a believer in Christ, i.e., a Jewish Christian, told Origen that the taw in the Old Hebrew script pre-dicted the mark which was to be placed on the foreheads of the Christians. Therefore the conception existed in Jewish Christianity of a cross mark, either literal or figu-rative, on the forehead, and this mark no doubt signi-fied, as the antecedent history of the sign suggests, that the person so marked belonged to the Lord and was marked for salvation. Since that mark in its earlier his-tory may have already stood for the name of the Lord or the Messiah, it may stand here also for the name of God or Christ. There is probably a direct reference to this mark, therefore, in the Shepherd of Hermas IX 13, 2 in the phrase, "bear the name," and in the Odes of Solo-mon 8:15 (Harris and Mingana II 254) in the statement, "And on their faces I set my seal." In both cases the thought of baptism is almost certainly implied. In the Shepherd of Hermas VIII 6, 3 Christian believers are ones who have received the seal, and in IX 16, 3ff. the seal is received in baptism. In the Acts of Thomas 120-121 (AAA II 2, 229-231; Klijn 129-130) Mygdonia requests, "Give me the sign of Jesus the Messiah" Δός μοι τὴν σφραγῖδα Ἰησοῦ Χριστοῦ), and the apostle proceeds to put oil on her head and to baptize her; and in another passage (157 AAA II 2, 266-267; Klijn 149) the anointing and baptism of a group are described: "And after he had anointed them, he made them go down into the water in the name of the Father and the Son and the Spirit of holiness" (cf. also chaps. 25, 27, 49, 132). In Greek the sign or seal is a σφραγίς, and this word means first of all an actual seal with which to mark anything. Therefore the above references probably mean that at baptism the candidate was actually marked with a sign on the fore-head which stood for the name of God or of Christ. Since this was done in a ceremony of anointing it was done with oil. Since it was done in connection with bap-tism, the word *sphragis* or "seal" became a term for bap-tism itself. Since this custom of the seal or the mark was widespread in Jewish Christianity in the time of the doc-uments cited, and since there was a comparable refer-

ence at Qumran, either figurative or literal, to the taw on the forehead, it seems very possible that in the inter-vening time and place, i.e., in the Jewish Christianity of Palestine prior to A.D. 70, a mark was used which stood for the name of God or Christ and conveyed the assur-ance of salvation, and that this mark was the taw.

The conception just observed in Jewish Christian writings is found also among the Valentinian Gnostics, and it is evident that Gnosticism preserved many ele-ments from Jewish Christianity. In the Excerpts which Clement of Alexandria gives from the Valentinian teacher, Theodotus, there is a discussion of baptism (77-86 GCS Clemens Alexandrinus III 131-133; Casey 86-91). Here too it is spoken of in connection with being "sealed (σφραγισθεῖς) by Father, Son and Holy Spirit" (80, 3). Then (86, 1-2) the saying of Jesus about the coin with Caesar's superscription (ἐπιγραφή) is recalled, and it is said: "So likewise the faithful; he has the name of God through Christ as a superscription. . . . And dumb animals show by a seal (διὰ σφραγῖδος) whose property each is, and are claimed from the seal. Thus also the faithful soul receives the seal of truth and bears about 'the marks (στίγματα) of Christ.' " Like the mark of ownership on an animal, the believer has a mark which shows whose property he is. Literally or figuratively he is marked with the name of God through Christ and, in-sofar as this mark is visualized or made actual, it must still be the taw of the early Jewish Christians. (Could this reference and allusion possibly be the "seal" which Jesus had in mind in John 6:27; cf. 3:33, "him hath God the Father sealed"? asks Professor Vardaman.)

In the foregoing quotations we have met not only the noun σφραγίς, meaning "seal," but also the verb σφραγ-ίζω, meaning "mark with a seal." In other passages, too, we find the same verb but without the connection with baptism which was characteristic of the preceding quo-tations. In the Acts of John 115 the action of the apostle immediately prior to his death is described in these words: "And having sealed himself wholly (σφραγισά-μενος ἑαυτὸν ὅλον), he stood and said: 'Thou art with me, O Lord Jesus Christ.' " Here the verb must mean that John marked the seal upon himself and indeed upon every part of his body, either literally or more probably figuratively in the sense of a gesture which traced the pattern of the seal. In other words "to seal" meant to make the sign that constituted the seal and, in accor-dance with what has been set forth hitherto, it meant to make a sign corresponding to a cross mark, i.e., to the taw. That such action was well known from the days of the earliest Jewish Christian church is, in fact, affirmed by Basil of Caesarea; he says in his work *On the Spirit* (27 NPNFSS VIII 41) (A.D. 375) that "to sign with the sign of the cross those who have trusted in the name of our Lord

349

Jesus Christ" is one of the practices in the Church which derive from unwritten tradition going back to the apostles.

THE CROSS AS REPRESENTATION OF THE STAUROS

IN THE FOREGOING we have evidence of the use of the cross mark as a "seal" in baptism and as a gesture of faith in Jewish Christianity, and of its probable employment in the primitive community in Palestine. The mark is still essentially the taw of the Semitic alphabet and of the passage in Ezk 9:4. It stands for the divine name and the eschatological salvation. In the quotation from Origen (*Selecta in Ezechielem* 9 MPG III 801) cited above (p. 786), however, his Jewish Christian informant told him not only that the Old Hebrew taw predicted the mark which would be placed on the foreheads of the Christians, but also that it resembled the cross (σταυρός). The *stauros* was an instrument of execution in the form of an upright stake often with a crosspiece at or near the top (Artemidorus, *Onirocriticon* II 53 Pack 183), and was the instrument of the death of Jesus (Mt 27:32, etc.). The statement of Origen's informant that the taw resembled the *stauros* is obviously correct, and the fact that this resemblance was noted in Jewish Christian thought is confirmed by allusions in various Jewish Christian writings. In the Jewish Christian Sibylline Oracles VIII 217-250 (Geffcken 153-157), for example, there is an elaboration of the famous early Christian acrostic, Ἰησοῦς Χριστὸς Θεοῦ Υἱὸς Σωτήρ, "Jesus Christ, God's Son, Savior," the initial letters of which words in Greek spell ἰχθύς, "fish." Here in the Oracles the word Σταυρός, "cross," is added to the formula, and then the letters in this entire sequence of words (the second word being spelled Χρειστός) were made the initial letters of the thirty-four lines of an acrostic poem. The last seven lines, corresponding to the word *stauros* may be rendered roughly in English as follows:

> Sign (σῆμα) then for all mortals, distinguished seal (σφρηγίς),
> The wood (ξύλον) shall be for all believers, the desired horn (κέρας),
> And life of devout men, but occasion of stumbling of the world,
> Ultimate illumination (φωτίζον) for the elect in the waters by means of twelve springs,

Rod of iron, which will shepherd and rule.
Our God, now portrayed and written above (προγραφείς) in the acrostics (ἀκροστιχίοις), is this one,
Savior immortal, king, the one who suffers for our sake.

In the multifarious allusions of this passage we hear again of the *sphragis* (in a slightly variant Greek spelling) or "seal," and of baptism (called φωτίζον, "illumination," in accordance with a widespread usage, e.g., Justin *Apology* I 61, 14 ANF I 183), and together with these we hear of the "wood" or "tree" (ξύλον, cf. Dt 21:22, Ac 5:30, etc.) which is the cross in the sense of the *stauros*. The *stauros* is also referred to as a "horn" (κέρας). Here comparison may be made with Justin, *Dialogue with Trypho* 91, 2 (ANF I 245), who sees in "the horns of unicorns" in Dt 33:17 (KJV) a type of the *stauros*. In form the cross has horns; in significance it is a manifestation of power, as the "horn" was a symbol of power in the OT. Concerning the form of the cross Justin writes: "For the one beam is placed upright, from which the highest extremity is raised up into a horn, when the other beam is fitted on to it, and the ends appear on both sides as horns joined on to the one horn. And the part which is fixed in the center, on which are suspended those who are crucified, also stands out like a horn; and it also looks like a horn conjoined and fixed with the other horns."

Also in the word προγραφείς the writer may mean not only to refer to what he has "written above" (cf. Eph 3:3, προέγραψα, "I have written above") in the entire acrostic, but also to allude to Gal 3:1 which speaks of how Christ "was portrayed on the cross" (προεγράφη ἐσταυρωμένος). This passage in the Sibylline Oracles is quoted, it may be added, by Eusebius (*Oration of Constantine* 18 NPNFSS I 574f.) in full, and by Augustine (*City of God* XVIII 23 NPNF II 372f.) with the omission of the last part about the *stauros* but with explanation of the acrostic "fish," which is left intact with that omission.

The Letter of Barnabas is another example of a writing emanating from a Jewish Christian atmosphere in which there is a statement about the *stauros*. The letter was written in Greek, and now it is not the Semitic taw but the Greek tau which is spoken of as representing the cross. Here (IX 8) Scripture is quoted as saying, "And Abraham circumcised from his household eighteen men and three hundred," which is a brief statement of the information provided by Gen 14:14 and 17:26-27. The eighteen is then explained as comprised of the Greek letters iota (= ten) and eta (= eight), which are the two first letters of the name of Jesus. As for the three hundred, it is the numerical value of tau, and therewith the cross is symbolized. "So he indicates Jesus in the two letters and the cross (σταυρός) in the other."

THE CROSS IN THE HELLENISTIC CHURCH

WHEN CHRISTIANITY MOVED into the area of Greek and Latin thought and language there was no doubt a certain shift in emphasis. The meaning of the Semitic *taw* and therewith the original understanding of Ezk 9:4 would naturally tend to fade out. Yet the idea of a ritual mark on the forehead, an idea so ancient and widespread in the history of religions, was of course known in the Gentile world too. Tertullian (*On Prescription against Heretics* 40 ANF III 262), for example, speaks of how in the kingdom of Satan, as he calls it, "Mithra . . . sets his marks on the foreheads of his soldiers." Here the concept may not be that of sealing eschatologically, as in Ezk 9:4, but the mark no doubt signifies belonging to the deity and being herewith under his protection. Tertullian himself, as we have already seen (p. 344), quotes Ezk 9:4, where "the mark Tau" was to be set upon the foreheads of the men of Jerusalem, and in respect to this quotation he continues immediately (*Against Marcion* III 22 ANF III 340f.): "Now the Greek letter Tau and our own letter T is the very form of the cross, which he predicted would be the sign on our foreheads in the true catholic Jerusalem." So the mark is still on the foreheads of Christians, literally or figuratively, but here in the Greco-Roman world it is not the Semitic taw but the Greek tau or the Latin t, and it has especially to do with the cross, i.e., the instrument on which Jesus died. In fact, this mark, which Tertullian elsewhere calls simply "the sign," was evidently traced upon the forehead, at least in a gesture, by the Gentile Christians upon every possible occasion. "At every forward step and movement," writes Tertullian (*The Chaplet* 3 ANF III 94f.), "at every going in and out, when we put on our clothes and shoes, when we bathe, when we sit at table, when we light the lamps, on couch, on seat, in all the ordinary actions of daily life, we trace upon the forehead the sign." Likewise Cyril says in his *Catecthetical Lectures* delivered in Jerusalem in A.D. 348 (XIII 36 NPNFSS VII 92): "Let us not then be ashamed to confess the Crucified. Be the Cross our seal made with boldness by our fingers on our brow, and on everything: over the bread we eat, and the cups we drink; in our comings in, and goings out; before our sleep, when we lie down and when we rise up; when we are in the way, and when we are still. Great is that phylactery (μέγα τὸ φυλακτήριον). . . . It is the sign of the faithful, and the dread of devils."

Like the Jewish Christians the Gentile Christians also found many types of the cross in the OT Scriptures, e.g.,

as Justin (*Dialogue with Trypho* 112 ANF I 255) and Tertullian (*An Answer to the Jews* 10 ANF III 165f.) tell us, in the outstretched hands of Moses (Ex 17:12), and in the brazen serpent on a standard (Num 21:9). They also recognized the cross in many objects in the world about them and Tertullian (ibid.) refers in this respect, for example, to the mast and the yard of a ship. Minucius Felix (A.D. 166) writes this (*The Octavius* 29 ANV IV 191): "We assuredly see the sign of a cross, naturally, in the ship when it is carried along with swelling sails, when it glides forward with expanded oars; and when the military yoke is lifted up, it is the sign of a cross; and when a man adores God with a pure mind, with hands outstretched."

The final comparison given by Minucius Felix may be compared with the statement of St. Nilus, a famous ascetic in Sinai at the end of the fourth century (SWDCB IV, pp. 43f.), who also explains (MPG LXXIX, Epp. I 86, 87 cf. III 132) that standing at prayer with arms outstretched is a figure of the cross as well as a testimony to the resurrection. Since the cross was compared, then, with a ship's mast and yard and with a person with hands outstretched in prayer, it is plain that the form of the cross was recognized not only in the T but also where the vertical member extended above the crossarm.

In summary to this point, we have seen that the Semitic taw, written + or ×, was a sign of salvation in the OT and Judaism, and also in Jewish Christianity. In Jewish Christianity already and also particularly in Hellenistic Christianity the same sign was connected with the instrument on which Jesus died (the *stauros*) and in such connection was used still in the form of the taw, +, but also in the form of the equivalent tau, T, and likewise in the form †. The Semitic taw also stood for the name of the Lord and of the Messiah. Written either erect or sideways it was recognized that the Greek chi was its equivalent, and indeed the latter was itself written both erect like a symmetrical cross mark and also in the more familiar form ×. Chi was of course the initial letter of the Greek word which translated "Messiah," namely, Χριστός, *Christos*. Therefore it was natural that, particularly in the Hellenistic church, the cross mark, written as a chi, was taken as standing for the name of Christ. As an example which almost certainly means this, we have the case cited by Eusebius (*Martyrs of Palestine* VIII 7 NPNFSS I 349 Schwartz GCS II 2, 926) of the martyr Valentina. When she was dragged into the midst of the court before the judge, she wrote on the honorable name of the Savior (καὶ τὸ σεβάσμον τοῦ σωτῆρος ἐπιγραψαμένη ὄνομα), which must mean that she inscribed the name on herself, probably on her forehead. Further, this must have been done by tracing a mark on herself, at least in a gesture, and this can hardly have been anything other than the cross mark understood as the letter chi and the initial letter and abbreviation of the name of Christ.

THE FORMS OF THE CROSS

THE FORMS of the cross mark considered in this survey of the literary evidence are, therefore: the equilateral cross, which is essentially the Semitic taw in upright position, which was still used widely in the Hellenistic church and is commonly known as the Greek cross; the tau cross (*crux commissa*), which corresponds in shape to the Greek letter tau and the Latin letter t, the letters which were the first equivalents in those languages of the Hebrew taw; the Latin cross (*crux immissa*), which is like a Greek cross but with the lower arm longer than the other three; and the cross which is like the taw written sideways, the Greek chi, and the Latin x or "ten," hence is known as the *crux decussata*. Originally this cross mark signified salvation and the divine name; even when the mark was connected with the instrument of the execution of Jesus it continued to express the saving power which works through his death.

Two other cross forms will also be encountered. One is the *crux gammata* or "gammadion," in which to each arm of an equilateral cross a further arm is attached at right angles, turning either to the left or to the right, until the whole can be described as like four Greek capital letters gamma joined at right angles. This is found widely in the history of religions, and is usually thought to have been originally a solar symbol or a sign of life or blessing. In India it is called *swastika* (from *su*, "well," and *asti*, "it is") when the outer arms are turned to the right, and *sauvastika* when they are turned to the left. The other form is the *crux ansata* or handled cross. This looks like a tau cross surmounted by a handle in the form of a loop. This is essentially the form of the Egyptian ankh, which may have been first of all a knotted amulet, and is found in the hieroglyphic writing as a sign meaning life and prosperity (cf. Nos. 339f.). Both of these forms, the *crux gammata* and the *crux ansata*, were adopted as forms of the Christian cross.

Goblet d'Alviella, "Cross," in HERE IV, pp. 324-329; John J. Collins, "The Archaeology of the Crucifixion," in CBQ 1 (1939), pp. 154-159; G. W. H. Lampe, *The Seal of the Spirit* (London: Longmans, Green and Co., 1951); Hugo Rahner, "Das mystische Tau," in ZKT 75 (1935), pp. 385-410; Maria Cramer, *Das altägyptische Lebenszeichen im christlichen koptischen Ägypten* (Wiesbaden: Otto Harrassowitz, 3d ed. 1955); Franz J. Dölger, "Beiträge zur Geschichte des Kreuzzeichens," in JAC 1 (1958), pp. 5-19; 2 (1959), pp. 15-29; 3 (1960), pp. 5-16; 4 (1961), pp. 5-17; 5 (1962), pp. 5-22; 6 (1963), pp. 7-34; Erich Dinkler, "Kreuzzeichen und Kreuz," in JAC 5 (1962), pp. 93-112; P. E. Testa, *Il*

simbolismo dei Giudeo-Cristiani (Jerusalem: Tipografia dei PP. Francescani, 1962); Jean Daniélou, *Primitive Christian Symbols* (Baltimore: Helicon Press, 1964), pp. 136-145; and Daniélou, *The Theology of Jewish Christianity* (London: Darton, Longman and Todd, 1964).

ABBREVIATIONS AND MONOGRAMS

IN THE WRITING of inscriptions and manuscripts, abbreviations were already employed in the last centuries before the Christian era, and increasingly in the Christian era (see Avi-Yonah, *Abbreviations*, for Greek abbreviations, and Cagnat pp. 399-473 for Latin abbreviations). A statistical tabulation of dated abbreviations by centuries shows the highest proportion of abbreviations to inscriptions in the second and third centuries of the Christian era and again in the sixth and seventh (Avi-Yonah, *Abbreviations*, p. 17). Abbreviation is usually accomplished by dropping some of the letters of a word so that one or more letters remain to stand for the whole word. Such abbreviations may then be indicated by adding a conventional mark, such as a horizontal line drawn over or through or under one or more of the letters, or by changing the position or shape of one or more of the letters. A special form of the last procedure consists in linking two or more letters so that a single compound character results. This is called a ligature or, as the representation of a name, a monogram.

With respect to the figure 318 in Gen 14:14, we have already noted (above p. 350) that the Letter of Barnabas (IX 8) says that the three hundred, which is expressed by the letter tau in Greek, discloses the cross, and says that in the ten and the eight, expressed by I and H, "you have Jesus (ἔχεις Ἰησοῦν)," i.e., you have the abbreviation of his name. Therefore this abbreviation, consisting of the first two letters of the name of Jesus in Greek, was familiar in the Jewish Christian circles represented by the Letter of Barnabas in the time in which it was written (probably between A.D. 70 and 132) and doubtless earlier too. If the iota and the eta, constituting this abbreviation, were written together, a simple monogram (HH) could result. At the same time this design could be considered to contain a plain equilateral cross standing erect between two vertical lines. This symbol may be seen in an inscription from Anatolia which is probably of pre-Constantinian date (W. M. Calder in ASR pp. 88-89 no. 10; see also Dölger I, p. 263).

The initial letters of the name Jesus and the title Christ, i.e., iota and chi, could also be written together. This would be essentially the combination of a cross mark and a vertical stroke and, in its simplest form, would look like a six-pointed star ($*$). This can be the abbreviation, in a ligature, of the name and title Jesus Christ. With the vertical line as the initial and abbreviation of the name of Jesus, the chi might also be considered as the mark of the cross. Examples are found in an inscription, probably of pre-Constantinian date, from Eumenia in Phrygia (Ramsay, *Phrygia*, pp. 526-527, no. 371), and in graffiti at the Vatican (see below, No. 329). In a passage preserved in two fifteenth-century manuscripts (Cod. 26 of Merton College and Har. 3049), Jerome mentions a monogram which appears to be composed of a cross and a Hebrew letter waw. Save that the vertical stroke is thus somewhat curved, the appearance of this symbol is much the same as that just mentioned. The waw, however, has the value of six in the Hebrew system of numerals. Since there are six letters in the Greek spelling of the name of Jesus ('Ιησοῦς), the waw can stand as a sign of that name. In that light this monogram expresses the idea of Jesus and the cross. It is also possible that the waw and the cross could be reminiscent of the brazen serpent on the standard in the wilderness in which Justin (*Dialogue with Trypho* 112 ANF I 255) saw a type of Jesus crucified (cf. p. 351).

That a numerical interpretation, such as that just suggested for the waw, is not far-fetched and could have been made even at an early period is shown by the numerical understanding set forth in the Letter of Barnabas (IX 8), as cited above (p. 352). Irenaeus (*Against Heresies* I 14-15) also mentions several numerical values which were connected with the name of Jesus Christ by the Marcosian Gnostics. Although this is a later reference than that in Barnabas, and the numerology is related to far-ranging Gnostic speculations, the Gnostics appear to have derived not a few elements of which they made use from Jewish Christianity, and it is possible that some of these other numerical observations come from that source too. Just as it was remarked in the preceding paragraph that the Hebrew waw ($=6$) could stand for the name of Jesus, so here in what Irenaeus reports it is observed that the name of Jesus consists of six letters and therefore the Greek character vau ($=6$) can stand for it. Like the other archaic characters, koppa ($=90$) and sampi ($=900$), which were used in the numerical system along with the twenty-four characters of the regular Greek alphabet, the vau was called an Episemon (τὸ ἐπίσημον, distinguishing mark or device [Herodotus I 195], from ἐπίσημος, having a mark, notable [cf. Rom 16:7]). So, Irenaeus tells us, in the usage of the Marcosian Gnostics, vau was the "Episemon number" and as such a sign for the name of Jesus. It is also observed here that the name Christ (evidently with the spelling Χρειστός) contains eight letters, and this would point to the possibility of its representation by the Greek letter eta, which has the numerical value of eight. Yet other observations

reported by Irenaeus in the same passage include the following: When Christ is called the alpha and the omega (cf. Rev 22:13) the number 801 is reached (A $= 1 +$ Ω $=$ V800 $= 801$). The same may be symbolized by the dove since the sum of the letters of this word is the same (π $= 80 + ε = 5 + ρ = 100 + ι = 10 + σ = 200 + τ = 300 + ε = 5 + ρ = 100 + a = 1 = 801$). Also if the numerical value of all the letters of the name of Jesus is reckoned the total is 888 (ι $= 10 + η = 8 + σ = 200 + ο = 70 + υ = 400 + s = 200 = 888$).

In addition to the initial letter, chi, as an abbreviation for Christ, the first two letters, chi and rho, could be used and could also readily be written together in the form of a monogram. The same two letters of course begin many other words too, and were written in monogram fashion as an abbreviation of other words. The chi-rho monogram, with the rho written vertically through the cross mark of the Chi, is found, for example, as the abbreviation of χ(ιλιά) ρ (χης), which means "commander of a thousand men" and is used as the translation of the Roman *tribunus militum* or "military tribune"; of χρ(ήσιμον), which means "useful"; and of χρ(όνος), which means "time" (Avi-Yonah, *Abbreviations*, p. 112). Accordingly the significance of the monogram, particularly if it appears in isolation, cannot always be ascertained.

In other cases, however, this monogram occurs in contexts which are unmistakably Christian. This may be seen in the inscriptions on two funeral stelae found in the district of Eumeneia in Phrygia. The rather long inscription of a certain Gaius is now judged to show plainly from its language that the author was a Christian. The date is probably around A.D. 200. In the last line on the front (A 11) of the monument we have the word Θ(εο)ῦ, "of God," written in the abbreviation of a monogram and, immediately after it, the monogram of which we are speaking, which must stand for Χρ(ιστοῦ), "of Christ" (JRS 16 [1926], pp. 61-64 no. 183). The less extended epitaph of a certain Glyconides, an inscription dating probably in the latter half of the third century, identifies him (in the first line on the shaft of the stela) as Εὐμενεὺς Χρ(ιστιανὸς) ἐπίσκοπος. Here, where the monogram occurs between the words which indicate that Glyconides was a citizen of Eumeneia and a bishop, it must be taken as an abbreviation for "Christian" (JRS 16 [1926], pp. 73-74 no. 200).

Other clues also may demonstrate the Christian significance of the monogram. At Dura-Europos (YCS 14 [1955], p. 194 no. 216) it is found as a graffito on a broken sherd of pottery, which is probably of the third century in date. Immediately beside the monogram at the left is a large capital letter alpha. This suggests the alpha and omega which are frequently written along with the chi-rho monogram (and also with the cross-monogram

which will be mentioned later). There are also other examples of the placing of the alpha alone alongside the
monogram (DACL 1:1, cols. 11-12). Standing alone with
the monogram the alpha could also have the significance
of the initial letter of 'Α(ρχή), "the beginning" (Testa
pp. 365-366 No. 22, p. 403 No. 1). "The Alpha and the
Omega" (τὸ ἄλφα καὶ τὸ ὦ) derive of course from Rev
1:8; 21:6; and 22:13. In the last two passages "the beginning and the end" (ἡ ἀρχὴ καὶ τὸ τέλος) stand in parallel
with "the Alpha and the Omega"; and in the first passage
(Rev 1:8) "the beginning and the end" is the reading of
Codex Sinaiticus instead of "the Alpha and the Omega."

Since context and accompanying clues do demonstrate in such cases as these just cited the almost certainly Christian usage of the symbol in the time before
Constantine, even when the monogram stands alone
and even in the pre-Constantinian period the possibility
of its Christian significance may often be considered.

In addition to the understanding of the chi and the
rho as the beginning letters of the names Christ and
Christian, other possibilities of interpretation arise in
the light of the numerical understanding of alphabetic
characters to which we have referred above. In the
Greek system of numerals the character rho has the value
of one hundred. Since Abraham was one hundred years
old when he received the promise of the birth of Isaac to
Sarah and himself (Gen 21:5; Rom 4:19f.), the combination of rho and chi (or also of rho and tau) could stand
for the fulfillment of the promise in the Cross. Ephraem
the Syrian (d. 373) attests another intepretation. He
says (ed. Assemani III p. 477c) that when the letter rho
is put above the cross it signifies (literally, "shows by a
sign") help, which is reckoned as one hundred (σημαίνει
βοήθεια ψηφιζόμενον ἑκατόν). The word βοήθεια, which
means "help," was also written βοήθια, which may be a
popular spelling corresponding to its actual pronunciation. In numerical value the letters of this word total one
hundred (β = 2 + ο = 70 + η = 8 + Θ = 9 +
ι = 10 + α = 1 = 100). Accordingly, as Ephraem leads
us to see, when rho was written with the cross (which
could be with either chi or tau) it was affirmed that "the
cross (is our) help" (RAE VI, pp. 84-85).

Another combination of Greek letters which resulted
in a monogram somewhat similar to the foregoing was
that achieved by the ligature of tau and rho to make the
sign ⳨. This occurs as an abbreviation of various words
in pagan inscriptions, e.g., of τρ(ιακάς) (Avi-Yonah,
Abbreviations, p. 105), which means the number thirty
and also the thirtieth day of the month. This sign is even
found on coins of Herod the Great dated to his third year
(see the discussion of this monogram on Herod's coins in
BA 26 [May 1963], pp. 48ff. [Vardaman]). But the combination of the two letters could also have Christian significance. When the word σταυρός, "cross," was written

in the abbreviated form, στρος, it was readily possible to
make the usual combination of the tau and the rho and
thus have the abbreviation σ⳨ος. This is actually found
in Christian manuscripts as early as A.D. 200 (see below
Nos. 336f.). At the same time the tau itself was recognized as a form of the Christian cross (see above p. 350),
and with this recognition it was possible to see the combination of the tau and the rho as constituting a cross-
monogram (⳨), as we may call it in distinction from the
Christ-monogram (☧) which was constituted by the
combination of the letters chi and rho. That the cross-
monogram had some similarity to, and might have been
influenced by the Egyptian ankh will be spoken of further
at a later point (Nos. 339f.).

With respect to the cross-monogram an epitaph found
at Rome provides a relatively early example. This inscription was connected with a burial loculus found in
the area between the Via Appia and the Via Latina and
inside the Aurelian Wall. Since burial was prohibited
within the walls of the city, this interment must have
been made before the time when Aurelian (A.D. 270-
275) built the wall which bears his name. The grave is
that of a certain Beratio Nicatora, whose name is given
in the first line of the inscription (BHPATIOYC NI-
KATOPAC). Beneath the inscription, which is in
mixed Greek and Latin, the cross-monogram occurs
twice, and beneath that are certain representations,
namely, of Jonah, the Good Shepherd, an anchor, and a
lion. The style of lettering agrees with the place of discovery in pointing to a date in the third century (Orazio
Marucchi in BAC 1886, pp. 15-17). Furthermore, both
forms of the monogram, ⳨ and P, have been found in
pre-Constantinian graffiti at the Vatican (M. Black p.
319, see below, No. 329).

According to a well-known account (Lactantius, Of
the Manner in Which the Persecutors Died, 44; Eusebius,
Life of Constantine, I, 28-31), Constantine saw a certain
sign in a dream or vision and inscribed it on the shields
of his soldiers or fashioned it into a labarum or imperial
standard, before his victory at the Milvian bridge (A.D.
312). Lactantius describes this sign as follows:

> A long spear, overlaid with gold, formed the figure of the
> cross by means of a transverse bar laid over it. On the top of
> the whole was fixed a wreath of gold and precious stones; and
> within this, the symbol of the Savior's name, two letters in-
> dicating the name of Christ by means of its initial characters,
> the letter P being intersected by X in its center.

From this we understand that the vertical lance with the
transverse bar on top of it formed what we have called a
tau-cross, while the two Greek letters at the top, the chi
and the rho written together, signified the name of
Christ, and all together we have both a cross-monogram
and a Christ-monogram, the combination of the two

forms also suggesting that both forms came out of Christian tradition from before the time of Constantine.

Not long after the date of Constantine's vision, the sign appears in a Roman funerary inscription (Diehl no. 3257) which is definitely dated *Severo et Rufino conss.*, i.e., when Severus and Rufinus were consuls, the year 323 (*Fasti consulares imperii*, ed. Willy Liebenam, KLT 41-43, p. 35). From then on it occurs frequently. But the evidence cited above shows that both the Christ-monogram and the cross-monogram must have had a long history before the time of Constantine.

All together, then, and already in the centuries before Constantine, we find the cross mark and the letters iota, eta, chi, tau, and rho used as abbreviations of Christian significance, and we find combinations of these forming monograms, notably ⵌ, ✳, ⳨, and ⳩ (cf. Dölger I, p. 386).

Germain Morin, "Hieronymus de Monogrammate," in *Revue Bénédictine* 20 (1903), pp. 225-236; H. Leclercq, "Monogramme," in DACL XI 2, cols. 2369-2392; Max Sulzberger, "Le symbole de la Croix (et les monogrammes de Jésus) chez les premiers chrétiens," in *Byzantion* 2 (1925), pp. 393-448; W. H. Buckler, W. M. Calder, and C. W. M. Cox, "Monuments from Central Phrygia," in JRS 16 (1926), pp. 61-74; Dölger I, pp. 353-386; M. Burzachechi, "Sull'uso pre-costantiniano del monogramma greco de Cristo," in *Atti della Pontificia Accademia Romana di archeologia* (serie III), Rendiconti XXVIII (1954-55), pp. 197-211; R. N. Frye, J. F. Gilliam, H. Ingholt, and C. B. Welles, "Inscriptions from Dura-Europos," in YCS 14 (1955), pp. 123-213; Matthew Black, "The Chi-Rho Sign—Christogram and/or Staurogram?" in *Apostolic History and the Gospel, Biblical and Historical Essays presented to F. F. Bruce on his 60th Birthday*, ed. W. Ward Gasque and Ralph P. Martin (Grand Rapids: Eerdmans, 1970), pp. 319-327; Vassilius Tzaferis, "Christian Symbols of the 4th Century and the Church Fathers" (Ph.D. diss., Hebrew University, 1971).

THE CROSS MARK IN RELATION TO FUNERARY CUSTOMS, JEWISH AND CHRISTIAN

IN THE FOREGOING DISCUSSION it has been established that the taw mark in the basic passage, Ezk 9:4, stands for protection and deliverance, and indeed in such a critical time as may be recognized as the end time of ultimate judgment. Furthermore, as also documented above, quotation of and allusion to this passage in Jewish (e.g., Damascus Document), Jewish Christian (e.g., Odes of Solomon), and Gentile Christian (e.g., Tertullian) sources show that understanding of the underlying eschatological significance of this sign lived on in all these areas, while specific connections with the cross of Jesus and the name of Christ were also introduced in Jewish Christian and Gentile Christian thought. Since the sign stood for salvation in the Last Judgment, it is evident that it was a mark particularly appropriate for use in connection with places of burial, and this could have been already true for Jews as well as later for Jewish Christians and Gentile Christians.

As for putting a mark or sign on a grave in Jewish custom we can cite the Assumption of Moses, probably the work of a Pharisaic author between A.D. 7 and 29. Here (11:1-6 CAP II, p. 423), Joshua is grieved that Moses is to die, and he asks: "What place shall receive thee? Or what shall be the sign that marks (thy) sepulcher?" As seen in examples already noticed in Jewish catacombs and on Jewish sarcophagi and ossuaries, in addition to such purely decorative designs as the rosette (Nos. 297, 299), it is such symbols as the *menorah*, *shofar*, incense shovel, *lulab*, and *ethrog* which are characteristically used (Nos. 259ff.). On the ossuaries there are also cross marks, and these can often be recognized as of purely secular significance. For example a cross mark on the side of the box and a corresponding one on the side of the lid can show the way the lid is to be placed to make a close fit, and a single such mark on the end of a chest can show the end which is to be inserted first into a burial niche (Rahmani in BA 45 [1982], p. 112). Other cross marks on ossuaries, however, especially if larger and more formal, but not necessarily only then, might surely be possible on Jewish ossuaries in the sense of the *taw* as the mark signifying protection and eschatological deliverance (Dinkler in ZTK 48 [1951], pp. 163-169; and in JAC 5 [1962], pp. 97-99).

For the custom of putting a mark or sign on a grave in Jewish Christian circles we can cite a reference in the first two chapters of II Ezra (IV Esdras), a portion of that work which was probably written soon after A.D. 150. Here (2:23) the Latin text of the Vulgate reads: *Mortuos ubi inveneris, signans commenda sepulcro, et dabo tibi primam sessionem in resurrectione mea.* The word *signans* can be referred to the *mortuos*, and this translation be made: "Wheresoever thou findest the dead, set a sign upon them and commit them to the grave, and I will give thee the first place in my resurrection" (Oesterley 11). Or, and with greater intrinsic probability, the word *signans* can be related to the *sepulcro*, and this translation be given: "When you find any who are dead, commit them to the grave and mark (or, seal) it, and I will give you the first place in my resurrection" (RSV). With respect to the connotation of *signans*, translated "mark," "seal," or "set a sign on," there can be little doubt that it refers to the mark of the cross (cf. above p. 350).

Another and even more explicit illustration in the same respect, still in the area of Jewish Christianity, is found in the account by Eusebius (*Ch. Hist.* II 23) of the martyrdom of James, the brother of the Lord, and the head of the church in Jerusalem (A.D. 61/62, cf. GCS *Eusebius* VII 182f.; Josephus, *Ant.* XX 9). James was thrown down from the pinnacle of the temple. "And they buried him on the spot," Eusebius writes (II 23, 18), "by the temple, and his monument (στήλη) still remains by the temple." At this point there is an additional note in one early Greek manuscript of the *Church History* (MPG XX 203, note 12), which reads: "This monument (στήλη) was an unshaped stone (λίθος . . . ἄμορφος), having as an inscription (ἐπιγραφήν) the name of the interred James. From which (example) even until now the Christians set up stones in their tombs, and they either write letters (γράμματα) on them, or they cut in the sign of the cross (τὸ σημεῖον τοῦ σταυροῦ)." According to this evidence, from the time of James on the customary marking on a Christian tomb monument might include the "letters" of the name of the deceased and the "sign" of the cross mark.

ILLUSTRATIONS OF THE CROSS MARK

WE PROCEED NOW to a series of illustrations of objects with the cross mark, together with occasional illustrations of related objects which are needed for explanation of some details. In the light of the references which have been given just above, it may be expected that the monuments on which the cross mark appears will often be those of a funerary character and this will be found to be the case. We begin, however, with examples where the cross mark appears to be only a conventional sign of purely secular significance. After that we look for examples of the cross mark in contexts where, particularly because of funerary relationships, some of the religious significance elucidated above may be believed to attach to the sign. According to the theoretical understanding worked out above, some of these may be Jewish Christian if circumstances point in that direction. If we do have examples of Jewish Christian cross marks in Palestine these will presumably be the earliest archeological evidences of the earliest Christian church. Finally, of course, we come to examples of the cross mark which are unmistakably Christian, and the survey is rounded out by noticing some of these and their most notable variations in Rome and in Egypt. Since in many of the earlier cases now to be cited we will be concerned with ossuaries at Jerusalem, it may be recalled (see above p. 336) that the use of ossuaries in and around Jerusalem is probably

to be placed in the period from about 50 B.C. to A.D. 70 or possibly 135.

THE TEL ARAD JAR

308. Jar from Tel Arad with Hebrew Inscription and *Taw* Mark

THE *TAW* APPEARS both as a letter of the alphabet in the inscription, and as a separate mark on the shoulder of this jar, which was found in 1962 in the excavation of Tel Arad, a large *tell* in the eastern Negev. The jar was on the floor of a room in a house in Stratum VI, which is dated to about the seventh century B.C. The inscription in two lines on the side, written in black ink in early Hebrew characters, probably reads as follows:

בשלשת	*bslst*	In the third (year),
ירח צח	*yrḥ ṣḥ*	the month Ṣaḥ.

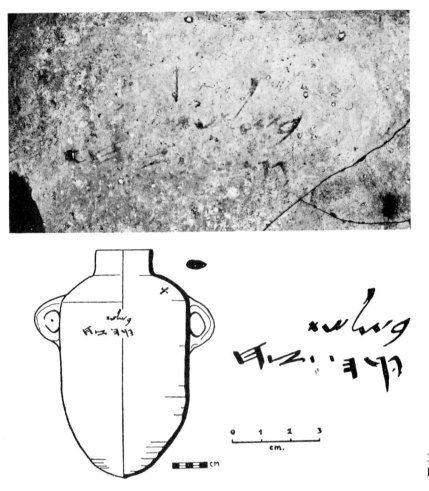

308. Jar from Tel Arad with Hebrew Inscription and *Taw* Mark

If this is the correct transcription and interpretation of the inscription, the *yerah Ṣah* is a previously unrecognized month in the Israelite calendar. It may also be mentioned in Is 18:4, where it could be translated "like the heat of the month of Sah," and must be a summer month. A guess as to the significance of the inscription is that the jar was for storage of perfume and the date is that on which the jar was filled. The alphabetic character *taw*, written as a cross mark in the sideways position, is the last letter at the left end of the first line of the inscription. The *taw* mark, again written as a cross mark in the sideways position, in black ink, and in larger size, also appears on the curve of the jar below the neck and near the handle. The significance of the latter mark is not evident but it provides an example of the use of the cross presumably as a merely conventional mark and of only secular significance.

Similar examples of the taw mark, written in ink and in charcoal, may be seen on storage jars found in the excavation of the storerooms of the fortress of Herod the Great on the rock of Masada. In this case the excavator, Yigael Yadin, interprets the mark as an abbreviation for the Hebrew word תרומה , *truma*, which is the "heave offering" and the priests' portion (cf. RSV) in Ex 29:27, etc. He draws the conclusion that the defenders of Masada were not only Zealots but also rigid adherents of the Law, adhering strictly to such commandments as tithing, in spite of the difficult conditions of life on Masada.

PEQ Jan.-Jun. 1963, pp. 3-4; Y. Aharoni and Ruth Amiran, "Excavations at Tel Arad," in IEJ 14 (1964), pp. 142-143; Yadin, *Masada*, p. 96. Photographs: courtesy Arad Expedition.

THE NICANOR OSSUARY

309. Inscription and Cross Mark on the Nicanor Ossuary

AT A SITE on the north end of the Mount of Olives, where there is a view directly across to the temple area,

309. Inscription and Cross Mark on the Nicanor Ossuary

an elaborate tomb with four independent groups of chambers was found in 1902. Seven ossuaries were obtained from the tomb, and the one dealt with here is now in the British Museum. It has painted red ornamentation in the form of rosettes on the front and zigzag lines on the back and lid and one end. On the other end is the inscription here shown. This is begun with some care but apparently executed with increasing haste and carelessness as it proceeds. The first three lines are in Greek, the fourth in Hebrew, as follows:

OCTATωNTOYNEIKA
NOPOCAΛEΞANΔPEωC
ΠOIHCANTOCTACΘYPAC
נקנר אלכסא

The first two lines may be read as: Ὀστᾶ τῶν τοῦ Νεικάνορος Ἀλεξανδρέως. Here it is possible that we have in the first word the plural contracted form of the Greek

word for "bones" (ὀστέα), and that between the second and third words we should supply an understood word such as "sons," "descendants," or "family." If this is correct the translation will be: "Bones of the (sons) of Nicanor the Alexandrian." It is also possible, however, that the first seven letters of the first line constitute a single word, namely, ὀστατῶν. Although it is not otherwise known, this word could be understood to mean a "receptacle for bones," and therewith be an equivalent of ὀστοφάγος (cf. above p. 216). In this case we would translate: "Ossuary of Nicanor the Alexandrian."

Confirmation that the latter is the correct interpretation may be seen in the Hebrew portion of the inscription. The first Hebrew word is *nqnr*, which is a Hebrew spelling of Nicanor, otherwise found also as ניקנור, *nyqnwr*. The second word is *'lks'*, which could be spelled out as Aleksa. This could be the Hebrew equivalent of Ἀλεξᾶς, which in turn could be a contraction of Ἀλεξανδρεῦς, meaning "the Alexandrian." Thus the

Hebrew probably simply gives the name of "Nicanor the Alexandrian," and thus tends to confirm the fact that this is indeed the ossuary of that person.

Concerning this Nicanor the third line of the Greek identifies him as the one

ποιήσαντος τὰς θύρας

who made the gates

In the Talmud (*Yoma* 19a SBT II, 5, p. 82) there is mention of the Nicanor Gate which was on the east of the Temple court, probably between the Court of the Women and the Court of the Israelites (see above No. 193). In contrast with the other gates, which were of gold (*Middoth* II, 3 SBT V, 6, p. 7), this one was of Corinthian bronze (*Yoma* 38a SBT II, 5, p. 175) and is doubtless the same one that is singled out by Josephus in these words (*War* V, 5, 3 §201): "Of the gates nine were completely overlaid with gold and silver, as were also their doorposts and lintels; but one, that outside the sanctuary, was of Corinthian bronze, and far exceeded in value those plated with silver and set in gold." Concerning the doors of this gate the Talmud (*Yoma* 38a SBT II, 5, p. 174) also states explicitly that Nicanor brought them from Alexandria of Egypt. The fact that certain miracles are also narrated here, with respect to the doors and their transport, at least attests the attention that was directed toward them. The conclusion seems entirely likely, therefore, that "Nicanor the Alexandrian who made the gates," according to the ossuary inscription, is this same Nicanor. That this man was buried across the valley on the Mount of Olives, at a place in full view of his famous gate, was very appropriate.

Interestingly enough, in the 1968 excavations at the south wall of the temple area (cf. above No. 189) some five burial caves were uncovered, three of which contained ossuaries, and on one ossuary there was a Hebrew inscription appearing twice which reads, "Simon, the builder of the temple." In addition to Nicanor, this is the only other man associated with the construction of Herod's temple whose personal remains have been found.

PEFQS 1903, pp. 93, 125-131 (Clermont-Ganneau, "The 'Gate of Nicanor' in the Temple of Jerusalem"), 326-332 (Gladys Dickson, "The Tomb of Nicanor of Alexandria"); 1905, pp. 253-257 (R. A. Stewart Macalister, "Further Observations on the Ossuary of Nicanor of Alexandria"); Frey II, pp. 261-262 no. 1256; Goodenough I, pp. 130-131; Erich Dinkler in JAC 5 (1962), p. 109 and pl. 5, b; *Biblical Museums Bulletin Eisenberg Issue* (Louisville: Southern Baptist Theological Seminary), Fall 1962, pp. 4-5, with additional bibliography. Photograph: courtesy Trustees of the British Museum.

310. Cross Mark on the Lid of the Nicanor Ossuary

AS MAY BE SEEN in the preceding illustration (No. 309), there is on the end of the Nicanor ossuary, beneath the lines of Greek text and to the left of the line of Hebrew text, a relatively large and rather irregular cross mark cut into the stone in a sideways position. In this photograph it may be seen that there is a very similar cross mark cut into the top of the lid of the ossuary very near one end. It is perhaps possible to hold that the cross mark on the end of the ossuary is intentionally related to the inscription alongside which it stands, and therewith perhaps possible to understand it as the Jewish *taw* mark which has been discussed above (p. 355). But in this case a simpler explanation may be more acceptable. In 1903, at which time she was in possession of this ossuary, Miss Gladys Dickson (see the Literature under No. 309) observed that the cross mark on the end of the ossuary and the cross mark on the end of the lid of the ossuary appeared to correspond, and she suggested that together they simply showed the proper way to turn the lid when placing it in position.

Photograph: courtesy Trustees of the British Museum.

THE OSSUARIES ON THE MOUNT OF OFFENCE

311. Inscription with the Name of Judah and Cross Mark on an Ossuary from the Mount of Offence

IN 1873 A ROCK-HEWN chamber was found on the Mount of Offence (cf. No. 143), to the southeast of Jerusalem, not far from the road to Bethany. This chamber gave the impression of being a storehouse for ossuaries collected from other burial places, for it contained at least thirty of these burial chests. Although the ossuaries were soon dispersed and many of them broken, Charles Clermont-Ganneau was able before this happened to make squeezes of their inscriptions and ornamentation and to compile a detailed description of the entire group. Most of the ossuaries had rosettes (cf. Nos. 297, 299) on one side, and many of them had inscriptions on a long or short side or on the lid. The inscriptions were scratched on with a sharp instrument, or painted with a pen, or written on with charcoal. Both Hebrew (or Aramaic) and Greek were found. As deciphered by Clermont-Ganneau the inscriptions contained the following names in Hebrew (or Aramaic): Shalamsion, the daugh-

311. Inscription with the Name of Judah and Cross Mark on an Ossuary from the Mount of Offence

310. Cross Mark on the Lid of the Nicanor Ossuary

ter of Simeon the priest; Judah, the scribe; Judah, the son (*bar*) of Eleazar, the scribe; Simeon, the son (*bar*) of Jesus; Eleazar, the son (*bar*) of Natai; Martha, the daughter of Pascal; and Salome, the wife of Judah; and in Greek: Jesus; Nathaniel; Moschas; Mariados (which could be a genitive meaning "of Marias"); Kyrthas; and Hedea. At least three of the inscriptions are accompanied by cross marks and the first of these, as copied from the squeezes of Clermont-Ganneau, is reproduced here. The Hebrew characters are undoubtedly to be read as יהודה, *yhwdh*, and so we have the familiar name, Judah. The same name occurs on another ossuary; on the lid of yet another there is a carefully cut inscription, "Judah, the scribe," and on a small end probably belonging to the same ossuary a carelessly made inscription, "Judah, son of Eleazar, the scribe." Eleazar is also a familiar name (e.g., II Macc 6:18) and is found in abbreviated form as Lazarus (e.g., Josephus, *War* v, 13, 7 §567; Jn 11:5ff.). On another ossuary and lid we have also the

name of "Salome, the wife of Judah." Carefully placed beneath the name of Judah in the present inscription, and therefore possibly to be taken as a symbol in some way connected with the name, is an equilateral cross.

C. Clermont-Ganneau in PEFQS 1874, pp. 7-10 and especially p. 8 no. 2; Clermont-Ganneau I, pp. 381-412; Frey II, p. 288 no. 1306. Photograph: Clermont-Ganneau I, p. 403 no. 11, courtesy Palestine Exploration Fund.

312. Inscription with the Name of Jesus and Cross Mark on an Ossuary from the Mount of Offence

HERE WE HAVE the name ΙΕϹΟΥϹ , which is presumably a variant spelling of Ἰησοῦς, Jesus. The same name occurs in Hebrew (or Aramaic) in one other of these inscriptions, where we read:

שמעון בר ישוע

In this case the well-known OT name Joshua (יהושע) occurs in the later form of Jeshua to which, in Greek, the name Jesus corresponds. The text reads, then, Simeon *bar* Jeshua, or, Simeon, the son of Jesus. In the inscription illustrated here, however, the name Jesus is written twice on the same line which is, at least, unusual (cf. Nos. 316, 317 below). At the left is also a cross-shaped mark of which the transverse bar runs somewhat obliquely and is relatively dim.

Frey II, p. 295 no. 1327. Photograph: Clermont-Ganeau I, p. 409 no. 22, courtesy Palestine Exploration Fund.

312. Inscription with the Name of Jesus and Cross Mark on an Ossuary from the Mount of Offence

313. Inscription and Cross Mark on an Ossuary from the Mount of Offence

THIS TEXT CONSISTS of only two Greek capital letters, eta and delta, cut deeply into the front of an ossuary. On another ossuary in the same group are the letters HΔHA, which could be a variant spelling of a woman's proper name, Ἡδέα, Hedea. Since the first two letters of this name are the same as the two letters in the text here illustrated, the latter could be an abbreviation of the same name. Or the two letters could have some totally different significance, but what that might be it is difficult to say. At any rate above the two letters, and also deeply cut in the stone, is a cross of which the vertical member is longer than the horizontal, i.e., a *crux immissa* or Latin cross (cf. p. 352). To Clermont-Ganneau (I, p. 404) this cross seemed to be unmistakably the Christian symbol and confirmed the probable Christian significance of many other of the marks on the Mount of Offence ossuaries. It also seemed to him (in PEFQS 1874, p. 10) not less than a "singular coincidence" that this whole group of inscriptions, found near the Bethany road and near the site of that village, contains nearly all the names of the persons in the Gospels who belonged to that place, namely Eleazar (Lazarus), Simon, and Martha. He therefore described these (in PEFQS 1874, p. 9) as "monuments belonging to the beginnings of Chris-

tianity, before it had any official position, coming from the very soil where it had its birth," and he wrote: "The cave on the Mount of Offence belonged apparently to one of the earliest families which joined the new religion. In this group of sarcophagi, some of which have the Christian symbol and some have not, we are, so to speak, assisting at an actual unfolding of Christianity." Needless to say, this interpretation has been contradicted by others, yet remains deserving of very careful consideration. It is also true that Clermont-Ganneau (I, p. 404) thought it necessary to put the latest of these monuments later than the reign of Constantine, but that can hardly be allowed in view of the opinion that the use of ossuaries at Jerusalem only continued up to A.D. 70 or 135 (cf. above p. 336). Whatever their significance, the inscriptions and the marks accompanying them are according to that dating not later than about the first century of the Christian era, and it is this early date which is important and remarkable if their Christian character can be substantiated. There may be support for that conclusion in comparison with the Talpioth (Nos. 315ff.) and more especially the Dominus flevit (Nos. 319ff.) ossuaries (cf. Bagatti, *Gli scavi del "Dominus flevit"* [cited in full below under No. 319], pp. 170f., fig. 39, nos. 7, 15, 16).

Clermont-Ganneau in PEFQS 1874, pp. 9-10; Clermont-Ganneau I, pp. 403f., 411f.; Goodenough I, p. 131; André Parrot, *Golgotha and the Church of the Holy Sepulcher* (New York: Philosophical Library, 1957), pp. 110f., 116, 118 n. 2. Photograph: Clermont-Ganneau I, p. 411 no. 29, courtesy Palestine Exploration Fund.

314. Inscription with the Name of Alexander on an Ossuary from near Silwan

IN THE SAME AREA of the Mount of Offence (No. 143), south of the village of Silwan, another rock-hewn chamber was found in 1941 by E. L. Sukenik and N. Avigad. In arrangement, there is a rectangular pit one meter deep in the floor of the chamber, and this forms three shelves along the walls except for the entrance wall, but there are no *kokim*. On the shelves and in part of the pit were bones, and on the shelf at one end were ten ossuaries and at the other end one ossuary (no. 11 in the excavator's report). It would appear that when the

313. Inscription and Cross Mark on an Ossuary from the Mount of Offence

314. Inscription with the Name of Alexander on an Ossuary from near Silwan

dead were buried they were placed on the shelves; later the bones were collected and put in the ossuaries. Pottery was scattered all over the chamber, and a so-called Herodian lamp and other items indicate a probable date in the first century of the present era. Pottery and all but one of the ossuaries were deposited in the Palestine Archaeological Museum; Ossuary no. 9 was brought to the Hebrew University.

The ossuaries have no decoration, but all but two (nos. 2 and 10) have inscriptions, eight inscriptions in Greek, one in Hebrew (no. 11), and one in both Greek and Hebrew (no. 9). All the inscriptions give names, and the name is undoubtedly that of the deceased person, which is the custom in almost all known ossuary inscriptions. As shown in the present photograph of the lid of Ossuary no. 9, the name of the person whose bones were placed here is Alexander. This name is incised neatly in both Greek and Hebrew on the lid of the ossuary (IEJ 12 [1962], p. 10, fig. 16 and pl. 4A). The same name is also written in green chalk (?) on the front of the ossuary, and scratched carelessly on the back, in both cases in Greek and together with the name of Simon. On the front the name Simon is in the nominative, but on the back it is properly in the genitive, and this Simon is evidently the father of Alexander. The inscription on the back is:

ΨΙΜΩΝΑΛΕ
ΑΛΕΞΑΝΔΡΟΨ
ΨΙΜΩΝΟΨ

Simon Ale
Alexander
(son) of Simon

Here the plainly inexperienced engraver has started by mistake with the name of the father Simon and the first three letters of the name of Alexander, then has begun again and written the names in proper order and with Simon's name properly in the genitive, thus identifying Alexander as the son of Simon.

Returning to the bilingual text on the lid of the ossuary as in the present photograph, the large line of Greek simply gives the name Alexander, but the lower line in Hebrew gives the same name in Hebrew, followed by קרנית, QRNYT. Although the reason for the final character (taw) is not fully understood, the first four characters surely provide a Hebrew transcription of the name of Cyrene (Κυρήνη in Greek), and the word probably designates the place of origin of Alexander, with which may be compared the name of "Philon the Cyrenian (Φίλων Κυρηναῖος)" in an ossuary inscription at Dominus flevit (Milik in Bagatti and Milik p. 81). Interestingly enough the nearby Ossuary no. 5 bears the name of "Sara (daughter) of Simon of Ptolemais." This Sara daughter of Simon must be the sister of Alexander son of Simon, and since the son was probably a Cyrenian, the daughter's home of Ptolemais was probably the Ptolemais in Cyrenaica. Thus we have here a family burial at least to the extent of two children of a certain Simon, and their place of origin was probably Cyrene. From Ac 6:9 we know that there was a synagogue of Cyrenians in Jerusalem, and in Mk 15:21 it was Simon of Cyrene (Σίμων Κυρηναῖος), the father of Alexander and Rufus, who was compelled to carry the cross of Jesus. It is surely a real possibility that this unostentatious tomb was the last resting place of the bones of at least two members of the family of this very Simon. That the members of the family became Jewish Christians is also a likelihood, for Mark's reference to Alexander and Rufus suggests that they were well known in Christian circles, and it is therefore also not unlikely that the Rufus of Mk 15:21 is the same as the Rufus who is greeted as "eminent in the Lord," together with his mother, by Paul in Rom 16:13 (John Knox in IB 9, p. 659.

N. Avigad, "A Depository of Inscribed Ossuaries in the Kidron Valley," in IEJ 12 (1962), pp. 1-12. Photograph: from IEJ 12 (1962), pl. 4A, after p. 76, courtesy Israel Exploration Society.

THE TALPIOTH OSSUARIES

315. Plan of the Tomb at Talpioth

THE TOMB REPRESENTED by this plan was found in 1945 near the Talpioth suburb south of Jerusalem and beside the old road to Bethlehem. The tomb is entered from a courtyard. In the main burial chamber (labeled I in the plan) a rectangular depression allows for headroom and provides a bench on three sides. In the walls are five loculi of the kokim type, two in the eastern wall, two in the southern, and one in the western. In the tomb were fourteen ossuaries. Three were taken out by the workmen who found the tomb. The other eleven were recovered by E. L. Sukenik and N. Avigad in an excavation conducted very soon after the original discovery. The places where the eleven ossuaries were found are indicated by the numbers 1-11 on the plan. There was evidence that the tomb had been entered once by robbers, who had broken into several loculi and had taken out several ossuaries. Evidently disappointed at finding nothing but bones, however, they left the other ossuaries as they were and thus the archeologists found them. In the tomb was a coin of Herod Agrippa I dating from A.D. 42/43. The pottery was Late Hellenistic and Early Roman. Thus the tomb appears to have been in use from sometime in the first century B.C. until no later than the middle of the first century of the Christian era. On three ossuaries are roughly incised inscriptions in Hebrew characters which may be read and translated as follows: on ossuary no. 1, שמעון ברסבא, Simeon Barsaba; on ossuary no. 4, מרים ברת שמעון, Mariam, daughter of Simeon; and on ossuary no. 10, מתי, Matai, which can be an abbreviated form of Matthias. On two ossuaries,

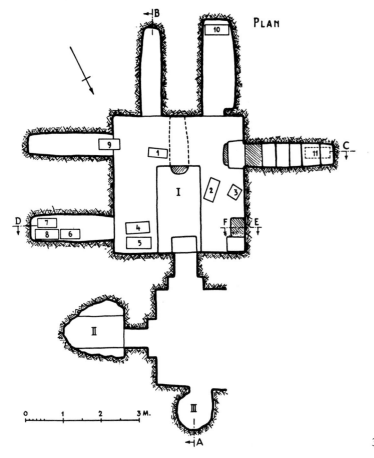

315. Plan of the Tomb at Talpioth

namely, nos. 7 and 8, are Greek inscriptions, and on one of these, namely, no. 8, are large cross marks. As may be seen in this plan, these two ossuaries were found side by side in what was evidently their original position at the back end of a loculus on the eastern side of the tomb. Both will be described more fully (Nos. 316, 317).

E. L. Sukenik, "The Earliest Records of Christianity," in AJA 51 (1947), pp. 351-365. Photograph: courtesy Department of Archaeology, The Hebrew University of Jerusalem.

316. Photograph and Tracing of Inscription on Ossuary No. 7 from Talpioth

THIS OSSUARY is decorated on the front side with carved panels and two rosettes, a type of decoration familiar on other ossuaries of the time (cf. No. 297). On the back is the inscription shown here, drawn in charcoal and written in Greek in a single line. As far as it can be seen plainly it reads:

IHCOYC IOY

Ἰησους ἰού

Jesus iou

Although in his facsimile drawing of the inscription (in AJA 51, p. 358) Sukenik shows a diagonal stroke to the right of the final upsilon, he says flatly (p. 363) that there are no more letters, and suggests that the term "iou" is the Greek exclamation meaning "woe." In classical Greek as an expression of sorrow and grief this exclamation is usually doubled, but it is also used as a single interjection (Aristophanes, *The Thesmophoriazusae*, 245 LCL III, p. 152). It is also a cry of joyful surprise (Aristophanes, *The Knights*, 1096 LCL I, p. 230), and a Scholiast says that it is written ἰοὺ ἰού when it is of woe but ἰοῦ ἰοῦ when it is of joy (Aristophanes, *The Peace*, 317, 345 LCL II, pp. 30, 32). Together, therefore, the two words are taken by Sukenik as a Christian lament for the crucifixion of Jesus—"Jesus, woe!"

316. Photograph and Tracing of Inscription on Ossuary No. 7 from Talpioth

Among many other interpretations, Hempel (ZAW 62, p. 274) notes the diagonal line to the right of the last upsilon and thinks a character stood there. Bagatti and Milik (p. 170, no. 17) think the diagonal line part of the letter alpha, supply a delta, and read the name of ΙΟΥΔΑ. If this were correct the whole could refer to a certain Jesus son of Judah, although the reading would be more unambiguous if we had Ἰησοῦς τοῦ Ἰούδα (cf. Lk 3:33) or Ἰησοῦς υἱὸς Ἰούδα (cf. Frey I, pp. 24-25 no. 31). Kane (p. 107), however, in the very careful tracing shown here sees the upper part of another upsilon below the upsilon of Ἰησοῦς, restores an omicron in this lower line, and reads the whole inscription as

Ἰησοῦς Ἰουδ
[ο] ῦ

Here the second name (as continued in the lower line) is taken as Judas (a name also otherwise very common in ossury inscriptions), and the reading is literally, Jesus of Judas, i.e., Jesus son of Judas.

For the bibliographies see under Nos. 317, 318. Photograph of ossuary: courtesy Department of Archaeology, The Hebrew University of Jerusalem. Copy of tracing of inscription from Kane in PEQ 1971, fig. 1 fac. p. 106: courtesy Palestine Exploration Fund.

317. Inscription on Ossuary No. 8 from Talpioth

THE INSCRIPTION is cut with a sharp instrument into the lid of this ossuary. It reads:

ΙΗϹΟΥϹΑΛΩΘ
Ἰησοῦς ἀλώθ

Jesus aloth

Here Sukenik (AJA 51, p. 363) very tentatively suggests derivation of "aloth" from the Hebrew and Aramaic אלה, which means among other things "to wail," "to lament," and thus the inscription could be understood to be of the same import as that with the word taken to mean "woe" on Ossuary no. 7 (No. 316). Among other interpretations of "aloth" it is suggested (Gustafsson) that the Greek word is a rendering of the Hebrew verb עלה in the infinitive form עלות. This verb is familiar in the OT where, in various contexts, it carries the idea of upward movement. In particular it is the verb found in Ezk 37:12-13 in the phrase, "raise you from your graves"; thus there could be an appeal here to Jesus that the deceased one might arise. Most probably, however, the word ἀλώθ transliterates the Hebrew noun אהלות, which means "aloes" in Song of Solomon 4:14, although where the same fragrant plant is mentioned in Ps 45:8

the LXX translation (44:8) is στακτή, a word which suggests how the plant's aromatic sap oozes out in drops, and in Jn 19:39 the word for aloes is ἀλόη. Whether with this derivation or not, perhaps the simplest interpretation is to see Aloth as a personal name and, in this case, as the personal name of the father, so that the whole name is Jesus son of Aloth (Kane pp. 106f.). Thus on both Ossuary no. 7 (No. 316) and the present Ossuary no. 8 it may be simply the name of the deceased that is there inscribed, and this is in accordance with the custom also otherwise attested in the inscriptions on almost all known ossuaries, which likewise give the name of the person whose bones were placed therein. The name Jesus is, of course, a very familiar name in this time, and if we read the present inscriptions as naming Jesus son of Judas and Jesus son of Aloth there is no connection with Jesus of Nazareth (Dinkler in ZTK 48 [1951], p. 156). At the same time it may be recalled (from above, No. 315) that on Ossuary no. 1 found in the main burial chamber at Talpioth there is the name Simeon Barsaba and, in contrast with the familiar name of Jesus, Barsaba is a family name which is otherwise known only from the NT (Ac 1:23; 15:22, Barsabas or Barsabbas).

E. L. Sukenik in AJA 51 (1947), pp. 363-365; Berndt Gustafsson in NTS 3 (1956-57), pp. 65-69. Photograph: courtesy Department of Archaeology, The Hebrew University of Jerusalem.

318. Cross Mark on Ossuary No. 8 from Talpioth

IN THE CENTER of each side of Ossuary no. 8 is a large cross mark, drawn with charcoal. The one shown here, on one long side of the ossuary, has bars of quite equal length. The other three have bars of somewhat irregular length. While it has been held that these marks were simply intended to show that the ossuary was in use (Willoughby in JBL 68 [1949]), this would hardly have been necessary in view of the original position of the ossuary at the back corner of a loculus and with its two exposed sides covered by two other ossuaries (nos. 6 and 7, see plan No. 315). The marks may have been drawn by the same person who wrote the inscription (No. 317), and their large size and prominent placement suggest some more significant purpose. If the cross marks are intended symbolically and if this is a Jewish family burial the marks could be the Jewish taw (Dinkler in ZTK 48 [1951], pp. 150f.). Bagatti, and Milik, however, compare the crosses with Judeo-Christian signs at Dominus flevit (p. 170 no. 6; pp. 173ff.), and Cornfeld sees the Talpioth chamber as the burial place of Jewish Christians, which seems the most likely view.

Carl H. Kraeling, "Christian Burial Urns?" in BA 9 (1946), pp. 16-20; Harold R. Willoughby in JBL 68 (1949), pp. 61-65; J. Simons in *Jaarbericht No. 11 van het vooraziatischegyptisch Genoot-*

317. Inscription on Ossuary No. 8 from Talpioth

318. Cross Mark on Ossuary No. 8 from Talpioth

schap *Ex Oriente Lux* (1949-50), pp. 74-78; J. Hempel in ZAW 62 (1960), pp. 273-274; Ethelbert Stauffer in ZNW 43 (1950-51), p. 62; B. S. J. Isserlin in PEQ 1953, p. 79; Erich Dinkler, "Zur Geschichte des Kreuz-symbols," in ZTK 48 (1951), pp. 148-172; and Dinkler, in JAC 5 (1962), pp. 109-110; Goodenough I, pp. 130-132; Duncan Fishwick, "The Talpioth Ossuaries Again," in NTS 10 (1963-64), p. 49-61; J. P. Kane, "By No Means 'The Earliest Records of Christianity'—With an Emended Reading of the Talpioth Inscription ΙΗΣΟΥΣ ΙΟΥ," in PEQ 1971, pp. 103-108; Cornfeld, p. 307. Photograph: courtesy Department of Archaeology, The Hebrew University of Jerusalem.

THE DOMINUS FLEVIT OSSUARIES

319. Plan and Sections of a Portion of the Cemetery at Dominus Flevit

WHEN A NEW wall was built at the Franciscan sanctuary of Dominus flevit (see above No. 161) on the

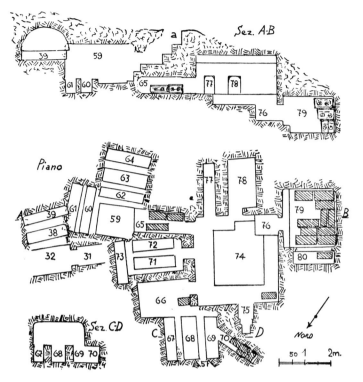

319. Plan and Sections of a Portion of the Cemetery at Dominus Flevit

Mount of Olives, a previously unknown ancient cemetery was discovered and, beginning in 1953, excavated by Father Bagatti of the Studium Biblicum Franciscanum in Jerusalem. The cemetery is very extensive and comprises more than five hundred known burial places. The evidence shows (Bagatti and Milik pp. 43-44, 163-164) that it was in use in two different periods. In the first period the graves were of the kokim type, the coins are from the time of the Hasmoneans to the second year of the Procurator Valerius Gratus, i.e., from 135 B.C. to A.D. 15/16, and the graves were used probably up to A.D. 70 (possibly A.D. 135) at the latest (cf. p. 336). In the second period the graves are characterized by arcosolia, the coins are from Gallus (A.D. 251-253) to the sixteenth year of Heraclius (A.D. 626), and the use of the cemetery was at its heights in the third and fourth centuries, especially the fourth. Besides the coins there were pottery lamps and jars and other objects of glass and stone. In the graves were seven sarcophagi and 122 ossuaries or fragments thereof, all from the first period of use of the cemetery. Inscriptions and signs on the ossuaries will be considered in what follows. The illustration represents only a small portion of the entire cemetery, lying near the southeast corner of the region excavated. In this area, shown here in both plan and sections, are the burial places numbered 65 to 80 by the excavators, which will be mentioned frequently below. The area comprises a central chamber (no. 74) from which there is access to burial places on all sides and notably, through a descent to the south, to a grotto (no. 79), measuring

2.2 by 2.1 meters, in which were stored no less than fourteen ossuaries (nos. 12-25 Bagatti and Milik pp. 52-53).

RB 61 (1954), pp. 568-570; A. Ferrua in RAC 30 (1954), p. 268; P. B. Bagatti, "Scoperta di un cimitero giudeo-cristiano al 'Dominus flevit,' " in LA 3 (1952-53), pp. 149-184; J. van der Ploeg in JSS 5 (1960), pp. 81-82; M. Avi-Yonah in IEJ 11 (1961), pp. 91-94; Bagatti and Milik p. 7 fig. 3. Photograph: courtesy Terra Santa.

320. Inscription with the Name Menahem from Dominus Flevit

MORE THAN FORTY inscriptions have been found on the "Dominus flevit" ossuaries (Milik in Bagatti and Milik pp. 70-109). They are either roughly incised or drawn in charcoal, and written in Hebrew, Aramaic, or Greek. There are fewer inscriptions in Hebrew, but about the same number in Aramaic and in Greek. As is customary in ossuary inscriptions (cf. No. 303), these ordinarily give the name of the deceased, and sometimes indicate a family relationship. Sometimes they also specify his work in daily life, as is the case in this inscription, no. 22. It was found on ossuary no. 83 in burial place no. 299, which is a considerable distance to the northwest of the group of burial places already mentioned, nos. 65-80 (above No. 319). The Hebrew text, incised in the stone, may be transcribed as follows:

מנחם   מן

בנא   יכים

כהן

The first word in the first line is the name Menahem, a name found also in Inscription no. 26. This name is known in the OT (ii K 15:14ff.) where, in LXX manuscripts (iv K 15:16), it is rendered Μαναήμ or Μαναήν. In the last form it is found in Ac 13:1. This Menahem in the present inscription is then identified as being from among the Bene Yakim, "the sons of Yakim," probably the family of Jachin (יכין LXX Ἰαχίν, Ἀχίμ) mentioned in i Ch 24:17. Finally in the last line he is described as a *cohen* or priest. While most of the ossuary inscriptions at Dominus flevit probably belong to the first part of the first century of the Christian era, this one is thought to come from before the turn of the century and to be one of the oldest of the entire group.

Bagatti and Milik p. 73 fig. 18, 1, pp. 89f. no. 22, tav. 29 fot. 85. Photograph: courtesy Terra Santa.

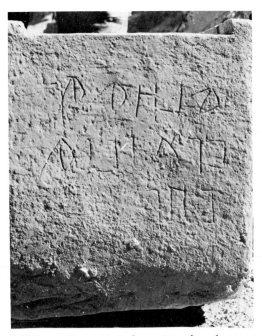

320. Inscription with the Name Menahem from Dominus Flevit

321. Inscription with the Names Martha and Mary from Dominus Flevit

THIS IS INSCRIPTION NO. 7 b on ossuary no. 27 in burial place no. 70 (see above No. 319). It is cut in large but shallow grooves on a long side of the ossuary. It is read by Milik as follows:

מרתה
מרים

Martha
Miriam

The first name is also found in Aramaic as מרתא and in Greek as Μάρθα. The second name is found as given here in both Hebrew and Aramaic. In Greek it is found in the same form Μαριάμ (indeclinable); with the *m* omitted to make Μαρία, Μαρίας; with a vowel added and the *m* sometimes doubled too, Μαριά[μ]μη, Μαριά[μ]μης; or with an *s* added to make Μαριᾶς, Μαριάδος. The same two Hebrew names are also found on the cover of the ossuary and on the other long side. In the last case we have the spelling מריה for the second name, corresponding to Μαρία, Maria.

Bagatti and Milik p. 75 fig. 19, 3, pp. 77-79 no. 7, tav 28 fot. 77. Photograph: courtesy Terra Santa.

322. Inscription with the Name Simeon Bar . . . from Dominus Flevit

THIS IS INSCRIPTION NO. 11 found written in charcoal on ossuary no. 19 in burial place no. 79 (see above no. 319). Milik reads the first five characters as shin, mem, 'ayin, waw, nun, and the next two as beth and resh written together. Thus far, then, we have:

שמעון בר

Simeon Bar

The last four characters are difficult to be sure of but could be yodh, waw, nun, and he, to give:

יונה

Jonah

Simeon and Jonah are Hebrew names of the OT, and Bar is the Aramaic "son." In the Greco-Roman period Simeon was a specially popular name, probably in part because of its equivalence to the Greek name Σίμων, Simon. In the Greek of Mt 16:17 we have Σίμων Βαριωνά (or Βὰρ Ἰωνά), which would be the exact equiva-

321. Inscription with the Names Martha and Mary from Dominus Flevit

322. Inscription with the Name Simeon Bar . . . from Dominus Flevit

lent of the above. It must be emphasized, however, that the reading of the last word in the ossuary inscription remains uncertain. The name Simeon occurs also in inscription no. 5 and on ossuary no. 8 in burial place no. 65, and in inscription no. 34 a and b on ossuary no. 107 in burial place no. 437.

In addition to the names just mentioned there are many other names in the Dominus flevit inscriptions which are familiar in the NT as well. A tabulation follows:

Name	Original Form	Inscription No.	Ossuary No.	Burial Place No.
Eleazar (Lazarus)	אלעזר	25	52	376
Jairus	Ιαειϱος	1	31	42
John	[Ιω]ανης	18	68	280
Jonathan (Ac 4:6 D)	יחונתן	16	36	80
Joseph	יסף	20	75	297
Judah (see below No. 278)	Ιουδα	13 a	21	79
Judas	Ιουδας	18	68	220
Martha (see above No. 274)	מרתה	7	27	70
Miriam (Mary) (see above No. 274)	מרים	7	27	70
Mattia (Matthias)	מתיה	3	33	55
Menahem (see above No. 273)	מנחם	22	83	299
Salome	שלום	8	29	70
Sapphira (see below No. 278)	שפירא	13 b	21	79
Simeon (see above No. 275)	שמעון	11	19	79
Yeshua (Jesus)	ישוע	29	93	425
Zechariah	Ζαχαϱ-ιου	30	95	431

In comparison with this list there may also be recalled the NT names found on the ossuaries from the Mount of Offence (see above No. 311) and from Talpioth (above Nos. 315-317):

Mount of Offence	Talpioth
Eleazar (Lazarus)	Barsaba
Jesus	Jesus
Judah	Judah (?)
Martha	Mariam (Mary)
Marias (Mary)	Matai (Matthias)
Nathanael	Simeon
Salome	
Simeon	

As for the frequency of occurrence of the several names on the ossuaries and in the NT, it is about the same.

Bagatti and Milik p. 83 no. 11, p. 86 fig. 22, 1, tav. 29 fot. 81; Milik in Bagatti and Milik p. 108. For the names seen as simply common names of the period see Rahmani in BA 45 (1952), p. 112. Photograph, courtesy Terra Santa.

323. Inscription with the Name Shalamsion and a Cross Mark from Dominus Flevit

THERE ARE ALSO a number of signs on the ossuaries which, like the inscriptions, are either incised or drawn in charcoal (Bagatti and Milik pp. 63-69). Some of these appear to have served only a practical purpose. In several cases, for example, there is a mark, perhaps a triangle or a curved mark, on the end of the chest and a corresponding mark on the end of the cover just above, these evidently being intended to show how the lid is to be placed on the chest (cf. No. 310) (see ossuary no. 64 from burial place no. 459, Bagatti and Milik p. 54 no. 64, p. 65 fig. 17, 17 and 18, tav. 27 fot. 74, and p. 100 inscription no. 43, tav. 37 fot. 117; ossuary no. 89 from burial place no. 301, Bagatti and Milik p. 55 no. 89, tav. 27 fot. 72; and ossuary no. 115 from burial place no. 437, Bagatti and Milik p. 54 fig. 16, 115, p. 57 no. 115, and pp. 97-98 inscription no. 37, p. 91 fig. 23, 6, tav. 34 fot. 105). But other signs, in the absence of any apparent utilitarian significance, appear to be intended as symbols. On ossuary no. 12 from burial place no. 79 there is a large, erect, approximately equilateral (the vertical and horizontal members measure 13 and 10 centimeters respectively) cross mark incised on the end of the chest, and a somewhat smaller cross marked incised in the sideways position on the end of the rounded cover (Bagatti and Milik p. 52 no. 12, p. 54 fig. 16, 12, pp. 64-66 fig. 17, 2, 8). This ossuary is otherwise undecorated and without any inscription, but in other cases a cross mark accompanies an inscription. The illustration shows inscription no. 17 on ossuary no. 1 from burial place no. 84 at Dominus flevit. The Hebrew name which is cut with deep, broad strokes into the upper right-hand portion of one long side of the chest, and repeated in somewhat smaller carv-

ing on the corner of the lid above, is read as follows: שלמצין

This name plainly incorportes the word *shalom*, meaning "peace," and the name of the holy hill at Jerusalem, Zion (spelled ציון in the OT, cf. No. 175). That it is indeed a personal name is shown by its occurrence in the same Hebrew form on an ossuary from the Mount of Offence (cf. above No. 311), where the name is followed by the designation, "daughter of Shimeon the Priest" (Clermont-Ganneau I, pp. 386-392). The same name in Greek is to be read, with restorations, on another ossuary from Dominus flevit (inscription no. 2 on ossuary no. 32 from burial place no. 42; Bagatti and Milik pp. 71-74, tav. 35 fot. 109): [Σαλα]μσι[ων]. In Josephus (*Ant.* XVIII 5, 4 §130) the same name occurs as that of the daughter of Herod the Great and Mariamme, Σαλαμψιώ. We may render the name, therefore, as Shalam-Zion or Shalamsion, and understand it as meaning etymologically, "Peace of Zion." Looking again at the name on the side of the chest in the photograph, we see that immediately under the lamedh and the mem is an approximately equilateral cross mark carved in the sideways position.

Bagatti and Milik pp. 67, 75 fig. 19, 6, pp. 87-88 no. 17, tav. 29 fot. 84. Photograph: courtesy Terra Santa.

323. Inscription with the Name Shalamsion and a Cross Mark from Dominus Flevit

324. Inscription with the Name Diogenes and a Cross Mark from Dominus Flevit

THIS IS INSCRIPTION NO. 21a on ossuary no. 81 from burial place no. 299 at Dominus flevit. The text is cut deeply into the cover of the ossuary, and reads:

ΔΙΟΓΕΝΗСΠΡΟСΗΛΥΤΟС
ΖΗΝΑ
Διογένης προσήλυτος
Ζηνᾶ

On the edge of the chest is the similar incised inscription:

Διογένης Ζηνᾶ π[ρ]οσήλυτος

This was, therefore, the ossuary of a man with the widely used Greek name, Diogenes, and he was probably the son of a certain Zena. He was also a proselyte, i.e., a convert to the Jewish faith (cf. Mt 23:15). In two other Dominus flevit inscriptions there is also mention of a proselyte, namely, in inscription no. 13 which will be cited below (No. 325), and in inscription no. 31 on ossuary no. 97 in burial place no. 432 (Bagatti and Milik p. 82 fig. 21, 6, p. 95 no. 31, tav. 32 fot. 97), which reads:

שלם הגירה

Salome the proselyte

Returning to inscription no. 21a with the name of Diogenes the proselyte, it may be noted in the present photograph that there is a cross mark, incised in the sideways

position, considerably below and to the left of the inscription. Likewise the similar inscription on the edge of the ossuary is followed by a similar cross mark.

Bagatti and Milik p. 89 no. 21, tav. 36 fot. 113. Photograph: courtesy Terra Santa.

325. Photograph and Drawing of Marks on Ossuary No. 21 from Dominus Flevit

OSSUARY NO. 21 (Bagatti and Milik p. 52) is one of the fourteen ossuaries found in burial place no. 79 at Dominus flevit (cf. above No. 319). It is painted in red with rosette decorations. On the center of the cover an inscription (Bagatti and Milik pp. 84-85 no. 13 b, p. 86 fig. 22, 3, tav. 29 fot. 82) is traced in charcoal with a single name:

שפירא

Sapphira

Inside the ossuary, below the edge of one long side, is a longer inscription in Greek (Bagatti and Milik pp. 84-85 no. 13 a, p. 91 fig. 23, 4, tav. 35 fot. 112):

ΙΟΥΔΑΑΝ̄ΠΡΟСΗΛΥΤΟ
ΤΥΡΑ

The name Ἰούδα with which the inscription begins can be the genitive of Ἰούδας, which can be rendered either Judah (cf. Mt 1:2, etc.) or Judas (cf. Mt 13:55, etc.). The abbreviation ν stands for νεώτερος, "younger." The next word is plainly προσήλυτος, "proselyte" (Mt

324. Inscription with the Name Diogenes and a Cross Mark from Dominus Flevit

23:15), in the genitive, lacking only the final upsilon. The word in the second line presents difficulties. If it could be read as Τύρου it could be the genitive of Τύρος, the city of Tyre, and could refer to the man's place of origin. The word is more probably τυρα, however, and one interpretation sees this as the genitive of τυρᾶς and the latter as a popular form of τυροποιός, which means a cheese maker. In this case the text reads:

Ἰουδᾶ ν(εωτέρου) προσηλύτο[υ] τυρᾶ

(Bones) of Judah the Younger, a proselyte, a cheese maker

This ossuary is of special interest for the signs, traced in charcoal, on one short end; the fragments bearing the signs are shown in this photograph and drawing. The sign at the left is scarcely to be made out in the photograph, but close inspection reveals it as reproduced in the drawing. It appears that it could be an eight-pointed

star or a monogram of some sort. If it is of Christian significance it could be the familiar combination of iota and chi to stand for Jesus Christ (cf. above p. 352) plus a horizontal stroke for the addition of a cross mark or, more simply stated, a combination of two cross marks, × and +.

The sign at the right is composed quite unmistakably of the Greek letters chi and rho written together as a monogram. Attestation of the use of this monogram as a Christian sign long before the time of Constantine has been presented above, and several possibilities of its interpretation in a Christian sense have been given (pp. 353ff.). We call it a Christ-monogram, for its most frequent occurrence seems to be as an abbreviation of the name of Christ, i.e., Χρ (ιστός); it may equally well mean Christian, i.e., Χρ (ιστιανός). Other understandings are also possible in a secular sense and some examples have also been given above. Here, however, on an ossuary the meaning of Christian is perhaps the most likely. This designation for followers of Jesus was used at Antioch about A.D. 44 (Ac 11:26) and at Rome about A.D. 64 (Tacitus, Annals xv 44, *Christianos*), hence was probably well known in many places by the middle of the first century. At both Antioch and Rome it was applied primarily to persons who had come from paganism (cf. Adolf Harnack, *The Mission and Expansion of Christianity in the First Three Centuries*, 2d ed. 1908, ii p. 126) and, according to the inscription inside this ossuary, this Judah was a proselyte, i.e., he had been a pagan before coming into Judaism and (if the monogram indeed indicates this) into Christianity.

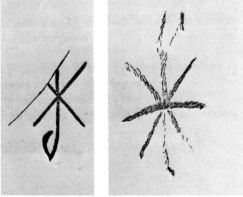

325. Photograph and Drawing of Marks on Ossuary No. 21 from Dominus Flevit

Burzachechi in *Atti della Pontificia Accademia Romana di archeologia, Rendiconti* xxviii (1954-55), pp. 200-201 no. 6; Bagatti andMilik pp. 64-65 fig. 17, 1, pp. 178-179, tav. 27 fot. 75, and frontispiece; Testa pp. 137-139 no. 25, pp. 401-402 no. 16; Dinkler in jac 5 (1962), pp. 96, 111; Margherita Guarducci, *Epigrafia Greca*, 4 vols. (Rome: Istituto Poligrafico dello Stato, 1967-78), iv, pp. 441-443, no. 1. Against recognition of the chi-rho as a Christian symbol, see A. Ferrua in rac 30 (1954), p. 268; R. de Vaux in rb 66 (1959), pp. 300f.; and M. Avi-Yonah in iej 11 (1961), p. 94. For the suggestion that the chi-rho monogram abbreviates χαραχθέν (from χαράσσω, to inscribe or engrave) and simply means that the ossuary has been "sealed," see Don Pasquale Colella, "Les abbreviations ʊ et ⳨(xr)," in rb 80 (1973), pp. 555-558. For the conclusion that the crude crosses and cross-like marks on the ossuaries are devoid of religious significance and almost always are of practical import (guides for matching lids to receptacles and the like), see Robert Houston Smith, "The Cross Marks on Jewish Ossuaries," in peq 1974, pp. 53-66. Although Kane (in peq 1971, p. 108) affirms that "No certain traces of a Christian presence have yet been found in any of the tombs of Jerusalem of this period," he mentions as "the most intriguing possibilities" the tomb of the Cyrenaican family including Alexander the son of Simon (No. 314) and this chi-rho mark at Dominus flevit. Photograph: courtesy Terra Santa.

326. Photograph and Drawing of Marks on Ossuary No. 18 from Dominus Flevit

OSSUARY NO. 18 (Bagatti and Milik p. 52) was also found in burial place no. 79 at Dominus flevit. Cut into the cover of the ossuary, near one corner, is the combination of marks shown in this photograph and drawing. Disregarding the crack toward the right, we see a roughly vertical and equilateral cross mark. From the right arm of this a stroke descends in two curves to complete what appears to be the capital letter beta. Then a diagonal stroke is cut deeply across the whole. All this together can be seen as a monogram comprising the letters iota, chi, and beta. In the light of parallels noted above (pp. 352f., 354), it can be understood as standing for Ἰησοῦς Χριστὸς Βοήθια, with some such meaning as "Jesus Christ (is our) help." For the concept of "help" (βοήθεια) reference may be made to Heb 4:16, and to the saying of Justin Martyr (*Dialogue* 30, 3): "For we call him Helper and Redeemer (βοηθὸν γὰρ ἐκεῖνον καὶ λυτρωτὴν καλοῦμεν), the power of whose name even the demons fear."

326. Photograph and Drawing of Marks on Ossuary No. 18 from Dominus Flevit

With respect to the items which have now been shown from Dominus flevit (Nos. 320-326) it is of interest to note that many of the signs which are capable of a Christian interpretation and many of the names which are also known in the NT come from the group of burial places nos. 65-80 and in particular from the one burial place no. 79 (cf. No. 319). In burial place no. 79 were ossuaries no. 12 marked with + and ×, no. 18 with iota, chi, and beta in a monogram, no. 19 with the name Simeon Bar . . . , and no. 21 with chi and rho in a monogram and the names Judah and Sapphira; while also in burial places 65-80 outside of 79 were ossuaries no. 1 with a cross mark accompanying the name Shalamsion, no. 27 with the names Martha and Mary, no. 29 with the name Salome, and no. 36 with the name Jonathan. Where there are, thus, signs that can be Christian, and names that are frequent or prominent in the NT and therefore might have been preferred by Christians, it surely comes within the realm of possibility that at least this area in particular is a burial place of Jewish families some of whose members had become Christians.

Bagatti and Milik pp. 64-65 fig. 17, 3, tav. 27 fot. 71; Testa pp. 396-398 fig. 145, 10, tav. 41 fot. 4. Against the conclusions of Bagatti and Milik, see Rahmani in BA 45 (1982), pp. 116f., but on Dominus flevit and in support of Bagatti, Testa, and Mancini, see Cornfeld, pp. 306-308. Photograph: courtesy Terra Santa.

HERCULANEUM

327. Wall Mark at Herculaneum

FOR COMPARISON and elucidation with respect to the marks that have been noted in Palestine, brief mention may also be made of some similar marks from outside of Palestine. In Italy the town of Herculaneum lies at the foot of the volcano Vesuvius and, like the city of Pompeii ten miles to the east, was destroyed by the eruption of that volcano in A.D. 79. Here in an upper room of the so-called Bicentenary House attention was attracted by the wall mark shown in the present photograph. It is a depression in a stucco panel and could be where an object of the same shape had been affixed to the wall and then removed. There are nail holes in the depression and also elsewhere in the panel. One theory sees the shape of the depression as that of a Latin cross (cf. p. 352), and supposes that if a wooden cross had been nailed to the wall at this point, then removed and a wooden covering nailed over the area, it would account for what can still be seen. In that case the upper room with this cross could have been a sort of private Christian chapel, and

327. Wall Mark at Herculaneum

the removal of the cross and the covering over of the area could have been done either by the Christians themselves or by others, and a likely time for this might have been during persecution such as that by Nero in A.D. 64. Other opinion, however, sees the place in the wall and the cross-shaped mark as simply where some practical object, probably a wall cabinet, was once affixed.

Amadeo Maiuri in *Rendiconti della Pontificia Accademia Romana di Archeologia* 15 (1939), pp. 193-218; L. de Bruyne in RAC 21 (1945), pp. 281-309; William L. Holladay in JBR 19 (1951), pp. 16-19; André Parrot, *Golgotha and the Church of the Holy Sepulchre*, p. 117. Photograph: courtesy William L. Holladay.

328. Stand at Herculaneum

THE PIECE of wooden furniture shown in this photograph stood against the wall beneath the panel with the cross-shaped mark in the upper room in the Bicentenary House at Herculaneum. When found it was entirely covered with the deposit of the volcanic eruption of A.D. 79. If the mark in the wall above is taken as a cross, then the stand below could be explained as a sort of altar. Otherwise the stand could have been of only utilitarian import.

L. De Bruyne, "La 'crux interpretum' di Ercolano," in RAC 21 (1945), pp. 281-309; Erich Dinkler in ZTK 48 (1951), pp. 158-159. Photograph: William L. Holladay.

328. Stand at Herculaneum

VATICAN

329. Graffiti in the Vatican Excavations

UNDERNEATH THE CHURCH of St. Peter in the Vatican in Rome, built originally by the emperor Constantine, excavations were conducted in 1940 and later

375

in the vicinity of the traditional tomb of the apostle. As learned in the excavations and with dates as given by Guarducci (*Tomb of St. Peter*, pp. 79-91, 95f.), a so-called Red Wall was built between about A.D. 146 and 161 to fix the boundary between a narrow street and gutter and an adjacent area of first and second century tombs. At the same time that the Red Wall was built (c. 160) a double niche was indented in it with two marble columns set beside the lower niche. This evidently formed a small shrine and was in all probability the "trophy" or grave monument of Peter, which is mentioned by Gaius of Rome about A.D. 200 (Eusebius, *Ch. Hist.* II 25; FLAP pp. 382, 514). In about 250, apparently to stabilize the area, Wall G (as the excavators call it) was built as a buttress perpendicular to the Red Wall. In about 315 Constantine enclosed the shrine and Wall G in a marble monument and then, beginning in about 322, built over the whole his great new basilica. In turn, above the

shrine and Constantine's marble monument was erected a sequence of superimposed altars, namely, those of Gregory the Great (590-604), Callistus II (1119-1124), and Clement VIII (1592-1605), the last being the present altar in the church.

On Wall G is a mass of graffiti, so thick that in places there are two or three layers one on top of the other. Almost all are in Latin, and they were obviously written by many pilgrims who visited this sacred spot. For the most part they are names and simple prayers for the spiritual well-being of relatives or friends, living or dead. In the light of the history just outlined the date of the graffiti is between about 290 and 315 (Guarducci, *I graffiti*, II, p. 443), and a great many of them are certainly earlier than the formation by Constantine of the "Constantinian" monogram in A.D. 312. As mentioned above (p. 354) in this connection, there are many examples in the graffiti of Wall G of the chi-rho monogram (☧) and one

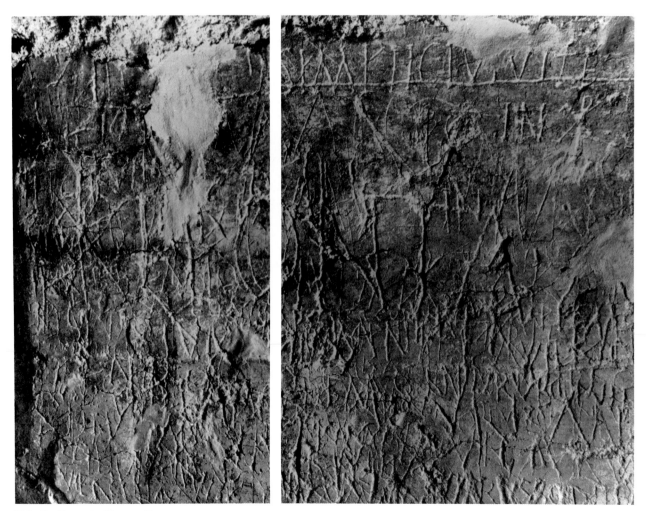

329. Graffiti in the Vatican Excavations

example of the cross-monogram (☧), as well as other abbreviations of the name of Christ such as ✕ and ✷ (Christ and Christ Jesus) (see the indexes in Guarducci, ibid., II, pp. 461f., 471f.).

The present overlapping photographs show a part of the upper left-hand corner of Wall G (sec. 1 and 2, and tav. 1 and 2 in Guarducci, ibid., III). About one-third of the way from the top and running across from the left margin of the first picture and to beyond the middle of the second picture is the large graffito which is traced as follows in its main components (Guarducci, ibid., II, p. 6): This is the name of a woman, Leonia, preceded by and connected with the chi-rho monogram of Christ. One arm of the chi is connected with the initial L of the personal name, and this may be understood to signify a desired connection between Christ and the person. That Leonia is a deceased woman is indicated by the wish written across the chi-rho (not shown in the tracing) i(n) vivis tu v(i)v(e) a(d) Pet(rum), "may you live among the living close to Peter." Without stopping with all the other signs which are woven in with the basic graffito, we note that at the end of the name a thin line runs over the top of the I between the N and the A, and the line on top of the I gives us here a T-cross; thus the name of Leonia is framed between the signs of Christ and of the Cross. The connecting of the N and A can also provide a contraction of the cry of victory (Greek νίκα, Latin nica), "conquer." A later graffito of the same import has also been written in above and to the right of the chi-rho preceding the name of Leontia. This inscription reads in two lines: HOC VIN(CE), "with this conquer," and in position next to the chi-rho must be a reference to the vision of Constantine on the eve of his battle at the Milvian bridge (above, p. 354, hence this upper garffito must be one of those on Wall G which are after that date (A.D. 312) (Guarducci, Tomb of St. Peter, pp. 112-118, 123-125; and I graffiti, II, no. 2, pp. 6-75).

The graffito with the cross-monogram (☧) is to be seen near the center of the upper part of Wall G (about one-third of the way from the top in Guarducci, I graffiti, III, sec. 3 and 4 and tav. 3 and 4; not shown in No. 329). In its basic form the inscription reads: NIKASI VIBAS IN ☧. The name is that of Nikasius, a common name in the Christian society at Rome in the first century, and the graffito expresses the hope and belief that this deceased person "lives in Christ." The K in the name was elaborated, however, to make a cross-monogram and then to make the lower part into an A, perhaps to suggest the alpha (and omega). Likewise additional signs were woven into the final chi-rho (Guarducci, ibid., II, no. 8, pp. 89-95).

Jocelyn Toynbee and John Ward Perkins, *The Shrine of St. Peter and the Vatican Excavations* (New York: Pantheon Books, 1957);

Margherita Guarducci, *I graffiti sotto la confessione di San Pietro in Vaticano* (Città del Vaticano: Librarie Editrice Vaticana, 1958); and Guarducci, *The Tomb of St. Peter, The New Discoveries in the Sacred Grottoes of the Vatican* (New York: Hawthorn Books, 1960). Photographs from Guarducci, *I graffiti*, III, tav. 1 and 2: courtesy Margherita Guarducci.

CROSS MARKS IN THE CATACOMBS

330. A Painted Inscription in the Jewish Catacomb in the Villa Torlonia

IN THE JEWISH catacombs at Rome (cf. Nos. 288-295) very few marks in the form of a cross are to be found, but this photograph shows one example. In the catacomb in the Villa Torlonia this inscription, painted in red, was found on a broken piece of stucco grave closure in a loculus at the point numbered 24 on the right side of the corridor letter C-G on the plan (above No. 293). So far as it is preserved the text reads:

ΠΑΓΧΑΡΙΟC   Παγχάριος
ΚΑΛΩC ΕΝΘΑΔΕ   καλῶς ἐνθάδε

How much more of the original inscription is lacking at the left or right or both is uncertain. By comparison with many other examples (above No. 289, etc.), it may be supposed that the word κεῖται was used, or may be understood, so that the translation can be: "Pancharios lies here honorably." In other examples, however, the word βιώσας is connected with the word καλῶς. Thus an inscription on a marble plaque in the Jewish catacomb in the Vigna Randanini on the Via Appia (Frey I, pp. 81-82 no. 118; cf. also nos. 9, 23, 82, 117, 119, 336, 353, 411, 509, 537) begins:

ΖΩΤΙΚΟC ΑΡΧΩΝ ΕΝΘΑΔΕ
ΚΕΙΜΕ ΚΑΛΩC ΒΕΙΩCΑC

Ζωτικὸς ἄρχων ἐνθάδε κεῖμ(αι) καλῶς β(ε) ιώσας

(I), Zotikos, an archon, lie here, having lived well (*or*, honorably)

By this analogy we could supply both words in the inscription shown above, to read: βιώσας] καλῶς ἐνθάδε [κεῖται and then the translation would be: "Pancharios, having lived honorably, lies here." Beneath the text are

330. A Painted Inscription in the Jewish Catacomb in the Villa Torlonia

three drawings also in red paint. The one at the left represents something which it is difficult to identify, but which may be a fruit, and, if so, perhaps an *ethrog* (cf. No. 289). The one in the middle appears plainly to be an ivy leaf, as is found elsewhere very frequently (cf. No. 289). The one at the right is a swastika or *crux gammata* with the outer arms turned to the right (cf. p. 352). These outer arms appear, however, to be painted in more lightly than the main branches of the cross, and the one at the bottom cannot even be made out with certainty. It could be surmised, therefore, that the outer arms were a later addition, and that there was originally here an equilateral cross. In that case the question could be raised as to whether this is an example of the Hebrew *taw* used with connotations of deliverance as an appropriate symbol to accompany a grave inscription (cf. p. 355). Also it could be asked if the alteration to a swastika was made after the original cross mark had been too widely recognized as a Christian symbol to be any longer appropriate in a Jewish catacomb.

Beyer and Lietzmann, *Die jüdische Katakombe der Villa Torlonia in Rom*, pp. 5-6, p. 32 no. 24, pl. 16 no. 24; Frey I, pp. 32-33 no. 48; Goodenough II, p. 43, Photograph: Beyer and Lietzmann, ibid., pl. 16 no. 24, courtesy Walter de Gruyter and Co., Berlin.

331. Rufina Inscription in the Catacomb of Lucina

Of the Christian catacombs at Rome the four oldest are those which have the names of Lucina, Callistus, Domitilla, and Priscilla, all of which probably originated at least by the middle of the second century (FLAP pp. 456ff.). In the Lucina catacomb the inscription shown in this photograph was found still in its original place on the closure of a loculus. It is a simple epitaph containing the name of the deceased ΡΟΥΦΙΝΑ, Rufina, a feminine

name (Preisigke, *Namenbuch*, col. 355), and the single word ΕΙΡΗΝΗ, peace. Beneath is an equilateral or Greek cross (cf. p. 352). The date is about the middle of the second century (Wilpert) or at the turn from the second to the third century (Styger).

De Rossi I pl. XVIII no. 1; Wilpert, "La croce," p. 5; DACL 3:2 col. 3056; Styger p. 28. Photograph: Styger pl. 5 fac, p. 32 (Berlin: Verlag für Kunstwissenschaft, 1933).

332. Irene Inscription in the Catacomb of Callistus

THIS INSCRIPTION was found in the oldest part of the Catacomb of Callistus and may date from the middle of the second century (Wilpert). The epitaph consists only of the name of the deceased, IRENE, but between the third and fourth letters and raised above the line is inserted a Latin letter t, corresponding to the Greek tau, and constituting a form of the cross. In this connection it will be remembered (above p. 351) that Tertullian (*Against Marcion* III 22) spoke of "the mark Tau" on the foreheads of the men of Jerusalem (Ezk 9:4), and added: "Now the Greek letter Tau and our own letter T is the very form of the cross."

De Rossi I pl. XLIII No. 14; Wilpert, "La croce," p. 13. Photograph: De Rossi, ibid. (1864).

333. A Cross in Anchor Form in the Catacomb of Domitilla

THIS BROKEN MARBLE plaque is found in the Catacomb of Domitilla. Here the cross is in the form of an anchor, with a fish on either side. In this case perhaps

331. Rufina Inscription in the Catacomb of Lucina

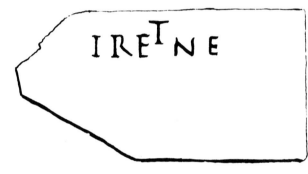

332. Irene Inscription in the Catacomb of Callistus

333. A Cross in Anchor Form in the Catacomb of Domitilla

the fishes are Christians caught by the cross. The circle on the upper part of the cross can be a sun disk. At the right can be also an alpha and omega combined with a cross.

Emil Bock and Robert Goebel, *Die Katakomben, Bilder aus der Welt des frühen Christentums* (Stuttgart: Urachhaus, 1930), p. 27 and no. 27. Photograph: JF.

334. Painted Sign in the Catacomb of Priscilla

THIS SIGN is painted in red on a tile found still attached to a loculus in the Catacomb of Priscilla. The date is probably the middle of the second century (Wilpert). What the marks at the right should signify is not evident. The marks at the left consist essentially of the letters iota and eta, the two first letters of the name of

379

Jesus in Greek. These are combined in a way somewhat like that in the monogram already mentioned (above p. 353), but in this case the letters may be considered to be set one after the other, with a horizontal stroke extended through and beyond both, resulting in the appearance of three Greek crosses set side by side and connected.

> G. B. de Rossi, "L'epigrafia primitiva priscilliana," in BAC 1886, pp. 34-171, especially p. 78 no. 101, p. 171 pl. XI no. 3; Wilpert, "La croce," pp. 5-6; DACL 3:2, col. 3056. Photograph: Wilpert, ibid., p. 6 fig. 1 (1902).

335. Trisomus Inscription in the Catacomb of Priscilla

THE OLDEST AREA in the Catacomb of Priscilla is the so-called Hypogeum of the Acilians. A grave for three bodies (*trisomus*) was dug in the floor of one passageway and must, therefore, represent a second period in the utilization of this area. The inscribed marble plaque shown in the illustration was found still in its original position over this grave. The date is probably still in the second century or in the third (de Rossi), but not as late as the fourth. In the following transcription of the Greek text spaces are left between words in correspondence with the

original, in which a small conventional sign marks the spaces in each case except the first (after the first two words). In the two cases where the connective καί occurs it is abbreviated with a stroke over the kappa. Ligature of nu and pi and nu and tau will be noted in the first line, and of eta and nu in the second line (three times). The inscription terminates with two signs of which at least the first, the chi-rho monogram, is to be read as a part of the text.

ΟΠΑΤΗΡ ΤѠΝΠΑΝΤѠΝ ΟΥC ΕΠΟΙΗCΕC K̄
ΠΑΡΕΛΑΒΗC ΕΙΡΗΝΗΝ ΖΟΗΝ K̄ ΜΑΡΚΕΛΛΟΝ
CΟΙΔΟΘΑ ΕΝ ☧

ὁ πατήρ τῶν πάντων οὓς ἐποίησες καὶ
παρελάβης Εἰρήνην, Ζόην, καὶ Μάρκελλον
σοὶ δόξα ἐν Χριστῷ

In spite of errors in the grammar, the inscription is quite evidently intended to say:

> O Father of all, who hast created and
> taken (to thyself) Eirene, Zoe, and Marcellus,
> to thee be glory in Christ.

334. Painted Sign in the Catacomb of Priscilla

335. Trisomus Inscription in the Catacomb of Priscilla

The sign which follows the chi-rho monogram is an anchor. According to Heb 6:19 hope is the anchor of the soul, and the anchor therefore became a symbol of confidence that the deceased was safe in the harbor of eternal peace. Like other appropriately formed objects connected with a ship (see above p. 351), the anchor was also recognized as a form of the cross. In this light the anchor says that the cross is the foundation of Christian hope. If, in the present inscription the anchor is to be read as a part of the text, the last line could be taken to say: "To thee be glory. In Christ (is) our hope." But if the last line is read as in our translation above, then the anchor can be taken as a separate sign, a mark accompanying many other epitaphs in the catacombs, expressive of the Christian hope, founded in the cross, that the deceased will arrive safely in the port of eternal peace.

De Rossi in BAC 1888-89, pp. 31-33; DACL 1:2, col. 2027; Styger pp. 104-105. On the fact that the cross mark is found in the catacomb inscriptions but scarcely at all in the earlier catacomb paintings, see Joseph Wilpert, *Die Malereien der Katakomben Roms* (Freiburg in Breisgau: Herder, 1903). Textband. p. 496. Photograph: Styger pl. 18 fac. p. 112 (Berlin: Verlag für Kunstwissenschaft, 1933).

THE CROSS MARK IN MANUSCRIPTS

336. A Page in Papyrus Bodmer II (P⁶⁶)

PAPYRUS BODMER II (P⁶⁶) is a manuscript in codex form with numbered pages which contains most of the Gospel according to John, Chapters 1-14, and fragments of the rest of the Gospel through Chapter 21. It was probably written about A.D. 200 if not even earlier. In the manuscript at most of the places where the noun σταυρός, "cross," and the verb σταυρόω, "crucify," occur an abbreviation of the word is employed in which the tau and the rho are written together to make the sign ⳨ (cf. above p. 354). The present photograph shows the extant fragments of page 137 (ΡΛΖ) in the codex. The beginning of line 3 contains that section of Jn 19:16 where it is stated that Pilate delivered Jesus "to be crucified." Here the verb σταυρωθῇ is abbreviated σ ⳨ θη. The initial sigma is badly preserved but the remaining

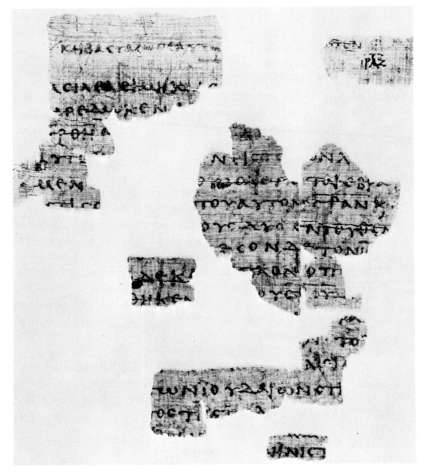

336. A Page in Papyrus Bodmer II (P⁶⁶)

letters are plainly legible together with the line over them which marks the abbreviation. Line 6 contains the mention of Golgotha in Jn 19:17, and continues with the opening words of Jn 19:18, "where they crucified him. . . ." Here the verb ἐσταύρωσαν is abbreviated $^\epsilon σ$ ⳨ $αν$, the initial epsilon being lifted above the level of the other letters as shown. Line 10 contains a portion of Jn 19:19 where Pilate wrote a title "and put it on the cross." Here, although it is more difficult to make out because of the break in the papyrus, the noun σταυροῦ is abbreviated $σ$ ⳨ $ου$.

Victor Martin, *Papyrus Bodmer II* (Cologny-Genève: Bibliothèque Bodmer. *Evangile de Jean, chap. 1-14*, 1956); *chap. 14-21*, 1958; Victor Martin and J. W. B. Barns, *Nouvelle édition augmentée et corrigée avec reproduction photographique complète du manuscrit* (*chap. 1-21*), 1962; Kurt Aland in NTS 10 (1963-64), pp. 62-79, especially p. 75, and note the rejection of Sulzberger's position on p. 79. Photograph Martin and Barns, ibid., pl. 133, courtesy Bibliotheca Bodmeriana.

337. A Page in Papyrus Bodmer XIV (P[75])

PAPYRUS BODMER XIV-XV (P[75]) is a codex which contains most of the Gospel according to Luke, Chapters 3-24 (Papyrus Bodmer XIV), and of the Gospel according to John, Chapters 1-15 (Papyrus Bodmer XV). The date of the manuscript is probably at the beginning of the third century, perhaps within the range A.D. 175-225. Thus it is of substantially the same age as P[66] (above No. 336), perhaps not quite as old. In this manuscript also the Greek words "cross" and "crucify" are abbreviated. In some places, but not in others, the abbreviation employs the ⳨ sign, the same as in P[66]. In the case of the Gospel according to John, Papyrus Bodmer XV breaks off in Chapter 15, and Chapter 19, in which are all the occurrences of "cross" and "crucify," is not available for inspection. The examples of the abbreviation are, therefore, all in the Gospel according to Luke, i.e., in Papyrus Bodmer XIV. The page of this papyrus shown in the photograph contains Lk 9:23-33. In line 8 is a portion of Lk 9:23 where Jesus says that if any man would come after him, "let him . . . take up his cross daily." Here the noun σταυρόν is abbreviated $σ$ ⳨ $ον$.

Victor Martin and Rodolphe Kasser, *Papyrus Bodmer XIV, Evangile de Luc. chap. 3-24* (Cologny-Genève: Bibliothèque Bodmer, 1961); Kurt Aland in NTS 11 (1964-65), pp. 1-21, especially pp. 1-3. Photograph: Martin and Kasser, ibid., pl. 19, courtesy Bibliotheca Bodmeriana.

338. A Page in the Gospel of Truth (Codex Jung)

THE GOSPEL of Truth (cf. FHRJ §§336ff.) is one of the works contained in the Coptic Gnostic manuscripts from Nag Hammadi. It is the second work in Codex I and was probably copied in the middle of the fourth century. Although the work has no title it begins with the words, "The Gospel of Truth is joy . . . ," and is therefore probably to be recognized as the book of that title which Irenaeus (*Against Heresies* III 11, 9), writing about A.D. 180, says had been composed recently among the Valentinian Gnostics. The pages of this codex are carefully numbered at the top, and this page, which is the *verso* of folio x, has the letter kappa which numbers it as page 20. In line 27 the text is making a statement, evidently based on Col 2:14, to the effect that when Jesus was crucified he also fastened the deed of disposition (διάταγμα) which came from the Father "to the cross." Here, as may be seen in this line in the photograph, the word "cross" is abbreviated C ⳨ OC.

Michel Malinine, Henri-Charles Peuch, and Gilles Quispel, *Evangelium Veritatis* (Zürich: Rascher Verlag, 1956). Photograph: ibid., f. x[v] p. 20, courtesy Rascher Verlag.

THE ANKH-CROSS

THE LIGATURE of tau and rho in the foregoing abbreviations (Nos. 336-338) forms a sign which, at least when it stands alone, we have called a cross-monogram (see above p. 354). As a sign by itself this is decidedly reminiscent of the Egyptian ankh sign which became a form of the cross and is known as the *crux ansata* or handled cross (see above p. 352). Because of this similarity, and because the tau-rho monogram occurs in the papyrus manuscripts just mentioned which must have been copied in Egypt, the possibility is suggested that this form of monogram may have originated in Egypt and under the influence of the ankh sign. Since the cross-monogram is found in the copy of the Valentinian Gnostic *Gospel of Truth* contained in the Jung Codex, the question could further be raised whether the development of this sign is to be attributed specifically to the Valentinian Gnostics. Since the sign is also used in the Bodmer papyri of the Gospels according to John (P[66]) and according to Luke (P[75]), however, it is probably not possible to narrow down the origin of the cross-monogram to so specific a point. At any rate we will turn now to Egypt to see there examples of the ankh (Nos. 339-340), of the cross-monogram (No. 341) and of the *crux ansata* which in Egypt, the land of its origin, we will call the ankh-cross (Nos. 342-344).

Jean de Savignac, "Chronique," in *Scriptorium* 17 (1963), pp. 50-52 (note that Savignac also criticizes the position of Sulzberger); Kurt Aland in NTS 11 (1964-65), pp. 2-3.

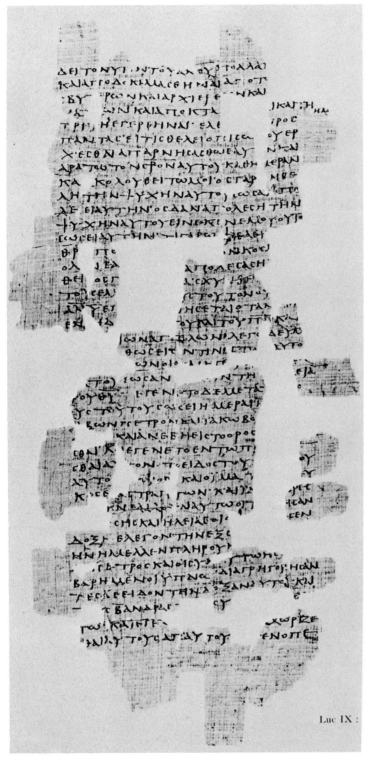

337. A Page in Papyrus Bodmer XIV (P75)

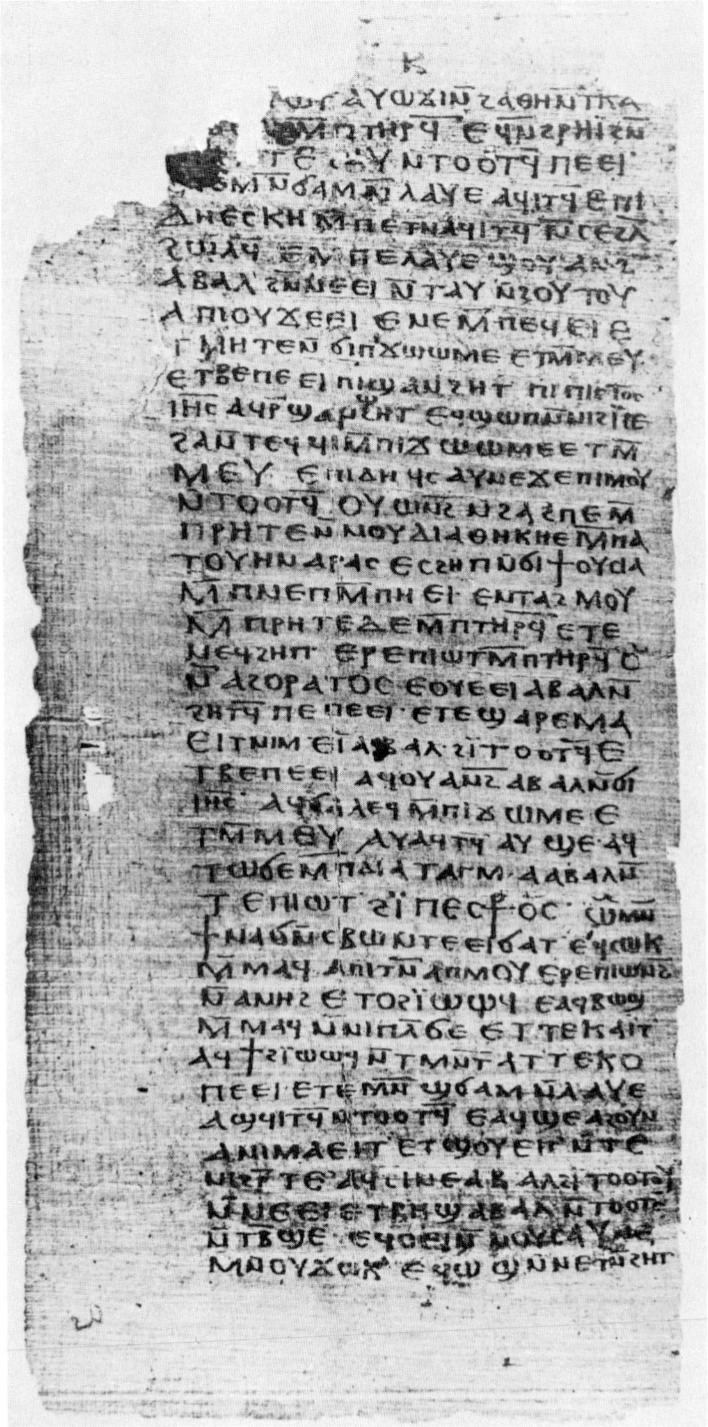

338. A Page in the Gospel of Truth (Codex Jung)

339. Slate Dish Embodying the Sign of the Ankh

THE ANKH is the name of a sign very widely found in Egyptian art and writing. From its form it appears to have been first of all a knot and then perhaps a knotted amulet. Used in hieroglyphic writing it is the sign ♀ and means "life." The slate dish in the photograph is from the Early Dynastic period; it embodies two hieroglyphic signs, and combines them to make a monogram. The raised back edge of the dish is continued around the two sides in the form of arms which terminate in hands. This is the hieroglyph for *ku* or *ka*, which probably designates the configuration of characteristics of a person and is sometimes translated "spirit." It does not concern us fur-

ther here. The other hieroglyph is the ankh. It is contrived to provide the handle and remaining side of the dish, and the circular portion of its interior. It looks like a knotted tape and appears to confirm the theory that the sign originated as a knot, perhaps the knot in a sandal strap or in a headband.

William C. Hayes, *The Scepter of Egypt* (New York: The Metropolitan Museum of Art, 1953), I, pp. 42-43, 79; Maria Cramer, *Das altägyptische Lebenszeichen* (Wiesbaden: Otto Harrassowitz, 1955). Photograph: courtesy The Metropolitan Museum of Art, Rogers Fund, 1919.

340. The Ankh Sign in Ancient Egypt

AS THE SIGN of "life" the ankh appears on the monuments of ancient Egypt in all periods. Here it is carved with other characters on a column of the famous terraced temple of Queen Hatshepsut (fifteenth century B.C.) at Deir el-Bahri in Upper Egypt. Elsewhere it is often held in the hand of a god or a king. In this its conventional form the ankh can be described most simply as like a Tau cross with a loop at the top. As such it lent itself to adoption by Christians as a form of the Christian cross. In its meaning of "life" it was also appropriate for such adoption. The connection between the cross and life is implicit in much of the NT and is brought out by Ignatius (*To the Ephesians* XVIII 1) in a passage in which there are

339. Slate Dish Embodying the Sign of the Ankh

340. The Ankh Sign in Ancient Egypt

manifold echoes of NT language and thought: "My spirit is devoted (περίψημα, cf. 1 Cor 4:13) to the cross (τοῦ σταυροῦ, cf. 1 Cor 1:18), which is a stumbling-block (σκάνδαλον, cf. 1 Cor 1:23; Gal 5:11) to those who do not believe (τοῖς ἀπιστοῦσιν, cf. 1 Pet 2:7), but to us salvation and life eternal (ζωὴ αἰώνιος, cf. Jn 6:54, etc.)." It is undoubtedly to this sign that Socrates (*Ch. Hist.* IV 17) and Sozomen (*Ch. Hist.* VII 15) refer when they tell how, at the destruction of the Serapeum in Alexandria by the patriarch Theophilus (A.D. 391), hieroglyphic characters were found which had the form of crosses, and pagan converts to Christianity explained that they signified "life to come" (ζωὴν ἐπερχομένην) (FHRJ §85). It is also hardly to be doubted that the potential of the ankh-sign for adaptation to Christian meaning had been observed and acted upon long before this. As noted just above (p. 381f.), the tau-rho abbreviation and cross-monogram may well reflect the ankh and are attested in Egypt at least by the third century in the manuscripts cited above (Nos. 336-338) as well as in the next inscription to be shown (No. 341). The ankh-cross itself appears on monuments for which dates are commonly held which push back at least into the fourth century (No. 343) and which, one suspects, could in some cases be even earlier.

DACL 3:2, cols. 3120-3123. Photograph: JF.

341. Inscription from Gabbari

GABBARI IS A SUBURB of Alexandria lying on the narrow strip of land between Lake Mareotis and the Western Harbor. On the seaside to the northwest of Gabbari a hypogeum was found in 1876 which appeared to go back to the fourth century and contained a Christian inscription. In the vicinity and even with the

341. Inscription from Gabbari

ground was an inscribed marble tablet, 19 by 21 centimeters in size, which is now in the Greco-Roman Museum in Alexandria (Inventory no. 11706) and is shown in the photograph. The character of the letters is judged similar to that in inscriptions of the time of the emperor Gordian III (A. 238-244). The Greek text is as follows:

KYPΙΟCΜΝΗCΘΙ
ΤΗCΚΟΙΜΗCΕΟC
ΘΕΟΔΟΤΗC
ΚΑΙΑΝΑΠΑΥCΕωC
ΝΙΛΑΜΜωΝΟC

In the last line (line 5) the first two or three letters can only be made out with some difficulty, and some have wished to read MΛ or MA instead of ΝΙΛ. The present reading appears to be correct, however, and gives a name (Νιλάμων) that is otherwise known (Preisigke, *Namenbuch*, col. 235), which is not the case with the other combinations. Furthermore a single word consisting of a single name at this point balances perfectly with the same in line 3. The Greek text may therefore be repeated and translated as follows:

Κύριος μνησθὶ
τῆς κοιμήσεος
Θεοδότης
καὶ ἀναπαύσεως
Νιλάμμωνος

Lord, remember
the repose
of Theodota
and the rest
of Nilammon

Beneath this text and comprising the sixth line of the inscription is the cross-monogram with alpha and omega on either side (cf. above, p. 354).

Lefebvre p. 5 no. 21; DACL 1:1, col. 1151. Photograph: courtesy Greco-Roman Museum.

342. Inscription from Tehneh

TEHNEH IS AN ANCIENT site on the east side of the Nile some ninety-five miles below Asyut and across from Minieh. At the foot of a mountain called Jebel el-Teir is a Roman necropolis and, to the north of this, a Christian necropolis, in which were found many funeral stelae with short inscriptions in Greek. One of these (Lefebvre no. 146 cf. p. xxv) is dated in the year 239 of the Era of the Martyrs (cf. FHBC §217), which is equivalent to A.D. 522/523. This suggests a probable date for the cemetery

342. Inscription from Tehneh

in the fifth and sixth centuries. In a number of the inscriptions small, plain incised ankh-signs accompany the text. They are probably from the fifth century (Cramer, p. 48). The inscription (Lefebvre no. 138) shown in the illustration is from this cemetery and is now in the Greco-Roman Museum in Alexandria (Inventory no. 27867). The piece of limestone, 27 by 18.5 centimeters in size, is only a fragment. It bears traces of red color.

ACETE
HKAI ♀

AMωNIΛ
HC L'IA
ϵN Kω
N ♀ IY

In line 3 and ending in line 4 we probably have the name Amonilla in the form Ἀμωνίλ[λη]ς (cf. Preisigke, *Namenbuch*, col. 29). This is followed by the angular sign for "year," or "years," and this by the number eleven (ι = 10 + α = 1). Then in line 5 we have, abbreviated, ἐν κυ[ρίῳ] "in the Lord"; and in line 6, also abbreviated, Ἰ[ησο] ῦ, "of Jesus." In addition, there is at the end of line 2 and prior to the abbreviated name of Jesus in line 6 the ankh sign which, in this context, may be recognized as the ankh-cross. Since the inscription is not more fully preserved it is not possible to tell whether this sign is simply inserted at places where the wording allows gaps in the lines or whether it can be read as a part of the text itself.

Gustave Lefebvre, "Inscriptions grecques de Tehnéh (Égypte)," in BCH 27 (1908), pp. 341-390 and especially p. 375 no. 118: Lefebvre p. 29 no. 138; Cramer p. 8 and abb. 2. Photograph: courtesy Greco-Roman Museum.

343. Inscription from the Vicinity of Armant

ARMANT, THE ANCIENT Hermonthis or On of the South (in contrast with On of the North, i.e., Heliopolis), is on the west bank of the Nile some fifteen miles above Luxor. On the edge of the desert to the west of Armant are many cemeteries which date from Predyn-

343. Inscription from the Vicinity of Armant

astic times onward, and among the finds are many Coptic tombstones. The stone (55 by 20 centimeters in size) with the Greek inscription shown in this photograph was said to have been found at Armant, was obtained in the neighborhood of that place, and was reported on to the Royal Irish Academy in Dublin in 1892. The text is cut into the stone inside an incised border and is accompanied by several signs. The date of the inscription is judged to be between the fourth and sixth centuries. The text, which is rather poetical in character, may be transcribed and translated as follows:

πρίν σε λέγειν ὦ τύμβε τίς ἢ τίνος ἐνθάδε κεῖται
  ἡ στήλη βοαᾷ πᾶσι παρερχομένοις
σῶμα μὲν ἐνθάδε κεῖται ἀειμνήστου Μακαρίης
  ὡς ἔθος εὐσεβέων γευσάμενον θανάτου
αὐτὴ δ' οὐρανίην ἁγίων πόλιν ἀμφιπολεύει
  μισθὸν ἔχουσα πόνων οὐρανίους στεφάνους

Before you say, O tomb, who or whose lies here, the stela
  proclaims to all who pass,
the body lies here of the ever-remembered Makaria; as is the
  custom of the pious, having tasted death,
she is herself busy in the heavenly city of the saints, having
  heavenly crowns as a reward of her sufferings.

The four signs which accompany the inscription are arranged inside the incised border, one at the left end of the last line of text and the other three underneath that line. From left to right they are a Christ-monogram (chi-rho), a cross-monogram (tau-rho), an ankh-cross, and another Christ-monogram (chi-rho).

Charles H. Keene in *Proceedings of the Royal Irish Academy*, Third Series, Vol. II 1891-1893), pp. 295-298 (Feb. 8, 1892), and pl. XI: Carl Schmidt in zÄs 32 (1894), p. 59; Lefebvre no. 423; Cramer pp. 8f. Photograph: *Proceedings of the Royal Irish Academy*, 1892, pl. XI.

344. Painting in a Tomb Chapel at the Oasis of Khargeh

FINALLY WE SHOW a painting found at Khargeh, an oasis 150 miles south-southwest of Asyut. There is a large Egyptian temple here dating from the Persian period, a smaller one from the Roman period and, in some distance to the north, a large Christian necropolis. The necropolis, known locally as el-Bagawat, comprises many hundreds of brick tombs. These structures are in fact tomb-chapels, each a chamber surmounted by a dome, with an apse that is apparent on the exterior, paintings in the interior, and sometimes with an antechamber too. The date of the paintings is probably not later than the late fourth and early fifth centuries. The finest preserved paintings are in a tomb-chapel on a bluff

at the south end of the necropolis. The dome painting in this tomb-chapel is shown in the photograph. It is divided into four concentric bands, separated from each other by rings of red; three bands are purely decorative, but the widest band shows biblical incidents and other figures. The names of the figures are written in Greek on the accompanying red ring. The subject first seen upon entering the room, at the bottom in our illustration, is Daniel in the lion's den. To the right is a tree and then a feminine figure identified as EIPHNH, Peace. In her left hand she holds a scepter or torch. In her right hand, precisely as if she were a figure on an ancient Egyptian monument, she holds a large, plainly drawn ankh which in this case must be an ankh-cross. Continuing around the circle of the paintings we find in succession: the Sacrifice of Isaac; Adam and Eve; Thecla and Paul, two early Egyptian saints; the Annunciation to Mary; Noah in the Ark; Jacob with arms lifted in prayer; then a symbolical figure representing Prayer, and finally another symbolical figure representing Justice holding a balance in one hand and a cornucopia in the other.

The fact that in Christian understanding the ankh-cross signifies "life to come" (cf. No. 340), means that, even though its external form is different, this form of the cross-sign is not unrelated to the primitive *taw*-mark of salvation. That mark, derived from Jewish background and perhaps already used by Jewish Christians on ossuaries in Palestine in the first century, stood for protection, for eschatological deliverance, and for the divine name; recognized also as a representation of the instrument of the death of Jesus it showed that death as an expression of divine help. With this meaning, the *taw* sign, vestiges of which may remain as the earliest surviving memorials of the earliest church, was the original basis of what became the many forms and significations of the sign of the cross.

C. K. Wilkinson, "Early Christian Paintings in the Oasis of Khargeh," in *The Bulletin of the Metropolitan Museum of Art*, New York. 23 (1928), pp. 29-36; Daniélou, *Primitive Christian Symbols*, pp. 141f., 145. Photograph: courtesy The Metropolitan Museum of Art.

344. Painting in a Tomb Chapel at the Oasis of Khargeh

INDEX OF SCRIPTURAL REFERENCES

INDEX